A BIOGRAPHY OF COURAGE

Chester

Dedication

'To Wilmot . . . the brother who carried around my dream of playing test rugby but never got to see it happen. You remain my inspiration.'

A BIOGRAPHY OF COURAGE

Chester

Mark Keohane

DON NELSON
Cape Town

Author's note

In an attempt to provide a personal account and a historical commentary of Chester's life and rugby career, I have alternated first and third party narration. The first person accounts by Chester, and the chapter by his wife Maria, are in 'roman typeface' while mine are in italics except for the afterword at the end of the book

ISBN 1 86806 209 0

First Edition 2002

Don Nelson Publishers
PO Box 18600, Wynberg 7824

Cover Photograph: Touchline Photo
Cover Design: Matthew Ibbotson
Photographs: Touchline Photo and Anne Laing
Typesetting by The Alpha Omega Studio, Cape Town
Colour reproduction by Virtual Colour, Cape Town
Printed and bound by Tandym Print, 25 Thor Circle, Viking Place, Thornton
Set 10.5 on 13 pt Palatino

Contents

The Author

A former detective, Keohane was educated at Fairmont High in Durbanville (where he was coached at under-15 level by none other than Nick Mallett). He started writing on rugby for the *Cape Argus* in 1991 and covered his first test match in 1992 when the Wallabies played the Springboks at Newlands. Since then he has reported on 103 test matches, including 93 involving the Springboks and covered two World Cups. He also worked as a rugby writer in New Zealand and Europe. In 2000 he left journalism to join Harry Viljoen's staff with the Springboks and continues to work with the Boks as the communications manager. This is his first book.

Keohane is married to Karin Schimke, a freelance journalist and former political writer of the *Cape Times*. They have a son, Oliver, and live in Vredehoek, Cape Town.

Acknowledgements

'The greatest thank you must go to Chester. He opened up on every front and it was his willingness to be honest about every situation that made this a rewarding project. I believe Chester's story was one that simply had to be told because it is as much a story about South Africa as it is about a Springbok rugby player. Fortunately I found an editor in Archie Henderson who shared my passion for this book. Thank you Archie for your support and professionalism.' – Mark Keohane

Many thanks to Touchline Photo for their co-operation and support with regard to the cover and many of the pictures used.

Foreword

Playing rugby gave me the opportunity to travel to many amazing countries. Representing the Wallabies enabled me to experience and understand cultures and people in places I never dreamed I would visit.

In 1985 I was invited to play in the Natal Invitation sevens at King's Park, Durban. Despite opposition from my government, friends and family, I took my stance as being dedicated to The Game, and saw this as an exciting opportunity in my rugby career. Not only would I play against some of the giants of world rugby, but it was also a chance to meet some of the legendary players.

After being crowned the World Cup champions in 1991, the Wallabies toured South Africa in 1992. The excitement and support for this tour was a far cry from the huge resistance against the 1985 visit and it showed how positively South Africans were responding to life after apartheid.

In 1993 Australia reciprocated and invited South Africa to tour Australia for a three-test series. It was during this tour that I met Chester Williams.

The first thing that struck me about Chester was his friendliness. Although he was an unknown at test level, it did not take long for the rugby world to identify his value, not only as a player, but also as a respected ambassador for South African rugby.

Unfortunately I played against Chester only once in the Super 10 tournament. Although I regret never having crossed paths with him at test level, his reputation as a first-class winger was evident. He impressed me so much that he was the only South African whom I invited to play in my tribute game in Australia in 1994.

The 1995 World Cup brought South Africa into the spotlight and Chester, along with the Springboks, played a style of rugby that the world will never forget. Chester embraced the opportunity and revealed a passion for rugby that encouraged respect from the rugby community, but more importantly, from the staunch South African rugby supporters.

Although Chester and I were opponents on the field, we continue to share a respect that far outweighs the boundaries of a rugby field. His continual involvement in the rugby sevens today and the success of the South African national sevens team is proof of his commitment and valuable knowledge of the game that is played in heaven.

David Campese

1995: How the World Cup was won

1

Part one: Flood, sweat but no tears

I don't believe Pienaar should have captained South Africa at the World Cup... but Pienaar's contribution that day was crucial to us being crowned world champions a week later

CHESTER WILLIAMS *was back. The Springbok wing who had been promoted as the new face of South African rugby ahead of the World Cup had had his dream shattered just nine days before the kick-off. Then, through a strange sequence of events, Chester was back in the team and ready to play a significant part in the denouement of South Africa's World Cup adventure.*

After missing all three of South Africa's first-round matches of the World Cup because of an injury, Chester returned for the quarter-final against Western Samoa and accompanied the team to Durban for what was to be the Springboks' most demanding game of the entire tournament.

But to reach that momentous game, Chester had endured pain and despair.

History will forever show that South Africa won the World Cup on June 24, 1995. But I believe the real victory came a week earlier, in conditions that were completely foreign to us and amid a backdrop of uncertainty and chaos.

Beating France in the World Cup semi-final in Durban still ranks as the most emotionally draining day in my rugby career. So much went wrong that Saturday – the weather, the false starts ...

First we were going to play, then we were told to wait, later we heard the match could be off. If the game was to be called off, we all knew the consequence of such a decision: South Africa would be declared the losers because of two players who had been suspended earlier in the tournament. Our indiscretions in a match of almost equally bizarre circumstances as the one we were about to play in Durban would come back to haunt us. We had had two players sent off against Canada in Port Elizabeth in a match where the floodlights had failed and where our tempers had got the better of us.

Those anxieties could have tortured us as we waited for a decision on the match in Durban, but Francois Pienaar, in the two hours before that World Cup semi-final, was brilliant. He showed calmness, composure and enthusiasm. He took the delay in his stride and made all the guys feel comfortable. He kept focusing on the occasion and he kept channelling all the energy towards the match. At no stage did he look rattled. He communicated what was going on as if it were all part of the master plan.

When the match finally got underway, he kept us focused on winning. He did not get carried away about the state of the pitch, the rain or the dreaded possibility that it could still be called off. His entire attitude had the effect of calming the players in what had been an unbelievably tense build-up.

I don't believe Pienaar should have captained South Africa at the World Cup. I don't think he deserved to be there as a player. He was not the best No 6 flanker in the country and he was not the kind of captain I took to. I had always thought he was too much flash and too little substance. My choice would have been Western Province's Tiaan Strauss. But I will never detract from Pienaar's contribution to our victory in the change-room that Saturday. It was pivotal to our attitude when we eventually got on to the field. It was crucial to us being crowned world champions a week later when we beat the All Blacks in the final.

The chance to play in the World Cup final was so nearly snatched from us that night in Durban. We all appreciated the enormity of the decision that Welsh referee Derek Bevan had to make. To play or not to play? To risk a player's life? The field was so badly flooded that a player could easily have drowned if he had been trapped under a ruck.

While we waited in the change-room at King's Park, team officials let us know that everything was being done to improve conditions on the field, which had begun to resemble a paddy field with all the water. Even a helicopter was called in and it hovered above the ground in a desperate attempt for the downdraught of its rotors to help dry the field.

Ground staff worked frantically to sweep away the water.

All we could do was wish for the rain and the water to go away. We prayed for the rain to stop, but even if it did not, we prayed that Bevan would be conservative in his decision-making and consider the huge implications of calling off a match of such importance.

Given the conditions, it would not have been an outrageous decision for any referee to cancel the game. Those conditions were the worst I have ever had to play in. The field was flooded, and in any other circumstances I don't think the game would have been played. Indeed, had it not been a World Cup semi-final I am sure the game would have been called off. But in this case it would have been a momentous decision for Bevan to have made. Even so, had he decided it was too risky to play, few would have argued against it. What would have made such a decision bold was the consequence. South Africa, the host nation, would have been knocked out of the World Cup on a technicality.

It would have been a massive decision. Bevan, though, was extremely calm throughout. We felt confident he would make the right call, which as far as we were concerned, was to play. In spite of the dangers, we felt any risk would be worthwhile that day. The uncertainty of it all, I have no doubt, helped psyche us up for that game while the French could not have cared less. If it was to be cancelled, they knew they would go through to the final and getting there on a technicality would not have bothered them.

So when Bevan gave us the okay to play France, it was as good as giving us the World Cup. I felt as if the World Cup had been taken away from us and then offered back again. That afternoon and early evening, during a time of indecision in Durban, it was as if someone greater had taunted us, simply to deepen our resolve.

I had known such a feeling before. It had been the story of my World Cup. I had been there, been part of South Africa's campaign, then I was gone and, through the most amazing set of circumstances, I was back again.

A central figure in my World Cup story was Kitch Christie. He was a special person and there was a quality about him that made me feel comfortable: he judged everyone on merit. There was no prejudice, no nonsense. He was straight up and down.

He told you what he thought, not in an aggressive or intimidating manner, but in an honest way. He earned the respect of his players through his honesty and his actions. He was a preacher of discipline. His successful Transvaal teams of the early 1990s were disciples of this gospel and they were fitter than most and generally better off for it.

When Kitch took over from Ian McIntosh as Springbok coach in 1994, he immediately instilled greater discipline and more demanding fitness levels. The Springboks in my time were never the most skilled side, but under Kitch's guidance there was no team in the world that could match us for tenacity and fight. We were fitter than any side, and if we were still in contention come the final 10 minutes of a game, we always felt we would win.

The training was intense. He was fanatical about fitness. He believed that if you were physically fit, your mind could manage anything. If your legs were still pumping at the 80th minute, there was no reason for your mind to go wandering. Even tighthead prop Tommie Laubscher could boast a decent heart-rate test time when he played in Kitch's Bok team – and that took some doing.

My introduction to Kitch was on a rugby field in 1994. It was everything I expected it to be – hard on the legs and testing of the mind and heart. He worked us physically and then instilled a belief in us that we could not be beaten on a rugby field.

Obviously I knew of him because his reputation had been legendary among the provincial teams. Transvaal had dominated the Currie Cup and won the 1993 Super 10 with Kitch at the helm. His reputation preceded him when he took over from Ian McIntosh as national coach.

My attitude towards Kitch was on par with that which I displayed towards any coach: total commitment and determination to succeed.

Kitch was also the only coach who never mentioned the word race to me. He never spoke of quotas, of me being under-privileged, or being from a disadvantaged background. These were the euphemisms all coaches in my experience had used to describe black players.

Kitch was different. He always treated me as just a player, as his left wing. I was, during his time as Bok coach, always the No 1 choice to wear the No 11 jersey. In turn, he demanded an attitude that gave everything to Bok rugby and one that put the team ahead of any individual aspirations. Because of his honesty, we enjoyed a wonderful professional relationship as coach and player. He regularly had one-on-ones with players and he was very up front about what was on his mind. Fortunately, I never experienced the 'harder' side of Kitch because I kept to the straight and narrow. If he said jump, my only response was: How high?

To come from a social and rugby environment of prejudice – not all of it intentional or malicious – and to be confronted with a leader who saw the merits in a black rugby player was just fantastic. Kitch brought the best out of me because he treated me as a rugby player. The only way I ever wanted to be judged was how I performed when I had a rugby ball in my hands.

Our one-on-ones were never lengthy discussions. He would always come to me and say: 'Chester, with you I don't have a problem at all. You are probably one of my best-disciplined players. When it comes to training you always give 100 percent.' He was the first coach with whom I felt totally comfortable. I could talk to him about anything. If I had a problem or a concern, I could easily communicate with him.

He knew how to work with people. His people skills were good. And because of this we were a very positive side in 1994 and 1995. Kitch instilled in us a belief that we were not inferior to any other team. He made us believe in ourselves. We had an attitude of winning.

Also, he tolerated no prima donnas. In Kitch Christie's team, James Small was just another player. I liked that because I had seen James dictate terms to Ian McIntosh and felt it unfair on all the other players.

Kitch was low key in his profile. He had never played for the Springboks and felt he was undeserving of a Springbok blazer. At first he refused to wear it. We players had to convince him that we respected that he was the Bok coach and that it was as great an honour for him to coach the Boks as it was for any of us to play for the team. For him it was about the players and the South African rugby team – and nothing else. I had huge respect for the man and would never dream of questioning any decision he would make.

In 1995 fitness played a major part in our World Cup build-up. I was as fit as I had ever been and feeling on top of my game. It was ironic, then, that this sense of well-being was soon to be replaced by doubts about my fitness.

We played Western Samoa in our only World Cup preparation test. We smashed them 60-8 and I scored two tries. I should have been elated but I was concerned after leaving the field with what I thought was a hamstring strain. I had felt a twinge in the hamstring and decided to come off.

The next few weeks would be hell as I tried to regain full fitness in time for the World Cup opening match against the champions, Australia, at Newlands. This was the match I had dreamed of: playing on my home ground against the world champions and in the company of David Campese, whom I considered to be the best winger of his generation.

I was determined to get to Newlands. I would do anything the medical team asked me to do. I don't know which was greater: my enthusiasm or my naïveté. I just wanted to train. I wanted to show Kitch that I was fit enough to play against Australia, but Kitch, always the thorough professional, left any decision on fitness to his medical team; he would never dream of interfering with them because they were the experts in their field.

Because of this I never spoke to Kitch about my recovery, or my concern about how the medical team were going about fixing me. I felt they were too demanding; they made me work when I believed I needed to rest the hamstring. I would do most of the exercises they gave me, but I could not sprint flat out.

The medical team did not share my concerns. They put me through a sprint test every day when all I wanted to do was rest. In fact, I wanted a week off from sprinting. I knew that I could be right for the opening game but it would mean leniency in their approach to me. There was to be none. They wanted certainty about my fitness and I could not give it to them.

James Small and I were the only wings in the squad. Perhaps they were aware of this and fearful of me breaking down in the opening match. I don't know because I never asked them why they were pushing me so hard. I believed they were just adding to the stress on the hamstring, but I did not have the confidence to challenge the team doctor, Frans Verster, and physiotherapist Evan Speechly.

Both had been involved with the Boks since South Africa's re-admission to international rugby and both were highly regarded within the team set-up. They were the experts and I accepted that. But I felt they had not managed me properly and I knew that my hamstring was not getting any better under the treatment I was being given.

The decision on how to treat my injury was theirs, but the big decision was mine: could I take part in the World Cup? It was a huge decision. My face had been sold to South Africa and the world as the face of the World Cup. Everywhere I went I would see huge posters with my face on them. I was flattered, but I also realised how big a decision it was to make. And the overwhelming thought was that my hamstring just would not come right.

I had to be honest: Could I do myself justice in the opening game? The answer at that stage was definitely no. I knew I was not 100 percent. I knew I would be holding back. The team would suffer so I went to see the Bok manager, Morne du Plessis, and Kitch. For the first time I spoke about the injury.

We spoke honestly. I told Kitch that I would be dropping the team if I played knowing I was not 100 percent fit. Kitch said he respected my honesty and my decision, but asked if I did not want to reconsider. He spoke about the magnitude of the tournament. He said he was prepared to nurse me through the early stages of the competition. He reminded me of the significance of the tournament and what I meant to the country. He said he would give me all the time I needed to recover. He did not want me to go, but he was not going to demand I stay either. I was adamant – I had to withdraw.

When I informed Francois Pienaar of my decision, the captain was desperate for me to stay on. He asked me where my pride was? He seemed agitated with me.

'Do you know how big the World Cup is?' he asked. I don't think he intended it to come out the way it did. He was disappointed that I would not be a part of it.

I said it was my pride that was forcing me to withdraw. I felt so much for the team and recognised the enormity of the tournament. I told him I was never going to play if I had an injury doubt. He asked me to stay on and fight through the pain. He said I could be nursed through the early matches. He emphasised what my presence would mean to the majority of South Africans, meaning black South Africans.

I was not prepared to be a political pawn and I was not going to play if there was any doubt about my fitness. I had to make a rugby decision. Given the pain I was experiencing and the emotional vulnerability that always haunts a player suffering from an injury, I knew the decision was not hard to make. It seemed bold because of the consequences, but it also seemed logical because of the reality of the situation.

Kitch and Morne accepted my decision and both then promised that they would draft me into the World Cup squad should the circumstance arise and my fitness allow for it. 'If I lose a prop, a hooker, or a lock, you will be my first replacement,' Kitch told me. It meant so much to me because it gave me a faint hope that the World Cup might still see Chester Williams. But at that point the hope was just a tiny flame. There was a hamstring to fix and I was convinced there wasn't enough time to get it right.

I was disappointed at the way in which the medical team had treated me. I questioned the treatment and felt they could have been more accommodating and more flexible. Even when I pleaded with them for me not to sprint, they drove me through another set of sprints. I felt driven out of the World Cup by wrong decisions; it was a time of great despair.

1995: How the World Cup was won

2

Part two: My finest moment

Nothing in that World Cup quarter-final surprised me, except for the four tries I scored. I would have settled for one. Four... Geez!

AFTER *Chester Williams had withdrawn from the Springbok team for the 1995 World Cup, no debate raged over the way the medical staff had treated him, but privately there was disagreement. It is still Bruce McLoughlin's medical opinion that Chester was poorly managed in the build-up to the tournament.*

McLoughlin is a Cape Town physiotherapist who worked with the Western Province rugby team from 1992 to 2000 and spent two seasons with the Springboks after the 1995 World Cup. He is convinced that Chester could have played against Australia in the opening match of the tournament, if only he had been treated differently. He disagrees with the treatment the Springbok medical staff administered and with their diagnosis of the injury.

McLoughlin believed that the treatment Chester received in the Springbok team stressed the injury instead of resting it. 'There was never time for recovery or effective treatment. It would be sprints day in and day out. Sprinting was the last thing Chester needed to be doing,' insists McLoughlin.

The Springboks had moved on without Chester and the team's medical staff began to concentrate on those players who were in the squad as opposed to someone now on the outside. Chester was uncertain about the seriousness of the hamstring and disillusioned about missing out on the Springboks' first World Cup match. He went knocking at McLoughlin's door. They had known each other professionally since Chester had become a regular in the Western Province team in 1993.

They shared a bond in the Afrikaans-dominated rugby world. Both were outsiders. Chester was black and McLoughlin was English-speaking. They were thrown together in a sporting environment that embraced Afrikaners and cynically accepted anything else.

'He was a loner as a player and I was pretty much in the same boat as the only English-speaking guy on the management. The players did not easily mix with me, and Chester, despite being popular within the squad, was never one of the squad. He clearly was different in the eyes of the players,' recalls McLoughlin.

The early association was professional. In 1995 it became personal and seven years on the two are still close. It is the events of 1995 that dominate McLoughlin's early memories.

'The first kind of linkage between the two of us started just before the World Cup when Chester withdrew because of the hamstring injury. He wanted professional advice from me. He also seemed desperate to confide in someone. He wanted trust and, most importantly, a professional capable of fixing his hamstring.'

The pressure on Chester at the time was phenomenal. McLoughlin remembers the rehabilitation sessions as if they were episodes in a television soap opera. No matter the time of day, television crews would be queuing. Everyone wanted an interview or an image. And if it was not the intrusion of the camera, it was the adulation of the fans.

'I have never experienced anything as hectic in my life. It was a crazy few weeks. I had not seen such a press presence in South Africa. It was the first time that Chester had been exposed to heaps and heaps of pressure for what was essentially a negative. He was injured. The media were not there to talk about a try he had scored. They were telling the world that this guy was out of the World Cup and they were attempting to detail his every move to get back. There were no guarantees it would end as a success story.

'There was phenomenal interest in Chester's rehabilitation, more so from the international media than in South Africa. Here was a guy who had been sold as the face of the World Cup and he was not going to be part of the tournament because of injury. The nature of his injury became hot news.'

McLoughlin, too, had never experienced the paparazzi to such a degree. He describes the first week of treating Chester as a stepping-stone for both of them in learning about the pressures of the media away from rugby. It was unrelenting, both from the media and local fans. Neither had been subjected to such press scrutiny before. In many respects they had no option but to trust each other.

'The trust component certainly started then. Chester started to confide in me. He started to tell me what was going on inside of him and what he felt had happened within the Bok camp. He was very hurt when he arrived at my door. He felt the Bok medical team had let him down. He did not believe they had managed him properly. He felt deserted and disillusioned about his prospects of playing in the World Cup,' says McLoughlin.

'I reassured him that we could get the hamstring right. I shared his views on the treatment he had been receiving. I felt it was not the right treatment. His biggest concern was that he felt he was now out of the World Cup. The physical aspect of the injury was a nonentity for him. I knew I could get him right and he knew he would be able to play if I got him right.

'The gist of the whole thing was hurt at how he had been managed and disbelief. Initially, he did not think he was going to get back. He thought the World Cup was over for him. After day three, he was a lot better. The emotion changed from being disillusioned to one of: "Fuck 'em. Let's show these guys". There was a definite defiance to prove the World Cup medical team wrong.'

Word of Chester's rehabilitation spread quickly in Cape Town. Chester was treated daily at (the Gamesman gymnasium in Claremont). His training runs were a few hundred metres away at a cricket oval in Protea Road, Newlands. There was no escaping the scrutiny and it forced McLoughlin to treat the hamstring between six and seven in the morning.

'If he arrived at the gym after seven in the morning, it would take him 45 minutes actually to get on the treatment table. He never said no to autograph-hunters. Unfortunately, the media presence was also an every day thing. To make sure there was minimal disruption, I had to treat him as early as possible in the morning.

'The poor guy could not move in Cape Town. You had to experience it first hand to appreciate the intrusion. We would walk across to the oval and cars would stop in the street, the drivers would hoot their horns, get out and run over to him for autographs. I have never experienced such adulation,' says McLoughlin, who remembers an unexpected visit to Grove Primary School in Claremont as another reminder of the pulling power of Chester Williams.

'I wanted him to do a few sprints and we popped over to a nearby school field. It was in the morning and the kids were in the classroom. I had not asked for permission from the school's headmaster because I

thought our time at the field would pass unnoticed. I was very naïve.

'A kid spotted Chester warming up and shouted to the rest of the class that Chester was on the field. Within five minutes, most of the school was next to the field watching his training run. We cut the session short and still the kids would not leave. They all wanted his autograph and he obliged as much as possible.

'I think he was as taken aback by the response as I was, but he was also very unsettled by a sarcastic comment passed by one of the teachers. As the teacher was walking past him, he made the comment. I can't remember the content, but it ruffled Chester. For the next few days he kept on quizzing me about the comment. He wanted to know what I thought the teacher meant by it? Why did he make it? It genuinely upset him.'

The media, too, were starting to get to Chester and he finally snapped during a morning session at the gymnasium. He screamed to an Italian television crew to leave him alone and to get out. It was the only occasion when he 'lost it'. McLoughlin was amazed that it had taken him so long to have a go at the prying TV cameras.

'He is not the confrontational type. Every morning he would ignore the media presence and just get on with his session. They were unrelenting and then he finally cracked. I have never seen him so upset. He let them know exactly how he felt.'

The Romanian World Cup side also let Chester know exactly how they felt about his treatment. They were most upset that McLoughlin, having been assigned to treat their squad, could also work on South Africa's celebrated winger. On seeing Chester leave McLoughlin's medical rooms, the Romanians refused to continue their treatment.

'It was among the more bizarre incidents at the time. Chester was leaving my rooms when the Romanian side arrived. Their security guard asked, in broken English, if that was Chester Williams. I said yes and he said: "That's it, we are gone." It took a day for them to come back. They could not grasp that I could treat their players as well as Chester. They were very suspicious of me after that.'

The Romanians appeased and the Italian media sorted out, McLoughlin and Chester could concentrate on the rehabilitation.

A day before the Springboks played Australia in the World Cup's opening match on May 25, McLoughlin put Chester through a fitness test. The player passed it easily.

'I have no doubt in my mind that Chester, if managed properly medically, should have played in that opening match. I spoke on one or two occasions to Evan Speechly. I never spoke to the team doctor. Evan had very different treatment techniques from mine. The diagnosis was also different. They were looking at Chester's injury as a soft-tissue and I

was looking at it as more neural. There was not a tear. They were stressing him with the sprints and that was making the hamstring worse. There was even the one session where he begged not to sprint and they said no.

'I was angry at how he had been treated. I also wanted to prove a point. I knew he could have been at the World Cup from the outset if he had been treated correctly. I saw it as a bonus that he had removed himself from the World Cup environment. It was to his benefit that he got to Cape Town, got the emotional support and got to gather his strength.'

Instead of playing against the Wallabies on May 25, it was just another day at the office for Chester. Being employed by the Western Province Rugby Football Union, Chester had to be at work on that day.

The union, as hosts of the match, seconded Chester to work with the Wallabies. He was usher to the Wallabies' substitutes bench. On an afternoon when he should have been terrorising the Australian defence and taking on the game's most celebrated wing of the previous 10 years in David Campese, Chester was looking after the needs of the Australian reserve players.

Ever since his withdrawal from the Springbok team, nine days before the big kick-off, there had been a national wave of sympathy for Chester. Even President Nelson Mandela felt moved to comment, calling Chester's absence from the Springboks a tragedy. There was also sympathy from an unlikely quarter: the Wallabies.

The coach of the Wallabies, Bob Dwyer, described Chester as a top rugby player and offered him the chance to be part of the World Cup – as a part-time Australian. Dwyer said the Australians would love to catch up with Chester, rope him in and make him feel part of the World Cup. Chester declined any offer to hang out with the Wallabies but, as an usher for their team at Newlands, he got as close to them as he would have had he been playing in the opening match. It was a frustrating substitute for the real thing.

The 'real thing' had a touch of irony. The man who had replaced Chester in the Springbok team, Pieter Hendriks, provided the turning-point in the match against the defending world champions. The Transvaal winger straightened the line, sized up Campese and took him on, one on one. Few players in world rugby had done this. Hendriks won the contest hands down and scored arguably the most memorable try of South Africa's World Cup campaign. The Springboks won handsomely and Hendriks was one of the stars.

In the build-up to the match, Hendriks had expressed sympathy for Chester. 'Not many will believe me but I feel terrible for Chester because I know exactly what it is like. When the Springboks went to France and England in 1992 I left as the first-choice left wing. I got injured in the opening match and lost my place for two years.'

The outcome of the opening World Cup game, a 27-18 victory for South Africa, lifted the spirits of the entire country and Chester was no exception. His defiance was starting to show all round. He was confident that the treatment on his injury was working and it made him more determined than ever to get back into the World Cup squad, but he knew he had no control over this. His inclusion could come only by way of a withdrawal or a suspension of a Springbok player. He had never thought the latter possible and his only chance back in would be at the expense of an injured teammate.

McLoughlin, confident that the winger was fit, ensured that Chester played a club match two weeks after treatment started. The sprint tests had not been a problem. McLoughlin now wanted Chester to get through 80 minutes of rugby. Now it was about getting confidence back, making a tackle and getting ball in hand.

'He had looked the part in one-on-one training. The only way we both would know for sure whether he could be available to play a part in the World Cup was if he made it through a match. The club match was the perfect test,' said McLoughlin.

On the Saturday that the Springboks would play Canada in Port Elizabeth, Chester started for his club, Northerns-Parow, against Hamiltons. He lasted 80 minutes in a pressure-free environment. He did nothing spectacular, other than survive the match. To the unusually large media contingent at the game and to the crowd, Chester had proved his fitness and all he could do now was wait. If he was to be called on, at least he knew he was fully prepared, fully fit, and raring to go. Then, 24 hours later, the call came.

There were times, I must admit, that I thought my chance would come. The World Cup is such a demanding tournament that it would inevitably take its toll on players. I never went on my knees and prayed for someone to get injured. I just wanted to make sure that if the call should come that I would be fit and ready to play.

But, strangely, that day when we played Australia at Newlands, I had no overwhelming sense of regret. Certainly, there was no self-pity. I was just pleased to be at Newlands – and to be a part of the occasion. Before the match I was introduced to the crowd amid the most amazing scenes and in a wonderful atmosphere. That was good enough for me.

I was working for Western Province. They needed every one of the staff to work at the opening match. On that day I was one of many on a work roster. If anything, I landed the cushiest of jobs, helping the Wallabies' bench. The Wallabies were very cool about it. I knew they were disappointed for me that I had been forced to withdraw. During the match there was very little communication between their bench and me. All they needed had been put in place. I was simply on stand by in case there were any additional requirements.

On the day they probably wouldn't have minded an extra player or two because they would have needed that to beat the Boks. We were simply brilliant and the final score was not a true reflection of our superiority in the game. They scored a late try when the contest was already over.

The occasion was magnificent. President Mandela's presence, as always, was inspirational and the Boks produced their finest display of the tournament. I rated the quality of play in that opening game as better than that produced in the final. It was a different occasion altogether but, sitting on the sidelines, I felt that we were destined to win.

Pieter Hendriks's try was a moment of brilliance. He backed himself and he won easily. All I thought at the time was 'Try, try'. Never did it enter my mind that it could have been me. I also never thought what I would have done in a similar position. That day at Newlands was about being South African and not only a Springbok.

On June 3, the day that Chester made his return to rugby, the Springboks took on Canada in their final first-round match of the World Cup. It was to be a dramatic evening from the start. The floodlights failed and so did the Springboks' discipline. They won 20-0 but it was a Pyrrhic victory, one in which they lost Pieter Hendriks and James Dalton for the rest of the tournament, the former for a kick for which he was later cited and the latter for fighting in the free-for-all that broke out during the game.

Dalton was sent off and Hendriks was afterwards accused of kicking an opponent, found guilty by a tribunal and banished for 90 days. It was the Springboks' worst performance of the tournament, and Canada were no better. But then Canada were hardly contenders for the title.

Hendriks was shocked and angry as he left the team. He admitted to being stunned by the decision of the tribunal, but saddened that the Springbok management had not put up a fight on his behalf. The team management accepted the Rugby World Cup judicial committee's verdict. There was understandable cynicism among the media, many of whom suggested the Bok management was delighted by the sudden vacancy. Chester Williams could now be brought back into the fold.

The Bok image tarnished, Chester arrived in Sandton as a publicity godsend and an integral part of the play-offs for the World Cup, which were to follow. His ability on the field was undeniable. His off-field charm in the week leading to the quarter-final against Western Samoa was equally powerful.

The chief executive of the South African Rugby Football Union, Edward Griffiths, who was also acting as the Springbok media officer at the World Cup, recognised that the world needed to see a smiling Springbok after the barbarism against Canada. Who else but Chester? After all, he was the smiling face of South Africa's World Cup campaign. He was the pin-up poster promoting the tournament.

Within a day Hendriks's banishment was relegated to a paragraph on the sports pages. The feel-good factor was that Chester was back. The Springbok management milked it, wheeling Chester out for a series of press conferences.

The South African media, desperate for good news, sucked on the image and inane niceties like kids given ice-lollies. They asked for more even though Chester said nothing dramatic. All he did was to put a smile on everyone's face. He had been well versed in giving the media a smile and no sensation.

The squad was down when I arrived. They were upset about the suspensions. The mood, however, was never going to have an adverse effect on the quarter-final against Western Samoa. We always felt that if we played to our potential we would win.

Kitch was very good in that week. He kept focus, maintained strict control and did not allow all the media hype around the suspensions and my recall to get in our way. Edward Griffiths and Morne du Plessis handled the media. We, the players, concentrated on the game.

I was very protected in the build-up. I did not know much of what was happening outside of the camp that week and in the following fortnight. I was totally oblivious of the impact my return had made, especially on the black community. Selfishly, all I was thinking about was the game. I just wanted to be a Springbok at a World Cup and test myself against the game's best.

Kitch Christie, as he had always done with Chester in the past, immediately included him in the starting XV. Throughout Christie's Springbok coaching career, a fit Chester was always a test certainty.

Tournament officials were relieved. South Africa's rugby bosses allowed themselves an extra smile in private. Chester was back, and of greater significance, was that the Springboks could no longer be branded lily-white – a justifiable criticism by politicians and rugby analysts who felt there was a need for greater representation of the new South Africa in the Springbok team.

Chester was coached to say very little and to smile a lot. He never entered the political debate. There were race questions, mostly from the foreign media. He politely deflected them and looked to manager Morne du Plessis to take charge of the conversation whenever these cropped up. The tiny winger with the biggest heart in world rugby simply wanted to play.

And play he did that Saturday evening at Ellis Park against Western Samoa, scoring four tries in the Springboks' 42-14 victory. He did not score another try in that World Cup, but those four tries put him in joint third place as the highest try-scorer of the tournament together with French centre Thierry Lacroix and fellow Springbok Adrian Richter. Inevitably, Jonah Lomu headed the final list with seven tries, a total he shared with his New Zealand teammate Marc Ellis. Gavin Hastings of Scotland and Rory Underwood of England were joint second with five tries each.

The win over Western Samoa was a wonderful Springbok victory, embellished by the romance of a Chester four-try comeback. But there was also controversy and Christie landed himself in the middle of it.

Western Samoa will never be considered among the elite of rugby union, but they rank as one of the more physically demanding outfits. Christie controversially referred to their defence as coconut tackles. Christie strongly denied there was ever a racial slur intended, but the New Zealand media in particular dined out on the remark.

Christie was commenting on the outrageous late and high tackles several of his players had suffered in the bruising quarter-final. The tackling by the Western Samoans had not been in the spirit of the game and Christie felt the situation needed to be addressed before a player suffered an injury that would cut short his career.

Stung by this criticism, the Samoans came with a riposte of their own: they alleged that the Springboks had racially abused them during the match. The Springboks denied the allegation and, rather predictably, Bok scrumhalf Joost van der Westhuizen defended himself by invoking Chester Williams.

With Chester back in the team, and the hero of the moment with his record number of tries in a Springbok jersey, the scrumhalf was able to claim, with angelic innocence, that Chester Williams was his best friend in the squad. In other words, with friends like Chester, how could he be accused of racism?

Chester still chuckles over that press conference. Whenever there was an accusation of racism, he was introduced as a star witness for the defence. He found it amusing because it was so predictable. He accepted it would always be the case. If someone questioned him, he said the right things at press conferences because it was in the interests of the team to do so.

Chester called his fiancée, Teresa Muller, after the victory over Western Samoa. They had become engaged the previous Saturday. One Saturday she had Chester all to herself, a week later she had to share him with a nation again. He would never be hers only.

Things get said on the field and a lot of it is gamesmanship. I know what some white South African players are capable of when it comes to taunting black players on the field. Nothing in that World Cup quarter-final surprised me, except for the four tries I scored. I would have settled for one. Four... Geez!*

I did not realise then that it was a record. I always thought Danie Gerber had scored more tries in a test for South Africa. No one said it was a record when I scored my fourth try. Afterwards, when I was sitting in the change-room, someone came up to me and said I had broken the Springbok try-scoring record and that the media would want to talk to me about the achievement. There were no great celebrations and there was not a lot of back-slapping. Some guys congratulated me. Others did not say anything.

The concern about injuries to Andre Joubert, in particular, dominated our feelings in the dressing-room after the match. At first we thought that he would be out of the tournament because of a suspected broken hand. We were worried because he was one of our key players.

But there was still a clear sense of being in the semi-final of the World Cup. Kitch was already looking towards that game and he was quick to emphasise to us the importance of staying humble. He made it clear that beating Western Samoa was not what we had to measure ourselves by. The semi-final would be against one of the big boys. We had to step it up, both in physical and mental preparation.

When I called Teresa after the game, she was calm and measured, as she always was about these things. She told me that she had never doubted me and that we would win the World Cup. She was very understanding of what the game of rugby meant to me. She knew the importance I had attached to making it back into the World Cup.

I went to bed that evening feeling relieved that my first match in the World Cup was over and that I had managed to add something to the Boks' campaign. That evening I would not appreciate that I had just recorded my finest chapter in my international career. Then again, which player ever recognises the day when it happens?

* Chester's record of four tries in a test stood until June 19, 1999, when Stefan Terblanche scored five in a test against Italy.

1995: How the World Cup was won

3

Part Three: Acrimony after victory

It was in Durban where it all happened ... not in Johannesburg. That day our destiny was decided: we would win the World Cup

VICTORY against Western Samoa had to be put in perspective. Kitch Christie reminded everyone that the quarter-final was one match the Springboks were expected to win, especially when they had beaten the same side so comprehensively just a few weeks before the World Cup in a warm-up test.

The coach was blunt with his players. The business end of the World Cup was only a few days away and France were proving to all that they had it in them to win the Webb Ellis trophy. Western Samoa did not represent a complete test of the Springboks' ability. It was merely a match that had to be played and won. Greater hurdles now awaited in the form of France and then one of New Zealand or England.

The belief within the Springbok squad, however, was such that they did not care whom they played against in Durban. The players felt they were good enough to win the World Cup. They believed they could beat anyone, their confidence further boosted by the surge of emotion from within the country. South Africans, many of them sceptical before the first kick-off, were now caught up in the euphoria of four successive victories.

Chester, back in the World Cup and immediately the toast of the *country after his record-breaking four tries against Western Samoa, was sheltered from too much media exposure. Christie, having consulted with Morne du Plessis and Edward Griffiths, wanted as little fuss made about his players as possible. The Springboks were not isolated from the media in the build-up to the semi-final, but Du Plessis was superb in deflecting the attention off individuals and focusing it on the support of the public and media.*

Objectivity among the South African media had become an afterthought in the final two weeks of the tournament. The Springboks, banned from the 1987 and 1991 World Cups because of apartheid, were two matches away from winning the World Cup at their first attempt. It was hard to be dispassionate in such an invigorating atmosphere of victory.

The rugby writers, regardless of publication, backed the Springboks. The radio and TV reporters, normally so scrupulous in not taking sides, became enthusiastic about the Springboks' chances. So when Francois Pienaar's Springboks arrived in Durban on the day of the test, few were willing to entertain the thought that the French might win the match.

When Chester stepped off the aircraft that had brought the Springboks to Durban, the weather did not seem out of the ordinary. The dark clouds and rain were a little unusual for June, but no one believed these elements would linger. Floods could be a problem in Kwazulu-Natal, but only in the summer for goodness sake.

The weather certainly didn't bother Chester, he was just grateful to be back in the Springbok team and still elated from having scored four tries in his comeback match. And when had a bit of rain ever spoiled a rugby test? Or so he and everyone else thought. But the weather in Durban on June 17, 1995, was no ordinary pattern. It was as if the elements had conspired to add to the drama of what was about to be an enormous moment in the history of Springbok rugby.

Perhaps Francois Pienaar and Du Plessis had a sense of the impending danger and they deliberately kept the arrival of the Springboks at a low key. Christie, a man of understated authority, had been urging humility. All three men realised that calmness in the team was essential. Emotions could easily get out of control in a situation where the Springboks were just two games away from becoming world champions.

The storms belted Durban all day and there was flooding in the streets as the Springboks' bus made its way to King's Park Stadium. The field was flooded and there were frantic attempts underway to sweep away the water.

In the dressing-room the Springboks were informed that the match could be abandoned because of the conditions. The implications of this call were dramatic: if there was no game, the winner would be decided on discipline. The team with the better record would go through, and France's record was impeccable.

The tournament ruling stated clearly that should the semi-final not be played because of conditions beyond the organisers'control, the team with the fewest suspensions would be declared the winner. France had no suspensions. The Springboks had two. Because of the bans imposed on Hendriks and Dalton for foul play, the hosts would be out of the World Cup on a technicality.

The Springboks wanted to play, regardless of the state of the pitch. They had no option. The French were happy to go with the referee's decision. They understood that a victory without a match being played might be hollow, but a week later no one would care.

All that mattered on this Saturday was making it to the final.

The rain stopped, then started again but the intensity of the storm had abated. The match referee, Derek Bevan of Wales, was undecided at the scheduled kick-off time of 4.30pm, but decided to postpone the start by 90 minutes. He was not going to risk the players' safety. It was not just the possibility that someone could drown so bad was the flooding, there was the constant danger of lightning.

But Bevan also appreciated the ramifications of a no-contest. He was going to give it the maximum time before making the decision. He consulted both teams. South Africa wanted to play and were desperate to get on with the game. The French were indifferent. With typical French composure, they shrugged their shoulders and let it be known that the decision was the referee's. Of course they wanted to play, but they would not have pushed too hard for the game to go ahead.

Finally, an hour after Bevan had made his first call to delay the kick-off, he gave the match the go-ahead. The game was a lottery. The conditions made it impossible to put together anything constructive. Whoever got the luckier on the day was going to win the match. Fortune was in South Africa's corner.

The Springboks won 19-15 and could have lost the match in the last minute. Every French rugby supporter will be convinced to this day that Abdel Benazzi scored for their side. Every South African will tell you otherwise. It would have been interesting if the video ref were in operation then. It was a close thing, especially in the wet where players do dive before the tryline and use the slippery surface to gain an extra metre or so.

South Africans also wanted the All Blacks to be in the final. It would be appropriate in the context of Springbok rugby history that the All Blacks be the opponents at Ellis Park on June 24. No two teams in rugby history have enjoyed the intense rivalry of the Springboks and All Blacks. Australia, during South Africa's international exile, appeared to have taken over the mantle as New Zealand's greatest foe. In 1995, however, the traditionalists were having none of it. South Africa versus

New Zealand in a World Cup final! It simply had to be.

The All Blacks did not disappoint and, inspired by the wing sensation Jonah Lomu, the men in black thrashed England 45-29, having led 36-3 early in the second half.

The corporate suites had got their dream final. Tournament organiser Rian Oberholzer could not have asked for more from the Springboks, nor from the semi-finals. If Durban was all drama, then Cape Town was all about sensation in the form of Lomu. The Auckland-born winger, only 20 years old at the World Cup, had crushed England with a record four tries. No one in the English media doubted Lomu would be as destructive against South Africa. Most of the English press corps expressed this opinion soon after England's humiliation. South African rugby writer Louis de Villiers dismissed the talk as that of supporters who felt as humiliated as their team.

'Don't compare us South Africans with you English,' bellowed De Villiers to every English journalist within earshot. De Villiers has a rasping voice that travels, so anyone within 100 feet would have heard him insult England and the English, at the same time boldly declaring everything good about a unified, new South Africa.

De Villiers epitomised South African optimism. Like virtually every rugby-lover in the country, he was convinced the Springboks would win the final. Chester is adamant the Boks felt the same way.

The Boks, playing in their first World Cup, beat New Zealand 15-12. The tournament had united a nation which unconditionally backed a team who had proclaimed throughout the tournament that they were one team playing for one country. Their captain emphasised this afterwards with his memorable comment about having won the World Cup for 43 million South Africans.

But as South Africans danced the night away, few were aware of the unfolding drama within the winning Springbok team. Coinciding with the World Cup finale, the once true-blue amateur game of rugby was entering a full professional era. The established rugby authorities had been caught in a blindside move by a group calling itself World Rugby Corporation with Australian Ross Turnbull as the front man. WRC was furtively going about trying to sign up all the top teams at the Rugby World Cup for a 'circus' similar to the one launched by Kerry Packer which cracked the monopoly that the blazered brigade once held on cricket.

Pienaar had been recruited by the WRC to persuade the Springboks to sign up. Most of the other teams had agreed to terms, but without the world champions, the WRC would be nothing. The actions of the Springbok captain would lead to a serious disagreement with Chester Williams.

The expectation was definitely there. Everyone who spoke to us, every kind of message we got and anyone whom we bumped into spoke of us winning the World Cup.

By the time we had reached the semi-final, this feeling of optimism had reached such a level that people did not seem to regard France as an obstacle. This worried us slightly, but it also gave us a huge boost to know how much the South African public rated our chances.

The players, reluctant to speak publicly about their confidence in going all the way, kept a low profile, said the right things in interviews and simply tried to keep the positive energy flowing. The last thing we wanted was to be portrayed as an arrogant team. Kitch Christie was not that kind of man. His teams were confident. They were not arrogant.

Humility was a characteristic he spoke about often. We had worked extremely hard to make it to the semi-final. He would not allow us to lose focus by believing we only had to arrive to win.

I believe that attitude helped us beat the French in Durban. Because of the weather, the playing conditions and the closeness of the result, it was one of tensest games I have ever played in. When Bevan declared that Benazzi was short of the tryline by a few centimetres it only added to the almost unbearable suspense. One more scrum followed ... our pack stood firm, Joel Stransky cleared the ball ... and the Springboks were in the final!

I was emotionally drained and physically exhausted. It had been the longest day of my life. We wanted to be happy in the dressing-room, to celebrate, but there was just this overwhelming sense of relief.

When I reflect on the World Cup, it was in Durban where it all happened and not in Johannesburg. That day, it seemed to me, our destiny was decided: we would win the World Cup. Morne du Plessis was convinced that there had been a greater force at play. Most of the team felt the same way.

It seemed that no matter what, we were going to win the World Cup. No player was that stupid to mention this to the coach. That would have been a sign of arrogance and, as I said earlier, the coach would not have tolerated such an attitude.

We were in the final. All we had to find out was whether we would play New Zealand or England. Most of us felt it would be the All Blacks.

It is easy to talk about predicted success once you have achieved it, but I promise you every single one of us in the squad felt we could beat New Zealand. We felt we were a fitter team, a better defensive team than any the All Blacks had had to face in the tournament, and physically we knew we could take them on up front.

Kitch never spoke to us about how to defend against Lomu. He did not single out Lomu nor devise a strategy around Lomu. He emphasised that Lomu could not be a factor if he never got the ball. The message was simple: tackle, tackle and tackle. Our centres, Hennie le Roux and Japie Mulder, were primed for the match. They had to cut off the ball supply. We had to pressure Andrew Mehrtens, and Joost van der Westhuizen told the team he would chase Mehrtens all day.

Within the team the talk was that if Lomu did get the ball then all of us would smash him. No one person felt it was his job alone.

I had seen Lomu at the 1995 Hong Kong Sevens. He was devastating and he had been impressive at the World Cup. Personally, I thought there were flaws in the make-up of his game in the tighter and more controlled 15-man environment and, nearly seven years on, I don't believe he is one of the great wings of his generation. He is an imposing physical presence, but he has limitations as a rugby player.

I knew he would not be the factor he was against England. Too many of the Springbok players wanted to have a go at him. Jeff Wilson's ability as a wing was more respected than Lomu's.

As a team, we did not fear New Zealand. They had beaten us 2-0 in a three-test series the previous year, but in the last test we had outscored them two tries to nil in an 18-all draw. We knew we could win if we did not miss our first-time tackles.

South Africans also expected us to win. Everywhere we went that week we got encouragement. The public never gave me the impression there was any doubt.

And after the drama of France in Durban, I shared everyone's enthusiasm. It was hard to argue with Morne when he said it was as if a greater force was guiding us.

The final was the biggest match I have played in when I think of the significance of the occasion. It was not the toughest, nor was it the most mentally demanding. I have watched the final a few times on video and I think, on balance, we should have won the game in normal time. We had more try-scoring opportunities than the All Blacks and I have no doubt Ruben Kruger scored a try for us early in the match.

Nelson Mandela's appearance in a Springbok No 6 jersey before the kick-off gave us another boost, the crowd noise added to the adrenalin, and Japie Mulder's big hit on Jonah Lomu is one of my highlights of the game. Another was my tackle on Jeff Wilson. I enjoyed making that one.

Statistically, the final goes down as one of the most dramatic because it was won by a drop-goal in extra time. Emotionally, I had more left at the end than in Durban the previous week.

After the final we had a team meeting before leaving for the official dinner. The meeting took place less than two hours after the final whistle. Edward Griffiths, the SARFU chief executive and Springbok media manager, addressed the squad. It was a strange meeting because so soon after winning the World Cup he was talking about us signing with SARFU and trying to rally excitement at how much money there would be for players to make in the South African game.

The game was going professional, said Griffiths. Then he cautioned us against signing with an unofficial breakaway rugby organisation before seeing what SARFU had to offer. He spoke of a television deal (with Rupert Murdoch) that would financially look after all of us. When Griffiths was finished speaking, Pienaar asked all the management to leave the room. He wanted to address only the players.

It was here that I heard for the first time about the World Rugby Corporation. Pienaar told us that there was another option available to us in rugby and that we would find out more about it in the next week. He, in turn, asked us not to sign with SARFU before we had seen the other offer.

There was a lot of secrecy all round. It was not the kind of mood you would associate with a team meeting following the winning of a World Cup. I did not give it too much thought at that stage. Subsequently, from what I have heard and read, a few of the players did know about the proposed breakaway some time before the final and that Pienaar had taken them into his confidence during the course of the World Cup tournament. I was totally unaware of any such plan. When Pienaar spoke about a rebel rugby circuit after the World Cup final at our team meeting, it was the first I had heard of it.

We eventually got to the official function a few hours late. Our late arrival was not appreciated and it was not a great evening. The president of SARFU, Louis Luyt, had apparently upset the New Zealanders with his speech and it certainly was not a festive occasion. We left within two hours of arriving and were back at the hotel close to midnight. Now I was exhausted, but emotionally on a high. Some of the guys went out, but Teresa and I went back to our hotel room.

I celebrated quietly. I had seen enough people for the day. I did not sleep much that night because the noise from the streets never stopped. Cars were hooting and people seemed to be screaming non-stop. That night South Africa hosted one big party – and when I got home to Paarl the next day, the party was still going on. It lasted nearly a week in Paarl and I am sure it was the same all around the country.

A week later the players and their partners were invited to The Palace at the Lost City. It was to be a thank you for the efforts at the World Cup, but it turned into a weekend of contract talks and one that would change the course of the game forever.

That Saturday evening Pienaar saw all of us individually and presented us with World Rugby Corporation contracts. I was reluctant to sign anything because I did not deal with that part of the game. I was ignorant of contract details and always referred the commercial side of my game to my manager, Frikkie Erasmus, who acted as my agent, adviser and lawyer.

I had complete trust in Frikkie's judgment. He was the person who was going to plot my rugby career and now I was asked to make a call on my own. I was very uncomfortable with the way things had been done. Pienaar told me that it was standard practice and that every Bok had signed. Every player had been sworn to secrecy.

I told Pienaar that I would not talk to anyone other than Frikkie. He was not happy with my stance but told me I had to do what made me feel comfortable.

That weekend the players talked among themselves and, as players do, figures were discussed. When I heard what some guys had been offered in their contracts I began to question the thing even more. I had been offered substantially less than some of the players and I thought this was unfair.

I had been the biggest marketing tool for the team during the World Cup and that value alone should have counted for something. I had also been a test regular since 1994. I had been offered just over R2 million for three years. Other players were going to be contracted for more than R3 million. I had never done any of my own negotiating, but you did not have to be an agent or lawyer to question why one player would be offered R3 million and another a million less. We all played our part in winning the World Cup. But in the end, I signed.

When I got back to Cape Town I told Frikkie everything. He agreed that it did not sound right and called Pienaar. He demanded that the contract be torn up, something Pienaar said I was entitled to do if I wanted to change my mind. *

It was Frikkie's belief (based on what I told him) that I had been pressured into signing the contract and that I did not want to be a part of any breakaway organisation. Pienaar, reluctantly, agreed to destroy my contract. He was not happy and it put a strain on our relationship.

Pienaar has denied in his biography that there was any pressure on

* Francois Pienaar, in his biography Rainbow Warrior, confirms that Frikkie Erasmus did call him and that he destroyed Chester Williams's contract. Erasmus also wanted proof that the contract had been torn up. Pienaar denies there was any pressure on Williams to sign the contract.

In Rainbow Warrior, Pienaar writes: 'There was no form of coercion or peer pressure during the meetings. Chester Williams did ask if he could take a contract to show his lawyer, but I said we could not afford to jeopardise the secrecy of the venture by showing the document to anyone outside the squad, and I reminded him of his option to have the contract destroyed any time he wanted.

'The players showed admirable calm, discretion and patience through the days that followed with the exception of Chester Williams, who was persuaded by his lawyer and agent, Frikkie Erasmus, to have his contract destroyed.

Footnote continues on page 34

me to sign and claims this distanced me from the squad. In a sense I was always separate from the squad. Had Francois Pienaar been a black player in the Springbok set-up he would understand what I mean. Did Pienaar ever go down to breakfast first and have no one join him at the table? I doubt it. Was Pienaar's playing pedigree ever questioned on the basis of his colour? Never. Was Pienaar ever called a product of development, a quota player or a token? Never.

My decision not to sign with a rebel organisation was based on a gut feeling and on the advice of my manager and adviser. I was not comfortable with what happened after we had won the World Cup.

Winning the World Cup in 1995 may have unified the nation for a week. It did not change my standing within South African rugby. I was a black rugby player and that somehow separated me from the squad. It was not my request to have my rebel contract destroyed that separated me from the team.

Footnote continued from page 33

'Upon their request, I ripped up the document and threw it away, but Erasmus called back several days later and he insisted on coming from Cape Town to Johannesburg and actually seeing the destroyed pieces of contract. Fortunately, my dustbin had not been emptied during the intervening time, so I hunted among the rubbish and was able to deliver the morsels of document to him.'

Pienaar claims that Williams's decision had the effect of 'somehow separating him from the squad and this scarcely endeared him to the other players'.

Getting a game with my dad

4

I never felt aggrieved or angry in my youth. All that bothered me was that there seemed to be toilets only for whites in public

GROWN *men chasing a ball after dark, in an arena lit up by car headlights, and with no protection from the cold wind.*

Ask Chester Williams about his earliest rugby memory and the image is not one manufactured by television. Nor is it of crowded stands, hot chips, pies and the one-sided chant of 'Western Province' at Newlands. It also is not of the Springboks.

When he digs deep into the memory bank, Chester comes up with cold nights spent waiting at an open field for his father's rugby training to finish.

Chester was five, perhaps six, he says, when he and his brother Wilmot would watch grown men turn a piece of empty, lifeless field into a theatre of dreams for two hours, three times a week.

Disciplined, the two boys would sit in the car and watch. If it wasn't too cold, Chester and the older Wilmot would take up another vantage point, bums on the grass, quietly passing the time. Neither boy would run wild; it was not the done thing.

The boys had little fun. They were not at the side of the field by choice. Chester admits that if he had had his way he would have been at home long before nature's lights went out and the car lights went on.

Circumstance meant that on his way home from work, Wilfred

Williams would collect the two boys from their grandmother's house in Amstelhof, drive to rugby practice, put in the necessary training and then drive the boys home to Langvlei.

Rugby, said to be in the family genes on dad Wilfred's side and mom Julene's, held no romantic sway for young Chester. These were long hours spent away from home when he would rather be doing something else.

Wilfred was a respected rugby player having represented the Federation team against the Lions in 1974 and the French in 1975. Chester, aged four when the all-conquering Lions toured South Africa, has no recollection of going to the games. Neither does he remember watching his dad play against France.

Perhaps I was taken along. If so, it made no impression on me. There is no flashback ... no memory of me watching my dad in these big matches. It has often been said that I was born to play the game because of the genetic mix of rugby on both my parents' sides. My dad played at the highest level available to a coloured player in the 1970s, his younger brother Avril played test rugby for the Springboks in 1984 and my mom's brother, Adam Dombas, also excelled at the game and, like my father, played for the Federation. But I did not grow up with rugby in my blood as such.

I played at junior school, then did not play in my early high school years and only started getting a love for the game when I started playing near the end of my Standard Nine year, my second last year at high school at Klein Nederburg Secondary.

My parents put no pressure on me to play rugby. My father loved the game, had achieved a lot as a player, but never pushed me towards rugby. Whatever I did was my choice. I got the backing for everything I did, but there was never an expectancy that I would have to play rugby. It made things very easy for me.

Discipline, says Chester, was non-negotiable in the Williams household. And both parents shared a passion for schoolwork in the sense that a lack of effort on this front would never be excused.

At a young age Chester knew he did not want to follow his father professionally. Wilfred is a master builder. He has been one all his working life. Chester, in his school days, had a taste of the workingman's world. It was never going to be for him.

Early on he wanted to be a lawyer. He cannot explain why, but it seemed the kind of profession that would command respect from within the community. It would give him status. In those teenage schooling years he liked the notion of dressing in a tie and wearing a suit.

Playing rugby, at best, would be a hobby. Building houses was what his father did. And, much to young Chester's relief, at no stage did his father express a desire that the master builder become the master builder and son.

My brother and I helped my father during weekday evenings and on weekends when we had no other commitments. It was a way to earn pocket money and it was also a way of learning discipline and a work ethic at a young age. It gave me an appreciation of the effort that went into my dad's working day.

It also convinced me very quickly that I was not cut out for this kind of thing. I had to mix the cement and do whatever labourer jobs there were. Wilmot, because of his health, had the easier of the physical workload, even though he was still required to put in the hours at weekends.

We worked hard, but it was never a case of my dad grooming us to join the trade. He wanted both of us to do well at our studies and academically be successful. Wilmot was the cleverer of the two. He got the better grades and it was in him that the family invested when it came to an education after high school.

Rugby, in my young days, was something my dad played. I was not that interested in the game. My dad was a rugby player and that's where it ended. I had no heroes, I did not support Western Province or the Springboks. I did not keep scrapbooks or follow the big games closely.

I have never asked a rugby player for an autograph. As a youngster I had no desire to have sporting heroes. When I was in high school I did not even know who was playing for Province or the Springboks. It really didn't matter and even when I started taking an interest in the game, what mattered was the club, Paarl League and the Federation. I would watch the Federation matches before I would want to watch any other team.

I was once a ball-boy at a Federation match and all I can remember is Wilfred Cupido, who would later play for WP League and Western Province, almost running over me. I had been sitting too close to the sidelines and was given a good talking to afterwards.

I think that was it for me as a ball-boy and despite my attempt at getting closer to the game, my interest wasn't great. Rugby was something people did for fun and something to do; not something I longed to do.

When I was 14, my uncle Avril got selected for the Springboks. It was on this day that I started to appreciate just what it meant to be picked for South Africa. Avril had come around to our house in Paarl for photographs. There were a lot of people from the community arriving unannounced to congratulate him. Everybody wanted their photo taken with him. It was a massive thing in our community and only in later years would I fully understand why.

Coloured and black players, ordinarily, were just not selected for the Springboks. I don't think it was ever written anywhere that black players had to be excluded. In apartheid South Africa it was taken as a fact that they would not play in the main white teams.

I never got a lesson in the history of the game or the politics associated with the game because my dad rarely spoke about it. He would talk about the joys of playing rugby and that is where it ended. There were no hard-luck stories, resentment or anti-white speeches. He played for Paarl League and the Federation and loved his rugby. Everyone spoke highly of him and he was popular at the club.

Our relationship was such that until recently we did not speak deeply about issues or life in general. We had a solid relationship but we were not as close as we are now. I did not question things. I accepted life the way it was, did not complain because I wanted for very little by way of love, support and wealth.

I knew we were not wealthy by definition, but there was always food on our table, we stayed in a house my dad had built and my basic needs were always looked after. As children we did not seek what we knew wasn't possible. There were no outrageous requests for things. My mom was there to bring comfort to our needs and my dad was there as head of the home – a provider who worked long hours and was respected within the community.

Alcohol was not banned in our house – my parents just did not drink. Because of this, we didn't drink. In magazine and newspaper articles, my family has been described as very religious, but this has created the impression that I come from a household in which religion dominated. It isn't true. Religion was part of the basic make-up. Mutual respect and basic family values were how we lived and that meant that religion was practised too.

It was nothing excessive and my parents don't drink because they have no desire to drink. It has nothing to do with religion. I hardly drink and while I can down a pint of beer in the blink of an eye, I don't like beer. I hate the taste of it and that's perhaps why I downed the things so fast during the team sessions in my playing days. By knocking it back fast I had no real chance of tasting it.

Indirectly, the family value system was passed down, which was both a positive and a negative. On the negative side, I rarely questioned things in life. I was grateful for what I had and I had been taught to work harder to achieve any kind of success. It was not good to judge others or to question the motives of others. We were a simple family, who saw the good in others and never took pity on the political situation or whatever restrictions there were with being black.

I remember thinking how odd the system was that we could only ride third class on the trains with the whites the only ones allowed in first class. Seeing signs that read 'Whites only' for toilets and beaches was something that puzzled me as a teenager. It all seemed wrong. Did I question it? Not a chance.

I accepted it and worked harder to be a decent person. Did I think about it? A lot of the time, but when I was growing up ours was not a family where you talked about these things. We didn't and still don't talk about the death of my sister or brother. There is the odd photographic reminder in my parents' house, but very little else. Perhaps it is because of the hurt and the sadness. I don't know. I have never asked my father. Our relationship is much stronger these days. We are more open with each other. Some subjects, though, still don't get touched.

Politically, I grew up oblivious to what had happened with the introduction of the Group Areas Act. My father, a young man with a young family, was kicked out of his home. My mom was pregnant with me when it happened. All he could afford at that time was rent in Magnolia Flats, an area where the gangster life was convenient and the daily grind was hard. My younger days were spent there. Funnily enough, my memories are not bad. Somehow you adapt, settle in and get on with things.

I felt loved as a young boy and that was enough. I had my mom and I had my dad, who was building the house my parents still live in today. I had no complaints, but I also knew that I didn't want to live in Paarl all my life. There was a bigger world that I wanted to explore.

There was something mystical about the way car headlights lit up a field and grown men took on the persona of schoolboys in their enthusiasm for running around for a few hours. But there was something also wrong with the fact that car headlights had to act as floodlights. I couldn't articulate it in my youth but there was always an uncomfortable feeling that it was not all right.

I never confronted the issues because I was never confronted with the reality of these issues. No one ever physically assaulted me, I never felt aggrieved or angry because of the actions of whites towards me in my youth. All that bothered me was that there seemed to be toilets only for whites in public. Where did we (coloureds) go if we felt the need to go?

Whites were not foreign to me. My dad did a lot of work for whites and there were many occasions when I went with him to earn some pocket money. I did not feel out of place in their homes. They acted like we did. Their mannerisms were the same and they, I assumed, experienced the same emotions as any coloured family.

My father was well liked by the people he worked for. They treated him with respect and he never spoke negatively about whites. The black and white thing was not an issue for me because all I knew was the simplicity of we lived here and they lived somewhere else.

That was fine, but it was the public-toilet thing that I could still not get my head around: 'Whites only?'

Despite the unanswered question, more prominent political incidents failed to trigger a deeper political consciousness in Chester.

Even violence, panic and death did not sear themselves into the young psyche, as did the simple question of where a coloured boy goes to pee when out in public.

With difficulty Chester dredged up two memories of the political climate in which he grew up.

I don't have any recollections of my parents discussing the political situation or of consciously joining the fight against the social and racial injustice prevalent in apartheid South Africa. I may be doing them a disservice and it could be that they did wage their own war, but believed it right not to shatter our world with the reality of theirs.

If I have got it wrong, Mom and Dad, I apologise. I also thank you for not crushing my world as a youngster when, despite our daily struggles, life still felt very good for me and home will always be home.

When I do think back to my early childhood, two incidents related to the political situation in South Africa stand out. The first involved our family, in particular my mom. The year was 1976, a time well documented because of the continuing uprisings by black people and the riots against the white militant order that ruled the country.

I have this image of my mother running from the police and army, being chased in the direction of our flat. She had been part of a large group of protesters who were stoning the police and army. This took place not far from our flat in Magnolia.

Magnolia, as I explained previously, was a poor place. Crime was not that rampant there because crime lived there. Gangsters dominated large sections of the area and because of the social circumstance in the area, if there was going to be trouble you would find it in Magnolia. Still today, it is sad to see the kind of poverty and ruin in the area.

The rioting had attracted everyone's attention in the Flats. I remember seeing burning tyres, flames and lots of smoke. The smell was also very unpleasant. The tyres were scattered across the streets like movie props, but this was real life.

My mom had been part of the stone-throwing and was being chased by the police. She ran in our direction, towards the flat. My dad was standing outside the flat, holding my little sister in one of his arms, my brother and I were standing next to him and he was motionless. All he could do was watch and see if she would make it.

I won't forget the look on both their faces when my mom made it to our flat. It was one of panic and shock. My dad hurried us all inside, amid the chaos of people running, police assaulting people and tyres burning.

Once inside, my parents quickly composed themselves, got us cleaned up and sent us straight to bed. The incident was not spoken about in front of us. It was never mentioned and, thankfully, I never again witnessed the sight of my mother in flight from the police. I was six years old at the time.

The other incident involved the killing of a close friend, gunned down by police in front of Chester's grandmother's house. Chester, 16 at the time, has no idea what his friend had done and whether it was mere coincidence that it had happened on his grandmother's doorstep.

Neil Moses, a friend since primary school at Nederburg in Paarl, had joined the political struggle against apartheid. As Neil's fight intensified, so too did the friendship with Chester drift apart. The two friends, inseparable as children, had become distant as teenagers in high school. Chester stayed clear of the politics. Neil did not. It would cost him his life.

We lived in the same street. We were always together in primary school. We were the best of friends at one stage. Then he changed and started to get involved with another group of friends. He had his friends and I had mine. We just got on with life, played our street cricket, messed around and steered clear of anything vaguely political.

Neil and I would talk every day when we bumped into each other on the street, but we had become distant. We did not share any deep secrets or hang out together any more. Then one day he was dead, shot in front of my grandmother's house. I don't know how it happened, or why he was shot. No one seemed to know.

A few days later Neil was buried. He was one year younger than I was. I was one of the pall-bearers. Strangely, I did not show a lot of emotion that day. It somehow did not seem real or perhaps I was not able to grasp what had happened. My sister had died some time before that and I had also not shown much emotion. I just got on with my life. I would do the same after Neil's death.

Rugby would creep slowly into Chester's life after Neil's death and the rugby field would be a place where he would find as much solace as he would experience pleasure.

In his formative years, however, rugby was secondary to the more intense and highly competitive street cricket league. Chester admits he was not an influential player, but he was a regular in the 'Rebels' team.

Nearly every day there would be a game. One street would challenge the next. We played anywhere and everywhere. We played on open fields, in alleys and mostly in the streets. You simply did not get beaten in your own street and you toured the neighbourhood playing against the best the other streets had to offer.

It was very competitive and while I was not a great player, I enjoyed the fact that we never played 'leg before wicket' when batting. It was one of the few luxuries I can remember as a batsman.

My friend Thinus Linee was the star. He was good at everything, cricket, rugby, telling stories and meeting girls. Thinus, even though he attended a different high school, was one of my closest friends. He was already a hero to the people when he was a schoolboy. He had all the confidence in the world. It never surprised me that he played more than 100 matches for Western Province and also got picked to represent the Springboks. He deserved to play test rugby, although his career high would be that of a midweek Springbok.

When we were kids our daily routine was very basic. Be home at 5pm so that when your dad arrived he could see you, say hello and make sure you weren't hanging out with the gangsters. You were then allowed to continue playing with your friends, but had to be home at 7pm for dinner. The older I got, the more relaxed the 5pm clock-in time became. I was allowed to stretch it a bit. I think it was because my parents knew that if Thinus was not at our house, then I was at his.

The neighbourhood in which Chester felt secure as a batsman in street cricket and first class as a citizen has not changed much. Chester goes there often and the faces are still familiar, if older. He stops whenever he can, chats and relives the school days and the street cricket.

I might have always dreamed of improving myself and experiencing more than my hometown, but it will always be home to me. I go there as often as I can, stop off at my parents' place, have a chat and occasionally a meal.

Sometimes I will stop off at an old school friend who still lives in the neighbourhood, take some beers and chat a bit. I don't drink the beer, but I will always give some of my time. I know I am different. I drive an expensive car and I live in a bigger house in a more affluent suburb. I have achieved a lot of things and because of my rugby profile I am easily recognised wherever I go. But I never forget where I came from.

Chester says he drives past his old primary school in Paarl once a week when he is in Cape Town. He has regularly given motivational talks to pupils of both the primary and high schools. Why the ritual? He offers no explanation, but the bond of a youth spent in Paarl is obviously one he does not want to keep just to himself.

I like to talk to the children. It is as if I am giving something back. I am always more emotional when it comes to talking to the little ones. I look at them and I see incredible poverty and the faces of children confronted daily with a hard life. I try to tell them that things can change if you are prepared to work hard and believe in yourself. I sat at the same old desk on the same old chair in an asbestos classroom. You can get out and experience something better. I am living proof of it.

Getting out of it, though, does not imply forgetting it. Chester's parents still live in the only house Chester knew between the ages of six and 18, when he enlisted in the navy and moved out. Since then, he has travelled the world, stayed in the most expensive hotels, dined with influential leaders and shaken the hand of royalty on more than one occasion. Rugby has taken Chester Williams to the greatest stadiums and into battle against the best in the game.

Rugby also gave him a moment that money could not – playing alongside his father in a club match.

There are three matches that Chester lists as his most significant: his test debut, the World Cup final and a club match he played when only 17 years old. What distinguishes this club game from any other is that it was the only time Chester played a match alongside his father. The deeper meaning of the occasion will never be forgotten.

One of the centres for Paarl League did not pitch up. I was 17 and my dad asked if I was prepared to play. I said yes without hesitation. How many children get to play a competitive match with their father?

It would be the only time we would play a match together. We nearly won that day, but the result is not what I took from the game. It was the hardness in approach that my dad displayed, especially towards me.

He watched as I stood up for myself and took the fight to guys a lot older and bigger. I knew he was there, but he wanted me to do it on my own.

There was just one occasion when he intervened, but it was not to have a go at an opponent. It was to get the best out of me. I scored a try and I got a knee in my back immediately afterwards. I lay there in pain. I couldn't get up. My dad ran over, pulled me up and told me in no uncertain terms to get on with it. I played the whole game in pain, but certainly not prepared to tell anyone.

I thought I played well. The team told me I had done everything I could have. My dad nodded his approval. There was an acceptance that I had never felt before then.

Afterwards, my dad announced his retirement. His reason: me. He told his teammates in the dressing-room: 'When you line up in the same team as your son then you know it is time to go.'

It was a lighthearted moment, but the words had the necessary impact on Chester. His dad had handed over the family rugby baton. Still, there was no pressure on Chester to run with it.

How James Small got me back to rugby

5

'You fucking kaffir … why do you want to play our game? You know you can't play it' – James Small to Chester Williams in a Currie Cup match

FOR *most of his time at high school Chester Williams stayed away from rugby. He loved the game and he watched it, but because of the great political divisions in his community, playing rugby was just not worthwhile.*

For Chester to add another chapter to the Williams family's rugby history in the Federation would mean sacrifices: he would be condemned at school as a sell-out, of being part of the oppressive and resented 'system'. It was better not to play at all.

Chester might have been politically unaware, but he lived in a part of South Africa that was deeply politicised. Outside of the comfortable white suburbs of Paarl, the politics of resistance were strong. During the uprisings of 1960 and 1976, Paarl's townships were among the national flashpoints. Political education might not have been officially on the curriculum of black and coloured schools, but there were none too subtle political lessons that were taught, often at the end of a cane.

Those teaching politics to the children of the oppressed saw it as an essential role in fighting 'the system' because 'the system' could be cunning as well as cruel. Black people, and especially young ones talented in sport, would be cynically manipulated to give the outside world the impression that apartheid South Africa was really a kind and uplifting place of racial harmony.

White South African society, rigidly separated from their fellow countrymen by years of prejudice and laws, was not ready to share the spoils but they could always give the appearance of doing so. They needed to project an image of sharing to the outside world. The ruling class, while not willing to live or play with their darker fellow South Africans nevertheless co-opted groups of them to give apartheid a semblance of legitimacy. At a governing level, the tribal homelands were cast as independent states of a commonwealth and the tri-cameral parliament was a futile attempt at democracy in action. On a recreational level, groups of black South Africans were lured into a compromise of mixed sport.

It was also a classic case of divide and rule and the South African Rugby Federation, for whom Chester's family played, was an example of this.

There had been divisive squabbling among black rugby authorities and, given the wink and a nod by the apartheid government, the white SA Rugby Board began to woo the Federation. The reason for this courting was that sports isolation was beginning to harm apartheid society.

The pressure exerted by the South African Non-Racial Olympic Committee on countries to boycott apartheid sport had started to have an effect. In the sixties South Africa was banned from the Olympics and international soccer, in 1970 the country was banned from test cricket and although rugby somehow survived for a while longer, visits by touring teams to the country were becoming fewer. After the demonstrations against the Springbok rugby team in Britain during the tour of 1969/70, there were also few places willing to host South African sports teams.

To overcome this growing hostility of the outside world, the establishment sports bodies and the government collaborated. If the Federation could be persuaded to throw in its lot with the SA Rugby Board, it would give the impression of multi-racial rugby. The president of the Federation, Cuthbert Loriston, saw it as an opportunity for his players to go beyond the organisation's parochial boundaries. For the president of the SA Board, Danie Craven, it was a useful political tool to impress the foreigners. To the president of the SA Rugby Union, Abdullah Abbass, it was a sell-out.

SARU had huge support among the non-racial sports bodies, unified under the South African Council for Sport (SACOS). This group would fight apartheid in sport at many levels, including the classrooms.

Chester's high school, Klein Nederburg Secondary, was run by teachers who were aligned to the non-racial fold. They saw their role as uncompromising commissars who would fight off the attempts by apartheid propagandists to recruit their youth.

It was in this political maelstrom that a teenage Chester Williams found himself in the turbulent eighties when the country was in the grip of a national uprising and the worst oppression in South Africa's history.

The decision to play rugby was not a simple one. If Chester decided to play for the Federation, he would incur the wrath of his teachers and even run the risk of being ostracised at school. If he played for SARU, he would break a strong family tradition.

It was better not to play at all, but the temptation remained and often Chester would sneak away and play a social game with some of the white kids. He saw it as just some fun; the commissars saw it as insubordination and on the Monday morning at school he would pay for it. After such games, Chester's Monday would invariably start with a caning for 'being a system and allowing himself to be turned on and off by the whites'.

The Williams family's tradition with the Federation was strong, however. Chester's father Wilfred played for the Federation at fullback, centre, flank and No 8. His uncle Avril went one better and was selected for the Springboks in 1984 against John Scott's England team.

Then in late 1987 all this changed for Chester. It was the year of the first Rugby World Cup. The Springboks were not invited, but rugby was the global talking-point. Interest was strong, even in isolated South Africa and the event would charm most rugby people, including those of Paarl. It would also force Chester into making a decision about his life and introduce him to the talents of James Small.

A few years later he would experience first hand the complexities of Small, as opponent and provincial and international teammate, but on this occasion he would only marvel at the man's rugby virtuosity.

The Craven Week (national high schools tournament) had everyone talking and even though I was not playing rugby I went to watch. That week I knew that I had to start playing regularly. Watching those guys play made me realise how much I wanted to be on the field. I also knew I was better than a lot of what I saw.

I had to make a decision about whether it would be with the Federation or SARU. Once I had convinced myself the time to play was right, it was always going to be with the Federation. It was a decision based on what had gone before me in the family. There was no political motivation in my decision.

Thinus Linee, Chester's good friend, was playing for Western Province League at the time. Black players of the Federation were not selected for the Western Province Schools team. The latter was exclusively white, as was the national schools side in those days. The black players of the

Western Cape represented either Western Province League or Boland League, teams made up almost exclusively of coloured players.

The visit to the Craven Week would encourage Chester to start playing seriously in 1988. It would also introduce him to South Africa's most controversial Springbok rugby player of the post-1992 era.

Thinus's match at the Craven Week had ended and later in the day we watched Transvaal. This guy came on as a substitute for Transvaal, wearing a No 17 jersey. He was the star of the match. He caught the ball, kicked it a long way, made tackles and ran hard. He was also very fast.

He played fullback and after the match everyone was talking about him. Everyone around me seemed convinced that he would become a Springbok great. His name was James Small and his personality dominated that match. I was very impressed with his performance.

The two would meet for the first time as players in 1993 when Chester played for Western Province against Natal, but six years earlier Small had entertained Chester with his footballing talents. It was the last time Chester would regard Small as purely a footballer.

James and I kept our distance on my first Bok tour in 1993. We rarely spoke and we never had a discussion of any substance. It was early days in transformation, both in rugby and in South African society. The first democratic elections were still a year away and 1993 in the Bok team might as well have been 1973. Thinus (Linee) and I were the only black players in the touring party to Australia. We were not treated poorly and there was no obvious hostility aimed at us. Clearly, though, we were black and that made us different.

I just wanted to play rugby. It was a great opportunity for me. Thinus and I had toured Australia and New Zealand earlier in the year with Western Province and I loved Australia. The people treated us with respect, spoke to us as if we were their equals and made us feel very welcome.

When I returned with the Boks I just wanted to justify my inclusion in the team and show the sceptics that I could play rugby. I loved the rugby we played on the tour, scored some tries and felt that I was making the necessary improvement to be a contender for the test team.

I think James and Jacques Olivier felt the pressure as the tour progressed. At the start of the tour they were the test wingers. I was there making up the numbers. They were aware of me, especially because I was playing well in the midweek side and scoring tries. I got the feeling they at first thought I was there in '93 because of the colour

With young friends and an older brother... *Chester Williams, aged five, third from the left, and brother Wilmot on the right.*

Friends and comrades? *Not exactly... Chester Williams embraced by James Small, but there was no love lost between the two. On the left are fellow Springbok wings Deon Oosthuizen in the raincoat and Jacques Olivier.*

A different game... *Chester tries his hand at golf during a break on tour.*

Backroom Bok men... *Morne du Plessis (middle) and Kitch Christie (right) watch with hands in their pockets. The manager and the coach were crucial to the Springboks' success at the World Cup in 1995.*

OPPOSITE TOP: **A farewell to arms...** *Chester Williams's final appearance in the green and gold, against the British Barbarians at Cardiff's Millennium Stadium in 2000.*

OPPOSITE MIDDLE: **A terrible test...** *Chester's only test match at Newlands – against England in 1994 – was marked by a poor performance – and concussion. Chester went off on a stretcher, but at least the Boks won to square the series.*

OPPOSITE BOTTOM: **A try to remember...** *With Welsh scrumhalf Rupert Moon his back, Chester scores at Cardiff Arms Park in 1994 to make the test safe. Chester regards this try as his most memorable.*

RIGHT: **Race against a rival...** *Chester, in the colours of Western Province, running against Jeff Wilson of Otago in a match at Newlands.*

Photos: Touchline Photo

Photos: Touchline Photo

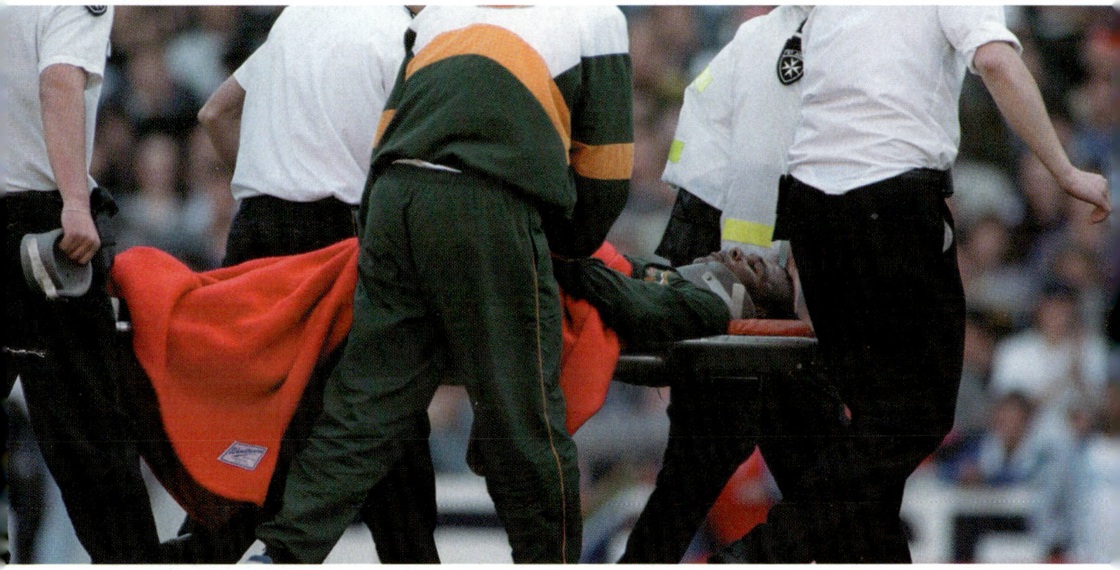

Photos: Touchline Photo

Twickenham touchdown... *Scoring a try against England in 1995, a year when the Springboks beat every top rugby country in the world. Behind Chester, saluting the score, is teammate Kobus Wiese.*

World Cup triumph... *at the end of the final in 1995 after the Boks had beaten New Zealand to win the World Cup. Chester is nowhere to be seen and photographs of him from this match, for some reason, are rare.*

of my skin, but they soon realised that I was a genuine threat to their wing positions.

The two of them were good mates and they hung out together. Jacques was the quieter of the two and very relaxed in his approach. James was all about James. I saw it in 1993, experienced it on the tours after that and even in his last few weeks in the Cats squad (in 1999). It was clear that all that mattered to James Small was James Small and not the team. For him it was never about the team.

On the 1993 tour to Australia, as with most of our tours, we hardly spoke.

It was this lack of communication that puzzled Chester the most. He accepted that the two of them would never be mates off the field, but he found it a struggle coming to terms with the fact that they could not be teammates.

Rugby is a team game. You play for each other. I always found James to be a player who played only for himself. Whatever he did had to suit him first. The team's needs were secondary. Because of this James also had a dominant influence on the Bok teams in which he played. He ran the show in the early days. He did as he pleased, especially in 1993 under Ian McIntosh. And he controlled the younger players, who were in awe of him and even afraid of him.

James does not lack confidence, but he is very manipulative and if he spots a weakness he will take over. Kitch Christie killed that dominance when he replaced McIntosh as Bok coach in 1994. Kitch was the first coach, at national level, to control James Small.

Small's personality, which Chester admits he never understood, did not allow for anyone else to take the podium, let alone share it with him. It is Chester's contention that Small resented his success and his following with the fans.

He hated it when I scored, or did something good on the field. It was as if he took it personally. He never said 'Well done' to me when I scored. It really used to upset him.

No team-like celebrations? No nod of approval or a handshake? 'Nothing,' says Chester. And he can laugh at it now.

You have no idea how much he disliked any success I might have had. It is weird. You had to be in the room to appreciate it. There has always been a distance. Even now. We were never friends and are not now.

Not long ago I was driving to George. A car passed me and I saw it was James. Now I am not the easiest guy to miss in a car. He glanced at me and just kept on driving. I chased after him because I wanted to greet him. He had been going through some difficulties that had been splashed in the press and I wanted to say 'Hi'.

He refused to acknowledge my waving. He turned off at a garage and I pulled up behind him. He refused to budge. He did not even look up. I got out of the car and walked over to his car window. Only then did he get out. It was a very strained conversation.

The on-the-field banter between the two, kept to a minimum, also reached bizarre levels, as Chester explains.

The last test we played together was against England at Twickenham in 1995. He was dropped for the test, but got on as a replacement. That day I scored two tries and had one disallowed. When I crossed for my second try, he got really upset that I had scored instead of passing the ball to him. As I was running back from scoring, he yelled: 'Fuck it, why didn't you pass?'

There was never a word of congratulations from him. Not on the field and not in the dressing-room afterwards. At Twickenham that day, I just ignored it and carried on running back. For him it was about breaking the record for tries. It was not about who else scored.

Provincially, the two men played against one another on only a few occasions, but each time the match was marred by controversy.

In 1994, Chester was playing for Western Province and he scored a try against Natal at Newlands. Small tackled him after Chester had touched down and the Newlands crowd turned on Small.

He certainly had decided that he was not going to waste the time he had spent in getting across to me, so he put in a dive after I had scored. I half expected it.

Some of the Newlands crowd at that end invaded the in-goal area and jumped on James's back. At one point during this fracas I thought someone was stabbing him, but it turned out to be only a piece of paper in someone's hands that looked like a knife.

He was furious and screaming. After the final whistle I went to shake his hand. He didn't want to take my hand. Instead, he wanted to fight with me in the tunnel area. I asked him what his problem was. He was very aggressive. His teammates took him away.

The next time the two opposed one other at provincial level, Chester left on a stretcher after colliding with Small's knee in chasing an up-and-under kick. It wasn't the collision that further soured the relationship. Television footage, replayed several times after the match, showed Small appearing to trample Chester's head.

Small, through the media, denied any malice and said he had lost his footing and was trying to find his balance. Chester dismisses the explanation as absurd.

I have watched the replay many times. If that was an attempt to find his balance, he has a funny way of doing it. Finding his balance that day was running on one spot, which just happened to be my head.

There was an up-and-under kick. I wanted to jump for the ball, but realised I was not going to get there. I didn't jump. He was already up in the air. My head connected his knee. I went down immediately. He came down on my head.

He obviously realised I was on the ground and he started to trample on me. The video shows how bizarre his claim was of finding his balance. Several blokes told me afterwards he had boasted about trampling on my head. It did not surprise me.

We never spoke about the incident. He never phoned to ask how I was. Then again, we hardly ever spoke. Even when we played test rugby, provincial and Super 12 rugby for the same team, discussion between us was limited. Before each game, without fail, I would go to him in the dressing-room and say 'Cover my back and I will cover yours'. I did this to ensure that our cover defence would be solid and to be sure that neither of us would be caught out of position. It was a ritual that I had for every match, regardless of who my wing teammate was. James would just stare at me without giving a response.

It never used to bother me. It used to baffle me because who knows what was going through his mind. All I know is we never clicked.

People may wonder why I devoted this space to James. The answer is two-fold. That day when I saw him play at Paarl in the Craven Week was hugely significant in my rugby career. It was the week in which I knew I wanted to play this game, and play it for a living. A young James Small helped me make that decision.

And the public seemed to connect James and I. Throughout my playing career I was asked one question constantly: 'What do you think of James Small? Are the two of you friends?' I never answered it. Now I have.

James and I never found a space where we could connect. I saw a teenage fullback carve up defences at the Craven Week in Paarl. That day in 1987 I admired his talent. I would never again feel the same way about James Small.

'You fucking kaffir ... why do you want to play our game?' screamed James Small at Chester Williams during a match between Natal and Western Province. 'You know you can't play it.'

That obscenity on the field did not shock me; I had been called the k-word many times in my rugby life. It was standard practice in most matches I played in the early 1990s and James had a reputation for being abusive and vocal on the field.

If I was going to let racial abuse get to me, then I was never going to succeed as a black rugby player in South Africa. The racial taunts were expected. If anything upset me it was the ignorant and arrogant belief that the game belonged to whites and that the black community had no right to show an interest in the game, let alone play it.

Robert du Preez, playing scrumhalf for Natal against Western Province that day, also had a go at me. He was another who saw my participation as an intrusion into a zone marked 'Whites only'.

On that day I put it down to psychological tactics. I didn't want to categorise any player as a racist and I also did not want to condemn an opponent for what they might well have believed was gamesmanship.

Yet six years later, any doubts I might have had about Du Preez's attitude were dispelled when he entered the Lions dressing-room after we had won through to the final of the Currie Cup.

Du Preez, representing the team sponsor, congratulated every Lions player personally. He walked straight past me. There was no handshake and not a word spoken to me. Six years on and, clearly to some, a black man had no place in South African rugby.

Race and the political shadow it cast were the two main reasons why I started playing rugby so late. The game was always close to me.

But the politics within our community scared me as a schoolboy. Politically, I was not very active. In fact, I am embarrassed to admit that politically I was very naïve in that I never had an appreciation of the magnitude of the struggle against apartheid.

I could also not understand why most of the coloured community in Paarl was so outraged that coloured people could willingly play with the white people and still allow themselves to be treated as second-rate citizens. I never considered myself second rate. We were a good, God-fearing family with honest values and a healthy respect for others.

We are a proud family and I delighted in all my father's achievements. In my eyes he had been successful. He had achieved all that a coloured player could at the time. He had made the SA Federation team and experienced international rugby.

In apartheid South Africa of the 1970s, blacks (and by that I classify any person not white) did not qualify to play for the Springboks. It had nothing to do with ability. Your colour classification would determine the level at which you played. Naïvely, I looked on my situation as a budding rugby player and not as a black citizen of this country.

The battles at school became very aggressive between those who aligned themselves with the South African Rugby Union and those who played under the SA Rugby Federation banner, the latter being part of the white South African Rugby Board.

My father had always been a Federation man. It was assumed that I would play Federation rugby. In that sense I was sheltered from being at the forefront of such rugby-related political battles. Those at school with me who were in the SARU camp knew about my father's standing in the Federation and at least they seemed to accept that I would be a Federation player. Very few of them ever confronted me, or challenged me politically. In that sense I was also protected from the realities of South African life as a black kid.

Frankly, for most of my senior school years, I steered clear of the fights and debates by opting not to play at all. Deep down I just wanted to play rugby, but it was not that simple. If you played for SARU, you automatically aligned yourself with the struggle against white supremacy. If you played for the Federation, you faced being labelled a sell-out.

Those who played for the Federation were called 'systems', the accusation being that the whites turned us on and off when they felt like it. It was an insult on a par with any four-letter word.

At the time I just couldn't get it. Rugby was only a game. I was very innocent in those days. A decade later I would regret not having been more politically active and not having resisted a rugby system that was cruel to the black player. Rugby in apartheid South Africa was a carbon copy of life in apartheid South Africa.

When I made the Springbok team in 1993 and played in the 1995 World Cup it seemed fashionable to brand me as this symbol of hope in South Africa. I was supposedly an example of what could be achieved by a black rugby player. But when I played my first test in 1993, for every person who supported me in my community there was one who detested me because they said I had sold my soul for the right to play with the whites.

I was never a symbol of black hope. I never saw myself as this. Before rugby unity there was not a widespread acceptance in the coloured community of my decision to play for the Federation.

I was a guy who loved rugby, was fortunate to be able to play it and wanted to play against the best in the world. To achieve this I had to play for the Springboks and that meant aligning myself with the

Federation. I am a rugby man and not a politician. However, 10 years of playing rugby in South Africa has made me realise what it means to be black in this country.

My story is not one of an under-privileged coloured boy who made it good. It is of a rugby player, of a young boy who dreamed of playing for his country once he had got a taste of rugby. All I ever wanted to be was a Springbok rugby player. All I ever was in South Africa was a black rugby player.

Four years after playing in a winning World Cup final I was excluded from a second World Cup because the coach, Nick Mallett, said he 'had enough quota players'. That remark hurt me. It shattered a belief that my performances in 1995 and thereafter had broken down prejudice and changed mindsets. All I ever wished for was to be judged on my playing talent.

The marketing men conveniently branded me a product of development and a sign of change in South African rugby. Nothing could have been more of a lie. I wasn't a pioneer. Other black players had been Springboks before me, one of them in my own family. More have followed me. They know the vibe. They have felt it and they have been demoralised by it.

All I ever was – and it was all I ever wanted to be – was a rugby player. It is my prayer that the next generation of South African black rugby players will be granted this. The game belongs to all South Africans. We have a right to play this wonderful game and we know how to play it.

Losing a brother

6

That night they told me I was going to play my first test was as much a celebration of Wilmot's dream as it was mine

WILMOT was the Williams family's favourite. He was, according to Chester, the good-looking one. The intelligent one. The stronger one. The popular one.

'My parents will never admit it, but every family has a favourite and in ours it was Wilmot,' says Chester. 'I don't mean it in a jealous way. The first-born usually has that advantage.'

Born first, even if only a year earlier, Wilmot always had the edge on his younger sibling. Everyone loved Wilmot. And Chester loved it that his older brother was who he was. Two brothers, both blessed with athleticism, in one family.

The rivalry should have been intense. It never was; the younger brother was too in awe of the elder one ever to want to compete. Instead, he would join the admiring queue. Resentment was never an issue. Wilmot's humility, despite his popularity, inspired his younger brother to want to be like him. Beating him was never a consideration; big brother was there as a motivation.

I admired everything he did because he was so successful. He captained every team he played in at primary school. He played for the provincial junior schoolboys rugby team. He was bigger than I was, better than I was and more skilled on a rugby field than I was. He even had my dad's good looks.

A defective heart valve ended Wilmot's rugby career before he got to high school. The setback was a minor irritation to Wilmot. His character continued to blossom even though his sporting ambition had been forced into retirement.

Wilmot applied himself to his studies, excelled in the classroom and comfortably made the transition from high school boy to a driven university scholar who was studying for his law degree at the University of the Western Cape.

The brothers remained close throughout their high school years, although their interests were no longer similar. Chester, having decided to play rugby in his last years of high school, knew he had the support of his brother. He did not know he had also earned the admiration of the brother he had idolised all his life.

He never spoke much to me about my rugby or athletics achievements. He was as supportive as everyone else in the family, but he never praised me or told me how good I was. He was always happy for me when I did well, but he never made me feel as if I was anything special.

At the same time, I never asked him what he thought of my ability as a rugby player. It always seemed inappropriate to want to talk about how good he was or how good I was.

Chester, having completed school, enlisted in the Defence Force. The decision had little to do with a belief that he had to keep the country's borders safe from whatever the propagandists said was going to threaten apartheid South Africa. It was a means to financial and job security. It meant an income and a way into the sophisticated and plush rugby structures. It also eased the financial burden on the family because part of Chester's monthly salary paid for Wilmot's university education.

Soon after school in 1989, Chester joined the navy, if only because that was where his uncle Avril had gone. But a fear of water, claustrophobia and a lack of rugby-playing opportunities soon persuaded him to change to the army. He was posted to the South African Coloured Corps in Eerste River, an infantry unit with battle honours which is now the Ninth SA Infantry Battalion. While he was a stores corporal there, he ran into his old friend Thinus Linee again. Linee was a drill instructor. Chester stayed in uniform until 1993 when he stepped back into civilian life. Life in uniform was not what Chester had in mind as a career, but it helped pay the bills.

Between Chester and his father Wilfred, Wilmot's financial commitments were met. It allowed the elder brother to focus on his studies – and the results were always pleasing to the family.

Chester's rise to prominence as a rugby player was rapid. In his first year of playing at high school he won provincial colours. But apartheid's discrimination meant that he could not be selected for the national schools team. Instead, Elmo Wolfaardt and Dan Hall were picked in 1988 as the country's best schoolboy centres. The coloured combination of Chester Williams and Thinus Linee had to settle for the South African Project XV – a kind of consolation prize handed out by the white rugby establishment.

Wilmot was pleased for his little brother, but never expressed an opinion on Chester's potential as a rugby player.

I always believed that Wilmot never wanted me to get a big head, so he rather said nothing. For all his academic achievements, he was very humble. And even though he was the family favourite, he never made me feel inferior because of it. It made me feel really good that part of my salary was going towards his university education.

I was playing a small part in his world. It made me feel important to him and that was a good enough feeling. I never wanted anything in return.

Then one day I was looking for something in his room. I saw his university satchel lying on the ground and when I went to move it, the black-ink writing caught my eye. What I read will stay with me forever. Thinking about it makes me feel as if I had read it a minute ago. It is that clear. Wilmot had written: 'Chester is the best centre. One day he will become a Springbok.'

I could not believe it. I stood there for a long time and read it again and again. It was the greatest gift he could have given me. It seemed as if he was carrying around my dream. He believed in my dream as much as I did.

I never mentioned it to him. He never said anything to me. I felt so proud that day and it is a pride I feel every time I think about that moment in my life. To know that my big brother, the guy I hero-worshipped, believed I was that good. It was the most unbelievable feeling. When I read that, I knew I would become a Springbok. There was no way I was going to fail. But Wilmot never got to see me play as a Springbok. Just 23 days before the Christmas of 1990 he died. He was only 21.

It left a void in my life. It was all so sudden. My family was shattered. I was stunned. My brother was there one evening and when I woke up the next morning he was gone forever.

Privately, I cried a lot. In my heart, I cried most of the time that year. Still today the sadness is there. It never leaves you. But I had to be strong. I had to take over his role. Now I had to be the big brother and be the one to look after my mother; to be there for my father.

Being in the army at that stage made it a bit easier. Physically, I worked my body to escape the pain. I was in a tough environment and there were days when I was too exhausted to think about what had happened.

I was not staying at home full-time, moving between the army, (my uncle) Avril's house in Strandfontein, which was close to work, and my parents' place in Paarl. Because of this I was not confronted with the family's emptiness every day. It made it more bearable because I determined when I would think about his death. Had I been at home every day in those first few months, it would have been a lot more difficult to handle.

I knew what my family was going through. The effect is still there today. That night our family lost something very big. Wilmot could never be replaced. I celebrate his birthday in my own way every year. I acknowledge the day (March 24) and think how old he would be. It is not something we talk about as a family.

I had to show strength, but it did not mean I did not feel helpless at times. I often wondered why it had happened to Wilmot. He was only 21.

Wilmot, initially diagnosed with Hong Kong flu, died of meningitis. Death had scarred the Williamses before. When Chester was 10 he lost his six-year-old sister Hybre to a blood clot on the brain.

When Chester was born, it was a difficult birth. His mother, Julene, thought death was going to crush her Chester in the first days after he was born. Severe gastric problems meant no weight gain for her new baby and for 48 hours the signs were ominous.

Chester admits he has little memory of what he felt when his sister died. Being so young, he could not articulate the loss. But 10 years later he understood what death meant – its brutality and finality.

Wilmot was so weak. He looked so frail. I had never seen him like that. He had been in hospital for a week and I had not been to visit him. I wanted to see him when he got home and when he was his strong self again. He had contracted flu (at least that was what the doctors at first thought) while I was touring Hong Kong with the SA Defence Force rugby team.

When I got back he was already in hospital. Our family joked that I must have given him the Hong Kong flu, but it frightened me when I heard my parents describe his condition. I don't know why I went to the hospital the day I did. I never for one moment thought he was not going to get better.

We all believed that he would soon get better. He was going to become a magistrate and then a judge. He was doing well at university. He had big ambitions and our family was so proud of what he was achieving.

That night at six o'clock I saw Wilmot. Our conversation was not meaningful and I don't even remember what we spoke about. All I recall is that we laughed a lot. The laughing hurt his body but, typical of his character, he laughed at my jokes and took an interest in my stories. I said goodbye when visiting hours were over, not ever thinking that I would never again say hello.

Later that evening Wilmot died. The next day his family found out he had passed his third year at university. Wilmot was taken away from them, but his enduring legacy would be the motivation he had provided for little brother Chester – the inscription of the satchel.

He backed my ability. I was never going to fail his faith in me. That Friday night of November 12, when they told me I was going to play my first test match the next day against Argentina in Buenos Aires, was as much a celebration of Wilmot's dream as it was of mine.

That test match memory remains an emotional one for me. That day I played for Wilmot and the writing on his satchel. I scored my first test try and in a soft whisper told him it was part of the thank you for believing in me.

I know he was smiling. I imagined how proud he must have been of me. His little brother was a test Springbok.

Fame and shame

7

I did not always sympathise with black administrators or players who were politically motivated. I was a simple kid who just wanted to play rugby

CHESTER WILLIAMS *still shakes his head in disbelief when he recalls one of the low points of his rugby career – being sent off the field for dirty play against Canterbury on his first visit to New Zealand in 1993.*

Young, innocent and desperate to become a regular member of the Western Province team, Chester wanted to use his introduction to Australian and New Zealand rugby as the springboard to greater things.

The 1991 and 1992 seasons had included seven starts for Western Province, but Chester's role in those two years was secondary to veterans Danie Gerber and Kobus Burger. When he left Cape Town in early 1993 as part of the Western Province touring team, Chester was eager to make an impact in Australia and New Zealand, but it would be one of the most frustrating and disappointing tours of his career.

His selection against Canterbury only came about because of an injury to Gerber. Chester believed the Western Province coach at the time, Dawie Snyman, did not rate him and he felt politics dominated a tour that should have been about promoting Western Province rugby.

Politics did indeed play a role. It had been only a year since all the rugby organisations in South Africa had unified into the South African Rugby Football Union. In Western Province the political scene was more complicated than anywhere else in the country. The white WP Rugby Union was strong in terms of players and facilities, but the Federation and the five SARU unions in Western Province (WP Union, WP Board, Tygerberg, City and Suburban and Somerset West) had to be accommodated in a new set-up where levelling the figurative playing fields would never be easy.

The Australian and New Zealand people were wonderful to us. The hospitality was amazing, but the rugby experience was not in the same class. I was very frustrated and expressed this to one of the senior black players in the squad, Jerome Paarwater. I complained that I was not getting an opportunity and felt that the coaching staff was simply paying lip service to the unification process by having included several black players in the squad.

There were quite a few of us black players on that tour, but it was obvious that Dawie Snyman did not think we were good enough to play in his team. He opted for players with whom he was comfortable and I found Snyman to be a poor communicator. In subsequent years I would get to know Snyman better and I would nurture a stronger relationship. He would, in the future, also back me as a player and keep faith in me when other coaches might have dropped me because of a poor performance.

But in 1993 on the tour to Australia and New Zealand there was not much communication between the two of us. He was an established coach and I was a youngster just starting out. I also felt I was not going to get a chance on that tour because Snyman was more comfortable with the players he knew.

I was never going to challenge any decision he made. I had learned at a young age that you win nothing as a player going head to head with a coach. You keep quiet, take on board whatever he says and try to prove, through performance, that you are good enough to play in his side.

Snyman, though, had his favourites and this was never better illustrated than when the team played against Auckland in the final tour game in New Zealand. We were getting smashed and were 39-0 down at halftime. We fought back well in the second half to make the score more respectable and Jerome played magnificently. He was up against the great Michael Jones and never took a step back.

The black players in the squad were delighted that Jerome had played so well. He had proved a point and when the New Zealand media made him the man of the match it was justification for all his efforts on the tour.

Snyman, however, speaking at the after-match function, made a point about the man of the match award. He said he disagreed with the selection and, as far as he was concerned, WP tour captain Tiaan Strauss was his man of the match.

All the players in the squad had the greatest respect for Tiaan and we all felt he was a fantastic leader, but I saw Snyman's comments as an insult to Jerome. The speech upset all the black players in the squad. We could not believe that he would embarrass Jerome in the way that he had. It showed a mentality that you still find in South African rugby today.

It also ended a week that was among the worst of my rugby career. One thing I pride myself on is that I always played the game in the right spirit. And in a career of 10 years I have never been the aggressor in any off-the-ball incident. I will always give it everything when defending, but there was never an occasion when I deliberately fouled a player.

That is why my sending-off against Canterbury came as such a shock. I dived to tackle a Canterbury player as he was kicking the ball. I made contact with him and the player gave an Oscar performance. The crowd started chanting 'Off, off'.

The referee gave them what they wanted to see. It was a home-town decision. I had no doubt at the time. Almost 10 years after it happened, nothing has changed my mind.

The referee, Mike Fitzgibbon, was unrepentant in his report after the match. His recollections, if anything, were more dramatic than the incident itself.

South African rugby historian Paul Dobson recorded the following, quoting Fitzgibbon's justification in sending off Chester: 'Province were unable to keep pace with the Canterbury team and they became surly, uncooperative and refused to communicate.

'Late in the first half, the Canterbury fullback, Anthony Lawry, received the ball near his own 22-metre line and counter-attacked along the grandstand touch. At about his 10-metre line he kicked ahead and swerved to clear an opponent. At least four sprinting paces after kicking, he was blown over by Chester Williams's torpedo.

'Chester had run at full pace towards touch, dived horizontally at Anthony with absolutely no attempt to use his arms, impacting with Anthony's right shoulder and head with sufficient force to knock him sideways more than four metres where he crashed into the advertising hoardings.

'Chester was so late he would have had time to send a telegram! I had absolutely no hesitation in ordering him off under Law 26 (3) (d). The action was dangerous in the extreme.'

Province hooker Dale Santon was also sent off and, for the first time in more than 100 years, Western Province had two players sent from the field in one match.

Canterbury won 54-32 and the tour ended three days later with a 46-24 defeat against Auckland.

Two wins in Australia (40-3 against Western Australia and 59-14 against Queensland Country), and a 12-12 draw against Queensland were packaged as the tour highlights. But the week in New Zealand still stands as one of the lows in Cape rugby history.

Chester learned more off the field on that 1993 tour than he did from any rugby-playing perspective. The rugby frustration aside, he still remembers the tour with a great deal of fondness.

I immediately fell in love with the country and the people. There are so many similarities to South Africa in appearance and climate, but I found the people to be particularly honest.

There was a fascination with the black players in the squad, especially by white girls in Australia. I found it very uncomfortable as I was not particularly confident with women, let alone an advance from a white woman.

We all got used to the advances and the attention we got as the tour progressed. The single guys had a great time. I was just blown away by the fact that so few of the Australians we encountered seemed to see us as black players ... as anything second rate or inferior as human beings. There was this fascination with us, but we were also made to feel the white person's equal.

Naturally, there were a lot of political questions and it was clear that there was a very simple understanding of the political situation in South Africa. To most Australian people I met, South Africa was about black and white. They could not comprehend that the problems could be black on black, coloured on coloured and white on white. Culturally, South Africa is blessed – and, I guess, cursed – because of its cultural diversity. There will always be questions and there won't always be answers.

I dealt with the political questions as best I could, but opted not to get involved in anything too political. There were several coloured players on tour and that was more because of unification than selecting the best squad available. It also showed in the starting XV selections. Few of the coloured players featured regularly on the tour.

I had always felt myself to be good enough to be selected in any team. I never wanted a political hand-out or a favour because of the colour of my skin. I was not politically very active, something I regret and a sentiment I will repeat often in this book, so I did not always sympathise with black administrators or players who were politically motivated. I was a simple kid who just wanted to play rugby and be acknowledged for his contribution on the field.

As a schoolboy player I knew that I could not be selected for the SA Schools team. Black players were not picked. It was that simple. I knew the rules and I dealt with them. But senior rugby was supposed to be different. My uncle had played for the Springboks. Many other coloured players had made it at provincial level. I never doubted I could make it. But I also never knew what kind of prejudice did exist in our senior rugby … from within the playing fraternity right through to the coaches and administration. I would find out with each year in senior rugby just how white the game was during my playing career.

In 1993 I thought I was good enough to play for Western Province and to be a regular. Opportunities were limited. I had played at centre, but was deemed too small, too slow and not aggressive enough in the tackle. Oh, I think my passing was also not up to standard.

So I was shifted to the wing, where I was still thought of as being too slow, too small and not particularly aggressive in the tackle.

Publicly, Chester said all the right things in 1993. He smiled for the cameras, spoke of how thrilled he was to be playing rugby and gave glowing reviews to the world about South African rugby.

Politically he was naïve. His parents confirm that there were few political discussions in their family. They were not a family who fought the struggle. They got on with life and were grateful for what they had.

It is why Chester detested any distinction being drawn between players because of the colour of their skin.

I was never made to feel inferior at home. My parents always encouraged me and my friends always backed me. I did not want to make a team because I was black and because white South Africa felt indebted to the black people of this country. I wanted to play because people felt I was the best rugby player in that position. If they did not consider this to be the case, then I did not want to be selected.

I never wanted to be used as a political weapon, by either black or white people. Unfortunately, my name was often linked to rugby politically. When I made it, I was supposedly a sign of development. That was nonsense. There have always been good coloured and black players in this country. All they ever wanted was an opportunity. Most of them were denied that opportunity.

That's all I ever fought for as a player – to be given a chance. My political education was such that I fought from the base of a rugby player and nothing more. I did not have the understanding to fight the bigger political fight. If a coach did not pick me and refused to give me a chance, I felt he was being unfair to me as a rugby player and a person. Initially, I never associated the lack of opportunity with being black. Later on in my career it would become patently obvious that colour came labelled with limited opportunity.

That first tour of Australia with the Western Province team in 1993 gave me a peek at the racial prejudice in our rugby. I was very frustrated, but I was also pleased by the support I got from a player like Jerome Paarwater. He told me I was good enough to make it. He kept on motivating me and pushing me to play so well that the selectors just could not ignore me.

Chester, despite the frustration within the Western Province structure, got his first taste of a Rugby World Cup in the form of the 1993 Sevens World Cup, played in Scotland.

Sevens rugby was foreign to South Africans. There was no great understanding of the game and South Africa's approach was that rugby was rugby, whether played by 15 or by seven.

The Springbok sevens team arrived in Scotland with a squad of brilliant players who, on natural ability, stunned sevens specialists Fiji and New Zealand before being edged out 7-5 by Australia and 14-7 by eventual winners England.

The 26-19 win against Fiji and the 31-12 demolition of the New Zealanders still ranks as one of Chester's career highlights, mainly because of the innocence of the squad and the magnitude of the results.

We went there to play rugby – not sevens. There was no great game-plan or thought that went into our challenge. We had some wonderful individuals, with a player like Andre Joubert absolutely brilliant.

We just hung on to the ball and enjoyed ourselves. To knock over Fiji and New Zealand was something very special when you consider how much emphasis gets placed on the sevens game in those countries. We were novices and perhaps that counted in our favour because we knew people did not expect us to win anything.

The World Cup sevens, in which Chester also earned rave reviews, prompted a call-up to the Western Province team. Chester responded with four tries against local rivals Boland and played in a 71-17 thrashing of Eastern Transvaal (now the Falcons). The latter match was significant because Chester and his old school friend Thinus Linee played together for the first time.

There were two 'international matches' for Chester before the end of June that year. He played for Western Province against France and for South Africa A against the French. In both matches he showed he was not out of his depth in top company.

France had toured South Africa and won a two-test series 1-0 (the other test was drawn). Chester did not feature in the test squad, but his performances for Province and the Springbok sevens put pressure on the national selectors to include him in South Africa's first tour to Australia since 1971.

Chester, at the time, would have felt his form justified his inclusion as a Springbok tourist. But there were many questions asked about his selection – and that of Linee's – when the squad was announced. Not one black player had featured in the test mix in 1992 and no black player had been used in the series defeat by France. Politically, however, South African rugby was being forced to face up to the realities of a changing country.

The black-dominated African National Congress (ANC) was still a year from being empowered as South Africa's first democratic government, but the signs were obvious to those who bothered to look. A black government would not tolerate a white national team, picked on racial guidelines that excluded black players while it embraced some mediocre white talent.

Williams and Linee had been added to the Bok mix and for the first time in Springbok touring history, two black players would represent South Africa.

Chester, selected in seven of the 12 matches on tour, was outstanding each time he played. He never threatened to break into the test side, however. James Small and Jacques Olivier were the test regulars.

I was not going to be picked in the test team. It was made very clear from the outset that I was part of the midweek team. And I got the feeling James Small and Jacques Olivier knew this. They were under no pressure from me at the start of the tour, but by the time the tour ended I thought I had done enough to be noticed.

The coach, Ian McIntosh, gave me a lot of opportunities in the midweek team and he was very supportive of me in that side. But he never told me that I was not in the test squad mix and I never asked. There are some things that don't need to be said.

I concentrated on my game, looked to maximise every chance and made a commitment to enjoy the tour. I had not had a great time earlier in the year with the Province team because of a lack of game time.

This time around I could not complain about not playing. Sure, I was not going to play in the three tests or the two main provincial games against Queensland and New South Wales, but I was being kept busy with the midweek team.

I was getting to see nearly every major city in Australia and I loved the tour. I was rooming with my good friend Thinus Linee and I felt part of everything. I had a mate, I was playing and scoring tries and the Australian people were very good to the two of us.

The standard of rugby in the midweek games was not good. We won most of them easily, but being in Australia with the Springboks felt good. I was a part of something national and Thinus and I believed we were representing the greater South Africa. We wanted to show that, as rugby players, we were good enough.

Politically, the questions were the same that we had been asked when touring with Western Province. Our answers were the standard 'No, we don't feel prejudiced against and, yes, we are accepted as players in the squad.' Publicly, we were never going to say anything to the contrary.

And, frankly, this time I did feel part of the tour because I had a good friend with me. Thinus and I kept to ourselves, but we had a great time, trained hard and played the best rugby we could. There was no need to look further than that.

I did not have much to do with the other players. I spoke very little to James Small and Jacques Olivier. They were fairly close and the wing positions in the test team were a closed shop. If fit, James and Jacques were always going to start. I made no attempt to get to know either of them.

My tour highlight was scoring three tries in the 78-3 win against Victoria in Melbourne. I had got my first taste of Springbok rugby, but until I played a test I would not consider myself a Springbok.

Still, Williams and Linee had shown up the racial injustice of South African society. The 'development' centre pairing of 1988 had successfully represented South Africa five years after apartheid had prevented them from reaching the very top of South African schoolboy rugby. Five years after they had been relegated to the SA Project XV, they were Springboks, while the SA Schools centres of that year in the all-white team, Elmo Wolfaardt and Dan Hall, were not even provincial regulars.

1993: A first test cap

8

I shouted to him (Tucuman wing Martin Teran), asking if this kind of fighting was usual. He said it happened all the time but that the crowd were even worse

WHEN *Chester Williams left with the Springboks on their tour of Argentina in late 1993, he was part of the second-string team – the dirt-trackers, as they are affectionately known all round the rugby world. The second-stringers were not guaranteed test places, but Chester wanted to use this tour to prove further that he belonged among South Africa's best rugby players.*

Linee had not made the touring squad and for the first time on an international tour Chester was the only black player in the squad. He roomed with Chris Dirks, Transvaal's full back, who did his best to comfort a homesick Chester. Dirks had been a good teammate on tour and he extended the hand of friendship when Chester needed it most.

It was an awful time and I was very lonely. Chris was very good to me and he tried to make me feel part of everything he did. Gary Teichmann, then only a midweek tourist with the rest of us dirt-trackers, was also very kind. He and Chris would make sure that I did not sit in the room on my own. They were always inviting me to go shopping or sightseeing. Even if they were going for a coffee, they would make sure I went along. They kept on telling me that it was not good to hang out on my own. It could only lead to more homesickness.

For many guys, touring is a lonely experience. As a black player I found it to be particularly lonely. I want to stress that there was no time that I was not made to feel welcome, but the mood was such that you always felt like an outsider.

To give some idea of how this loneliness affects you, I will give Bruce McLoughlin as an example. In 1996, when I was out of the Springbok team because of injury, I telephoned Bruce, who was a good friend and at that time was the physiotherapist with the Springbok team.

I called him to find out how it was going with the Boks. I also wanted to know how he found the experience of being involved with the Boks since he was quite new to it. He sounded very down and told me that it was an incredibly lonely experience. He was English-speaking and the management was predominantly Afrikaans. Most of the players were also Afrikaans-speaking. Bruce said he felt uncomfortable and not part of the team set-up. He said it was terrible being on tour because he felt like an outsider. I joked: 'Join the club'.

He had told me that when joining a table at meal times there would be silence and he assumed it was because of his presence. I had experienced exactly the same thing. I told him that if he wanted to know exactly where he stood in the team, he had to be seated at the breakfast, lunch or dinner table at least half an hour before the rest of the squad. That way it would be up to others to join him. He would quickly know whether he was the reason for the silence at previous meals.

Bruce decided to try this and I called him a few days later. 'How's it been going?' Bruce laughed: 'Great … I got to breakfast half an hour early, sat on my own and watched as every squad member arrived for breakfast … I ate alone!' I laughed out loudly … 'Join the club … I've had a few of those 'table for one' breakfasts myself.

The Springbok rugby culture has many good things that one can look back on. There are others that are best confined to the past. Bruce never felt welcome and neither did I entirely feel I belonged in this South African rugby brotherhood. It is changing now with the introduction of more aggressive and politically sussed black managers. It is a recent change and Springbok rugby is starting to embrace all South Africans and not just a select minority.

Dirks and Teichmann eased the pain of touring by not only joining Chester at the dinner table but also by encouraging him to force his way into the test side.

Chester scored in the opening match of the tour, an easy win against Cordoba. He did not play in the Springboks' next match, a shock 28-27 defeat by Buenos Aires. He returned for wing duty in the brutal showdown against Tucuman – a match that still stands as one of the most unruly involving a Springbok team.

Chester went over for a try in the 40-12 win, but whoever scored was secondary to who got sent off. Efrim Sklar, a referee from Buenos Aires, showed red cards to Springbok players Keith Andrews and Hannes Strydom, as well as local players Luis Molina and Pablo Buabse. A few more Tucuman players were carried off in a match that had more boxing than rugby.

Andrews, a jovial Bok tighthead prop who was the consummate tourist, had been warned about the probability of violence in Tucuman. And the locals were true to their reputation.

'Ja, a good mate of mine, the former French flanker Laurent Cabannes, had warned me about playing in Tucuman,' recalls Andrews. 'He told me to "Watch out for those guys. Be prepared for a fight from the start and watch out for the crowd. They are vicious".'

The Springboks had not visited Argentina in more than 10 years and were largely unaware of Tucuman's brutal reputation that had been earned during that time. It was just as well that Andrews had come forewarned and he passed on this intelligence to the rest of the players.

'Laurent had told me that the crowd could be more intimidating than the team, who have a reputation for beating up international opponents. When the French played there, the power lines were cut at half-time and a section of the crowd broke down the fence, invaded the pitch and beat up two French players.

'I told the Boks about it, especially the coach, Ian McIntosh. He made it clear that we should not stand back and allow ourselves to be physically intimidated. Our intention was not to fight or to start anything. But if they hit, we had to hit back.

'Deep down you knew that you were going to be hitting early on. These guys did not have a reputation for nothing. I think every Bok had prepared himself for a brawl.

'When we arrived at the stadium you could sense that there would be a fight. The crowd was hostile. There was lots of heckling, spitting and swearing. Henry Honiball's kick-off to start the match went straight into touch. Less than a minute into the game it all started at the first scrum. Even before we made contact I got head-butted and then I was hit. BANG … I responded. There was a free-for-all,' says Andrews.

'All you could do was run and hit and try to ensure you did not get a "trap shot" (a punch from behind). There was aggro everywhere. They were snorting and grunting. I was speaking English, Afrikaans and French and they were not the kind of words you would find in the family dictionary. In any case, the only words these guys would understand were those delivered by way of a fist.'

Andrews reckons that in the process he got in what was the best punch he ever threw in a Springbok jersey.

'What happened was that I had been hit from the side and gone down. I got up and turned to cover myself from a front-on attack. I saw

this guy moving past me and let rip with an open-fisted roundhouse that landed just under his nose. The next thing he was out cold, lying next to Chris Dirks (a Springbok player).

'The referee went crazy. He screamed at me to go, and even chased me from the field. The crowd were as crazed, baying for my blood. I have never been as charged up in my life; as I walked towards the crowd I grabbed at my groin and shouted: "Suck on this!"

'The next day the local newspaper's main picture was my "salute" to the crowd. The headline, translated from Spanish to English, read: "Andrews shows genitals to the crowd".

'It was hectic that day. The two most bizarre memories are my punch and Chester Williams seemingly in gentle discussion with his opposite number. It was the most unbelievable contrast on a rugby field. Fourteen guys were trashing each other and Chester was having a chat some distance away from the action.'

Williams admits he was going nowhere near the kitchen in Tucuman.

I have never been a fighter on the rugby field. I knew that this game was going to get ugly. There had been a lot of talk in the media about how Tucuman would deal with us. They had a reputation for fighting and Keith Andrews had told Mac that they were going to come for us.

As Keith says, it all started within the first minute. When the first fight broke out, the Tucuman wing Martin Teran and I were far away from the action. We both stood our ground and watched. He could speak some English and I shouted to him in English, asking if this kind of fighting was usual.

He was not aggressive in his approach to me and I saw no reason to be aggressive because of this mass brawl going on in the middle of the pitch.

He was not at all surprised by what was going on and said it happened all the time, but he added that the crowd were even worse than the players. He showed no interest in getting involved and we agreed that it made no sense to injure ourselves in a fight that had nothing to do with either of us.

So, while everyone else was beating each other up, we stood on the side of the field and chatted about rugby in general. We were to meet again when I was up against him in the second test match.

Of course, I did not know then that I would win a place in the test team, but he knew he was going to be picked for the Pumas so it made no sense for him to get involved in a fight where he ran the risk of getting hurt and missing a test cap. You could say we made a pact to leave it at 14 fights 14.

The other Boks teased me about it afterwards, but it did not make sense for me to get involved. Watching from the sidelines was more fun than being in the middle. And I can tell you that Keith Andrews's punch was huge. The guy dropped immediately. He went straight down!

When it happened, Martin and I shook our heads – a kind of acknowledgement that we had made the right decision to stay out on our wings.

It was a good decision in view of the upturn my rugby career was about to take. I wanted to play test rugby and my chance would finally come in the second test because of the illness of Jacques Olivier.

The Boks had been unconvincing first-test winners, edging out the Pumas 29-26 after leading 29-10 at halftime. I did not play in the first test, but got game time against Rosario in a 40-26 win the following week. Jacques had not been well all week, but he still trained with the test squad.

Mac got me to run with the test squad, but there was no guarantee that I would play. They were going to give Jacques the maximum time to recover and this annoyed me a bit. I felt Mac did not show any confidence in my ability to cover for Jacques.

Every player will tell you that there is no worse feeling than not knowing if you are going to be playing by the Friday morning of a test match. I was desperate for the coach to make a call, but I was not going to go to him and demand he make a decision. I waited and waited.

I badly wanted to play but I never wished for Jacques to be forced to withdraw. It is not in my nature. I believed that if I got a chance it was because it was meant to be.

Jacques did not recover sufficiently and on the Friday night Mac told me that I was in. It was now official and I was determined to make an impression. It was a big day for me and for someone who had been a very special person in my life, my brother Wilmot. I dedicated my first test to him and nine minutes into my test career, I managed to give him the gift of a first test try.

1994: All things black and beautiful

9

I was playing for the Springboks. That meant more to me than who I was playing against. I did not have this love affair with – or hate for – the All Blacks

THERE *has been no bigger year for South Africa than 1994. The nation celebrated its first democratic elections, a historic moment that would redefine the country's image and radically alter its persona.*

White dominance was officially over, the change symbolised by President Nelson Mandela's inauguration at the Union Buildings in Pretoria where he was accompanied by the generals of a military machine that had previously upheld apartheid South Africa.

South Africa, once banished from the global village, was no longer a dirty word. On the contrary, it was now fashionable to be a South African, especially a liberated one who embraced change and accepted the principles of equality and freedom.

On the surface, South Africa in 1994 was a fairytale story. Fears of a violent right-wing backlash had amounted to little more than isolated bombing incidents. The white supremacists of the Afrikaner Weerstandsbeweging had been talked out of their pitiful rebellion by no less a person than General Constand Viljoen, a former commander of the apartheid military and a darling of the political right.

Black South Africans rejoiced in their new freedom by queuing for hours at the polling booths. Their white fellow voters showed signs of relief rather than resentment. White South Africans could again look the world in the eye and the benefits of freedom were obvious. International sports tours, for one thing, were coming and going. The All Blacks, the

Wallabies and the French had been here briefly to resume rugby ties and the country had been to an Olympic Games again, winning a wonderful silver medal through the running of Elana Meyer, whose lap of honour with the winner, Derartu Tulu of Ethiopia, appeared to signal a new beginning not only for South Africa, but the continent, too.

On the rugby field, South Africa faced its toughest season since international readmission in 1992. The Springboks would host England in a two-test series before travelling to New Zealand for the first tour there in 13 years.

The last time South Africa had sent a rugby team to New Zealand, Chester Williams had been only 11 years old and hardly interested in following the fortunes of the Springboks. Street cricket in Paarl was then a greater priority.

The Springboks were competitive in 1981 and fielded many outstanding players in Naas Botha, Danie Gerber, Carel du Plessis, Johan Heunis, Ray Mordt ... Errol Tobias. Tobias, the first black man to wear a Springbok jersey, was kept out of the test team on the tour by the gifted Botha, but others would say that old South African prejudice played a role too. The critics of the team dismissed Tobias's presence as window-dressing but he would prove his international class three years later against England when Botha had gone to seek fame and fortune in American football.

South Africa lost the first test on that tour, won the second convincingly and in the third Mordt scored three tries, but the Springboks lost 25-22 to a dramatic – and disputed – penalty by fullback Alan Hewson in extra time.

But the 1981 tour was memorable for what happened off the field rather than on it. During the final test, an apartheid protester flew a light aircraft dangerously close to Eden Park, even threatening to crash the plane into the grandstand. The pilot, however, opted for a more symbolic protest, dropping flour bombs on to the pitch. It was serious stuff at the time, but in the wake of September 11, it is now cast in comic relief.

More serious was the effect the Springboks had on New Zealand society. The tour divided the nation, disrupted New Zealanders' tranquillity and scarred the country for many years. It was also of short-term interest to South Africa because the fall-out of the tour would lead to the Springboks' expulsion from international rugby.

The tour only came about because of a series of political miscalculations. In the age of Thatcherism, the prime minister of New Zealand, Robert Muldoon, eager to project a strong image and wanting to be seen as someone defending the freedom of choice, decided not to prevent a Springbok rugby tour. Unlike previous governments, he would not stand in the way of a New Zealand Rugby Football Union invitation to the South African Rugby Board.

The rugby men, notoriously insensitive to the politics of the time, could see nothing wrong with inviting a team who represented white supremacism. They also ignored the clamour of protest from other countries, especially those in the Commonwealth. In South Africa, the rugby men of the SA Board saw the invitation as heaven sent. The last time they had been allowed to visit New Zealand was 1965 when they had suffered a humiliating defeat. They saw the invitation as an opportunity to set the record straight; they also knew that this time they had the players with which to do it.

The South African government was delighted. Sending a Springbok team to New Zealand would be a propaganda coup in the face of the apartheid country's increasing isolation. They might also have miscalculated on the effect the images of New Zealand would have on South Africans.

On previous tours to Britain in 1969/70 and to Australia in 1971, the extent of the opposition to the Springboks, through the huge demonstrations against apartheid, was less obvious than it would be in 1981 when New Zealanders and police clashed violently. During those earlier visits, South Africans did not even have television; in 1981 virtually every white home had a TV set and the images from New Zealand were not pretty. Apart from the rugby, white South Africans would realise just how much they were loathed as a people. Who knows what effect it had on white society and what role it played in finally persuading it to ditch apartheid?

White South Africa's relationship with New Zealand had always been uneasy in spite of the intense rugby rivalry. A former South African prime minister, Hendrik Verwoerd, widely credited as the architect of apartheid, had infamously refused Maoris to be part of any All Black touring team, and New Zealand authorities in the past had been at pains to accommodate South African racial prejudices. It was only a selfish rugby ambition that kept the two nations close; neither would be acknowledged as the best in the world unless they regularly beat the other. And New Zealand still rankled over the 1937 victory by the Springboks in New Zealand. Until 1996, it was the only time when one of the two countries had scored an away win over the other in a rugby test series.

Against this historical backdrop, with its rich sporting heritage and heavy political baggage, the first Springbok rugby tour in 13 years would take place. And South Africa managed to cock it up right from the start with the selection of the Springbok team.

In 1994 South Africa was a unified nation, but it sent a Springbok téam to New Zealand that was anything but united. Politically, questions *were still being asked about the white-dominated make-up of the squad, provincially the squad was divided and culturally the English and Afrikaans element still created more confusion than cohesion.*

The South African government was also still undecided about the future of the Springboks. There had been endless debate over the green and gold colours of the national team and its identity as Springboks. Many outside of rugby felt that the colour and name were associated with apartheid South Africa.

Former Springbok players implored the government to allow the team still to be called Springboks. The South African Rugby Football Union president, Louis Luyt, fought for the right to keep the name, arguing that the Springboks represented the best of South African rugby and were not a reflection of apartheid.

Luyt's resolve to keep the Springbok was not weakened when cricket decided to forego the Springbok emblem for the Protea.

Luyt, in 1994, was in constant communication with the government about rugby's identity and rugby's role in helping shape a new South Africa.

The government did not enforce any change. The decision would have to be rugby's and despite New Zealanders promoting the test series in 1994 as one to be played between the All Blacks and Proteas, South Africa arrived in Auckland wearing green and gold blazers and they were called the Springboks.

The team, coached by Ian McIntosh and led by Francois Pienaar, was a sad reflection of the country's rugby talent. Provincial politics played more of a role than player ability when the final squad of 30 was selected. Seven selectors had picked the team for McIntosh. The coach would later admit that he would have taken a very different team to New Zealand had the choice of players been his alone.

If the selectors were confused in their thinking, it was understandable. They had been required to pick a team in the wake of an unexpected defeat by England and there was uncertainty in their minds. To be safe, each selector opted for the players he knew best and, once more, South African rugby fell back on provincialism.

The shock to South Africa's rugby system had come early in 1994 when the England touring team arrived. To the average observer, they seemed to be the usual cannon-fodder from the northern hemisphere. A strong enough side to test the Springboks, who were eager to sharpen their game ahead of the more challenging tour to New Zealand, but no real threat to the home team. South Africans had already forgotten a similar lesson of 22 years before.

In the games before the first test at Loftus Versfeld in Pretoria, the English were beaten by Natal, South Africa A and Transvaal (now the

Lions). The only doubts in the minds of the home supporters were whether these visitors could give the Springboks a good game in the two test matches.

There was a carnival atmosphere in Pretoria on the day of the first test match. President Nelson Mandela attended and introduced himself to each player. After the anthems and pleasantries, the capacity crowd settled down for what they expected to be a regulation Springbok victory at one of their team's favourite venues.

But this time the Springboks were the ones to take a beating. Even before President Mandela had time to make himself comfortable in his grandstand seat, the Springboks were down 20-0. They lost the test 32-15. It still ranks as one of the most emphatic defeats ever suffered by a Springbok team at home and evoked memories of a similar shock when an underrated England team under John Pullin beat the Springboks at Ellis Park in 1972.

England, having won at altitude, were favourites to win the second test too. It was played in Cape Town at a Newlands stadium that was undergoing reconstruction for the following year's World Cup where the venue would host the opening match.

Newlands would suit the tourists even better than Loftus Versfeld, argued the critics. But then the Springboks, faced with the possible humiliation of a series defeat by England at home, roused themselves and won 27-9, a convincing victory marked by a well constructed try scored by Hennie le Roux that emphasised the home team's superiority on the day.

The game, however, was not one of Chester Williams's finest moments on a rugby pitch. He dropped the ball with the tryline open to him and was also concussed in a tackle. Of his 47 Springbok matches, this was the least memorable. Making it even sadder was that it would be his only test at his home ground.

The Springboks had salvaged some pride, but the second-test win was not enough to allow for clarity of thought in the minds of the seven selectors. The shock of Loftus was still too vivid and they came up with some strange selections in the 30-man squad for New Zealand. Some very ordinary players were among those who boarded a flight to New Zealand in the guise of Springboks.

Chester Williams, despite not being part of McIntosh's initial training squad, had played against England in Pretoria and survived for the second test in Cape Town. Politically, it would have been courting disaster to drop him, although he never felt his selection was based on politics.

Besides, Chester came in useful when the tricky questions were asked at press conferences. It was Chester's innocence that allowed him to be used as a spokesman whenever the issue of team identity was put to the squad.

'We all want to be called Springboks,' was the common response. 'Ask Chester, see what he thinks.' Chester would then be asked and he would repeat the line with great conviction: 'I have always wanted to be a Springbok and wear the green and gold.'

It was no lie. When Chester decided to turn to rugby in high school, his burning ambition was to become a Springbok. He never associated the rugby team with apartheid South Africa. Chester's answer was good enough for the rugby world. A black South African wanted to be a Springbok. All had to be well in unified South Africa.

All, however, was not well in South African rugby. Not that Chester was even dimly aware of it at the time.

Chester, like most players, was oblivious to the usual behind-the-scenes manipulation and influence that had characterised South African rugby for more than 100 years. Typically, he just wanted to play rugby and steer clear of the politics.

New Zealanders, though, wanted to talk as much about politics as they wanted to know about Springbok rugby. Chester was black and it was wrongly assumed he spoke on behalf of the black community in South Africa.

I did not have the knowledge to speak about the political situation. I could only offer my opinions, which were very simple and based solely on a guy who just wanted to play rugby. The New Zealand people, because I was black, took a liking to me.

Perhaps they saw me as some kind of victor in white South Africa. Perhaps they took pity on me as being the only black player in the South African squad. I never asked them why they liked me … I was just grateful that they backed me and gave me support throughout the tour.

The media in New Zealand were kind to me. I got good reviews and the people were as generous in their acceptance of me as a rugby player. I was flattered by this because there had been a lot of talk back in South Africa that it was an achievement to be acknowledged as a quality rugby player by New Zealanders.

Politically, the questions were not complicated, it was just that I was not able to do justice to the answers. The questions included: How had South Africa changed for me as a black person? At that stage it hadn't. How did it feel to be accepted as part of the world? I had not been in a position where I had felt the world had excluded me. I was too young to have experienced isolation.

Most commonly, I was asked how it felt to be treated as an equal. Honestly, I could not answer that because while the government was changing the country's constitution, it had no power to change minds which had been set in their ways for 300 years.

In time I would feel the positive influence of change in South Africa. In time I would feel that white South Africans saw me as their equal. In 1994, very little had changed in this regard. I was a Springbok rugby player, but to many in the squad I was there to keep the politicians quiet.

Chester had been concussed in the second test against England at Newlands and could not play for the first two weeks of the New Zealand tour. It meant he could not take part in any contact training and it isolated him from the team at practice.

This at first led some New Zealand journalists to believe that Chester was being victimised on the basis of colour. The question was put to Chester. He quickly rebutted it.

The squad did not make me feel like an outsider. Had I not been concussed I would have trained with the team. I told the New Zealand media this and they accepted my explanation.

It was a very strange tour. Provincialism ruled the tour. The Transvaal guys were used to playing under Kitch Christie. They loved him and ideally wanted him to be the Bok coach. They were the dominant provincial team in South Africa and there was a strong contingent of Transvaal players in the Bok squad. They played to win, but they were not totally supportive of Ian McIntosh.

Balie Swart and Kobus Wiese, in particular, were players who sulked if they did not get their way with Mac. They spoke up the Transvaal thing a lot. I couldn't get a grip on Pienaar's feelings during that tour. He gave little away and played the captain's role well. He appeared to give Mac the backing you would expect from a captain to a coach.

The Sharks players did as they pleased, especially James Small. Mac had no control over him. Both are very emotional characters and James's opinions counted for a lot when it came to certain decisions.

I had been worried about the influence some players had over the coach and was not very confident about my own situation in the squad. I had been injured against England and could not play in the early part of the tour. That was not the ideal way to start.

I also did not know how much Mac rated me, if at all. I played down suggestions that my selection was politically motivated because I always believed I deserved to be in the test team. I felt I was a good enough player, but I would be lying if I did not admit that I started wondering about everything during that first fortnight on tour.

I did not have the confidence to go to Mac and ask him about my position. Cabous van der Westhuizen, the Sharks winger, was playing on the left wing. Cabous, like James Small, was a Mac man. I was concerned that I would lose out because of provincialism.

I went to see the team manager Jannie Englebrecht. I told him I was worried that I would not make the test team because I had not played in the first few matches and that Mac might opt for his provincial combination of Cabous and James.

Jannie told me not to worry. He said he also picked the team and I could count myself as a certainty if I was fit. He said my only concern should be my fitness. If I was fit, then I would play. I felt better about the situation and relieved. Jannie did have a major say in selections and he was also a dominant presence in the management structure. He had told me he would look after my interests. I passed a fitness test, played against Southland and the Hanan Shield XV and was selected for the first test against New Zealand in Dunedin. The test was my third match in 10 days.

There was a lot of interest in my showdown with the legendary All Blacks right wing John Kirwan. All week Kirwan's name dominated the newspapers and in interviews it was the first time I was not asked about being a black player in South African rugby. The New Zealand media wanted to know how I was going to cope with a player they rated as their best wing ever.

I had only ever seen Kirwan play on television. I had never played against him or even stood next to him. The only image I had was of what I had seen on television. I had never given it much thought.

I was playing for the Springboks. That meant more to me than who I was playing against. I also did not have this love affair with – or hate for – the All Blacks. In apartheid South Africa most of the coloured players I knew loved the All Blacks because they represented a team that included black players. White South African players hated the All Blacks because they represented the ultimate opponent.

I started playing rugby only in my second-last year of high school. I had not followed the rivalry between the two countries. I was not in awe of the All Blacks' strip and neither was I in love with it. My approach was very simple and it probably was to my advantage.

Kirwan, to me, was not a legend and the remark has nothing to do with a lack of respect. I had not followed Kirwan's career. There was nothing for me to be in awe of because I did not know enough to feel that way. Playing the All Blacks also was not as significant as it was to a lot of the other players.

My preparation that week centred on my role as a wing. I wanted the ball. I wanted to attack, but in Mac's team you only saw the ball as a backline player once the pack had totally dominated.

We were never going to steamroll the All Blacks pack, so I knew I had

Photos: Touchline Photo

In his sights... *Chester takes aim. At the time he was an NCO in the quartermasters stores in the army.*

Top of the Table... *Chester Williams and Joel Stransky fool around with a rugby ball on Table Mountain during a Springbok excursion in Cape Town during the 1995 World Cup.*

Lost opportunity... *Chester and an employee during his foray into business as a cooldrink supplier in Paarl. The deal later turned sour.*

Photo: Anne Laing

Photo: Anne Laing

Photo: Touchline Photo

TOP LEFT: **A step up...** *At a Bok training session in Bellville. Alongside is Brendan Venter.*
MIDDLE: **Packing for Pacific...** *Getting ready for the tour to New Zealand in 1994.*
TOP RIGHT: **Turning-point try...** *Pieter Hendriks, who took Chester's place in the Springbok World Cup team of 1995, on his way to scoring against Australia at Newlands.*
BOTTOM LEFT: **Coming through...** *Beating Jonah Lomu, a fellow winger whom Chester does not rate as highly as he does Joe Roff or Jeff Wilson.*
BOTTOM RIGHT: **World Cup inspiration...** *Nelson Mandela in his famous appearance at the World Cup final in 1995. He and Chester formed a close bond during that time.*

Photo: Touchline Photo

Photo: Touchline Photo

TOP LEFT: **In a class of his own...** *Springbok fullback Andre Joubert, whom Chester picks in his fantasy Bok and World XVs.*
TOP RIGHT: **Making friends...** *Rivals on the field, Jonah Lomu and Chester Williams are mates off it after the World Cup final of 1995..*
BELOW: **A first...** *Chester scores against Argentina in 1993, the first of 14 tries in 27 tests.*

Photos: Touchline Photo

A taste of gold at last... *Holding the Currie Cup after victory with the Lions in the final against Natal in 1999.*

to make my tackles and take whatever opportunity came my way. I was not going to get the ball too often.

Mac, as a coach, had some very good qualities. He was passionate about the game, had a very good knowledge and was tactically astute. He did, however, believe that his 'direct rugby' approach was non-negotiable. You win the battle up front, you dominate the opposition and you suck in defenders before you take the ball wide. Mac believed in numbers. You play 15 on seven. You tie up their defenders and you attack with numbers. This direct approach can win you games, but against the best teams it can also leave you looking unimaginative and stereotyped. Mac's teams, if they did not get forward domination, were in trouble. In New Zealand, in those first two tests, we were in trouble.

The big confrontation with Kirwan never happened. I made one tackle on him in the game and I don't even know if he had to make a tackle on me. I hardly saw him because the ball did not come our way. I know he was at the end of his career, but I expected him to be quicker and to be more creative.

He did not get as involved as I thought he would. Given all the hype surrounding him, I expected him to make a greater impression.

He did score a try against us in the first test and it proved the difference as they won 22-14. Mac was furious afterwards. He was very down that we had lost and he was never one to hide his emotions.

His lack of emotional control is probably the biggest criticism I have of him as a coach. During those times I did not get close to him because he never asked for input from me. He had certain players he would go to and those did not include me.

His emotional outbursts and his behaviour did not instil the greatest confidence in a player. Often he appeared to be out of control and that was probably the big difference between Mac and Kitch Christie. Kitch was strict, unruffled and always in control of the situation. Mac could be all over the place.

There was a lot of sympathy for Mac when he was axed as Bok coach. I shared those sentiments because he was given a raw deal. He was not allowed to pick his own team and he had to deal with provincial divisions that would have freaked out most coaches. But he also had to take responsibility for his approach to the game. It was too one-dimensional and I found him to be too emotional as a test coach. I don't know if we would have won the World Cup under Mac, purely because I don't believe he would have handled the pressure.

The Springboks lost the series 2-0 in New Zealand after going down 13-9 in the second test to the All Blacks in Wellington. The third and final test was drawn 18-18 in Auckland.

Again a series result was overshadowed by controversy. Springbok prop forward Johan le Roux was cited and sent home for biting the ear of All Blacks captain Sean Fitzpatrick in the Wellington test where the series was decided.

In subsequent years there has been regret expressed by the Springbok management and players that they allowed themselves to be intimidated by the New Zealanders in sending Le Roux home. The front-ranker was banned from the game for 18 months, a suspension that effectively ended his international career.

Chester does not share the sentiments of those who believe Le Roux was hard done by.

There was incredible emotion in the week of that test. James Small had been cited after the Waikato win and he had been given a one-match suspension. It meant he could still play in the test match. Off the field, things were not operating smoothly. Mac gave us the impression that we were under siege and that the New Zealand public and media were out to get us.

There was a lot of pressure on us. We felt it, and Mac let us know that there would be no second chances. We had to win in Wellington to keep the series alive. We lost and I thought Le Roux's actions were disgraceful. You don't bite an opponent, just as you don't kick an opponent in the head.

I have heard those defending the action saying that he did not take a big bite out of Fitzpatrick's ear. Nevertheless, he took a bite and his intention was clear. I thought the decision to send him home and ban him was the right one in the context of the game. It was not a good decision for us as a team because we lost a good prop. But, from a rugby perspective, you cannot argue the decision.

I believe our Bok management acted correctly and in the interest of the sport. Johan le Roux was no angel. It would be hypocritical to add my voice to those who believed we were hard done by because of Fitzpatrick's alleged gamesmanship. There was blood from a bite and I don't think the issue is the amount of blood.

The Springbok tour, into its last week, continued to prove controversial. Rumours abounded that McIntosh would be sacked. The discipline of the squad was questioned and the tour selectors dropped James Small for the final test, more because of his poor discipline than his playing performance.

The Springboks drew the last test 18-18 and Chester still blames himself for the team not getting a win.

I made a try-saving tackle on Michael Jones, but I was in a position to do so, so it should not count as anything special. I also gave away a penalty for hands in the scrum. It was plainly poor discipline. The penalty I gave away and the one that Brendan Venter conceded when he reacted to Fitzpatrick's tug of the jersey cost us six points and the match.

We had deserved to win the test, but in international rugby all that matters is the score. We lost the series 2-0 and that's all the public were interested in. We knew there would be changes when we got home. No one could have thought the changes would come the moment we arrived back in South Africa.

As the Springboks walked through customs at Johannesburg International, Ian McIntosh was greeted with the news that he had been sacked.

* * *

Uli Schmidt threw into a short lineout from 50 metres out ... Mark Andrews tapped it back to Hennie le Roux, who took it into a maul. From the maul Joost van der Westhuizen broke, then passed to Andre Joubert. He made good distance and then he off-loaded to me. My run-in to the tryline was not much more than 10 metres, but the Welsh scrumhalf Rupert Moon was coming across at top speed.

I caught the ball and just went straight for the line. I have run a lot further for tries in my career, but I don't recall a more frantic dash over 10 metres. All I remember is Moon on my back, the thud into the ground and the silence of the Cardiff Arms Park crowd. I had scored. The test was safe. In the context of the match, it was one of the most memorable tries I have scored in my test career.

We were leading 13-12, there wasn't a lot of time left and Wales were giving it a full go. We needed something special to break the match open. I scored the try, but the movement was the spark we were looking for. I was just fortunate to be the last recipient of Andre's pass. Hennie kicked a great conversion from the touchline and we won the game 20-12.

It was also one of the most spontaneous team celebrations I had been a central part of in my international career. The guys just jumped on me. There was elation within the squad. I got hugs from players. I have never been so happy to score a try.

There had been personal triumphs in the past, like my first test try against Argentina. This try was different. This one was significant to the outcome of the match. I was the lucky guy to have scored it. The way the squad celebrated, all that mattered was that someone had managed to get over for five points.

The test had been as tough as they got and we had triumphed. I found that match to have been tougher than any of the three tests I had played in New Zealand. There was a passion about the Welsh that was hard to describe. And we had throttled it. The Welsh players were beaten. Their crowd was silent.

The tour had been a success. We had beaten Scotland easily and now we had overcome a spirited Welsh team. The atmosphere at the Arms Park was intense. The Welsh were pleading for a win from their team and for 60 minutes it looked as if they would get it. In the last 15 minutes we got it together as a team and took our game up to another level.

Kitch Christie was not a man who got carried away by victory, but this time he clearly showed his delight. Not only had we won, but we had also shown a resolve that had been missing in previous tests. When pushed to the limit, the Boks responded as a team and not as individuals in a team.

I believe that the win at the Arms Park that day was the start of our march towards greater things the following year. The New Zealand tour had been an experience for all of us and the better team had taken the series. But we now had a new coach, who instilled discipline and who was not there to be liked or to be a friend of the players. You either called him coach or Mr Christie. You did not dare call him Kitch. You also never assumed he was your friend. He was your coach and as a player I responded well to the discipline and mutual respect.

Kitch Christie had taken over from Ian McIntosh following the Springboks' 2-0 series defeat in New Zealand. Christie's record at Transvaal was unrivalled. He had led the team to Currie Cup wins, Lion Cup success and the 1994 Super 10 title.

The Christie-led Springboks operated on realism. The coach believed in simplicity, honesty and basic values. He did not tolerate players who deemed themselves to be bigger than the game. He did not pick players who lacked discipline.

In his first two tests in charge of the Springboks, the South Africans comfortably beat Argentina at home. Chester, picked on the left wing for both tests, scored two tries in the 2-0 series win. Argentina had been kind to him. His first test try was in Buenos Aires. His first test try at home was against the men from the Pampas.

What impressed Chester the most about Christie was that he acted more than he spoke.

There were no idle threats. When he said something he meant it. When he said he did not tolerate a player being late, the player who arrived late was punished. He never spoke about it, he simply acted on his belief that discipline in the team was not something to be debated.

I was pleased by the way in which the James Small matter in 1994 was handled. Again, there was sympathy within the team for James's axing from the squad after he had been involved in a fight in a Port Elizabeth bar.

I did not share the views of the James Small apologists. The incidents involving James had been too numerous in the two years I had been playing for the Boks. He was allowed to do as he pleased, regardless of the impact it had on the team.

Kitch did not tolerate such behaviour. He dropped James for the second test and refused to pick him for the tour to Wales and Scotland. It was this type of approach that had been lacking in 1993 and 1994. James was one of those players who was a law unto himself under Ian McIntosh. With Kitch, James would be forced to put the team interests first. A failure to do so would mean a failure to make the test team.

The tone had been set for the assault on the World Cup. Only the most disciplined and committed would make the side. You also had to fit into the coach's plans. He did not want complications, as Small found out. He did not want conflict, as Tiaan Strauss learned when Christie sacrificed the Western Province captain because of a possible clash of personalities with Francois Pienaar.

If he took to a player, Christie backed that player. Chester found himself taken to and favoured – all because of his ability to play rugby. It was refreshingly new to Chester and it encouraged him greatly. It was strong evidence that the Springboks could win the World Cup the following year. The win against Wales had confirmed the maturity of the Springboks. Playing at home would be an added advantage.

The biggest gain, though, was the introduction of Kitch Christie. The Springboks once again had discipline, and a disciplined Bok team was a champion team.

End of 1995: Triumph at Twickenham

10

The English have a way of boosting themselves and we felt the year would not have been complete without beating them

SOUTH AFRICAN television news bulletins showed the incident over and over. They slowed it down, cut it frame by frame and replayed it in super-slow motion. What the producers were telling viewers was: 'You be the judge.'

James Small, controversial Springbok and Natal winger, was in the dock for what appeared to have been a deliberate trampling of Chester's head during a Currie Cup match in Durban. The media slammed Small, who denied any intent to harm his Springbok teammate.

'I know it looked bad, but I was getting pushed around and didn't have much control. I would never hurt a mate like that,' Small pleaded to the media.

For all Small's protests of innocence, the volatile Bok winger was fair game to the country's media, and not only the pro-Chester press fan club in Cape Town. If the Cape press spared Small nothing, accusing him of playing the man and not the ball, other commentators were not far behind.

Gary Lemke, a Durban sports columnist at the time, was blunt in his assessment. 'Whichever way you look at things, James Small was guilty of trampling Chester. Otherwise referee Tappe Henning would not have reversed a Natal penalty and awarded it to WP ... What makes his trampolining of Chester appear that more callous was because it happened when the WP wing was lying unconscious on the King's Park turf.'

Cape Argus senior rugby writer Gavin Rich urged the South African Rugby Football Union to investigate the matter and backed up his request with detailed comment from Western Province president Ronnie Masson.

Province, as a union, wanted a full SARFU investigation. If found guilty, WP wanted Small suspended and ruled out of the test match against Wales, to be played in Johannesburg.

Chester had been concussed in an accidental mid-air collision with Small. It was not the collision that had led to the outrage, it was Small's alleged trampling on an unconscious Chester immediately thereafter.

Chester remains convinced that Small's action was deliberate. Masson, backing his player at the time, wanted justice done and the Cape media called for Small to be dropped for the test against Wales.

Cape Argus sports editor Archie Henderson asked for an official inquiry to be conducted and for the process to be open to the public.

'If it had been anyone other than James Small using Chester's back as a trampoline, we could have had second thoughts about what really happened out there on the King's Park turf,' wrote Henderson. He added that Small's threat to leave the country if the incident was investigated smacked more of a guilty conscience than an assertion of an innocent man unfairly persecuted.

Masson demanded action and took up the fight with the game's governing body, the SA Rugby Football Union. 'Technically, we are not able to cite a player for foul play once an incident has been acknowledged by a referee. But we think this incident is serious enough to warrant our sending an official letter of complaint to SARFU for further investigation,' said Masson.

The Province president also wanted SARFU to add substance to a promise from its chief executive Edward Griffiths that the governing body would take a hard line on foul play. SARFU cleared Small to play against Wales and said it would continue to investigate the incident, but added that no immediate action would be taken.

Griffiths said SARFU would deal with WP's request to further investigate the matter, but, predictably, in keeping with an apparent unwillingness on the part of the national body to deal with foul play, Small was later cleared of any wrongdoing. Not that it changed Chester's view.

James told the media that it was not intentional, but he never took the time to ever phone me and tell me the same story. He never spoke to me about it and when we toured together at the end of 1995 it was never mentioned. I know what I saw and it is my opinion that it was not an accident.

Chester, his rugby on hold for three weeks because of the concussion, turned his attention to things more glamorous – dinner with Nelson Mandela, president of South Africa and the inspiration of the Springboks' World Cup success earlier that year.

The contrast in Chester's movements – from knocked-out rugby player to VIP guest at the President's house – summed up his roller-coaster 1995 season: in the World Cup, out of the World Cup, back in and an instant success, a World Cup winner, a victim of concussion, out of another test, an invitation to dine with the President, later a losing Currie Cup final and the climax of the year, a glorious 80 minutes against England at Twickenham.

In August, 1995, Chester arrived at President Mandela's Cape Town residence, Genadendal, his head still sore from the clash with Small and the visit to Twickenham still two months away. He left with his head in the clouds and even more determined to play against England in the final test match of the year.

Chester and his fiancée Teresa had been invited to a private dinner at which the other guests were Errol Tobias, the Springbok flyhalf of the eighties and the first black player to wear the green and gold in rugby, and Tobias's wife Sandra.

To Chester's relief, President Mandela did not ask about the Small incident. Instead he spoke about attitudes, of role models and of South African sporting achievements. He described Chester as a leader of South Africa in the global sporting world and challenged the winger to add to what he had already achieved.

It was a pleasant evening. The invitation had come a few weeks before the incident with James Small so I would hate people to think it was based on the publicity following the game. It was not an invitation to ask me how my head was. We never even spoke about the incident.

Mr Mandela is a unique person and it is always inspirational to be in his company. We had struck up a kind of rapport during the World Cup and he would occasionally phone me to find out how things were going. He still calls me every now and then, just to catch up for a few minutes.

That evening he congratulated Errol and I on what we had achieved, despite the obvious hurdles of growing up black in apartheid South Africa. He is a rugby fan so he gets passionate about the Springboks. He congratulated us and, in my case, encouraged me to continue proving to the world that black players had the ability to be the best in the world.

It was a very low-key and laid-back evening. Soon after he started chatting, you forgot you were listening to the President of the country and a man who is acknowledged as one of the great leaders of the last century. I felt extremely comfortable. It was a bit like chatting to my grandfather. It was very relaxed. He has a good sense of humour and I, for one, found it easy to relax in his company. He wanted me to continue doing well. He impressed on me that winning the World Cup was only the start. I now had to take my performance to another level. He never spoke about humility, but his actions were a reminder of the power of humility.

The 1995 season had brought the Springboks unrivalled success. They were unbeaten in eight tests (six of them at the World Cup) and they were the champions of the world. All that remained in the year was a one-week stop-over in Rome en route to a season-ending finale against England.

Sceptics had questioned the benefit of playing England in London at the end of the World Cup year. The Boks had everything to lose. The players did not think so. They had not played against England at the World Cup because the All Blacks had beaten the English in that Lomu-inspired semi-final at Newlands.

While the South African public would have been content to end the international season after the World Cup final, the Boks wanted that one last game because it was England.

The English have a way of boosting themselves and we (as players) felt that the year would not have been complete without beating them. The World Cup worked out in such a way that we did not play them on our side of the draw. The trip to London would provide us with a chance of knocking over all the top teams in one year.

We had beaten Australia at Newlands, France in Durban and New Zealand in Johannesburg. England, in London, would be like the dessert after the main course.

The fear among rugby supporters and critics was that the Boks could be suffering from post-World Cup blues by the time they got to Twickenham. Defeat would devalue the year and would deprive the Springboks of their greatest season since returning to the international fold.

For about an hour in Rome, these fears appeared justified as the Springboks struggled to subdue a passionate but average Italian team. During those 60 minutes the Italians had taken the lead. Only a late flurry of points gave the Springboks a flattering win.

Chester and Small struggled more than most. Chester, in particular, had a horrible day. One mistake followed another.

If he had been dropped on the basis of that test, Chester would not have had reason to complain. But Kitch Christie was to remain true to his word: Chester would always be No 1 for No 11. While Chester would play against England, Small would not; Christie preferred Jacques Olivier on the other wing.

The axing of Small and the arrogance of the English squad, in particular South African-born flyhalf Mike Catt, set the tone for the week of the Twickenham test.

The senior Springboks were jolted by Small's omission from the starting team, but Christie had come to win; he would not tolerate anything but total commitment. This was to be no World Cup honeymoon. As far as Christie was concerned, this was an extension of the World Cup. Beat England and the Springboks could rest. Lose and lose the 1995 season.

The Boks were motivated and not in the mood to be ridiculed. Catt, new to the England squad, misread the situation. He targeted Pienaar in the English media, suggesting that the Springbok captain was a limited player and an average international.

Christie, usually composed and unflustered, could not hide his fury. He told the South African reporters covering the tour that it was a disgrace. Catt and the English would be made to pay.

It was not the wisest of comments to make. Kitch fired up the guys and got a bit extra out of them at training that week. It had been a long season, an emotionally draining one and, physically, the players had taken a beating. If some of the guys needed a spark, Mike Catt gave it to them in that week.

England coach Jack Rowell admitted after the test that Catt had learnt a valuable lesson: don't ever be that stupid again. The Springboks won 24-14, scored three tries to one and should have had a few more.

Chester got two, had a third disallowed by Scottish referee Jim Fleming and Joost van der Westhuizen scored one of the great individual tries in Twickenham's history.

Fleming had made it uncomfortable for the Springboks with the penalty count favouring England 28-7. But he could do nothing to suffocate the presence of Chester and Van der Westhuizen. He could also not help an England pack out-muscled, out-thought and out-played.

The Springboks won easily. England were scalped. Life, it seemed, could not get better on a rugby field. For Chester, it never would. There were more international highs, but mostly the next five years would be a time of frustration, reflection and an appreciation of the magnitude of what had happened in 1995.

1996/97: 'Chester is down'

11

I turned to chase a ball. As I turned I felt the knee go. I hobbled towards the ball, picked it up and threw a pass to James Small. I then just slumped on to my back and rolled over to the sideline

FOR Chester Williams, the 1996 season lasted 33 minutes. His next five years in rugby would be a constant struggle to overcome the effects of two knee injuries that threatened to bring his career to an end.

But the time he would spend on crutches would teach him about people, about rugby, about relationships and, most pertinently, about himself. In some acquaintances he found true friendship and in supposed friends he discovered fair-weather acquaintances.

If 1995 had been a roller-coaster, 1996 came packaged in a plaster cast and a set of crutches. A pre-season friendly against New Zealand's Canterbury Crusaders turned out to be Chester's only rugby activity of the year. With about 15 minutes gone in the game, Chester turned to chase a ball. He felt something go in his right knee, but carried on running.

The more he ran, the better the knee felt. But whenever he stopped running he felt as if the knee was going to give in. Nevertheless, he continued to play, trying out a few exercises to ease an increasing feeling of numbness in the knee. A quarter of an hour later he stopped again, and this time it felt as if the knee was going to cave in altogether. He walked off the field. He had torn the knee's cruciate ligaments, those two elements which play a significant part in keeping the joint stable.

The message that the cruciate ligaments sent to the muscles that day *was not good. Chester would need surgery which would put him out of rugby for at least six months, perhaps even longer. His season was over.*

He took a philosophical view, telling himself that the rest might even do him some good after an exhausting 1995 season. This reasoning also helped him come to terms with sitting at home for six weeks and hobbling around on crutches. He had to stay off the right leg for six weeks.

I was a very good patient in the beginning. The doctors said stay off the right leg because they feared sideways movement. I listened to what they said and tried to be disciplined while trying to get around.

Those first six weeks took a long time. It was a very difficult period because I was mostly confined to being at home, watching television and being dependent on others if I wanted to go anywhere. I had always been very independent and active during the day. Sitting around, to my mind, was wasted time. Gee, it was frustrating and you could not help but feel disillusioned. Those close to me would try to talk me up, but I knew that my recovery was about being patient. I had to count down the days and the hours and do exactly what the doctors told me.

The first six weeks were the worst because I was in a plaster cast. The most tempting time came when the doctors removed the cast and put me on a go-slow recovery programme. The temptation to run before I could walk was huge. It was a bit like being given a bicycle when you were used to driving a car at 100 kilometres an hour. Those first six weeks were an emotionally challenging experience.

Chester kept himself busy by getting involved in a series of community activities, including anti-crime and anti-drug campaigns, talking at schools about recycling (yes, it's a topic close to his heart), getting involved in raffle draws and generally staying in the public view.

He also visited the island of Reunion in late April 1996 to open a rugby stadium in the capital of St Denis. Chester might have been injured but he was far from forgotten.

He opened a cooldrink distribution depot in Paarl on the advice of his agent and lawyer Frikkie Erasmus. The business venture proved a disaster. Chester, however, also signed contracts with Shell, Adidas, BMW and Spur Steak Ranches. As far as he was concerned, financially he was set up for life.

He had signed a three-year contract with Western Province instead of signing with the South African Rugby Football Union.

Erasmus handled all Chester's business interests. The player never studied any contracts, he did not know the details of these contracts and did not ask about the finer points. He simply signed on the advice of Erasmus.

I trusted Frikkie with my life ... in later years I would find out how wrong I had judged the situation.

The television diet was over once the plaster cast came off and Chester set about the tedious task of getting his right leg strong again and finding some fitness along the way. Rebuilding the right leg was the main event in the early part of 1996. Watching the Super 12's inaugural year had convinced Chester that he still wanted to play rugby and he most definitely wanted to share the stage with the likes of Lomu, Cullen, Wilson and Joe Roff in this new southern-hemisphere competition.

The recovery schedule was standard: jogging five kilometres twice a week, three days of gymnasium work and check-ups with physiotherapist Bruce McLoughlin every two weeks.

Over and above that, the big event in Chester's life that year was his wedding to Teresa Muller. It was a grand affair, with 250 guests at the Spier wine estate near Stellenbosch. President Nelson Mandela was the special guest and Chester admits that, with hindsight, it was a mistake to invite such an icon to his wedding.

I was flattered that he accepted the invitation to attend, but the wedding became about the President of the country and not so much about Teresa and I. Getting married is a nerve-racking experience. Having the most revered man of the century as the guest of honour turned the entire afternoon into quite a drama. Security was tight, guests had to have special passes to get in. It turned into a state-like event when it was meant to be our wedding. I would learn from the experience.

The President spoke at the reception and wished us well. But his speech was a general one and not directed at Teresa and I. Many of the guests - and you cannot blame them – were more interested in President Mandela than they were in the two of us, the couple who were getting married. It made it a different day from the one Teresa and I and our families had envisaged.

You grow up planning your wedding day. It should be the happiest day of your life. It should be the day when you have the most fun. Your friends, your family and the woman you have committed yourself to are all there. It should have been one big party. Instead, my wedding day, on December 7, 1996, was one of the most nervous days of my life. I stood on ceremony most of the day, I was too nervous to speak and I was overawed by the occasion. I felt as if I was in this vacuum and the day was carrying me along, instead of me carrying the day.

Chester's mother, Julene, shares her son's recollection of what was supposed to be his big day.

'I felt like a movie prop being shifted around all day. Then we had to move here, then we had to go there. Then there was a scurry because the President was coming. The security ... ah ... I just wanted to see my son get married and have a fun day. It was a very formal affair ... very stiff. Never again, not like that.'

Chester and Teresa were married in Paarl and the media covered the event as if the couple were royalty. It was front-page news in the papers that weekend and exclusive wedding pictures were sold to a South African magazine.

A year in which Chester had played only a little rugby ended with the player's smiling face emblazoned across a magazine cover. Surely this was a portent for a better future after a dismal 1996? The famous smile hid the story of the setbacks in a year when Chester played only 33 minutes of rugby, committed himself to a business venture that flopped and sealed a marriage vow that in time would have to be broken.

The year also ended with Andre Markgraaff, a noted Chester Williams admirer, concluding his first year in charge of the Springboks. Markgraaff had succeeded Kitch Christie as coach of the Springboks. Christie, who had long suffered from leukemia, was retired as coach because of ill health, although he would hint in his biography that he had been worked out of the position.

Christie, in contrast to the resilience he had shown in the World Cup, went without a fight and his health took a severe beating during the Lions' unsuccessful debut season in the Super 12. He left the Lions in 1996 and, although he was tempted to help out with the Bulls in 1997, he could not see out the Super 12 season because of ill health. Christie, South Africa's saviour in 1995, died on April 22, 1998, after a battle with cancer which had lasted more than two decades.

Markgraaff, in succeeding Christie in 1996, struggled at first in the job as Springbok coach. His record of eight wins in 13 starts was average when compared with Christie's 14 successive wins. The start to the new era was inauspicious: Markgraaff's teams began by losing four of their five tests against the All Blacks and for the first time the Springboks lost a home series to New Zealand.

During that time Markgraaff brought Francois Pienaar's international career to an end and gave the captaincy to Gary Teichmann. The new coach also looked to rid himself of many of the 1995 World Cup-winning squad. Many players from that team were still suffering from a World Cup hangover and Markgraaff decided to put his trust in younger players who still wanted to win a World Cup medal instead of those who would rest on the laurels of having already done so.

Nevertheless, there was a mood of optimism. At the end of 1996, Markgraaff took a young team to Argentina, France and Wales and played some outstanding rugby in winning all five tests.

The Springboks beat Argentina 2-0 in a series, flew to France and completed a 2-0 series win and then concluded the year with a wonderful exhibition of total rugby in beating Wales 37-20 in a test at the Arms Park.

Chester, injured for the entire 1996 season, was excited at the prospect of forcing his way back into the test squad the following year. He knew it would not be easy, especially after the team had been so successful late in the year, but Markgraaff let Chester know early on that all it would require to get back in by 1997 would be the passing of a fitness test.

Even before Chester had played a match in 1997, Markgraaff included the winger in his national training squad. Chester was delighted, but he wanted to prove his inclusion was warranted.

Chester was part of Harry Viljoen's Western Province pre-season squad in 1997 and he worked hard at getting back to his best. The training went well, but the crunch would come in a match. Chester had not played for 12 months when Viljoen picked him to start an away game against the Falcons. Province won easily and Chester made it through 80 minutes. He took a few tackles, put in a few runs and scored a couple of tries.

Chester had experienced the euphoria before of making it through 80 minutes of rugby with his body intact. He had been there in 1995 when a seemingly unimportant club match provided him with the comfort that he was fit enough to play in the World Cup. He felt as good in the early part of 1997 as he had in 1995 when he had fought his way back from injury to get into the World Cup.

The 1996 rehabilitation had lasted almost a year. Chester had kept to the programme, had done everything the doctors had asked of him and had resisted the temptation to fast-track his recovery. His conscientious approach had paid dividends. In the February 1997 issue of South African Sports Illustrated magazine, Chester was featured on the cover, declaring that he would again play test rugby for South Africa. Other players had fought their way back from knee surgery, among them All Blacks flank Michael Jones and Wallabies centre Tim Horan. Chester wanted to add his name to the list of international stars who had fought off injury demons and returned, some even better than before.

There were the usual sceptics, some who questioned his lack of pace in the opening match against Eastern Transvaal. Chester just laughed it off. 'I have never had pace. Read the reports of my career,' he said to the media. 'How does a slow wing lose his pace?'

Province hosted Griqualand West in their first home match of the 1997 season. Chester was back at Newlands, starting for the first time since his 33-minute stint against the Crusaders the year before. This time his match lasted slightly longer, but he did not make 80 minutes. In another freak accident, his left knee's cruciate ligaments tore.

I turned to chase a ball. As I turned I felt the knee go. I hobbled towards the ball, picked it up and threw a pass to James Small. I then just slumped on to my back and rolled over to the sideline. Bruce McLoughlin came running over. I gave him one look. We both knew that we should expect the worst. I said to him: 'Bruce, my left knee's cruciate ligaments have torn.' He said that we did not know for sure. I said I knew. I had experienced the feeling before. I knew the knee was gone.

McLoughlin's memory of the sight is slightly more dramatic.

'Andrew Aitken, playing for Western Province, alerted me to the injury. I thought it was another player. He said: "Chester's down." My world collapsed for a moment. I took one look at him lying on his back and feared the worst.

'All I could think of was the rehabilitation of 1996. The guy had been through so much. He had fought so hard to get back and now he seemed to be gone again. I had not seen him involved in any contact. I did not even see him go down.

'When I got to him he was adamant that the cruciate ligaments were torn. Within 30 seconds – the time it took for him to go down and for me to arrive – he seemed to have rallied himself for the next year of recovery. When I got there, he said we simply had to start all over again.

'I think I was more shattered initially than he was. Perhaps it was his way of coping with the disappointment, but I kept on thinking how difficult it was going to be to start all over again. I underestimated Chester's fighting qualities and his desire to play rugby again. He had often told me that he would retire only on his terms, when he felt the time was right and he was ready to go. No one and no injury were ever going to determine his fate. He seemed pretty sure about that.'

Province won the match 27-14 and went on to win the domestic Nite Series (a forerunner to the Vodacom Cup) and Currie Cup that year, but Chester would spend the first six months of Province's domestic dominance limping between the gymnasium, McLoughlin's rooms and the athletics track.

'He was as motivated as ever,' remembers McLoughlin. 'You had to admire his resolve and self-belief. Everyone was writing him off. His epitaph had been written in most newspapers. The condolences were pouring in. Very few people expected him to be back. I would pick up the morning paper and read that Chester could not come back. Professor Tim Noakes (a noted Cape Town sports scientist) was quoted as saying

Chester had only a 40 percent chance of recovery. It was going to be a huge effort for him to play top-class rugby again, but Chester never seemed to doubt that he would be back.

'I would go from a mood of wondering if he would come right to knowing he would come right. He would arrive at my practice, oblivious to those who had written him off. He was upbeat and determined to get back. His strength of character is something I have yet to see the equal of in another rugby player. He fought prejudice, social injustice and injury. I don't think the average supporter can truly appreciate the magnitude of Chester's comeback. You had to work with him every day to know how hard he worked to make it back.'

Chester, in the months following his second knee operation, kept a low profile. This prompted Edward Griffiths to claim that Chester had been poorly managed and advised by Erasmus.

Griffiths, who had been fired as chief executive of the SA Rugby Football Union by Louis Luyt, had become head of SABC Topsport and was an occasional columnist. There was a history of disagreement between Griffiths and Erasmus.

While he had been chief executive of the SA Rugby Football Union, Griffiths had wanted Chester to sign for the union after the World Cup in 1995. Erasmus advised Williams not to and Chester ended up agreeing only to a three-year contract with Western Province that gave him complete control over any individual endorsements.

Griffiths, in a column written in 1997, launched a scathing attack on Erasmus's management of Chester. Griffiths cited specific examples of Erasmus's alleged mismanagement, claiming that Chester had 'disappeared' from the public eye.

'He is simply not there, not in blue and white, not in green and gold, not even on television, not on the radio, not in the newspapers. 'Gone,' wrote Griffiths. Among the missed opportunities to which Griffiths referred was a weekly appearance on a Topsport rugby programme. Erasmus had turned it down.

Erasmus, in the Cape Times on May 13, 1997, denied the accusations.

'Williams, having just renewed deals with Adidas and Spur Steak Ranches, continues his involvement with Telkom, contributes to water conservation in his capacity as a patron of the Department of Water Affairs and Forestry, visited Kenya as a guest of their inaugural sevens, was invited to the May 24 World XV match at Twickenham and has been asked to visit Australia and New Zealand to speak as a guest prior to the Tri-Nations matches.

'He writes a weekly column for the Cape Times and is actively involved in game development.

'Chester's welfare, his public profile and his future are my priorities. I

will act in Chester's interests as I have always done. Edward's public attack is a result of a history that exists between the two of us, and it includes me advising Chester not to sign with SARFU following the World Cup. It is a decision both Chester and I believe was vindicated by subsequent events.

'When Chester returned from Sun City after the World Cup and disclosed to me the events of Sun City and the proposed Kerry Packer breakaway, I contacted Griffiths and informed him that Chester would take no part in such a circus. I also did not believe it was in his interests to sign with the South African Rugby Football Union.

'Edward became very negative about my involvement with Chester and this was compounded by a previous dispute involving South African Airways.

'After the World Cup, Edward wanted Chester to be a part of a Bok team advertisement featuring the airline. As Chester was not contracted to SARFU, I requested payment. This led to a dispute and threat from Griffiths that the ad would go ahead without Chester. I told him the airline would not be happy as Chester was a client of theirs. When Griffiths would not relent, I suggested that Chester could always do an individual ad with rivals Sun Air if no agreement could be reached.

'This soured personal relationships and they got worse when I confronted Edward about allegations made to Chester about me. This was done in the presence of Chester and SARFU president Dr Louis Luyt.

'Griffiths reneged on what was said to Chester and, in Chester's presence, denied statements made. At that meeting he even threatened Chester, saying that if he did not sign with SARFU, he would not be picked for the Boks. Luyt took him to task immediately for the outrageous threat.

'When Luyt fired Griffiths as chief executive, I successfully acted for Luyt in resisting Griffiths's attempts to be reinstated. He has never forgotten that.

'Topsport wanted Chester to fly to Johannesburg every Saturday and do player profiles. They were not prepared to pay for his services and a broadcasting representative told me that there was no money available to pay him. I refused, saying Chester had to be paid.'

Erasmus also rebutted allegations that Chester had not wanted to be involved in the promotion of Cape Town's Olympic bid. He also gave his side of a dispute over a portrait of Chester that would be auctioned.

'Griffiths claimed the proceeds from the auction would go to development. There are few more committed to development than Chester. He does not need a television crew around each time he promotes development.

'The incident of the portrait involved Chester calling me on the eve of

the auction and telling me Edward wanted him to sign the portrait. I spoke to Edward and expressed my disappointment that there had been no prior consultation. Because Chester was not contracted to SARFU, I asked what he would be getting paid.

'Griffiths said he would get nothing; I requested a 15th of the auction fee. Griffiths then threatened to publicly let it be known that Chester did not care about development. I informed Chester not to sign the portrait. It was auctioned, unsigned, and Chester received no money for it.

'As far as the Olympic bid proposal was concerned, an agency phoned me and asked if they could use Chester as part of their campaign. When I asked what fee they had in mind, they said "None". When I asked if they were getting paid, they said "Yes". That was the end of our discussion. Chester, like many Capetonians, was undecided about the bid at that stage.'

Chester, in the same newspaper article, defended Erasmus: 'I have enormous respect for Mr Erasmus. We have developed a special bond since our relationship started in 1994 and I have great trust in every decision he makes.

'He has always put me first and because he does not accept a fee, it was I who said I would always want him involved in any future ventures. He guided me at a time when I needed it most, just after the World Cup. He acted for me and not himself. He continues to do so.'

Chester, in years to come, would not offer as flattering an overview of his relationship with Erasmus. The apology, in time, would go to Griffiths. In 2002 Chester severed all ties with Erasmus and took control of his own business interests.

Chester, through his weekly columns in the Cape Times, was still being profiled. His opinions mattered and he kept rugby followers informed about his recovery and expected comeback.

In August, 1997, Williams wrote: I leapt for joy when I heard the prognosis this week. I am back. My knee is fine. And in two weeks' time I will be in the rolling mauls and brawls in a club game for Stellenbosch University against Ceres.

I was very nervous going to see knee specialist Spike Erasmus for the final examination. He is happy that my knees will hold up to competitive rugby.

My physiotherapist, Bruce McLoughlin, is thrilled with my condition. I feel as if I am about to play for the first time; it is like starting all over again.

I will see how it goes in club matches. If everything runs according to plan, then I will be looking to play in the Bok sevens squad that will play in Punta del Este in Uruguay at the end of the year.

Chester's declaration that he was back enlivened newspaper copy and the headline on August 27 read: 'Chester to make his comeback … for Stellenbosch thirds.'

The next headline was ominous: 'Chester comeback put on hold.' It spoke about a hamstring strain, but the assumption was obvious. There would be no comeback. Chester Williams's career was over.

Chester tried to explain the delay and the cause of the hamstring strain.

Bruce (McLoughlin) said it was caused by the removal of a tendon from my hamstring to replace part of the ligament in my injured knee. He was not too surprised that my hamstring would play up a bit. I am delaying the comeback by a week or two, more as a precautionary measure. Believe me, I will be back.

Finally, Chester did make his comeback, playing for Stellenbosch's third team, the Cravens, against Parow NTC, the same club (with a slight name change) for which he had played in his comeback match in 1995.

Stellenbosch's senior team were playing in the national club championships and Chester wanted to be part of their build-up to the finals. But to be considered for the first team, he had to show he could make it through 80 minutes of club rugby.

Somehow he managed to do so and in the space of two weeks he played three matches: for the Cravens, for the Victorians (the club's second team) and for Stellenbosch senior team in the semi-final of the national club championships. Stellenbosch beat Vaal Reefs in the semi-final and Chester found himself preparing for a final at Newlands on October 25.

On the same day that Province hosted Free State in the Currie Cup final, Chester played for Stellenbosch in the curtain-raiser against Rand Afrikaans University.

I had wanted to play in the Currie Cup final on October 25. That was my intention when the season started. Now I was just grateful to be playing at all on that day.

I felt I had achieved something really big to be back on the field before the end of the season and to be playing in a club final was a bonus. Victory meant I had a medal to show for my 1997 season. It may only have been a club medal, but under the circumstances it was a medal that would symbolise a great deal to me during the remainder of my career.

I had been told I was finished and that I would never play again. I had proved people wrong. I knew I needed game time and I wanted to be in the best shape of my life in 1998. I wanted to make it a year that counted … one in which I proved to everyone I could play at the highest level again.

Quite unexpectedly, Chester got an offer to play club rugby in Italy at the end of 1997. It would be for only a few months, but it would mean that Chester would get much-needed match practice ahead of the 1998 season. Chester was desperate to play, especially if it was to be in a pressure-free environment.

He signed a three-month contract with Italian Second Division club Casale in the north of Italy. But if he thought there would be no pressure on him, he was wrong.

News spread quickly in Casale that a rugby legend would be playing for the local club. Casale president Giovanni Maggiore told the media: 'I have a container business and contacts with South Africa. I asked around if there was a good player available to come to our club for a few months. The name that came forward was Chester Williams. When I told our coach who I was bringing, he nearly fainted.'

Chester, too, was surprised to find out how much attention he attracted on arrival.

Casale played at the Eugenio Enrico Stadium. The capacity of the stadium was 2 200. Nearly 1 000 people turned out to watch my first training session. I was stunned at how much interest there was.

The people were wonderful. Everyone wanted to talk to me. The Italians are passionate people and they love their rugby. I played in my first match after only the one session and we lost to Parma. I did not know anyone's name, I could not speak the language and it was chaos on the field. No one seemed to care. They were playing and I was playing for them.

Even though we lost, it didn't mean that fewer people came to watch us train the next week. The people were great, but the weather was terrible. I had only been to Rome before and thought that the whole of Italy was like Rome.

When I got to Casale, it was raining; there was a lot of fog around and it was freezing. I did not enjoy the climate or the conditions in which we played. The people made up for the climate with their warmth. My only regret was that I was not in better physical shape.

I was into my second month of competitive rugby after a virtual two-year lay-off. They were understanding of my situation, but I still wish they had seen me at my best.

I only played three or four matches because the national Bok sevens selectors picked me for a tournament in South America. Sevens would again be my way back into the South African rugby fold. I was determined to show the world I could play rugby at the highest level. What I needed now was game time and lots of luck. The last real rugby I had played was in 1995. The 1998 season could not come quickly enough.

1998: Getting a new start

12

I just wanted to play. When you have played in three matches in two years and finished in only one, you don't really care where you start

ON a Friday night in late February 1998, Cape Town was pulsating with late summer heat, the bustle of thousands of tourists – and rugby.

The city that was passionate about the game had missed an entire season of the new Super 12 competition because its beloved Western Province had failed to qualify in 1997 by finishing outside the top four in the Currie Cup the year before. But on this night, the Super 12 returned to Cape Town, even if it was in a new form called the Western Stormers.

The Western Stormers was part of a new concept in South African rugby: regionalism. The country had been divided into four regions to ensure that all the top players would get a chance to play in the southern hemisphere's regional competition against teams from New Zealand and Australia. South Africa's four regions were the Western Stormers, the Sharks, the Cats and the Bulls.

The Stormers were presented that night to a Newlands crowd who found it hard to reconcile their love for the blue and white stripes of Western Province with this alter ego in muddled pyjama-looking jerseys. In time they would come to love an all-in-black Stormers team as much as their own WP, but on that February night it was pure love of rugby that helped them put aside their traditions and watch this notion of a home team play the Wellington Hurricanes.

They would even find mitigation for their new team's 45-31 defeat. Nothing could make them miserable; after all, it was still summer and, on a balmy night at Newlands, they were watching an international game of rugby that included a superstar in All Black and Hurricanes fullback Christian Cullen.

Much of the anticipation that night was based on a residual excitement from less than six months before when Western Province had won the Currie Cup. So, even if regionalism had not been introduced, Western Province would have been in the Super 12 of 1998. And anyway, this team made up of players from WP, Boland and South-Western Districts had a strong Province flavour. It was also coached by Harry Viljoen, who had taken WP to Currie Cup glory in his first year with the team in 1997.

The South African Rugby Football Union had opted for regionalism as a means to ensure that the country's 120 leading players were involved in the Super 12, a competition featuring five teams from New Zealand, three from Australia and four from South Africa. The Super 12 would be a stepping-stone to test rugby, which was why South Africa was eager that all its top players take part.

The Super 12 aside, the other talking point that month was Chester Williams. The darling of the successful 1995 World Cup, Chester had missed the 1996 and 1997 seasons because of knee injuries. In 1996 he had torn the right cruciate knee ligaments. A year later the left knee caved in. Medical opinion was divided on Chester's ability to play again. Cape Town's respected sports scientist Professor Tim Noakes gave Chester no more than a 40 percent chance of again playing top-class rugby.

At the start of 1998, Western Province had sent Chester to Adelaide in Australia for a sevens tournament in an attempt to ease him back into first-class rugby. Typical of the player, Chester responded brilliantly, playing in all the Western Province team's nine matches, scoring 10 tries and being named runner-up as player of the tournament.

Western Stormers coach Viljoen included Chester in the initial Super 12 squad, but it was only to make up the numbers. Chester had missed the Stormers' pre-season camp in Hermanus because of sevens duty and on his return he found himself training more with the Western Province Vodacom Cup team than with the Super 12 side.

The Vodacom Cup had been launched in 1998 as a South African competition to be held at the same time as the Super 12 to accommodate players who had failed to make the 120-man draft, and to identify latent talent.

One of the main purposes of the Vodacom Cup was to stimulate black rugby, and teams agreed to select more black players in order to speed up the process of bringing black talent into provincial rugby.

Teams in the south of South Africa were required to field at least three black players in their starting line-ups. Teams in the north needed a minimum of two as there was a belief that black players were fewer in that part of the country.

At the start of the season Chester was not looking at the Vodacom Cup for his comeback because he had made the initial Western Stormers pre-season squad, along with left wings Pieter Rossouw and Breyton Paulse. The right wings were James Small and McNeil Hendricks with Justin Swart covering at fullback and wing. But when Viljoen whittled down his squad, Chester lost out, as did Boland's Hendricks, who was drafted by the Bulls.

Chester, having started in only three matches in South Africa since his 1995 World Cup year ended in triumph against England, was prepared to settle for a place in the Western Province Vodacom Cup team. What he was not prepared to stand for, however, was being used as a political pawn by coaches who continued to baulk at picking black players. Some white coaches selected only the bare minimum of black players while others distorted the spirit of the agreement.

It was ironic that in 1998 South Africa's only black player at the 1995 World Cup needed to use a tournament designed to promote inexperienced black players as his means back into the international fold – six years after unity of black and white rugby had been achieved in South Africa with the specific aim of encouraging young black talent.

Even in the Vodacom Cup, Chester's provincial return was not without controversy.

To identify the black talent that South African rugby was seeking, the players were classified as coming from under-privileged areas (UPA). In the interests of political correctness, the definition changed within days to players coming from a previously disadvantaged area (PDA). Some cynics simplified the tag to 'quota players' or 'development players'. What was meant to be uplifting became pejorative.

The Western Province Vodacom Cup team of 1998, coached by Anton Chait, fielded six black players, including two Springboks in Chester Williams and Thinus Linee, in the opening match against Griquas.

Chait, young as a provincial coach and seemingly ignorant of the sensitivities involved, described Williams and Linee as being among his required 'development players'. He believed he was covering himself for a match where he needed at least two black players on the field at all times. But to the two Springboks, it was an insult.

To compound the insult, Chait then claimed the moral high ground against Griquas coach Andre Markgraaff, who had selected only three black players in his match squad of 23.

Markgraaff was no stranger to racial controversy in South African rugby. He had become coach of Griquas almost a year after vacating his position as coach of the Springboks in February 1997 following a revealing tape-recording of him making racist remarks against prominent South African rugby officials.

Markgraaff admitted that it had been his voice on a tape-recording containing outbursts of racial abuse and other obscenities. The remarks were made during a conversation with Griquas player Andre Bester, brother of a well-known right-winger Piet Bester, who had played for Griquas and Free State. Unknown to Markgraaff, Bester had tape-recorded the interview.

Bester then leaked the tape-recording to the SABC, South Africa's national broadcaster, and the transcript to various newspapers. Once transcripts of the tape-recording became public, Markgraaff resigned in disgrace from the Springboks.

Bester, a disgruntled player, had gone to see Markgraaff to renegotiate his playing contract and had hidden a tape-recorder in his pocket. During their discussions, the two men spoke about South African rugby in general. Markgraaff was scathing in his opinion of individuals such as Springboks Francois Pienaar and Andre Joubert. He also lashed out at blacks in rugby, referring to them as 'kaffirs'.

In his resignation speech on television, a tearful Markgraaff maintained that he was no racist and that he had been set up by what he described as 'one of the ugliest incidents in sport'.

More than a year after that damning incident, Markgraaff's name was linked to another racial controversy in South African rugby, albeit of a different nature – the contentious issue of quotas in rugby and specifically how these applied to the Vodacom Cup match between Western Province and Griquas.

The dispute over quotas between the two teams came against a background of political tension in South African rugby at the time.

The game was under attack, especially from the politically aware youth who wanted to see growth and transformation in South African rugby, a sport which had once been claimed exclusively by the white minority as its national pastime.

At the same time, rugby was trying to shed its image as the apartheid regime at play and it was sensitive to criticisms that it could not adapt to a new South Africa. The last thing it needed was unnecessary controversy over the selections – or the lack of them – of black players.

Chait's assumption that Williams and Linee could be part of his minimum black representation was seen as a cynical expedient and he was condemned for it. His attempts to cast the blame in Markgraaff's direction, for picking three black players – and all of them on the wing – were met with scorn.

All this happened just as black players began to speak out for the first time – with their criticism not only aimed at white coaches.

Stanley Raubenheimer, selected for the Western Province team in 1993 but never given an extended run at scrumhalf, slammed black and coloured administrators for not looking after the interests of black players. Five years after WP had selected seven coloured players to tour Australia and New Zealand, the Western Province team that won the 1997 Currie Cup final was all white.

Raubenheimer lashed out at the WP selectors. On February 6, 1998, he told the Cape Times: 'I want the WP selectors to know that coloured and black players have dignity and the will to achieve. I also want people to acknowledge that we have played the game for as long as the whites have.

'We are not second-rate players. Apartheid robbed us of structures and opportunity. Unity promised the latter, but our own officials have not been prepared to walk with any former South African Rugby Union player.' SARU had been the non-establishment rugby body which was affiliated to the South African Council of Sport and had been one of the organisations at the forefront of the struggle against apartheid. Raubenheimer's implication was clear: some black administrators were sell-outs.

'We can blame the provincial presidents and coaches until we are blue in the face, but our own people have let us down since unity. The administrators are only looking after themselves.'

Black politicians who wanted to know why the pace of transformation had been so slow also began to apply pressure on the black rugby community. Six years after white and black rugby had united in 1992, white players still dominated representative teams.

Also in February 1998, the then Minister of Sport, Steve Tshwete, touched the nerve of white South African rugby – the cherished Springbok emblem. He hinted that there could be a change of emblem if the national rugby team continued to remain exclusively white.

Tshwete had been a strong supporter of the unification process in South Africa's racially divided sport. Indeed, he had often played a key role in bringing together rival elements, earning the name 'Mr Fixit' by helping to reconcile apparently irreconcilables. Now he, too, was getting tired of an obvious resistance to transformation.

Tshwete's comments followed National Sports Council president Mluleki George's outspoken views on the lack of transformation in the South African game. George had threatened to call for an international rugby boycott of South Africa if the provincial unions did not recognise the need for teams to reflect all the rugby talent in the country, and not just the white part of it.

Tshwete questioned the commitment of white officials to change after only four black players were among the 121 selected for South Africa's four Super 12 teams in 1998. It was a testing time for South African rugby.

South Africa's regional and provincial coaches, all of them white men, still did not seem to appreciate the seriousness of the situation and made little attempt to ease the tensions. A case in point was the Eastern Province winger Deon Kayser, who had made a strong claim for regional inclusion.

Kayser missed out on the initial squad of 120 players. He was added to the Sharks squad of 30 after black politicians condemned his exclusion. Instead of dropping a white player to accommodate Kayser, the selectors simply added a black number to the mix. Kayser would go on to become a distinguished Springbok.

This lack of recognition for black players was typical of South African rugby in the 1990s. Coaches and administrators played a numbers game. It annoyed the politicians, none more so than Tshwete.

Furious at the lack of opportunities for black players, Tshwete asked whether South African rugby's 'lily-white teams' deserved to be playing international rugby. 'Do they deserve to wear the Springbok? Do they deserve to be competing with international teams in the light of the scenario that is developing in this country?' he asked.

At the same time, between February and March of 1998, Tshwete and President Nelson Mandela were locked in a bitter High Court battle with the game's national governing body, the South African Rugby Football Union, which had been formed after unity and had brought together the disparate elements of rugby in the country.

The battle had come about after a court challenge by the rugby union to a government intention to appoint a commission of inquiry into the sport.

The government, impatient with a lack of change in rugby, had announced in August 1997 that the commission was to be set up. It would be chaired by a senior Johannesburg advocate, Jules Browde.

But rugby, led by SARFU president Louis Luyt, decided in October 1997 to challenge the government's right to investigate the union. SARFU maintained that the government had no right to interfere in an independent organisation and that the union had protection under the constitution.

Legally, the game's governing body had two legs to stand on, but morally it was legless. Rugby's defiance of a government inquiry and its insistence, during the hearing, in forcing President Mandela to the witness stand proved to be among the most self-defeating moves it played in the 1990s.

Through all the infighting and political manoeuvring, the Vodacom Cup, the tournament of opportunity, was seen as a bright light in the unified South African game in spite of some selection distortions.

The focus of the Vodacom Cup was on how many black players would get opportunities. Actions had to show a clear intent to change. Quotas were introduced, but it was hoped that coaches would look beyond these and spontaneously pick more black players than the minimum laid down by regulation.

It was naïve, however, to think that 100 years of prejudice in South African rugby would disappear in a few seasons. Even in February 2002, in the first round of the Vodacom Cup, only one province in 14 exceeded the revised quota of five black players in southern teams and three black players in northern teams.

In this political turmoil, Chester Williams, a test Springbok in 1993, a sevens Springbok since 1993, a World Cup winner in 1995 and the darling of Western Province rugby, used the Vodacom Cup as his way back from two career-threatening knee injuries.

He was excited about playing again. His goal was to play Super 12 rugby in 1998 and test himself against the southern hemisphere's best. He knew that his only chance back into the test squad would be through the Super 12.

But to break into the Western Stormers Super 12 squad, he would first have to make an impression in the Vodacom Cup. Stormers coach Harry Viljoen, on arriving in Cape Town in 1997 to coach Western Province, had shown he did not select on reputations.

Chester was prepared to take the long road back. He took the Vodacom Cup campaign seriously.

I just wanted to play. When you have played in three matches in two years and finished in only one, you don't really care where you start. It is just about getting a start. I had no problem working my way back in the Province Vodacom Cup team. I didn't regard the team or the competition's status as second rate. Playing rugby is all I wanted to do and the competition was an opportunity for me to do so.

In the week leading up to the tournament's opening fixture between Griquas and Western Province, Chester found himself at the centre of a row that emphasised white coaches' reluctance to pick black players.

WP coach Chait said he would protest if Griquas were unable to maintain their quota requirement of two black players on the field at all times.

'We have got six black players in our squad total and Griquas are taking a huge risk. If they lose two, they will be unable to maintain the quota and WP would then protest,' said Chait.

Markgraaff retorted: 'You cannot regard Chester Williams or Thinus Linee as development or under-privileged players. They're both Springboks. WP, by picking these two as UPA players, are taking a bigger chance and not playing in the spirit of the competition.'

The dispute over semantics and what constituted a UPA player only showed up the racial bias that even today haunts post-apartheid rugby in South Africa.

Chester, having always shied away from the racial politics associated with the game in South Africa, went public with his condemnation of the UPA tag. At the time of the controversy, these were his words...

I find it insulting because development always refers to coloured or black players. In my case, particularly, there are a few misconceptions that need to be put right.

I am not a product of any development system. I fought my way through the structures by playing club rugby for Defence and provincial rugby for Western Province League and Western Province. I made the Springbok team on merit and my record justifies my selection.

I do not come from a socially disadvantaged background. I consider my upbringing to have been good. My parents worked hard to give me the best. My financial circumstances now are very healthy and as a citizen of this democratic country I have the right to vote.

I also played in a winning World Cup final against the All Blacks and, having marked a player of Jeff Wilson's quality, I would like to ask the authorities and coaches, how much more developing do I need?

Chester added that the constant reference to coloured and black players as development and UPA products was not only embarrassing but an oversight of the individual social circumstances of rugby players, irrespective of their colour.

I am a test Bok who, financially, is not struggling. But I am coloured and am classified a UPA player. In our WP team Martin van Schalkwyk is a 21-year-old white student who supports himself by working as a barman. He is considered a Western Province player!

People really need to start looking at the merits and not the colour of each player.

WP Rugby Union president Ronnie Masson responded publicly and positively to Chester. Embarrassed by the ignorance of his provincial selectors, Masson declared that Williams and Linee would never be seen as anything but rugby players. They had represented their country and would be given the necessary recognition.

The match, unlike the build-up, passed without incident. Chester completed the 80 minutes, rarely saw the ball and Province were hammered 55-26. Of greater importance to Chester was that his comeback was on track. The knees felt strong. The mind had always been strong.

The determination, amid the racial turmoil, would once more prove that he was worth his place as a player and could never be classified a black player in need of special treatment.

Super 12 remained his goal and the daily grind at Vodacom Cup was a means to get there. Every week Chester put in the necessary slog and each weekend was another step closer to the Super 12 and possibly even the national squad.

Rugby, though, was taking a pounding in its scrap with the government. SARFU president Louis Luyt had taken on Nelson Mandela. It might have been bold; it might have been constitutionally correct. Given the political sensitivities in South Africa, it was an act of self-destruction for Luyt.

On March 19, 1998, Mluleki George, NSC president but now wearing his cap as president of the Border Rugby Union, urged all of rugby's provincial unions to distance themselves from Luyt and SARFU's decision to challenge a government-sanctioned commission of inquiry into rugby.

'It is clear Luyt is leading rugby to a disaster,' read a statement, signed by George. 'We are calling on all provinces to come out openly and distance themselves from this Louis Luyt fiasco. The President (Nelson Mandela) went out of his way to mobilise the nation to be behind the national squad during the World Cup. To thank him for his efforts, Luyt summons our beloved President to be interrogated and humiliated in front of the High Court of this country.'

Luyt's action, said George, was indicative of a calculated campaign to undermine and embarrass the democratic forces which had opened the way to international sports arenas. 'While the other codes have been engaged in transformation, reconciliation and nation-building, Louis Luyt has actively shown his intention to maintain the status quo of the old apartheid order.'

SARFU dismissed George's accusations, countering his argument with a curve ball of its own. 'The SARFU decision to oppose the proposed Browde commission of inquiry in court was taken by the full SARFU executive and not Dr Luyt. This was done at a meeting in Johannesburg on August 5, 1997.

'On this occasion, prior to the appointment of the proposed commission, Mr George was adamant in stating SARFU should use all legal means at their disposal to protect their rights,' said the statement.

'The decision to oppose the proposed commission in court was accepted and ratified by the SARFU annual general meeting and the 14 provinces in Cape Town on November 4, 1997. Both of these decisions have been submitted as evidence in the court action. For Mr George now to attempt to blame Dr Luyt for a decision he was party to, is unacceptable.'

The public spat between SARFU and the government and within SARFU made for sensational newspaper copy, but it was suffocating the game. Weekly threats of international boycotts made players edgy. Players' agents scouted overseas because of the fear of new isolation. Rugby sponsors called for emergency meetings.

The game had to be put before personal agendas and no individual could be seen to take priority over the game. Luyt, South African rugby's tycoon, was under siege. He stood firm, however, his defiance applauded by the rugby conservatives. He questioned every motive behind the calls for an investigation into rugby.

Emotion proved more powerful than fact and while rugby (Luyt in particular) was condemned, the government did not cover itself in glory. Mthobi Tyamzashe, at the time director-general of sport, admitted to the court that he had not exactly been truthful in a statement to the press quoting President Mandela as saying that if Tshwete wanted a commission appointed to investigate rugby's affairs, then he would get one.

It was a potent admission. A proposed commission of inquiry was said to have had the backing of the President. Now Tyamzashe was telling the court that the President had never actually expressed this support.

Many of South Africa's newspapers failed to see the significance in this admission. After Tyamzashe's appearance in the witness stand, the government could suddenly find no copy of the press statement. SARFU, however, obliged by finding its copy.

Tyamzashe was asked to explain the statement but, under cross-examination, could not. All he had wanted to do, he admitted, was give rugby a fright and get it to co-operate with the inquiry. It was, he said, just part of the tactics to make SARFU nervous and to comply.

Tshwete further acknowledged, also in court, that he had learned in time that Tyamzashe had not spoken to the President. But he did not consider it serious enough to take action against his director-general. There would be no disciplinary measures and no retractions.

Rugby's bosses challenged the government's decision to appoint a commission because they felt there were no grounds to justify an inquiry.

The Cats were asked to include Chester in their squad. The Sharks and the Bulls inquired about his availability. All of a sudden Chester Williams was in demand again. Finally the call came, although the circumstances could have been better.

The Western Stormers returned to South Africa after a four-match beating in Australia and New Zealand. The results included a record 74-28 hammering by the Blues.

The Stormers squad was in disarray, coach Viljoen had offered his resignation, injuries had weakened the squad and morale was at a low after Van der Linde had been sent home and banned from rugby for his racial insults of the woman in the Christchurch bar incident.

Chester, desperate to play in the Super 12, let it be known he would play for any team. The Cats, Sharks and Bulls all wanted him. So, too, did the beleaguered Stormers, who had first option.

The Stormers invited Chester to their first training session after returning from tour and picked him on the right wing. He took the position which had been held by James Small. Small had been injured and his return from injury would be limited to the substitute's bench.

Chester's first match for the Stormers was against the Highlanders from New Zealand. No more than 14 000 turned up at a soaked Newlands to watch a Stormers team that in the following years would average a home crowd attendance of more than 40 000. The Highlanders won 36-15, with All Blacks winger Jeff Wilson and Jeremy Stanley each scoring hat tricks.

The only positive for Western Province and South African rugby was that Chester Williams was on fire. He scored two tries, played aggressively and looked a class act again.

After the match, Stormers coach Harry Viljoen was asked whether he had made a mistake by writing off Chester earlier in the year. 'I have new respect for Chester Williams,' Viljoen replied. 'I have always admired him as a player, but this year he has shown that as a person he is deserving of as much respect. He is the most committed and courageous player I have ever seen. I can only compliment him on his comeback and say "Well done". Clearly, you don't write off Chester Williams.

'To be honest, I didn't think Chester was ready. But he has proved me wrong; in all my years in rugby I have never worked with a player with such determination and spirit to succeed.'

Those words stayed with Chester, who was seated two places away from Viljoen at the press conference.

It meant a lot to me that he publicly acknowledged my comeback. In the years to follow we would always have a healthy and honest relationship.

The euphoria of his first match for the Stormers soon ended for Chester. The following week he limped through 80 painful moments of Super 12 rugby at Ellis Park.

A Stormers team, di[illegible]led and disjointed, made up the numbers in [illegible] of the season against the Cats. Their coach [illegible]e squad was injured and a luckless Johnny [illegible]ormers' captaincy.

Chester, playing on the wing, strained a hamstring but had to stay on the field because there were no more replacements available on the bench.

We got smashed by 40 points. There was absolutely nothing going on. There was nothing to play for. I don't think I have ever experienced a match in which a team was at such a low going into the game.

I ended up playing scrumhalf because I could hardly walk; James Small simply walked from the field shouting at Alan Solomons, the assistant coach, and every one of the squad counted down the whistle.

For the record, the Cats won 41-7 in what was only their second victory in the competition that season.

The ring announcer at Ellis Park screamed at the 22 000 die-hards to stay off the field. Instead, they screamed back at him to open the gates; they wanted to get out of the park, and not on the field. It had been that kind of game.

Chester, his hamstring hurt again, knew he had three weeks in which to recover. There would be little domestic rugby until June. Rehabilitation was again a word used to describe Chester's daily routine.

Chester, on the mend, knew that it was unrealistic to expect international recognition on the basis of a two-try burst against the Highlanders and one-legged makeshift performance at scrumhalf against the Cats.

He was not overly concerned at initially missing out on the test squad. He did not deserve to be picked on form. All he cared for was that there would be no international boycotts. His dream of playing test rugby again would not be thwarted by politics. Knees and hamstrings perhaps, but not boardroom and courtroom confrontations.

It was game on for the Springboks, even though Chester accepted that there had not been enough Super 12 game time to warrant inclusion in Mallett's test squad to play Ireland. Other wingers had been playing well. Stefan Terblanche had made an impression, McNeil Hendricks was the black wing flavour of the season and Pieter Rossouw and James Small had been regular internationals in the two years that Chester had watched from the sidelines.

I did not expect to get into the team. There had not been enough games. My focus had to be on taking the next step back through the Currie Cup.

Surprisingly, on June 30, Springbok coach Nick Mallett drafted Chester into an extended squad of 26 for the single test against a weakened England in Cape Town. There were whispers that Chester's recall had to do with race and black numbers in the Springbok squad, but Mallett focused on the ability of a player who boasted a World Cup winner's medal.

Mallett told the media: 'Chester has always been among the wing candidates and we need cover for the back three. It is good to have him back in the framework. He is a widely respected Springbok, within the squad and the opposition. Full credit to him for the way he has battled through two injuries that wiped out two years of his career. He put in the hours at the gym and was prepared to play club, sevens and Vodacom Cup rugby to get back. Now he has got his reward.'

Chester, his last test match against England at Twickenham in 1995, was desperate to make it into the squad of 22. It was not to be. There were two little Chester cameos in the month of July, both as a blood replacement in the Springboks' historic away wins against Australia in Perth and New Zealand in Wellington. The minutes Chester spent on the field in Australia and New Zealand can be counted on both hands, but he had the taste of Springbok rugby again.

To get a bigger helping, he would have to play for Western Province in the Currie Cup. What had once been a formality for Chester was going to prove a challenge in 1998. Province had a new coach in Springbok assistant Alan Solomons – and Solomons was ready to trade in the Chestermobile for something faster, more exciting and much newer.

'Scrap the Chestermobile'

13

I had gone on record saying that they wouldn't even have to pay me to play for WP. However, it was quite clear that Solly was never going to pick me

RESPECTED *South African rugby writer Gavin Rich, in speculating that Chester Williams might leave Western Province, described Newlands without Chester as Cape Town without Table Mountain.*

In 1998, however, it seemed inevitable that the colossal presence of Chester Williams would not be seen in the blue and white hoops at Newlands again. New Western Province coach Alan Solomons looked to a WP future which he believed did not need the stabilising influence of the World Cup winger.

Solomons, who replaced Harry Viljoen as WP coach in mid-1998, was a great believer in the qualities of WP and Springbok wing Pieter Rossouw. Solomons also spoke favourably of the potential impact a young Breyton Paulse could make on the game. Chester and fellow test wing James Small were contracted to Western Province for the duration of the 1998 season, but from the outset Solomons made it clear that Small would not feature in his plans for the 1999 season.

Small was offered no contract and tried unsuccessfully to rejuvenate his career at the Lions in 1999. Chester was determined to prove he had a future at Western Province. Solomons had given him assurances that he was still in the mix, but would give him no guarantee that he would start in the Currie Cup campaign in 1998.

I was in a difficult position because I had not played much Super 12 rugby. I could make no demands nor claim any position as my own. I had to rely on opportunities, which I felt were going to be limited.

Solomons had made no secret that he felt Pieter Rossouw was his number one wing and he was beginning to speak highly of Breyton Paulse as a class player. All I could offer Solly was my commitment that I would give him my best.

Anyway, Chester's Currie Cup ambitions were put on hold because of national sevens commitments at the Commonwealth Games in Kuala Lumpur in 1998. He had been made captain of a South African team that included Western Province stars Rossouw, Paulse and Bob Skinstad.

The sevens call-up came at an awkward time and Chester believes events at the tournament might have killed off any prospect he had of making it at Western Province during the Solomons era.

Skinstad, a phenomenon in South African rugby in 1998, had been appointed Western Province captain. Solomons rated Skinstad the best rugby player in the world and the best South Africa had produced in two decades. The relationship between the two was very close.

Chester feels he may have closed the door on his WP career because of an on-field altercation with Skinstad at the Commonwealth Games.

We were playing Samoa in the quarter-finals and we were awarded a penalty. Skinstad had the ball and I felt he was showboating. I screamed for him to tap the ball and pass it. He didn't respond. I screamed at him to 'pass the fucking ball'. I was really upset and used the f-word in the heat of the moment.

The game continued and there was a break at a lineout. Skinstad ran over to me and told me to never, ever scream at him again. I told him that I would scream when I felt it necessary and if he wasted time again I would react in the same way.

He then threatened to the leave the field. I told him to go, using the f-word again. I got quite heated and screamed at him. If he did not like it, then it was best that he went. He stayed on the field, but the incident obviously upset him.

That night I walked into his room and he was on the phone to Solly. I heard my name mentioned and when he looked up I was standing there. He ended the call. We sorted the thing out, but who knows what was said to Solly.

When we returned to South Africa the following week I was the only Western Province player who had competed at the Commonwealth Games who was not required for Province's Currie Cup match against the Lions. Solly told the media that I was tired and needed a break after the sevens. But he picked Breyton, Bobby and Pieter. How could I have been more tired than they were? I believe it was felt that I would undermine Bobby's captaincy because of what happened in Kuala Lumpur.

I never took on Solly about his decision as it was not my style to confront coaches who did not pick me. When the media called me, all I told them was that I was fit and eager to play. If the coach felt I needed a break then that was his opinion. Mine was that I could have played.

Chester was included in the Province match squad of 22 for the latter part of the Currie Cup campaign and he was instrumental in taking Solomons's WP team to one move away from a Currie Cup final win against the Blue Bulls.

An injury to fullback Percy Montgomery meant a backline reshuffle for the Currie Cup final against the Blue Bulls at Loftus. Rossouw and Paulse, both capable fullbacks, shared the No 15 responsibility and Chester took his place on the right wing. He scored a try, running on to a kick through from flyhalf Christian Stewart, and in the final moments of the game he was put away by a Paulse pass for what would have been the match-winning score... except that referee Andre Watson ruled the pass to have been forward. Chester felt the pass had been good.

I was the one running off Breyton. All my life I have heard that I don't have pace. How could I have been ahead of Breyton? Seriously, I thought it was a good pass and that I was behind the ball.

It was Andre's call, but it could so easily have been called good. When I look at the video replay it was a very close thing. I believe it was good. On another day the referee might have let it go and Western Province might have been another Currie Cup richer.

Chester's performance in the final showed his career was back on track, but it had come too late to make it into Nick Mallett's 1998 Springbok team for the tour to the United Kingdom and Ireland.

The following year would be massive. It was World Cup time and Chester accepted that to make the 1999 World Cup team he would have to play regularly at the top level. But he was not even sure of getting a chance to play regularly for Western Province with Solomons in charge. If his career was going to include international rugby, then Chester would have to move.

I was disappointed that Solly did not want to use me in the 1999 season. He offered me a poor contract, almost half of what I was on, and made it very clear that unless there was an injury, he would not pick me in his starting line-up.

Solly did not have faith in me. He was concerned about my durability after the two knee injuries and felt that it was not in his interests to continue with me. He was honest with me: he told me that he was not going to pick me; he had Breyton and Pieter and he felt he wanted to use the younger guys as back-up to them.

I respected his decision and it forced me to make a business decision. I just wish he had been as open with me when I had got back from Kuala Lumpur. I would have respected him even more if he had then told me he thought I wasn't good enough, instead of telling the media I needed a break.

Chester insists that if it had been possible, he would have stayed in Cape Town.

All my career I had maintained that I would never leave Western Province. I had gone on record saying that they wouldn't even have to pay me to play for WP. However, it was quite clear that Solly was never going to pick me.

Moving to Johannesburg was never a personal choice. I had to make a move if I was going to win back the Bok test jersey. The Lions provided me with a positive career move.

I never regretted the decision and I don't think Solly ever regretted letting me go. You could say it worked out for both of us. Solly will feel vindicated because of what Breyton and Pieter did for him and I won a Bok recall on the basis of my performances with the Lions and Cats.

In the two years that he was in Johannesburg, Chester would play only once against Paulse and once against Rossouw. The first match, between the Cats and the Stormers at Newlands in May 1999, was the more emotional of the two victories.

It was strange to arrive at Newlands and walk towards the visitors' change-room. Everyone was very good to me. People who worked at Newlands came up to me and chatted before the game. Everyone who came up to me wanted me to do well. They wanted me to score tries, but they wanted the Stormers to win. It felt very good to know they still supported me. It gave me a boost to get that kind of response.

When they went on to the field before the kick-off for the customary pre-match walk around the park, the Cats players were booed, and when they ran on for the game a while later, the jeering was even louder. But when he ran on last, Chester was cheered as if he were still playing for Western Province and the Stormers. Even when he took to the field as part of the opposition, the crowd reserved a special welcome for him. His jersey colour had changed. His popularity had not.

One of the superstitions when I run out on to a field is to always go out last, about three metres behind the fullback. So the team goes and a few seconds later I leave the tunnel. When I came out there was a very positive reaction. It made me feel as if I had never left.

Newlands, home to so many Chester Williams tries, tackles and breaks, had also been a ground of torture for the winger. Twice he had been carried from the field with torn cruciate knee ligaments and in his only test at Newlands he was carried off with concussion.

On this particular day, the ground would be kind to him. His homecoming was celebrated with a win: the Cats, 11th in the Super 12, shocked the league-leading Stormers.

It was a special match for me and one we badly wanted to win. We had come back from a month in Australia and New Zealand and had not got a win. The Stormers were crushing every team and playing some superb rugby. There was a lot of needle in the match and there were a lot of guys in the Cats squad who wanted to prove a point.

Among those were Chester, former Western Province under-21 halfbacks Dave von Hoesslin and Gaffie du Toit, former Western Province conditioning coach Chris van Loggerenberg, and the Cats assistant coach Dick Muir, who captained the Western Stormers in 1998.

The match turned out to be a nail-biter with the Cats outlasting the Stormers 18-16. Chester and Paulse hardly had a run at each other with the match played mostly among the forwards and in the midfield.

I have always rated Breyton very highly. I played most of my career with him so I can't say much about him from the view of the opposition. I imagine he must be very difficult to play against because he has such good footwork. In the match against the Stormers, neither of us saw much of the ball.

A year later, the Cats again beat the Stormers, only this time the match was played in atrocious conditions at Ellis Park with the game nearly called off because of lightning. In that match Chester opposed Pieter Rossouw, Solomons's first-choice wing and a good friend of Chester's.

Again, there was much antagonism in the build-up to the match.

Chester, having been part of the team to put one over Solomons's Stormers in 1999, was at it again in 2000. Impressive in all aspects of the game, Chester rounded off his performance with a fine individual try. In a show of gamesmanship, he presented Rossouw with the ball once the try had been allowed. The act was a response to the sledging Chester had received during the match.

Pieter and I are good mates and we chat often. When I was injured he was one of the few guys who would always call to see how things were going and to keep me up to date with the team news. I appreciated the calls.

That day when I scored, I showed him the ball as if to ask 'What do you say now?' Pieter, very uncharacteristically, had chirped me a bit during the game. He is not the kind of player who does a lot of chirping on the field so I was a bit surprised, but then again you have to put it down to the pressure of the match.

When I scored I gave him the ball as my response. It was my chirp. There was no malice in the gesture. You could say we were playing mind games. He chirped me and my best response was to score. Afterwards we had a good laugh about it, but I think we both felt a bit embarrassed by our actions on the field.

Chester, though, had reminded Stormers coach and Springbok backline coach Alan Solomons that he could still play rugby. More importantly, he had forced his way back into the test frame through quality performances. Like him or not, rate him or not, Springbok coach Nick Mallett was going to find it increasingly difficult to leave out an in-form Chester Williams.

1999: A World Cup snub

14

In that week I saw just how the Stormers and Western Province players are despised by the teams from the north

CHESTER WILLIAMS *was primed for the 1999 season. It was World Cup year and he felt that all he had to do to make Nick Mallett's Springbok squad was play well in the Super 12 and Currie Cup.*

The decision to leave Cape Town had pretty much been made for him. Western Province and Stormers coach Alan Solomons did not rate Chester, but the player was comforted by the appointment of Andre Markgraaff as head coach of the Cats. Markgraaff was someone who held Chester in high regard.

Markgraaff had always believed in Chester's ability. In 1997 Markgraaff, while still Springbok coach, had included Chester in his pre-season test squad of 27. The fact that Chester had not played any rugby in 1996 because of a knee injury had not deterred Markgraaff at the time. Chester was his man and as far as the Springbok coach was concerned, the only thing that would keep Chester out of test rugby would be a lack of fitness or injury.

But Markgraaff could never call on Chester; the winger broke down in February 1997 with another knee injury and by the time Chester had recovered, Markgraaff had left the international stage, a disgraced individual whose achievements would always be clouded because of a racist outburst in which he called blacks 'kaffirs'.

In 1999 the two finally got to work together. Markgraaff had been forgiven by the black rugby authorities, if not by the black community, and was reintroduced into South African rugby through Griquas at provincial level and the Cats in the Super 12.

Chester, his career as a Western Province and Stormers player over, had gone to live in Johannesburg and would play for the Cats in the Super 12 and the Lions in the Currie Cup.

Seeing Chester in the Cats strip was not strange at the time because the Super 12 regional teams were still in their infancy. The Cape traditionalists, however, would struggle to come to terms with Chester in the red and white of the Lions rather than the blue and white of Western Province. For close on a decade, Chester had worn only the colours of Western Province; now he was part of the enemy.

Markgraaff was confident he could get the best out of Chester and played him in the Cats' first Super 12 match, with James Small – another rugby refugee from Solomons's WP – on the other wing. The two wings, who had played together often for the Springboks, would play their last game as a wing partnership in the match.

The Cats won, but there were no heroics from either of the two wings. A hamstring injury forced Chester out of the next match, against the New South Wales Waratahs in Bloemfontein. This was to be Small's last Super 12 game; he left the field shortly before full-time never to return. After two Vodacom Cup matches for the Lions and two Super 12 matches for the Cats, Small limped away from South African rugby in August 1999. It was a sad way for him to go.

Chester continued in the squad, playing six of the 11 matches in that Super 12 season. It was a frustrating season, with wins a rarity. There was the injury-time defeat against the Waikato Chiefs in a match when Chester played against New Zealand's giant winger Jonah Lomu for the first time in four years. But there was the win against the Stormers in Cape Town and a captain's debut against the Queensland Reds in Brisbane.

It was also a season in which Chester saw South Africa's bitter north-south rivalry from a different perspective.

I have a lot of time for Markgraaff. I think it is because of his passion for the game and because I always knew where I stood with him … well most of the time.

The oddest week I had playing under him was when he made me captain against the Reds and then hardly spoke to me all week, opting rather to relay his strategy to Andre Vos. It was strange … then again that season was all a bit strange.

No one could doubt Markgraaff's commitment. He had the respect of the players and he certainly let them know he was in charge.

I found him intelligent in his analysis of the game, but I also felt his approach in 1999 to be counter-productive to getting wins. He wanted to play direct rugby, with the emphasis on 'pick up and go, drive, recycle and then play the ball to the same side'. It is an effective way of playing, but to be successful you have to be super fit. We just didn't have the legs to survive the pattern. We were not conditioned to play 80 minutes of rugby like this, let alone week in and week out in the Super 12.

This was never better illustrated than when we played the Crusaders in Nelson. We were up by 30 points at half-time, but I think we all knew we were never going to win the game. We had nothing left in the last 20 minutes. Everyone's legs felt like jelly. We knew it and the Crusaders knew it. They scored 50 points, most of them in the last 30 minutes, to beat us.

Markgraaff's season, though, seemed to revolve around just one match – against the Stormers in Cape Town.

The Cats had lost all four matches in Australia and New Zealand, but there was nothing lacking in their spirit when they arrived back from Sydney to play the Stormers. Markgraaff was bullish at press conferences and the Cats players made it clear they had arrived in Cape Town to get the win.

If you just looked at the results, you would have thought we were at a low. We weren't. We had not won on tour, but we could easily have won three of those matches. We dominated the Auckland Blues but were beaten. We lost in the final minute to the Waikato Chiefs and lost by six points to the Queensland Reds. So while the record looked bad, we were not disillusioned when we got to Cape Town to play the Stormers, who were top of the log.

It was a game every Cats player felt we could win. We felt we were the equals of the Stormers and we were more physical. Markgraaff had emphasised all week that we had to be extremely physical if we were to unsettle them and get early momentum. We also had to score early to keep the crowd quiet. The Newlands crowd, as wonderful as they are, do go quiet quickly if Province or the Stormers struggle.

Our week was very gentle. We went through all our structures. We trained at the False Bay club in Constantia, but the training was low key. We had only two sessions the entire week. The one session we walked through our moves; the next was the captain's run.

Markgraaff was more motivated than I had ever seen him. We all wanted to beat the Stormers. In that week I saw just how the Stormers and Western Province players are despised by the teams from the north. When I was playing for WP we were always aware of the rivalry, but only in that week did I begin to appreciate how the hatred of the Cape players plays a part in the build-up to a game.

The Cats also saw the Stormers as the glamour boys of South African rugby and as Mallett's boys. It was a feeling that was justified because Mallett chose 11 Stormers in his test team to play England.

There was more north versus south than English versus Afrikaans in the motivation. We knew that the Stormers guys had the advantage when it came to national selection because the Stormers coach Alan Solomons was also the Bok assistant coach.

Markgraaff used this as motivation. He also challenged the Cats players to prove to South Africa that they were better than the Stormers, who at that stage were basically the Springboks wearing black.

I found the whole hatred thing odd, but I must confess I was motivated to win. I held nothing against Solomons, but I wanted to show him he had made a mistake in not using me in his teams when he had the chance.

It was like a test match in our change-room before kick-off. It was the most psyched-up I had ever seen that Cats team. Our guys saw it as an opportunity to upstage the national team selection, even though we knew that Mallett would not be influenced by one game.

Krige, Fleck, Montgomery, Paulse and Rossouw were among the Stormers that day. They were all regular test players. We felt as if we were playing against the Bok team. There was a lot of hatred going into that game. Players were very personal about the opposition. We weren't playing just the Stormers, we were playing individuals. Before the match our guys were privately outspoken about what they were going to do to 'this player and that player'. It was a very physical match.

Our game-plan was simple: hammer them up front, give the halfbacks 'go forward' ball and get them to kick to the corners. We were going to play the percentages all day and not take any risks. Trying to play the Stormers at their game would be playing to their strengths. We wanted to negate their backs, and that meant not even get into a contest with them. We backed our defence to shut them out, but it was on attack where we were wary. One mistake, one turnover and they were the sort of team who made any side pay.

Markgraaff's philosophy was straightforward: 'No mistakes and all out aggression up front.' It all worked out brilliantly on the day. Dave von Hoesslin (scrumhalf) and Gaffie du Toit (flyhalf) played probably their best matches for the Cats that season. They controlled the game after our forwards had won the contest up front.

Afterwards you would have thought we had won the Super 12. Markgraaff was ecstatic. He could not stop smiling or talking. He was very proud of the team and asked us to autograph one of the jerseys for him. It was an achievement for him to beat the Stormers in Cape Town.

He told us that it was among his career highlights as a coach and that the memory would stay with him forever. I must admit I, too, felt it was a special win.

With the Super 12 over, the next objective was the Currie Cup. For Chester, selection in the Super 12 under Markgraaff was a foregone conclusion; there would be no such certainty from Lions coach Laurie Mains in the Currie Cup.

Mains, who had coached the All Blacks at the 1995 World Cup, had been hired in 1999 by Louis Luyt to take over the coaching Luyt's Lions after a few dismal seasons for the team. Soon after the Super 12 ended, Chester also signed for the Lions but it was no guarantee that Mains would select him.

The appointment of Mains seemed bizarre. Mains had blamed the defeat of the All Blacks at the 1995 World Cup on food poisoning, which had led to him being ridiculed virtually everywhere except in New Zealand. Back in 1995 there had been no love between him and Luyt, who was the president of the South African Rugby Football Union at the time.

More precisely, there was little love for Luyt from any of those All Blacks. In a speech, variously described as typically bombastic or uncharacteristically tongue-in-cheek, Luyt had remarked that South Africa would have also won the World Cups of 1987 and 1991 if only they had been allowed to play. The All Blacks, who had won in 1987 but lost in the semi-finals of 1991, fumed with indignation. After their defeat at Ellis Park only a few hours before, they felt deeply offended at the time.

But four years later, any ill feeling between Luyt and Mains had apparently disappeared. It was another example of what made Luyt successful. He put aside any lingering dislike for the former All Blacks coach and appointed the man from Otago because he believed Mains could bring out the best in the Lions. Luyt had made a business decision and from the moment Mains got the Lions to win matches, the relationship between the two men flourished. But it would be only temporary.

Luyt wanted an iron fist to take charge of a team which had won no trophies since Kitch Christie's glory days in the early 1990s. Mains, his no-nonsense approach legendary in New Zealand rugby, came armed with a huge reputation. With his early success, and his close relationship with Luyt, Mains was even touted as a candidate to coach the Springboks.

Mains, for all his faults and peculiarities, got the results that Luyt and the Lions wanted – and he got them quickly. Within eight months the

Lions could claim ownership of both domestic trophies, the Vodacom Cup and the Currie Cup.

Chester, along with the Lions contingent playing in the Cats' Super 12 side, were keen to get involved in the Currie Cup campaign. The Lions had started the season well by winning the Vodacom Cup, which is run concurrently with the Super 12.

Mains's Lions team had been destructive in their domination of the competition. They beat Griquas 73-7 in the Vodacom Cup final, a year after Griquas had beaten them 57-0 in the final of the same competition. Mains had achieved a 123-point turnaround. His managerial shortcomings were excused; he got wins and he had won a cup. That was what Luyt and his executive committee wanted.

The players, however, were wary. They were too afraid to question the coach, who ruled by fear a team that had previously gone soft on the early riches of professionalism. Chester admired any coach who could instil a winning culture, but he did not like Mains.

I knew almost immediately that we would not be sharing too many drinks. When I linked up with his squad after the Super 12, I asked for a week off to finalise my move from Cape Town. He was not exactly thrilled and although he let me go, I was not surprised to find that I had not made his team for the first Currie Cup match of the season against Eastern Province.

The Cats had not done well in the Super 12 while the Lions had won the Vodacom Cup. Mains rewarded the Vodacom Cup players with places in the Lions team for the opening Currie Cup match. He phased in the Super 12 players, an approach with which I had no problem.

He also made it very clear that he would tolerate no player who thought he was above the game. This signalled the end for a guy like James Small, who hung around for a while, played a few Vodacom Cup matches before the Currie Cup and then packed it in.

Laurie Mains, discipline and fitness his key principles, ruled by fear. When he spoke the players listened; he did not take easily to spontaneous player input. He spoke to players, but only to the players he wanted to speak to and I was not on this list, despite being one of the most senior backs in the squad.

I never questioned him. It was not my style to ruffle feathers or to take on coaches. I just got on with playing. I desperately wanted to go to the World Cup. I thought I had shown enough in the Super 12 to be in contention. What I needed was a good Currie Cup campaign.

To do this I needed to play. To play I needed to shut up, ignore Mains's lack of people skills and look to his coaching positives. In that first year, life in Johannesburg was lonely. I had a friend in Pretoria with whom I spent a lot of time, but Johannesburg was foreign to me, Mains was foreign to me and I was still feeling my way around among the squad. To add to this, my home life was taking serious strain.

I was commuting between Johannesburg and Paarl and I sensed that my marriage was taking a beating. I am not someone who talks easily about personal problems and I had no one to confide in. It was a difficult time and rugby was my only saviour. It was the reason I left Cape Town. I just wanted to play rugby.

Laurie gave me no indication that I was his first-choice wing. I did not play the first game, played the second on the left wing, played the third on the right wing and was on the bench for the fourth game.

Thinus Delport had started as fullback and Dean Hall, one of the stars of the Vodacom Cup, played on the other wing. Hall, a youngster with loads of potential, was Mains's pet project. He rated Hall highly and made it known that the big wing could become a test player. He liked the physical approach of Hall.

I assumed Mains was using the first few matches to find his best Currie Cup combination. I bided my time when on the bench and never questioned whether he picked me at right wing or left wing.

By round five of the Currie Cup, Mains had settled on a combination. He moved Delport to left wing, dropped Hall to the substitute's bench and played me as right wing. He never spoke to me about it, or to us collectively as a back three. As I said, there were some players he spoke to and others he ignored.

That year the Lions were disciplined, physical and effective in everything they did on the field. Mains had turned the Lions into a New Zealand team. The forwards were good, the backs workmanlike and the overall attitude was one of hardness.

Chester played as well as he ever had. With each game, he assumed he was challenging for a World Cup position. He was also aware of the political pressures.

Then in June, 1999, there came another upheaval in South African rugby. Springbok coach Nick Mallett told South African journalist Gavin Rich that he would not be dictated to on selections. The question had been asked to gauge the coach's reaction to growing pressures for more black players to be included in the national team.

Mallett said he would pick on merit only and said it was his belief that there was not a black player good enough to make the Springbok starting XV.

Two days after his comments to Rich, Mallett dropped black wing Breyton Paulse from the team to play Wales at the opening of the Millennium Stadium, the venue for the World Cup later that year. The reaction was predictable: the conservative white minority backed Mallett; the rest of the country saw his actions as a snub to black players.

The South African Rugby Football Union was put out. It was trying to forge an unlikely coalition among a disparate group of men who, only a few years before, had been implacable foes. Now one of its employees had thrown a spanner in the delicate workings of the union.

It also did not make marketing sense: trying to sell a game played at the highest level only by white men to a country where most of the people were black. The seeds of Mallett's demise as the Springbok coach were probably sown in Cardiff that week rather than in Durban the following year when he criticised the price of test tickets.

Rian Oberholzer, the chief executive of the SA Rugby Football Union, was in Cardiff too that week. It had been a visit planned months before to join the celebrations of the opening of the new Welsh rugby showpiece. Instead of a leisurely week away from the office in Cape Town, Oberholzer's visit took on a greater significance for South African rugby. He would have to explain to the Springboks why the team could never again be an all-white one, in spite of what Mallett had said and done that week.

It was a difficult moment for Oberholzer. According to some of those who were present at the meeting, there was resentment from some white players, who believed their places in the team would be threatened by affirmative action. Elsewhere in South Africa, however, the dearth of black players in the team was blamed on white coaches and white selectors ignoring obvious black talent.

Mallett responded to the criticism of his all-white team that played against Wales with a baffling selection in the weeks that followed: he drafted in Kaya Malotana of Border, a centre who had scored five tries in nine Vodacom Cup matches. Malotana had not made it into any of the four South African Super 12 squads, but Mallett picked him for the Tri-Nations, which followed the test in Cardiff. It was blatant window-dressing. The player was done a disservice, as were Chester and other black players who were more deserving of a call-up.

That was probably the first definite sign that I was not going to feature in the World Cup of 1999. I was playing well in the Super 12 and I was settling in nicely in the Lions Currie Cup team. I was powerless to change the national coach's mind. He had his views on selection and even though he had included me in his Tri-Nations squad in 1998, it seems I had been there merely to add colour to the mix and make up numbers.

Publicly, Mallett told the media how well I had done to get back into the test squad after my injuries. Publicly, he said all the right things. Privately, he never spoke to me.

Chester's rugby, however, was on track again. Mains gave him regular game time, even if it was out of position on the right wing. Chester's personal life was not as settled, however. The commuting between Johannesburg and Cape Town was not working; he and his wife Teresa were growing apart more quickly than Chester had ever imagined.

Chester had left Cape Town in an attempt to resurrect his rugby career. He wanted to play international rugby again. He felt he was a good enough player. In Johannesburg he got the opportunity to re-establish himself, even though the national recognition did not come as easily as his acceptance had happened at the Lions.

The Lions also had beaten most of the other Currie Cup teams. A Vodacom Cup/Currie Cup double looked likely in spite of defeats against Free State and the Natal Sharks.

Internationally, the picture was bleak. Mallett's team had lost four matches in a row, including record defeats by the All Blacks and Australia. Chester, although outstanding in the Currie Cup, found no international reward.

Meanwhile the South African Rugby Football Union, now fed up with the provinces' apparent unwillingness to encourage black talent, introduced a quota system in the Currie Cup. The need to change the face of South African rugby would be forced on the provinces by making them select a certain number of black players.

Chester, however, did not regard the quotas as applying to him. He was confident that the Springbok selectors would be forced to pick him on his form. But Mallett had already let Chester's agent know that the winger was not going to be considered. Chester, now all of 28 years old, would apparently have age and his lack of pace counted against him.

For probably the only time that I can remember I was angry and disillusioned about my Springbok prospects. I knew I was good enough to go to the World Cup; I also knew I was playing well enough. I was too old, but Deon Kayser (the same age) was not. And with all respect to Kaya, I refused to accept I was a poorer option.

The omission from the World Cup squad gave me added motivation for the Currie Cup final a week later against the Natal Sharks in Durban. It was going to be an emotional occasion because Gary Teichmann, Henry Honiball, Andre Joubert and Ian McIntosh were all saying goodbye to Natal and South African rugby. Laurie Mains turned this emotion into a positive for the Lions.

At least, this was Laurie's intention. I have never been one who needed to get hyped by a coach or captain. I have my focus. I know what I need to do, but Laurie was fired up for this final.

We got together in Johannesburg a few days before the final and

Laurie started psyching the team. It was typical Laurie stuff – a lot of swearing, a lot of who did they think they were? … Honestly, it bored the hell out of me, as it did players like Rassie Erasmus and Werner Swanepoel.

Laurie knew the three of us didn't take his speeches seriously. They were the same words before every match. It might have had an effect on some guys. I was not among them.

The final was an anti-climax. The Sharks scored first, but were never in the game. Our forwards got on top and systematically we edged closer to victory. I scored a try, which pleased me in the light of the Currie Cup final the previous year. In 1998 I had scored one try and should have been awarded a second, which would have ensured a Western Province victory. This time there was no controversy and a lot of satisfaction.

With about eight minutes to go, the final had been decided. I walked from the field, pretending to be injured and told Dean Hall to enjoy a few minutes of what was his first final. Nothing is worse than being in the squad for a final and then to have played no part in the victory on the field. Dean had been on the bench in the latter part of the season, with Thinus Delport and I starting on the wings. I know he appreciated the gesture because it at least gave him a feeling of having contributed to the win.

The Lions under Mains had won the domestic double. I felt relieved that I had got through the season in one piece, although the Currie Cup final win did little to make up for my omission from the World Cup squad. After two failed attempts with Western Province, I had a Currie Cup winner's medal, but it did not ease the pain of being left behind for the World Cup.

Many people have also asked if it meant less to me winning the cup with the Lions than it might have done if I had been playing for WP. I felt that the Lions were my team then and that it felt wonderful. I did not think for one minute that it could have been a better feeling had I been wearing Province's colours. WP will always be dear to my heart and the memories can never be taken away, but I was a Lion now. The union had been good to me. They had been prepared to back me when others in Cape Town wrote me off. I felt good that I could have played a part in the success of the Lions. I had rewarded the faith that Louis Luyt and the Lions chief executive Johan Prinsloo had shown when signing me.

Laurie was euphoric. It was the happiest I had seen him. It was the first time I had seen him smile and enjoy the moment. It was also the last time.

Mains, the Lion King in 1999, would not again be king of the Lions. There would be no more silverware in 2000 and the New Zealander would find out that there was only place for one king at the Lions ... King Louis.

The success of 1999 would not be repeated. Mains would stay in charge of the Lions for 2000 and coach the Cats to successive Super 12 semi-finals in 2000 and 2001. But his relationship with the Lions and Luyt would end abruptly in October 2000 after it became public that Luyt had been tapping Mains's phone calls and was taking the Big Brother concept to the extreme.

Mains quit the Lions at the end of the 2000 Currie Cup season in October. Ironically, in the same month, Luyt severed all ties with the union he had transformed into one of the most successful in South African rugby.

There would still be a Super 12 campaign for Mains and a last push from him to be reinstated as Cats coach for the 2002 season. But with senior players like Chester, Rassie Erasmus and Werner Swanepoel refusing to support an extension on his Super 12 coaching career in South Africa, Mains returned to New Zealand to once again coach in Otago.

2000: Dying for the cause

15

I believe that if Monty had not heard me that day, I would have drowned. Monty saved my life

WHEN *the Springboks started preparing for the 2000 season, Nick Mallett took them again to Plettenberg Bay. It would be a time for training and team-building in the relaxed atmosphere of one of South Africa's most exclusive resorts. But for Chester Williams it would be a holiday resort from hell.*

I took one look at the sea and every grain of fear that is in my body jumped to the fore. I was petrified. I stood there wondering how I could get out of this exercise.

Going on a boogie board in the ocean was not my idea of fun. It was not the way I bond with teammates or build team spirit. I was scared out of my wits.

As the point of the exercise was being explained to the Springbok squad, all I could think about was why I hated the sea, the terrible memories I associated with the ocean and the concept of forcing people to do things with which they clearly were not comfortable.

I wanted to play rugby. That is what I was good at. I wanted to train, do whatever fitness drills were necessary and test my defensive skills against the biggest and best. I did not want to go into the sea.

Those of you who have a phobia will understand exactly what was going on in my head. To those who pass through life fearless, count yourselves very lucky.

I had enlisted in the navy in 1989. My brother Wilmot was the cleverer of the two of us. He was going to university and he was going to become a magistrate. My dad's income alone could not sustain Wilmot's university fees, so I had to find a job and help pay the way.

I also had a future in rugby and it was accepted that a good rugby player could use the South African Defence force to further his career. At the same time it ensured me a basic salary. It meant I could contribute towards Wilmot's studies.

I chose the navy, not because of a love of the ocean or the uniform or because of any romantic association. My uncle Avril was in the navy. Because he was there, it seemed logical for me to go to the navy. All I really wanted to do was finish my basics and then play rugby.

I was sent to Saldanha Bay on the Cape West Coast to do my basics. The fear I felt the first time I stood on a ship, looked down at the water and waited to jump was the same I felt at Plettenberg Bay as I looked at the ocean and asked myself why I had to prove anything to anyone and go on a boogie board. The anxiety is hard to describe. I can only try to tell you how scared and nervous I was, but it does not convey the full extent of my fear.

Back in my navy days, I told the instructor that I could not swim. He did not seem to be interested in my concern that I could drown. 'You have a lifejacket on,' he said. 'And if you don't come up, there are navy divers who will find you.' If I had been scared before, his 'reassurance' frightened me out of my mind.

I jumped from the ship. I had to. I came up, struggled to stay afloat and was eventually guided to the safety of dry land.

My rugby career at Saldanha Bay was not much better. I tried out to make the local starting XV, but failed. 'Whites only' was still the requirement then to play in the first team. That was the end of my rugby during basics so I just concentrated on finishing my training there and getting a transfer to the naval base in Simon's Town.

This did not come quickly enough but once in Simon' Town I lived in constant fear of being sent to sea. I was seconded to a group working with the submarines, which only aggravated my fear. Apart from a natural fear of water, I had a tendency to feel claustrophobic too. Each day I had to face the prospect, not only of going to sea, but the possibility also of going to great depths in a very small craft. I did not want to be part of a submarine crew.

I was lucky. My only contact in six months with submarines, as it turned out, was on dry land. Never once did I have to take part in a dive. When I transferred to the army I did not have to worry about submarines again.

All those anxieties returned that day in Plett during a Springbok training camp. In the name of fun, I awaited my turn on the boogie board. I would be required to paddle out and paddle back in. The Bok management knew that I could not swim, but they were confident that nothing could happen. No lifejackets were worn because they felt nothing could happen in a fun event such as a simple boogie-board paddle. I knew differently.

I had nothing against the 'building team spirit' theme. Many of the events were fun and they certainly did bring the guys together. But this one particular event had me scared from the moment we were told about it.

I was in a state of panic before it started. I was nervous. I tried to be brave, attempted to show no obvious fear to anyone, but inside I was terrified of drowning.

I knew I could not swim. I knew I could not handle myself in the water. I had no confidence in my ability to survive in the water and because of this, I was never going to be relaxed.

But when my turn came, I paddled out, using my arms, just as I had seen the other guys do. With each paddle the uncertainty intensified. We did not have to go far, but each metre felt like a metre closer to a danger I could not handle.

My mind was a mess at that stage. I was only a few metres out before I felt myself slipping off the board. I did not know what to do. Everyone else was going as fast as they could. The event, even though it was meant to be fun, was a competitive exercise. All events that involve rugby players naturally turn into a striving for superiority. In my case, however, this event was different. The others were going for victory; I was just trying to stay on the board and stay alive.

I find it hard to articulate just how I felt when I started losing my grip on the board. To say I was terrified just seems so inadequate. I certainly panicked. Everything I feared was happening. I was falling off the board and I knew that I was going to drown. I felt myself sinking and knew I had no control.

The more I panicked, the more I felt I was sinking. I started to scream, but no one seemed to hear me. My screaming got louder and I felt as if I was going to blank out.

I kicked frantically in the water. It was a natural reaction to just hang on. I screamed, half in a daze and felt as if these were my last moments alive.

Then I saw Percy Montgomery swimming towards me. He had heard me and he had obviously realised I was not playing the fool. He knew I was in serious trouble.

He got to me and immediately got me back on to the boogie board. He did not say anything, or if he did, I cannot remember. He just continued swimming, pulling me to the shore on the board.

I believe that if Monty had not heard me that day, I would have drowned. Monty saved my life. I don't think he knew just how much difficulty I was in. I don't think anyone present knew what I had just experienced.

It was one of the most awful moments in my life. I thought it was the end.

As you would have guessed, I am not one for team-building activities that include swimming in the sea. I am more a traditionalist. You get the guys fit on the rugby field, you concentrate on the basics of the game and you don't send a guy off on a boogie board when he can't swim.

Chester, recalled to the test squad for two brief appearances in 1998, did not get the chance to play an international match in 1999 – a season he describes as his best since the 1995 World Cup year.

He missed out on the 1999 World Cup because the national coach, in selecting four black players in 30, had enough quota players. The Springbok coach, Nick Mallett, had also thought Chester to be too old in 1999. In 2000, though, Chester (a year older) was considered young enough to make a contribution to the Springbok squad.

By 1999 Chester was accustomed to making up black numbers in teams. He was never selected to be part of the starting XV; he was there as a back-up to Breyton Paulse and Deon Kayser, the two black wingers who made the trip to the 1999 World Cup ahead of him.

Contact between Chester and Mallett was minimal.

Mallett did not speak much to me. Solly was the backline coach and if there was anything to be said, then I heard it from Solly. Mallett would ignore players with whom he did not want to communicate. Joost van der Westhuizen, in 2000, hardly said anything to Mallett.

Joost was furious. In 1999 he had captained the Boks at the World Cup and six months later he was sitting on the bench and treated as a back-up player.

Mallett rated himself as the best, was very confident about his own ability and surrounded himself with people who did as he told them. He had his favourite players. I was not among them.

Nothing would change this. Again, when I got selected for the 2000 season Springbok training camp, I just gave it my best shot.

I did not talk about my omission from the 1999 World Cup and it was not something that the management ever spoke about to me. Even though I was shattered not to make the World Cup squad, I never went public with my anger. Throughout my career, I never used the media as a forum to discuss my disappointments or used them to fight my fight.

I was always of the belief that a player got short-term gain from speaking his mind through the media. In the end it just gave the coach another reason not to select the player.

I never criticised Mallett publicly for not taking me to the 1999 World Cup. I knew I was good enough to go and I also believed Gary Teichmann was still the best option to captain the Boks at the World Cup.

I held nothing against Mallett in the 2000 season. I saw my squad call-up as the chance to play for South Africa again. I was motivated to play for my country, not to play under Nick Mallett.

The international season of 2000 started with a test against Canada in East London and then a two-test series against England. I did not start in any of the tests, but came off the bench in all three of them, playing at fullback!

We easily beat Canada, although we did not play well and we drew the series one-all against England. I thought we played well for 30 minutes of the English series and then we were outplayed. We were lucky to get away with a drawn series, but we could still have won the series 2-0 had the ball bounced my way in the final minute of the second test in Bloemfontein.

We scored against the run of play, through Joost, to be within five points of the English, who led 27-22. Then, in the final moments of the game, I chased a kick ahead. The ball bounced past me. Had it bounced back into my hands, I would have jogged over for the try and the conversion would have given us a victory.

It was a match the English dominated, yet somehow we could still have won it. I remember the series for a tackle I made on Dan Luger when I showed good pace to run him down.

Opportunities were minimal for me in that series. I had been through enough disappointment in the past few years to even think about complaining. I took every minute of test rugby that came my way.

I felt I had a good year left in me, perhaps even two, and I wanted to go out on a high. My Currie Cup and Super 12 form in 1999 had been very good. I thought I had done reasonably well in 2000, but I was taking nothing for granted. Each time I got picked for a squad, I just said a quiet thank you.

Chester, despite not starting in the three home tests of 2000, was selected in an extended squad to play two away Tri-Nations tests against Australia and New Zealand as well as a second encounter against Australia in Melbourne for the newly introduced Mandela Cup challenge. But again he knew he was just making up the numbers.

We played in Melbourne first. We got there a week before the test and Mallett selected me on the bench. He had Breyton Paulse, Pieter Rossouw, myself and Thinus Delport as wingers in the squad. Pieter was his favourite and he also rated Thinus.

Personally, I felt Breyton was the best winger in the squad. He was the one player capable of cutting up defences, yet Mallett never used his attacking potential. He picked him, but never backed him and this was most noticeable when we played Australia in Sydney during the 2000 Tri-Nations.

On departure for Australia and New Zealand, where we would play three tests (two in the Tri-Nations and the Mandela Cup against Australia), the plan, according to Mallett, was to play all of us in the first two tests and by the third he would pick whom he considered to be the two best wingers.

Well, my opportunity came in Melbourne. Mallett sent me on with two minutes – it might even have been one – left on the clock. We were down 37-23 and I had just got on to the field. Australia won an attacking ball on our 22 and Stephen Larkham kicked an up and under on to my wing. I turned to catch the ball on our tryline but Stirling Mortlock beat me in the air. He gathered the ball and fell over for the try.

Mortlock had done exceptionally well to get up and collect the ball and he is probably the best wing chaser of a high ball in the game. The Australians are the masters of the kick and chase and the kick undid us.

The match ended after the conversion and Australia had scored a record 44-23 win against us. As I was walking to the change-room, Mallett walked past me. He was very upset and, as I had become used to, he was never one to hide his emotions. 'How could you let him score … that gave them a record score against us,' he said in an aggressive and annoyed tone.

I was taken aback by his comment. Why did I let him score? I certainly did not do it deliberately. I never even responded. He was angry that we had lost and he was even more upset because it had been a record score.

That one minute I got proved to be my opportunity in the three test matches. We went to Couran Cove, an island resort about an hour's drive from Brisbane, for the next 10 days to prepare for the Tri-Nations test against New Zealand.

All we did for 10 days was fitness, contact, fitness and more contact. It was physically a very demanding time, but I never minded training that hard. Physically, I felt I could do whatever he wanted me to do.

What frustrated me was the lack of playing time. I knew I was not going to feature on the remainder of the tour. I was very much an extra at Couran Cove and that made it a difficult time to be with the squad. I was not alone. Other guys, also not in the match 22, were as frustrated. Mallett barked a lot during those days at Couran Cove.

There was huge pressure on the team to perform well and everyone felt it. Mallett made it clear that we had to win in New Zealand and Australia. He was furious that we had lost so badly to Australia in Melbourne. In his usual way, he took out his anger during the video session. There were some players he never attacked, there were others he never left alone and there were those of us he never seemed to acknowledge.

Mallett was a typical bully. He hammered those he perceived to be weak and he backed off against players with strong personalities or intelligent players, like Andrew Aitken.

Guys like Henry Honiball and Gary Teichmann got respect from Mallett. He treated them as his equal. I also remember only one occasion when he took on Andre Venter, but he apologised to him later. Others were easy targets for him.

As a rugby coach, he has many strengths. Technically, he is very good and he has a good understanding of the game. He can be an excellent motivator and he definitely is a better individual to work with when the team is winning. But he has no respect for players and treats them poorly. I found this surprising after all that he had gone through as a player.

His confrontations with the rugby administration are well known and I thought he would have been a player's coach above all else. He wasn't. In my time of playing under him, he did not communicate well and he did not deal with defeat very well.

Mallett also never showed any faith in the black players in the squad. This was never better illustrated than when he picked the test team to play Australia in Sydney. He picked Pieter and Breyton as the two wingers, then involved Pieter in all the plays and told Breyton to just stick to his wing.

He never showed any confidence in Breyton and I found that to be the most disappointing. Breyton, if managed properly, can be one of our most explosive players. If you don't show him you back him, you won't get the best out of him.

The time in Australia was not easy and there were a lot of unhappy players.

For all the high intensity training we did at Couran Cove, we never came close to beating New Zealand in Christchurch. We lost 25-12 and failed to score a try. All our points came from Braam van Straaten's boot.

Mallett was fixated with the Australian way of playing, or more specifically the Brumbies style. He wanted us to play like the Brumbies, but then he never selected individuals with the attacking skills to do so.

The return match against Australia in Sydney was probably the most disappointing of the lot on that tour.

After the down of Melbourne and the torture of another defeat in Christchurch, we showed precious little improvement as a team in the 26-6 defeat against the Wallabies. The tour showed up the vulnerabilities of Mallett and our rugby had not advanced much.

But I was at the stage of my career where I just didn't let it get to me any more. I had good company in my Lions teammates Rassie Erasmus and Werner Swanepoel. I got on very well with these two guys from the time I moved to Johannesburg. On Bok and Super 12 tours when they were around, I mixed more, felt a lot more comfortable and enjoyed the tours a lot more.

I could speak to Rassie and Werner about anything, from rugby to relationships, to cultural differences … anything. Rassie, in particular, is an exceptional rugby player with a better understanding of the game than a lot of coaches. He analyses videos all the time, thinks about the game and knows what he wants. He is a very strong character and this has put off some coaches, but it also meant that very few treated him poorly.

Mallett rated Rassie and Rassie rated Mallett. Rassie would speak favourably of Mallett, even during those tough days at Couran Cove. He backed Mallett as a coach and felt he was good for South African rugby.

I was not as convinced. I knew he was a good coach, but I doubted he was the right man for the job in 2000. I believed he should have gone after the 1999 World Cup. Our rugby needed a change then and Mallett had enjoyed a good run between 1997 and 1999.

I knew that while Mallett was coaching South Africa, my chances would be limited. I was frustrated on that Tri-Nations tour in 2000, but I was not depressed about the situation. I felt liberated because I had made a decision regarding my marriage. I was content with my social situation in Johannesburg and there was nothing more I could do to convince a Springbok coach he had to pick me.

I was past taking guys like Nick Mallett too seriously. If he picked me, I would give him my best. If he did not select me, there was no reason to feel bitter. I was not going to change his personality or his take on who could contribute what to Springbok rugby.

I found it odd that Mallett, whenever he was asked about me publicly, would always be fairly flattering. But he never backed this up with selections or with direct conversation.

The Springboks lost all three matches in Australasia, by 21 points in Melbourne, 25-12 to the All Blacks in Christchurch and by 20 points to

Australia in Sydney. Mallett, however, kept his job for the home leg of the Tri-Nations, although he knew that nothing other than two victories at home would see him continue as Springbok coach. There were whispers that even two wins would not be enough to ensure this.

The Springboks won 46-40 against the All Blacks in Johannesburg. Chester had started the test and started the All Blacks' rot with an early try. He also denied Jonah Lomu a first try against the Springboks with a crunching cover tackle.

Personally, the test was a triumph for Chester. He showed he could still compete against the likes of Cullen, Umaga, Lomu and Wilson. He did everything that had been expected of him.

I had done nothing different from the month in Australasia. I was surprised to find myself in the starting XV. I think there was pressure from the government and South African rugby's administration to pick more black players.

I was thrilled when I got selected and what made the night even more memorable was that my best friend, Maria, flew to Johannesburg to watch me play. We had known each other for four years and she had never watched a live game.

It was a great night and I rate my try as probably the best I scored in test rugby because of the quality of the opposition. My try against Wales in 1994 was very special, but this one was probably my try-scoring highlight in test rugby.

The game was a thriller. We won 46-40 with Werner Swanepoel giving us the lead with only a few minutes to go. The final minutes were frantic. They attacked in the latter part of the match and I have never played in a test match where the Boks defended as heroically as that night at Ellis Park.

This was a very different mood to the World Cup final. We were desperate. We had lost four tests in a row, one against England and three in Australasia. The All Blacks threw everything at us. We all made great tackles. We all put our bodies on the line.

I remember crashing into Lomu as he was headed for the tryline. I just never believed he was going to get past me. There was one moment when they were attacking frantically that there was a stoppage for injury. Andre Vos, captain at the time, called us into a huddle and said that there was no way they could score against us. Everything we had worked for was on the line. He was incredibly passionate and he led by example. He said we would never forgive ourselves if we let them back into the match.

We just tackled and tackled. Eventually, we forced the mistake, kicked the ball through and chased the All Blacks back into their half.

Right then we knew we had won the match. They had thrown every single thing at us and our defence had not broken.

The mood in the change-room afterwards was one of relief. After the defeat against England in Bloemfontein and the three losses in Australasia, we had finally won a test. It felt better than good.

There had been big pressure on the team and on Mallett and Solomons. Mallett was on a high. He was determined to win in Durban and so too were the team.

There were a lot of players who did not back Mallett as coach and there were those who believed he was the only guy good enough to coach South Africa. The one thing about Springbok players is that they play for the jersey and for the country. I experienced test rugby with Ian McIntosh, Kitch Christie, Nick Mallett and Harry Viljoen as coaches. It did not matter who coached the team, the guys went out and gave it everything.

I never heard one Bok say to another: 'If we lose we can get rid of the coach.' I have heard Boks say to one another that they dislike the coach, that they don't rate him. But I have never played with a Bok who did not give everything to win a test.

And that's exactly what happened in Durban against Australia. We went out to win, for ourselves and for the country. Not too many people gave us a realistic chance of winning, but we felt we had a psychological advantage over Australia in South Africa.

Just as there seems to be a belief among South African players that they cannot beat Australia in Australia, there is an equally strong conviction that they cannot lose a test against Australia in South Africa.

I thought we had won the test at 18-16 when Braam van Straaten kicked the penalty from 50 metres with a minute to go. Then they got a penalty in injury time and won it 19-18.

We were shattered, but still very proud of our effort. Mallett was also fair towards the team. He acknowledged the desire of the Boks to win and told us we had done everything to win the game. Some things were not meant to be and the post-match team session was an emotional one for the coach and players.

Our 2000 Tri-Nations campaign had come to an end. We had not been successful and Mallett told us that there was a good chance he would be forced out as national coach. I felt sorry for him that night. He was hurting, but then so were all of us. No individual is bigger than the game and in South African rugby no individual is safe in the game.

I was just happy to be getting home. I was dating a lovely woman named Sue, I was settled in Johannesburg and I was looking forward to being in a less pressured environment.

Photo: Anne Laing

Saying goodbye... *Chester and his first wife Teresa. This was in 1993 when Chester was leaving on his first Bok tour.*

Marrying Maria... *Chester in a mock proposal with his wife Maria at their wedding. Maria's son Ryan is on the right.*

All in the family... *Chester's wife Maria on their wedding day with mom-in-law Julene, left, and Chester's Aunt Ida*

11

Photos: Touchline Photo

LEFT: **World Cup comeback...** *Chester on his way to scoring one of his four tries against Western Samoa in his first match of the 1995 World Cup.*

ABOVE LEFT: **New colours...** *Chester in the colours of the Cats after Alan Solomons would not pick him for the Stormers.*

ABOVE RIGHT: **End of the game...** *A moment of relief at the end of another Springbok victory.*

ABOVE: **The Great Campo...** *Australian winger David Campese, for whom Chester Williams had enormous respect. The two never met in a test match.*

Happy among friends... *Chester is 'fed' a beer by teammate and friend Jerome Paarwater during a light-hearted moment on Western Province's overseas tour in 1993. On the right is his great friend Thinus Linee*

Photo: Anne Laing

Bok buddies... *Chester with three of his big Springbok buddies, from left, Tiaan Strauss, Fritz van Heerden and Keith Andrews.*

2000: A farewell to arms

16

I scored two tries... the second with Cullen too late to stop my dive for the line. That's a decent memory to keep. I walked from the field and the applause was thunderous. I felt honoured. I felt complete

NICK MALLETT resigned as Springbok coach after the Tri-Nations series in 2000 and Harry Viljoen, who had been out of rugby since quitting the Western Stormers in 1998, was appointed to succeed him. The appointment was controversial because Viljoen had not coached for two years nor had any contact with the rugby world in that time.

Viljoen, wealthy and not in need of an income from rugby, took on the challenge of coaching the Boks. In time he would admit that Viljoen the 30-year-old accepted the job, but that Viljoen the 40-year-old arrived to tackle the assignment.

Perhaps if Viljoen had been made Springbok coach in 1992, when many thought he should have been given the job, it might have been different. Ultimately, his tenure would end in failure when he resigned after only 15 months in charge.

Before that was to take place, however, and only in his first month of the job, Viljoen called Chester Williams and offered him a position as Springbok backline coach. Chester was still playing for the Lions in the Currie Cup and he was the incumbent test right wing, having played against the All Blacks and Wallabies in Nick Mallett's last two tests in the No. 14 jersey with Breyton Paulse switched to the left wing in place of the axed Pieter Rossouw.

I was playing good rugby. My performances in the last two tests of the Tri-Nations convinced me that I still had a good year left in the game at the highest level. Laurie Mains, the Lions coach, had spoken to me about my future during the Currie Cup. He had asked me what I intended doing in 2001. I was undecided and he urged me to continue playing for another season. He said that I would be important to his Super 12 campaign and that I had a big role to play.

It was during the run-in to the Currie Cup play-offs that Viljoen was appointed and soon afterwards he phoned me. I was very flattered by his approach and the prospect of coaching the Springboks was very tempting.

He was very open with me. He said he had a proposition for me. He told me that he rated my knowledge of the game and that he felt I had the potential to coach South Africa one day. He also said that I was nearing the end of my playing career and the offer was to become involved with him in a coaching capacity. He insisted that I should not interpret the advance as a sign that I would not make the side.

He told me to relax, think about the situation and that I would definitely tour as a player if I decided to continue playing. If I wanted to retire at the end of the Currie Cup season, he would draft me into his coaching team immediately.

I asked him to give me a few days to think about the offer. I called my adviser and agent Frikkie Erasmus and he told me that it was too early to retire. He also felt that the time was not right and that I had another year of playing the game still left in me.

During the week that I was thinking about the offer, there were reports in the South African media that Harry had approached me. Laurie probably spoke more to me in that week than he did in the entire season. He said I would be crazy to take on the job and align myself with Viljoen. He said Viljoen would be a disaster and that he was not a good appointment for Springbok rugby. Laurie said that if I went with Viljoen I would destroy any chance of a coaching career before it had a chance to develop.

Laurie also said that he wanted to use me in the Super 12 and that it was too early for me to go into coaching. He added that if I retired after the 2001 Super 12 season, he would make sure that the Lions Rugby Union looked after me from a coaching point of view. He would organise something for me at the Lions.

I was very tempted to be involved in coaching because I felt my future was as a coach more than anything else. But I wanted to make one more tour for the Boks. I wanted to go out on a winning note and not as a good loser.

I phoned Harry and told him that I had given everything a lot of thought, but that I felt it was too early for me to be involved in coaching, especially at such a high level. He was very good about my decision. He said not to worry. He again confirmed that he would pick me in the touring squad. Mains was pleased that I had turned down the approach. He said it would be good for my career.

Chester played out the Currie Cup 2000 season and was picked to tour Argentina and the United Kingdom in a squad of 40. Viljoen had impressed on him that he was part of his test plans and that his involvement would be with the test squad and not the midweek campaign.

Harry had been straight with me and he seemed to think that I was playing good rugby. He sat down all the test wingers on tour – me, Breyton Paulse and Pieter Rossouw.

He told us that he would give us all a chance to play our way into the starting XV for the England test. He saw this as the climax to the tour. Stefan Terblanche and Deon Kayser would start the tour as part of the midweek squad, but he also let us know that both of them would be considered for test selection if our performances were not good enough.

I had heard a similar speech from Nick Mallett earlier in the year and was not going to be taken in by the words. Mallett had promised everyone a chance in Australasia and I had got only one or two minutes.

Viljoen, to his credit, gave us all an equal chance. I played the first 40 minutes against Argentina, but pulled up at half-time with a hamstring strain. Breyton started and Pieter replaced me in the second half.

In the second test match, against Ireland in Dublin, Pieter and I started and Breyton was rested. In the third test against Wales, Breyton and Pieter started, but Pieter got injured early on and I replaced him on the wing. Viljoen had given us all a chance, but I was confident I had done enough to play one more time at Twickenham.

Not for the first time in his international career, Chester's confidence was misplaced.

It was later said of Chester's swansong that it was perfectly scripted: two tries against a star-studded Barbarians team, a rapturous ovation from 70 000 at Cardiff's Millennium Stadium and an integral participant in one of the most memorable Barbarians games – a match in which the Springboks had come from 31-12 behind to win 41-31.

It was the kind of send-off Chester Williams deserved, but the image was incomplete. That week in Cardiff was one of the emptiest and most depressing the winger had ever experienced.

A week before the Barbarians match, the Springboks completed their

2000 international season against England. They lost 25-17, Chester warmed the bench and never got a taste of action. He and hooker Charl Marais were the only substitutes not used. He was not angry. He was disappointed because he felt he could have made a contribution that day. Harry Viljoen thought otherwise.

Chester did not have to guess Viljoen's actions or try and make light of the thinking. He knew exactly what was going on in the coach's mind. Earlier in the week of the England match, Viljoen had asked Chester to see him in the privacy of his hotel room.

The Springboks were based in the picturesque town of Windsor, an hour outside central London. The surrounds were of ducks on the Thames River and of misty tranquillity. It was a sleepy afternoon.

Chester, on his way to Viljoen's room, had to leave his section of the Sir Christopher Wren Hotel, cross the sidewalk, round the corner and wait for a few minutes until the intercom system clicked open the door. It was drizzling lightly and the skies were more black than grey. The omens were not good and Chester was nervous.

It is not the norm for a coach to invite a player to his room during the late afternoon for a chat about the weather. Viljoen's tone had suggested it was more serious. Chester had a suspicion it would have to do with his test selection for the England game. The media had speculated about his position after the Springboks had scrambled a 28-18 win against Ireland in Dublin.

The press had written that Chester looked average. Defensively, he seemed to be wanting in his positional play. Video footage would suggest that the defensive naïveté of his inside backs contributed more to Chester's indifferent display than the winger's own perceived inadequacies. Again his pace was the main criticism. The unanimous belief was that Chester had lost his pace. The critics felt he was too slow to be a factor at test level.

Chester arrived at Viljoen's room, expecting to hear that the coach had not been happy with his performance against Ireland. He was prepared to listen, adamant that he would work harder and confident that the coach would entrust him with the wing duties against England.

It bothered him that the coach had called the private meeting at that time of the day. He did not expect a bombshell, perhaps just a timely reminder that no player could take test selection for granted. It entered Chester's mind that the coach might relegate him to the bench.

But when Viljoen spoke, the words weighed a ton. Not only did he drop Chester, he retired him from international rugby, saying he would never again pick Chester in a test for the Springboks. Viljoen had seen enough on the tour to satisfy himself that Chester was finished as a test player. Viljoen did not make the decision easily. Once before he had written Chester's epitaph, only for the winger to rise from the ashes.

In 1998, Viljoen had publicly apologised to Chester for prematurely retiring him as a Super 12 player. This time he was convinced that the winger was past his best. He had called Chester to his room, sat him down and told him that he had played his last test match. Chester was shattered.

There had been media speculation that I was too slow. It was a line that I had read for 10 years. I did not take much notice. I had never had express pace at test level when you compared my speed with some of the sprinters in the game. I had other qualities that made up for this shortcoming.

Now the Bok coach was telling me I had lost my pace and that because of this, my best years had gone. He said these were the reasons why I would not make his test team. I respected his honesty and his frankness, but I was not going to accept anyone telling me when to go. I was going to retire myself. Nobody had the right to retire me from the game.

I did not argue any point with him. I did not plead to be in the test team. I simply told him I did not believe it was the end for me. I would fight my way back. I had proved everyone wrong on numerous occasions. I wanted to go on my terms, when I felt I was ready to leave the game. I still backed myself as a player. I had the hunger and the will to play test rugby.

I left the room feeling low. I took a walk down past the river. It was a quiet afternoon and I walked for a while, contemplating what had just happened. It was a lonely time for me. Generally I am a loner when on tour. I keep to myself and don't mix too much. There was no one who I could go to, or wanted to go to. It was not the greatest afternoon to be in Windsor, even though the place did offer me some solace through its peacefulness.

Viljoen, not the confrontational type, attempted to soften the crushing blow by promising Chester a coaching job. There was nothing available within the national coaching structure, but Viljoen said he could arrange for Chester to be included on the coaching staff of a Super 12 franchise.

The Springbok coach had huge respect for Chester. He envisaged a coaching career for the player whose international one he had just ended. Viljoen had often spoken highly of Chester to the Bok management on the tour. He had also expressed his admiration of Chester at speaking engagements and in media interviews.

Chester was not interested in taking up a coaching position. He viewed it as second prize; a thank you after the fuck you.

Viljoen, also aware of the political considerations when picking his Springbok team, included Chester on the bench for the test against England. If anything got to Chester, it was the fact that he had again been used for his colour and not ability.

If he did not think I was good enough, then fine. That was his opinion and I had enough experience of coaches not rating me in my career. You don't argue the point, you try to get back on to the field and you hope the opportunity is there to prove them wrong.

He told me I was finished as a player. On that basis I should not have been involved in the test match at all. He had just told me my international career was over. I knew that he was not going to put me on the field out of choice.

Then I was picked as a substitute. It had nothing to do with the coach thinking I was good enough and that I would add value. There I was, five years after being a part of a winning World Cup team, making up the standard two black players in a Springbok match 22 – a number that had become synonymous with test selections ever since politicians had threatened international boycotts if the Springbok team selection remained exclusively white.

I would have preferred him to leave me out rather than pick me as a token, but deep down I held out hope that I might be needed in the test against England. I had experienced one of my best days in rugby against England at Twickenham in 1995. Five years later, I would sit through 80 minutes that symbolised the most heart-breaking reality of my career: I was still being used as a black player making up the numbers. Ten years after playing my first match for Western Province League, after a World Cup final and three Currie Cup finals I was simply a black player warming the bench for South Africa. It hurt more than it angered me.

Viljoen included Chester for the Barbarians match, more as a tribute to the player's career than a belief that Chester was the best wing in the touring team. Chester accepted the challenge to show up Viljoen's decision a week earlier – that of retiring him.

The media and public were dismissive of the relevance of the Barbarians match. It was a festival occasion, a kind of semi-contact run around.

The Springboks took the match very seriously. They needed to return home victors and they were wary of the make-up of the Barbarians. Most of the squad were southern hemisphere players and the side would be coached by Australian legend Bob Dwyer and former All Blacks coach John Hart.

Viljoen and his management team had every reason to believe the

Baabaas were as serious about the match. Three days before the match, the managements of the two teams dined together. It was at the dinner that Hart and Dwyer told Viljoen that the match was one too far for the Boks. They were not in a good enough physical condition to win.

Viljoen rallied the tired Boks with the words of Hart and Dwyer. Chester did not need to be motivated. Viljoen's words the week before in Windsor had been powerful enough. The winger, who was no longer needed as a test player, wanted to respond in the only way he knew – through his match performance.

I was not angry with the coach. I had been down that road too many times to feel anger. I had wanted to complete the tour, reassess my position in South Africa and then make a decision on my future.

I wanted to be the one to go to the provincial and national coaches and say it was over. I had already spoken to the SARFU chief executive Rian Oberholzer about coaching possibilities. His positive response was encouraging and I was certainly thinking about retiring in the new year.

Now I was determined to prove I could still play with the best and the occasion provided me with a test as good as I could have asked for had the match been an official international. The Barbarians backline included Christian Cullen, Chris Latham, Matthew Burke, Daniel Herbert, Brian O'Driscoll, Carlos Spencer and Agustin Pichot. In my test career I had never lined up opposite a backline with so much talent and pedigree.

I scored two tries, the first from a kick through, the second with Cullen too late to stop my dive for the line. That's a decent memory to keep. I was substituted with about 20 minutes to play. I walked from the field and the applause was thunderous. I felt honoured. I felt complete. Internationally, I had made my last run and scored my last try. I had done so on the same stage as some of the game's modern-day greats.

I had experienced a special moment against Wales at the Arms Park in 1994 when I scored the try that won us the test against Wales. Six years later, at the new Millennium Stadium in Cardiff, I felt a similar elation. I had left on a high even though I was still prepared to go on my terms and not on the decision of the Springbok coach. No coach was going to retire me. I would decide when it was time to say goodbye.

A celebration of black rugby

17

A black South African team, like the New Zealand Maoris, would highlight that blacks can play the game and have done so for many years... I would love to coach such a team

EVER since South Africans started playing test rugby, 729 individuals have represented the country at that level. This statistic includes the Springboks' 2002 Tri-Nations test against the Wallabies in Johannesburg. Of the 729, only 15 have been black players.

Chester was the first black player to represent the Springboks since the unification of rugby in South Africa, he was the first black player to score a test hat trick, the first to play more than 10 tests, and he was the first black Springbok to play in a winning World Cup final – in 1995 when the Springboks beat the All Blacks 15-12.

In 1998 he was also the only black player in the Springboks' first overseas Tri-Nations success, although his contribution was limited to a few minutes as a blood-bin replacement. Fellow winger McNeil Hendriks, another black player, started that campaign but was injured before playing a match.

Chester, however, was not the first black player to wear the Springbok green. That honour belongs to Errol Tobias, who toured New Zealand as a midweek Springbok in 1981 and played two tests against England in 1984. Tobias owed his test place in 1984 to the absence of legendary Springbok flyhalf Naas Botha, who was dabbling in American football at the time, but the black player distinguished himself in the Springbok No 10 jersey.

Tobias aside, the only other black player to represent the Springboks before unity was Chester's uncle Avril Williams.

Before unity in South African rugby, which was officially declared a done deal in 1992, two black Springboks had intruded in the white majority of 593. Since unification, the number has increased dramatically, but 13 black test Springboks out of 134 is still only a trickle. The biggest breakthrough only came after the 1999 World Cup with seven of the 33 new Springboks until 2002 being black.

Of the 13 black Springboks since 1992, only Chester Williams, Breyton Paulse and Deon Kayser have played more than 10 tests. This will surely change in the future as Conrad Jantjes, Bolla Conradie, Lawrence Sephaka and Adrian Jacobs continue to make strides in Springbok rugby.

Springbok test statistics, however, don't tell the full story of the hardships in the struggle to transform South African rugby.

At the end of 2001 there were 694 registered professional rugby players in South Africa. Of this number, 130 were black. This is fractionally less than 20 percent of the playing total, an under-representation when it is considered that of the estimated 300 000 players at all levels in South Africa, more than 120 000 are black.

The biggest concern since unification has been the slow pace of change at domestic level. Coaches, given the benefit of the doubt, baulked at picking black players and it was only in 1999 that South African rugby officialdom opted for decree to speed up transformation.

The catalyst for their decision had been Nick Mallett's remarks in Cardiff that he would not be instructed whom to pick. He followed this up by selecting an all-white team to play against Wales in the same week that he uttered his remarks. The official response to Mallett's defiance was quotas. This was officially declared later that year and became part of the South African scene in 2000.

Those politicians who were eager to see some progress in transformation, but who were frustrated by the slow pace of change, started playing the numbers game. But their good intentions were misdirected; instead of focusing on the domestic structures of the game, their emphasis was at a national level.

This only harmed the fight by black players for equality in South African rugby and it abetted the absurd notion that blacks could not play test rugby. Black players were used as political pawns in the middle and late 1990s to deflect government pressures – and those players were the ones who suffered the most.

Black players such as Owen Nkumane (1998), and Thando Manana (2000) were picked to play for the midweek Springbok team, while Kaya Malotana had a solitary outing on the wing against Spain at the 1999

World Cup. This hurried window-dressing neither helped the cause of black rugby, nor did it encourage any progress.

By 2002, however, the situation had improved dramatically, not only in numbers but also in expectations. Five black players were included in the Springbok test squad of 22 to play Samoa – and the figure hardly rated a mention in the press. The reason was that all five had excelled in the Super 12 competition of that year and in the Currie Cup during the previous year. The players had been given an opportunity and they had proved they were good enough to play test rugby.

Some lost their test places, but so too did some white players from that match squad. When black players were dropped, there was, for the first time, consensus that the decisions had been made on playing performances and no one pointed a finger at racism.

Although 2002 has proved to be a watershed for black representation at national level, the numbers of black players taking part in the Super 12, Currie Cup and Vodacom Cup are still strikingly low and remain a problem for South African rugby.

The Vodacom Cup, a competition aimed at promoting black talent, was introduced in 1998 and was the first senior competition to insist on a minimum number of black players in a team.

The Currie Cup followed in 2000, with three black players in a match squad of 22 the requirement for coastal teams and two in 22 for northern teams, the reason for the disparity being a belief that there were more black players in Western Province, Boland, South-Western Districts, Eastern Province and Border capable of making the Currie Cup teams than elsewhere in the country.

In 2002, the lack of black players getting game time in the Super 12 meant that the South African Rugby Football Union had no alternative but to impose an unofficial quota of four black players in each Super 12 squad. That such decisions were made was an acknowledgement, within the corridors of the national governing body, of the slow rate of change – and resistance to change – at a provincial level.

What also cannot be ignored is that no team exceeded the quota in the Super 12 of 2002, and only two out of 14 provincial teams consistently exceeded the quota in the Currie Cup and Vodacom Cup during that time. At senior club level, where there is no quota system, not one black player featured in the semi-finals at the 2002 national championships.

For these reasons, South African rugby authorities cannot avoid enforcing a quota system. The downside is that black players will continue to suffer the indignity of being labelled quota players as they fight for equal opportunities in the game.

I absolutely hate the term 'quota player'. It is a negative one, which, for all of my playing days, was used exclusively to identify black players in any South African team.

My distaste for the association of 'quota' with black was that it implied black was inferior to white. It meant that in the early part of my career, I confused the necessity and effectiveness of the quota system with the word quota. It led me to denounce the quota system without ever appreciating the role it had to play in South African rugby.

Often journalists would ask me if I supported the quota system and I would reply that I did not. It always made headlines and, innocently, I would state that a player should be selected only if he were good enough. Colour, I argued at the time, should never be a consideration for team selection.

That was how I felt about the situation when I started playing rugby. I did not want any hand-out, nor did I want to feel as if I were being done a favour on the basis of my skin colour. I wanted to make the team because the coach and selectors believed I was the best in the position. My teammates had to believe in my ability and see me as a teammate and not a black player keeping a white player out of the team.

Unfortunately, during most of my playing days in South Africa, there was never an understanding among players of what the quota system was about. White players generally regarded it as a hand-out to black players. They saw it as a token gesture to black players, usually at the expense of one of their white teammates.

In all my playing years, most white South African players believed that a black selection weakened the team. My experience was that only a minority of the players I was associated with looked at a black player's ability and not the colour of his skin.

Quotas were brought in because of a lack of opportunity for black players and since their introduction at senior level, they have had positive results.

I have experienced first hand how inherently racist the mindset of coaches can be in this country. There is very little malice in their actions. They were simply of the opinion that a black player was inferior to a white counterpart. It never seemed to occur to them that a black player could be a better rugby player than a white one.

Decision-makers in the South African game have been mostly white. This is something that has changed only since 2001. In the same way, a black player's role was mostly confined to the wing position.

In the past year there has been a dramatic shift from within the South African Rugby Football Union and SA Rugby Pty Ltd (SARFU's business arm) and there has been an unrelenting and quickening of the pace in what is meant by transformation within the game.

Transformation should not be confused with development. The latter is the nurturing of talent, and talent identification should never have a colour coding.

Transformation is about opportunity, and while I was fortunate to play regularly at all levels during my career, I was in a minority group. There were several other black players who were just not given a chance to prove their worth as rugby players. White players were given opportunities every weekend while a black player was given only one or two chances to make an impression.

There was resistance from within the South African game to change and it came as much from players as it did from conservative administrators and coaches. In a way, this was understandable: you don't change an individual's thinking in the space of five or 10 years.

I remember sharing a room with Springbok and Lions wing Pieter Hendriks. At the time, Stanley Raubenheimer, a black scrumhalf and a former teammate of mine, was going out with a white woman. The two are now married and have been together for the best part of seven years. Hendriks, who had never treated me poorly, offered an opinion on Stanley's relationship. He told me he could not believe that a coloured player could have a white girlfriend. It upset him and he felt it was just not right. I was amazed at how strongly he felt about the situation.

Listening to Hendriks talking so passionately about his perceived wrongs of a mixed relationship, it never entered my mind that one day I would also fall in love with a woman who happened to be white. But I did, and I married her too.

Perhaps Hendriks has moved on in his thinking; I wouldn't know. But his attitude at the time was just one example of what South African society was like during the apartheid days. Conservative whites grew up thinking a certain way because of what they had been taught at home and at school. Much of the indoctrination was based on the belief that being white in South Africa somehow made you superior to anyone born black. It would be unrealistic to think that hundreds of years of such preaching could be erased in five or six years.

I have seen individuals change their attitudes, socially and on the rugby field. It has not happened overnight, and it is important to acknowledge this. But the word 'kaffir' is still used on the rugby field.

South African society did not go from being abnormal to normal in one democratic election. Similarly, our rugby did not embrace the concept of unification just because we now all played under one banner. There was an acceptance of unity because that was the reality; embracing the change was not as easy to put into practice.

I resisted a quota system because I felt that it was abnormal. In time I would realise that it was necessary to normalise a situation that had always been abnormal in our society.

The unfortunate thing about a quota system is that it labels black players. It creates the perception that if it were not for the quota system then the player would not be good enough to take his place in the team. It can have a negative effect on black players, who can become unsure about the coach's true opinions of them. Such doubts can include whether the coach really rates the player or whether he is being forced to pick the black player.

The only person who can erase the doubt is the coach. If our coaches are committed to selecting the best possible players in South African rugby, then there would not be a colour issue and the matter of quotas would disappear in time.

I realise now that quotas are necessary in South African rugby. Without the quota system there would still be limited opportunities for black players. Black players, for the next few years, will have to learn to deal with the stigma and they will need to focus on the positive aspect: that they now have a chance to show what good rugby players they really are.

Once they have done this, the rugby element will take over in the public's mind. I already sense it with the emergence of some fine black players in recent months. There is an acceptance that black players in the Springbok squad of 2002 were there on merit and national coach Rudolf Straeuli's willingness to select them against New Zealand and Australia was confirmation that they are good enough to play with and against the best in the world.

The reality is that until the new order dominates the running of the South African game, quotas will be a necessity at provincial level. And by 'new order', I mean businessmen and administrators who are interested only in the growth of the game and not the colours of those involved.

There has to be a healthy pool of black players competing at provincial and Super 12 level on a regular basis. From this pool those good enough to make the national team will do so. You will never need a quota system applied to the test team if the quota system is effective at provincial level. The black players will stand up and be picked at the highest level because they are good enough.

No test team that I played in was ever weakened because of the inclusion of a black player. And I don't know of any test match in which the selection of a black player led to that team losing the game.

If it was not for a quota system at provincial level, the likes of Breyton Paulse, Bolla Conradie, Quinton Davids, Conrad Jantjes, Adrian Jacobs, Ricardo Loubscher and Deon Kayser would not have been given sufficient exposure in which to prove their worth as rugby players.

Lawrence Sephaka and Gcobani Bobo are more recent examples of players who have benefited from the quota system at provincial level. They were both good enough talents to make provincial teams, but they suffered because of a belief that white players were better, purely by virtue of their skin colour.

It was only in my last few years as a player that I began to see, and feel, the racial prejudice that did exist in the South African game. There have been huge changes in the South African Rugby Football Union's approach since 2000 and words have been given substance because of actions. Black players are now being given an opportunity because those who run the game in South Africa are demanding this change. And black players, in return, are showing that they can make a contribution to South African rugby at all levels.

I was not surprised by a recent written attack from conservatives on the running of the South African game. Their comments that quotas were weakening our rugby did not surprise me. It is in keeping with a view that might never change. There is a part of our rugby that will have to die a natural death. We cannot force the death.

I know that to make a positive contribution I have to fight harder for the rights of the black player. I never did as a young player because I was trusting of the human values associated with team selection: the best man plays.

The fight is worth it because black players add value to South African rugby. They give our game another dimension and the performances of the South African under-21 squad at the World Cups in 1999 and 2002 are proof that black players don't weaken national teams. We beat the game's best with our best combinations; some happened to be white and others black. Quotas have forced coaches to pick black talent and at a national level these players have mostly been successful.

I have taken a sevens squad through a World Series and a Commonwealth Games. I have played in a World Cup and a Commonwealth Games. Black players involved in those tournaments and competitions have not weakened the side. Neither have the white players.

In 2002 we finished second to New Zealand in the World Sevens Grand Prix and we certainly were not content with finishing second. We want to be the best at sevens rugby and I know we can achieve that goal. We won a bronze medal in the 2002 Manchester Commonwealth Games in sevens and all that weakened our squad was the unavailability of players who had been chosen from our squad to play test rugby that weekend.

South African rugby, if it puts aside individual agendas, prejudice and provincialism, can consistently be the best rugby-playing nation at every level of the game. We have the talent and this has never been better illustrated than in the sevens and at junior rugby, where we won the under-21 World Cup twice and made the under-19 semi-finals in 2002. Some great youngsters are getting an opportunity and they are taking the chances being offered to them.

You have to only look at the quality of rugby played by the 2002 Springboks to know that our rugby is strong. The future of South African rugby is healthy from a playing perspective, but it is still going to need a change of mindset across the board at provincial level. The South African Rugby Football Union and SA Rugby Pty Ltd have recognised the areas in which our game has been struggling and, through the much-publicised Accenture report, they have acted to rectify the shortcomings.

I have been in the South African rugby system for 10 years, mainly as a player and in the last two years as a sevens coach. It has only been in the last two years that I can truly feel things are changing. Actions, for the first time, are matching words.

There is a sense that we have to move forward and I find that hugely encouraging. But to move forward we also have to recognise the past and accept the realities of our history as a rugby country.

There was division and there was the sidelining, through apartheid, of black rugby aspirations. It is sad that so little is known about South African black rugby. It is disappointing that there seems to be a reluctance to acknowledge the place black rugby has in the South African context.

I am a black player who knew very little about the history of the game among the black rugby-playing population. I knew the basic things – that there were a variety of different unions, that not everyone played under the same banner and that there was as much division within black rugby as there was between black and white rugby. It is a fact of our rugby history and we cannot shy away from it.

It was only during the writing of my life story that I started to find out more about black rugby. I read Manie Booley's 'Forgotten Heroes', which is a history of black rugby from 1882-1992. I learned a lot from his book.

I also learned something when reading Cape Argus rugby columnist Andy Colquhoun. He wrote about quotas and the popular belief that these meant white players were the victims. He argued that no white player had ever been victimised because of quotas. I cannot agree with him more.

He wrote of black players who had been forced to give up the country of their birth to pursue their rugby talents. Two he mentioned I had never heard of: David Barends and Green Vigo, players who excelled at rugby league in England. Barends left South Africa in 1960, signed for Wakefield Trinity, and played rugby league for Great Britain against New Zealand and Australia.

Colquhoun highlighted a Vigo hat trick that features in '101 Great Rugby League Tries'. He also mentioned Enslin Dlambulo, Goolam Abed, Winty Pandla and John Newman. These were all players who looked to the north of England or to Australia to play professional rugby league. They left because they were denied an opportunity in their own country.

I knew none of these names. I had never heard of them. They are black players who deserve to be honoured in the South African game. They are a reminder to me of what sacrifices were made in an age when white South Africa was telling the world that blacks did not play rugby.

I am embarrassed to admit that I know more about the history of white rugby than I do about black rugby. I am sure, however, that I am not the only black player with a red face.

I believe we should celebrate the history of black rugby and honour those heroes who fought greater social fights than we ever did in order to redress the obvious wrongs that happened in our country during apartheid.

A few years ago, I read an article proposing that a South African team made up entirely of black players be selected, something like the New Zealand Maoris. The article caused much debate and I was surprised at how strongly rugby's black administrators were against the proposal. There were suggestions that the idea was racist, but I disagree.

I feel there is a place in South African rugby for such a team and that it should play selected matches against touring teams. If that team plays two or three matches a year it would serve a purpose and it would be an investment for South African rugby, as well as a reminder to South Africa of the traditions of black rugby.

Our black players are crying out for opportunities and for match time in competitions like the Currie Cup and Super 12. The situation is improving, but it is still a struggle and the fight will continue for a few more years. As I keep saying, you can change a constitution, but you don't change a mindset as easily.

For those who are selected to a black South African team, the experience should also be a cultural education. So little is known, or acknowledged, about the 100 years of black rugby history. We need to change this if we are ever to appreciate what battles were fought to ensure normalisation of our rugby and unification within South African rugby.

I started looking seriously at the injustices in rugby only during my final few years when it became obvious to me that too many in the rugby fraternity still saw me as a black player and not a South African player.

The black players of today and the future must learn the history of the game in this country. It will give them a greater understanding of the new South Africa. Things were not always as they are now. Our future players need to know this.

A black rugby team, selected to play on specific occasions, would celebrate the efforts of those who were denied the opportunity in the past. It would definitely not be segregation. It would be a salute to a history that we should never allow our children to forget. It would also present opportunities. Even in a unified South African rugby context, these have been scarce for black players. Behind the bland statistics, presented earlier in this chapter, are stories that tell of enormous hardships.

As a player, I saw from close up the struggles that guys like Deon Kayser, Breyton Paulse and Conrad Jantjes had to wage. I was not politically conscious enough in my younger days for it to have affected me. I had a simplistic view of the situation: play well enough and they have to pick you. I was fortunate. Many coaches actually liked me and they also seemed to enjoy it that I did not challenge the system. They rated me as a player and gave me a chance. Other black players, more outspoken than I was, were not as lucky.

Jantjes, one of the country's most gifted sportsmen, was mentally tired of all the talk of quotas and the constant doubting of a black player's ability. At 20 years old, when his career should have been nurtured, he was challenging a coach to pick him on ability and not because of the colour of his skin. No 20-year-old should be fighting such emotional battles.

In 2001, the situation at the Cats, where I was playing at the time, had become desperate. Laurie Mains was coaching us and I did not believe he gave the black players a fair chance. The unofficial quota in the Super 12 was that two black players should be included in the match squad of 22. Mains never exceeded the quota. At times he did not even pick two in his 22.

Conrad was upset that he was being used as a political convenience. He was included in a squad as a black bench-warmer. There was little opportunity on the field and yet he was required to train as hard as everyone else, even though he knew that his role in the match would be just to sit on the bench.

He did not want to tour Australia and New Zealand in the Super 12 because he knew he would be wasting his time. He wanted to play for a team in which his services were valued. It was at just that time that he was selected for the national sevens team.

It was also a time when I had reached the end of the road with Mains and the coach's bias against black players. Mains never said anything insulting to me, he simply did not select black players in the Cats team. You only have to go through the team lists during his time in South Africa to know this.

I was fed up with Mains and his selection policy. I felt that I was being used to make up black numbers. Mains had urged me to continue playing in 2001 and had told me that I would play a big role in his campaign. I never did. I only added colour to the mix. I felt the same as Conrad did. We were being used.

Conrad had been drafted into the squad during the course of the Cats' away leg of the Super 12 in New Zealand and Australia. I had told Mains that I was struggling with an injury and Conrad was called up to take my place on the bench. In spite of being called up by the national sevens team, Conrad's contract obliged him to accompany the Cats to New Zealand and Australia for the Super 12, even though he knew he would not get to play. Conrad was not thrilled.

I decided to complain to the Cats team manager, Mac Hendricks, about Mains. I was not the only black player or management member to express such dissatisfaction, so Hendricks arranged for a meeting of the black players and the management on the tour.

Hendricks told Mains that the black players felt they were being unfairly treated and that they were made to feel second rate when it came to selection. Hendricks, a no-nonsense individual who had fought the black struggle in rugby, pulled no punches. He told Mains the black players (myself, Conrad, Clarke Roberts and Wylie Human) believed he was a racist.

Naturally Mains denied this, then countered our accusation with one of his own. He said he had received complaints from the white players that we refused to mix with them. He wanted to know what our issue was with the white players.

During all my years of playing rugby, I had kept quiet and taken the sarcastic and racist jokes on the chin. I had dismissed the attitudes of those many racists in our rugby as one of ignorance and not of malice. Now I was being questioned about not mixing with whites.

I challenged Mains on the accusation and he said that the white players felt the black players all sat together during meal times and did not want to mix. I snapped. I raised my voice: 'That's fucking bullshit Laurie. Why must we always make the effort? We are the first to arrive at the meal room and you expect us to get up and go over and join the white guys when they arrive. Why don't they ever come over and join us?'

Mains was taken aback by my outburst. He did not have an answer.

He apologised, saying he was not aware that was the case. He said he would take it up with the white players. I don't know if he ever did and I really did not care. I was disillusioned and fed up that after 10 years of giving everything to South African rugby, this was what I was being subjected to. I was not alone.

After all these years, I was a black player making up quota numbers. I had lost my desire to be a part of the set-up under Mains. I went to see Mac Hendricks in the week during the build-up to the match against the Blues in Whangarei, a lovely town about two hours' drive from Auckland.

I asked Mac to book me a flight home. I told him that I had a knee injury and it was not getting better. Mains asked me to stay and play. I told him I was not fit enough to play. I got on a plane, arrived home with a month still to be played in the Super 12 and, a few weeks after the completion of the competition, I announced my retirement.

It was not the way I wanted to leave rugby and I certainly did not want to go with such pained feelings about the injustices in our rugby. I felt my career deserved more and that the black players of the future deserved a better deal.

Part of a better deal must be to celebrate our past. We cannot ignore the history of black rugby or deny the prejudice that black players have had to endure. We have to know more about all this to appreciate its true value.

Only recently have I started to try to educate myself. I believe it is something all our players should do. They should know what has gone before them, both black and white.

Acknowledging black rugby by means of a black team would be a major boost for the game in the black communities. It would also provide an additional opportunity for black players.

My view will be seen as controversial because there will be those who say it promotes segregation. I don't believe it does. If anything, a resistance could be interpreted as denial of the truth of our country's rugby history.

Such a team would highlight the fact that blacks can play the game and have done so for many years. The New Zealand Maori side is an example of how you can promote the game culturally. Why should South Africans be different?

I would love to coach such a team. I want to give back as much as possible to rugby because the game gave me direction in my life and gave me the chance to experience the world in a way that would never have been possible had I stayed in Cape Town and lived my life as a soldier in the South African Defence Force.

More than that, I want to promote the game among the black

communities, and for this to be done successfully those communities need to see black players in action. They certainly would identify with a black team that played two or three times in a season. As a player, I was too naïve to think this way. My view has changed and as a coach I would have the chance to back up my ideas with action.

I look at the black talent in South Africa and it excites me. The future of our game is safe if we can all accept that the dynamics have changed in the make-up of those playing rugby in South Africa.

For the purposes of this book, as an indication of what is possible and with the hope that one day I may get to do it, I have selected a black invitation team to play two matches a year as black South Africans celebrate their place in the history of the South African game.

In doing the exercise, I imagined how we would play, where we would play and against whom. I also pictured the response and the positive impact it could have on all of us who are trying to deal with the past.

There is a lot of black talent starting to make an impression on South African rugby and that has happened because people have fought for the opportunities for those players. Our under-21 and sevens teams are producing quality black players and there is an exciting breed of backline player who can only strengthen South African rugby at the highest level.

When looking at selections for a Black XV, I was spoilt for choice in most areas, especially among the backs.

There was a feeling less than 18 months before I decided to tell my lifestory that South Africa lacked good backline players. The talent has always been there. It just had not been acknowledged or nurtured.

Imagine a backline that included Conrad Jantjes at fullback, Breyton Paulse and Egon Seconds on the wings, Deon Kayser and Gcobani Bobo or Wayne Julies in the midfield, Adrian Jacobs at flyhalf and Bolla Conradie at scrumhalf. I think that is a backline that will excite any rugby-lover.

If I opted for a combination like that, it would mean there would be no places for Ricardo Loubscher (Springbok), Ian Fihlani (Sevens Springbok), Gavin Passens (Springbok), McNeil Hendriks (Springbok), Jeffrey Stevens (Sevens Springbok), Fabian Juries (Sevens Springbok), Ashwin Willemse (SA under-21), Dewey Swartbooi (SA under-21), Chumani Booi (Sevens Springbok), Monwabisi Mdyesha (SA under-23), Norman Jordaan (SA 'A'), Enrico Januarie (SA under-21) and Eugene Francis (Sevens Springbok). And you can be sure there are others who will soon force their way in as contenders.

Black backline play is very strong in South African rugby, even if it has not always been reflected in the make-up of provincial and Super 12 teams. The depth of backline play is greater than among the forwards, but it is not to say you could not field a very competitive pack.

Matches celebrating the history of black rugby would give these forwards greater exposure and possibly influence the merits of their selections when it comes to picking provincial and Super 12 teams.

It has to be a huge plus to black rugby that there is an all-black front row currently doing well in the domestic game with an average age of 23. Lawrence Sephaka (loosehead), Hanyani Shimange (hooker) and Eugene Maqwelena (tighthead) would be an efficient unit. Back them up with SA under-21 prop Guthrie Steenkamp, Sharks tighthead Ettiene Fynn and you certainly won't take a step backwards. As for the hooker back-up, the veteran Dale Santon and Germaine Brinkhuys offer reassuring reserves in that department.

There are not many black locks who are playing provincial and Super 12 rugby and opportunities need to be created for players in these positions. Again, an invitation team such as the one I have suggested would force the selectors to pick black locks. They might be surprised to find that the talent is there. Because of the high quality of the white locks in our country, the position is one where few black players have excelled since 1992.

I would go with Springbok lock Quinton Davids and the experienced Bolander Randile Julies as a combination. Bandile Ncunyana, a former SA under-21 lock, is another who has suffered because of a lack of opportunity.

The loose-forward mix in my team would be Boland's Henley du Plessis, the Bulls' Denzil Frans, Puma's Clarke Roberts, sevens Springbok Wayne van Heerden and the Lions' Sean Plaatjies. They will be capable of holding more than their own. Solly Tybilika of Griquas is another who impressed in the past two seasons.

The point of this exercise is to illustrate that, despite limited opportunities, black players are making an impression. They do play the game and they do have a love for rugby.

An unfair and wrong political system meant that South Africa was robbed of a talent base that included players from all backgrounds. In a unified South Africa you would think that this is no longer the case, but for our rugby to be truly unified in selection, the quota system has to remain in force until we start seeing the quota exceeded at domestic level.

There is no quota system within the test team and I don't believe there will ever be a situation where this is necessary. The problem is not with the test team, it is at the lower levels. Until the situation changes domestically, black players will have to live with the added weight of being labelled quota players.

These black players need to see the positive side of the system. Quotas give them a chance and that is more than thousands of black players had for 100 years in South African rugby.

New life for sevens

18

Brent Russell, with 46 tries, was our star. He is not unique. There are other Brent Russells out there, black and white, who have never been given the chance

TOLD to listen, shut up and play, Chester Williams did just that as a Springbok sevens player. It did not help to challenge a South African mindset in which coaches were gods and players were meant to be obedient mortals.

Chester, desperate to get game time, shut up. It was in keeping with an attitude that helped make him an accepted member of the South African rugby fraternity. His refusal to challenge those entrusted with the power probably ensured he broke into the white-dominated South African game and survived for just under a decade.

As a player, Chester said very little to spark controversy or to upset the influential decision-makers. He had played in two sevens World Cups, a Commonwealth Games and more sevens matches than any other South African player. His experience was unrivalled, yet he remained muzzled as a player, forced to play a secondary role to whoever had been given the job of coaching the sevens Springboks.

Finally, when given the coaching role in late 2001, he knew how to rectify this. He was going to do things his way and he would try to address the imbalance of the coach/player relationship. The naïveté associated with Chester the player had been replaced with a confidence that some would interpret as arrogance.

Quite simply, Chester questioned things. He attributes a lot of the change in his personality to his second wife Maria. She encourages *debate, inquires instead of accepts and backs her man all the way.*

She told me to express myself, to have the courage to do what I felt needed to be done instead of accepting what others believed was the best for the team, or for me.

I had lived with incredible frustration while playing sevens. Then I was given total support within South African rugby by the managing director of SA Rugby Pty Ltd Rian Oberholzer to implement whatever was needed to make South Africa a force in sevens. I had to show the confidence in my approach that someone like Rian had shown when appointing me.

Even though Rian had backed me, he had given me no hand-out. When I was appointed my salary did not differ from that of my predecessor. I challenged this and felt that my profile would add value to the sevens brand and that I deserved to be paid more.

Oberholzer is a tough negotiator. He refused to budge on the salary issue. He said he rated me as an individual with the potential to become a very good coach. But he refused to pay me what I wanted because I had no coaching track record. He would give me the opportunity to coach South Africa at sevens. If successful, his door would always be open for renegotiation.

He made it clear that I would be rewarded if I backed my ability with results. He was desperate for sevens in South Africa to improve, but he was not going to throw cash at sevens without knowing he had a winning product.

I accepted his decision. I knew I could make a difference. I wanted South Africa to play sevens rugby and not an abbreviated version of 15-a-side. In all my years of playing sevens, I felt that no national sevens coach understood that it was a different game from 15-a-side. These coaches would pick quality 15-a-side players based on what these players did in that form of the game. And invariably South Africa would fail to do well.

There was no respect for the green jersey in sevens. We were always the team there to make up the numbers. We were a name that teams would claim as a tournament upset, but realistically it was not an upset when the likes of Canada and Argentina beat us. They were picking a sevens squad. We were selecting players we thought could play sevens because they were good footballers in the 15-a-side code.

Unfortunately, our players believed they were not good enough to win big tournaments in sevens. If they made a quarter-final, they were happy. Everyone seemed to accept that was our lot. I never did. We have some great athletes, players who can be up there with the best.

The lack of fitness of our sevens players was my biggest concern.

There was also no sevens structure. We were picking guys who were being conditioned to play 15-a-side rugby. Sevens is a completely different game. It requires a different attitude and a totally different emphasis on fitness. I needed players who were 'sevens fit'.

I wanted an approach that was focused totally on sevens rugby. It meant revisiting our sevens campaigns and being honest about why we failed. Fitness was non-negotiable. To be competitive you have to be the fittest. Then you can start with skills and then a game-plan. I also had to identify players who were suited to sevens. In the past we had relied on name players from the 15-man code who were perceived as sevens players but were not.

Emotionally, the South African sevens teams of the past few years were also vulnerable. They were weak, never backed their own ability and never believed they were capable of winning, let alone playing the final.

I was a part of those teams. Beating New Zealand or Fiji in the final was not something that was ever viewed as a possibility. It was a case of 'let's make the quarter-finals and then try and win a tournament'.

I had an advantage in that the opposition did not respect us at the outset of the 2002 season. We were the guys who never made it past the quarter-final. It had always been New Zealand, Fiji and on the odd occasion Australia. But when it came to pre-tournament talk about winners, South Africa never featured in media reports based on player views. We were not a factor.

Chester, outside of a rigorous month-long schedule dominated by fitness, put off-the-field systems in place. He wanted a working management team where every individual was aware of his responsibility.

The physiotherapist had to acknowledge his role, the manager had to take control of off-the-field issues and the players had to take ownership of how they played. Chester wanted to be in a position where he could focus on coaching the team. He also wanted a sevens team and not a squad made up of 'name' players.

Once I had got the guys fit, then I could work on the skills. The beauty was finding a sevens squad. I knew what I was looking for in a particular player and it certainly had nothing to do with any preconceived ideas based on a player's performance in 15-a-side rugby. I found myself working with players and not names. That immediately produced a freshness within the squad.

Being competitive was the first goal. Making a semi-final was next on the checklist and winning a final completed the three-pronged approach

Chester instilled in his players as a 'must' if they were to be taken seriously.

You cannot just want to make a final. If you are in a final, you have to believe you can win it. But I couldn't talk of finals when we had hardly ever made it beyond the quarter-finals.

The players had to believe they could beat those viewed as the best. They had to back themselves to win on the field. It meant that the physical preparation had to be good. They had to be fit, they had to be skilled and they had to play to an effective pattern.

In 12 tournaments, Chester's sevens Springboks won one of them, played in seven finals, advanced to two semi-finals and played in three quarter-finals. Their second position in the World Grand Prix circuit in 2002 was a championship high for South Africa, beating their previous best of fifth.

It was still not good enough to beat off New Zealand and that was why Chester asked for a two-year extension of his sevens contract; a confirmed appointment that puts him in charge of South Africa's sevens World Cup campaign in 2004.

Ultimately, my goal is to coach in the Currie Cup, Super 12 and at the highest level. But coming second in a world series is not the goal I set myself. Winning one tournament was also not good enough. I feel there is unfinished business.

We have started something in sevens, we are showing the world we have naturally talented athletes as good as anyone you will find in Fiji, New Zealand, England and Australia.

Winning in New Zealand was a major breakthrough. South African teams generally struggle to beat New Zealand teams in New Zealand, be it schools rugby, provincial or Super 12 games. Psychologically, it was big to win in Wellington and what made it even more impressive was the fact that we knocked over New Zealand in front of their home crowd.

We had made it to the final in Argentina, but inexperience cost us that match against Fiji. The lessons were learned, however. We had beaten Fiji in the group stages, but when it came to the big game they were more composed. They played finals' rugby. We played as if we were just happy to be there. It meant there was still one step to take and that was knowing you could win the final and not just be content with an appearance in the final.

We almost made the mistake in the final in Wellington. We had played superb sevens rugby to beat Australia and New Zealand in the quarter-finals and semi-finals. We played Samoa in the final, were well placed and then tried to defend the lead. They came close to scoring in the final minute.

We had a bit of luck in the final, but then it was long overdue. It was an important lesson to the youngsters. Never defend the lead. Attack it and close out the game.

Even in a winning final, there were plenty of lessons.

New Zealand sevens guru Eric Rush paid Chester and his team a compliment after the Wellington sevens: 'Any team who wants to win in the remaining tournaments will have to beat South Africa. They are fast, strong and hot at the moment.'

The Fijians have even started talking about South Africans in the same breath as New Zealand. Chester chuckles when he recalls the Fijian manager's comments to him after the Wellington win.

'So now we have to watch you guys as well,' the Fiji manager said, his tone one of surprise and even the hint of regret.

They fear us now. Both Fiji and New Zealand know we have youngsters who are not in awe of them. We have a well-balanced team who have pace and are very physical in their approach. Some outstanding players are coming to the fore.

Brent Russell's success story in being picked for the Springbok test team is a sevens success story. It has probably done more for sevens than winning tournaments could have done. It has shown young players out there that sevens is a stepping-stone to playing test rugby. Springbok coach Rudolf Straeuli has given the sevens game a massive boost by picking one of the sevens stars in his test team.

Brent had not played Super 12 rugby, nor had he played Currie Cup rugby when he was picked for the Springbok sevens team. He was overlooked by every Super 12 franchise. But he was our star and in every tournament he made an impression. His 46 tries were the most scored by an individual in the World Series, and don't forget that he missed the last two tournaments because of test commitments.

He is the kind of footballer that we have in South Africa. He is not unique. There are other Brent Russells out there, black and white, who have never been given the chance because of perception and a conservative belief that focuses on what the player apparently cannot do as opposed to what he can do.

Brent is a wonderful athlete and he is equally comfortable passing left and right. Anton Pitout was superb in Wellington and is very physical; Paul Treu is the senior statesman in the side while Fabian Juries and Jean de Villiers have been consistently good. Ask me about the team of 2003 and I am sure there will be a few new names being spoken about.

I was encouraged in 2002 when Rudolf contacted me to discuss players I felt had the potential to play test rugby. It was obvious he valued what sevens can mean to the development of a player and I was flattered by his approach. I was even more flattered when, after another meeting, he invited players to the national trials.

I had discussed Brent with Rudolf and his assistant Tim Lane. Both had seen video footage of him and were impressed. What counted against him was that he had never played a senior match at Currie Cup or Super 12 level.

They both asked me: 'Is he good enough to play test rugby and where would you pick him?' I said: 'Yes. His kicking game needs to be worked on and he will have to learn to play off other players and not always make the play himself. But definitely, he is special. I would pick him at flyhalf, fullback, wing ... anywhere actually.'

In May, just before the start of the 2002 test season, Straeuli arranged a Springbok trial and invited Russell to join the other trialists. Chester was not surprised that Russell was one of the day's big attractions.

Chester had given Russell a chance when everyone else had overlooked his talent. Now Russell was giving Chester and the shortened-version of the game a boost.

Sevens was indeed becoming a talking point in South African rugby. Wins against Fiji in Argentina and handsome back-to-back wins against Australia and New Zealand in the quarter-finals and semi-finals in Wellington were examples of the impressive statistics associated with the Springbok sevens squad.

Two seasons before it was commonplace to hear of South African defeats against minnows like the Cook Islands, Chinese Taipei, while Canada, Samoa and Argentina had also knocked over the South Africans. Those days are gone. And if Chester has it all his own way, so are the days when the coach is god and players are merely meant to follow.

They have to have an input. I will make the decisions, but there has to be buy-in from everyone. My players back my approach and game pattern. It is only right that I back their right to have a say.

I experienced too much frustration as a player to make the same mistakes as a coach. I know what used to upset me as a player: dishonesty from the coach, a lack of communication from the coach, racial prejudice from the coach and very little game time.

If a player is not good enough, then a coach has to tell him. Being honest does not always make a coach popular, but it does earn him respect from his players. I am sure there are players I have coached at sevens who won't invite me around for drinks, but I doubt any one of them would be able to say that I was not honest with them.

I give all my players a voice, but their performance is what will make the lasting impression.

Chester again does not take it as a compliment that his sevens squad brought home a bronze medal at the 2002 Commonwealth Games held in Manchester.

He admits a bronze beats a fourth-place, but he believes that the way the sevens Springboks played at the Games, a silver or gold medal would have been out of place.

It was always going to be a very difficult competition because we had some players who were injured and had also lost Brent to test rugby. I believe if Brent had played at the Commonwealth Games we would have made the final.

We lacked his exceptional pace in the play-off matches and I think the six-month season had caught up with some of the players. They gave it everything, but they were struggling to recapture the energy usually associated with the 2002 sevens Boks.

The likes of Jorrie Muller and Jean de Villiers had experienced the high of winning the under-21 World Cup and perhaps they were a bit drained emotionally at the Commonwealth Games.

We lost 17-7 to Fiji in the semi-finals after leading 7-5 at half-time. They probably deserved the win, although they were always going to struggle against a very impressive New Zealand team and I was not surprised that the Kiwis won the final easily.

New Zealand, at the completion of the 2002 season, still dominated sevens rugby, but they know there is a new challenger in South Africa.

The sevens game now also has a greater profile in South Africa because of Brent's explosion on the test scene.

I know that my business in sevens is unfinished. I have committed myself to sevens for the 2003 and 2004 seasons.

My goals, in the next two years, include making South Africa a dominant sevens force, winning the World Grand Prix in 2003 and winning the 2004 World Cup.

And it is imperative that sevens keeps on producing players who can take the step up into test rugby.

Our best players in recent years have come through the sevens system. It is why we can never again afford to neglect the value of sevens in the development of the best test squad in the game.

My marriage breaks up

19

Teresa ... understood my desire to play again ... but she was not going with me. She had a life in Paarl. She was not going to be a rugby widow in a foreign city.

IT *was the hardest decision that Chester Williams would make: to end his marriage to Teresa. He admits now that he knew when it was over. The two of them hardly spoke. It was, he recalls, 'a terrible time'.*

I was commuting between Johannesburg and Paarl once a week. My marriage was being dismantled with each day apart. I knew it, but I didn't know how to confront it, or even admit it to myself. Each week I would come home, hopeful that I would feel differently. Sadly, I never did in those last 12 months.

I had made a promise to my dad to give my marriage another go, but in the first year of commuting between Johannesburg and Paarl in 1999 I became convinced that there was nothing to go home to.

Teresa and I had grown apart. She was doing her own thing. My focus was rugby. My life was in Johannesburg. Hers was in Paarl. She was not prepared to move to Johannesburg while I resurrected my career. I was not prepared to stay in Paarl, play club rugby in Cape Town and simply grow old. I knew I still had something to offer the game.

Western Province coach Alan Solomons had made it clear at the end of 1998: I could stay in Cape Town the following year, but he was not going to pick me. There were rugby offers from up north. Staying in Paarl was not an option for me; I was not going to give up the chance to continue playing professional rugby.

Teresa was equally adamant that she was not going to leave Paarl.

She understood my desire to play again. She recognised the passion I had to make it back to the top and she gave me her blessing to go. But she was not going with me. She had a life in Paarl and while she had become accustomed to being a rugby widow in the early part of our relationship, she always had the comfort of her home and her friends to fall back on. She was not going to be a rugby widow in a foreign city.

I understood her reasons for not moving to Johannesburg. We searched for a compromise and it appeared that this was for me to commute once a week. But our lives grew apart, more quickly than I ever imagined it could have happened.

Often I forced myself to remember the good times – the night we met, by coincidence, the drive home and the love that unfolded soon afterwards.

I had been dumped by my girlfriend at the time, but I had already accepted an invitation to attend her sister's 21st. Single again and allowed to look, I spotted Teresa at the party. She was also single and we got chatting. I had known her in the Nederburg junior school where we had been classmates, but she had attended a different high school. We saw each other on the odd occasion during our high school years, but there was nothing by way of a relationship between us.

Then we met again at the 21st that I had not wanted to attend, but had felt obliged to because I had said I would be there. At the party Teresa and I started chatting and I asked to walk her home. It was the start of a relationship I thought would last forever.

At the time she seemed everything I wanted in a woman. She was kind, sensitive, shy and very much her own person. Despite being small in stature, she had a strong personality and that reassured me. I was never the most confident person away from the rugby field and it was comforting to be in the company of Teresa.

We started dating and soon afterwards we became engaged. Rugby, though, dominated my life at that time. I wanted to be the best player in my position in the world and I would make whatever sacrifice was necessary to achieve that ambition.

Teresa was very supportive of my desire to play for Western Province and South Africa. It was a time in my life when I took my relationship for granted. I also took it on face value. Teresa was there and we were a partnership. There was no time for any kind of relationship insightfulness. I had been exposed to little socially and nothing had tested my relationship.

Ours was a courtship that seemed strong to everyone, myself included. I never thought for one moment that I was not going to marry Teresa.

At the same time I never expected our wedding to be such a big social event, but it was because President Nelson Mandela was among the guests.

We had invited the President because of the support he had given me during the 1995 World Cup and even afterwards when I suffered my first knee injury. His words had always been inspirational to me and it seemed only right to invite him to what was one of the most special days for me. I was surprised when he accepted the invitation. Both of us were very excited that he would witness our wedding.

It was, of course, an honour to have him as a guest and I was flattered by his acceptance of our invitation, but his awesome presence had a strange effect on many of the guests. Instead of the attention being focused on the bride and groom, it was on the President of South Africa.

I felt lost, nervous and intimidated. I was very emotional at the time; too emotional even to thank him publicly or any of the other guests. Teresa got up and made the thank-you speech.

It was an incredible day in so many different ways, but it was also a weird day. I felt like a guest at my own wedding and a few years later I would feel like a stranger in my own house.

Four years after we had been married, I knew it was over. I had battled with the emotion for more than a year. I had taken my dad's advice to try again. This time I knew I had to be true to myself and I had to make a decision. It was my second year of playing for the Lions and it was also my second year of commuting between Johannesburg and Paarl.

Our relationship was very strained. We hardly spoke. I would arrive in Paarl and I would see a stranger in my life. Teresa would look at me as if I was something from the past. I was lonely, unhappy and very sad.

I could not lie to myself or to Teresa any more. I had spoken to my father about my unhappiness, but the person I had confided most in was my best friend Maria. She encouraged me to do what was best for me. 'Look after your own happiness first,' she said, but it was not that easy. Teresa had been in my life, seemingly forever, but she had hardly been a part of it. Maria knew more about me than Teresa did. I spoke more to Maria than I did to Teresa.

I confided in Maria, trusted her with my emotions and believed in her as my best friend. She was always there to listen and where possible to give guidance. She was undemanding and uncomplicated. Life was fun to her. Life was lonely for me.

I had to make a decision about my marriage. I had to confront the issue. I finally flew to Cape Town to see Teresa. I told her that it was over and that I wanted a divorce. It was a very traumatic evening. She cried. I cried.

She refused to accept it. She was prepared to continue with our living

Photos: Anne Laing

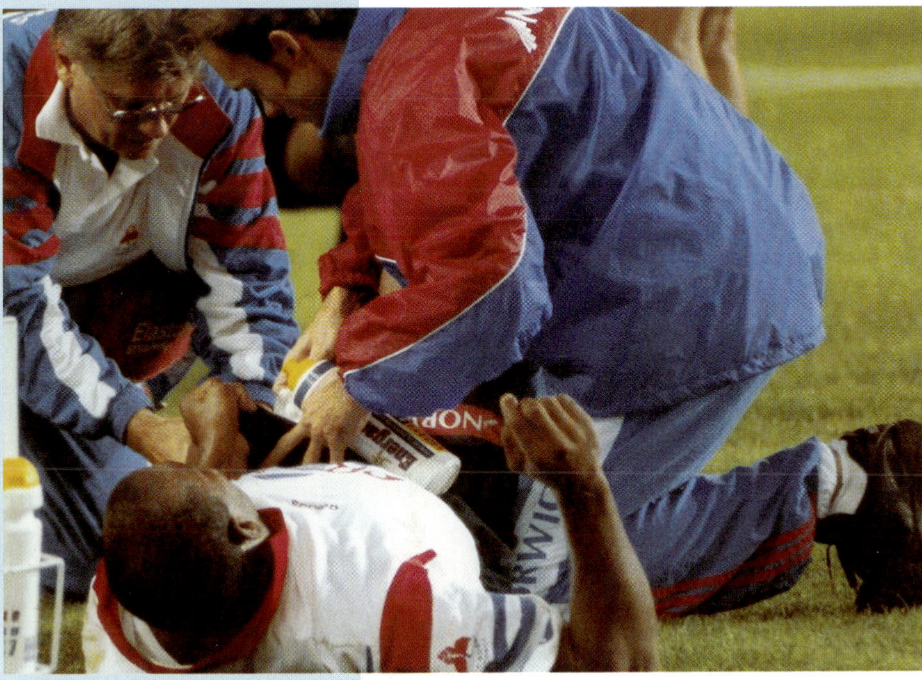

Chester is down... *Western Province team doctor Francois Malan and physiotherapist Bruce McLoughlin attend to an injured Chester Williams in a match against Griquas at the start of the 1997 season. Chester had just recovered from a knee injury the year before and, after this injury, spent much of 1997 on crutches too.*

Time for a fan... *Signing the scrapbook of a young admirer.*

Soft landing... *Chester is dragged by a parachute during a rehabilitation exercise after knee surgery.*

A last hurrah... *Chester Williams breaks past Christian Cullen (above) to score his last try in test rugby, a touchdown at Ellis Park against the All Blacks in the Springboks' 46-40 win in 2000.*

LEFT: **Changing colours...** *Chester, in the red and white of the Lions, plays against his old team, Western Province, in the 2000 Currie Cup and hands off WP flyhalf Chris Rossouw.*

RIGHT: **A star in stripes...** *Chester Williams, as the Newlands fans will always remember him – in the blue and white.*

Photos: Anne Laing

Waiting his turn...
On the bench for the Cats in the 2000 season.

arrangement. She had her crèche. She had her environment and there was enough going on in her life to cut out the loneliness of me not being at home on a regular basis. But there was no way I could continue like that any more. I told her that we had grown apart and that we were like two strangers. It hurt, as you cannot imagine. It was a most difficult time; I had battled with this feeling for nearly two years.

I felt a heavy guilt weighing on me, not because there had been anyone else in my life, but because of how our two lives had turned out. We had been married and I thought it would last a lifetime. It hadn't. Teresa did not accept it.

I called her parents and my parents and arranged to meet all of them. She refused to go with me. I told them about my decision. Her mother was very upset. My parents were equally unhappy at the decision, but they accepted it and gave me their support.

My dad was very clear in his view. He did not encourage my decision, but he also did not know what was going on in my relationship. The decision, he said, had to be mine. He also said that I had to be true to myself and to Teresa. It did not help that I lived a lie to keep up some kind of pretence.

I started divorce proceedings, against Teresa's will. It would take two years for the divorce to be finalised and unfortunately the two-year battle killed off whatever little affection that might have remained. We hardly speak now.

During this time I met Sue and we dated for six months. She was white and I was nervous about introducing her to my family. I told my mom that I had a girlfriend, but did not elaborate. I was torn between two feelings. I really liked Sue and was enjoying the freedom of the relationship, but at times I still felt guilty about getting divorced. In those lonely moments I thought of the sacrifices Teresa had made as a rugby widow.

I never shared my mixed emotions with anyone but Maria. She was my best friend. We had known each other since 1996 and we had always been there for each other. In four years we had not so much as kissed each other hello. Ours was a friendship and not a relationship.

I talked a lot to Maria about the situation with Teresa. I knew I had made the right decision, but I was no longer smiling; Teresa was not smiling. We were strangers in a marriage. I wanted a friend. I wanted to be with someone every day and I wanted that someone to be with me.

People grow older. They change. I know it's a cliché and it certainly is not an attempt to defend my decision. I had to do what was right for me. I had to end the marriage.

Rugby, somehow, helped me cope with the uncertainty and the loneliness. It was the same when my brother Wilmot died. I dealt with the pain through rugby. My rugby actually improved because I threw everything I had into the game.

I would train to take away the pain of his death. Now I would simply train harder to ease the loneliness I was feeling. My marriage was over. I was relieved that I had made the decision, although the emotions still varied from relief to guilt.

Sue had come into my life. It was enjoyable but it was not as if we ever spoke about marriage. We were dating and taking it day by day. Our relationship lasted less than six months. Ironically, we broke up the day after I introduced her to my family. It had taken me nearly six months to pluck up enough courage to take a new girl to meet my parents. It was going to be very difficult to explain to them that the new girl was now an ex-girl.

On the surface I was not in love with any woman. As I was to discover later I had been in love with someone for some time and she was about to turn my world upside down.

Maria's story

20

I have found the man of my dreams after discovering the friend of my dreams

CHESTER'S path and mine crossed for the first time in 1994. I was organising a promotional activity and the sum total of our conversation was a 'hello'. He made no impression on me at the time and I doubt if I made one on him. Naturally, I knew who he was, but the introduction in 1994 was too brief to form an opinion.

Two years later I met him again. Once more our professions accounted for the occasion, if you could call it an occasion. I was doing an educational promotion and Chester was there as one of the VIP guests. A Cape Argus representative, Diane McMahon, was there for the event and she asked me if it would be possible to have a rugby ball signed by Chester. It seemed no big deal and I prompted her to approach Chester and ask him. She did so and I was stunned by the response. He was polite but said he had to phone his agent before he was allowed to sign anything. Then he made a call to Frikkie Erasmus and the two of them spoke.

Frikkie told Chester to put Diane on the line and he quizzed her about her intentions. She made it clear she did not want to make money out of the signed ball and that it was for a fundraiser.

All of this took the best part of 20 minutes. I couldn't believe it. Eventually Chester signed the ball. This time I would remember meeting Chester, but the impression had not been a good one.

After he had signed the ball, we spoke briefly. He gave me his phone number and said if I ever needed him to help with any charity or promotional activity I should call. At first I was quite excited at his offer, but he then qualified it with a reminder that I had to work through his agent.

I had never met Frikkie but decided to give it a go. I was busy with a promotion for a chocolate brand called Sweetie Pie and decided to telephone Frikkie about getting Chester involved. He told me to put the proposal on paper for consideration. I did so and subsequently contacted him a few times to see if Chester would be available.

Each time I called, he would refer to me as 'Miss Sweetie Pie'. He said that no decision had been made and that I should visit his offices. 'Don't forget to bring a few Sweetie Pies,' is how he ended the conversation.

I was keen to have Chester involved and visited Frikkie's offices, armed with the Sweetie Pies. Frikkie still did not give me an answer and the proposal was never again officially discussed.

At the time, part of my freelance promotional and marketing work involved giving the Western Province rugby players Energade – an energy drink. I got on very well with all of them. They were a great bunch of blokes, who would visit frequently, either on their way to training or whenever they were in the area.

Chester never collected his sponsored Energade. In the beginning I would give his allotment to the other players to pass on to him. It bothered me that he never collected his energy drinks. I had only met him on a few occasions and during those times I had found him to be shy. He lacked confidence and was very much in the background, despite all the fuss the public made about him.

One day in 1996 I called him up: 'It is time you collected your Energades,' I jokingly mocked him. Then I invited him to lunch. Surprisingly, he agreed, but he said he would have to be accompanied by his agent, Frikkie Erasmus.

I found this odd, but the initial request to have his agent present for our lunch outing was not as bizarre as the appointment itself. We both went to Frikkie's office first and then went to lunch at the Parliament buildings near Frikkie's office.

I felt like a schoolgirl with a date and a chaperon. It was the strangest of lunches and what struck me most was Chester's insistence in calling Frikkie 'Mr Erasmus'. Not once did he address him by his first name. It is something that would bug me for the next five years.

The lunch itself was like something out of a movie. I would ask Chester a question and before he answered he would look to Erasmus for a nod of approval. Once Chester had answered the question, he would look to Erasmus for confirmation that everything was okay.

And when Erasmus spoke, Chester hung on to his every word. I had never seen anything like it in my life. There was total domination in the relationship. Chester did not think for himself. Erasmus talked and Chester listened.

A while later, once our acquaintance had begun to develop into a friendship, I jokingly asked Chester if he had to phone Erasmus before he went to the toilet. It was early on in our friendship and he was still getting to know my sense of humour. He thought I was serious. 'No', was his retort. I said: 'Thank God … it isn't that bad yet.'

Our friendship, strictly platonic, started slowly. Chester intrigued me because of his shy demeanour and the fact that I had never been privy to a relationship like the one between him and Erasmus. I would mock him a lot about the control Erasmus had over him. He would always defend Erasmus, whom Chester believed to be an intelligent man. He said their relationship meant everything to him professionally.

Chester and I, after the initial three's-a-crowd lunch, started to get to know each other well. However, it was a very strange relationship that was developing. It was different to any kind of friendship I had previously known. It had started with me phoning this guy and saying it was time to collect his energy drinks and then a few months later he would visit me regularly at the office. He did not come to collect the Energades, just to say hello. And that was about all he would say.

He would speak Afrikaans, I would speak English and I would do most of the talking. I think he probably found me to be good entertainment value. I was different to anyone he had known – loud, on the move and operating at 100 miles an hour. I think I used to amuse him. It was free entertainment. He was so shy and reserved and I was the complete opposite.

He would sit there and say very little. One day, when I had to visit a Cape Town newspaper office, I said: 'Hey, I have to go to Die Burger,' and he said: 'Okay, I'll come along.' Weird, I thought, but what the hell. 'Hop in the car,' I told him. So he tagged along and I started to tease him about being so shy. My teasing never stopped him from coming to visit.

The more he visited, the more English he spoke, the more Afrikaans I learned and the more our friendship grew. He would tell me about his family and he always spoke about his fiancée, Teresa. I had never met her and we would meet only a year later.

I was like his best friend, but in another world. I was his escape from everything he was involved in relationship-wise. He would stop at my work or phone and say he needed to get his mom a present … or one for his fiancée. I would help him shop for the gift. I would be his sounding board and we would just have fun together. It was our friendship. No one got a look in and it was a very private world. There was my world, Chester's world, and our world as friends.

In 1997 he injured a knee in only his second match after recovering from a similar injury the year before. He was booked into the Panorama Clinic in Plattekloof for the operation and recovery period. I stayed only two minutes away from the hospital so I visited Chester several times a day.

I did what any good friend would do. I would try to make him laugh, cheer him up and spoil him with home-cooked food. He used to love my visits because they livened up his day. The poor guy was lying in hospital, flat on his back and pretty down about another enforced lay-off.

I would try to start his day with a home-cooked breakfast, then a few stories, a bit of a laugh and I was out of there. I would be back for lunch and I'd pop in just before the family and friends used to visit in the evening.

Our friendship was extremely strong at that stage, but still I had never met his fiancée or his parents. One morning, during his stay at the hospital, he asked if I could go to Paarl to fetch his fiancée and bring her to visiting hours. She could not drive and did not have transport.

I had no problem giving her a lift, but it was a very uncomfortable drive. She said nothing throughout the 40 minutes the journey took. Being opinionated, outspoken and generally very loud, I tried to make conversation. It was not very successful. She just nodded occasionally but she said nothing.

When we arrived at his hospital room, she was very subdued and it struck me that when she entered the room she did not even kiss him hello. There was a very formal greeting. There seemed to be little affection.

I left and his fiancée got a lift home with a friend. It was the first time we had met and it was the first time that I had a glimpse into Chester's world. His parents were still off-limits, as was his other world, which remained very private.

Chester really did operate in different worlds – there was the rugby player who could compete with the best, the puppy dog around his agent, the innocent and good son in the eyes of his parents, the solid fiancé and the unshackled Chester, who used to hang out with me and was becoming my best friend.

I adored him – the simplicity and decency and the fact that he could want a friendship with a woman and that there was never an advance of any kind, outside of friendship.

I was also intrigued by his relationship with his fiancée. It seemed so distant. The biggest contrast was that of the player on the field and the player in the company of his agent. He went from being a giant on the field to a helpless puppy dog when around his agent. It always bugged me. It used to irk me that he always called Erasmus 'mister' and that he allowed himself to be treated as inferior to Erasmus.

Erasmus did not enjoy my presence in Chester's life. I questioned things. I questioned the dominance of one person over another. Chester would always change the subject, take it away from Erasmus and talk about the lighter things in life.

I was never invited to Chester's wedding in 1996. I was this imaginary friend in his world. His mom would later tell me that he had mentioned me on occasion, but for the most part I existed in his other world. We had our own special place: two friends who loved life.

I admit that I tried to talk him out of marriage. It had nothing to do with me wanting in. As I have said, ours was a friendship and nothing more. I just knew he was not ready for marriage. There was a Chester screaming to get out, yet there was a Chester committed to the traditional things of life: a proposal at a young age and the obligation to go through with the marriage. At least, that's what I thought.

I told him: 'Marry when you are 30 … enjoy life … your best years are ahead of you.' But any attempt to deter him was futile. The wedding had been arranged; Chester was marrying his fiancée. It would be a grand event and even President Mandela would be there.

At the time, Chester never spoke to me in great detail about the wedding nor about his marriage. He used to mention his family and wife when he wanted to buy gifts and the two of us would go shopping for these presents.

When we were together the focus was on our friendship. I also respected the fact that he did not feel comfortable talking about his wife. Our friendship was very strong, but I never abused this by prying into his other world.

Then, one day in 1998, he visited me on his way to training. While he was there, he got a call from his wife, who needed to go shopping. Chester had to drive from Cape Town to Paarl (a journey of between 30 and 40 minutes), pick her up, take her shopping and then drive her home. I thought this was madness and told him so.

'Teresa doesn't have a licence,' he said.

'Well, then let's get her one,' I said and I volunteered to help Teresa with driving lessons.

Chester told Teresa that I would teach her to drive and she accepted the offer. In 1998 we started having regular contact for the first time, through the driving lessons. I found her a difficult person to get to know and even more private than Chester, which I thought was not possible.

If I had experienced Chester as lonely, she was even more of a loner. She kept to herself, never let me into her life and treated my offer to teach her how to drive a car in a professional way.

Chester, in the latter part of 1998, had spoken to me about his intention to move to Johannesburg if he could not further his rugby career in Cape Town. He loved Western Province and home to him will always be the Cape. But he was disillusioned with the set-up at Western Province.

He told me that the coaching staff at WP did not rate him and that he would be wasting his time playing in Cape Town. There was the possibility of a move to Johannesburg, and while he did not want to live there, he knew it was the only way to continue playing professional rugby.

His move, in 1999, did not affect our relationship. It may even have made it stronger because we used to phone each other daily, SMS each other a lot and talk for a long time. Being apart was difficult because I loved his company so much, but it was still fun chatting every day.

In 1999 I hardly saw Chester, even though we spoke to each other every day. He was playing rugby again and excited about the chances of making it back into the national team, but he was extremely lonely. He was not socially happy and his marriage was taking serious strain.

He would commute at weekends when it was possible to be with his wife. When he had a few days off from rugby, he would visit his wife in Paarl. Those visits were precious to him and I never saw him. He would phone to say he would be in Paarl, but that he needed to spend time with Teresa.

Telephonically, we would talk on a regular basis and he spoke for the first time in great detail about how much trouble his marriage was in. There were no other women in his life and no men in hers, but he felt they had drifted apart. I did what friends do: I listened, offered my bit of advice and tried to cheer him up.

All I cared for was my friend's happiness. Chester was my friend. There were people in his life who were not. I hardly knew any of them.

The unhappiness over his relationship lasted quite a while. Then at a point, between six months and a year later, it reached an unbearable point. Chester phoned me to tell me that he was going to ask Teresa for a divorce.

It was a massive decision for him and he had agonised about it for a long time. He had spoken to his father and to me at different times. I think my advice was similar to that which he got from his father, which was to do with his own happiness and sanity.

Chester flew to Cape Town, went home and confronted Teresa with the news. She did not accept it and refused to grant him the divorce. It was not going to be an easy separation, but Chester was confident that he had made the right decision. He immediately seemed a different person. He laughed a bit more and it seemed as if a huge weight had been lifted from him.

He was still the Chester I had always known – very shy in company, still in awe of Erasmus and still a different soul when the two of us were alone.

Emotionally, we were close and our relationship was special. Physically, we had never even kissed each other hello and I don't think either of us had given it much thought. We had known each other since 1996 and in four years we had never even given each other as much as a peck on the cheek, let alone the lips.

Chester was now officially separated, even though Teresa was not going to easily give him the divorce. Despite the divorce complication, he was relaxed, he was playing great rugby (at least that's what everyone said because I had still never been to watch him play) and he was happy.

By the middle of 2000 he called to tell me he had met someone else. He was more excited on the phone than I had ever heard him. He had met an air hostess named Sue.

I was as excited for him. I had seen him go through some very lonely and empty stages and to hear him sound so upbeat immediately gave me a kick.

I told him how happy I was and I wanted to see him. I arranged to go to Johannesburg to watch him play for the Springboks against the All Blacks. It turned out to be a wonderful weekend. The Springboks won, Chester scored a try and he clearly was happy about having met Sue.

Chester couldn't stop talking about Sue. She was attractive, intelligent and everything he seemed to want. She gave him a buzz, he said.

The two dated for a few months and the Chester who spoke to me on the phone was content and happy. Now, bear in mind, that in four years of our wonderful friendship, there had never been a hint of any romance. I know it sounds boring and something of a cliché, but we were like a brother and sister. We shared a wonderful bond, but there was no hint of the friendship ever developing romantically.

Chester was on tour with the Boks in Europe and I called him to say I would be in Johannesburg on business. My visit to Johannesburg overlapped with his return from London. We arranged to meet and he said he wanted to bring Sue along for me to meet her.

I'll never forget that day when I saw him. I had hardly spent time with him that year because he had been in Johannesburg and I had been in Cape Town. He was confident, cool and very much in control. He oozed confidence. He strutted as opposed to walked.

It was wonderful to watch. I said hello to him and when he introduced me to Sue, I greeted her with a kiss on the cheek. He chirped me: 'Hey where's my kiss … is it only Sue that gets a kiss hello.' It was very unlike Chester and he caught me off-guard. He had never shown this kind of confidence in front of a woman.

In four years we had never kissed each other hello. I did not know whether he was joking or serious. I said okay and went over to give him a kiss and a hug. I don't know why, but I was nervous and we tripped over each other. It was a clumsy attempt at an innocent hello kiss and one of the most embarrassing moments of my life. Everything about the hello kiss seemed awkward. Needless to say, I didn't offer a goodbye kiss and he never asked for one.

That meeting took place early in December, 2000. Later that month Chester and Sue were going to Cape Town. She had never met Chester's parents. For the record, neither had I.

In four years I had never been introduced to his parents. I had once popped into Chester's house for a quick visit on his birthday. He was having a party and I was not invited. I helped Teresa prepare some food and then left. I saw his parents, but there was not the opportunity to say hello. I left as everyone was arriving.

Chester was nervous about taking Sue to his parents' house. It was a big thing for Chester. Sue was white and while he had told his parents about this new love in his life, they had never met.

Sue and Chester spent Christmas Day at his parents' house. On Boxing Day, Chester arrived at my place alone and told me that his relationship with Sue was over. I was quite surprised, but he seemed indifferent to it all, disinterested about it and a bit distant. He told me that it had been coming for a while and that the romance had run its course. He never spoke negatively about Sue. He just said it was over.

The last thing I needed on Boxing Day was Chester moping around my place. 'Bugger this', I told him: 'We'll find you someone else.' He just laughed.

We spent a hectic few days socialising. I introduced him to friends of mine, but the quiet and reclusive Chester had returned. He seemed totally uninterested. He just wanted to chat, have fun and enjoy our friendship as he had in the past.

It was great having him all to myself as a friend. It was just like it was before he had moved to Johannesburg. We always felt comfortable in each other's company.

But I wasn't going to give up without a fight. On December 31 we went out to celebrate the new year with a few of Chester's friends, among them rugby players Conrad Jantjes and Thando Manana. We ended up at 69 on Long Street, a jazz club and restaurant.

We had a wonderful time that evening and we laughed a lot. We were so happy together. The New Year clock had already done its thing and we were dancing and chatting. I don't know what prompted it and I cannot remember any particular incident in the build-up to the moment … but we kissed. Not a peck … a kiss … the real deal.

It was amazing. Probably for the first time in our friendship I said nothing. Not for the first time, Chester also said nothing. We seemed to just go with the moment. I had remembered an earlier discussion that evening when I asked him what he wanted in a girlfriend: He had answered: 'She has to be like you.'

I had never taken any notice of it. I had assumed he was talking about an outgoing personality and someone who wanted to live life and not moan about it. Now we were kissing, holding hands and being very intimate. I thought I was going to regret this forever. I was worried that this one moment was going to destroy four years of friendship.

Chester stayed at my house that evening. He slept on the couch and while neither of us said anything once we got home, I feared for the worst in the morning. I shouldn't have. In the morning, the way we felt a few hours earlier was merely confirmed. There was nothing to feel guilty about. We both smiled and kissed each other good morning. This time, we did not trip over each other in a clumsy embrace.

There was one problem. Chester did not know how to tell his parents that he had broken up with Sue. It had taken him six months to introduce her to them. A day after he had taken the big step, they had broken up.

I told him to relax. 'I will tell them,' I said. This made him even more nervous. In four years he had not yet taken me to meet them. Now he would be taking home a second white girl in five days and the second girl would be telling his parents that the first girlfriend was no longer on the scene.

He did relax, we did visit his parents and after four years I wondered what all the fuss was about. We got on easily and the fact that Chester had broken up with Sue was a decision his parents respected. It was his life, they told me. He must make choices that determine his happiness.

Subsequently, Chester's dad has told me that on that day he told Chester's mom that there was something between Chester and me. At the time neither of them said anything. I guess it must have been obvious, but Chester and I were playing it cool.

Since then our love has become stronger, our bond has become more united and the romance has added to our relationship and not detracted from it.

Chester has also parted ways with Erasmus. Formally, he has severed all business ties and emotionally he has broken the shackles in that he has dropped the formal 'Mr' greeting. He now refers to Frikkie by his first name … and it is a name that we try to mention as little as possible.

Chester's divorce was made official in 2002 and we married on May 10. Only 30 people attended our wedding. A few close friends and our immediate family. My son Ryan, from my first marriage, handed me over to Chester. It was a moving and symbolic moment because Ryan has also accepted Chester into his life.

For Chester and I, it is our second attempt at marriage. God willing, it will be our last. I have found the man of my dreams after discovering the friend of my dreams.

My Springbok XV

21 

Deon Kayser's selection ... will surprise many ... but to those who have played with and against him it will not be a shock. In another era, playing under coaches with different mindsets, Kayser could have got his real reward

THE most frequently asked questions during my playing career were those relating to teammates and the opposition. Which world team would I pick as the best of my era? Which Springbok team would I select as the best of the 1990s? Who was the best wing I played against? Who was the easiest to defend against? Who was the quickest? Who was the smartest?

In some instances I could easily cop out of a debate by saying I had never played against the player. It was never good enough. My friends would then still ask me for an opinion on these players.

In picking my two fantasy teams – Bok and World – I restricted my combinations to the years between 1992 and 2001 – my era, that is. Some players were at the end of their careers when I came on the scene, others had only started theirs when I retired. In certain cases, a player's impact was such that I felt he did more in a few matches than others had done in a 10-year career.

My first-class career lasted 10 years, from 1991 through to 2001. During this time I played with and against some of the game's greats. My World team may have a southern hemisphere slant to it because I played so much rugby against guys from New Zealand and Australia.

I judged the northern hemisphere players on appearances I made against them or on what I saw of them as international players. My experience of them at club level was limited.

My Springbok team has no provincial prejudice, but it does have a provincial feel to it in the sense that there were certain players whose talents were never given the necessary international recognition. I believe if they were given more international exposure they would have made a greater impact on the world game.

Here is my test team, including the reserves bench...

Fullback (No 15): Andre Joubert

Joubert's selection was one of the easiest I had to make. I played against Andre, I played in the same team and there were many occasions when I watched from the sidelines with admiration. He was one of the most natural athletes I have ever seen on a rugby field and he was equally effective at sevens and in the 15-a-side version of the game.

He always had time when fielding the ball, which is the trademark of a good player. His vision on the field was without comparison; his left boot was among the best in the game; and he had a presence on attack.

One of his greatest strengths was that he could counter-attack effectively with the boot. The manner in which he used to mix up his grubber kicks with his running counter-attacking always meant the opposition was in two-minds when kicking the ball to him.

I know his critics point to a defensive vulnerability. As a wing who played test rugby with him, I never felt for one moment that he was not up to it defensively. He was an excellent communicator. He played off his wingers effectively and got them to play off him very well.

There were too many wonderful performances from Juba to single out just one. I will, however, always remember his courage in playing out the World Cup with a broken hand. It showed his commitment to the team. The contrasting matches he played in the 1995 World Cup quarter-final against Western Samoa and the semi-final against France underlined his class.

In selecting a Springbok fullback of my time, he was in another class to any other fullback in the country.

Right wing (No 14): Deon Kayser

This is a selection that will surprise many people, but to those who have played with and against Kayser it will not be a shock. In another era, playing under coaches with different mindsets, Kayser could have got his real reward. It is unfortunate that his international career will be recorded as that of a winger who played a bits and pieces role for the Springboks. It should have been much more.

He is a player who has never been given a hand-out in South African rugby. He has fought for every bit of recognition. He has had to fight harder than most to get club, provincial, Super 12 and finally test recognition.

Many others were picked ahead of him, but he has outlasted them. I cannot recall him having too many mediocre games in South African rugby. I don't remember a poor test match.

Deon was one of the most consistent performers and it is for this reason that I choose him above Pieter Rossouw, who was one of the most lethal players when on form, but in his career there was too much inconsistency. An in-form Rossouw is up there with the best of them. An out of form Rossouw is not the best of sights on a rugby field.

Kayser gives me the comfort of always delivering. On balance, I pick him ahead of Rossouw as a right wing. I always thought Pieter was a better right wing than a left wing, even though he played most of his wing career in the No 11 jersey.

Kayser's defence, more so as a wing than a centre, was always outstanding. He gives away nothing in defence, in marking one on one, and his pace was as good as any wing playing the game in South Africa in the 1990s and early 2000s.

Defensively, I will always remember two tackles he made on Tana Umaga and Jonah Lomu in a Super 12 match (for the Sharks against the Hurricanes) in the 2001 season.

If he was white, he would have been given greater opportunity and he would have played many more test matches. Kayser was a victim of being a black player in the immediate post-isolation era. If he had played in the decade 2001-2011 I would probably not have to convince too many about his ability.

We never played against each other, wing against wing. I played against him when I was on the wing and he was at outside centre. It is among my regrets that we never got to play against each other more often because you always want to measure yourself against the best – and I believe he could have held his own in any company.

Outside centre (No 13): Danie Gerber

Frik du Preez was recently voted the South African player of the century. Not only do I believe Gerber was the player of his generation, I also rate him as the South African player of the last 100 years, ahead of Du Preez.

Gerber had everything. We played together when he was in the twilight of his career, but it did not make him any less dangerous on attack. He commanded a presence on the rugby field. His aura was unrivalled in this country and the only player who shades him in world rugby is the French great Philippe Sella. I would loved to have seen Sella play inside centre with Gerber on his outside – now that would have been a lethal combination.

Gerber, in a South African context, is without comparison. He was at his best from broken play. His feel for the game was unmatched and he was an incredible try-scoring force as an outside centre.

I think many people will share my view that the world missed out on seeing one of the best during South Africa's isolation. Gerber, had he enjoyed an extended international career, would be spoken of in revered terms in every rugby-playing country.

Inside centre (No 12): Hennie le Roux

Le Roux was the most valuable backline player of the Springboks' successful 1995 World Cup campaign. He was the master tactician at the World Cup. He was the pillar around which our defensive pattern was built. He was the strength in uniting the Bok backline.

He had the advantage of having played flyhalf for much of his career, but inside centre was his most effective position. He marshalled defences from the No 12 position and any No 10 playing on his inside had the advantage of tapping into one of the best sets of eyes playing the game in the 1990s.

Hennie's defence was rock solid and many an opponent made the mistake of trying to intimidate him because of a perceived lack of size. He was compact and strong in defence. He had a useful boot, could kick at the posts if the team needed it (as the Boks did in the win against Wales in 1994) and on attack he read the game perfectly.

One of England's strengths in the 2000 season was playing Jonny Wilkinson at flyhalf and Mike Catt at inside centre. I felt the Springboks had a similar luxury at the 1995 World Cup when Joel Stransky was at flyhalf and Hennie le Roux at inside centre. Le Roux, in tandem with Stransky, was a very effective combination, although I believe the Le Roux and Henry Honiball match-up was never allowed to reach its full potential. Le Roux at No 12 also instilled confidence in the inside backs as well as those on his outside.

He was a difficult guy at times and he is a complex personality. This should not detract from his ability as a player. He called things as he saw them. He was not afraid to speak his mind and his knowledge of the game is very impressive.

Left wing (No 11): Breyton Paulse

What a wonderful attacker. What an athlete. Paulse, when fit and confident, is a breath of fresh air for our rugby. He also had to fight prejudice in the mid-1990s because of being black. In any other country they would have recognised his rugby ability before seeking out any vulnerabilities.

His lack of size should never have been an issue in his rugby. To too many South African coaches it was used as an excuse not to select him. I will have a fit Breyton in my team every weekend of the season. What he gives you on attack far outweighs any defensive shortcomings. He will score you four tries and give away one. I'll take the plus-three ratio every time.

Traditionally, our coaches don't pick attacking wings. They will go the conservative route and select a guy who is defensively strong even if he offers little on attack.

Paulse's defence is not the greatest, but he has worked hard on this aspect of the game. He is not afraid to make the tackle, as was highlighted when he stopped Wallaby strongman Nathan Grey in the Springboks' 14-14 draw against Australia in Perth in 2001.

He has worked on his defensive positional play. He knows that teams will kick the high ball on to him and that they will always run at him one on one because they feel he is weak on defence.

On attack, he is one of the most dangerous players. He has acceleration that carves up defences; he backs himself to have a go; and he has a feel for the game. He is most dangerous when he attacks the defence from close in. His feet play tricks on defences.

Paulse's inclusion, like Andre Joubert's, was one of the easiest to make. I picked him at left wing even though he played most of his test rugby at right wing. Being a natural left-footer, I think he is better suited to the left side.

Flyhalf (No 10): Henry Honiball

He has been called King Henry – and rightly so. I believe All Blacks flyhalf Andrew Mehrtens went up to Honiball after the 1999 World Cup and thanked Henry for retiring! Opposition players admired Honiball. They respected him and in many instances they feared him. I don't know of many who liked playing against him.

He redefined the role of the flyhalf when playing for South Africa. Other countries picked teams to counter him. They focused on him and not the ability of their own player. When a team shows you that kind of respect, then there has to be a special quality about you.

Honiball, defensively, was in a league of his own as a flyhalf. He shut down an attacker, be it a fullback, wing, flank or lock. He cut the opposition down and very few flyhalves ever tried to attack his channel.

Defensively, he was any coach's dream and don't underestimate his attacking ability. He had a good kicking game, was an effective goal-kicker when called on to do so and he was particularly effective when attacking the gain line. He would stand flat and wide, which gave him the freedom to run at space, and to put the defence in two minds.

I always talk about great players having time and presence on the field; he had both. It was unfortunate that injury ruled him out of most of the 1995 season and that he was not selected for the 1995 World Cup squad. I also believe that his absence from the majority of the 1999 World Cup matches was the biggest setback to the Springboks. With Honiball at flyhalf, the results might have been a lot different.

As well as Jannie de Beer kicked in the quarter-final against England at the 1999 World Cup, I would have played a fit Honiball in the semi-final against Australia. He would have commanded a respect from the opposition that De Beer, through no fault of his own, never did get in the semi-final.

Scrumhalf (No 9): Joost van der Westhuizen
I pick Joost, not because I thought he was an outstanding scrumhalf, but because he was probably the best of a decent bunch (by international standards). During the 1990s South Africa produced good scrumhalves, but nothing that could be classed great.

If you picked Joost you sacrificed the composure and kicking authority that a Johan Roux provided. If you swapped them around, you gave up the athleticism of Van der Westhuizen.

Joost was a great athlete. I believe he was a limited scrumhalf who covered up his shortcomings with naturally blessed athleticism and a brilliant attitude towards the game. He is a fighter, a competitor and a guy with whom you can comfortably go to war.

His passing was inconsistent and lacked authority. He was not comfortable kicking with either foot and his pass was not equally strong from both sides. He favoured one side and that is a weakness in the armoury of any scrumhalf.

Yet he gave his team a lot on attack and on defence. He made some great tackles in his time and he scored some fabulous tries. He was not in the class of some of the scrumhalves playing international rugby in the 1990s, but he would never let any team down.

I pick him ahead of Johan Roux in my fantasy team because of his athleticism and predatory instincts.

No 8: Gary Teichmann
I find it appropriate that Teichmann is the most celebrated Springbok captain in the past century. He holds the record for the most capped test No 8 and the most consistent Bok captain in the past 100 years. He did not play in a World Cup and that was a great injustice.

As a leader, Teichmann was the quiet and stern type. He demanded respect through his approach on and off the field. He led in the way he played – from the front. There was nothing flash about him, but there was plenty of substance to him as a player and a leader.

I found him to be an outstanding individual and a quality person. I was fortunate to get to know him as early as 1993 when we played together in the midweek Springbok team during the tour of Argentina. He treated every player as his equal. He was never aloof, even when he became a test regular and South Africa's most successful Bok captain.

He maintained humility throughout his playing career and his contribution to the Bok team never varied in its outstanding consistency. He was another who played few bad games.

There was nothing spectacular about the way he played or his approach to the game. He did the basics well, gave the team his all and instilled a belief in his players that anything was possible. He was not a leader in the Francois Pienaar or Bobby Skinstad mould. There were no sideshows with him and he was not big on the hyped motivation. He led and the team followed.

As a player he typified the traditional No 8 role. He took the ball up, invariably broke the first tackle and never minded getting dirty. His anticipation in falling back to help the back three, and his ability to make the cross-cover tackles were among his strengths. He makes my team because of all those good points, but he does not captain the team because I believe there was someone better in South African rugby during the 1990s.

No 7 flank: Johan (Rassie) Erasmus

There are those coaches who believe Rassie is a better No 8 than a 7 flank. I don't share this opinion. During the 1990s Erasmus stood out as a loose forward and the choice came down to Erasmus or Bobby Skinstad. As with Erasmus, I don't believe Bobby's best position is No 8. I also think he is better suited to playing No 7 flank and playing off a strong No 8.

Rassie gets the nod ahead of Bobby because of his work rate and the fact that physically he takes on more responsibility. Bobby is the more skilled of the two, but Rassie works harder at his game.

During my two years at the Cats and Lions I was enormously impressed with Erasmus's knowledge of the game. His analysis is of the best I have experienced and he is a player who thinks about the game all the time.

Injuries hampered his career in 2000 and 2001 but when on form he is an asset to any team. As is the case with Hennie le Roux, Erasmus is not the easiest person to have in a squad because he questions and challenges coaches.

His playing pedigree, though, is beyond dispute, as is his all-round game. He is an intelligent footballer, who knows his limitations when it comes to out and out pace. He knows he lacks speed but compensates for this with an outstanding feel for the game. Physically he also does not stand back to anyone.

Skinstad, if he stays injury free and realises his potential, could become one of the best loose forwards in the game in the next few years, but based on my experience of the 1990s I select Erasmus.

No 6 flank: Tiaan Strauss (captain)

Contrary to what many believe, this was one of the easier choices to make in the pack. Tiaan stands out above any of the other contenders, who include the 1995 World Cup-winning flank and captain Francois Pienaar.

I would not have picked Pienaar for the 1995 World Cup. He was not the best No 6 flanker in the country. I can understand why Kitch Christie made the decision. Kitch was comfortable with Francois, whom he had coached for three years at Transvaal. Most of that World Cup squad were Transvaal players, so it would seem logical to get Pienaar to captain the side. It made sense even if it was not a true reflection of who was the best No 6 in the country. Strauss played a lot of his rugby at No 8, but it is my belief that he was better suited to the No 6 role.

I also enjoyed his captaincy more than I did Francois's. The strength of Strauss was that he led from the front. He took the blows and the scars he carried because of it were more powerful than any motivational speech. Pienaar, when going forward, was outstanding, but he did not command the same presence when the match turned against his team.

Strauss, whether you were up by 10 or down by 10, was the same. Pienaar was more about words. He was very good in motivation. I am one of those players who is motivated by the occasion and not by the words of a captain. I want my leader to be out there putting it on the line first. Strauss did most of his talking through grafted deed.

I really felt for him when he did not make the 1995 World Cup squad. He played his heart out in the final 'trial' game at Newlands when Joel Stransky dropped a goal to save the Shadow XV the embarrassment of losing to the Strauss-captained Western Province President's XV.

He was the best loose forward on the field that day, but Kitch and the selectors chose Robbie Brink. There was no comparison.

Strauss did not make the side because Kitch feared a clash of personalities. Again, I can understand the selection philosophy even though I will never agree with it. Instead of risking division, Strauss was omitted.

I was happy for Tiaan that he decided to return to rugby union and played test rugby for Australia. He is a player who should have represented South Africa in many more tests. He got to a World Cup and played a part in a winning campaign. It was unfortunate that it was not in the colours of South Africa. He deserved to be the Bok captain at the 1995 World Cup.

Locks (No 5): Victor Matfield

In the past 10 years I don't think I have seen a lock as naturally talented in the South African game. Matfield has everything going for him. He is athletic, he is the best lineout jumper we have in this country and he is the most skilled lock in South Africa.

His attitude has been questioned and I have heard critics knocking his apparent lack of physical presence. But put him in the right environment and he can develop into a figure as imposing at test level as John Eales was for Australia and Ian Jones was for New Zealand.

Naturally, he has to work on his game and he will develop further with experience. As a ball-winner in South Africa, only Albert van den Berg compares. Victor's all-round game is better to start a test, with Van den Berg the ideal impact player.

Locks (No 4): Johan Ackermann

For the second lock position, I considered Ackermann and Mark Andrews. Ackermann is the one I opted for and it was not a particularly difficult decision.

There will be those who argue that Andrews has been there and done it all at test level. I just don't think Ackermann ever got the same opportunity. National coaches were also reluctant to show as much faith in him as Laurie Mains did at a provincial and Super 12 levels.

Ackermann's career was disrupted because of a two-year ban for taking anabolic steroids, but when he returned he was as imposing as the player who made his test debut in 1996. He has incredible strength, has the ability to wrap up any player in the tackle and provides the perfect foil to a combination that includes Victor Matfield.

Physically, Ackermann is the most potent lock with whom I played. He was particularly impressive when playing lock in the Laurie Mains-coached Lions and Cats teams. Mains got the best out of him and played to his strengths.

Tighthead prop (No 3): Keith Andrews

There were stronger tighthead props in the 1990s, but there was not one prop who had the kind of game Andrews produced week in and week out.

He was a converted flanker, so he knew what to do with the ball in hand. He had mobility and was strong enough to stand up to his man. Put a bloke like Ackermann behind him in the set-pieces and you won't see him going back to any loosehead.

It was his mobility and skill level that gave him the edge over other tighthead contenders, the best of whom was Cobus Visagie. Given the way I would want my team to play, having a tighthead with skill would be a major advantage.

Keith also provides leadership and he is one of the best team guys you could hope to have in a squad. He is also not afraid to mix it and I'll never forget the punch he threw to knock out the Tucuman No 8 when the Boks played them in the 1993 game, notorious for one of the most brutal fights I have ever seen on a rugby field.

Hooker (No 2): Uli Schmidt
This was one of the most difficult choices I had to make, but I opted for Uli ahead of a current Springbok hooker John Smit on the basis that Smit must still reach his peak, whereas I had seen first-hand an Uli Schmidt at the height of his career.

Smit, in years to come, will become one of South Africa's greats. He has all the attributes to become the dominant hooker in world rugby in the next five years. His lineout throwing has to become more consistent, but I am sure this will come in time.

One of Uli's strongest points was his accuracy in throwing in. His calmness under pressure was the best in South Africa and his skill level added a dimension to any pack he played in. A neck injury probably cut two years off his career, but it did not rob him of making his mark in South African rugby. He went out while at the top of his game and he is another of those gifted players who played average, good or great games. It is not easy to recall bad matches, although he would probably admit to a few.

He was very aggressive and physical in his approach. He did not stand back for anyone and his adventurous approach did not mean he neglected his basics. Had he played more international rugby he would have made an even greater impact. During the 1990s he was my pick as the most influential and effective hooker in South Africa.

Loosehead prop (No 1): Os du Randt
This was without a doubt the easiest of my choices in the forwards. Os du Randt, in a short time, became the best loosehead prop in the world, let alone South Africa. He was magnificent at the World Cup in 1995 and had it not been for injury, he would still be a dominant force in the game.

He had everything a prop could ask for. He had size, mobility, a great appreciation for the game and an imposing presence. And he could tackle. Just ask Australian Matthew Burke. I think Os cut short Burke's Super 12 season twice with crunching tackles.

Os also had courage. I don't buy the story that he left the field against the All Blacks in 1996 because he had had enough. It was not in his nature. He was one of the most committed and courageous players I had the pleasure of knowing.

He suffered badly from knee injuries and he showed guts even to play in the 1999 test season. He gave it everything at the 1999 World Cup, even though the nature of his injuries did not allow him to operate with maximum fitness.

The bench

Forwards

Hooker: John Smit
A dynamic player, he would provide immediate impact. He can also double as a loosehead.

Prop: Garry Pagel
By all accounts the strongest prop in South African rugby in the 1990s. Garry's biggest asset was the stability he brought to any scrum. He was a specialist loosehead but was reasonably comfortable at tighthead. He was not the most mobile, but that is not why I would pick him.

When the going got tough, Pagel got stuck in. He is the kind of prop you want in your team and not as part of the opposition.

Lock: Albert van den Berg
He is probably the one lock in South Africa who can perform the role of specialist impact lock. He is a brilliant lineout jumper and dynamic around the field. When the game opens up, he is at his most devastating.

Loose forward: AJ Venter
I saw the potential in AJ when he played No 8 for the Lions in the 1999 Currie Cup season. He was superb. He has added more aggression to his game and after an initial struggle has found the balance between his athleticism and his aggression.

He is the most versatile loose forward in the country. He can play No 8, flank and lock. It is at lock where he will probably complete his career. Currently, he would make a contribution to any team playing in any one of those three positions.

Scrumhalf: Johan Roux
Roux's kicking game was unrivalled in South Africa. He was particularly effective in wet conditions. He was also a very smart player

and a fine passer of the ball. He warms my bench because of the stability and sanity he would bring to any pressure situation.

Midfield: Brendan Venter
Brendan can play at inside or outside centre. He is a master tactician and it has not surprised me at all that he achieved such success as a coach with London Irish.

His knowledge always impressed me and as a player he was a fantastic communicator. Some would say he probably talked too much, but I don't think any player with such insight can be guilty of saying too much.

Defensively, he is solid, but his greatest attribute is his intelligence on the field.

Utility back: Conrad Jantjes
This selection will probably surprise a number of people because Conrad was only 22 years old in 2002 and until then had played only one season of test rugby.

I worked with Jantjes for two years at the Cats and he is the most talented back I have played with in the past 10 years. He can play fullback, on either wing or at flyhalf. He is one of a rare breed of natural footballers.

My concern is that he does not work half as hard as he should and that it could take him time to come to terms with the week in and week out demands of test rugby. I envisage a great future for him in South African rugby, if he is managed correctly and if he puts in the necessary hours.

My choice for the final position was between Percy Montgomery and Jantjes. Percy is even more versatile, having played fullback, wing, centre and flyhalf in his 50-odd test matches.

Potentially, I believe Jantjes can be better and that is why I opted for him.

My World XV

22

Lomu is a marketing man's dream, but he is a limited international wing ... he lacks the all-round class of Joe Roff

Fullback (No 15): Andre Joubert (South Africa)
I won't repeat myself about the virtues of Andre Joubert as a rugby player. I have already detailed why I felt he was the best in South Africa in the 1990s. I also considered him to be more of a complete fullback than the likes of Matthew Burke and Christian Cullen, two of the star performers during my career. So, in my book, he was the best fullback playing international rugby in the 1990s. There was not a more graceful sight than Juba at the peak of his powers.

Right wing (No 14): Philippe St Andre (France)
I will pick him on the right wing because he simply has to make my side. I found him to be the most underrated of all the international wingers I played against and one of the more creative players.

Whenever I would play Australia or New Zealand, the talk was of Kirwan, Wilson, Lomu, Roff and Tune. I played against John Kirwan in his final season of test rugby in 1994 and in his final test for New Zealand at Auckland's Eden Park. He hardly saw the ball. His contribution was minimal and he did not leave much of an impression on me. Yet, even in the 1994 series between the Boks and All Blacks in New Zealand, you would always read about Kirwan in the previews.

People would stop and ask me how I was going to counter Kirwan. The game itself did not match the hype. In the three tests he saw very little of the ball. He did score against the Boks in the first test in Dunedin, but there were few opportunities for him to do anything spectacular and he was controversially dropped from the All Blacks team after the Boks left New Zealand.

When Kirwan departed from the stage, the hype was transferred to Jeff Wilson and Jonah Lomu. But it was St Andre who made the biggest impression on me. He was a clever winger who knew how to finish and maximise whatever ball came his way.

He looked for work, had pace and was an aggressive player. He had that wonderful French flair, the kind that only the French seem to possess. He was a wing who could create something out of a seemingly hopeless situation, just as he did when he won the series for France against New Zealand in 1994 with the 'try from the other side of the world'.

Ben Tune is very unlucky to miss out. He is one heck of a wing who runs hard and is pacy. I just feel he lacks a bit of the all-round genius of St Andre.

Outside centre: (No 13) Philippe Sella (France)
If any player can be selected ahead of Danie Gerber, then it has to be a struggle to find words that adequately describe such a talent.

I would love to have seen Sella play regularly at No 12. At inside centre, I think he would have been an even greater danger to France's opponents on a rugby field than was the case at outside centre.

Inside centre: (No 12) Tim Horan (Australia)
For 10 years Tim Horan dominated world midfield play. The Australian selectors played him in nearly every backline position in his last few years, from flyhalf to wing. But it is at inside centre where he made his name at the 1991 World Cup and it was in this position where he fittingly guided Australia to the 1999 World Cup triumph.

He took the outside gap as if it were a door that had been opened for him. He did it regularly and with ease. I thought his performance in the 1999 World Cup semi-final against the Boks was one of the best I have ever seen.

Defensively, he was like a brick wall. He survived a career-threatening knee injury, played in three World Cups and came away with two winners' medals. There is not much more I can say, other than he had to be a certainty in my World XV.

Left wing: (No 11) Joe Roff (Australia)
I came on to the scene when David Campese was at the tail end of his career. Campese, the winger whom I admired the most when I first played at test level, would have been my pick for the winger of the 1980s. In the 1990s, the time that coincided with the major part of my career, the wing who stood out was Roff.

I think he is the most complete winger in world rugby. He is intelligent, he is big and strong, runs magnificent lines, is equally comfortable at left wing or fullback and possesses a decent boot. He has also never had a problem with defence. Imagine him playing off Juba and vice-versa? I would pity any opposition's defensive system.

Roff, somehow, played in the shadow of Lomu during most of his career. Lomu is a marketing man's dream, but he is a limited international wing. No one will deny Lomu's brute strength and his ability to break tackles, but I found him a good wing to play against, without ever being great, both at Super 12 and test level. He is a nice guy and he has always been pleasant to me. But he lacks the all-round class of a Roff.

Flyhalf (No 10): Henry Honiball (South Africa)
England's Jonny Wilkinson has been impressive in the last two years and Australia's Stephen Larkham has matured into a more complete flyhalf than when he started in that position. Nevertheless, my pick still goes to South Africa's Henry Honiball. He instilled fear in the opposition and neither Wilkinson nor Larkham possess that special quality.

Scrumhalf (No 9): Agustin Pichot (Argentina)
If Pichot played for the more fashionable teams like South Africa, Australia, New Zealand, France or England, he would long ago have been acknowledged as one of the best in the world. Playing for Argentina, he just does not get the global recognition to which I believe he is entitled.

He is a fantastic scrumhalf who can cause chaos when in possession. He keeps the opposition guessing all the time, has a great service and is very aggressive on the pitch. I love his attitude to the game and his ability to come good when it counts. He played against the Boks in 2000 and he also played for the Barbarians against the Boks in 2000. On both occasions he was superb.

No 8: Zinzan Brooke (New Zealand)
I thought about Toutai Kefu, but in the end Brooke was a comfortable winner in my book. He embodied everything that is classy about a quality No 8. He created, he was physical on attack and in defence and he had skills I have never seen in another No 8. The drop-goal against England in the 1995 World Cup semi-final at Newlands and the one against the Boks at Loftus in 1996 were illustrations of the genius of Brooke.

Flank (No 7): Josh Kronfeld (New Zealand)
I often read about coaches who singled out Kronfeld as the difference between winning and losing when their teams played against the All Blacks. He was that good.

He was one player who never seemed to play a poor test match. There are some who suggest he played outside the laws of the game; I don't agree. I think he was the master of his profession. He was a brilliant player who also knew when to say goodbye to international rugby. That takes a special quality. He walked away from test rugby on his terms when he was only 28 years old.

Flank (No 6): Tiaan Strauss (South Africa)
Who else, but the Kalahari Kid!

I am a huge fan of Strauss, of his ability as a player and a leader. I played with him until his departure for Australia at the end of the 1995 season. In my world team he and Kronfeld would both play fetcher roles and Brooke (at No 8) would feed off their ball-winning dominance. Defensively, there weren't too many more aggressive in the tackle than Tiaan.

Lock (No 5) John Eales: (Australia)
Eales was the complete lock and along with Zinzan Brooke probably the most complete forward I encountered during my career. He won everything as a player and a captain and he was instrumental in securing many of those famous Australian victories.

His leadership will take some replacing with the Wallabies and so too will his presence on the field. Off the field, he was also one of the game's great ambassadors. When you talk about greats of the game, Eales stands taller than most.

Lock (No 4): Ian Jones (New Zealand)
I found Jones and Eales to be the dominant locks of their playing generation. Each was magnificent in the lineout and more than capable in the loose.

Jones's physical approach was not always acknowledged because of his lanky appearance. Believe me, he was very tough and aggressive at the breakdown. In tandem with Eales, I can think of no one better to secure lineout ball against the rest of the planet.

Tighthead prop (No 3): Olo Brown (New Zealand)
A no-frills front-ranker who just got down and did his job every time. The Boks had enormous respect for him and I know the South African teams in the Super 12 always spoke highly of Brown's ability. When our

teams played against the Auckland Blues, Brown always figured among key opponents in the planning for the game. He was consistently good during a career that spanned longer than most test front-rankers.

Hooker (No 2): Sean Fitzpatrick (New Zealand, captain)
Fitzpatrick captains my World XV, with his record as captain giving him the inclusion above Ireland's Keith Woods. I think Woods is a fantastic player, but Fitzpatrick had something very special about him as a player and a leader. New Zealand only truly realised what they had in Fitzpatrick when he was no longer available. Like Eales, he was one of the great statesmen of the game in the 1990s.

Loosehead prop (No 1): Os du Randt (South Africa)
Os is Afrikaans for Ox. He certainly was as strong as an ox, but he also had incredible mobility for a man of his size. When Os was playing you always felt a lot more confident about the match.

The bench

Forwards

Prop: Pieter de Villiers (France)
He has been the form prop for France since 2000. The move to France from South Africa was the best thing he could have done. His career was going nowhere in South Africa. I don't think he would ever have played at the highest level here because of a lack of opportunity. He went overseas, took his chance and impressed the right people. He can play either loosehead or tighthead so he is the ideal replacement in any match squad. A powerful scrummager, he also has mobility and decent handling skills.

Hooker: Keith Woods (Ireland)
I doubt there is a more passionate player than Woods. He was magnificent for the Lions in South Africa in 1997 and equally good against the Wallabies four years later. At times he seems to carry the entire Irish pack.

His skills are very good for a hooker and his defence is one of his strengths. I remember him making a tackle on Robbie Fleck in our test against Ireland in 2000. I couldn't believe that he got to Fleck. It was a brilliant piece of defending.

I think he would be incredible coming off the bench after a player like Fitzpatrick had softened up the opposition for 50 minutes.

Lock: Abdel Benazzi (France)
Thank goodness he was not an inch taller, otherwise France would have been the team playing in the 1995 World Cup final. Benazzi dived for the tryline and I think every one of us feared the worst, although none will admit he ever thought Benazzi scored.

He was an imposing player and he added a dimension at lock and loose forward during his career. In my fantasy team, he can do a job in the loose forwards or as an impact lock.

Loose forward: Michael Jones (New Zealand)
Injury changed the course of Michael Jones's career, but he was still a magnificent player. In the late 1980s he was sensational as a ranging flanker, but after a serious knee injury he bulked up and took on a more physical approach, playing No 8 and No 6 effectively. I admire him as a person and have enormous respect for him as a player, especially when you consider what he went through with all his injuries.

Backs
Scrumhalf: George Gregan (Australia)
Gregan is not as dynamic as Pichot, but he will take control of any game when his pack is dominant or at least competitive. He is vulnerable when harassed and when operating behind a beaten set of forwards, which has not happened too often in his career. His discipline is not always the greatest but he is a very influential player. He has great vision for the game and an amazing defence for someone his size.

Centre: Brian O'Driscoll (Ireland)
He covers both centres. If he remains injury free he will become the most dynamic midfielder in the next five years. He probably is already the best centre in world rugby. I thought he was brilliant for Ireland in the 2000 and 2001 seasons and he confirmed his class when playing for the Lions against Australia. There is a bit of Horan, Gerber and Sella in him – and that's some pedigree!

Wing: Jeff Wilson (New Zealand)
Wilson is a superb athlete, who is at home playing fullback, left wing or right wing. He is a class player with good pace and has a wonderful understanding of the game. When looking for versatility I felt he was in a league of his own.

Afterword

By Mark Keohane

A lot of players concern themselves only with their own positions and performances. They cannot put a match into perspective. Chester was clearly beyond that, a thinker who had big opinions on the game

PERHAPS the greatest misrepresentation in South African rugby during the 1990s was the story of Chester Williams.

He was the black guy who got an opportunity. He was the symbol that a suspicious and fragile nation looked to in times of rugby's adversity and indifference. He was the conscience of the conservative white South African rugby traditionalist. He was the indicator of change in a sport whose politics were as crass and non-negotiable as that of the apartheid government itself.

Chester was the image white rugby bosses sold to the world ahead of the 1995 World Cup. Remember those eyes, spread across metres of billboard advertising? The big ones that greeted visitors to the country. Remember the smile? The beaming expression, allegedly of a nation freed of racial discrimination.

Chester was a godsend to white South African rugby. He spoke only when spoken to, which was not often. He knew his place. He was not caught up in politics. He had no emotional baggage. He was not complex and he certainly was not a black troublemaker. He was a rugby player and he could score tries. White conservatives could live with such a black guy in their rugby team.

Chester, with seeming complicity, gave white rugby the escape it sought in the early 1990s as the game's conservatives revelled in the freedom of international acceptance and delighted in keeping the game as white as possible. South African rugby in the 90s might not have had many black faces in the crowd, but at least it had one on the field, dressed in green and worth a ton of gold.

Those in Auckland, Sydney and London, regarding themselves as great liberals with knowledge and insight of South African rugby, claimed Chester to be the symbol of hope for the new country. Chester was proof that South African blacks could play the game and were accepted within the white fold. He was the tangible in transformation.

Unfortunately, it was never that simple for Chester in a society still in transition, despite the symbolic significance of apartheid's demise in 1994.

'Tell me about Chester,' my wife Karin asked. 'What makes him this inspiration to you?'

I had never thought of Chester as an inspiration before. I had tended to identify inspirational people as those who had paid a heavy price in their fight for justice. What price had Chester paid? There was no visible torture to Chester. Naïvely, I considered Chester one of the fortunate black sportsmen in South Africa. He was talented and he was playing rugby for his country. He had achieved more than most young rugby players in South Africa. But he was just another rugby player. He seemed to have no hang-ups.

We met in 1992 during my first year as a rugby writer at the Cape Argus and his second as a provincial rugby player in Western Province. He was polite, always greeted me at training, but never sought out the journalists for a chat.

For those of us in the rugby media, there are three kinds of players: the ones who hate rugby writers, those who seek out rugby writers to manipulate them and those who end up becoming rugby writers.

Chester, except for a bit of newspaper column-writing during his injury lay-off in 1997, was neither a talker nor a hater. He was one of those guys who would have been described as a neutral because he rarely said anything. He never thanked me for a flattering review and he never questioned a report that was critical of his performance. He would arrive at training, smile and greet. That was Chester.

The only time I remember him ever probing the thoughts of journalists about his own performance was in 1993 when Western Province had played Namibia in Windhoek.

Chester played the worst game I would see him play over the next eight years. He could not catch a ball all day. He must have dropped half a dozen, although he recalls it being more like a dozen. Had Western Province coach Dawie Snyman axed him after that match, there would have been no complaints.

Chester, having bumped into me at a nightclub on the Saturday evening after the match, greeted and chatted about the game. Province had won in the last minute, thanks to a Lance Sherrell penalty. Chester was praising Lance's kick and the win, which certainly had been no thanks to the butter-fingered winger. Then he half-inquired about his own game.

'I thought you were terrible,' I told him. 'If you are sensitive, don't read the paper.' He laughed and nodded. He added that he had never played so poorly in his life. He did not know what had happened.

We hung out together that evening and returned to the hotel at the same time. My room was next to one occupied by Freddie Hendriks, who worked in the Afrikaans Sunday press for Rapport. As we walked past Hendriks's room, Chester saw that the door was slightly open. Hendriks wasn't in, but his laptop computer was on the desk.

'Do you know what Freddie wrote about me?' inquired Chester.

I was blunt with my answer. 'No, but I doubt it was good.' I reminded him again how awful he was.

'Let's see what he wrote,' said Chester with a naughty grin. 'How does this thing work?'

We tried to crack Freddie's password to find the match report. We struggled for about 10 minutes and then decided, why bother? Chester accepted that everyone had thought he was terrible.

The next day we saw Hendriks on the plane back to Cape Town. Chester had finally got to read what Hendriks had written, in print. It was not flattering. He went up to Hendriks, put his arm around him and said: 'Hey, I wasn't very good was I?' We all had a good laugh.

Chester survived the drop in form and his season improved. He played test rugby later that year, against Argentina, and he scored the first of 14 test tries in an international career robbed of its best years by two knee injuries.

It was during 1997 that I finally got to know a bolder Chester – one who spoke with confidence about the technicalities in rugby. And it was only in writing his biography that I finally obtained an insight into the real Chester – a man who has been misrepresented in the media.

I was working for the Cape Times newspaper in 1997 and we had signed up Chester as a columnist. Getting players to write columns was a good marketing ploy and Chester's appeal was huge in Cape Town. Although he had played only 33 minutes of rugby since the end of the 1995 international season, he had not been forgotten. Even the Springbok coach at the time, Andre Markgraaff, had not forgotten and he included Chester in a training squad early in the year.

There was no doubt in my mind that Chester would play for the Boks in 1997 and he would give us an 'in' at the Springbok camp through his columns.

As it turned out, Markgraaff resigned in February because of a racial scandal and Chester was injured in his comeback match at Newlands. His season was over and he had written only one column. We took an editorial decision to keep him as a columnist, but to shift the focus of his columns: he needed to be more technical in his analysis and he needed to take a stand on issues.

He responded on both fronts and while I ghosted the columns, the ideas, analyses and views were all his own. I was impressed with his reading of the game and his overall understanding of it.

In 10 years of writing on rugby I found that not every player can articulate the technical aspects of rugby. Many players concern themselves only with their own positions and performances. They cannot put a match in perspective. Chester was clearly beyond that, a thinker who had big opinions on the game.

He enjoyed writing the columns and would phone in advance with ideas. We would debate the merits of his ideas and I know that one particular column annoyed Nick Mallett, who was coaching Boland at the time.

Boland had enjoyed good results in the Nite Series and were scheduled to play Western Province at Newlands. Chester, in his column ahead of the game, was critical of Boland's style of play. He wrote that it was too predictable to beat Western Province and too one-dimensional.

Mallett, speaking to the reporters after the match, raised the content of the column and was dismissive of Chester's opinion. Province, however, had beaten Boland on the night.

Who knows if Mallett even remembers the column or what effect it had on his thinking as a Springbok coach, but he would never fully embrace Chester's talents.

Chester, in speaking to me about Mallett, was not flattering of what he called Mallett's people skills. 'I always found him to be more about himself than anything else,' Chester told me on several occasions between 1998 and 2002.

Mallett had drafted Chester into his Springbok set-up in 1998 and 2000 but never entrusted him as his regular first-choice left wing. Ironically, when he did finally select him for the 2000 Tri-Nations home test against the All Blacks at Ellis Park, Chester scored a stunning try to open the scoring and played a crucial part in a thrilling 46-40 win.

When Mallett first selected Chester in 1998, it was only as a back-up player. Chester, however, accepted this as he had just returned from a two-year injury lay-off. In 1998 Chester was happy to be a part of international rugby again. It was the snub in 1999 that got to Chester.

It was the first time that Chester had talked himself up in conversation with me. I phoned him about his exclusion. He said he knew he was good enough to have been selected and that his form that season had warranted World Cup inclusion.

I asked him if he could be quoted. He didn't want a story written about it. 'I am telling you that I should be there. I don't want a media story out of it. I just wanted you to know.'

I asked him if he had spoken to Mallett. He hadn't, but his agent at the time, Frikkie Erasmus, had inquired why Chester had not been picked. Mallett is alleged to have told Erasmus that he had enough 'quota' players.

Mallett had included four black players in his World Cup squad: Breyton Paulse, Deon Kayser, Wayne Julies and Kaya Malotana. The only player who would be a regular in the match 22 was Kayser. I called Mallett and asked him why he had taken Malotana and not Williams. His response: 'Picking Chester Williams would be a step backwards.'

In 2000, Chester made it into the squad. Mallett had obviously had a rethink, although again the player was not rewarded with any decent game time in the early matches. He came on as a substitute against Canada and in the two tests against England and then played only two minutes in the Mandela Cup against Australia.

Chester, in the build-up to the Mandela Cup test, was despondent about getting a fair chance. He would call at my room regularly and chat about the tour, his future prospects and rugby in general. It was never a moan session. I found it informative and insightful to understanding the squad's dynamics at that time.

He said he knew Mallett did not rate him, nor did the coach rate Breyton Paulse. It was clear in Mallett's attitude towards them at training, he said. Mallett wanted Thinus Delport and Pieter Rossouw to be his wings, and Percy Montgomery to be his fullback.

Mallett had told me a similar story. In Melbourne, before the Mandela Cup, Mallett told me that, if he could, he would pick Rossouw and Delport and use Paulse only as an impact player. He would not include Chester in his match 22.

This was borne out as the Tri-Nations unfolded. Mallett never had faith in Paulse's ability to play against Australia and New Zealand. He worried about Paulse's size and he felt Chester was too slow and not up to standard.

I listened to Chester and did not let on that I knew Mallett did not want to pick him. I just listened.

After the Melbourne test, the squad spent 10 days at Couran Cove near Brisbane. It was an intense camp and Mallett cracked the whip. He was unrelenting in his criticism of the Boks for losing to Australia.

The players were on edge during the stay, but they never complained. They put their heads down and gave it everything at training. But there were individuals who would rather have been elsewhere.

We stayed in luxury apartments and while the players shared two to an apartment, the journalists had the privacy of being alone in an apartment. Chester would visit and chat to me, but not in great detail. He was very conscious of who was watching and he did not want to be perceived as a player running to the media.

One evening I invited Chester and Rassie Erasmus to my apartment for a drink. Beers at the resort were seven Aussie dollars each but I had gone to the mainland that day and bought 30 beers for only A$31. I felt it would be a good investment: get a few of the players to my room and get a bit of insight into the workings within the camp.

No player wants to spend A$7 on a beer. Invite him to your room and tell him the beer is on the house and after a while most start talking about their frustrations. If there is an issue in the squad, the beer will get it out of the player.

Chester and Rassie were together a lot. Mallett was a big supporter of Rassie and the player was equally convinced of Mallett's ability as a coach. Chester's views were the opposite. I found it a fascinating evening chatting to the two because both showed how technically clued-up they were about the game.

They were probably two of the brightest thinkers in the team. Rassie had one advantage: Mallett asked him for an opinion and Erasmus was never shy to voice it. Chester, frustrated at being a passenger on the tour, spoke freely when in the company of Rassie and me. He never did so in the presence of Mallett.

I asked Chester if I could to do a story about his frustrations. Once again he didn't want any negativity to detract from the team's build-up to the test against New Zealand in Christchurch. He knew he would not be involved, but held out hope that he would play in Sydney on the following week.

He never did play in Sydney and it was in the week of the test against Australia when Chester and Breyton Paulse popped into my room to have a chat. Breyton had brought his laptop along and asked me if I could have a look at a fault in the computer. I know how to use a laptop, but I don't know how to fix one. But the reason for their visit was more about having a chance to talk about frustrations than it was about fixing laptops.

Breyton had been picked to play against Australia, but told me it was a case of 'stay on your wing and stay out of trouble'. He had expressed his disappointment to Chester and to me.

Chester was more bemused than annoyed. I thought it would make a good story. I told them I would write it. Both of them said it was not worth it. They did not want to be seen as troublemakers. It seemed to be the story of Chester's career.

In 2000 I was aware that Chester's marriage was on the rocks, but he seemed to be coping well enough. The truth is I was not in a position to make a judgment. As I would discover in writing the biography, the Williamses are not a family who talk easily about their feelings and they certainly don't seek sympathy for apparent hardship. Chester, all his life, had accepted his lot and tried to make the most out of it.

But there was a change in his willingness to speak about his frustrations, both at test and provincial level. He also started speaking to me for the first time about the plight of black players in South African rugby.

Early in his career he never became embroiled in political arguments. Now he was telling me about the prejudice in South African rugby, and the unwillingness on the part of some to change that. He was not bitter, but he had become aware of what it meant to be a black player.

He felt he was being used as a political pawn, but not by the politicians. Coaches in South Africa were categorising him as a black player, one who could be used to satisfy quota requirements and the like. It was getting to him.

There was an air of resignation about being seen as a black rugby player instead of just a rugby player. I think it got me more riled than it did him.

I champion the cause of black rugby players in South Africa because I believe they have been done a disservice. I was outspoken in my writing about the prejudice of our coaches towards black players. I had been privy to too many conversations and had spoken (in confidence) to too many coaches. South African rugby in the 1990s was not changing because those who selected teams at all levels were not capable of looking at a player's ability. Colour always seemed to play a part.

Whereas Jonah Lomu, Michael Jones, Olo Brown, Jason Robinson, Toutai Kefu, Andrew Walker, Mark Ella and George Gregan, to name a few, were quality international players, South Africa's quality black players were merely 'quota' players.

In 2001 Chester started speaking more to me about this issue and I encouraged him to write a book about life in South Africa as a black player. Was there prejudice? Or was everything about embracing change? I felt he owed it to himself more than anyone else to document his feelings and tell his story.

He said he would consider a book but his agent, Frikkie Erasmus, told him the time was not right to talk about his life. I challenged

Chester on this and said he should give it serious thought. The time, more than ever, was right for him to let people know what life was like as a black rugby player in South Africa in the 1990s.

In the meantime, I had left journalism to take up a position as adviser to Harry Viljoen, who had been appointed Springbok coach at the end of 2000.

Viljoen, in offering me the job, enticed me with the issue of transformation. He said I had beaten the transformation drum in the media for so long and was now giving me an opportunity to make a difference from the inside. He wanted advice on the transformation issue and he was committed to making it happen.

Many stories did the rounds that Viljoen had got me out of journalism because he feared that I would be too critical of him. Perhaps he did, but it did give me a chance to make a noise about the black players' issue from inside the tent. I had been on the outside looking in for 10 years, now I could make a difference. I had the ear of the national coach.

Viljoen had a high regard for Chester. He had written him off as a player before, only for Chester to embarrass him with a remarkable comeback. He was not going to make the same mistake again.

Viljoen also enjoyed Chester's character. He described him as intelligent, technically good and respected internationally for his ability as a rugby player. Viljoen believed that Chester had the ability to coach South Africa, but he was concerned that Chester's best days as a player were over.

He felt Chester was playing good rugby, but he did not think it could get any better. He asked me to give Chester a call and sound him out about being the Boks' backline coach. Chester was surprised at the call, but excited. I had only wanted to know if he would be interested. He said he definitely was.

Viljoen then called him directly, and a few other people at SA Rugby were made aware of the offer. It leaked to the media and Laurie Mains then became involved, telling Chester he would be stupid to take on the role.

Chester and I spoke on a few occasions in the week after the newspaper story. He wanted in on the coaching side, but he also wanted to end his career with one last tour. Viljoen said he would pick him as a player, but then he couldn't guarantee that the offer as backline coach would still be available in 2001.

Chester was not influenced by Mains's negativity towards the Springboks. He told me Mains couldn't stand Viljoen or myself, and that he knew that had been the basis of the New Zealander's argument.

Chester had to make a decision he would not regret. He had to trust his instincts and it became clear on speaking to him that what he wanted to do was finish on a high as a test player.

England were to be the Springboks' last test in 2000 and I think he wanted to close the book on the five-year period following his brilliant performance against England at Twickenham in 1995.

Financially, he also stood to lose a lot if he gave up his provincial contract with the Lions. He knew that what he would earn as an assistant coach could not match what he was getting as a player. He made the decision to tour and he was full of enthusiasm in the early part of the tour.

He enjoyed a good relationship with Viljoen, spoke quite easily with the coach and talked often to me about his performances and the prospects for 2001.

If anything, I provided him with a few comforting words and answers where possible, but both of us knew that my loyalty was to Viljoen. The coach had hired me and he was paying my salary.

Then came probably the most difficult few days that I have experienced with Chester in the 10 years we have known each other. The Boks had beaten Ireland 28-18 and the media had been critical of Chester's performance. Viljoen shared their sentiments. He felt Chester had been poor and that he was no longer good enough; a substitute's role the next week against Wales served only to further the opinion that Chester was finished as a test player.

Viljoen spoke to me about it and told me that he was going to drop Chester for the England test. He said he would speak to Chester the moment we got to Windsor. He would then make a decision about playing Chester against the Barbarians.

Viljoen said that the player deserved a decent send-off, but he did not believe the player was capable of producing at the highest level. I knew he was going to drop Chester and knew that it would not be ethical to warn him. Also, Viljoen did have a habit of changing his mind and it would not have surprised me if he had called Chester in to drop him, then been swayed to keep him after discussing the issue with the player.

Chester knew that I would know whether he was in or out and he seemed to be seeking me out to get some kind of answer. I just had to avoid him until the coach had met with him.

Once the squad had been announced, I went to him and said 'Hard luck'. He shrugged his shoulders, but he said he would fight back. I knew that no matter how hard he fought, Viljoen was not going to pick him.

I kept my distance from Chester that week and was pleased when Viljoen did pick him to play against the Barbarians in Cardiff the week after the England test. He now had the chance to put the record straight.

I don't know if he can claim to have done this, but at least he heard the applause one last time in what was an amazing contest. The Boks won 41-31 after trailing 31-12.

Afterwards I congratulated Chester, but I got the feeling he knew he had played his last international game. He was content without being overjoyed.

In 2000 I thought I knew Chester, but I didn't. I had known only a personality I had been reporting on in my writing. I respected him, but I was not inspired by him. Now that I have had an insight into his life story, the respect is greater and the inspiration is undeniable.

For all his loneliness, frustration and emotional hardships, he keeps on dreaming of living in a country where he will be judged, not by the colour of his skin but by the content of his character.

Chester Williams's career in the Springbok jersey

	Opponents	Date	Venue and Result	Scoring
1	Western Australia	July 14, 1993	Perth. Won 71–8	1 try
2	South Australian Invitation XV	July 17, 1993	Adelaide. Won 90–3	
3	Victoria	July 21, 1993	Melbourne. Won 78–3	3 tries
4	New South Wales Country	July 27, 1993	Orange. Won 41–17	
5	Australian Capital Territories	August 4, 1993	Canberra. Won 57–10	2 tries
6	Queensland Country	August 11, 1993	Mackay. Won 63–5	1 try
7	Sydney	August 18, 1993	Sydney. Won 31–20	
8	Provincial XV	October 27, 1993	Cordoba. Won 55–37	1 try
9	Tucamán	November 3, 1993	Tucumán. Won 40–12	1 try
10	Provincial XV	November 9, 1993	Rosario. Won 40–26	
11	**ARGENTINA**	November 13, 1993	Buenos Aires. Won 52–23	1 try
12	**ENGLAND**	June 4, 1994	Pretoria. Lost 15–32	
13	**ENGLAND**	June 11, 1994	Cape Town. Won 27–9	
14	Southland	July 2, 1994	Invercargill. Won 51–15	
15	Hanan Shields Districts	July 5, 1994	Timaru. Won 67–19	1 try
16	**NEW ZEALAND**	July 9, 1994	Dunedin. Lost 14–22	
17	Waikato	July 16, 1994	Hamilton. Won 38–17	
18	**NEW ZEALAND**	July 23, 1994	Wellington. Lost 9–13	
19	Canterbury	July 30, 1994	Christchurch. Won 21–12	
20	**NEW ZEALAND**	August 6, 1994	Auckland. Drew 18–18	
21	**ARGENTINA**	October 8, 1994	Port Elizabeth. Won 42–22	1 try
22	**ARGENTINA**	October 15, 1994	Johannesburg. Won 46–26	1 try
23	Cardiff	October 22, 1994	Cardiff. Won 11–6	
24	Llanelli	October 29, 1994	Llanelli. Won 30–12	
25	Swansea	November 5, 1994	Swansea. Won 78-7	1 try
26	Scottish Combined Districts	November 12, 1994	Glasgow. Won 33–6	
27	**SCOTLAND**	November 19, 1994	Edinburgh. Won 34–10	1 try
28	**WALES**	November 26, 1994	Cardiff. Won 20–12	1 try
29	Barbarians	December 3, 1994	Dublin. Lost 15–23	
30	**WESTERN SAMOA**	April 13, 1995	Johannesburg. Won 60–8	2 tries
31	**SAMOA**	June 10, 1995	Johannesburg. Won 42–14	4 tries
32	**FRANCE**	June 17, 1995	Durban. Won 19–15	
33	**NEW ZEALAND**	June 24, 1995	Johannesburg. Won 15–12	
34	**ITALY**	November 12, 1995	Rome. Won 41–21	
35	**ENGLAND**	November 18, 1995	London. Won 24–14	2 tries
36	**AUSTRALIA**	July 18, 1998	Perth. Won 14–13	
37	**NEW ZEALAND**	July 25, 1998	Wellington. Won 13–3	
38	**CANADA**	June 10, 2000	East London. Won 51–18	
39	**ENGLAND**	June 17, 2000	Pretoria. Won 18–13	
40	**ENGLAND**	June 24, 2000	Bloemfontein. Lost 22–27	
41	**AUSTRALIA**	July 8, 2000	Melbourne. Lost 23–44	
42	**NEW ZEALAND**	August 19, 2000	Johannesburg. Won 46–40	1 try
43	**AUSTRALIA**	August 26, 2000	Durban. Lost 18–19	
44	**ARGENTINA**	November 12, 2000	Buenos Aires. Won 37–33	
45	**IRELAND**	November 19, 2000	Dublin. Won 28–18	
46	**WALES**	November 26, 2000	Cardiff. Won 23–13	
47	Barbarians	December 9, 2000	Cardiff. Won 41–31	2 tries

Appendix

Chester Williams's test career

Tests:	27 appearances (14 tries)	
Tests:	Won 20 with one draw	= 74 percent success rate

All matches in a Springbok team

Won 39. Drew 1. Lost 7 = 83 percent success rate

Provincial career

Western Province League :	7 appearances (1990-91)
Western Province:	1991-1998 (62 appearances, 39 tries and one drop-goal)
Lions:	1999-2000 (23 appearances, 11 tries)
Super 12:	Stormers (2 appearances, 2 tries)
Super 12:	Cats (20 appearances, 7 tries)

Other representative matches

South Africa A	(one appearance and one try)
SA trials:	1993 (one appearance and two tries)
SA Forces:	1994: (one appearance and no try)
SA Defence Force:	1991/2: (3 matches, no try)
SA Development XV:	1992: (one match, no try)
SA Permanent Forces:	(2 matches, no try)

First-class record

170 matches, 89 tries and a drop goal = 447 points. At the start of Chester's career a try counted four points and was later increased to five.

Sevens Springbok since 1993

World Cup in 1995 and a Sevens World Cup in 1993 and 2001

Index

A

B

C

D

E

F

G

H

J

K

L

M

N

O

P

R

S

T

CAMBRIDGE STUDIES ON THE AMERICAN SOUTH

Series Editors:

Mark M. Smith, *University of South Carolina, Columbia*
David Moltke-Hansen, *Center for the Study of the American South, University of North Carolina at Chapel Hill*

Interdisciplinary in its scope and intent, this series builds upon and extends Cambridge University Press's long-standing commitment to studies on the American South. The series not only will offer the best new work on the South's distinctive institutional, social, economic, and cultural history but will also feature works in a national, comparative, and transnational perspective.

Titles in the Series

Robert E. Bonner, *Mastering America: Southern Slaveholders and the Crisis of American Nationhood*
Ras Michael Brown, *African-Atlantic Cultures and the South Carolina Lowcountry*
Christopher Michael Curtis, *Jefferson's Freeholders and the Politics of Ownership in the Old Dominion*
Louis A. Ferleger and John D. Metz, *Cultivating Success in the South: Farm Households in the Postbellum Era*
Luke E. Harlow, *Religion, Race, and the Making of Confederate Kentucky, 1830–1880*
Ari Helo, *Thomas Jefferson's Ethics and the Politics of Human Progress: The Morality of a Slaveholder*
Susanna Michele Lee, *Claiming the Union: Citizenship in the Post–Civil War South*
Scott P. Marler, *The Merchants' Capital: New Orleans and the Political Economy of the Nineteenth-Century South*
Peter McCandless, *Slavery, Disease, and Suffering in the Southern Lowcountry*
Johanna Nicol Shields, *Freedom in a Slave Society: Stories from the Antebellum South*
Brian Steele, *Thomas Jefferson and American Nationhood*
Jonathan Daniel Wells, *Women Writers and Journalists in the Nineteenth-Century South*

Cultivating Success in the South

Farm Households in the Postbellum Era

LOUIS A. FERLEGER
Boston University

JOHN D. METZ
Library of Virginia

CAMBRIDGE
UNIVERSITY PRESS

CAMBRIDGE
UNIVERSITY PRESS

32 Avenue of the Americas, New York, NY 10013-2473, USA

Cambridge University Press is part of the University of Cambridge.

It furthers the University's mission by disseminating knowledge in the pursuit of education, learning, and research at the highest international levels of excellence.

www.cambridge.org
Information on this title: www.cambridge.org/9781107054110

First published 2014

Printed in the United States of America

A catalog record for this publication is available from the British Library.

Library of Congress Cataloging in Publication Data
Ferleger, Lou.
Cultivating success in the South : farm households in the postbellum era / Louis A. Ferleger, Boston University, John D. Metz, University Library of Virginia.
pages cm. – (Cambridge studies on the American South)
Includes bibliographical references and index.
ISBN 978-1-107-05411-0 (hardback)
1. Farm produce – Georgia – History. 2. Households – Georgia – History. 3. Farm risk – Georgia – History. 4. Georgia – Economic conditions. I. Metz, John D. II. Title.
HD9007.G4F47 2014
338.109758'109034–dc23 2014001856

ISBN 978-1-107-05411-0 Hardback

For Nancy

For John, Paul, and Cara

Contents

Acknowledgments

Louis A. Ferleger: Many people have read parts of this book and provided me with valuable comments and suggestions. Several stand out: Peter Coclanis, Stanley Engerman, Jay Mandle, David Moltke-Hansen, and Mark Smith. Lewis Bateman provided considerable advice and assistance over the years, and I appreciate his support. It is hard to acknowledge others who in ways unbeknown to them have contributed to the narrative and arguments presented in these pages, but I am very grateful for their encouragement, support, and criticisms. Virginia Shardon and Rosemary Hynes significantly contributed to my initial efforts at the Georgia State Archives to locate and secure numerous documents, especially probate and tax digest records. Sarah Phillips and Jennifer Green helped initially assemble the data, for which I remain very grateful. John and I owe a special gratitude to Matthew Pressman, whose excellent editorial suggestions led to substantial improvements in both style and content. My children, Ali and Max, have inspired and encouraged me tremendously. I dedicate this book to Nancy Scherer, whose love, patience, and support were critical to completing the project.

John D. Metz: I owe a debt of gratitude to many people who had a hand in shaping this project through to completion. The incredibly able staff of the Georgia State Archives and the Library of Virginia made research a joy. A number of professional colleagues shared their interest, intellect, and good cheer, including Marley Brown, Jon Kukla, Gabrielle Lanier, Gloria Main, Kurt Russ, Jessica Sewell, Brent Tarter, and Sandy Treadway. John Burrison deserves a special mention for patiently answering my questions on the potters of Crawford County and North Georgia. I must also recognize the help of Ann Mercer of Jasper and Mona Lowe of Crawford, who were enthusiastic ambassadors of their respective counties. Most important, none of this would have been possible without the patience, love, and unflagging support of my sons, John and Paul, and my wife, Cara: it is to you that I dedicate this book.

Abbreviations

AH	*Agricultural History*
AHR	*American Historical Review*
AJS	*American Journal of Sociology*
AQ	*American Quarterly*
EEH	*Explorations in Economic History*
GDA	Georgia Department of Archives and History
GHQ	*Georgia Historical Quarterly*
GPO	U.S. Government Printing Office
HM	*Historical Methods*
JAH	*Journal of American History*
JBS	*Journal of British Studies*
JEH	*Journal of Economic History*
JIH	*Journal of Interdisciplinary History*
JSH	*Journal of Southern History*
RCG	*Report of the Comptroller General for the State of Georgia*
SEJ	*Southern Economic Journal*
SSH	*Social Science History*
WMQ	*William and Mary Quarterly*

Introduction

Contesting the Myth of the Backward Southern Farmer

Like any good son, D. W. Hancock, an African-American farmer in Franklin County, Georgia, took care of his father's estate following his death in 1896.[1] Doc, as he was often called, had always worked closely with his father and his brothers on the family farm.[2] Barney Hancock had died in June, but Doc and his brothers were anxious about settling the estate so early in the growing season, when it was difficult to predict how well the cotton crop would fare. After all, Georgia law gave them up to twelve months to settle affairs. The past few years had been rough; the economy was depressed, and it was simply not safe to bet on the weather or the market. Moreover, the Hancocks knew that any essentials the family needed in the coming months would be purchased on credit and paid off once the cotton had been sold. So they decided it was best to wait to begin the probate process until fall, when the crops would be in and they would have a better idea of what the profits and the debts would be.

Barney Hancock's estate entered probate on October 2, 1896, when Doc traveled to the county seat in Carnesville to appear before the Clerk of the Court of Ordinary for Franklin County and submitted a petition asking to be appointed administrator of the estate, because his father had died without leaving a will. Despite Doc's effort, the court appointed A. W. McConnell, a white man from Carnesville, to be responsible for "collecting and paying the debts because of and owing by the estate and for the purpose of making distributions thereof among the heirs."[3] While discrimination against African

[1] Barney Hancock was one of fifteen African-American decedents identified in Crawford, Franklin, and Jasper counties for the period between 1880 and 1910, representing 6 percent of the 228 estates used in this study.

[2] U.S. Bureau of the Census. *Tenth Census of the United States, 1880: Population.* Gunnels District, Franklin, Georgia, Roll 147, Page 527B. Enumeration District 28, Image 0338.

[3] "Application of D. W. Hancock for Letters of Administration on the Estate of Barney Hancock, dec'd," 7 October 1896 (Atlanta: Georgia Department of Archives and History, hereafter, GDA).

Americans in the South was pervasive during this era, race may not have been a major factor in the case of the Hancocks, as many white estates were treated similarly. In any event, Doc and his family were keen to ensure careful oversight of the estate, since they estimated the land and personal possessions to be worth \$2,000 – roughly three times the value of the average white farmer's estate in Franklin County, and over fifteen times the value of the average black estate.[4] While Barney Hancock's success is impressive by any contemporary standard, it is exceptional given that he was African American.

Barney was born into slavery, probably in Franklin County or its environs, while his wife, Harriett, was born across the border in South Carolina. Barney and Harriett appear to have been together as early as the mid-1850s, since their two oldest daughters, Lucy and Ann, were born in 1856 and 1857, according to the enumerator's notes in the 1870 Federal Census.[5] By the end of the 1860s, the family lived in the Bold Spring district of Franklin County, located approximately ten miles southwest of Carnesville. Barney initially worked as a hired farm laborer to support his wife and their six children (Lucy, Ann, Nancy, James Neal, Doctor, and George) while Harriett kept house. By the time of the 1880 census, however, Barney's family consisted of five girls and six boys, ranging in age from three months to twenty-five years.[6] Although Ann had left the household, the family now included Henrietta, Harriet, Columbus, Charles, and three-month-old John. At the time of his death 16 years later, Barney owned 210 acres of land in 2 tracts, as well as 4 mules, 8 hogs, and a 2-horse sulky plow. The land, the livestock, and the ability to acquire the latest farming implements were clear indicators of hard-earned success.[7]

The Hancock family returned to court on November 2, 1896, to make certain that Harriett and her three minor children received the household possessions and twelve months of financial support from the estate guaranteed

It is unclear why the court appointed McConnell as administrator of the estate in spite of the application of D. W. Hancock. It is possible that the court was acting out of racial prejudice or felt that there was some benefit to an alternative appointment (e.g., McConnell was literate and Doc Hancock was not). There may have even been dissension among family members over which of them should serve as administrator. Unfortunately, court appointments rarely if ever include such details.

4 William A. Wright, *Report of the Comptroller General for the State of Georgia (hereafter, RCG) for the Year Ending September 30, 1895* (Atlanta, GA: Franklin Publishing House, 1895), 132, 137, 147, and 152.

5 *1870 Federal Census*, District 210, Franklin, Georgia, Roll M593–150, Page 15B; Image: 247. The 1870 census listed Barney as "Barnet."

6 *10th US Census*, 1880, *Franklin, Georgia*. Roll 147, Page *527B*, Enumeration District *28*, *Gunnels*, Image *0338*.

7 The average white farmer in Franklin County had an average of \$78.13 in livestock, while Barney Hancock's four mules alone were appraised for a total of \$202.00. Likewise, Hancock's sulky plow was valued at \$10.00, representing a little more than half the \$19.13 average for tools that white farmers in the county possessed; Wright, *RCG* (1895), 132, 137, 147, and 152.

for widows under Georgia law. The court appointed five "discrete and proper persons" to appraise the estate and return a "true and perfect" inventory of Barney Hancock's personal possessions.[8] The appointees, all white men, were neighbors of the Hancock family who acted quickly and returned the appraisal within eight days of being selected.[9] The Warrant of Appraisement lists the items selected by the widow, amounting to one-third of her husband's personal estate, which included 250 pounds of corn, 8 hogs, 6 bushels of wheat, 25 gallons of sorghum syrup, feed and fodder for livestock, and the sulky plow, in addition to nearly all of the household goods. Besides the beds, chairs, and cooking stove that Harriet chose from the household goods to sustain her family in the coming year were a desk and a "lot of books," which suggests, contrary to the enumerator's notes for the 1870 and 1880 censuses, that at least some in the Hancock family could read and write.[10]

Once the widow received her distribution from the estate, Georgia law dictated that the remainder be sold at auction to provide the cash needed to pay creditors, with any surplus cash being divided equally among Barney's adult children.[11] A small group of family and neighbors gathered at the courthouse in Carnesville on December 3, 1896, to witness the sale of what remained of Barney's personal estate. While cash was always helpful, the opportunity to buy healthy livestock and good tools cheaply may have been more important to farmers like the Hancock boys. In the end, Doc and two of his brothers purchased twenty-one of the twenty-six lots auctioned off that day. Doc got his father's two best mules, the red heifer, and the two-horse wagon. George was able to buy the sand-colored yearling cow, a mule, and farm tools, while Charles purchased a drawknife, the cultivator, a turning plow, and a set of harness. Two of the appraisers, Jessee T. Holbrook and William Y. Holbrook, also participated. William was the successful bidder for the saddle, while Jessee won the lot of boards. William's son, W. N. Holbrook, got the best deal of the day with the double buggy he acquired for $18 less than the appraised value. In fact, nearly all of the prices realized at auction that day were bargains, ranging from 10 to 90 percent lower than the appraised values.[12] Six months later, A. W. McConnell concluded the administration of Barney Hancock's estate when he appeared at the July session of the Court of Ordinary to certify the

8 "Petition of Harriett Hancock, widow of Barney Hancock, dec'd. for twelve months support out of estate of said dec'd and order appointing appraisers for selling a part of same," 2 November 1896 (GDA).

9 "Warrant of Appraisement, with Oath, for the Estate of Barney Hancock, dec'd.," 10 November 1896 (GDA). While the documents associated with Barney Hancock's estate reflect the typical range of estate issues faced by executors, heirs, and survivors in Crawford, Franklin, and Jasper counties at the turn of the century, it should be stressed that the Hancock family's level of success was a rarity among African-Americans in Franklin County for the period under study.

10 *1870 Federal Census*, Roll M593–150, Page 15B; *1880 Federal Census*, Roll *147*, Page: *527B*.

11 "Sale Bill of Barney Hancock's Personal Property," 24 July 1897 (GDA).

12 Ibid.

bill of sale for the auction, listing the items sold, the names of the buyers, and the prices paid.

We can tell the story of Barney Hancock because of the information carefully recorded in a series of seemingly mundane probate documents: an application for the administration of an estate, the petition for twelve months of support for a widow and her dependents, an inventory of the personal possessions owned at the time of death, and a bill of sale for the items auctioned off at the end of the process. This complex method of dispersing an estate at death, as demonstrated by the example of Barney Hancock, was standardized and well-established in Georgia law by the end of the nineteenth century in order to ensure the proper distribution of land, possessions, and capital from one generation to the next.

While this story from Middle Georgia may seem insignificant at first, closer scrutiny of probate inventories reveals critical details about the type of "ordinary" Georgia farmer who is frequently silent in the historical record. From the inventories we learn that Barney Hancock was typical of most Georgia planters in the 1890s in that he worked hard to be self-sufficient – producing enough corn, hogs, and cane syrup to sustain his family – while pinning his fortunes on the prospects of the cotton he grew for market. While he spent conservatively, he saw the potential in new technology and invested hard-earned cash in a sulky plow that would allow him to put more land into cultivation. Likewise, his household possessions were mostly utilitarian (including an outmoded spinning wheel), but he also owned books, a desk, and a fairly expensive cookstove. Perhaps most significantly, we learn from the probate documents that this African American achieved an impressive level of economic success at a time when racial and economic circumstances prevented most farmers of color from escaping tenancy and achieving any economic freedom whatsoever.

Most Southern yeomen, whether white or black, owned little. However, the items listed in the probate inventories of Barney Hancock and his contemporaries suggest that Georgians were shrewd consumers who focused on acquiring those things that would give them a productive edge. Likewise, the persistence of seemingly antiquated items like spinning wheels and looms, despite the availability of cheap cloth on the market, suggests a lingering perception among farming families that self-reliance remained the surest way to hedge one's bets against poor harvests and unpredictable downturns in the cotton market. The Hancock story, along with the stories of many other black and white Georgians to be discussed in subsequent chapters, calls into question the long-standing notion of an impoverished postbellum South characterized by a stagnating economy, political turmoil, and racial tension. Barney Hancock achieved a considerable degree of success in spite of the racist society in which he lived, and clearly his family was eager to achieve that same level of success for themselves, as indicated by the fact that the bulk of his estate was purchased at auction by kin. In this way, the Hancocks were similar to many white farmers who purchased their relatives' belongings at estate auctions. Indeed, auctions were a very common part of the estate-settlement process. Their prevalence suggests the development of a vigorous secondary market in used goods – hardly surprising in a region where cash was tight and farmers were constantly striving to increase their production.

Because such people left behind few written records, the stories of the Hancock family and other Southern yeomen like them are often lost to history. But they were the backbone of the South's agricultural economy, and their stories are crucial to understanding the development of the region and nation. Using probate records, census returns, and county-wide tax data allows us to explore the world of goods yeoman farmers inhabited in Middle Georgia between 1880 and 1910. The information contained in these records may appear mundane – inventories of farm tools, kitchen utensils, livestock, and the like – but it can reveal valuable insights into people's economic strategies and motivations, as well as their aspirations and values.

How did Georgia's yeomen respond to the challenging circumstances of the late nineteenth and early twentieth centuries? How did they adapt their traditional means of agriculture and system of labor to become more fully engaged in the market economy by the early twentieth century? What did it mean to farmers to be successful in the postbellum South? Our answers to these and other questions challenge the notion of the New South as a culturally stunted and economically stagnant society. Identifying patterns in the way that goods were acquired, used, and disposed of, we find that Southerners employed rational, sophisticated strategies to minimize economic and social risks and to maximize their chances of success and prosperity. The yeoman farmers of Middle Georgia were, more often than not, forward-thinking and hopeful actors. Like their urban counterparts, they were active and eager consumers, but they consumed in very different ways and for very different reasons.

Poverty and economic complacency came to be considered hallmarks of the South soon after the Civil War. Northern writers frequently viewed Southern economic hardship through the lens of social and cultural differences, leading them to depict the region as both peculiar and pathetic.[13] Southern writers like Thomas Nelson Page, on the other hand, lost no time in recasting adversity as genteel decay, which helped to create the image of crippled nobility associated with the "Lost Cause" interpretation of the Civil War.[14] Joel Chandler Harris's observations fell somewhere in between.

Born and raised in the Middle Georgia town of Eatonton, Harris came of age during the closing years of the Old South, the tumult of the Civil War, and the dawn of the New South. While he is best known as the popularizer

[13] Edward L. Ayers, *The Promise of the New South: Life After Reconstruction* (New York: Oxford University Press, 1992), 25.

[14] David Blight, *Race and Reunion: The Civil War in American Memory* (Cambridge: Belknap Press, 2001), 222.

of "Uncle Remus" folktales, he was also a journalist and short-story writer. In his fictionalized versions of the South, Harris eschews any pretense of nobility, instead offering vignettes that portray Southern society in all its threadbare richness, featuring characters (both white and black) who are wry, shrewd, and self-effacing, and who struggle to do their best with what little they have. In the short story *Free Joe*, Chandler offers a succinct view of the economic challenges facing the New South. Describing the fictional Middle Georgia town of Azalia, he explains, "There was room for improvement, but no room for progress, because there was no necessity for progress.... They were satisfied with things as they existed, though they had an honest, provincial faith in the good old times that were gone."[15] While neither the Northern writers, nor Page, nor Harris quite captured the full complexity of economic life in the New South, Harris came closest.

In our effort to understand the lives of common people in postbellum Georgia, we use a wide range of primary documents, but we rely most heavily on probate inventories. Probate inventories are lists of a person's material possessions owned at the time of his or her death. Inventories from Georgia, like those from many other states, list only moveable objects, not land or buildings. Under state law, an estate was subject to probate in the absence of a will, in situations where inheritance was in dispute, or in cases of insolvency. Typically, the district court appointed two or three appraisers familiar with the occupation of the deceased to compile an inventory of the decedent's possessions and to assign a fair market value to the personal estate.[16]

Historians have long been aware of the importance of probate documents to understanding the material lives of a broad spectrum of society. They provide a snapshot of a moment in time, a peek inside the barns and cupboards of people who lived in previous centuries. Moreover, information from probate inventories can be quantified and measured in a number of ways. Scholars have become quite adept at teasing out data about economic and social development from these documents by focusing on the presence or absence of certain items, their quantity, the frequency with which they are mentioned, when they appear in or disappear from the historical record, their location in the home, and the ways in which they are described.[17] It is also possible to quantify change over

[15] Joel Chandler Harris, *Free Joe and Other Georgian Sketches* (New York: Charles Scribner's Sons, 1887), 165, http://docsouth.unc.edu/southlit/harrisj/harris.html.

[16] Lois Green Carr and Lorena S. Walsh, "Inventories and the Analysis of Wealth and Consumptions Patterns St. Mary's County Maryland, 1658–1777." *HM*, 13(2) 1980: 81–104.

[17] Lois Green Carr and Lorena S. Walsh, "Changing Lifestyles and Consumer Behavior in the Colonial Chesapeake," *Of Consuming Interests: The Style of Life in the Eighteenth Century*, edited by Cary Carson, Ronald Hoffman, and Peter J. Albert, 59–166 (Charlottesville: University of Virginia Press, 1994); Gloria L. Main, "Probate Records as a Source for Early American History," *WMQ* (33) 3, 1975:88–99; Lorena S. Walsh, "Urban Amenities and Rural Sufficiency: Living Standards and Consumer Behavior in the Colonial Chesapeake, 1643–1777," *JEH* 43(1), 1983:109–117; Paul A. Shackel, *Personal Discipline and Material Culture: An Archaeology of*

space and time by comparing patterns of probate data from different regions and years. While this finer level of analysis is common for earlier periods of American history, probate-based studies of individuals and discrete groups are virtually nonexistent for the postbellum South.

The material possessions listed in inventories also reflect a person's consumer choices, values, and world view. Changing ways of thinking become evident when individual inventories are compared to those from a different area, socioeconomic class, ethnic group, gender, or time period. The patterns of material culture that these records reflect provide important clues about how consumption differed between groups in a given era, as well as how consumption habits shifted over time in response to altered social and economic conditions.[18]

To be sure, inventories have their drawbacks as primary sources. First of all, how the information is presented can vary greatly from one appraiser to another. This makes it difficult to judge both the quantity and quality of goods in some inventories. For example, appraisers rarely listed every single item, often referring to groups of objects instead, such as "one lot of earthenware." And "one plow" could refer to any number of varieties used by Georgia farmers in the late-nineteenth century. Second, probate inventories do not reflect a reliable cross section of society. The poorest and richest segments of society are barely represented, because estates worth less than $500 were not subject to probate, and the very wealthy usually left a will. Those who disposed of their property prior to death are also missing from or misrepresented in probate records.[19] Third, inventories may be deficient in many types of data. For example, details concerning clothing, food, debts owed by the deceased, and everyday objects of little value often do not appear in the inventories. Appraisers also may have omitted heirlooms, possessions bequeathed in a will, goods given prior to death, and objects belonging to others in a household.[20] As we will show in Chapter 2, however, there are ways of accounting for and overcoming these gaps and biases in probate records.

Our work is concerned with production and consumption among yeoman farmers in the Georgia Piedmont during a period of tremendous change, as they

Annapolis, Maryland, 1695–1870 (Knoxville: University of Tennessee Press, 1993); Carole Shammas, *The Pre-Industrial Consumer in England and America* (Oxford: Clarendon Press, 1990).

18 In a landmark study of the standard of living, self-sufficiency, and the increasing importance of consumer culture in colonial Maryland, Lorena Walsh observes that, "One does not learn of these changes much from letters, diaries, or other personal records… One finds most of the answers to such questions in probate records." See "Urban Amenities and Rural Sufficiency," 109.

19 Mark Overton, Jane Whittle, Darron Dean, and Andrew Hahn, *Production and Consumption in English Households, 1600–1750* (New York: Routledge, 2004), 27–28.

20 As Mark Overton argues, "the omission of some goods from an inventory has no effect on the accuracy of unit valuations (prices) for example, but would lead to an undervaluing of the moveable goods of the deceased." Ibid., 32.

made the transition from self-sufficiency to market dependence. We dispute the timeworn assertion that Southern yeomen were desperately poor and did little to improve their condition. Examining shifts in the pattern of goods ownership, we can see the resourceful ways in which farmers adapted to profound economic and social changes. These same patterns allow us to understand the factors that prompted farmers to assume greater risk in order to improve their lot in life, as well as those factors that stood in the way of progress. Additionally, we look for evidence to determine when, how, and to what degree Georgia farmers engaged in the "consumer revolution." Focusing on the household as the primary unit of analysis, we test what seems to be a reasonable hypothesis: farmers who were risk-averse diversified their productive capabilities in order to guard against economic disaster, while those who focused intensively on a single crop (cotton) were confident enough in the stability of the market to put all their efforts into a single pursuit.

While many studies of the postbellum South focus on county-aggregate data to reveal the evolving patterns of land tenure, agricultural production, and reliance on store credit, the wealth of data from the three rural counties we examine makes it possible to reveal specific trends in household assets over time, by linking sales and tax data with probate inventories.[21] Specifically, our investigation draws from a sample of 228 estates from the counties of Crawford, Franklin, and Jasper between 1880 and 1910. Each decedent was verified independently and cross-verified through census data (the household had to have been recorded in the 1880 census as living in the same location as at the time of death), annual state tax records (the individual had to have been recorded as paying Georgia taxes for at least five years prior to his or her death), and other primary sources. Although 90 percent of the probated estates used for this study belonged to white males, African Americans accounted for 6 percent of the decedents, and women for 7 percent. Given this, we consider both race and gender at length.

The Middle Georgia counties of Crawford, Franklin, and Jasper are especially fitting for an investigation through probate records of the material world of yeoman farmers engaged in cotton production. Each county has a rich body of historical documents to work from, and all three have always been on the periphery in Georgia, geographically, economically, and socially.[22] Crawford

[21] See, for example, Louis Ferleger, "Capital Goods and Southern Economic Development," *JEH*, XLV (June 1985): 411–417; –, "Self-Sufficiency and Rural Life on Southern Farms," *AH*, 58, (July 1984): 314–329; Jay Mandle, *The Roots of Black Poverty: The Southern Plantation Economy After the Civil War* (Durham: Duke University Press, 1978); William N. Parker, "The South in the National Economy, 1865–1970," *SEJ* 46 (April 1980): 1019–48; Gavin Wright, *The Political Economy of the Cotton South* (New York: W.W. Norton, 1978); and Roger Ransom and Richard Sutch, *One Kind of Freedom: The Economic Consequences of Emancipation* (New York: Cambridge University Press, 1977).

[22] Franklin County, named for Benjamin Franklin, was settled in 1784. Jasper County, located southwest of Franklin, was established in 1807 as Randolph County and renamed in 1812 for

and Jasper counties are situated in the Lower Piedmont, while Franklin County is in the northeast corner of the state, in an area of the Upper Piedmont known as the Uplands (Figure 1.1). Crawford County was among the first Piedmont counties to be drawn into the cotton economy when planters from the older cotton-producing region known as the Black Belt moved northward in the 1830s and 1840s, in search of fresh farmland. Jasper County also became integrated into the cotton economy well before the Civil War, yet it retained economic similarities to the more remote Upland counties because of its location on the northern margin of the Lower Piedmont region. Franklin, on the other hand, was located squarely in the Uplands, where conditions were more conducive to smaller farms practicing mixed agriculture. Landowners there were typically smallholders or middling farmers who produced corn for the local market and wheat, small grains, peas, beans, and potatoes for home use. While cotton had been grown for home and local consumption in the Upper Piedmont ever since whites settled in the area, it was not commercially viable until the widespread adoption of fertilizers and the arrival of railway service following the Civil War.[23]

Chapter 1 establishes the broader historical context necessary for understanding our analysis of production and consumption in Crawford, Franklin, and Jasper counties. We begin by describing the conditions on the eve of the Civil War and go on to discuss economic change from the Reconstruction period through the first decade of the twentieth century. Here we show how the Southern yeomanry transitioned from subsistence-level conditions to more intensive involvement in commercial agriculture and fuller engagement with a national economy. The impact of this transition was greatest in regions such as Franklin County, which had existed on the margins of the cotton economy prior to the Civil War.

Chapter 2 delves into our methodology, stressing the importance of probate files as the most representative documentation available to permit a comprehensive analysis of yeoman households in the postbellum period. The detailed inventories created as part of the probate process, listing the possessions of individuals at various wealth levels, make it possible to explore farm families' domestic organization, their degree of self-sufficiency, and the ways in which they defined success. The household was the locus of most production-related activities throughout Georgia in the late-nineteenth century, and virtually every family member was involved in agriculture in some way. Similarly, most craftwork and manufacturing took place in the home or in dependencies located

William Jasper, a Revolutionary War soldier killed in Savannah in 1779. Crawford County was formed in 1822 and named for William Harris Crawford, President of the United States Senate, minister to France, and Secretary of War and the Treasury; Marion B. Holmes, ed. *Georgia Official and Statistical Register* (Atlanta: Perry Communications, 1978), 1117, 1122 & 1112.

23 Steven Hahn, *The Roots of Southern Populism: Yeoman Farmers and the Transformation of the Georgia Upcountry, 1850–1890* (New York: Oxford University Press, 1983), 79.

on the home property. Therefore, the household was the most important economic unit in Middle Georgia. We examine how changes in household organization and family composition relate to the transition of the regional economy toward more intensive levels of cotton cultivation, arguing that the scale and scope of production were typically limited by family size or by the ability of kin groups to work together.

Chapter 3 considers the full range of productive activities carried out on yeoman farms, including production for home use, production for market, and by-employment, in order to provide a more holistic view of production and self-sufficiency in the three counties. We contend that farmers in Middle Georgia balanced the high-risk strategy of cotton monoculture by engaging in other productive activities whenever possible – not only farming but also trades and crafts. These additional sources of income allowed farmers to diversify their earnings and remain as self-reliant as possible, thereby limiting risk.

In Chapter 4, we focus on the role of the household as part of a farm operation, and on how household possessions reflect consumption practices. Our analysis of probate inventories and estate sales (auctions) suggests that Middle Georgia farmers at all wealth levels were eager and active consumers. They made farming and productive by-employment priorities over consumption and the purchase of domestic amenities, but they also followed the latest product and fashion trends as they took hold in urban centers. Likewise, Southern farmers understood the ways in which material goods and the act of consumption communicated one's station in life and position in the community. Unlike in urban areas, agricultural implements, production-related items, and laborsaving devices appear to have been linked more strongly to affluence than were domestic refinements. While the goods listed in the inventories imply something about purchasing decisions and patterns of acquisition, the records of estate sales conducted as part of the probate process provide perhaps the broadest and best insight into the buying habits of Georgia yeoman farmers. We conclude Chapter 4 with a discussion of how estate auctions created a robust secondary market in used goods, providing Georgians with an alternate source for acquiring the things they wanted or needed. While many aspects of the Georgia estate-sale system are enigmatic, the auction process served a clear purpose: it offered quick access to cash and the equitable division of assets without contention. Many heirs likely preferred this arrangement to spending the considerable time and energy required to attempt to divide possessions equally among survivors. A sale held "at public outcry," after all, offered the beneficiaries of the estate the potential of exceeding the value assigned to goods in the inventory, while those attending the auction had the opportunity to acquire a cultivator, a stove, or a mule at a discount.

Chapter 5 explores questions of wealth and status as they are represented through land tenure and goods ownership. We find that the rural, agriculture-based economy of postbellum Middle Georgia was every bit as complex, dynamic, and viable as the contemporaneous urban model characterized by increasing industrialization and higher levels of consumption. Farmers acquired a broad range of items, most of which were utilitarian or production-related; farmers in all wealth categories tended to invest their assets first in farm stock, tools, and implements, then in livestock, and lastly in household possessions. Still, small and middling farmers often owned luxury items such as books and clocks, while many wealthier families possessed expensive pieces like parlor organs. The wealthiest households strove for increased economic success by purchasing advanced technologies like steam-powered cotton gins, or labor-saving devices such as stoves or rotary washing machines. While many of these trends are apparent across the sample population, we also consider how patterns of asset ownership varied by county and by race.

In the conclusion, we find the meaning behind Joel Chandler Harris's characterization of Middle Georgia as a place where there was "room for improvement, but no room for progress." Without a doubt, farmers living and working in the postbellum South faced considerable challenges as they worked to refashion an economy and a society in a world without slaves, a world where cotton was a king of a different sort. But Harris may have been exaggerating when he wrote that there was "no room for progress." While Georgia farmers were above all practical-minded, the historical record shows that they were keenly aware of the consumer culture taking shape in the country's urban centers, and they found ways to buy in on their own terms.

1

Different Crops, Different Cultures

The Evolution of Three Georgia Counties

The loan application submitted by James Jefferson Bowman in 1890 provides a glimpse into the aspirations and realities in the life of a typical yeoman farmer living in the Georgia Piedmont in the late nineteenth century.[1] This Crawford County farmer sought a loan to pay for extensive improvements on his property. All indications suggested that the time was right to expand: cotton production in Georgia had increased from 143 pounds per acre in 1885 to 170 in 1889, while the average price of cotton over the same period remained steady, at $0.085 per pound.[2] Moreover, credit was fairly easy to secure from merchants and other lenders who saw similar opportunities for profit from the encouraging trends that Bowman and other farmers had noticed. On the application, Bowman provided a detailed financial history and answered a list of questions about the character and scope of his farming operation.

The thirty-nine-year-old farmer owned 101.25 acres valued at $900, with 40 acres under cultivation and 50 in timber; 51.25 acres were enclosed with rail fences.[3] Bowman, his wife, and their three sons and two daughters lived in a new frame house with two large common rooms, two bedrooms, and front and back verandas. He had also built a new two-room frame duplex with a central chimney for his tenants. While the application does not list the number of tenants, the eighteen-by-twenty-four-foot dimensions and the center

1 "Application of James J. Bowman to C. P. N. Barker, Atlanta, Georgia, to negotiate a loan of $350 for five years at 8 percent interest, October 1890." Crawford County, Miscellaneous County Offices, Miscellaneous Original Documents, 1826–1928, Record Group 139, Subgroup 12, Series 10 (GDA).

2 USDA, *Cotton and Cottonseed: Acreage, Yield, Production, Disposition, Price, Value by States, 1866–1952* (Washington, DC, 1955), 10; from U.S. Bureau of the Census, *Historical Statistics of the United States from Colonial Times to 1970, Part I*, Series K (Washington, DC, 1975), 517–518.

3 Ibid.

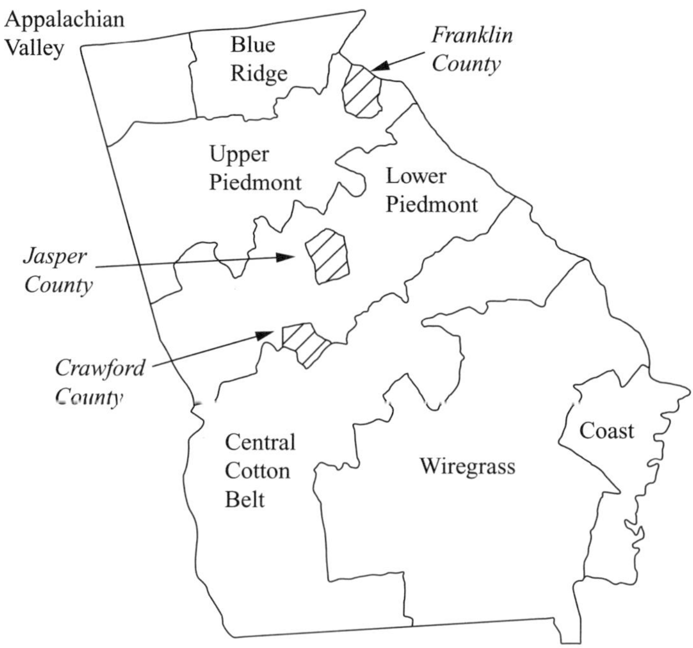

FIGURE 1.1. Map of Georgia showing the location of Crawford, Jasper, and Franklin Counties in relation to the location of the Lower and Upper Piedmont physiographic regions (Metz).

chimney configuration are typical of the two-family design that developed as a means for housing slaves during the antebellum period and remained popular for quartering white and black laborers throughout the South into the early twentieth century.[4] Other outbuildings included a sixteen-by-eighteen-foot barn with an attached stable, a sixteen-by-eighteen-foot "driving barn" to shelter wagons and buggies, and a cotton house measuring twelve feet by fourteen feet. In all, the buildings were valued at $300 in 1889 (for taxation purposes).[5]

And what did Bowman manage to produce on this farm? According to the application, cotton was his primary crop, and in 1889 his output included eight 500-pound bales of cotton and 240 bushels of cottonseed. Reporting on the pending harvest, he was guarded, writing that "the crop is not so good as last year," but he added optimistically that "the prospect is evening

4 Edward A. Chappell, "Slave Housing," *Fresh Advices: A Research Supplement* (Williamsburg, VA: Colonial Williamsburg Foundation, November 1982), i–iv.

5 Bowman, "Application of James J. Bowman to C. P. N. Barker," 1890, 2; "1880 FC," Crawford County, Georgia, Township 573, Family 263, page 26. Crawford County, Miscellaneous County Offices, Miscellaneous Original Documents, 1826–1928, Record Group 139, Subgroup 12, Series 10. GDA, Morrow, Georgia.

up."[6] Like most farmers in Crawford, Bowman worked to be as self-sufficient as possible by growing a host of additional crops, including corn, wheat, oats, peaches, peas, peanuts, potatoes, and sorghum. While it does not appear that Bowman grew enough grain or vegetables to be considered a truck farmer, the amounts listed in the loan application are large enough to suggest that he was able to provide for the needs of his seven-person family and his livestock, perhaps with some left over for local exchange. However, he also produced several bushels of peaches and peanuts that may have been grown for market.

The final question on the application asked for information about any items of importance not mentioned previously or "any special improvements made in the neighborhood" of the applicant.[7] Where Bowman gave succinct answers to nearly all of the other questions, here he decided to be more effusive. He called attention to the location of his farm within half a mile of the Atlanta & Florida Railroad line, "two good grist mills," several churches and schools, and a number of sawmills, ending with the hopeful observation that "the section is rapidly improving in many aspects."[8]

James Bowman was in many ways the quintessential Georgia Piedmont farmer in 1890. His 101-acre farm was slightly under the average holding of 138 acres, yet he owned more land than over half of the farmers in the county. Like most other farmers, he had most but not all of his acreage in cultivation, and he had the ability to hire tenants to help increase his productive capacity. He was ambitious, as the money he invested in new buildings attests. His loan application places the value of all of the improvements made to his farm, including the new buildings, at $900 – the improvements alone would be worth roughly 37 percent more than the total value of buildings and other structures on an average Crawford County property, and they would increase the value of Bowman's property by 75 percent.[9]

Bowman looked with pride at the churches, schools, and small industries that had appeared in his neighborhood in the past decade, and he saw the new rail line passing through the county as a sign of hope and progress. His ambition, however, came at a cost – the loan he received to help pay for his new construction placed him in the growing ranks of debt and dependency, like countless other Southern cotton farmers. Ultimately, his bid to succeed as a self-sufficient farmer failed. By 1900, Bowman and his family were renting a farm in nearby Houston County, and by 1910 he had left farming to work as a carpenter.[10]

[6] Ibid.

[7] Ibid.

[8] Ibid.

[9] "Census Data for 1890, Agriculture," *Historical Census Browser (hereafter HCB)*, retrieved December 10, 2010, from the University of Virginia, Geospatial and Statistical Data Center: http://fisher.lib.virginia.edu/collections/stats/histcensus/index.html.

[10] U.S. Bureau of the Census, *Twelfth Census of the United States, 1900: Vol. 1–2, Population.* Prepared under the supervision of William C. Hunt (Washington, DC, 1901–1902), Houston

FIGURE 1.2. The landscape of cotton farming in the Georgia Piedmont during the postbellum period. A typical rural home near the town of Roberta in Crawford County, circa 1885. Courtesy of Georgia Archives, Vanishing Georgia Collection, image number crw005.

The Bowman loan application illustrates many of the ambitions of yeoman farmers in the Georgia Piedmont during this era, as well as the challenges that sometimes thwarted those ambitions, such as debt, cash shortages, and low cotton prices. Crawford, Jasper, and Franklin were all cotton counties by 1880. Middling farmers who owned their property and held between 20 and 175 acres accounted for the majority of the population. While cash tenants and sharecroppers certainly existed in each of these counties, owner-operators outnumbered renters by at least two to one. Each county had a sizeable black population, ranging from 21 percent of the population in Franklin (in 1880) to nearly 50 percent in Crawford and Jasper. The residents of each county remained hopeful about their economic future, seeing glimmers of prosperity in every new church spire, school bell, and mile of railroad track. They worked hard to develop towns, promote industry, and attract the railroads that would

County, Militia District 528, roll 205, page 10A; U.S. Bureau of the Census, *Thirteenth Census of the United States, 1910: Vol. 1, Population.* Prepared under the supervision of William C. Hunt (Washington, DC, 1913), Houston County, Militia District 528, Roll T624-195, Page 18A.

connect them economically and socially to the wider world beyond the county line. Crawford, Jasper, and Franklin counties would all struggle with the incessant rise of debt and tenancy for both blacks and whites. But despite these similarities, the differences in environment, history, and demographics among the three counties resulted in their traveling profoundly different paths to cotton monoculture.

King Cotton was a relative latecomer to the Georgia Piedmont, not fully embraced as a staple crop until the 1850s. In fact, settlers and planters considered much of the state a frontier land as late as the 1820s, despite the fact that the first pioneers had pushed inland from the coast beginning in the late eighteenth century. Established as a Protestant refuge under the leadership of James Oglethorpe in 1733, and declared a Crown colony in 1752, the Georgia settlement for the first thirty years of its existence remained confined to a narrow strip of coastline between the Savannah and Altamaha rivers – the British colonists were hemmed in by Creek and Cherokee settlements inland, and by the fear of rival European powers attacking from the south (the French from the Caribbean or the Spanish from their Florida possessions).[11] These fears were allayed with the signing of the Treaty of Paris in 1763, which brought an official end to the French and Indian War. Soon after, British settlement extended southward along the coast to where the St. Mary's River formed a border with Florida.

While slavery was initially banned in Georgia under Oglethorpe and his trustees, it became legal once the Crown assumed governance of the colony. Even so, slaveholdings remained small until the 1770s, when rice developed as Georgia's first major staple crop and the need for cheap mass labor became clear. Within a decade, planters increased cultivation of sea island cotton in addition to rice. Although labor-intensive, cotton could be raised with simple tools, and its cultivation involved a series of fairly repetitive tasks that could be easily taught and supervised.[12] Green-seed or short-staple upland cotton had been grown in limited quantities since before the American Revolution, but it was not considered a viable cash crop because of the difficulty in separating the seed from the fiber. This changed in the mid-1780s, with the introduction from the West Indies of long-staple, black-seed cotton, whose seeds could easily be removed from the boll. Like rice, however, the long-staple varietal could be cultivated only in a narrow, 50-mile-wide swath along the coast of South Carolina and Georgia, where the growing season was longest.[13]

Settlers initially acquired land in Georgia through a headright system that granted 200 acres to every head of household, plus an additional 50 acres

[11] Kenneth Coleman, ed., *A History of Georgia* (Athens: University of Georgia Press, 1977): 101.

[12] Willard W. Cochrane, *The Development of American Agriculture: A Historical Analysis* (Minneapolis: University of Minnesota Press, 1979): 69–71.

[13] Lewis Cecil Gray, *History of Agriculture in the Southern United States to 1860*, Vol. I. (Gloucester: Peter Smith, 1958): 26–27.

for every dependent and slave (up to a maximum grant of 1,000 acres).[14] As a result, grantees could quickly accumulate vast holdings that were perfect for the type of large-scale cotton plantations that developed in the Black Belt region of Central Georgia.[15] The headright system was intended to prevent land speculation by requiring that grantees actually live on the land, but fraud nevertheless became common in the rush for pensions and land bounties following the Revolution. This prompted the adoption of a land lottery system early in the nineteenth century. Under the lottery system, the state established counties and divided each one into parcels ranging between 200 and 400 acres.[16] Designed to thwart rich land speculators and attract yeoman farmers and their families, the lottery enabled any prospective settler who could prove citizenship and had paid annual taxes in Georgia to submit his name on a slip of paper for a drawing. Those whose names were drawn could each purchase a 200-acre plot for $0.04 an acre.[17] The seven lotteries for public land held in Georgia between 1805 and 1833 roughly correspond with the forced cessions of Creek and Cherokee lands that eventually drove both Indian nations from the state.[18] Jasper County, for example, was created in 1805, following the Creek cession of 1804, and Crawford County was established in 1822, following the Creek cession of 1821.

While the lottery system expanded the ranks of landownership to include some yeoman farmers, it proved susceptible to speculation and fraud, much like the headright system it replaced. For example, those who had already received headright grants were still allowed to participate in the lottery, and wealthy individuals could easily defraud the system by paying others for their lots.[19] Once again, land speculators and large planters found ways to purchase huge amounts of land, thereby creating the basis for large-scale slaveholding in Middle Georgia.[20]

[14] Ibid., 106.

[15] The Black Belt, named for the band of rich, dark soil stretching from central Georgia through Alabama and up through northeast Mississippi and into Tennessee, was identified as prime land for short-staple cotton production beginning in the 1820s. The region quickly became characterized by large-scale, plantation-based cotton monoculture. The name quickly took on a demographic connotation, referring to counties where blacks outnumbered whites because of the heavy reliance on slave labor.

[16] Frederick B. Gates, "The Georgia Land Act of 1803: Political Struggle in a One-Party State," *Georgia Historical Quarterly* 82, no. 1 (Spring 1998): 1–2. The land lotteries were first authorized by the legislature in May, 1803, and began with Wayne County, which was divided into 450-acre plots, and in Baldwin and Wilkinson Counties, where 202.5 acre-plots were awarded.

[17] Enoch Marvin Banks, *The Economics of Land Tenure in Georgia* (New York: Columbia University Press, 1905): 15–17.

[18] Between 1805 and 1833, the state of Georgia conducted eight land lotteries, one each in 1805, 1807, 1820, 1821, 1827, and 1833, and two in 1832. Indian land cessions for the same period occurred in 1802, 1804, 1817–1819, 1821, 1825–1827, and 1835.

[19] Steven Hahn, *The Roots of Southern Populism: Yeoman Farmers and the Transformation of the Georgia Upcountry, 1850–1890* (New York: Oxford University Press, 1983): 17–18.

[20] Banks, *Economics of Land Tenure*, 18–20.

Georgia's inland cotton-producing area initially centered on the Lower Piedmont, a region extending from eastern Georgia into western South Carolina. But by 1840, cotton growing had expanded into an area that stretched from the southern border of North Carolina down along the Appalachian foothills – a strip of rich farmland known as the Black Belt, which continued westward through Alabama and Mississippi. By 1860, cotton was being cultivated as far west as the Red River in Texas, down into Louisiana, and up the Mississippi River to Arkansas and Tennessee.[21] The crop's increased range expanded the extent of slavery and the planter society it sustained farther than ever before. Because of its great wealth, the planter elite quickly came to dominate Southern society, despite being few in number. In Georgia in 1860, only 5 percent of the white population owned twenty or more slaves and could rightly be counted among the planter elite. Most slaveholders owned fewer than six slaves, and non-slaveholders accounted for nearly two-thirds of Georgia's population.[22] Within the Black Belt, the incidence of slaveholding was much higher, typically exceeding 50 percent of the households. In 1860, for example, 60 percent of the households in Crawford County owned slaves, as did 68 percent of households in Jasper County (Table 1.1).[23]

The small group of elite planters shaped exchange networks by dealing directly with cotton factors – credit merchants – along the coast or in inland market towns such as Augusta and Macon.[24] The factors not only handled the sale of cotton for export but also arranged for the purchase of supplies and luxury goods that could not be acquired locally. Before the days of mail-order companies, therefore, the planters' connections to factors made much of the community dependent on them – even more so because only the planter elite possessed the capital to invest in gins, mills, and other machinery needed to sustain an agricultural community. Additionally, large slaveholders were able to maintain a workforce that typically included tradesmen like carpenters, blacksmiths, and weavers, who enhanced the self-sufficiency of the estate beyond the production of food crops (and who could be hired out to poorer farmers).

Yeomen living in the Black Belt, on the other hand, did not possess the resources to produce all that they needed on their farms. They sold their crops and purchased (or bartered for) necessary supplies through local merchants, itinerant peddlers, and credit merchants, or through wealthy planters eager to

21 Gray, *History of Agriculture*, 26–37.

22 Numan V. Bartley, *The Creation of Modern Georgia* (Athens: University of Georgia Press, 1983): 20; Coleman, *A History of Georgia*, 184–86; Hahn, *The Roots of Southern Populism*, 17.

23 "Census Data Year 1860," (2004). *HBC*. Retrieved December 10, 2010, from the University of Virginia, Geospatial and Statistical Data Center: http://fisher.lib.virginia.edu/collections/stats/histcensus/index.html.

24 Hahn, *The Roots of Southern Populism*, 33; Joseph P. Reidy, *From Slavery to Agrarian Capitalism in the Cotton Plantation South: Central Georgia, 1800–1880* (Chapel Hill: University of North Carolina Press, 1992): 18–19.

TABLE 1.1. *Distribution of Slaveholding in Franklin, Crawford, and Jasper Counties, 1860*

County	Slaveholding Groups	Number of Slaveholding Households	% Slaveholding
Franklin	5 or fewer	132	57
Crawford	5 or fewer	186	48
Jasper	5 or fewer	193	37
Franklin	5–9	61	27
Crawford	5–9	82	21
Jasper	5–9	103	20
Franklin	10–19	31	13
Crawford	10–19	62	16
Jasper	10–19	108	21
Franklin	20–49	4	2
Crawford	20–49	46	12
Jasper	20–49	89	17
Franklin	50–199	2	1
Crawford	50–199	12	3
Jasper	50–199	22	4
Franklin	Total	230	100
Crawford	Total	388	100
Jasper	Total	515	100

Source: "Census Data Year 1860," (2004), *HCB*.

establish an economic monopoly within a region.[25] The arrival of rail service in some communities, beginning in the 1830s and 1840s, brought traveling factors or buyers who added a new dimension to local exchange. White smallholders and yeomen often resented the power of the planter elite, and being able to deal directly with factors lessened these small farmers' dependence on their wealthy neighbors. While railroads introduced greater value and variety in the goods that could be acquired from beyond their counties, yeomen knew they still had to rely on the planters for milling and ginning services, as well as for help getting their cotton to market. They also shared a racial connection that intensified in the 1830s, as enslaved blacks began to outnumber whites in many Black Belt counties.[26]

Plantation slavery lent a distinctive character to patterns of landownership and slaveholding in the Black Belt during the 1850s and 1860s. Landholding became increasingly concentrated, as the biggest planters gobbled up more and

[25] Hahn, *The Roots of Southern Populism*, 33.

[26] Reidy, *From Slavery to Agrarian Capitalism*, 32–35, 56; Jeffrey Robert Young, *Domesticating Slavery: The Master Class in Georgia and South Carolina, 1670–1837* (Chapel Hill: University of North Carolina Press, 1999).

more acreage. In 1850, planters who owned 500 acres or more controlled 35 percent of the land in the Black Belt; by 1860, they controlled 60 percent.[27] Likewise, slaveholding became more concentrated by 1860, when nearly 70 percent of white households in the Black Belt owned slaves. Within the ranks of the slaveholders, 50 percent owned ten or more, and one-fifth of the households included more than twenty enslaved people.[28] Eventually the voracious appetite of the planter class for large landholdings – and their propensity to overproduce and exhaust the soil – forced smallholders and newcomers to look elsewhere for fresh cotton land and a chance to succeed. While some headed west, others pushed the boundaries of the Black Belt northward, moving into the backcountry, where they came into contact with Georgians of another sort.

The climate, topography, and culture of the Georgia Uplands proved resistant to the encroachment of cotton monoculture for more than fifty years after whites first began to the settle there. The Piedmont is a wide, sloping region that stretches southward from the base of the Blue Ridge Mountains in North Georgia. The Upper Piedmont, or Uplands, is a broad plateau crisscrossed by rivers and streams. This gives way to the gently eroded hills of the Lower Piedmont before terminating along the fall line, where the mountains meet the extensive plain of the Georgia Tidewater. Farmers who settled in the Uplands beginning in the late eighteenth century had to clear the heavy growth of hardwoods and yellow pine to plant the fertile clay soils. The climate differs just enough from that of the Lower Piedmont to affect crop choice; because temperatures can be as much as twenty degrees cooler, the Upland growing season can be up to thirty days shorter than in the area near the fall line.[29] The Uplands also receives as much as eight inches more precipitation a year than do regions to the south.

The backwoods pioneers who settled in Franklin County, in the Uplands, were of a different stock than those who established themselves in the Black Belt, and the pattern of settlement that developed differed as well. First, white smallholders predominated from the earliest days, and the minority who

27 Gavin Wright, *The Political Economy of the Cotton South: Households, Markets, and Wealth in the Nineteenth Century* (New York: W. W. Norton, 1978): 30; Hahn, *The Roots of Southern Populism*, 41.

28 "Census Data for Year 1860," (2004). *HCB*. Retrieved December 10, 2010, from the University of Virginia, Geospatial and Statistical Data Center: http://fisher.lib.virginia.edu/collections/stats/histcensus/index.html; Hahn, *The Roots of Southern Populism*, 25.

29 Sam Bowers Hilliard, *Atlas of Antebellum Southern Agriculture* (Baton Rouge: Louisiana State University Press, 1984): 11–17. Temperatures in Upper Piedmont range from forty degrees in the winter to eighty degrees in the summer with an average of 210 frost-free days, while the Lower Piedmont is up to ten degrees warmer with as many as 240 frost-free days. Precipitation varies from around sixty inches annually in the Franklin area to an average of fifty-two inches a year in Crawford and Jasper.

brought slaves held them in smaller numbers than did settlers in the plantation belt. This dynamic persisted throughout the antebellum period, even as the cotton economy expanded northward and took hold of Lower Piedmont counties such as Jasper.[30] The terrain and climate in the Uplands were amenable to smaller farms practicing mixed agriculture, not plantations. Second, cotton never became king. Some Upland farmers grew cotton in small quantities, for home consumption and local exchange, but it was not adopted as a market crop on a wide scale until its price reached record levels in the 1850s, making it profitable despite the transport costs involved. Even as late as 1850, grain accounted for about 90 percent of the cropland and about 80 percent of the total crop value in the Uplands.[31]

The rugged terrain and the grain-based economy of the Uplands contributed to the formation of a relatively insular society that relied more on local exchange than on extra-local contact. The landscape defined by hills and shallow, rocky streams did not encourage road construction, nor did the trade in corn and grain, which, unlike cotton, did not transport well and spoiled easily. The remote location and lack of good roads were not conducive to the development of towns either. In many cases, yeomen who grew crops for market had to trade with neighbors, conduct their business locally in the county seat, or travel by wagon over ill-maintained country roads to one of the regional market towns in Middle Georgia, such as Atlanta, Columbus, Athens, Macon, or Augusta. Given the environmental impediments, it should come as no surprise that rail service developed later in the Piedmont than it did south of the fall line, where the landscape was more amenable, economic networks were far more developed, and the demand for contact with the outside world was greater and potentially more lucrative. As a result, the Uplands retained its backwoods character well into the antebellum period.[32]

While planter society dominated the Black Belt, the yeoman farmer defined the Uplands. Almost without exception, those who settled the Upper Piedmont identified themselves as farmers, even if they practiced additional trades like blacksmithing or wagon making.[33] These farmers were highly self-reliant, raising most of what they needed to sustain their families and producing a small surplus to sell at market or to exchange for the services or goods they could not produce themselves. Census data from 1850 provide an indication of the extent to which Franklin County farms differed from those in the Cotton Belt. In 1849, Franklin grew $18,082 worth of garden produce, among the highest in the state, while the agricultural schedule indicates there was no market

[30] Ibid., 20; James C. Bonner, *A History of Georgia Agriculture, 1732–1860* (Athens: University of Georgia Press, 2009): 42

[31] Ibid.

[32] Robert Preston Brooks, "The Agrarian Revolution in Georgia, 1865–1912" (PhD diss., Madison: University of Wisconsin, 1914): 74–76; Hahn, *The Roots of Southern Populism*, 20.

[33] Hahn, *The Roots of Southern Populism*, 21.

garden produce in either Crawford or Jasper.[34] At the very least, the value of the produce grown in Franklin shows a difference in crop regimes, and it may suggest the extent to which the Upland farmers provided for themselves.

The agricultural report prepared for the eighth federal census in 1860 reveals the differences in farming between the Upland counties and those involved in cotton production.[35] Both Crawford and Jasper produced in excess of 9,000 pounds of cotton in 1859, which was slightly less than average among Georgia's cotton-producing counties. Franklin, on the other hand, produced only 793 pounds, suggesting that the cotton was likely intended for home use. Corn production in Crawford and Jasper also reflected the predominance of cotton monoculture – a process in which corn was essential for food, feed, and forage. Crawford County reported 274,645 bushels of corn harvested, and Jasper reported 327,214. Franklin County produced 30 percent less corn than did Crawford, but the difference is not great enough to suggest a dramatically different agricultural pattern – unlike the difference in wheat, where Franklin County produced nearly three times as much as Crawford (24,053 bushels). Surprisingly, Jasper deviated from the Uplands–Cotton Belt pattern with a large harvest of 36,682 bushels of wheat in 1859. Whereas farmers in Franklin and Jasper produced on average between twenty and thirty bushels of wheat per household, Crawford averaged only three or four.[36]

Also among the census data are indicators of cultural difference between the Upland farmers and those in the developing cotton areas of the Lower Piedmont. One was tobacco. On the eve of the Civil War, enumerators for the census reported that farmers in Franklin County harvested 3,412 pounds of tobacco in 1859.[37] Jasper, located in the northernmost section of the Lower Piedmont, reported 1,100 pounds, while none was recorded for Crawford. Many of the families that settled in the Franklin and Jasper areas came from states like Virginia and North Carolina, where tobacco culture was prominent even among backwoods farmers.

Farm size is another indicator of the yeoman influence in the Georgia Uplands. While plantations of between 100 and 500 acres characterized the Black Belt, smaller farms were the norm in the upcountry where landholding was linked more closely to the amount of land that a family-based workforce could effectively work.[38] Over time, the size of landholdings decreased

[34] "Census Data Year 1850," (2004), *HCB*. Retrieved December 10, 2010, from the University of Virginia, Geospatial and Statistical Data Center: http://fisher.lib.virginia.edu/collections/stats/histcensus/index.html.

[35] U.S. Bureau of the Census, *Eighth Census of the United States, 1860, Agriculture*. Compiled from the original returns of the Eighth Census by Joseph C. G. Kennedy (Washington, DC, 1864), 21–23.

[36] Hilliard, *Atlas of Antebellum Southern Agriculture*, 60–61.

[37] *Eighth Census of the United States, 1860, Agriculture*. Kennedy, 23.

[38] "Census Data Year 1860," *HCB*. Retrieved December 10, 2010, from the University of Virginia, Geospatial and Statistical Data Center: http://fisher.lib.virginia.edu/collections/stats/histcensus/index.html.

TABLE 1.2. *Distribution of Landholdings in Crawford, Jasper, and Franklin Counties, 1860*

County	Farms 3–9 Acres	Farms 10–19 Acres	Farms 20–49 Acres	Farms 50–99 Acres	Farms 100–499 Acres	Farms 500–999 Acres	Farms 1,000+ Acres
State Average	7	21	103	107	143	20	7
State Median	4	17	94	96	131	10	2
State Min.	0	0	6	11	3	0	0
State Max.	52	120	350	322	420	100	71
Crawford	2	3	47	96	171	35	9
Jasper	0	1	26	73	211	77	25
Franklin	2	24	242	215	110	2	1

Source: "Census Data Year 1860," (2004), *HCB*.

in Upland counties like Franklin, perhaps reflecting population pressure or an adjustment toward a more optimal level of acreage given the crops grown, the level of production, and the average number of people in a farming household (Table 1.2). By 1860, 81 percent of the 596 farmers in Franklin County owned fewer than 100 acres. Around 30 percent of the farmland in Franklin had been improved, compared to 45 percent in Crawford County and more than 60 percent in Jasper, attesting to the greater resources – in particular, more slave labor – that farmers in the plantation counties possessed.[39] In comparison, the households that farmed more than 200 acres in the Upland counties of Jackson and Carroll relied on slaves and were more likely to be involved in the production of cotton for export, while the farms with fewer than 200 acres in those counties typically owned no slaves.[40] Ultimately, the higher percentage of improved land suggests a greater intensity in cultivation in counties where cotton was the primary cash crop.

Uplands–Cotton Belt contrasts are even more pronounced if you compare Piedmont counties to those in the heart of the Black Belt (Table 1.3). For example, only 30 percent of the Piedmont households owned slaves, compared to 70 percent in the Black Belt located south of the Piedmont, and blacks comprised one-fifth of the population statewide in 1850.[41] While slaveholding increased by nearly 15 percent in Crawford and Jasper between 1850 and 1860, it decreased by 3 percent in Franklin over the same period. By 1860, slaves represented less than 30 percent of the population in Franklin County, while they represented more than 50 percent of the population in Crawford and Jasper.[42] The pattern of slaveholding also differed significantly in the Uplands, where half of those who owned slaves held between one and five bondsmen.

39 Hilliard, *Atlas of Antebellum Southern Agriculture*, 39.
40 Hahn, *The Roots of Southern Populism*, 27.
41 Ibid., 24–25.
42 Hilliard, *Atlas of Antebellum Southern Agriculture*, 30.

TABLE 1.3. *Total Population of Crawford, Jasper, and Franklin Counties, 1860*

County	Total Households	Free Pop.	Slave Pop.	% Slaves	Number of Slaveholders	% Slaveholders
Crawford	619	3,423	4,270	56	369	60
Jasper	733	3,789	6,954	65	496	68
Franklin	1,313	6,080	1,313	18	217	17%

Source: "Census Data Year 1860," (2004), *HCB*.

The wealthiest tenth of the population, on the other hand, held 60 percent of the slaves, reflecting a situation where slaveholding was concentrated among the richest citizens – unlike in the Black Belt, where slaveholding was more broadly distributed.[43]

The Georgia Piedmont was in the midst of great economic and social change in 1860. Much of the Lower Piedmont had been incorporated into the Georgia Cotton Belt beginning in the 1830s. Counties like Crawford, located near the heart of the cotton-producing region, were dominated by a planter class that pinned its fortunes on acquiring land and slaves to produce a single staple commodity. Franklin County represented the opposite extreme. Located in the Georgia Uplands and settled by backcountry yeomen from Virginia and the Carolinas, Franklin was rugged and remote enough to encourage self-reliance and the development of a local exchange network. As a result, Upland farmers engaged in mixed agriculture and raised a variety of crops and livestock as a safety-first strategy, whereby they worked to provide for their families before trying to acquire any necessities or niceties that were beyond their skills to produce. Jasper, situated in the Lower Piedmont near the Upland region, was somewhere in between. The expanding cotton economy had arrived and taken hold, although farmers in antebellum Jasper still raised small grains and tobacco, as their predecessors had done. But the record prices cotton was fetching at market as 1861 approached suggested that Georgia's cotton culture would continue to expand and would draw the Piedmont into its orbit as far north as the soil and climate would allow. The war, however, changed everything.

The devastation of the Civil War extended far beyond the battlefield and those who were killed or maimed. For Georgia, it meant $275 million in losses because of the destruction of industry, railroads, and other infrastructure, while property was devalued by nearly 55 percent.[44] In addition, Georgians would have to renegotiate economic and social relationships with their former slaves to accommodate the freedmen's newfound rights (or, sometimes, to try to take

[43] Wright, *Political Economy of the Cotton South*, 24–49; Hahn, *The Roots of Southern Populism*, 25.

[44] Hahn, *The Roots of Southern Populism*, 138.

away those rights). Renewed demand for cotton from abroad, however, presented farmers, both black and white, with an attractive opportunity to succeed in agriculture. For blacks especially, cotton represented a path to landownership and self-sufficiency.[45] With cotton prices outpacing those of most other agricultural products in the early 1870s, cotton production expanded rapidly. This expansion was fueled by the increasing availability of fertilizers that made it possible to grow cotton farther north, beyond its original range, as well as by the efforts of communities throughout the Piedmont to build market towns and railroads to promote the efficient export of the staple.

All of this came at a cost, however, and those who had little or no capital to start a farm were forced into a world of credit and tenancy that took a variety of forms around cash rent and sharecropping. Cash tenants agreed with the landlord at the beginning of the year on a set price to rent fields for the duration of the growing season, whereas those who agreed to a "standing rent" established an amount of the crop that would be provided as payment to the landlord at the end of the season. Renters who entered into an agreement on "Thirds" or "Fourths" received use of land and a house in exchange for giving the landlord one-third or one-quarter of the harvest, depending on what equipment or supplies the renter brought to the arrangement. Sharecropping, the most common form of tenancy for African Americans, was increasingly utilized for those who had no collateral nor anything else to recommend them beyond their labor; it meant theoretically that the crop would be split evenly with the landowner in exchange for everything needed to farm, including land, seed, fertilizer, a mule, housing, and even the provisions needed to sustain the sharecropper's family.[46]

With chronic cash shortages in the South, landlords needed credit too, and they typically agreed to crop liens from the merchants who provided the seed and fertilizer that landlords in turn provided to tenants and croppers. Although the system of tenancy that developed in the South in the early postbellum period theoretically allowed a landless farmer to proceed gradually toward landownership and economic independence, few succeeded – inconsistent cotton harvests, bad credit arrangements, and the long economic depression that began in 1873 and lasted into the mid-1890s made it exceedingly difficult. By 1880, thousands of whites and blacks had failed to meet their quota in crops or had defaulted in some other way; they slipped down the tenancy ladder to swell the

[45] Joseph P. Reidy, "Slavery, Emancipation, and the Capitalist Transformation of Southern Agriculture, 1850–1910," in *Agriculture and National Development: Views on the Nineteenth Century* (Ames: Iowa State University Press, 1990): 229; Gavin Wright, *Old South, New South: Revolutions in the Southern Economy since the Civil War* (New York: Basic Books, 1986): 11.

[46] Edward L. Ayers, *The Promise of the New South* (New York: Oxford University Press, 1992): 195–197; Douglas A. Blackmon, *Slavery by Another Name: The Re-Enslavement of Black Americans from the Civil War to World War II* (New York: Doubleday, 2008): 24–32.

TABLE 1.4. *White and Colored Population in Crawford, Jasper, and Franklin Counties, 1860–1910*[47]

	1860		1870		1880	
	White	Colored	White	Colored	White	Colored
Crawford	3,407	4,286	3,284	4,273	3,940	4,716
Jasper	3,771	6,972	3,884	6,555	4,258	7,593
Franklin	6,308	1,355	6,034	1,859	8,906	2,547
	1890		1900		1910	
	White	Colored	White	Colored	White	Colored
Crawford	4,159	5,156	4,550	5,818	3,388	4,922
Jasper	5,392	8,487	5,388	9,645	5,067	11,484
Franklin	14,760	3,298	13,496	4,204	13,920	3,974

Source: "Census Data Years 1860–1910," (2004), *HCB*.

ranks of sharecroppers.[48] The cropping phenomenon would survive well into the twentieth century, until the Great Depression and the Second World War that followed created a new environment of change.

Farmers throughout the Piedmont experienced the full spectrum of this transition to an ever-greater reliance on tenants and sharecroppers. At the time of the 1870 census, the region was still crippled from the aftereffects of the war; according to the census, property values were down by 25–30 percent and agricultural production had dipped by 40 percent.[49] Major demographic shifts, however, did not occur until later: they are reflected in the 1880 and 1890 censuses, with the number of inhabitants growing slowly in Crawford County, increasing more steadily in Jasper, and fairly exploding in Franklin, which more than doubled in population from 1870 to 1890. Despite these different rates of overall population growth, each county maintained roughly the same ratio of white to black residents (Table 1.4).

Apart from the demographics, the 1870 census indicates that profound change was already under way. Shifts in land-tenure patterns were among the most significant developments (Table 1.5).[50] In Crawford, the tenure group

47 The archaic term "Colored" is used here to accurately reflect the language used reporting census data throughout the period under consideration.

48 Hahn, *The Roots of Southern Populism*, 139; Wright, *Old South, New South*, 69–70; Ayers, *The Promise of the New South*, 195–197.

49 *Eighth Census of the United States, 1860, Agriculture.* Kennedy, 22–29; U.S. Bureau of the Census, *Ninth Census of the United States, 1870, Agriculture.* 120–127. Unlike other Georgia counties, Crawford, Jasper, and Franklin did not experience significant boundary changes after the Civil War.

50 U.S. Bureau of the Census, *Ninth Census of the United States, 1870, Agriculture*, 127.

TABLE 1.5. *Distribution of Landholdings in Crawford, Jasper, and Franklin Counties, 1870*

County	Farms 3–9 Acres	Farms 10–19 Acres	Farms 20–49 Acres	Farms 50–99 Acres	Farms 100–499 Acres	Farms 500–999 Acres	Farms 1,000+ Acres
State average	25	21	166	139	133	11	3
State median	8	17	138	115	120	6	1
State min.	0	0	3	11	1	0	0
State max.	616	120	886	467	402	74	25
Crawford	6	9	78	113	180	13	2
Jasper	6	34	257	176	176	0	1
Franklin	22	98	384	205	86	0	0

Source: "Census Data Year 1870," (2004), *HCB*.

of 100–499 acres was still the most common one: before the war, nearly 60 percent of the farmers had fallen into that group; in 1870, less than half did. Jasper represented an even more marked example of the same trend: 76 percent of farms had been larger than 100 acres before the war, and 73 percent were smaller than 100 acres in 1870. In Jasper, the most common tenure class shifted from 100–499 acres to 20–49 acres. Although Franklin County also showed a downward shift in parcel size among farmers, it was not as dramatic as in Crawford or Jasper. In 1860, 80 percent of parcels in Franklin were smaller than 100 acres, with landholdings in the 20–49-acre range being the most common. The twenty-to-forty-nine-acre tenure class remained the norm following the war, but the number of farms operating with fewer than twenty acres grew significantly. While the pattern of land tenure in the Uplands had always favored smaller holdings, these data suggest the entry of new farmers into the local economy.

By 1880 the pattern of landholding had changed yet again, with a significant increase in the total number of farms in each county: a 55 percent rise in Crawford County farms, 41 percent in Jasper, and 52 percent in Franklin. Like the decrease in average farm size, this may reflect the number of black farmers who had been able to establish farms over the previous decade. A new pattern had also developed in all three counties, wherein more than 60 percent of landholdings fell into two tenure classes: 20–49 acres and 100–499 acres (Table 1.6). In virtually every case, the number of farms in the twenty-to-forty-nine-acre tenure class more than doubled. More surprising is that the 100–149-acre class grew by 53 percent in Crawford, 65 percent in Jasper, and an astounding 84 percent in Franklin between 1870 and 1880. Although there was convergence in the overall pattern of land tenure, the average farm size in 1880 reflected the earlier pattern differentiating the Cotton Belt counties from the Uplands. The average farm in Crawford and Jasper operated with 188 and

TABLE 1.6. *Distribution of Landholdings in Crawford, Jasper, and Franklin Counties, 1880*

County	Farms >3 Acres	Farms 3–9 Acres	Farms 10–19 Acres	Farms 20–49 Acres	Farms 50–99 Acres	Farms 100–499 Acres	Farms 500–999 Acres	Farms 1,000+ Acres
State average	1	23	63	267	190	391	51	25
State median	0	12	39	223	173	381	46	19
State min.	0	0	3	7	6	35	7	0
State max.	14	396	308	1,460	575	920	152	23
Crawford	2	12	24	242	179	387	48	9
Jasper	2	10	68	236	217	500	57	23
Franklin	6	61	278	472	240	554	58	9

Source: "Census Data Year 1880," (2004), *HCB*.

180 acres, respectively, while Franklin county farms averaged 120 acres.[51] While the pattern of two predominate tenure classes persisted into the twentieth century, the average size of landholdings continued to decrease, likely reflecting the impact of the economic depression that persisted into the 1890s.

These patterns in land tenure, including their racial components, are evident in state tax reports as well as in the federal census – particularly after 1890, when the worst effects of the economic depression were beginning to be felt (Table 1.7). Crawford and Jasper show a similar pattern: the number of white polls – taxable individuals – remains fairly steady between 1890 and 1910, while the average acreage and land value dip until 1905, rebounding through 1910. This reflects the overall trend in the economy, with a period of decline through the turn of the century and the beginnings of a recovery shortly thereafter. There is a different pattern in Franklin County, where the number of polls increased until 1910, when they dipped slightly, but the average property size and value declined consistently over the entire period.

The tax data for African-American taxpayers from Crawford, Jasper, and Franklin counties display the stark differences in wealth between them and their white neighbors (Table 1.7). While the number of black taxpayers (polls) in each county fluctuated, as it did for whites (reflecting slight changes in demography and the tax base), the average parcel among black landowners in Crawford and Franklin in 1890 was roughly twenty times smaller than the average parcel size countywide; in Jasper, African Americans' farms were almost fifty times smaller than the average. Similarly, the property of black landholders was worth twenty-three times less than that of whites in Crawford and Franklin, and was worth almost forty-four times less than white-owned property in Jasper County. The situation improved slightly by 1910, when the

[51] Roland M. Harper, "Development of Agriculture in Upper Georgia from 1850 to 1880," *GHQ* 6, no. 1 (1922): 3–27. The average throughout the Georgia Piedmont was 178 acres.

TABLE 1.7. *Comparison of Land Tax Values of White and Colored Property Owners in Crawford, Franklin, and Jasper Counties, 1890–1910*

County	Race	Year	Polls	Total Acres of Land	Average Acreage Per Owner	Total Value of Land	Average Land Value
Crawford	White	1890	694	180,224	260	$475,783	$686
Crawford	Colored	1890	663	8,674	13	$19,438	$29
Franklin	White	1890	1,740	196,913	113	$1,048,640	$603
Franklin	Colored	1890	429	2,287	5	$11,318	$26
Jasper	White	1890	911	221,936	244	$770,730	$846
Jasper	Colored	1890	1,078	5,389	5	$20,053	$19
Crawford	White	1895	751	184,385	246	$507,210	$675
Crawford	Colored	1895	716	9,291	13	$23,265	$32
Franklin	White	1895	1,998	191,447	96	$932,314	$467
Franklin	Colored	1895	449	3,657	8	$13,985	$31
Jasper	White	1895	1,033	214,784	208	$703,921	$681
Jasper	Colored	1895	1,157	5,550	5	$19,351	$17
Crawford	White	1900	853	189,878	223	$550,107	$645
Crawford	Colored	1900	685	9,048	13	$26,321	$38
Franklin	White	1900	2,247	192,553	86	$948,033	$422
Franklin	Colored	1900	586	2,626	4	$9,539	$16
Jasper	White	1900	1,014	221,561	219	$746,142	$736
Jasper	Colored	1900	1,032	5,534	5	$20,454	$20
Crawford	White	1905	769	198,459	258	$638,099	$830
Crawford	Colored	1905	869	12,579	14	$47,386	$55
Franklin	White	1905	2,383	192,356	81	$1,125,639	$472
Franklin	Colored	1905	538	3,915	7	$16,072	$30
Jasper	White	1905	1,036	216,454	209	$799,306	$772
Jasper	Colored	1905	1,439	11,518	8	$41,121	$29
Crawford	White	1910	639	191,230	299	$680,745	$1,065
Crawford	Colored	1910	608	17,491	29	$59,689	$98
Franklin	White	1910	2,137	146,202	68	$1,198,145	$561
Franklin	Colored	1910	379	2,867	8	$24,229	$64
Jasper	White	1910	1,010	210,045	208	$898,457	$890
Jasper	Colored	1910	1,725	17,364	10	$80,685	$47

Source: William A. Wright, General Manager, *RCG*, 1890; William A. Wright, General Manager, *RCG*, 1900; William A. Wright, General Manager, *RCG*, 1910.

average black farmer in Crawford and Franklin controlled one-tenth as much land as his white neighbors (and black-owned land was worth on average one-tenth as much). The average African American in Jasper County worked a piece of property that was twenty times smaller than the average white landholding and worth eighteen times less.

TABLE 1.8. *Improved Acreage in Crawford, Jasper, and Franklin Counties, 1890–1910*

	1890	1895	1900	1905	1910
Number of improved acres					
Crawford	188,918	193,676	198,926	211,038	208,721
Jasper	227,325	220,334	227,095	227,972	227,409
Franklin	199,200	195,104	195,179	196,271	149,069
Aggregate value of improved acreage					
Crawford	$495,221	$530,475	$576,428	$685,485	$740,434
Jasper	$790,783	$723,272	$766,596	$840,427	$979,142
Franklin	$1,059,958	$946,299	$957,572	$1,141,711	$1,222,374
Average value of improved land by acre					
Crawford	$2.62	$2.74	$2.84	$3.24	$3.52
Jasper	$3.47	$3.28	$3.37	$3.69	$3.39
Franklin	$5.32	$4.84	$4.71	$5.82	$8.15

Note: Poll numbers come from the Comptroller General reports for the State of Georgia, while Population numbers are from the federal census for the years 1890 through 1910.

Source: Harrison, *RCG*, 1890; Harrison, *RCG*, 1895; Harrison, *RCG*, 1900; Harrison, *RCG*, 1905; Harrison, *RCG*, 1910.

The changes in landholding in the Georgia Piedmont are indicative of shifts in labor and in agricultural focus as more farmers began to grow cotton as a staple. Planters in Crawford and Jasper who had previously relied on slave labor condensed their holdings to a size that was economically feasible to operate with a reduced labor force comprised of family members, tenants, croppers, or hired laborers. The price of cotton relative to the value of other crops also encouraged the change – especially in the Upper Piedmont, where mixed agriculture had been the long-standing practice. Cotton provided an attractive alternative to grain and other crops for farmers in the Uplands because it was cheaper and easier to transport to market, and it held out the possibility of considerable profits when prices were high.[52] As a result, tenant farmers, sharecroppers, and yeomen dedicated ever-increasing amounts of their acreage to the crop (especially when prices went up), and the cotton yield in Georgia increased.[53] The significant uptick in the amount of improved acreage on farms in Crawford, Jasper, and Franklin counties, as well as the rising value of that land, suggests that farmers were maximizing the amount of land in cotton (Table 1.8).

[52] Hahn, *The Roots of Southern Populism*, 141–143; Frederick A. Bode and Donald E. Ginter, *Farm Tenancy and the Census in Antebellum Georgia* (Athens: University of Georgia Press, 1986): 79.

[53] Willard Range, *A Century of Georgia Agriculture, 1850–1950* (Athens: University of Georgia Press, 1954): 116.

TABLE 1.9. *Cotton Production in Crawford, Jasper, and Franklin Counties, 1880 and 1910*

County	Year	Land Area (sq. miles)	Acres	Acres in Cotton	Bales Produced	Bales Per Acre
Crawford	1880	340	53,531	24,754	6,765	0.27
Jasper	1880	380	87,203	27,600	6,741	0.24
Franklin	1880	330	61,117	16,901	5,723	0.34
Crawford	1910	340	53,531	23,011	8,424	0.37
Jasper	1910	380	87,203	68,168	25,848	0.38
Franklin	1910	330	61,117	43,595	19,312	0.44

Note: Agricultural schedules for 1880 and 1910 set the bale weight at 475 pounds.
Source: Loughridge, "Report on the Cotton Production of the State of Georgia," *Tenth Census, June 1, 1880*. Washington, DC: GPO, 1882, 269–270; U.S. Bureau of the Census, *Thirteenth Census of the United States, 1910, VI, Agriculture, 1909 and 1910: Alabama-Montana* (Washington, DC: GPO, 1913), 361–365.

Dr. R. H. Loughridge's report on cotton production in Georgia, included as part of the agricultural schedule of the 1880 federal census, suggests how important cotton had become to Franklin County farmers and to the local economy since the end of the war (Table 1.9).[54] Cotton was grown on nearly 28 percent of tilled land in Franklin in 1879, while 31 percent of the fields in Jasper and over 46 percent in Crawford were devoted to cotton production. The statistics also provide some indication of the relative fertility and productivity of the soil among the three counties. All three fell near the middle of the curve in terms of cotton production among the fifty-five Middle Georgia counties, where the output ranged from a low of 2,635 bales (Glascock County) to a high of 18,655 bales (Troup County, where cotton was farmed intensively). The traditional Cotton Belt counties (Crawford and Jasper) each produced slightly more than 6,700 bales on about 25,000 acres, while Franklin County farmers harvested 5,723 bales from 16,901 acres. Whereas the two Cotton Belt counties outproduced the Upland county by 15 percent, the output per acre in Franklin was greater – more than one-third of a bale, compared to about one-quarter of a bale in Crawford and Jasper. Not only had cotton become more important in Franklin, its future looked more promising to the Upland farmers than it did to those in the traditional Cotton Belt counties. The greater output per acre in Franklin was almost certainly because cotton was just being introduced into the county's crop regime and the land had not yet experienced the soil exhaustion prevalent in counties where cotton had been grown for decades.

54 U.S. Bureau of the Census, *Tenth Census of the United States, 1880*, "Report on the Cotton Production of the State of Georgia, with a Description of the General Agricultural Features of the State" (Washington, DC, 1882), 269–270.

By 1910, the amount of land devoted to cotton in Crawford County had diminished by 7 percent, yet the overall output increased by nearly 2,000 bales. Productivity had climbed to well over one-third of a bale per acre, probably reflecting the more intensive use of guano and other fertilizers (Table 1.9). In Jasper County, farmers increased their cotton output to nearly 26,000 bales in 1909, representing a 74 percent rise over the 1879 harvest. They had increased the amount of land in cotton by 60 percent, and the average yield per acre was up by 38 percent. Jasper County farmers were confident enough in the crop to devote more than 80 percent of their fields to it. Franklin County also shifted to cotton in a major way from 1879 to 1909, with production up by 70 percent and cotton accounting for nearly three-quarters of the tilled acreage in the county, where less than a third had been in cotton in 1879.

As Piedmont farmers became more engaged in cotton in the 1870s, they began to understand the critical need to acquire railroad access and to develop market towns offering a wide variety of trades, services, and amenities, especially in the Uplands. Railroads promised an efficient, cost-effective way for farmers to connect with the national and international cotton markets on which they now placed their hopes for success. While Georgia had more extensive rail development than most other Southern states prior to the war, there was no rail access to Crawford, Jasper, or Franklin. Following the war, boosters in the three counties worked feverishly to lobby the railroad companies and woo investors, hoping to convince them in each case that this particular locality held great economic potential. Franklin County promoters, for example, encouraged the developers of the Seaboard Railroad to build their line through the heart of the county, with a stop at Carnesville (the county seat), on its way north along the Atlantic coast.[55] When these efforts failed and the Seaboard decided to lay its track just north of the county, entrepreneurs from Franklin and neighboring Hart County developed a plan to build a connector from Royston (on the border of the two counties) to Toccoa, in Stephens County, where the main Seaboard line would have a stop. Local boosters began construction of the connector, called the Elberton Air Line, in 1875, after having attracted investors and secured the permission of Seaboard management to make a connection with their rails in Toccoa. Once completed in 1878, the Elberton Air Line began service with two locomotives, two passenger cars, fourteen boxcars, and six flat cars, offering daily freight and passenger service.

Crawford and Jasper counties succeeded in getting rail service with slightly less effort. In 1886, the Atlanta & Florida Railroad completed its tracks through

[55] Sam Bowers Hilliard, "The Rails Come to Town," in *Lavonia, Georgia: Then & Now, 1880–2005*. Compiled by the Lavonia Historic Preservation Commission and the Franklin County Resource, Conservation, and Development Council (Franklin Springs, GA: Lavonia Historic Preservation Commission and the Franklin County Resource, Conservation, and Development Council, 2005), 116.

Atlanta and Fort Valley with a whistle stop at New Knoxville in Crawford County, while the Covington and Macon Railroad began building the first rail line through Jasper in 1885 and completed the project three years later.[56] The 106-mile connector from Athens to Macon, with stops in the Jasper towns of Adgateville, Minneta, Machen, and Madison, provided three daily trains, including a through freight, a local freight, and the Fast Mail.[57]

Rail access proved to be a critical element in the development of towns following the Civil War. Shady Dale, in Jasper County, is a case in point. The only incorporated town in Jasper before 1900 besides Monticello (the county seat), Shady Dale was on the road from Covington to Milledgeville, the state capital until 1868. It began to languish once the capital was moved to Atlanta – that is, until the train came through in the late 1880s. What had been a sleepy crossroads developed into a vibrant depot town, with a cotton gin, a grocer, two general stores, two blacksmiths, and two sawmills. In Crawford County, by contrast, city leaders refused to allow the Atlanta & Florida Railroad to pass through Knoxville, then the county seat.[58] Railroad-company planners therefore decided to create a town called New Knoxville a short distance away and built their rails there. By 1900, the town, renamed Roberta, had outgrown its reluctant neighbor.[59]

The arrival of the railroad also led to the county seat being eclipsed in Franklin. Carnesville had been the center of the county since its founding, but its inhospitable terrain worked against it when it came time to build a railway connector. Instead, the Elberton Air Line was routed from Royston, at the southeast corner of the county, up through Aquilla on the way to the Toccoa junction. Aquilla was renamed Lavonia once the railroad came through, and it quickly grew to be the largest town in the county. By the turn of the century, Lavonia could boast a cottonseed-oil mill, a flour mill, the Lavonia Gin Company, the Lavonia Cotton Mill, Stevenson's Brick Mills, and the Mason, Randall & Company lumber and sawmills, in addition to two hotels, two churches, a school called the Lavonia Institute, and the Bank of Lavonia.[60]

A great deal had changed in the Georgia Piedmont by the time James Bowman of Crawford County submitted his loan application in 1890. Upland

[56] Hilliard, "The Rails Come to Town," 116; Emmie Carnes Bankston, *History of Roberta and Crawford County, Georgia* (Macon: Omni Press, 1976): 13.

[57] Bankston, *History of Roberta and Crawford County, Georgia*, 20; Marcia Hayes Carnes, John P. Harvey, and Irene Roberts Malone. *History of Jasper County, Georgia* (Fernandina Beach: Wolfe Publishing, 1984): 44–45.

[58] The city leaders were afraid of the noise, the filth, and the rabble that they felt the railroad would introduce into their community, so they assumed that they could reap the benefits of the railroad by letting an adjacent community serve as the rail stop.

[59] Carnes, *History of Jasper County, Georgia*, 44; *Crawford County Sesquicentennial, Roberta, Georgia*, 16–17.

[60] Anna Belle Little Tabor. *History of Franklin County, Georgia* (Fernandina Beach: Wolfe Publishing, 2004): 366–367.

farmers did not share all of the traditions of their neighbors to the south, but they too had turned to cotton as their crop of choice, as those in the Lower Piedmont had done decades before the Civil War. The increased availability of fertilizers extended the range of cotton production northward, extensive rail service throughout the Piedmont made it feasible to transport the crop cheaply, and credit was widely available to provide farmers, even those who had little or no capital, with the opportunity to earn enough to buy their own farms.

While cotton cultivation expanded into the Uplands, the culture and land-tenure patterns of the Uplands expanded into the Lower Piedmont. The realities of the New South economy led to an expansion of the ranks of yeoman farmers, who worked smaller plots and struggled to balance self-sufficiency with the ability to grow enough cotton to produce a profit. The Upland yeoman tradition of self-reliance had become the measure of success for cotton farmers throughout the Piedmont. Indeed, they worked like James Bowman: they looked for ways to expand cotton production while growing enough of staples (such as corn, oats, potatoes, and sorghum) to sustain their family and livestock through the growing season, and they looked for opportunities to diversify production, which would provide a fallback for the family in bad years as well as an opportunity to capitalize on other opportunities and markets when times were good.

2

Land, Households, and Race in the Georgia Piedmont

The Big Picture

In the early 1880s, many farmers in Georgia were anxious to make sense of the South that had emerged in the years following the Civil War. They were learning to adapt to a world without slavery but found it difficult to define the place in society for freed men and women who would now ostensibly enjoy the same rights and opportunities that whites knew. Moreover, they hoped to distance themselves from the image of the Old South even as an increasing number of Georgians were being pulled into the cotton economy that served as the basis for Georgia's antebellum plantation culture. There were those who, like the journalist Henry Woodfin Grady, saw an opportunity in courting Northern capital and were eager to proclaim the death of a South "of slavery and secession" and the birth of a New South of "Union and Freedom." This New South, Grady wrote, would be characterized by "a social system, compact and closely knitted, less splendid on the surface, but stronger at the core – a hundred farms for every plantation, fifty homes for every palace – and a diversified industry that meets the complex needs of this complex age."[1]

Then there were those who, like the poet Sidney Lanier, looked suspiciously on the lure of increased commercial and industrial ties with the North, as well as on the expansion of King Cotton's dominion. He declared, "the New South means small farming," and he articulated a vision of an agricultural system in which yeoman farmers were completely self-sufficient – there would be "no notes in the bank," everything needed on the farm would be "made and sold (instead of bought)," and farmers would produce "a hundred other items all representing income from a hundred sources."[2] Finally, there were those

[1] Henry Woodfin Grady, *The Speeches of Henry W. Grady with a Short Biographical Sketch of His Life* (Atlanta: Charles P. Byrd, 1895): 9–18.

[2] Sydney Lanier "The New South," in *Retrospects and Prospects: Descriptive and Historical Essays*, 2nd ed. (New York: Charles Scribner's Sons, 1899); 104, 110.

who, like the Populist leader Tom Watson, believed that Georgia lawmakers should do everything possible to promote the interests of small farmers no matter what they produced, and that Georgia should resist Northern business interests at all costs. At a meeting of the State Agricultural Society in Atlanta in 1883, Watson made an impassioned speech in which he urged his fellow Georgians to compete with the Yankees "in everything but their religion and morals," exhorting them to "Get rich! Sell everything marketable and live on the culls . . . and Georgia . . . will not only be the empire state of the South, but in less than half a century will be the empire state of the whole union."[3]

Grady, Lanier, and Watson may have disagreed on the role of industrialization, commercial development, and Northern involvement in Georgia's future, but each agreed that the small farmer was crucial to the success of the New South. This allegiance may have stemmed from the fact that all three were born and raised in the Georgia Piedmont, where yeoman farmers owning fewer than 175 acres comprised the majority of the farming population.[4] While it is difficult to say how the farmers themselves struggled with and reconciled these competing visions, historians of the postbellum South generally agree that farmers in many areas became more engaged in cotton following the Civil War and moved away from mixed agriculture.[5] As the focus on cotton production intensified, farmers became less self-sufficient, as they produced fewer crops for home consumption and became increasingly reliant on outside sources for food and supplies. The intensification of cotton monoculture, in turn, was hastened by farmers with few resources who often chose to invest entirely in the crop that promised the greatest financial reward. Landlords and furnishing merchants reinforced this pattern when they extended credit to farmers on the condition that they devote the majority of their production to cotton, in order to maximize the return on loans.

Historians have established the broad contours of this transition, in large part, through the use of census and tax data aggregated at the county level. This approach has proven to be useful for characterizing economic and social conditions down to the local level, as well as for demonstrating change over time; however, it does little to elucidate how individual farmers struggled

[3] C. Vann Woodward, *Tom Watson: Agrarian Rebel* (Savannah: Beehive Press, 1973): 118–119.

[4] Henry Grady was from Athens, Sydney Lanier was born in Macon, and Tom Watson was raised thirty-five miles west of Augusta, in a part of Columbia County that is now McDuffie County.

[5] Ferleger, "Self-Sufficiency and Rural Life on Southern Farms"; Roger Ransom and Richard Sutch, *One Kind of Freedom*, 151–56; Gavin Wright and Howard Kunreuther, "Cotton, Corn, and Risk in the Nineteenth Century," *Journal of Economic History* 35, no. 3 (1975): 526–527; Gavin Wright, *Political Economy* (New York: W. W. Norton, 1978), 164–166; Peter Temin, "Patterns of Cotton Agriculture in Post-Bellum Georgia," *Journal of Economic History* 43, no. 3 (September 1983): 661–674; David F. Weiman, "The Economic Emancipation of the Non-Slaveholding Class: Upcountry Farmers in the Georgia Cotton Economy," *Journal of Economic History* 45, no. 1 (March 1985): 71–72.

with and attempted to resolve questions concerning the risks and rewards in achieving self-sufficiency, diversifying production, or specializing in the production of a single staple crop. Probate inventories provide an opportunity to sharpen the focus of historical inquiries to the household level by providing a relatively precise accounting of household assets at the time of death. The power and potential of probate inventories lie in the meticulous detail they provide about household possessions, which is very often sufficient to determine the particular types of tools and equipment used on a farm, the varieties of crops and livestock raised, and the condition of the assets. This fine-grained level of description allows for informed judgments about how decedents invested their resources. By using inventories in conjunction with countywide tax assessments, decennial census data, and other probate documents, such as estate-sale records, it is possible to identify trends in household and farm assets across a population and over time.

The possessions revealed through estate inventories provide a glimpse into the ways in which individual farmers from a variety of wealth levels in Middle Georgia optimized their chances of success under challenging circumstances. The items they accumulated offer clues to the farmers' range of production, their level of self-sufficiency, and the strategies they employed to maximize output and limit risk. Probate inventories provide crucial details on how farmers organized their household economies to provide some insurance against disaster even as they struggled to succeed. Furthermore, they indicate the degree to which farmers in the Georgia Piedmont employed new technologies and labor-saving devices to gain a productive edge that would free them from creditors and the need to pay for additional labor. Examining these lists of household possessions, we can define patterns of acquisition and use within regions as well as trends across time, allowing us to more fully assess the extent of change that occurred in the Georgia Piedmont in the early years of the New South. It is important, however, to first determine the degree to which the probate records for the three Piedmont counties are representative. Establishing the proper context for the probate data from Crawford, Jasper, and Franklin is possible using demographic data provided by the decennial federal censuses and focusing on the variables of age, race, gender, and family size, as well as the patterns of land tenure and mortality as reflected in the probate sample.

A probate inventory is simply a list of possessions compiled on behalf of a deceased person by an estate administrator who was either preselected by the decedent and named in a will or, more commonly, appointed by a local court. From a historian's perspective, probate inventories can be quantified and measured effectively, since they often list the number of items as well as an appraised value, and they record with considerable accuracy a person's possessions at a given point in time. It is also possible to quantify changes in the assets present in households by comparing patterns of data from different years. Moreover, the goods listed in inventories reflect a person's consumer choices,

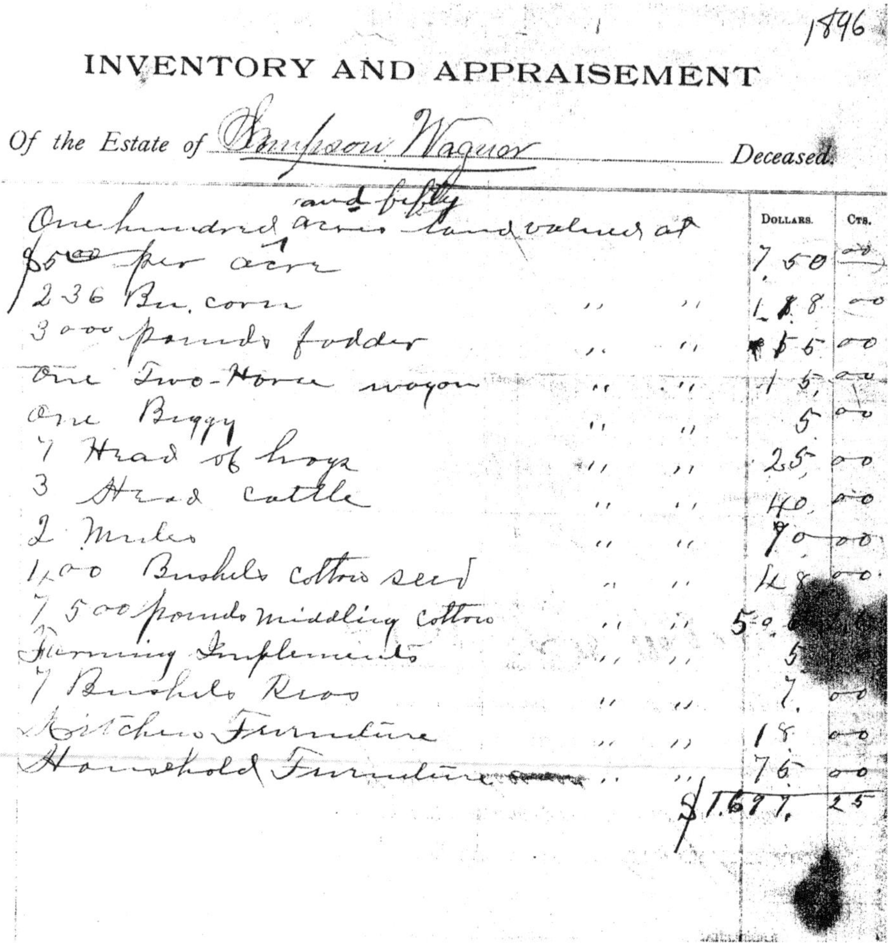

1896

INVENTORY AND APPRAISEMENT

Of the Estate of Sampson Wagner *Deceased.*

	Dollars.	Cts.
One hundred and fifty acres land valued at $5.00 per acre	750	00
236 Bu. corn " "	188	00
3000 pounds fodder " "	55	00
One Two-Horse wagon " "	15	00
One Buggy " "	5	00
7 Head of hogs " "	25	00
3 Head cattle " "	40	00
2 Mules " "	70	00
1,200 Bushels cotton seed " "	48	00
7500 pounds middling cotton " "	59[illegible]	[illegible]
Farming Implements " "	5	[illegible]
7 Bushels Peas " "	7	00
Kitchen Furniture " "	18	00
Household Furniture " "	76	00
	$1.697.	25

FIGURE 2.1. Inventory and appraisement of the estate of Sampson Wagner of Jasper County, deceased, 1896. From the collections of the *Georgia Archives, Morrow.*

values, and worldview. Changes in these ideals are often difficult for scholars to discern, but they become evident when individual inventories are compared to others from different regions or time periods. That is, "One does not learn of these changes much from letters, diaries, or other personal records . . . one finds most of the answers to such questions in probate records."[6]

Although inventories typically offer consistent types of information, they have their weaknesses. The level of detail, for example, varies widely among inventories even within the same time period and region. Given that most

[6] Lorena S. Walsh, "Urban Amenities and Rural Sufficiency," *Journal of Economic History* 43, no. 1 (March 1983): 109.

administrators were not legal professionals – usually they were family members, acquaintances, or neighbors – they often provided just enough description to meet the needs of the court in assigning value to the estate. Some item-level descriptions are so brief that it is difficult to say much, if anything, about the object. "One plow," for instance, tells us nothing of its type or condition. Moreover, appraisers deemed some items so mundane that no elaboration was called for, as in the case of "one box," or "cans." Appraisers throughout Georgia also lumped possessions together whenever possible, listing such things as "bedroom furniture," "household goods," "one lot of books," or even "plunder," a term commonly used throughout the Piedmont to refer to the low-value miscellanea that accumulate in virtually every household. Undervaluation reflecting age, quality, or condition is another variable that is difficult to detect, especially when the appraiser failed to use a modifier or to provide other, more specific descriptive information.[7] Inventories also regularly omit certain categories of goods, especially personal items such as clothing, jewelry, heirlooms, pets, and toys. Nor would goods given prior to death, bequeathed in a will, or belonging to the decedent's spouse show up on a probate inventory.

Another drawback of probate records is that they are not necessarily representative of society as a whole.[8] Scholars estimate that the proportion of the population represented through probate records varies widely, ranging from 10 to 80 percent depending on regional conditions and legal tradition.[9] While some might believe those statistics should deter historians from using probate inventories to generalize about entire populations, others argue that entry into the probate process was "neither random nor unsystematic."[10] For Crawford,

[7] Alice Hanson Jones, "Estimating Wealth of the Living from a Probate Sample," *Journal of Interdisciplinary History* 13, no. 2 (Autumn 1982): 275–276.

[8] Carole Shammas, "Constructing a Wealth Distribution from Probate Records," *Journal of Interdisciplinary History* 9, no. 2 (Autumn 1978): 297.

[9] Kenneth Lockridge, "A Communication," *William and Mary Quarterly*, 3rd ser., 25 (1968): 516–517; Alice Hanson Jones, "Wealth Estimates for the American Middle Colonies, 1774," *Economic Development and Cultural Change* 18, no. 4, part 2 (July 1970): i–x, 1–172; Daniel Scott Smith, "Underregistration and Bias in Probate Records: An Analysis of Data from Eighteenth-Century Hingham, Massachusetts," *William and Mary Quarterly*, 3rd ser., 32, no. 1 (January 1975): 100–110; Lockridge estimates that 10 to 80 percent of inventories survive in the Northeast, while Alice Hanson Jones argues that 71.8 percent of the decedents in the Middle Colonies were probated while only 32.7 percent of New Englanders were probated in 1774. Daniel Scott Smith's finding of 36 percent of male decedents and 6 percent of female decedents having been probated in eighteenth-century Hingham, Massachusetts, conforms to Jones' findings for New England.

[10] Holly V. Izard, "Another Place in Time: The Material and Social Worlds of Sturbridge, Massachusetts, from Settlement to 1850" (PhD diss., Boston University, 1996), 59. Izard found that decedents were represented in the probate record in Sturbridge, Massachusetts if they had written a will, owned real property at the time of death, left minors in need of support, had notes due on their estate, or if they were insolvent. Ultimately, the involvement of an estate in probate was due to the "expressed intent [of the testator or the administrator] to settle the financial affairs and distribute the material effects of the deceased." See page 67.

Jasper, and Franklin counties between 1880 and 1910, the probated population is not entirely representative, in that it excludes the very poor (who had little or no money and few possessions of value) and the very wealthy (who relied on wills to specify their wishes as to the transmission of their property, or who disposed of the bulk of their estates prior to death). Yet a broad cross section of Piedmont society is represented in probate cases, including most if not all of the wealth classes in each county between 1880 and 1910. Nevertheless, it is necessary to attempt to establish context and detect bias. Scholars who use probate inventories routinely employ tax lists and census records to determine the representativeness and wealth of the probated population relative to the broader population, and we follow that approach as well.[11]

The household and farm possessions represented in inventories can be measured in a number of ways. The simplest method is to count the frequency with which objects appear in order to show the introduction, acceptance, and spread of new goods, such as clocks, sewing machines, and steam engines. Alternatively, because consumption is a cyclical process, the same method can demonstrate when objects become obsolete or fall out of fashion. Historians have also looked at the values listed in inventories to infer wealth and expenditure patterns. This is risky, however, since the relationship between consumption costs and the value ascribed to goods in an inventory is unclear.[12]

Another approach to using probate inventories is to note the increase in quantity of certain items. For example, the number of specialized dishes and eating utensils increased rapidly over the course of the eighteenth century, as Georgian ideals of symmetry and gentility took hold in Anglo-American society.[13] Whereas the yeoman farmer living in the seventeenth century ate his entire evening meal off of a single trencher using a knife, the genteel American wife of the early nineteenth century entertained with elaborate place settings where a different dish was provided for each course and guests were given multiple utensils, each fulfilling very specific functions.[14] Likewise, the farm family of the late nineteenth century had far greater access than its eighteenth-century counterpart to a burgeoning world of consumption, once mass

11 Gloria L. Main, "Probate Records as a Source for Early American History," *William and Mary* Quarterly 3rd ser., 32, no. 1 (January 1975): 98–99; Smith, "Underregistration and Bias in Probate Records," 110; Jones, "Estimating Wealth," 279; Shammas. "Constructing a Wealth Distribution from Probate Records," 297.

12 Overton et al., *Production and Consumption in English Households, 1600–1750* (New York: Routledge, 2004): 88.

13 Cary Carson. "The Consumer Revolution in Colonial British America, Why Demand?" in *Of Consuming Interests: The Style of Life in the Eighteenth Century* (Charlottesville: Published for the United States Capitol Historical Society by the University of Virginia Press, 1994): 483–700.

14 James Deetz, *In Small Things Forgotten: An Archaeology of Early American Life* (New York: Anchor Books/Doubleday, 1976); Richard Bushman, *The Refinement of America* (New York: Knopf, 1992), 1–5; Cary Carson, "The Consumer Revolution" in *Of Consuming Interests*, 483–485.

production brought costs down and new distribution networks made goods easier to transport.

Inheritance laws vary considerably by region, and Georgia, like anywhere else, had its own practices and traditions. Under English common law, a decedent's entire estate passed automatically to the eldest male heir (the primogeniture system), and this was the case in Georgia until 1777, when the newly established state legislature introduced a system that favored a more equitable transfer of wealth among heirs.[15] Another change was the practice of separating the real and the personal estate during probate. Although both forms of property could be used to satisfy debts, land passed immediately to the heirs, unless otherwise directed, whereas all other property was probated for distribution to heirs and creditors.[16] Legislators also appointed a register of probate in each county and created a lower court called the Court of Ordinary, or the Court Ordinary, to handle the administration of estates within the localities.[17] The Courts Ordinary were empowered to direct distribution of assets among heirs, oversee the accounting of estates, hear and resolve disputed claims, divide land, and direct the sale of possessions to satisfy debts.[18] Decisions made in these courts could be appealed to a superior court.

Those who died with a will were "testate," while those who failed to provide a last testament were "intestate." Georgia law concerning wills was very permissive prior to the twentieth century, and there was wide latitude in what constituted a will – it did not have to follow any prescribed form or directives on wording, it just had to be written. Although the legal age of majority in Georgia was twenty-one, state law allowed individuals aged fourteen and older to make a binding will. In fact, any free person could make a will unless he or she suffered some disability arising "from a want of capacity, or a want of perfect liberty of action."[19] A will took effect immediately upon the death of the testator, and the deceased's directives were to be carried out by an executor or executrix named in the will.

Settling an estate was much more involved in cases of intestacy. Representatives of the deceased were urged to enter the estate into probate as soon

15 Lee J. Alston and Morton Owen Schapiro, "Inheritance Laws Across Colonies: Causes and Consequences," *Journal of Economic History* 44, no. 2; – ," The Tasks of Economic History," (June 1984): 278.

16 Richard H. Clark, Thomas Read Rootes Cobb, and David Irwin, *The Code of the State of Georgia* (Atlanta: Franklin Steam Printing House, 1867): Pt. 2, Tit, 6, Chap. 3, Art. 2, §1782 & §2371.

17 Lewis M. Simes and Paul E. Basye, "The Organization of the Probate Court in America, I," *Michigan Law Review* 42, no. 6 (June 1944): 992; Simes and Basye, "The Organization of the Probate Court in America, II," *Michigan Law Review* 43, no. 1 (August 1944): 119.

18 Simes and Basye, "Probate Court in America, I," 992.

19 Richard H. Clark, Thomas Read Rootes Cobb, and David Irwin, *The Code of the State of Georgia* (Atlanta: Franklin Steam Printing House, 1867): Pt. 2, Tit, 6, Chap. 3, Art. 2, §2359–§2371.

as practicable, but they had up to a year to begin the process. One initiated probate by appearing before the Court Ordinary to submit a letter of administration seeking the appointment of an overseer, or administrator, for the estate. The spouse of the deceased typically had the right to be administrator; if there was no spouse, then the order of preference descended through the next of kin, from children to parents and then siblings. In cases where there were no close relatives, or none willing to serve as administrator, the judge, known as the Ordinary, selected an acquaintance or a creditor "with the greatest interest in the estate."[20] Once the selection was made, the court published a citation announcing the appointment in a local newspaper for thirty days, in order to provide sufficient time for anyone to challenge the decision.

After thirty days without objection, the appointed administrator was sworn in and posted a bond worth up to double the value of the estate – a security deposit to ensure that the duties of administrator would be faithfully executed according to the law. Once this was done, the administrator typically submitted a petition for the support of the widow in cases where there was a surviving spouse or minors, which allowed the widow to draw support from the estate until an appraisement could be made and a distribution calculated "according to the circumstances and standing of the family previous to the death of the testator or intestate, and keeping in view also the solvency of the estate."[21] The Ordinary also issued a warrant of appraisement directing five "disinterested" freeholders within the county to "fairly and justly" appraise the value of the personal and real property of the deceased; their appraisement was to be presented to the administrator within sixty days.[22] The administrator was then required to take the appraisement and produce the inventory, which had to be submitted to the court within four months of the date of the warrant. For many intestacy cases the probate process ended at this point, given the statutory directive that estates worth less than $500 were provided in their entirety to the widow and her children.[23] Those appraised for more were subject to the lengthy rules of inheritance and distribution.

According to Georgia law, the rules of descent in cases of intestacy dictated that the husband was the sole heir of his wife's estate, whereas the wife only enjoyed lifetime use of her husband's land and possessions. In cases where there were no children, she became the sole heir and inherited all of the property. If there were children, the wife and each child were entitled to an equal share. She could, however, elect to take her dower, which provided her with the use of one-third of the land for the remainder of her life.[24] In the absence of a living spouse, inheritance proceeded to the children and the father of the deceased, then the lineal descendents of the children, and then on to the siblings of

20 Clark, Cobb, and Irwin, *Code of Georgia*, Pt. 2, Tit, 6, Chap. 3, Art. 2, §2459.

21 Ibid., §2632.

22 Ibid., §2477–§2479.

23 Ibid., §2530.

24 Clark, Cobb, and Irwin, *Code of Georgia*, Pt. 2, Tit. 6, Chap. 4, Art. 2, §1753.

the deceased, uncles, aunts, and cousins. The rules governing the more remote degrees of relation were determined by the dictates of the canon law as adopted and enforced in the English Courts prior to July 4, 1776.[25]

Administrators were also responsible for sorting out the financial situation of the deceased, satisfying debts, and settling accounts. The law allowed for twelve months to meet financial obligations, unless the administrator could provide proof of extenuating circumstances, for instance, timed payments as part of a contract.[26] Administrators typically began by informing creditors of the need to submit their claims against the estate prior to the impending settlement; this announcement would be made by placing an advertisement in one of the local newspapers for six consecutive weeks, or by posting notices in three different public places. Priority in the payment of debts began with funeral expenses, followed by support of the family, administrative expenses, unpaid taxes or other debts due the state or federal government, judgments, mortgages, liens, debts due for rent, payment of promissory notes, and, finally, open accounts. While the entire estate, beyond that provided for the support of the widow and children, was eligible for use in paying debts, perishable property was sold first, followed by personal effects. Real estate was sold last, and even land that had been transferred to heirs could be recalled for payment of debts if needed.[27] The personal estate was sold at auction, although land could be sold either at auction or through private sale.

Once the debts were paid, distributions could be made to the heirs. The order of distribution was the same as that used for ranking administrative rights to an estate, following kinship from spouse through the blooded relations. This process was well documented, with the administrator required first to submit a petition to initiate each phase, and then to report the results in a series of inventories that listed not only possessions and debts but also the names of debtors, creditors, and buyers at auction, the prices realized, and sometimes even which heirs received money in the final distribution. The probate process culminated once the administrator appeared before the Court of Ordinary to attest to the execution of all necessary steps in settling the estate, and to submit the appraisements, inventories, and sales bills generated during the settlement process (including receipts for the expenditures incurred during administration). The administrator received payment of 2.5 percent of the value of the estate as compensation for services rendered.[28]

While drafting a will could be an expensive undertaking, the administration of an estate in cases of intestacy was expensive as well. The papers related to the administration of the estate of Joseph H. Edwards, submitted to the Court of Ordinary in Franklin County in June 1889, provide an indication of how complex and costly probate could be. Edwards died in the fall of 1887, leaving

[25] Clark, Cobb, and Irwin, *Code of Georgia*, Pt. 2, Tit, 6, Chap. 3, Art. 2, §2448.
[26] Ibid., §2491–2493.
[27] Ibid., §2513–§2515.
[28] Ibid., §2486 & §2548.

a wife and two minor children.[29] A. J. Neal was appointed administrator of the estate in October 1887 and spent the next year and a half settling Edwards's affairs and providing for his widow. Among the papers Neal submitted to bring the administration of the estate to a close in June 1889 was a bill that detailed the fees he paid out of the estate throughout the probate process. To begin, he paid $2.00 in fees in October 1887 for the application for letters of administration, the citation to publish his appointment, and the printing and recording of the citation and other proceedings. On December 5, 1887, he returned to pay seventeen additional fees amounting to $14.50, for issuing the letters of administration, warrant of appraisement, and order of appraisement, and for a petition to sell Joseph Edwards's land. All of these documents had to be issued, copied, and officially recorded in the county probate files.[30] In the end, the $16.50 in administrative fees Neal paid for the estate nearly equaled the value of the two fattening hogs ($12.00), 150 bushels of fodder ($2.25), ten bushels of cottonseed ($1.25), and four chairs ($0.50) listed among Joseph Edwards' possessions in the inventory recorded in December 1887.[31]

For this study we identified a total of 228 decedents from the counties of Crawford, Jasper, and Franklin whose inventories provided enough detail to conduct analysis of the changes that occurred in the Georgia Piedmont between 1880 and 1910. In order to ensure that the decedents were not recent transplants to the area, the pool was limited to those individuals who could be linked to their respective county through the 1880, 1900, or 1910 federal census. We also cross-referenced them using state and county records – specifically, agricultural censuses and tax digests, in which the decedents must have appeared for at least five years prior to their death.[32]

The federal census data include details ranging from the age, gender, ethnicity, and occupation of household members, to the size and value of properties, to capital invested in machines and tools. Similarly, the Georgia state tax rolls typically list a taxpayer's occupation, the amount of land owned, the type and

[29] U.S. Bureau of the Census, *Tenth Census of the United States, 1880, Population*. NARA Microfilm T9, Roll 147, Grimlog Militia District, Franklin, GA, Enumeration District 30, Page 568.

[30] "Receipt for payment of fees related to the administration of the estate of J. H. Edwards, 29 June 1889." Franklin County, Probate Court, Marriage Records, 1806–1905. Record Group 159, Subgroup 2, Series 3 (GDA).

[31] "Warrant of appraisement for J. H. Edwards and petition for twelve months support. Book Six, Folio fifty seven, 10 January 1888. Franklin County, Probate Court, Marriage Records, 1806–1905. Record Group 159, Subgroup 2, Series 3 (GDA).

[32] The 1890 census could not be used for this study since many of the schedules were destroyed or damaged beyond recovery in a catastrophic fire at the Department of Commerce in Washington, DC, in 1921. Fragmentary data survives for only eleven states, including Georgia; however, Crawford, Jasper, and Franklin are not among the counties represented. The manuscript returns were destroyed once the mandated retention period expired in 1932; Jason G. Gauthier, *Measuring America: The Decennial Censuses from 1790 to 2000* (Washington, DC: U.S. Dept. of Commerce, 2002), 210.

number of crops produced, and in some cases information on investments, industrial ventures, and merchandise. The values listed in the 1880 state agricultural census recorded in each county provide a baseline against which to measure changes in holdings of household and farm equipment, livestock, and crops in subsequent decades. With these rich sources of information from the federal, state, and county levels, we can craft a remarkably detailed understanding of farm households and how they changed over time.

The availability and reliability of this data helped determine the time frame we established for this study: 1880 to 1910. Although each county had a significant number of probate inventories from the 1870s, it proved difficult to establish five years of residency for many of the decedents, especially African Americans. The 1870 federal census was largely excluded from the household analysis because of the well-established concerns about the accuracy of the returns – particularly the under-recording of as many 1.26 million African Americans across the South.[33] While there are some concerns about the 1880 census as well – enumerators might have under-counted the number of tenant farms, and estimates of secondary-crop production in some areas seem low – the population schedules are believed to be reasonably accurate.[34] Likewise, the county-level tax assessments executed under the direction of William A. Wright, who served as comptroller general for the state of Georgia from 1879 until his death in 1929, are considered very reliable. One caveat that Wright often mentioned in his annual reports is his concern that taxpayers (unsurprisingly) reported the bare minimum of what they actually possessed.[35] That said, the evidence suggests that the entire population of taxpayers engaged in that practice, so it does not skew the statistics for any one group or region inordinately.

Of the 228 estates identified for use in this analysis, 56 were from Crawford County, 61 from Jasper, and 111 from Franklin (Table 2.1). While the representation from Franklin is nearly double that of the other two counties, it was nearly 100 square miles larger than Crawford County and 42 square miles larger than Jasper – until 1905, that is, when the state legislature divided Franklin County nearly in half and incorporated the northern portion into the newly established Stephens County.[36] Moreover, Franklin had the largest

[33] Henry Gannett, "The Alleged Census Frauds in the South," *International Review* 10 (1881): 459–467; Francis A. Walker, "Statistics of the Colored Race in the United States," *Publications of the American Statistical Association* 2, no. 11/2 (September–December, 1890): 98; W. Stull Holt, *The Bureau of the Census: Its History, Activities, and Organization* (Washington, DC: Brookings Institution, 1929): 20; Gavin Wright, "Note on the Manuscript Census Samples Used in These Studies," *Agricultural History* 44, no. 1 (January 1970): 95.

[34] Thomas Allen Scott, "Cobb County, Georgia, 1880–1900: A Socioeconomic Study of an Upper Piedmont County" (PhD diss., University of Tennessee, 1978), 6, 15, 210.

[35] Ibid., 211.

[36] Crawford County was 328 square miles from 1870 to 1915, while Jasper County encompassed 377 square miles for the period under study. Franklin County included 428 square miles from 1859 until 1905, when 162 square miles at the northern end of the county was combined with land from Habersham to create Stephens County; John H. Long and Peggy Tuck

TABLE 2.1. *Distribution of Decedents from Crawford, Jasper, and Franklin Counties Over Time*

County	1880–1885	1886–1890	1891–1895	1896–1900	1901–1905	1906–1910	Total
Crawford	10	14	9	11	6	6	56
Jasper	21	12	12	10	4	2	61
Franklin	22	30	25	34	0	0	111

population of the three in 1880, although Jasper surpassed it by 1900. The number of estates involved in the probate process was greatest in the 1880s and gradually diminished over the next thirty years in Crawford and Jasper. That trend, however, was reversed in Franklin, where the number of probated estates increased between 1880 and 1900, at which point it abruptly dropped to zero, suggesting that the county's probate documents are lost or have not yet been processed by the Georgia State Archives.

Many historians stress the importance of identifying age bias within probate samples, as this can have important implications for interpreting patterns of asset ownership and wealth. Those who are in the prime of their lives, actively raising families and earning a living, are likely to have possessions very different from those of the elderly, who are not as actively engaged in productive activities and who may already be transferring land and possessions to the next generation.[37] By the same token, middle-aged adults generally own more than younger decedents, who are just starting out and have not had as much time to accumulate possessions. Without taking age and station in life into account, one might mistakenly explain these differences solely in terms of wealth and poverty.

The age distribution in the Crawford, Jasper, and Franklin probate cases is relatively even, increasing gradually over time (as might be expected in healthy communities) (Table 2.2). The youngest decedent was seventeen and the oldest ninety-five. The average age of death in the sample population was fifty-eight in Crawford, sixty-four in Jasper, and sixty in Franklin. Among the fifteen African Americans represented in our probate cases, the average age of death was fifty-five, while for the eighteen women it was sixty-two. The youngest age cohort in the sample was decedents aged fourteen to thirty-nine. This group never accounted for more than 16 percent of the decedents from any of the

Sinko, eds., *Georgia: Atlas of Historical Boundaries* (Chicago: Newberry Library, 2010), http://publications.newberry.org/ahcbp/, 306, 450–451, 650, and 1031 (accessed January 5, 2011).

37 Jones, "Estimating Wealth of the Living," 274; Gloria L. Main, "Personal Wealth in Colonial America: Explorations in the Use of Probate Records from Maryland and Massachusetts, 1650 to 1720," *Journal of Economic History* 34, no. 1 (March 1974): 289-293; Main, "Probate Records as a Source for Early American History," 96; Shammas, "Constructing a Wealth Distribution from Probate Records, 297.

TABLE 2.2. *Age Distribution of Crawford, Jasper, and Franklin County Decedents*

County	15–19	20–29	30–39	40–49	50–59	60–69	70–79	80–89	90–99
Crawford	1	1	5	11	11	14	8	5	0
Jasper	1	3	4	5	12	9	9	15	3
Franklin	0	7	11	16	18	17	24	14	4

counties, suggesting that most of the young adults in the Georgia Piedmont had not yet invested the time and energy necessary to amass estates valuable enough to require a will or administration. Whereas 64 percent of the decedents in Crawford were technically in the prime of their lives, falling in the forty-to-sixty-nine age bracket, those older than seventy accounted for only 23 percent of the group.[38] The decedents were a bit more evenly distributed between the middle and upper age brackets in Jasper and Franklin counties, where between 43 percent (n = 26) and 47 (n = 51) percent were between the ages of forty and sixty-nine. Forty-four percent of the decedents in Jasper (n = 27) and 39 percent in Franklin (n = 42) were older than seventy.

The vast majority of the decedents from the three counties were white males, as might be expected (Table 2.3). In Crawford County they accounted for fifty-one of the fifty-six decedents, representing 91 percent of the total estates from the county. Among these estates, 82 percent owned land (n = 42), 94 percent had inventories (n = 48), and one-third wrote wills. A total of fifty-three of the sixty-one estates from Jasper belonged to white men, representing 82 percent of the group. Eighty-five percent of these men owned their land (n = 45), one-third had wills, and inventories were prepared for 81 percent of their estates (n = 43). White men in Franklin accounted for 86 percent of the decedents (n = 96). Eighty-six percent of these men owned land (n = 83), 99 percent of the estates were inventoried (n = 95), and 17 percent had wills (n = 95).

Although the overwhelming majority of the decedents in the three counties between 1880 and 1910 were white males, women and blacks were represented in the sample. Women accounted for 8 percent of the total number of decedents from the three counties combined (Table 2.4). This number is small, but the proportion of female heads of household in these counties declined from 15 percent in 1880 to 10 percent by 1910. Five of the female decedents were from Crawford, four from Jasper, and nine from Franklin. The five women from Crawford, one of them an African American, represent 9 percent of the total sample population from that county. All were landowners, and each appears

[38] Ansley J. Coale and Norfleet W. Rives, Jr., "A Statistical Reconstruction of the Black Population of the United States, 1880–1970: Estimates of True Numbers by Age and Sex, Birth Rates, and Total Fertility," *Population Index* 39, no. 1 (January 1973): 15–18; Michael R. Haines and Richard H. Steckel, eds., *A Population History of North America* (New York: Cambridge University Press, 2001): 312–333; Herbert Klein, *A Population History of the United States* (New York: Cambridge University Press, 2004): 107–145.

TABLE 2.3. *Characteristics of the Estates of White Male Decedents from Crawford, Jasper, and Franklin Counties*

County	Total Probate Sample	Number of White Males	White Male Landowners	White Male Wills	White Male Inventories
Crawford	56	51	42	17	48
Jasper	61	53	45	18	43
Franklin	111	96	83	16	95

to have been widowed by the time her estate entered probate. Four decedents from Jasper were women, accounting for 7 percent of the county sample. All were white, and all but one, Mary Ragland, owned land. Franklin's probate cases included nine women, eight of them white, representing 6 percent of that sample population; all owned land except for the one African American, Tildy Wheeler. It goes without saying that these statistics demonstrate the inferior status of women as property holders in the Georgia Piedmont, given that they constitute such a small percentage of the probated decedents despite near-equal ratios between the sexes throughout the period under study. Moreover, the evidence suggests that most if not all achieved any status they did have as property holders through the death of a spouse.

African Americans are even less well represented in the probate samples from Crawford, Jasper, and Franklin counties, confirming their marginal position as property holders in the Georgia Piedmont (Table 2.5). Despite being in the majority of the population in Crawford and Jasper through 1900, and growing from one-fifth of the Franklin population in 1880 to one-third by 1900, blacks accounted for only 7 percent of the combined total of the probated estates captured in the sample. Five of the fifty-six estates from Crawford County belonged to people of color, representing 9 percent of the group. Census records identified three of them as "Negro" and two as "Mulatto." Three were listed as landholders, while the two without land had assets significant enough to

TABLE 2.4. *Characteristics of the Estates of Female Decedents from Crawford, Jasper, and Franklin Counties*

County	Total Probate Sample	Number of White Females	Number of Black Females	Female Landowners	Female Wills	Female Inventories
Crawford	56	4	1	5	1	5
Jasper	61	4	0	3	5	2
Franklin	111	8	1	8	1	9

TABLE 2.5. *Characteristics of the Estates of Black Male Decedents from Crawford, Jasper, and Franklin Counties*

County	Total Probate Sample	Number of Black Males	Black Male Landowners	Black Male Wills	Black Male Inventories
Crawford	56	4	2	1	4
Jasper	61	3	1	2	2
Franklin	111	6	4	2	6

warrant making a will (as in the case of Samuel Lowe) or completing an inventory and appraisement (as was done with the estate of Joe Danielly).

Three black men were included among the Jasper County decedents, representing 5 percent of the estates in the sample. Only one of the three, William Thomas, owned land, although Allen Clark felt the need, like William Thomas, to write a will. Finally, the Franklin County dataset included seven African-American decedents, representing 6 percent of the sample. Inventories were made of each estate, with the bulk of the possessions left by David Brawner and Barney Hancock being sold at public auction. Four of the seven owned land, and two of the landowners, Jack Bellamy and James Brown, left wills – however, their estates entered probate anyway, meaning that there were likely significant debts or other complicating factors.

While it is important to know the age, racial, and gender characteristics of our probate population, it is also critical to understand their household and family structures. Naturally, a decedent whose estate was large enough to be subject to probate was usually the head of a household. In fact, the vast majority of the individuals in the sample were identified as heads of household in at least one of the three federal censuses available for the period under study. Ninety-one percent of Crawford County decedents (n = 51) were listed as a head of household, as were 98 percent of those from Jasper (n = 60) and 95 percent of those from Franklin. One exception was Thomas Hines Williford – his wife Nancy was listed as the head of the household in 1880. She was sixty-seven and her husband was seventy-six, suggesting that he was infirm by the time of the federal enumeration.[39]

Not all households were nuclear families, as the data from the Georgia Piedmont reveal (Table 2.6). Although more than half of the individuals in our sample whose household composition could be determined lived in family units consisting of a husband, wife, and children, other arrangements abounded.

[39] U.S. Bureau of the Census, *Twelfth Census of the United States, 1900: Population*, Microfilm T623, Roll 190, Crawford, GA, Enumeration District 2, Militia District 494, Page 47B.

TABLE 2.6. *Household Size Represented Among the Crawford, Jasper, and Franklin County Decedents, 1880–1910*

County	Average Household Size	Median Household Size	Average Single Family Household	Median Single Family Household	Average Composite Household	Median Composite Household
Crawford	6.1 (n = 56)	6.0	4.8 (n = 30)	5.5	7.5 (n = 26)	8.0
Jasper	4.2 (n = 61)	6.0	4.1 (n = 55)	5.5	5.5 (n = 6)	6.0
Franklin	5.9 (n = 111)	6.0	5.9 (n = 78)	6.0	6.3 (n = 33)	6.0

Thirteen households were extended families that included at least one grandparent, a sibling of the husband or wife, or a nephew or niece attached to the household under guardianship or by some other legal means. Pleasant Bellamy's Franklin County household, for example, included a goddaughter and a male whose surname differed from the rest of the household and whose relationship to the others was not specified in the census.[40] As for Charles Harrison of Crawford County, he was a married father of one but was not listed as a head of household – instead he lived with his in-laws, John and Rebecca Sharp.[41] This model of household formation, in which a couple lives with parents and assumes control of their farm after the elders become too aged or infirm to manage the operation themselves, was not uncommon. Unmarried people occasionally formed their own households. In at least ten cases, households consisted of only one person or of two or three unrelated individuals. Servants could also be considered part of the household. Six of the households in our sample had a single servant, while two others had two servants. In all but two cases, the servants were black. To take another example, the household of William C. McEntire consisted of ten people in 1880: William, his wife, their four children, his father-in-law, a nephew, an African-American farm laborer, and an African-American cook.[42]

The average married couple in the three-county aggregate sample had between three and four children living at home, although one family listed nine (Table 2.6). Crawford had the largest average family size, with 6.1 members, and Franklin was next with 5.9. The average family in Jasper County

[40] U.S. Bureau of the Census, *Tenth Census of the United States, 1880: Population*, District 812, Franklin, GA, Roll T9 147, 544.4000, Enumeration District 28, Image 0372.

[41] U.S. Bureau of the Census, *Twelfth Census of the United States, 1900*: Population, Militia District 497, Crawford, GA, Roll T623–190, Page 17B.

[42] U.S. Bureau of the Census, *Tenth Census of the United States, 1880: Population*, District 26, Carnesville, Franklin, GA, Microfilm Roll T9–147, Page 471.1,000, Image 0225.

was considerably smaller, with 4.2 members, mainly because 90 percent of the Jasper households were nuclear families, averaging 4.1 members each. The extended-family, or composite, households in Jasper, accounting for the remaining 10 percent, had an average size of 5.5 individuals. The Franklin County sample also included a high percentage of nuclear families (n = 70%), but there the average nuclear family had 6.0 members. Composite households in Franklin averaged 6.3 members, meaning that unlike in Jasper, the difference in size between a nuclear household and a composite household was negligible. In Crawford County, a little more than 50 percent of the households were nuclear families, which averaged nearly five members (n = 4.8), while the size of an average composite household was 7.5. These differences suggest the persistence of regional variation into the postbellum period. They reflect the plantation tradition of the Lower Piedmont, where larger landholdings prevailed, and the Upland pattern of family-based units subsisting on smaller parcels of land.

It can be difficult, however, to make generalizations about the size and structure of the probate population's households, because the decedents included in the sample were at various stages of life. The 1880 census listed just three people in the household of James and Elizabeth Bruce of Franklin County, both of whom died in 1885; yet the 1860 census indicated that their household consisted of twelve members.[43] The case of Crawford Elliot is equally confusing. Elliot was listed as living in his grandfather's household in 1880; however, in 1900 he was recorded as the head of his own household, which included a grandson named Manton Tague.[44] Finally, John Weatherby of Crawford County is a rare example within the dataset of an elderly parent who resided with his daughter's family in the final years of his life. The 1880 census saw Weatherby living with his daughter, her husband, and their five children. His occupation is listed as "widower," suggesting that he no longer worked.[45]

For this study we divided the decedents into six classes based on land tenure – that is, the amount of acreage they owned or farmed (Table 2.7). We determined land to be the most valid way to define social and economic class within the three counties, as virtually everyone farmed and land was generally the most precious asset they owned. The primary variable, therefore, in defining one's position in society was the number of acres under one's control,

43 U.S. Bureau of the Census, *Tenth Census of the United States, 1880: Population*, District 812, Franklin, GA, Roll T9 147, 578.4000, Enumeration District 30, Image 0440; U.S. Bureau of the Census, *Eighth Census of the United States, 1860: Population*. Microfilm Roll M653–121, Franklin County, Page 648, Image 649.

44 U.S. Bureau of the Census, *Twelfth Census of the United States, 1900: Population* (Washington, DC: National Archives and Records Administration, 1900). T623, Roll 190, Crawford, GA, Enumeration District 2, Militia District 497, Page 23B.

45 U.S. Bureau of the Census, *Tenth Census of the United States, 1880: Population*. NARA Microfilm Roll T9_142, Enumeration District 45, Page 659D.

TABLE 2.7. *Distribution of Inventoried Crawford, Jasper, and Franklin County Decedents Among Tenure Classes, 1880–1910*

County	Farms 1–49 Acres	Farms 50–99 Acres	Farms 100–149 Acres	Farms 150–499 Acres	Farms 500–999 Acres	Farms 1,000+ Acres	Total
Crawford	2	2	9	20	7	6	46
Jasper	5	3	4	17	7	2	38
Franklin	11	10	17	67	11	3	119

whether or not the land was improved. The tenure classes used here were based on those the federal government used in the census, except that we grouped together the tenure classes with fewer than fifty acres, since few decedents whose estates went to probate had so little land. The first tenure class, those who owned between one and forty-nine acres, included eighteen individuals. The next group, owning anywhere from fifty to ninety-nine acres, numbered fifteen. The 30 households in the third class held between 100 and 149 acres. The fourth and most numerous group, those with 150–499 acres, consisted of 104 landowners. In the fifth class were 25 people owning 500–999 acres, and in the final tenure class were 11 individuals who held more than 1,000 acres. Fifty-six of the decedents could not be placed in a tenure class, either because no record exists of their having owned or rented land, or because of inconsistencies in the acreage that different sources attribute to them.

Comparing these land-tenure patterns with the census figures indicates that our sample is skewed toward larger landholders (Table 2.7). Of the 46 decedents from Crawford, 91 percent owned more than 100 acres of land. In the overall population of the 3 counties, by comparison (Table 1.6; Table 2.8), half of the farms in 1880 were smaller than 100 acres. Looking at the number of farms of 500 acres or more reinforces the impression that large landowners are overrepresented in the probate sample. According to the census data, landowners in this class accounted for 7 percent of those with real estate in Crawford and Jasper counties, and 4 percent in Franklin (reflecting the traditional pattern of smaller landholdings in the Uplands). In the probate sample, however, such large properties are far more common: 28 percent of Crawford farms, 23 percent of Jasper farms, and 12 percent of Franklin farms fall into the 500-acre category. The probate data and the census data are in accord on a different question: each confirms that landholdings in the Lower Piedmont counties of Crawford and Jasper were larger on average than those in Franklin County, in the Upper Piedmont.

The skewing in the middling range of 100–499 acres was not nearly as dramatic in Crawford and Jasper Counties as it was for the tenure classes above and below this range. Sixty-three percent of the probated decedents in Crawford fell into this category, compared to 42 percent of households in

TABLE 2.8. *Comparison of Tenure Classes Among Inventoried Crawford, Jasper, and Franklin County Decedents and the Data from the 1880 Census*

County	Farms 1–49 Acres	Farms 50–99 Acres	Farms 100–499 Acres	Farms 500–999 Acres	Farms 1,000+ Acres	Total
Crawford estates	2	2	29	7	6	46
Probate	4%	4%	63%	15%	13%	
1880 census	31%	20%	42%	5%	2%	
Jasper estates	5	3	21	7	2	38
Probate	13%	8%	56%	18%	5%	
1880 census	28%	19%	45%	5%	2%	
Franklin estates	11	10	84	11	3	119
Probate	9%	8%	70%	9%	3%	
1880 census	48%	14%	33%	3%	1%	

the 1880 census. In Jasper, the difference was just 11 percent – 56 percent of the individuals in our sample owned between 100 and 499 acres, while the census figure was 45 percent. Franklin County, however, displayed an almost 40 percent disparity between the probate and census data, with 70 percent of estates probated between 1880 and 1910 coming from this middling tenure class, whereas only one-third of the general population had landholdings of that size according to the census. Overall, the landholding patterns revealed through the probate samples from each county corroborate the observation that the bias within probate samples is systematic. The explanation for that bias is straightforward: those whose estates were probated had significant assets to protect but saw no need to go to the trouble and expense of writing a will, since the process under law, properly executed, ensured that their immediate family would be provided for, their debts and other outstanding financial obligations resolved, and their assets distributed equitably among the remaining heirs.[46]

Comparing the landholding patterns from the probate sample with those from the 1880 census provides a good indication of potential skewing in the data. Further comparison between the two data sets, however, provides a more complete picture of how representative the probate sample is. The federal mortality census schedules for 1880 are especially helpful.[47] The mortality schedules reported all deaths at the county level for one year prior to June 1880, providing information on the age, sex, race, and profession of each

[46] Izard, "Another Place in Time," 59, 67; Alston and Schapiro, "Inheritance Laws Across Colonies: Causes and Consequences," 279.

[47] John S. Billings, *Report of the Mortality and Vital Statistics of the United States as Returned at the Tenth Census (June 1, 1880): Part I: Mortality and Vital Statistics* (Washington, DC, 1885), T655, Reel 10.

TABLE 2.9. *Comparison of General Population and Mortality Figures Reported for Crawford, Jasper, and Franklin Counties in 1880*

County	Total Population	Head of Household	Mortality Reported	Adult Mortality	Sample[a] Probate Average, 1880–1889	% Probated Adults
Crawford	8,679	701	123	46	2 (14)[b]	4 (30)[b]
Jasper	10,219	2,151	145	58	3	5
Franklin	11,099	2,570	122	46	4	9

Note: [a] The Sample probate average is the yearly mean of all probated estates included in the study calculated for the decade between 1879 and 1889. [b] The entry for Crawford includes an average of all wills and administrative bonds submitted to the Court of Ordinary for probate every year between 1879 and 1889.

Source: United States Census Mortality Schedules for Crawford, Jasper, and Franklin Counties, 1880; Henry, *Miscellaneous Estate Records of Crawford County*; Wilder and Henry, *Wills of Crawford County Georgia.*

decedent, along with the date of death, cause of death, and length of illness prior to death. The 1880 mortality schedule for Crawford reported 123 deaths, while Jasper reported 145 and Franklin 122, representing around 1 percent of the population in each county (Table 2.8). In each county, roughly 60 percent of the deaths were children younger than twenty-one, who were legally considered minors in Georgia during the late nineteenth century; removing them leaves forty-six adults who died in Crawford, fifty-eight in Jasper, and forty-six in Franklin.

We can use the mortality census to estimate what proportion of estates entered the probate process in Crawford, Jasper, and Franklin counties.[48] In Crawford in 1880, five wills and eleven administrative petitions were submitted to the Court of Ordinary, while the mortality schedule lists the deaths of forty-six adults, suggesting that 35 percent of estates entered probate that year (Table 2.9).[49] This figure closely matches the estimates of scholars who have

[48] The tenure classes are defined by those used in the 1880 federal census; Eugene W. Hilgard, *Report on Cotton Production in the United States: Also Embracing Agricultural and Physico-Geographical Description of the Several Cotton States and of California* (Washington, DC, 1884).

[49] Data are not available on how many wills and administrative petitions were submitted in Jasper County or Franklin County, but our research suggests that the proportions were roughly the same as in Crawford; Billings, United States Census Mortality Schedules for Crawford County, 1880; William R. Henry, *Miscellaneous Estate Records of Crawford County, Georgia: Guardians Bonds, 1874–1906; Administrator's Bonds Book "2," 1874–1898; Appraisement and Sale Bills, Volume III* (Warner Robins: Central Georgia Genealogical Society, 1989); Sunnie Wilder and William R. Henry, *Wills of Crawford County Georgia: Wills Book "A," 1835–1852; Wills Book "B," 1852–1894; Wills Book "C," 1894–1948 III* (Warner Robins: Central Georgia Genealogical Society, 1989).

studied probate records for colonial America.[50] The statistics differ, however, for those estates where inventories and appraisements were completed. For example, only two of the estates in Crawford were inventoried in 1880, representing 4 percent of the total number of adults who died that year. Likewise, the sample set from Franklin County includes an average of four estates for each year between 1879 and 1889 – equal to roughly 9 percent of the forty-six adults who died between June 1879 and June 1880. The figures for Jasper are lower, with an annual average of three estates per year inventoried, representing 5 percent of the fifty-eight adults included in the 1880 mortality census. As indicated by the Crawford data, many more estates entered probate than were subjected to inventory and appraisement. The remainder of estates may have been exempt from these further steps because a single heir inherited everything, with assets having been transferred prior to death, or because the estate was worth less than $500.

Probate records are among the most representative primary sources available to scholars interested in studying historic populations. Like all sources, however, they are subject to bias, which must be identified and accounted for in order to allow accurate and meaningful analysis to proceed. The 228 probate case files from Crawford, Jasper, and Franklin that provide the basis for our study of Piedmont farmers between 1880 and 1910 are no exception. Fortunately, accurate census data and tax lists exist for postbellum Georgia; these serve as a control and provide a means of determining the extent to which the probate samples are representative of the population at large.

The sample includes 56 estates from Crawford County, 61 from Jasper, and 111 from Franklin. Although the sample thus appears to be skewed toward Franklin and Jasper, those counties had more land and more people. Decedents ranged in age from seventeen to ninety-five, and the number of decedents increased gradually over time for each county. The average age of death among the sample population was fifty-eight in Crawford, sixty-four in Jasper, and sixty in Franklin; across the three counties, the average age of death for women was sixty-two, and for African Americans fifty-five. Eighty-five percent of the decedents were white males, 8 percent were female, and 7 percent were African-American. These figures underscore the minority status of women and blacks as property owners in postbellum Piedmont society – especially considering that there was a nearly equal gender balance in the three counties for the period under study, and that blacks were in the majority in Crawford and Jasper (and their proportion of the Franklin County population increased from one-fifth to one-third between 1880 and 1910).

50 See the estimates Alice Hanson Jones provided for the middle colonies in 1774 and what Daniel Scott Smith calculated for Hingham, Massachusetts, in the early eighteenth century. Jones, "Wealth Estimates for the American Middle Colonies," 160; Daniel Scott Smith, "Underregistration and Bias in Probate Records," 105.

In terms of family composition, the data from the three counties mirror trends in the federal census returns. Nuclear-family households were more prevalent in Franklin and Jasper counties, where 70 percent and 90 percent of decedents, respectively, lived in family units composed solely of the immediate family members. Extended-family units including parents, grandparents, siblings, nephews, or nieces, and composite family groups with extra-familial associations, accounted for nearly 50 percent of the estates represented in the Crawford sample. The average household size was largest in Crawford, where the typical household included 6.1 members, followed by Franklin at 5.9, and Jasper with 4.2. The pattern of family composition and size as reflected in county samples demonstrates the persistence of smaller, family-based households in the Upper Piedmont, while larger, composite households were more prevalent in the Lower Piedmont.

More than 90 percent of all decedents were listed as the head of a household, which reinforces our interpretation of the probate process as a means of protecting possessions and ensuring the orderly transfer of assets to beneficiaries at death. In addition, 87 percent of the decedents in the sample owned land, and the pattern of land tenure reveals a bias toward larger landholdings than is the norm in the census data. The average decedent in our sample owned between 150 and 499 acres of land, whereas the census data indicate that half of the landholders in the region owned fewer than 100 acres. Despite the disparity between sources on some matters, the probate data validate the interpretation that landholdings in Crawford and Jasper were larger on average than those in Franklin. The prevalence of estates in the middling tenure classes indicates that yeoman families were more likely than wealthier ones to engage in the probate process in order to protect estates and to direct the intergenerational transmission of assets.

3

Production in the Piedmont

More Than Just Cotton

Many Georgia farmers looked forward to Bill Arp's weekly "Country Philosopher" column in the *Atlanta Constitution* throughout the last quarter of the nineteenth century. After all, Bill Arp was one of them – a resilient North Georgia country boy who knew the joys and hardships of farm life, and who possessed the quick wit to depict them with humor and wisdom.[1] His anecdotes softened the harsh realities of cotton farming, where weather, pests, poor credit terms, and a fickle market frequently conspired against all efforts to realize even a small profit. He good-naturedly likened farming to fishing: "every time you start out you can just see yourself catchin' 'em but after tryin' every hole in the creek you go home sorrowfully, with a fisherman's luck."[2] Not one to complain, Arp was quick to point out that Georgians could weather the bad times, because good farmers were self-reliant enough to have "wheat enuf for biskit every day and light-bread on Sunday, and a few bushels to spare for them angels that's to come along unawares sum of these days."[3] He knew that the persistent hope for "them angels" and for the sweet convergence of favorable circumstances were the motivations that kept most farmers doggedly committed to trying cotton year after year. He also understood that farming was "a precarious business all around," and that most farmers looked constantly for

[1] Bill Arp was the pseudonym for Charles Henry Smith, who was born in Gwinnett County and owned a farm during the last thirty years of his life. Smith began his career as a humorist in 1861, when he wrote a letter to a newspaper in Rome from the perspective of a homespun Georgia country boy named Bill Arp commenting on Lincoln's response to the shelling of Fort Sumter. From that time, Smith regularly played the role of social commentator, speaking through Arp until his death in 1903.

[2] Bill Arp, *From the Uncivil War to Date, 1861–1903: Memorial Edition* (Atlanta: Hudgins Publishing, 1903): 142–143. See also David B. Parker's *Alias Bill Arp: Charles Henry Smith and the South's "Goodly Heritage"* (Athens: University of Georgia Press, 1991).

[3] Ibid., 143.

ways to make their luck by finding additional means of support. That might mean making investments, diversifying crop and livestock production to meet local needs, or developing other skills and services; Arp called such pursuits "a sorter side-show to my circus."[4]

Bill Arp's observations leave little doubt that Georgia cotton farmers gave a great deal of thought to the concepts of self-sufficiency and risk. They knew the difficulties inherent in cotton farming, and they understood that success often depended on the providential alignment of favorable conditions. Although a farmer's immediate goals were to emerge from the season with enough money to provide for his family and pay off the debts he had incurred in order to bring the crop to market, he also hoped to make enough profit to buy the supplies needed for the next season. Farmers wanted to do well enough to make improvements to their operations, or to invest in machinery or livestock that would enhance their ability to succeed even if the cotton crop failed or the prices realized at market fell below expectations. In many cases, the potential advantages of making improvements or investments appeared so promising that farmers were willing to seek credit where their own finances fell short. Like James Bowman of Crawford County, who secured a $350 loan to increase his productive capacity by adding additional work structures and housing for labor, many farmers viewed the path to success as straightforward and achievable, so to them the risk of taking on debt seemed acceptable.[5]

The proper balance between self-sufficiency and risk would arguably have been most evident to farmers in the Upper Piedmont, where, because of limited market involvement and the absence of dependable transportation networks, self-reliance had been the way of life before the Civil War. The situation changed dramatically in the years following the war, with the expansion of rail lines that linked once-isolated rural areas with national and world markets. This, coupled with the introduction of fertilizers, brought the Upper Piedmont squarely into the cotton economy. Many scholars have focused on macro-economic aspects of this transition, such as the role of credit terms in promoting the increase in cotton production, the reduction in self-sufficiency as demonstrated by the decline in local production of foodstuffs, and the increasing social and racial disparities linked to the rapid increase in credit and tenancy. While this broad approach has revealed important overarching trends, it often imparts the sense that the transformation of the cotton South during the last quarter of the nineteenth century was monolithic and all-encompassing. Far fewer scholars have sharpened the focus of their investigations to explore the micro-level details that clarify and provide insight into the discrete mechanisms

[4] Ibid.

[5] "Application of James J. Bowman to C. P. N. Barker, Atlanta, Georgia, 1890." Crawford County, Miscellaneous County Offices, Miscellaneous Original Documents, 1826–1928, Record Group 139, Subgroup 12, Series 10; Ferleger, "Self Sufficiency and Rural Life on Southern Farms," 314–329.

involved in the social and economic transformation.[6] Moreover, studies examining the relationship between sharecropping and low rates of mechanization in Southern agriculture, and those exploring the impact that the availability of fertilizer had on crop choice, have shown that the type and degree of transformation in the South varied significantly by region. Because of the diverse circumstances and traditions that shaped the culture and economy in different areas, they transformed in different ways.[7]

Our exploration of economic and social change in the Georgia Piedmont focuses on the productive capabilities of farm households. The household was selected as the primary unit of analysis because most Southern farmers organized themselves in family-based household units in the nineteenth and early twentieth centuries (although there was a fair amount of variability in the composition of family units).[8] Furthermore, the household was the primary locus of production in the rural South throughout the nineteenth century, and virtually every family member was involved in agriculture in some way. Even most craft production was organized around the household in the rural agricultural sectors of the South. Focusing on agricultural households in the Georgia Piedmont offers the potential to characterize the type, range, and extent of productive activities as well as the scale and scope of production. In some cases, it is even possible to make a distinction between market-oriented production and production intended for home use or exchange.

A total of 199 probate inventories were identified from Crawford, Jasper, and Franklin counties from the period between 1880 and 1910 that contained enough detail to facilitate an analysis of production at the household level. From these data, we explore the full range of activities carried out on postbellum Piedmont farms. In addition to crop and livestock production, we look at by-employment, the use of technology, attempts at diversification, economic organization of households, and gender roles. Together, these considerations address the concepts of self-sufficiency, risk, and the definition of success in the Georgia Piedmont.

Information about occupations and production activities in Georgia in the late nineteenth century is available from a number of different sources, including

6 For example, see Roger Ransom and Richard Sutch, "Debt Peonage in the Cotton South after the Civil War," *Journal of Economic History* 32, no. 3 (September 1972): 641–669; Peter Temin, "Patterns of Cotton Agriculture in Post-Bellum Georgia," 661–674.

7 Louis Ferleger, "Sharecropping Contracts in the Late-Nineteenth-Century South," *Agricultural History* 67, no. 3 Summer (1993): 31–46; J. William Harris, "Crop Choices in the Piedmont before and after the Civil War," *Journal of Economic History* 54, no. 3 (September 1994): 526–542.

8 For example, nuclear family and extended family; conjugal, consanguine, and non-consanguine relations; and, primary, secondary, and tertiary kin. On the role households played in Southern history, see the seminal work by Elizabeth Fox-Genovese, *Within the Plantation Household: Black and White Women of the South* (Chapel Hill: University of North Carolina Press, 1988).

TABLE 3.1. *Professions Listed in the 1880, 1900, and 1910 Federal Census Data for the Decedents from Crawford, Jasper, and Franklin Counties, 1880–1910*

	Farmer/Farming	Farm Laborer	Keeps Gin Mill	Blacksmith	Carpenter	Physician	Dentist	Merchant	Lawyer	School Teacher	Laborer	Keeping House	Domestic
Crawford	46	4		1						1	1	3	
Jasper	40	3				1		1	1		2	3	
Franklin	101	4	1	1	1		1	1	1		2	6	1
Total	187	11	1	2	1	1	1	2	2	1	5	12	1
N = 227													

Note: Occupations listed are based on the most recent listing within the census data. Occupational descriptions are those used by the enumerators and reflected in the manuscript census data. This chart includes the twenty-nine decedents for which there were not sufficient records to facilitate household-level analysis of material goods.

Source: US Census of Population, 1880; *12th US Census, 1900*: 1–2, Population; *13th US Census, 1910*: 1, Population.

federal census data and county-level agricultural censuses and tax assessments. It is even possible to infer a decedent's occupation from a probate inventory, although probate and other court documents rarely state professions explicitly. Still, the federal census data recorded after the Civil War generally provide the most accurate and comprehensive record of primary occupation, especially for individuals listed as the head of a household. In our three-county sample, the overwhelming majority of the 199 decedents listed farming as their primary occupation – 86 percent, according to the 1880, 1900, and 1910 federal census returns (Table 3.1).[9] That proportion increases to 93 percent if individuals whom census enumerators consistently recorded as "keeping house" are included, as most of these women were part of farm households. Of the twenty-eight decedents whose primary occupation was not listed as agriculture, twelve were listed as "keeping house," five were identified as laborers, four were educated or trained professionals, three were employed in crafts and services that existed to support farming, and the remainder included two merchants, a schoolteacher, and a domestic. The pattern changes little when the counties are considered individually – including homemakers, Jasper had

[9] The enumerators for the 1880, 1900, and 1910 censuses consistently identified several types of farming occupations, although the official instructions for enumerators do not describe the differences. The agricultural occupations identified include "farmer," "farming," "farm hand, "farm laborer," and "works on farm."

90 percent of its population involved in agriculture, Crawford had 94 percent, and Franklin topped the three at 96 percent.

The 12 percent of decedents who were identified as working outside of farming included, in addition to the twelve homemakers, two blacksmiths, two merchants, two lawyers, a carpenter, a physician, a dentist, a schoolteacher, and a domestic. Crawford had the lowest number of non–farm-related positions among the three counties, with one blacksmith, one laborer, and a schoolteacher, while Franklin had the most, with two laborers, one blacksmith, one carpenter, a cotton-gin proprietor, a dentist, a merchant, and a domestic. The non-farming occupations represented in Jasper included a physician, two lawyers, and a merchant, in addition to two laborers. Only one African American had an occupation that fell outside of farming or homemaking: Barney Martin of Crawford County, who died in 1896, was identified as a blacksmith. While only women were identified as "keeping house," five were recorded in the 1880 census as having other occupations. Rebecca Hammack, who died at the age of seventy-six in Crawford County, was identified as a farmer, whereas Rena Jordan, an African-American woman from the same county, was listed as a farm laborer. Mary Lazenby and Mary Ragland from Jasper County also fell outside of the homemaker category. Lazenby was identified as a farmer, while Ragland, who died in 1893 at the age of eighty-five, was identified simply as "elderly" and appears to have been incapable of work. Elizabeth Bruce from Franklin County was listed as "farming," while Caroline Sewell of the same county declared her occupation as a "domestic," indicating that she worked in another household.[10]

The tax assessments recorded within the counties each year often included details about occupations and productive activities that provide insight into taxpayers' additional means of income or support. These documents recorded information on investments, industrial ventures, and merchandise in addition to land, crops, livestock, and other possessions. Often these figures make it possible to determine a household's main productive activities, the scale of those activities, and their development over time. For example, Van Buren Horn of Crawford County was listed as a farmer in the 1880 census, but the annual state tax assessment provides a finer level of detail, showing that he primarily raised cattle. According to the tax records, his livestock was typically worth between $800 and $900, and the amount he invested in plantation and

[10] Like the terms used to identify farmers and other agricultural laborers, enumerators used a variety of terms, primarily for women, including "keeping house," "housekeeper," and "domestic," which may or may not refer to a woman's role as a homemaker. The family situations of the women identified as "keeping house" and "housekeeper" suggest that they were homemakers, while Caroline Sewell was recorded as single and living alone in 1870 and 1880, making her profession as a hired domestic more plausible; *Ninth Census of the United States, 1870*, District 370, Franklin, Georgia; Roll M593, 150, Page 91, Ancestry.com (accessed September 30, 2008).

mechanical tools increased consistently, from $50 in 1877 to $1,200 in 1890, suggesting that he may have become involved in other productive activities.[11]

Overall, the 1880 tax assessments reveal that the median property size among the individuals in our 3-county sample was 268 acres, and the median land value $1,000. They reported on average $350 in farm products, $165 in livestock, $50 in household possessions, and $10 in tools. The median value for farm products in the Crawford assessment in 1879 was $525, while Jasper's was $400 and Franklin's $305. The size of landholdings reported in the 1880 tax assessments reflects the pattern of larger parcels in the Lower Piedmont and smaller ones in the Upper Piedmont. The median parcel size in Crawford was 405 acres, compared to 247.5 acres in Jasper and 224.5 acres in Franklin. This pattern extends to livestock as well, with a median value of $240 invested in livestock in Crawford and $150 in Jasper and Franklin. The assessed value of household possessions was fairly equal across the three counties, with a median value of $60 in Crawford and $50 in Jasper and Franklin. Tools were similarly balanced, averaging $10 in each county. To sum up, the amounts listed in the 1880 tax assessments suggest that the value of household goods, livestock, and tools per household was more or less equal across the dataset, but that there were larger variations in land values, the size of landholdings, and the value of crops produced. The differences in real estate were particularly stark, as the median holding of 405 acres in Crawford County was nearly twice the median parcel size in Franklin and Jasper. While the disparity in parcel size between Crawford and Franklin clearly reflects a Lower Piedmont–Upper Piedmont dichotomy, the similarity between landholdings in Franklin and Jasper may indicate that Jasper in 1880 resembled the Upper Piedmont more than it did the heart of the Cotton Belt.

A review of the 1880 tax assessments reveals that eight of the twenty-eight individuals recorded as being employed outside of agriculture in the 1880 federal census actually had significant investments in land, tools, and livestock, suggesting that they were involved in agriculture of some sort, even if what they produced was intended entirely for home use. It stands to reason that the two blacksmiths would be involved in farming, since much of their work consisted of providing shoes for mules and horses, and fixing iron tools and equipment. However, while the two men shared the same occupation, they differed greatly in wealth – the estate of the white blacksmith, John Tabor, was worth nearly twice as much as the estate of Barney Martin, an African-American blacksmith. Tabor's property was assessed at $1,150, with $50 in tools, $200 in livestock, and 100 acres of land valued at $700.[12] Martin, on the other hand, had an estate worth $648, with $15 in tools, $158 in

[11] Van Buren Horn, *Tax assessment*, 1877–1890, Crawford County, Militia District 497, Property Tax Digests, 1877–1910, (GDA).

[12] Crawford County, *Property Tax Digests*, 1877–1910 (GDA); Franklin County, Property *Tax Digests*, 1878–1910 (GDA).

livestock, and 100 acres of land worth $200. Given that the median value of all the estates in the sample was $185, Martin could certainly be considered successful. However, he had 70 percent less invested in tools than Tabor, and about 20 percent less invested in livestock, yet both men were assessed for $300 in agricultural produce. Finally, both men owned 100 acres of land, but Tabor's was worth over 70 percent more than Martin's, suggesting that the property of the African-American blacksmith was marginal compared to Tabor's. While this is but one example, the disparity between the Tabor and Martin estates illustrates the inequality between races in the South during the late nineteenth century.

The other men who farmed in addition to their primary occupations also did well compared to their neighbors.[13] Newton Teat, a Franklin County carpenter, was assessed for a total of $925 in land, household possessions, tools, and livestock in 1880. He owned 175 acres worth $600, and he reported $175 in livestock, $25 in tools, and $800 in crops grown in 1879. Jasper county merchant Michael McDowell produced $900 worth of crops on 80 acres of land and was assessed $100 for livestock. William Royston, a merchant in Franklin County, was by far the most successful of those in our sample who were not primarily farmers, owning land, household possessions, and livestock valued at $3,845. The bulk of Royston's wealth must be attributed to his mercantile enterprise, however – while he reported holding 200 acres of land, he had only $175 worth of livestock and produced only around $200 in crops (indicating that the land might have been a speculative investment).

Three women from the sample were among those who reported significant assets associated with farming in the 1880 county tax assessment.[14] Michal Allen of Crawford County, who produced $430 in crops, owned 125 acres, $10 worth of farm tools, and $250 in livestock, while Avoline Peurifoy of Jasper was assessed for land, household goods, livestock, and tools amounting to $1,060. While she had $185 in animals, the bulk of her wealth rested in the 375 acres she owned, worth $800. She also produced $400 in farm products. Most intriguing is the domestic from Franklin County, Caroline Sewell, who was assessed in 1880 for 125 acres worth $800, $75 in livestock, and a mere $3 in tools – despite owning considerable personal property and real estate, she continued to work in someone else's house. It bears mentioning that each of these women was widowed with children, and the land and possessions for which they were assessed in 1880 appear to be the residue of their husbands' estates. These assets likely represent the share they were legally entitled to enjoy for the remainder of their lives – the assets would be transferred to the next generation of heirs upon each woman's death. The small number of female

[13] Franklin County, *Property Tax Digests*, 1878–1910; Jasper County, *Property Tax Digests*, 1888–1892, Vol. 2, 2252 (GDA).

[14] Franklin County, *Property Tax Digests*, 1878–1910; Jasper County, *Property Tax Digests*, 1888–1892; Crawford County, *Property Tax Digests*, 1877–1910 (GDA).

property holders demonstrates a significant disparity between the world of women and that of men in the Georgia Piedmont.

While valuable, the tax assessments do not provide the detail necessary to analyze the types of activities farmers engaged in or the level of intensity of those pursuits. The best way to identify primary occupations, by-employment, and other production activities is from the goods listed in the inventories. Most inventories include a thorough record of goods related to production, such as tools, equipment, crops, and livestock. For example, Henry David's Franklin County inventory, recorded in 1892, lists a drawknife, axe, adze, hammer, chisel, and a number of additional carpentry tools, suggesting that he may have worked as a carpenter, cabinetmaker, or builder in addition to his primary occupation as a farmer.[15] Production information can also be deduced from the context in which an inventory item appears. In some cases, items are grouped according to where they were stored; in others, the space is not directly identified, but it is often possible to determine the location on the property or within a structure on the basis of which items were grouped together. For example, butter churns listed with stoves, tables, and earthenware were probably functional pieces located in the kitchen. On the other hand, a churn listed at the end of the inventory in association with a trunk, a spinning wheel, and old quilts may refer to a storage area such as an attic. Functional groupings within an inventory also present the possibility of identifying the varied aspects of household production. This is particularly important with regard to women's tasks such as dairying, sewing, and spinning, which often go unmentioned in more conventional historical texts.

However, the utility of inventory data depends not only on the level of description but also on the presence of enough specialized equipment to hint at an occupation other than farming.[16] For instance, occupations that required few if any specialized tools may be difficult to identify. In this case, groups of items listed together often provide clues about specialized activities. The club, froe, and 1,000 shingles grouped together in Lilborn Wright's inventory suggest that he or someone working on his farm was involved in riving shingles. The huge number of shingles, moreover, may be indicative of production for sale or use beyond the Wright property.[17]

Like the federal census data and the state agricultural censuses, the items listed in the inventories from Crawford, Jasper, and Franklin leave no doubt that farming was by far the most important occupation in each county. Just as 93 percent of the decedents were identified as farmers (or homemakers in farm

[15] Henry David, *Inventory and Appraisement*, 1892, Franklin County, Probate Court, Estate Records, 1786–1916, Record Group 159, Subgroup 2, Series 1 (GDA).

[16] Overton et al., *Production and Consumption in English Households*, 35.

[17] Lilborn H. Wright, *Inventory and Appraisement, 1892*, Franklin County, Probate Court, Estate Records, 1786–1916, Record Group 159, Subgroup 2, Series 1 (GDA).

households) in the census and tax records, fourteen of the twenty-two categories of production-related tools, equipment, and supplies in the inventories were explicitly agricultural or necessary to support farming. For the purposes of this study, farm tools and equipment were sorted by function, by crop, and then, if necessary, by more inclusive general categories (if the equipment was used for a broad range of activities). Functional categories within agriculture include plows, harrows, planters and cultivators, harvest-related equipment, and processing machinery, such as cotton gins. Crop-related categories include items used specifically for the cultivation or processing of cotton, grain (including corn), or sorghum, as well as items used for logging and milling. More general agricultural categories include farm tools and supplies, harnesses, wagons, wagon-related accessories, and power engines that were used almost exclusively with gins and threshers. Non-agricultural categories include items related to crafts or trades outside of farming, such as blacksmithing, building, carpentry and cabinetmaking, shoemaking, textiles manufacture, and dentistry.

A Piedmont farmer's growing season began in February, when the fields were first plowed to turn the soil, plow under plant stubble or a cover crop, and to allow the winter rain and the frost-thaw cycle to break down the soil so that it could be cultivated more easily. Once the cotton and corn were planted, by the end of April, plows were used regularly to break up the soil to allow air and rain to penetrate, to build up the soil at the base of the plants, and to thin plants and control weeds. Although Southern farmers generally opted for shallow cultivation, they used a wide variety of plows and specialty plowshares for specific applications.[18]

Appraisers identified sixteen types of plows and plowshares in use among the decedents in the three counties, including Dixie, double, fore, foot, gopher, jack, pony, scraper, scooter, shave, shovel, square, sulky, sweep, Syracuse, and turn plows. Some of these, such as Dixie and Syracuse, referred to well-known brands. The Syracuse was a popular and sturdy steel-beam plow produced in New York, whereas the lighter, wood-beam Dixie and Dixie Boy plows were designed specifically for cotton farming and produced in Richmond, Virginia. Both were variations on the time-tested walk-behind moldboard design, with an iron plowshare attached to a wooden or iron beam. The fore, gopher, jack, scraper, scooter, shave, shovel, and sweep plows were all more specialized. Scrapers, scooters, and shave plows had lighter, shallow-draft blades that allowed farmers to plow close to crops to remove weeds and "cut out" or thin plants to prevent crowding.[19] Gopher plows had a vertical disc that was used to cut through roots.[20] Double, sulky, and turn plows were more advanced implements. The double plow had two plowshares and required the power of

18 Gray, *History of Agriculture*, 700–701; Charles S. Aiken, *The Cotton Plantation South since the Civil War* (Baltimore, MD: The Johns Hopkins University Press, 1998): 98–101.

19 Ibid.

20 Range, *A Century of Georgia Agriculture*, 19.

FIGURE 3.1. Typical steel beam turn plow with chilled wearing parts from the last quarter of the nineteenth century. *Lynchburg Chilled and Hillside Plows*, p. 22, Courtesy of the Library of Virginia.

two mules or horses – it could work twice as much land in a day as a standard plow. As for turn plows, they saved time because they had a reversible share that could be turned at the end of a row so that the plowman could return through the field in the opposite direction while throwing the furrow in the same direction. Sulky plows represented the most advanced models available in the late nineteenth century, because the plowman actually rode the implement through the field.[21]

A total of 294 plows were identified in the sample, with 129 households owning at least 1 – the median number of plows was 3 per household, and Jesse Power of Franklin County owned the most, with 28.[22] Eleven of these were identified as gopher plows on the administrator's sale bill for Power's estate, and the remaining seventeen were listed generically as "plows."[23] Overall, the plows were distributed among decedents from the 3 counties, with 213 in Franklin, 45 in Jasper, and 36 in Crawford. Fourteen Dixie and Dixie Boy plows were listed in the inventories, with seven in Crawford County, five in Franklin, and two in Jasper. Seven decedents had double plows – six in Franklin and one in Crawford. Finally, Barney Hancock, an African-American farmer in Franklin County, owned a sulky plow. In fact, he was the only decedent from any of the three counties, white or black, who owned a technologically

21 R. Douglas Hurt, *American Agriculture: A Brief History* (West Lafayette: Purdue University Press, 2002): 194–195.

22 It is unclear why Jesse Power owned so many plows at the time of his death in 1900, although he may have worked as a blacksmith in addition to farming, judging from the $12 in blacksmith tools listed in his inventory.

23 Jesse G. Power, *Administrator's Sale Inventory*, December 1, 1884. Franklin County, Probate Court, Estate Records, 1786–1916, Record Group 159, Subgroup 2, Series 1. GDA, Morrow, Georgia (GDA).

advanced plow of this type.[24] Overall, the data on plows from the three counties suggest that only 5 percent of the decedents with plows invested in the more advanced implements. Three percent purchased the lighter Dixie plows that were designed for cotton farming, while 2 percent acquired double plows that would cut plowing time in half. The data also suggest that farmers in Franklin County were more likely to invest in more advanced implements than those in Crawford or Jasper. The value of an estate with at least one plow averaged $892.

A total of thirty-four harrows were identified among the decedents from the three counties, with eight harrows in Crawford, eighteen in Jasper, and twenty-eight in Franklin. Only 16 percent of Crawford County decedents owned harrows, compared with a quarter of Franklin County estates. The highest incidence of ownership among the three counties occurred in Jasper, where the eighteen decedents who owned harrows represented 45 percent of the sample. Harrows were used to break the soil, pulverize clods, and smooth the surface. They differed from plows in that they were designed to work at very shallows depths and were not intended for turning the soil. Because of this, harrows were often used after plowing to create a consistent planting bed, and after planting to cover newly sown seeds with a thin layer of soil. Appraisers were often quite specific when listing harrows in inventories. The types represented among the estates include rudimentary iron-tooth, two-horse, and side harrows, as well as the more advanced Terrell, Thomas, and cutaway models. The harrows made by H. D. Terrell and Company of Conyers, Georgia, were well-made iron-and-wood tooth harrows, while the Thomas harrows included smoothing and reversible types made by the Herendeen Manufacturing Company of Geneva, New York.[25] Charles Aiken of Jasper County owned a cutaway harrow, the most advanced and expensive style available, with steel construction and rotating disc blades.[26] The average wealth of a farmer owning a harrow was $986, slightly more than the average of $893 for a plow-owning decedent.

Like harrows, cultivators were used after a field had been plowed to pulverize clods and prepare a smooth seedbed. However, while harrows disturbed the full extent of the soil over which they passed, cultivators provided for greater precision in breaking the soil and could be used in tight areas close to the crop to remove weeds.[27] Cultivators featured a series of shovel blades or teeth set in a tight pattern, which allowed the plowman increased control and made for a good close-quarters tool. They were also used throughout the season and saved considerable time and effort. By the 1870s, many companies were

[24] Barney Hancock, *Sale Bill*, 24 July 1897, Franklin County, Probate Court, Estate Records, 1786–1916, Record Group 159, Subgroup 2, Series 1 (GDA).

[25] Farm Implement News Company, *Farm Implement News Buyer's Guide, 1888* (Chicago: Farm Implement News Company, 1888): 31, 94.

[26] Ibid., 114.

[27] Hurt, *American Agriculture*, 141–142.

FIGURE 3.2. "The 'Continental' Disc Cultivator for Corn and Cotton Culture" promised to "Make a perfect bed for your cotton rows," circa 1899. *The Watt Plow Co.*, p. 28, Courtesy of the Library of Virginia.

producing walk-behind and riding models. Fifteen households in the sample owned cultivators. While the average decedent with a cultivator owned only one, one decedent, James Mathews of Crawford County, owned four (two others each owned two – James Cobb and Joseph Ayers of Franklin County). The 1885 agricultural census indicates that Mathews owned 1,454 acres, which likely explains his need for 4 cultivators.[28] The average value of an estate listing at least one cultivator was $1,054.79, suggesting, perhaps, that wealthier farmers acquired these implements to increase their speed, efficiency, and capacity beyond that which plows and harrows could afford them.

Thirty-three decedents owned planters of some sort. The types of planters available to American farmers expanded exponentially in the mid-to-late nineteenth century, a period of rapid innovation for agricultural tools, implements, and supplies. Planters varied according to the type of seed to be planted,

[28] James N. Mathews, Crawford County, *Property Tax Digests*, 1883–1887, Vol. 3, 3133 (GDA).

FIGURE 3.3. Cotton planter pulled by a horse, circa 1883. J. W. Fitz, *Profitable Farming in the Southern States*, p. 308, Courtesy of the Library of Virginia.

and they ranged from handheld to horse-drawn riding implements. They also differed by how the seed was sown – available models included drop planters, drills, and broadcast seeders.[29] The inventories suggest that farmers in the Georgia Piedmont were selective in the range of planters they purchased and employed. Appraisers were quite succinct in their descriptions of planters, but they listed corn, cotton, and pea planters, handheld as well as animal-powered. In all, forty-seven planters were identified in the inventories. Thirteen of the decedents in Crawford County owned twenty-seven of the planters included in the data set. Although this group averaged two planters per farm, Crawford Elliot owned three and Van Buren Horn owned four.[30] Of the fourteen planters found in Jasper County, William Campbell owned the most, with three, and at the opposite end of the spectrum James Doster owned a one-third share, valued at $1, in a planter, suggesting that he was part owner of a more elaborate horse-drawn planter.[31] Finally, ten decedents in Franklin County owned one planter apiece, ranging in value from $0.23 to $3.00.

29 Hurt, *American Agriculture*, 193–195; "Farm Implement News," 71–79.

30 Crawford Elliot, *Inventory and Appraisement*, 1902, Crawford County, Ordinary Court Minutes, Book B (GDA); Inventory of Van Buren Horn, 1900, Crawford County, Ordinary Court Minutes, Book B.

31 William Campbell, *Inventory and Appraisement*, 1896, Jasper County, Probate Court, Estate Case Files, 1809–1907, Record Group 179, Subgroup 2, Series 3 (GDA); James Doster, *Inventory and Appraisement*, 1889, Jasper County, Probate Court, Estate Case Files, 1809–1907, Record Group 179, Subgroup 2, Series 3.

The tools and equipment owned by farmers in the Georgia Piedmont can also be classified according to the crop grown. Naturally, cotton-related items accounted for a large percentage of the overall agricultural assemblage. Piedmont farmers used purpose-built cotton sowers and planters to get the seed in the ground. The light, wooden, shallow-draft Dixie Boy plow was designed specifically for plowing and cultivating cotton.[32] During the season, farmers used cotton knives and cotton choppers to thin the plants, while bags and baskets were essential when it came time to harvest the crop. Once the crop had been brought in from the field, it was often stored in a cotton house built on the property, and a farmer might well have a cotton balance and calculator to estimate the value of his harvest before he took it to market. Larger farms might even have a cotton press or screw to form the crop into 500-pound bales.

The more self-sufficient or entrepreneurial planters often acquired a gin in order to process cotton. A total of thirty-six gins were owned by twenty-eight households in the probate sample. Eighteen gins were identified in Crawford County, while Jasper had eight and Franklin ten. Proportionally, nearly a quarter of the Crawford County decedents owned gins, 15 percent of those in Jasper, and 6 percent in Franklin. The wealthiest people in the sample were all involved in ginning cotton. Sixteen of the decedents who owned gins had estates worth in excess of $1,000, while the twelve remaining gin owners had estates averaging $319. The presence of high-value items, such as gins, in seemingly modest estates may indicate that the decedents distributed or disposed of some of their possessions prior to death. Given the relatively even distribution of cotton-related tools among the three counties, the lower incidence of gins in the Uplands may suggest that the cotton culture was still in the process of taking hold in the Upper Piedmont, or alternatively that farmers relied on gins from unidentified sources.

Forty- and fifty-saw gins appear to have been the most common, and the brands represented include Miller Centennial, Excelsior, Massie, Pratt, and Winship – the latter produced by the Winship Machine Company of Atlanta, Georgia.[33] Parts such as gin belting, shafts, and condensers indicate that some of these gins were powered by steam or animal traction. The prices indicate that most were major installations designed to process cotton for a large farm or for many farms in the locality. While the cheapest gin, valued at $0.15, was likely a small hand-crank model, obsolete, or broken, the average value of a gin was $32.80 – a sum that could buy a decent mule or horse. The most valuable gin, appraised at $152.50, belonged to William Addington of Franklin County.[34]

[32] Ferleger, "Sharecropping Contracts," 9, 16; Farm Implement News Co., *Farm Implement News Buyer's Guide* (Chicago: Masonic Temple Publishers, 1888): 200, 410, 420.

[33] Algernon L. Smith, *The Story Of The Continental Gin Company, 1900–1952* (Birmingham: Birmingham Publishing, 1952): 48.

[34] William M. Addington, *Inventory and Appraisement*, 1894, Jasper County, Probate Court, Estate Case Files, 1809–1907, Record Group 179, Subgroup 2, Series 3 (GDA).

FIGURE 3.4. Franklin Bowers (left) and Byron Bowers (right) seated beside the Climax Cottonseed Culler, which Byron invented and Franklin marketed through the Bowers Machine Work Company. Franklin County, Georgia, 1900, circa 1900. Note the steam traction engine in the background. Courtesy, Georgia Archives, Vanishing Georgia Collection, image number fra152.

Gins required power, and while the smaller ones were hand-cranked, larger gins needed a steady, dependable source of energy. Although a horse treadle was certainly an option for farmers in the late nineteenth century, portable steam traction engines offered an attractive alternative, albeit for a price. The first viable portable steam engines entered the market in the 1840s, although they remained relatively uncommon until the mid-1880s, by which time their quality had improved enough and their cost had decreased enough to spark a boom in consumer demand that continued until gas powered engines took over the market in 1912.[35] Eleven engines were identified among the estates in Crawford, Jasper, and Franklin. The fact that John Miller of Crawford owned a gin at the time of his death in 1885 suggests that he was among the first to acquire one of these mechanical wonders as they surged in popularity in the 1880s.[36] He was not alone; Crawford County farmer James Mathews had

[35] Stewart H. Holbrook, *Machines of Plenty: Pioneering in American Agriculture* (New York: Macmillan., 1955): 55–57.

[36] John A. Miller, *Inventory and Appraisement*, 1885, Crawford County, Ordinary Court Minutes, Book B (GDA).

a steam engine by the time he died in 1888, as did Elbert Baynes of Jasper at the time of his death in 1886.[37] Five of the six large gins were powered by engines, although only three were described in any detail. William McEntire and John Miller of Crawford both used steam engines, although James Mathews had arguably the most advanced technology with an eight-horsepower engine. Ironically, the second-wealthiest farmer involved in ginning, James Darden of Jasper, had not made the investment in a power engine and still relied on a horse-powered gin.[38] He died in 1881, four years earlier than Miller and seven years before Mathews, which may suggest that engines began to replace horses in powering gins in the Georgia Piedmont between 1881 and 1885.

The average value of engines in the sample was $122, while the highest was $300. The decedents from Crawford and Jasper who acquired engines typically owned twice as much land as the average decedent in their respective counties. In Franklin County, however, the 3 farmers who owned engines held an average of 650 acres, 3 times the 207-acre average among the 109 Franklin County decedents. The engines listed in the inventories ranged from one horsepower to twenty horsepower, with one variable-speed, four-to-six-horsepower engine. The variable-speed Frick owned by Elbert Baynes was the only brand name machine mentioned by appraisers.[39] Most owned a single engine, while John Miller of Crawford and Joseph Edwards of Franklin owned two. Franklin County decedent Micager Martin's 50 percent share in an engine was valued at $300, indicating that the engine itself was worth twice that much.[40] Likewise, James Williams of Crawford owned a 25 percent share valued at $15, which presumably meant the engine was worth $60.[41]

Gins were not the only pieces of equipment Piedmont farmers needed to power. John Miller's inventory lists a steam engine and a gin on the same line, while his sale bill lists an engine and a saw together, which suggests that he operated a sawmill in addition to farming and operating a gin.[42] While the engine-powered gin may have been used to process cotton from his own 1,080-acre property, it is more likely that he was following his entrepreneurial instincts to meet the lumber and ginning needs in his area. James Williams, however, appears to have used his steam traction engine to process grain,

37 James N. Mathews, *Inventory and Appraisement*, 1888, Crawford County, Ordinary Court Minutes, Book B (GDA); Elbert W. Baynes, *Inventory and Appraisement*, 1886, Jasper County, Probate Court, Estate Case Files, 1809–1907, Record Group 179, Subgroup 2, Series 3 (GDA).

38 John Darden, *Inventory and Appraisement*, 1881, Jasper County, Probate Court, Estate Case Files, 1809–1907, Record Group 179, Subgroup 2, Series 3 (GDA). The total value of Darden's personal estate was valued at $3,784.24 at the time of this death in 1881.

39 Elbert Baynes, *Inventory and Appraisement*, 1886.

40 Micager W. Martin, *Inventory and Appraisement*, 1889, Franklin County, Probate Court, Estate Records, 1786–1916, Record Group 159, Subgroup 2, Series 1 (GDA).

41 James M. Williams, *Inventory and Appraisement*, 1898, Jasper County, Probate Court, Estate Case Files, 1809–1907, Record Group 179, Subgroup 2, Series 3 (GDA).

42 John A. Miller, *Inventory and Appraisement*, Crawford County, 1885.

FIGURE 3.5. The "'Peerless' Portable Steam Engine on Wheels" and the two to four horsepower "Domestic Steam Engine" designed for the farm, circa 1899. *The Watt Plow Co.*, p. 73, Courtesy of the Library of Virginia.

since his inventory lists an "engine & separator" together, as was common in the Midwest.[43] Likewise, grain threshers identified in all three counties could

[43] James M. Williams, *Inventory and Appraisement*, 1898, Jasper County, Probate Court, Estate Case Files, 1809–1907, Record Group 179, Subgroup 2, Series 3 (GDA); Holbrook, *Machines of Plenty*, 56–57.

have been powered by portable steam engines. In fact, the inventories for each of the nine decedents who owned engines included either grain-processing implements or logging equipment in addition to gins. These individuals were evidently maximizing the return on their investment in a steam engine, as well as reducing their need for labor, by adding machine power to more than one crop or productive activity. Moreover, the presence of gins, engines, threshers, and separators in the same inventory suggests that these farmers were willing to take a risk and invest in several state-of-the-art implements.

The probate samples from each of the three counties provide considerable evidence for the continued importance of corn and small-grain production throughout the period under study. While corn was equally important to all three counties, the inventories from Franklin and Jasper counties reveal more wheat- and small-grain-related tools and equipment than in Crawford County, which supports the generally accepted pattern of crop preference in the counties and may speak to the higher level of effort required to harvest and process wheat, oats, and similar grains. In addition to corncribs, corn knives, and corn shellers, there was a great variety of small-grain-related items listed. Virtually all of the tools for small grains were associated with the harvest and post-harvest processing. Scythes, oat cutters, grain cradles, and cradle stocks were tools for harvesting small grains. While scythes were sometimes acquired for mowing hay and grass, cradle-scythes were designed expressly for cutting sheaves of wheat and "cradling" – keeping the sheaves together until they could be gathered into shocks in the field.[44] The persistence of grain cradles throughout the period under study leaves no doubt that Piedmont farmers remained committed to the cultivation of wheat and oats, even if the overall production numbers declined over time.

Grain fans, threshers, thrashers, separators, vibrators, and wheat sieves were used to process the grains once they had been harvested. First developed in the 1830s and 1840s, wheat fans, vibrators, and separators were hand-cranked machines designed to separate the wheat from the chaff once the wheat had been brought in from the field. Threshers and vibrators, on the other hand, were horse-drawn and designed for use in the field as the grain was harvested. Early threshers simply mechanized the cutting process, but by the 1840s they had begun to combine harvesting with separating the wheat from chaff and stalks. Once the wheat was cut, it fell onto a canvas belt, which dumped the wheat into sieves that separated the grain from waste. By the 1870s, threshers had become even more sophisticated. Engine-powered threshers called vibrators reduced the amount of time and labor required at the end of the season by combining many of the harvesting and processing steps, making it easier to process the crop in the field immediately after it was harvested.[45] Other examples of advanced

44 Hurt, *American Agriculture*, 58–59, 152–153.
45 Holbrook, *Machines of Plenty*, 51–51, 64–68.

harvest-related equipment listed in the probate inventories include pea thrashers, horse-drawn mowers, horse-drawn rakes, and combination rakes.

Although farming was the primary occupation in each of the three counties, the probate inventories provide evidence that the decedents practiced a number of additional productive activities. Such activities might include blacksmithing, building, cabinetmaking, jug making, logging and milling, shoemaking, tanning, and weaving. These are endeavors that people undertook as a sideline to the household's main occupation. Often times, therefore, the presence of an item in the inventory suggests that a certain trade was being practiced; however, the scarcity of functionally related items implies that the activity was limited in scope.[46] Evidence for some of the trades is elusive and consists of a single tantalizing clue, such as the "tanner's rubbers" listed in Elijah Purcell's 1890 Franklin County inventory, or the "jug wheel" listed among the odds and ends belonging to William Sandefur's Crawford County estate.[47]

Although Barney Martin and John Tabor were the only individuals in the sample identified as blacksmiths by the federal census, sixty-nine of the 199 estates included blacksmith-related tools and equipment, and ownership of such items was spread fairly evenly among the three counties. In Tabor's estate inventory, his tools were appraised at $28, while the inventory for Martin, an African American from Crawford County, did not include any blacksmith tools. In fact, Martin's entire estate consisted of 250 acres of land, a small number of livestock, and a few household items valued at $25, suggesting that his estate was largely dispersed prior to his death. The 1880 agricultural census supports this interpretation, as Martin reported owning $25 worth of tools in 1879, which correlates to the level of Tabor's investment.[48] Overall, the average value of blacksmith equipment among the sixty-nine estates was $9.55. These decedents typically owned more than 200 acres, with the average being 469 acres.

Eleven of the estates had metalworking assemblages valued between $15 and $38, which suggests that these individuals, like Martin and Tabor, had enough tools and equipment to provide blacksmithing services beyond what a small-to-middling farm would need (mainly repairing equipment and shoeing draft animals). The three decedents who owned the most metalworking equipment in terms of dollar value were all identified as farmers in the 1880 census. Two of

46 Overton et al., *Production and Consumption in English Households*, 65.

47 Elijah Purcell, *Inventory and Appraisement*, 1890, Franklin County, Probate Court, Estate Records, 1786–1916, Record Group 159, Subgroup 2, Series 1 (GDA); *Inventory and Appraisement*, 1881, Crawford County, Probate Court, Miscellaneous Records of the Inferior Court, 1822–1900, Record Group 139, Subgroup 2, Series 1. (GDA).

48 John Tabor, *Inventory and Appraisement*, 1887, Franklin County, Probate Court, Estate Records, 1786–1916, Record Group 159, Subgroup 2, Series 1. (GDA); Barney Martin, *Inventory and Appraisement, 1896*, Crawford County Property Tax Digests, 1877–1910 (GDA).

them, Elbert Baynes and Thomas Dickson, owned more than 1,000 acres and had estates valued in excess of $1,900, suggesting that their substantial investment in smithing was to support large farming operations. The third, Franklin County farmer Elisha Mitchell, owned 153 acres and had a personal estate valued at $314, yet he had $30 in blacksmith tools, constituting 10 percent of his assets outside of real estate. Mitchell's investing such a large proportion of his wealth in smithing tools indicates that he may have engaged in metalworking as a form of by-employment, providing a valuable service to his neighbors. For the sake of comparison, the two decedents who worked primarily as blacksmiths had personal estates in which tools represented between 4 and 7 percent of the total value. One other estate reflects a pattern like Mitchell's, which suggests that a farmer practicing a side business as a blacksmith was not a total anomaly. James Chapplear of Franklin County owned 500 acres and died possessed of a personal estate valued at $435.[49] That estate included $22.50 in blacksmith tools, representing 4 percent of the total value. Jane Mitchell, Elisha Mitchell's widow, also had smithing tools representing 4 percent of her personal wealth; however, this likely represents the wholesale transmission of her husband's estate to her upon his death in 1888, since it was valued at less than $500 and thus was exempt under Georgia law from use in the payment of debts. Jane possessed the bulk of the estate, including the blacksmith tools, when she died in 1892.[50]

The pattern of ownership of carpentry tools is more difficult to decipher. A total of 135 estates, representing 68 percent of the sample, included carpentry tools of some sort. As with blacksmith tools, carpentry tools appeared in roughly the same proportion of inventories across the three counties – 72 percent of Crawford decedents, 65 percent of Jasper decedents, and 67 percent of Franklin decedents owned woodworking tools of some sort. This is not unexpected, since repairs and small-scale building projects are a regular part of farm life even today. To be sure, plenty of common tools appear in the inventories, from hammers and chisels to saws, drawknives, and drills. However, the decedents in our sample owned a striking number of specialized carpentry tools as well, such as spoke augers and fellows saws (for wagon-making), cooper's adzes and scorps (for barrel-making), and froes and shingle mills (for making shingles).[51] Likewise, several estates contained the more refined and precise tools required to do the detailed handwork in cabinetmaking,

[49] James H. Chapplear, *Inventory and Appraisement*, 1894, Franklin County, Probate Court, Estate Records, 1786–1916, Record Group 159, Subgroup 2, Series 1 (GDA).

[50] "Petition of Mrs. Jane Mitchell, widow of E. Mitchell, dec.d, for 12 months support, 15 December 1880," Franklin County, Probate Court, Estate Bond Books, 1853–1880, Record Group 159, Subgroup 2, Series 37 (GDA), page 59; Jane Mitchell, *Inventory and Appraisement*, 1892, Franklin County, Probate Court, Estate Records, 1786–1916, Record Group 159, Subgroup 2, Series 1 (GDA).

[51] Graham Blackburn, *Traditional Woodworking Handtools: An Illustrated Reference Guide for the Woodworker* (New York: Gramercy Books, 2000): 285–288.

including chisels, planes, compasses, gauges, ratchet drills, tack hammers, and wood vises.[52]

The value of each estate's collection of woodworking tools ranged widely, from $0.25 to $115.65; the average was $10.00, and the median $4.30. Jasper County had the highest average at $15.02, followed by Crawford County at $12.73, and then Franklin at $6.87. Ironically Franklin County, despite having the lowest average tool value among the three counties, was home to the only decedent in this study whose primary occupation was listed as "carpenter" in the federal census: Newton Teat, who was described as a carpenter in the 1880 census, and who had an estate valued at $595.81 at the time of his death in 1889.[53] His woodworking tools were valued at $9.50, representing a mere 2 percent of the total estate value. The agricultural census of 1880, however, reveals that he owned $75 worth of tools in 1879, representing 5 percent of an estate then valued at $1,500 – we can assume, therefore, that Teat gave away most of his estate, including his carpentry tools, prior to his death (either that or he suffered an economic catastrophe).[54]

Ten individuals in the sample owned assemblages of woodworking tools valued at $20 or higher. Of these, Thomas Dickson of Franklin County had the most invested in tools, at $115.65, representing 7 percent of the total value of his estate, followed closely by John Dent of Crawford County, who had 11 percent of his wealth invested in tools appraised at $114.00 in his 1880 inventory.[55] Likewise, the $64.31 that John Tomlinson held in tools represented 12 percent of his overall worth, while Crawford County farmers John McElmurray and Thomas Sanders each had 4 percent of their wealth invested in tools, at $37.95 and $23.99, respectively.[56] Given the large amounts of money Dickson, Dent, McElmurray, Tomlinson, and Sanders invested in carpentry tools relative to their overall worth, it is possible that these men were engaged in carpentry or cabinetmaking at a level beyond home use, possibly representing by-employment to their primary occupation as farmers. Furthermore, Dickson's considerable investments in carpentry, blacksmith, and sawmill tools

52 Ibid., xvi–xx.

53 Newton Teat, *Inventory and Appraisement*, 1889, Franklin County, Probate Court, Estate Records, 1786–1916, Record Group 159, Subgroup 2, Series 1 (GDA).

54 Franklin County, *Property Tax Digest*, 1878–1882, Vol. 3, 1354 (GDA).

55 Thomas Dickson, *Inventory and Appraisement*, 1900, Franklin County, Probate Court, Estate Records, 1786–1916, Record Group 159, Subgroup 2, Series 1 (GDA); John W. Dent, Inventory and Appraisement, 1880, Crawford County, Probate Court, Miscellaneous Records of the Inferior Court, 1822–1900, Record Group 139, Subgroup 2, Series 1. (GDA).

56 John R. McElmurray, *Inventory and Appraisement*, 1886, Crawford County, Probate Court, Miscellaneous Records of the Inferior Court, 1822–1900, Record Group 139, Subgroup 2, Series 1. (GDA); John D. Tomlinson, *Inventory and Appraisement*, 1891, Jasper County, Probate Court, Estate Case Files, 1809–1907, Record Group 179, Subgroup 2, Series 3. (GDA); Thomas J. Sanders, Inventory and Appraisement, 1887, Crawford County, Probate Court, Miscellaneous Records of the Inferior Court, 1822–1900, Record Group 139, Subgroup 2, Series 1. (GDA).

and equipment suggest the intent to diversify his farming operation by developing capabilities in three closely related crafts.

Several of the inventories also listed tools or materials suggesting that the deceased produced building materials or was involved in the building trades. John Franklin of Jasper, Crawford County's James Mathews and John Miller, and (once again) the entrepreneurial Thomas Dickson of Franklin, all had steam engines listed with saws, suggesting large-scale logging and milling operations.[57] The lumber, 4,000 shingles, and 500 bricks owned by John Miller strongly suggest that he was a builder or a producer of building supplies. Each of these individuals had personal estates worth between $800 and $5,000, making them some of the wealthiest men in the three counties. Furthermore, each owned between 900 and 1,500 acres, so they likely had forests and woodlots that could support profitable logging and milling operations.

Activities associated with textile production, including sewing, spinning, and weaving, were also well represented in the probate records, and textile production appears to have been an important form of by-employment for women. In all, sixty-four inventories offer some evidence of textile-related activities. Twenty-one of those sixty-four households had a sewing machine, with twelve in Franklin County, five in Jasper, and four in Crawford. Eight decedents possessed a spinning wheel, a loom, or a flax wheel. The five who had spinning wheels included Fred Weaver of Franklin County, who also owned sheep and sheep shears.[58] Four owned at least one loom, and two had a loom and a spinning wheel. Milly Voiles of Franklin County appears to have produced textiles on a scale beyond home use – she had a spinning wheel and four looms.[59] Similarly, Pleasant Bellamy's Franklin County estate included a loom and two spinning wheels.[60] The inventories with evidence of textile production, like the ones with blacksmithing and woodworking tools, generally fall in the middling wealth categories. These individuals typically owned around 214 acres and had estates averaging $2,725 in value, which suggests they had the resources to engage in additional productive activities that would reduce their dependence on merchants or craftsmen.

In addition to the two decedents whom the census identified as merchants (Michael McDowell of Jasper County and William Royston of Franklin), one

[57] John Franklin, *Inventory and Appraisement*, 1886, Jasper County, Probate Court, Estate Case Files, 1809–1907, Record Group 179, Subgroup 2, Series 3 (GDA); Thomas Dickson, *Inventory and Appraisement*, Franklin County, Probate Court, Estate Records, 1786–1916, Record Group 159, Subgroup 2, Series 1 (GDA); James N. Mathews, *Inventory and Appraisement*, 1888, Crawford County, Ordinary Court Minutes, Book B (GDA); John A. Miller, *Inventory and Appraisement*, 1885, Crawford County, Ordinary Court Minutes, Book B (GDA).

[58] Fred A. Weaver, *Inventory and Appraisement*, 1891, Franklin County, Probate Court, Estate Records, 1786–1916, Record Group 159, Subgroup 2, Series 1 (GDA).

[59] Milly P. Voiles, *Inventory and Appraisement*, 1884, Franklin County, Probate Court, Estate Records, 1786–1916, Record Group 159, Subgroup 2, Series 1 (GDA).

[60] Pleasant Bellamy, *Inventory and Appraisement*, 1885, Franklin County, Probate Court, Estate Records, 1786–1916, Record Group 159, Subgroup 2, Series 1 (GDA).

of the farmers in the sample might have been involved in a mercantile venture. The probate inventory for William Rampley of Franklin County, who died in 1896 at the age of seventy-eight, included an "office clock," a safe, and $900 in "merchandise."[61] Given that these three items were listed together, we can assume that the safe was not a food safe, a common piece of furniture in many nineteenth-century homes.[62] Unfortunately, the inventory provides no details about what the merchandise might have been. The 1880 census identifies Rampley solely as a farmer, although he was able to employ a married black couple, David and Milley Dooley. Milley worked as a servant, and the census identified David as a farm laborer.[63] The $2,202 in cash listed in Rampley's inventory may be another indication of mercantile activity – it could represent profits he made through the sale of merchandise.

In order to assess the full context of production, it is necessary to know what crops the farmers in Crawford, Jasper, and Franklin counties cultivated, as well as how they intended to use those crops. Doing this allows us to better understand the ways in which these farmers worked to maximize production, and how they balanced their desire for self-sufficiency with the need to take risks in order to succeed. Overall, the probate inventories reveal a narrow range of crop diversity among Piedmont farmers. Although a wide variety of garden produce was available for them to choose from, the produce they grew reflects a preference for the more durable and marketable field crops, such as cotton and corn, to the exclusion of more perishable garden vegetables, fruits, and berries (cotton, of course, was the most important crop by far in all three counties).[64] Certain products associated with home consumption, such as smoked meats, sorghum syrup, and fodder, appeared in the inventories of many decedents; however, these were more durable than most other garden produce, and they held their value longer. Some variation in the types of crops found in inventories, we must bear in mind, results from the time of year when the death occurred (although produce of some sort was evident in virtually all of the estates, suggesting active involvement in farming year-round). The estate of Barney Hancock is an excellent example. Hancock died in June 1898, early in the growing season, and his family waited until fall to begin the probate process;

61 William Rampley, *Inventory and Appraisement*, 1898, Franklin County, Probate Court, Estate Records, 1786–1916, Record Group 159, Subgroup 2, Series 1 (GDA, Georgia).

62 Overton et al., *Production and Consumption in English Households*, 35–36.

63 U.S. Bureau of the Census, *Tenth Census of the United States, 1880, Population*, Franklin County, Georgia, Township 264, Family 17, page 2.

64 William N. White, *Gardening for the South, or How to Grow Vegetables and Fruits* (New York: Orange Judd, 1868): 161–433; Dr. A. Oemler, *Truck-Farming at the South: A Guide to the Raising of Vegetables for Northern Markets* (New York: Orange Judd, 1910): 119–251; John Frederick Duggar, *Southern Field Crops* (New York: Macmillan, 1911): 422–547; Louis Ferleger, "Science, Technology, and Farm Implements: Agricultural Research at the Alabama Experiment Station," *Agricultural History* 62, no. 2 (Spring 1988): 208–224; Sam Bowers Hilliard, *Hog Meat and Hoecake: Food Supply in the Old South, 1840–1860* (Carbondale: Southern Illinois University Press, 1972): 173–82.

had they begun the process in June, the estate would likely have included far less cotton and other produce.

It comes as no surprise that cotton was the most commonly listed and most thoroughly described field crop in the inventories, given its place as the primary focus of the Piedmont economy. The cotton season was long – it began in February, when the ground was first plowed and manured, and stretched late into fall, when the pickers made pass after pass through the fields to collect each successive round of opening bolls.[65] After the fields were plowed in late winter, they were allowed to sit for several weeks so that frost and rain could break down the soil and smooth it out. Planting typically occurred in mid-to-late April in the Piedmont region and could last into June.[66] Once the cotton seedlings broke through the soil – about ten days after planting – farmers began running light plows between the rows to thin the weeds and extraneous cotton plants, as well as throwing successive layers of soil toward the center of the beds to "hill" the cotton seedlings. They would hill the plants at least once every two weeks until early August, when the first bolls began to open. During this time, farmers used hoes to thin or "chop out" cotton plants, leaving clumps of three or four together to promote more vigorous growth.[67] Picking typically began in late August, peaked in October, and continued through November and sometimes into December.

Appraisers frequently described a decedent's cotton crop in ways that left no doubt as to where it was in terms of the season. Seed cotton, or cottonseed, usually referred to the seed that was removed during ginning to be set aside for next year's planting; once collected, cottonseed could be sold to be pressed for oil, kept by the farmer to fertilize fields, or fed to pigs and cattle to fatten them for slaughter.[68] Appraisers specified "cotton in the field" or "unpicked cotton" to designate a crop under cultivation. They would sometimes even chance an estimate of "bales of cotton in field" if the crop was closer to harvest. "Picked cotton," "cotton in the seed," and "cotton in house" referred to newly harvested cotton that was stored on the farm, often in purpose-built cotton houses, to dry out until enough had been picked to make a trip to the gin worthwhile. Once cotton had been ginned in December and January, appraisers would list it as "cotton lint" or "lint cotton." Finally, the cotton lint was pressed into bales ranging from 300 to 500 pounds, depending on the market destination.[69] Several of the inventories from the three counties differentiated between "new cotton bales" and "old cotton bales," suggesting that bales were not always sold promptly once the cotton had been processed.

[65] Joseph B. Lyman, *Cotton Culture* (New York: Orange Judd, 1868): 23–42; Aiken, *The Cotton Plantation South*, 99.

[66] Lyman, *Cotton Culture*, 18–19; Duggar, *Southern Field Crops*, 377.

[67] Lyman, *Cotton Culture*, 24.

[68] Duggar, *Southern Field Crops*, 459, 531.

[69] Duggar, *Southern Field Crops*, 51–59.

The only qualitative designation for cotton appearing in the probate inventories was "middling cotton."

Although cotton was the primary staple grown in the three counties, corn was a close second. It was raised for human consumption as well as to provide a cheap, high-protein feed for working stock during the growing season and for fattening livestock destined for slaughter in the colder months.[70] Far fewer designations for corn appeared in the inventories of Crawford, Jasper, and Franklin counties than for cotton. Most often, appraisers referred simply to "corn" – "white corn" was the only specific variety mentioned. "Corn in the ear" represented whole ears placed in a corncrib to dry for later processing, corn that had been shelled was listed as "corn seed," and the appraisers even listed "refused corn" on occasion, suggesting that it had been deemed unfit for milling or market. Appraisers also listed corn meal, indicating that the corn had been ground for table use.

Perhaps the most telling indicator of corn's importance to the cotton economy and to the self-reliance of farmers is that it competed directly with cotton for resources and care. Corn's season largely coincided with that of cotton, and it had many of the same needs that occurred at about the same time. As a result, corn was often neglected, since it was hardier than cotton. Farmers could begin planting corn in March, a bit earlier than cotton, but they often delayed doing so until the pre-season preparation of cotton fields had been completed and the cotton crop safely put in.[71] Like cotton, corn benefited from frequent plowing between the rows in June and July to thin plants, to allow greater penetration of air and water, and to gradually hill the plants, which reinforced the base of the stalks and helped the nutrients in the soil make their way to the roots. Corn ripened and was ready for harvest at the same time as cotton, so corn and corn fodder were pulled between late August and early October, when the cotton harvest was in full swing. As a result, farmers frequently harvested whole ears and placed them in corn cribs unshucked and unhusked, to be processed later.[72] The average harvest per acre in three counties in 1900 ranged from 6.5 bushels in Jasper to 8.8 in Crawford, and 10.5 in Franklin.[73]

Field peas (often referred to as cowpeas) were also important to farmers' efforts to remain as self-sufficient as possible. Field peas were likely favored over beans and green peas because they represented an effort-maximizing crop that could be inter-planted with corn, required minimal attention, and could be used either for human consumption, as feed for livestock, or as a fertilizing cover crop. Southern farmers traditionally sowed cowpeas among the corn when it was planted, so that the peas would grow and mature over the course

[70] James Oscar Morgan, *Field Crops for the Cotton-Belt* (New York: Macmillan, 1917): 201–202.

[71] Hilliard, *Hog Meat and Hoecake*, 152–154.

[72] Duggar, *Southern Field Crops*, 181.

[73] Le Grand Powers, U.S. Bureau of the Census, *Twelfth Census of the United States, 1900: Vol. 5–6, Agriculture; pt. 2, Crops and Irrigation* (Washington, DC, 1901–1902), 158.

of the growing season. Once the peas had been harvested, the vines were plowed under to provide nitrogen to the soil.[74] In addition, peas of all sorts could be sown for hay, pasture, or green manure – they would be plowed under early in the growing season (prior to planting) to provide an extra dose of nitrogen, which was especially beneficial in the northern parts of the Cotton Belt like Jasper and Franklin counties.[75] Crawford County produced 2,000 bushels of cowpeas in 1879, while Jasper and Franklin produced more than 4,000 bushels each.[76] The peas represented in the inventories include several variants of the cowpea, such as clay peas, field peas, and white peas. Speckled peas were likely a variant of the genus *dolichos* – actually a type of bean but usually called black-eyed peas. Rough peas and ground peas, on the other hand, were similar to cowpeas in their appearance and growth patterns but were likely a variant of wild pea that was cultivated for forage, hay, or green manure.[77]

Small grains listed in the inventories included wheat, oats, and rye. Rye was seldom grown for food in the South and was most often sown as a cover crop, to be plowed under at the end of the season to fix nitrogen in the soil.[78] Jasper County cultivated the most rye of the three counties, producing 250 bushels on 48 acres in 1900. Oats were also grown primarily as a nitrogen-fixing cover crop and to prevent erosion, but farmers also used them to provide feed for horses and as a late-winter pasture crop, particularly in the southern Uplands.[79] Several inventories listed "rustproof oats" – a supposedly rust-resistant variety that could grow well in the hot and humid South – or "sheaf oats," which simply referred to oats that had been bundled after harvest.[80] Once again Jasper produced the most, with 38,480 bushels from 1,921 acres (an average of 20 bushels per acre); the 1,842 acres in oats in Crawford yielded 22,010 bushels (12 bushels per acre).[81] While wheat was not commonly grown in the Lower South because of the perception that the hot, humid climate was not conducive to successful cultivation, it was more prevalent in the Georgia Uplands, although it was primarily grown for home consumption, with perhaps some for local exchange.[82] This pattern is apparent in the 3 counties under examination here, with Franklin County in 1899 producing 39,910 bushels on 8,105 acres (a per-acre average of 4.9 bushels) and Jasper producing

74 Duggar, *Southern Field Crops*, 212.

75 Gray, *History of Agriculture*, vol. 2, 823; Morgan, *Field Crops for the Cotton-Belt*, 288; W. F. Wright. *The History of the Cowpea and Its Introduction into America* (Washington, DC, 1907): 12–14.

76 *Tenth Census of the United States, 1880 Agriculture: 1880*, 265.

77 Hilliard, *Hog Meat and Hoecake*, 125.

78 Ibid., 6, 50.

79 Gray, *History of Agriculture*, 820.

80 Mark Alfred Carleton, *Lessons from the Grain Rust Epidemic of 1904* (Washington, DC, 1905): 16.

81 Powers, *Crops and Irrigation*, 158.

82 Gray, *History of Agriculture*, 816–818.

20,300 bushels for a 3.7 bushel-per-acre average; Crawford, by comparison, grew wheat on a mere 4,620 acres in 1899.[83]

Cane syrup and molasses were also important to households in the Piedmont. While sugarcane had long been grown in the Lower South, sorghum was a Chinese import introduced to the United States in the 1850s.[84] It became popular as a sugar substitute that could be grown in the northern areas of the South, where frost prevented sugarcane cultivation. In addition, sorghum cane, like many other Southern farm crops, could be used as fodder for livestock. Although sorghum could be planted several weeks after the earliest corn, most was planted in May, and planting could extend into July if the crop was meant to provide fodder.[85] Both syrup and molasses were produced from sugarcane and sorghum cane, although the appraisers usually failed to identify which plant was used. The inventories simply listed "cane," "molasses," "syrup," and "cane syrup." Thankfully the federal agricultural census of 1900 provides some insight into the relative volume of sugar and sorghum. Crawford grew only sugarcane, producing 12,086 gallons of cane syrup and 3,260 gallons of cane molasses.[86] Jasper produced both sugarcane and sorghum, with 956 gallons of cane syrup, 5,423 gallons of cane molasses, and 7,454 gallons of sorghum syrup.[87] Franklin, on the other hand, was located too far north for sugarcane to be viable and had to rely solely on sorghum; Franklin County farmers produced a total of 22,703 gallons of sorghum syrup in 1899.[88]

In addition, inventories listed garden crops intended primarily for home use, including potatoes, peanuts, pickled cucumbers, fruits, and tobacco. Unfortunately, appraisers provided minimal description of these crops, making it difficult to determine what varieties were favored or even the intended use of the crop. Potatoes, for example, were listed simply as "potatoes" or "banks of potatoes," with no distinction among white, Irish, or sweet potatoes, all of which were grown in the Piedmont.[89] Likewise, the reference to a "seed garden" provides no indication of whether the seeds were intended to start field crops, garden crops, or a product intended for home use, exchange, or sale. In some cases, the modifiers appraisers used provide a fairly clear picture of

83 Powers, *Crops and Irrigation*, 158.

84 Gray, *History of Agriculture*, 829; Hilliard, *Hog Meat and Hoecake*, 52, 179; Peter Collier, *Sorghum: Its Culture and Manufacture Economically Considered as a Source of Sugar, Syrup, and Fodder* (Cincinnati: Robert Clark & Company, 1884): 16; Louis Ferleger, "Cutting the Cane: Harvesting in the Louisiana Sugar Industry," *Southern Studies* 23, no. 1 (Spring 1984): 42–59; Ferleger, "Farm Mechanization in the Southern Sugar Sector after the Civil War," *Louisiana History* 23, no. 1 (Winter 1982): 21–34; Ferleger, "Productivity Change in the Post-Bellum Louisiana Sugar Industry," in *Time Series Analysis* (New York: North-Holland Press, 1981): 147–171.

85 Duggar, *Southern Field Crops*, 268.

86 Powers, *Crops and Irrigation*, 218, 481.

87 Ibid., 219, 481, 484.

88 Ibid., 484.

89 Gray, *History of Agriculture*, 826–828 Hilliard, *Hog Meat and Hoecake*, 173–175.

the ways in which farm families preserved fruits and vegetables to extend the use of garden products throughout the year. Several inventories from all three counties included dried fruit, pickles, and apple vinegar. Peanuts were listed among several estates in all three counties. It is almost certain that these were some variant of the smaller Spanish peanut that accounted for 90 percent of the peanuts grown in the United States before 1940. Peanuts in the South were intended primarily for cattle and pigs, although many progressive agriculturalists promoted their cultivation for human consumption. The herbaceous part of the plant was used as a forage crop or dried as hay, while the peanut itself was excellent for fattening hogs and cattle.[90]

Like crops, livestock are another subtle indicator of the choices farmers made in the area of production, particularly in terms of diversifying their operations. In the inventories from Crawford, Jasper, and Franklin counties, a large majority of the livestock-related items consist of bridles, harnesses, and the gear used with plows and wagons. Inventory items related to the daily care of livestock included currycombs, brushes, and troughs. Spaying needles and spaying knives were the only veterinary equipment among the decedents' possessions – they would have been used for sewing up lacerations, spaying animals with diseased ovaries, or castrating draft and food stock.[91] Several decedents had tools and equipment related specifically to goats and sheep, which may indicate an effort to diversify production, even if only for home use. Goat bells were used to signal the location of ranging goats, and goat collars were used to tether the animals. Sheep shears and wool cards were almost certainly production-related, especially in Franklin County, where the persistence of spinning wheels and looms in the probate record suggests that certain farmers continued to produce their own textiles even as these items became cheaper and more widely available to consumers throughout the United States.

As with garden crops, the probate sample suggests that the range of livestock held by yeoman farmers in the Georgia Piedmont was limited. Cattle, horses, mules, goats, sheep, swine, and farmyard fowl were all represented in the inventories, conforming to the general consensus among historians about the narrow range of husbandry practiced by cotton farmers in the last decades of the nineteenth century.[92] With the exception of a handful of Jersey cattle and peafowl, livestock were listed in catch-all categories as mules, horses, oxen, cows, bulls, hogs, sows, chickens, and ducks. Whereas this generic type of identification may indicate a lack of familiarity with or interest in the specific breeds, it is

90 B. W. Jones. *The Peanut Plant, Its Cultivation and Uses* (New York: Orange Judd, 1885): 44, 58, and 61–62; Gray, *History of Agriculture*, 828; Hilliard, *Hog Meat and Hoecake*, 100.

91 Wales E. Van Ame, *Veterinary obstetrics* (Fort Wayne: Wales E. Van Ame, 1903): 55; J. Russell Manning, *The Illustrated Stock Doctor and Live-Stock Encyclopedia* (Guelph, Ontario: World Publishing, 1881): 322, 462, 478, 485.

92 Range, *A Century of Georgia Agriculture*, 103–107; Julius Rubin, "The Limits of Agricultural Progress in the Nineteenth-Century South," *Agricultural History* 49, no. 2 (April 1975): 366–367.

much more likely that the Georgia farmers in the sample population raised livestock for home consumption or local exchange, and that few were involved in breeding, where maintaining thoroughbred or "blooded" animals would be much more important. Furthermore, the ways in which appraisers inventoried livestock suggest that they were keenly aware of the value and function of a whole range of an animal's characteristics apart from breed. Specifically, the modifiers that appraisers used to identify or differentiate animals provide a great deal of insight into how livestock was perceived and valued. Modifiers denoting color, age, breeding condition, market intent, location, and seasonality were all used to categorize animals.

Swine provide an excellent example of how appraisers made distinctions within a large and broadly defined category. A manual on selecting and raising hogs published by the Georgia State Commissioner of Agriculture in 1877 encouraged farmers in the state to consider using thoroughbred brood stock, such as Berkshire, Essex, Poland China, Guinea, and Jersey Red hogs, to elevate the quality of production in the state.[93] The manual, however, clearly indicated that it was fighting to overcome the common perception that half-breed or mixed-blood "common" hogs were best suited to the practice among Georgia farmers of allowing the animals to forage in woods and harvested fields prior to penning and fattening them at the end of the season.[94] The probate data suggest that the state's advice on hog breeding continued to fall on deaf ears during the last two decades of the nineteenth century. Swine were the second-most-common farm animal in the three counties during the period under study, accounting for 1,536 of the approximately 3,700 animals listed in the inventories and reflecting the continued importance of pork to the Southern diet in the postbellum period.[95] Within the swine category, the 1,109 hogs outnumbered the 428 sows by almost 3:1. In all, 63 percent of the estates inventoried (n = 125) listed hogs among the possessions, while 28 percent of the decedents owned sows. The median holding for sows and hogs was five.

Although none of the inventories identified specific breeds of swine, descriptions of individual pigs were often quite specific, suggesting that these animals were indeed very important to Piedmont farmers. Appraisers frequently made note of color, which might be red, black, blue, dun, mouse, or sandy – or a combination, such as black-and-white or spotted. Darker varieties predominated, in accordance with the Southern practice of selecting for dark-colored swine that would be less likely than lighter ones to suffer from sunburn, mange, or other skin diseases – especially because the stock ranged free and foraged for most of the season.[96] Age distinctions were limited to mature adults (listed as sows, boars, hogs, and pigs), while the only juvenile designation used was

93 Thomas P. Janes, *A Manual on the Hog* (Atlanta: James P. Harrison and Company, 1877): 20–31.

94 Janes, *Manual on the Hog*, 31.

95 Gray, *History of Agriculture*, 206–209; Hilliard, *Hog Meat and Hoecake*, 42, 58, 92.

96 Janes, *Manual on the Hog*, 10, 20, 90.

shoat, which is a weaned pig less than two years old. Breeding descriptors included "brood sow," "boar," "open hog," and "open sow" – boar refers to full-grown, uncastrated male swine, an open hog is one that has been bred only once, and an open sow is one that has given birth to a single litter of piglets.[97] Other modifiers were used to denote the purpose for which hogs were raised, such as "pork hog," "fat hog," and "fattening hog," all of which indicate that the hog was destined for the table, whereas "choice" and "first choice" hogs may have been intended for breeding or for the market. Finally, the modifiers that appraisers used to describe hogs sometimes provided an indication of how they were fed and cared for. "Hogs in the range" and "pigs in the woods" referred to foraging swine, while "pigs in pen" or "fattening hogs" referred to the practice of penning hogs later in the season, to control feeding in order to maximize weight gain prior to slaughter.

Mules and horses accounted for 12 percent of the livestock listed in the inventories. A total of 284 mules were included among the estates; horses appear to have been less important, numbering only 165. Scholars have long recognized the crucial role of mules in Southern agriculture, where they were highly valued for their agility, stamina, intelligence, resistance to disease, and suitability to work in hot climates.[98] A horse mule results from crossbreeding a male ass, known as a jack, with a female horse.[99] The horse provides the size, speed, and power, while the donkey contributes calmness, intelligence, and stamina to the hybrid. In most cases, mules are infertile. Most mules in Georgia were bred out of state in Kentucky, Missouri, and Tennessee, and most breeders recognized a class of plantation mule that was especially popular in the South.[100] Plantation mules were smaller than the standard draft mules commonly found in the Northern and central states; subcategories of plantation mules included the large, dependable sugar mule and the lighter cotton mule.

The probate data from Crawford, Jasper, and Franklin counties indicate that 44 percent of the decedents (n = 107) owned mules, with a median holding of two mules. Appraisers specifically identified mules, horse mules, mare mules, and mule colts among the holdings. The animals' ages ranged from less than four years (colts) to twenty-eight. Appraisers also specified a wide range of colors among the mules, including bay, black, chestnut, mouse, roan, sorrel, and a chestnut-and-sorrel mix. Frequently, mules were identified by given names, among the most popular of which were Alex, Beck, George, Jane, Kate, Mary, Mike, and Mollie. Twenty-three percent (n = 66) of the mules listed in the

97 Denver Ewing Baughan, "Tarheel Talk," *American Speech* 32, no. 4 (December 1957): 286.

98 Charles S. Plumb, *Judging Farm Animals* (New York: Orange Judd, 1919): 87–195; Martin A. Garrett, Jr., "The Mule in Southern Agriculture: A Requiem," *Journal of Economic History* 50, no. 4 (December 1990): 925–927.

99 The correct term for the result of a crossbreed between a jackass and a horse mare is "horse mule," although most refer to the hybrid simply as a "mule."

100 Ransom and Sutch, *One Kind of Freedom: The Economic Consequences of Emancipation* (New York: Cambridge University Press, 1977): 50; Plumb, *Judging Farm Animals*, 193–194.

probate sample were named, compared to 11 percent of horses (n = 19) and 2 percent of cattle (n = 28). Among animals that farmers named, mules were the most likely to have human names.[101] Only 11 percent of the names given to mules were based on the animal's characteristics – for example, Boney, Leader, or Pep – whereas 26 percent of named horses and 36 percent of named cows were called by such non-human monikers. The higher degree of anthropomorphism in the naming of mules suggests just how closely farmers worked with these draft animals, and the bond that developed through the need to understand their personalities and habits. Donkeys were far less common than mules, and in the entire sample only three specific descriptors were given for donkeys: two were identified as jacks, two as jennies, and one as a fourteen-year-old bay-colored mare.[102] There is no indication that either of the jennies was used for breeding mules.

A total of 100 decedents from Crawford, Jasper, and Franklin counties owned horses, representing 53 percent of all the estates. Within this group, decedents averaged one horse per household, and slightly fewer than half (n = 46) owned at least one mule as well. Appraisers gave more generic designations to horses than to mules; however, they did identify younger colts, fillies, and an eight-year-old mare, in addition to specifying which animals were brood stock (mares, stallions, and studs). Colors among the horses ranged from white and clay-colored to sorrel, bay, gray, and black. Only nineteen horses were named, representing 11 percent of the total from the three counties. As with mules, human names predominated, including Allen, Bob, Charlie, George, Fannie, Ginnie, and Maud. Non-human names for mares included Rocket and Bounce, while Parrot, Tuck, and Black were among the male horses' names.

The cotton-growing South was never considered cattle country, but, surprisingly, the 1,712 cattle listed in the inventories accounted for nearly half (n = 46%) of all livestock in the three counties. Holdings ranged from a minimum of 1 to a maximum of 133 (owned by John W. Dent of Crawford County), with a median holding of six head of cattle. Moreover, the probate data reveal that 84 percent of the decedents had at least one cow.[103] Following its establishment in 1874, the Georgia Department of Agriculture made many efforts to promote diversity in the state's agriculture. One of its earliest successes was in convincing Georgians to invest in livestock, particularly cattle – farmers might have been receptive to this idea because of the prevailing notion that livestock required less labor than field crops. As a result, the number of cattle increased from around 700,000 head in 1870 to 900,000 head in 1880, a

101 "Anthropomorphic" names were determined to be those that appeared as given names at least once in the 1880, 1900, or 1910 census for Crawford, Jasper, and Franklin counties.

102 Male donkeys are correctly called "Jacks" while females are called "Jennets" or "Jennies;" Plumb, *Judging Farm Animals*, 175.

103 John W. Dent, *Inventory and Appraisement*, 1880, Crawford County, Probate Court, Miscellaneous Records of the Inferior Court, 1822–1900, Record Group 139, Subgroup 2, Series 1 (GDA).

number that remained relatively stable into the first decade of the twentieth century.[104] As with hogs, purebred cattle were slow to catch on in Georgia and never accounted for a significant percentage of the cattle raised in the decades bracketing the turn of the century. According to one estimate, only 28,000 of the 900,000 Georgia cattle in 1890 were high quality, and only about 4,000 were purebred stock.[105]

The probate data from Crawford, Jasper, and Franklin show each of the three counties matching this pattern. Virtually all of the cattle included in inventories were given minimal descriptions – they were listed simply by sex (cow or bull), age (yearling, heifer, or numeric age), color, size (big or small), the presence of horns ("butt-headed," no horns, or horns), or the intended use (milk cow, beef cattle, or stock cattle). The inventories included twenty Jersey cows and a one-quarter interest in a Jersey bull (held by William McEntire of Franklin County, who died in 1887). Jersey cows were introduced into Georgia from Pennsylvania in 1876 in the hope of promoting dairying in the state.[106] As such, it can be assumed that the Jersey cows owned by Crawford, Jasper, and Franklin County farmers were dairy stock, while McEntire's Jersey bull was used to breed with native stock. The vast majority of the cattle in our sample were destined for the slaughterhouse and were not given names; farmers were more likely to name their breeding stock (like the bulls named Charlie and Oscar) or dairy cows (whose names included Belle, Bess, Cherry, Chessie, Isrelight [Israelite], Jule [Jewel], Sillie, Speck, and Star).

Among the bovines in our samples were sixty-eight oxen, representing nearly 5 percent of the cattle owned by decedents in the three counties. The census data suggest that ownership of oxen was greater in the general population, as oxen constituted 11 percent of the total number of cattle for the three counties reported in the agricultural schedules of the 1880 federal census.[107] Oxen were most often held in working pairs, or yokes, and described almost exclusively in terms of their size: big, large, and small. The three-county sample also included one yoke of steers and several steers listed singly. Whereas oxen and steers are both male bovines castrated before they reach four years old, steers differ from oxen in that they are raised for beef; therefore, they are typically castrated earlier than oxen and left untrained. Despite this distinction, the appearance of yokes of steers implies that these were trained working pairs, and that the terms "steer" and "oxen" may have been used interchangeably on occasion. While the persisting value of oxen in the postbellum South is often overshadowed by the predominance of mules, Nathan Joeday Newsom, a successful farmer in Washington County, Georgia, stressed their importance in 1885, when he wrote that "every well regulated farm should have a good

104 Range, *A Century of Georgia Agriculture*, 102–03.
105 Ibid., 104.
106 Ibid., 104–105.
107 *Tenth Census of the United States, 1880, Agriculture, 1880*, 147–148.

yoke of Oxen and Cart, and a man ought to be as particular in selecting a yoke of Oxen."[108] Research suggests that oxen were actually favored by small planters with holdings of up to thirty acres, because they cost less to purchase and maintain than did mules or horses.[109]

Goats and sheep were also listed in significant numbers in inventories from the three Piedmont counties. Appraisers were succinct in their descriptions, listing simply "goat," "goats," "sheep," or "head of sheep" without any further elaboration on breed, age, color, size, or gender. They did, however, frequently add "first choice" through "fifth choice" to the listing for both types of animal, indicating a grading system for differentiating quality and assigning market value. Because mutton and goat meat were not typically eaten in the South, it appears that the sheep were raised for wool and the goats kept for their milk and hides. In fact, there is some indication that milk goats were a cheaper alternative to cows among poorer farmers.[110] Unfortunately, some of the inventories grouped sheep and goats, making it impossible to provide an accurate count for the sample group. The 1880 and 1900 census data provide reliable aggregate figures for both types of animal. In 1880, Crawford and Jasper farmers owned a little more than 1,100 sheep, while Franklin County farmers had slightly more than 3,000.[111] Over the next 20 years, the sheep populations in Crawford and Franklin grew to 1,269 and 5,984, respectively, while the population dropped to a mere 428 in Jasper. Instead, Jasper showed an increased preference for goats, which numbered 1,048, compared to 350 in Crawford and 150 in Franklin.[112]

The only other livestock included in the estates were bees and farm fowl. Apiarian evidence consisted of bee gums, beehives, and bee stands. Fourteen hives were distributed among four estates in Crawford County, while ninety gums were listed among seven estates in Jasper County. The probate evidence suggests that beekeeping was much more important in Franklin County, where thirty-two decedents owned a combined total of more than 200 gums, implying a greater degree of self-reliance in home production of foodstuffs in the Upland county. Farm fowl, on the other hand, were more evenly represented across the three counties. Farm birds were often grouped within the inventories, making it difficult to determine exact holdings. Appraisers identified a small variety of fowl, including chickens, peafowl, pigeons, ducks, and geese. The only

108 Kenneth Coleman, "How to Run a Middle Georgia Cotton Plantation in 1885: A Document," *Agricultural History* 42, no. 1 (January 1968): 59.

109 Martin A. Garrett, Jr., "Evidence on the Use of Oxen in the Postbellum South," *Social Science History* 22, no. 2 (Summer 1998): 244.

110 Hilliard, *Hog Meat and Hoecake*, 59, 144; Plumb, *Judging Farm Animals*, 467.

111 *Tenth Census of the United States, 1880, Agriculture*, 147–48.

112 Le Grand Powers, U.S. Bureau of the Census, *Twelfth Census of the United States, 1900*, Vol. 5–6, *Agriculture, Part I: Farms, Live Stock, and Animal Products* (Washington, DC, 1902), 278–279. The 1900 federal agricultural census was the first to count sheep and goats separately, and it appears that these two categories were combined for the 1880 census.

elaborations in descriptions were among the chickens – some were identified as roosters and others as "grown" chickens, indicating age.

Among the animal products listed in the probate inventories were wool, sheep hides, "beef" hides, tallow, and meat. The small amounts of wool and hides recorded suggest that they were used for home consumption. Likewise, the tallow rendered from the fat of slaughtered sheep and hogs was used on the farm to make candles and soap. Meat was the most prevalent animal product in the inventories, and although mutton was represented in small amounts in Franklin County, pork accounted for the majority of the meat in all three counties. Providing meat to the household was problematic in the days before refrigeration – particularly in the South, where the heat and humidity hastened decomposition, it was an expensive and labor-intensive process. Hogs, cattle, and chickens represented significant assets that were carefully managed and raised to the point of maximum return on the investment. Farmers looked at their livestock and weighed the idea of a Sunday chicken dinner against the value of having a consistent supply of eggs. Hogs were allowed to forage for themselves for most of the year until late in the fall, when they were penned, fattened, and carefully assessed for peak weight gain in order to provide the best meat for curing once the weather turned cold enough.

While chickens and beef were generally eaten fresh on the rare occasions when they were slaughtered for the table in the South, pork became the meat of choice because it could be most easily preserved.[113] Hog killing was a fairly standardized practice for farmers throughout the United States by the late nineteenth century, and it differed little in the Piedmont South. Above all, it was necessary to wait for the weather to become consistently cold enough to allow for the several weeks needed to effectively cure the meat so that it could last for a year or more without refrigeration, even under hot and humid conditions. Once the animal was slaughtered, great care was taken to select and prepare the various cuts for curing. The inventories from Crawford, Jasper, and Franklin counties provide an excellent indication of the interest that farmers in Middle Georgia took in the meat they preserved. Listed among the decedents' possessions were bacon, sides of meat, shoulder meat, hams, "middling" cuts, and lard, showing that little of the animal was wasted. The inventories also reveal how meat was cured, with frequent references to smoking or "smokehouse contents." In this technique, the butchered cuts were placed in a meat box, where they were covered with salt to draw out the blood and excess moisture. After several weeks, the meat was removed, washed, and hung over a smoldering fire within the airtight confines of a smokehouse to allow the nitrates in the smoke to slowly infuse the meat, acting as a preservative.[114] Several inventories

[113] Hilliard, *Hog Meat and Hoecake*, 42–43.

[114] Mary Randolph, *The Virginia House-wife* (1824; reprint. New York: Dover, 1993): 49; Rosemary Brandau, "The Butchering and Processing of Pork in Eighteenth-Century Williamsburg, Research Report RR-31" (Williamsburg: Colonial Williamsburg Foundation, 1984).

also referred to "pickled pork," which could actually be prepared in warmer weather without fear of spoilage.[115] Pickling involved soaking the butchered meat in casks filled with a brine solution. While this technique was as effective as smoking – and it was better for preserving difficult cuts like the head – the pickled meat often had to be soaked in successive baths of fresh water to draw out enough of the salt preservative to make it palatable.

Overall, the farmers in Crawford, Jasper, and Franklin counties sought to use the most advanced technology available to them within their means; they tried to diversify wherever possible; and they organized production in ways that maximized their ability to maintain a healthy household, even during down times.

The stories told here illustrate the degree to which two questions defined the postbellum farming experience: how to achieve self-sufficiency without assuming a dangerous level of risk, and how to measure success. In the Georgia Piedmont, cotton dominated, but households keenly sought to broaden their economic horizons. The wide range of tools, equipment, supplies, crops, and livestock that households possessed attests to those efforts; and indeed, farmers who diversified their economic pursuits were more likely to succeed than those who eschewed such a strategy. The probate records clearly show that some non-cotton farm production – specifically, smoked meats, sorghum syrup, and homespun textiles – employed many women and helped increase the possibility of achieving success over the years.

During the year that followed an estate holder's death, his or her survivors attempted to keep the household intact and continued to engage in farming activity in order to protect valuable crops, animals, and products until the probate process was complete. As Bill Arp would remind readers of his newspaper column, success still depended on some degree of luck and fortitude. Changing circumstances often required a change in production – perhaps altering the household's productive activities to meet local needs, if possible. Juggling a desire for self-sufficiency and an aversion to excessive risk was difficult; however, many more households were successful than previous work has acknowledged. The following chapter highlights those households that were capable of mixing market-oriented production and production intended for home use or exchange.

[115] Hilliard, *Hog Meat and Hoecake*, 43.

4

The Material World of Piedmont Farmers

In early fall 1909, Magnolia Wynn Le Guin was devastated by her husband Ghu's decision to build the new cotton house so close to their home. She loved nature, and she treasured the views she had of the landscape surrounding the house. She confided in her diary that "the natural groves around our old home are grand, but Ghu has *spoiled* one view to my sorrow. He doesn't love nature as well as I." She continued, "It is with deep regret that I daily look at this building.... I would be proud of the large roomy cotton house if it was down in or near the horse lot or the old buggy house."[1] Although disappointed, Magnolia knew that Ghu had made the right decision – she conceded that the new cotton house "saves many steps for him; and he works *so very* hard and takes so many steps."[2] She also understood that the new cotton house and its placement on the property were vitally important to their strategy for success as cotton farmers, whereas beauty and personal desires were secondary indulgences. Above all, she knew the essential role of the household in relation to the farm: while her husband and sons worked the fields, she worked to support her large family by keeping them fed and clothed. She frequently lamented in her diary that despite her love of nature and outdoor life, hers was "the home concealed life," and she was "compelled to live most of the time in doors – housekeeping and family affairs: sewing, cooking, ironing, patching etc., etc., etc., etc., etc., etc."[3]

Magnolia Le Guin was an ordinary Georgia Piedmont farmwoman during her lifetime, but in the historical record she is quite extraordinary: she was one of the only people in her socioeconomic class who recorded daily events and

[1] Magnolia Wynn Le Guin, *A Home-Concealed Woman: The Diaries of Magnolia Wynn Le Guin, 1901–1913* (Athens: University of Georgia Press, 1990): 312–313.

[2] Ibid., 313.

[3] Ibid., 70.

frequently expressed her thoughts in diaries (or, at any rate, she was one of the only such people whose diaries were preserved). Because economically disadvantaged rural Southerners like her are conspicuously silent in the historical record, they have long been depicted as poor, uneducated farmers who were conservative in mind and manner and resistant to change.[4] Magnolia Le Guin's diaries suggest otherwise. She and her neighbors were intelligent, creative, and resilient in their efforts to balance the needs of the family and the farm during a period of economic hardship and profound change. Her journal entries reveal the importance of the household in supporting the market-oriented productive efforts of the farm. While men in the farm household typically focused their productive efforts on cultivating crops for external markets, women were more internally focused, working to provision the farm and provide for the household's needs. In addition to cooking, cleaning, sewing, and child-rearing, farmwomen were often responsible for making butter, maintaining the vegetable garden, caring for farmyard fowl, overseeing food preservation, spinning, and weaving. In many households, women even provided the additional labor needed in the fields at harvest time, and the butter, garden vegetables, and textiles they produced were used for local market exchange.[5] Magnolia Le Guin's diaries amply demonstrate the contention that the household, "although structurally and often in practice subordinate to the farm operation, was nonetheless tightly integrated with it."[6]

Historical sources that detail the daily life of farm families, like the Le Guin diary, are rare, but probate inventories and the sales listings from estate auctions are far more common. As snapshots of the material world of decedents at given points in time, inventories offer a holistic view of the domestic economy, providing rich insight into the range and diversity of household production and consumption. Although they might simply be considered lists of possessions, on a deeper level they reflect consumer practices and patterns. The assemblage of possessions represented in a probate inventory implies a conscious effort to acquire certain objects through purchase or exchange, or a conscious decision to keep an object if it was inherited or received as a gift.[7] In essence,

4 Woodward, *The Origins of the New South 1877–1913* (Baton Rouge: Louisiana State University Press, 1951): 176–177; Steven L. Barsby, "Economic Backwardness and the Characteristics of Development," *Journal of Economic History* 29, no. 3 (September 1969): 449–472; Ayers, *Promise of the New South*, 25–26.

5 Elizabeth Fox-Genovese, "Women in Agriculture during the Nineteenth Century," in *Agriculture and National Development: Views on the Nineteenth Century* (Ames: Iowa State University Press, 1990): 269; Nancy Grey Osterud, "She Helped Me Hay It as Good as a Man": Relations among Women and Men in an Agricultural Community," in *"To Toil the Livelong Day": America's Women at Work, 1780–1980* (Ithaca: Cornell University Press, 1987): 87–97; Adams, "The Decoupling of Farm and Household: Differential Consequences of Capitalist Development on Southern Illinois and Third World Family Farms," *Comparative Studies in Society and History* 30, no. 3 (July 1988): 458–459.

6 Adams, "Decoupling Farm and Household," 467.

7 Overton et al., *Production and Consumption in English Households*, 88.

consumption is a dynamic process that involves deciding how to spend time and money. Items consumed may be durable goods (such as hoes, furniture, or jewelry), disposable or perishable things (such as food), or even services and entertainment that have no real material presence.

Studies of the consumer revolution in America, particularly those examining the nineteenth century, usually focus on urban residents and luxury goods.[8] Mid-to-late-nineteenth-century farmers are typically neglected in these studies because, as a group, they were more conservative than their urban counterparts in what they purchased, choosing to spend money primarily on items related to farm production.[9] However, while farmers may have bought fewer luxury items, the decision to invest in fences, to build a cotton house, or to purchase a more advanced piece of equipment still represented a consumer choice, albeit of a more utilitarian nature. The consumer experience took hold in rural areas differently than in urban contexts because of the tradition of self-reliance, along with well-developed family and community networks that allowed them to resist the allure of the expanding consumer market; farmers did not feel the need to obtain new and better products as strongly as their urban counterparts did.[10]

This began to change as American agriculture became more specialized. The developing commitment to production of a single staple crop undercut the tradition of self-reliance. In the new cotton economy, farmers were rewarded for putting as much of their effort and resources into cotton production as they possibly could, which worked at counter-purposes to the safety-first strategy of mixed agriculture that yeomen had long practiced. As the commitment to staple production increased, so did reliance on the consumer market, which, in turn, greatly increased the need for cash income. But even as farmers participated in and came to depend on the consumer culture, "it was an incomplete process in which farm people resisted, modified, and selectively used these technologies to create new rural cultures, new forms of rural modernity – many of which

[8] See, for example, Richard Wightman Fox and T. J. Jackson Lears, eds. *The Culture of Consumption: Critical Essays in American History, 1880–1980* (New York: Pantheon, 1983); Kenneth L. Ames, *Death in the Dining Room and Other Tales of Victorian Culture* (Philadelphia: Temple University Press, 1992); Richard Bushman, *The Refinement of America: Persons, Houses, Cities* (New York: Knopf, 1992); Katherine C. Grier, *Culture and Comfort: Parlor Making and Middle Class Identity, 1850–1930* (Washington, DC: Smithsonian Institution Press, 1997); Eleanor Thompson, ed., *The American Home: Material Culture, Domestic Space, and Family Life* (Winterthur: Winterthur Museum, 1998).

[9] Sally McMurry, *Families and Farmhouses in Nineteenth Century America: Vernacular Design and Social Change* (New York: Oxford University Press, 1988): 145; Adams, "Decoupling Farm and Household," 462; Ronald R. Kline, *Consumers in the Country: Technology and Social Change in Rural America* (Baltimore, MD: The Johns Hopkins University Press, 2000): 9–19; Hal S. Barron, *Mixed Harvest: The Second Great Transformation in the Rural North, 1870–1930* (Chapel Hill: University of North Carolina Press, 1997): 1–16.

[10] Kline, *Consumers in the Country*, 18.

TABLE 4.1. *The Distribution of Farm Stock, Livestock, and Household Goods by County*

	Farm Stock	Livestock	Household	Total Assets
Crawford				
Total	$21,007.28	$15,215.00	$5,778.67	$42,000.95
Average	$386.34	$338.11	$115.57	$840.02
Median	$239.25	$220.00	$47.54	$550.43
Cases	48	45	33	48
Jasper				
Total	$20,351.55	$11,133.71	$7,774.51	$39,259.77
Average	$494.14	$292.99	$194.36	$981.49
Median	$184.50	$197.50	$56.90	$517.58
Cases	39	38	32	39
Franklin				
Total	$23,231.16	$15,256.00	$11,058.26	$49,545.42
Average	$202.35	$150.74	$101.45	$454.55
Median	$133.75	$112.50	$63.50	$346.34
Cases	107	103	89	108

were individual modernities."[11] The pattern of goods ownership among rural households in the Georgia Piedmont between 1880 and 1910 shows the extent to which consumer culture pervaded the lives of farming families, how they mediated between market dependence and self-sufficiency, and how they chose to adapt urban middle-class sensibilities to meet their needs and aspirations.

The pattern revealed through probate inventories indicates that the rural, cotton-based economy of the Piedmont was every bit as dynamic as the urban model characterized by increased consumption. Farmers appear to have acquired a broad range of goods. While many of the items in the estate inventories were utilitarian or production-related, it is clear that farmers were influenced by urban middle-class domestic ideals; many acquired the latest labor-saving devices for the home and even indulged in purchasing a luxury item from time to time. Although farmers of all wealth categories placed most of their assets in farm equipment and supplies, followed by livestock, the household possessions inventoried at death frequently represented a significant accumulation of assets (Table 4.1). Moreover, the median values for household assets in the probate sample match closely with the median values of household assets calculated from the Georgia State Comptroller's tax data for the years 1890, 1900, and 1910, indicating that the probate sample is highly representative of the population at large (Table 4.2).

[11] Kline, *Consumers in the Country*, 7–8.

TABLE 4.2. *Average Value of Household Goods for Tax-Paying Households in Crawford, Franklin, and Jasper Counties, 1890–1910*

County	Polls (White & Black)	Household & Kitchen ($)	Avg. Household ($)	Clocks, Watches, Jewelry, Silver Plate ($)	Avg. Clocks, Watches, Jewelry, Silver Plate ($)
1890					
Crawford	1,357	42,626	31.4	2,723	2.0
Franklin	2,169	83,897	38.7	3,441	1.6
Jasper	1,989	75,991	38.2	6,271	3.2
1900					
Crawford	1,538	48,315	31.4	2,094	1.4
Franklin	2,833	81,472	28.8	3,151	1.1
Jasper	2,046	72,194	35.3	5,362	2.6
1910					
Crawford	1,247	50,227	40.3	1,987	1.6
Franklin	2,516	92,918	36.9	3,376	1.3
Jasper	2,735	100,335	36.7	5,665	2.1

Source: William A. Wright, General Manager. *Report of the Comptroller General for the State of Georgia for the Year Ending September 30, 1890*. Atlanta: George W. Harrison, 1890. *RCGG, September 30, 1900*. Atlanta: George W. Harrison, 1900. William A. Wright. *RCGG September 30, 1910*. Atlanta: Charles P. Boyd State Printer, 1911.

The average decedent from Crawford, Jasper, or Franklin County had household assets representing about 20 percent of the overall value of the estate. Those who owned more land generally had more valuable possessions as well; however, the wealth gap between large and small landowners varied from one county to another. Decedents owning more than 200 acres in Crawford owned an average of $57 worth of household goods, while those owning fewer than 200 acres had household goods valued at $14. In Jasper, estates with more than 150 acres of land typically had household goods valued at $28, while those with fewer than 150 acres owned $14 in household items on average. Franklin County showed the least amount of disparity, with estates that were 150 acres or larger averaging $23 invested in household assets, while the figure for those with fewer than 150 acres was roughly $14.

A total of 155 (n = 78%) of the estates from the three counties contained at least some household goods. Forty-four estates, however, were without household possessions of any description, despite the presence of farm-related items and livestock. Eight of these decedents, including Rebecca Hammack of Crawford County and John Franklin of Jasper, had wills that provided instructions for the distribution of household material and other select items prior to the appraisement of the remainder of the estate.[12] Eight others were elderly and lived with relatives, including Uriah Miller of Franklin County, who died in 1886 at the age of 92 – a widower, he had resided with his daughters Ludicy and Nancy since at least 1870.[13] The vast majority of estates missing household goods (n = 24), though, represent situations where distributions were made for the benefit of a widow or dependents prior to formal appraisement. In these situations, the items separated from the estate for the use of the widow or dependents were excluded from the formal appraisement of the larger estate. In the case of Barney Hancock, for example, his wife Harriet received one-third of her late husband's assets as stipulated by law.[14]

Only 4 of the estates showing no household assets in the inventory represent cases where the estate was valued at $500 or less, and the appraisers directed that it be transferred in its entirety to the widow without listing specific household possessions. One such case was that of Robert Walton of Crawford County, who was forty-three years old and married with nine minor children at the time of his death in 1897.[15] He owned no land and appears to have been a tenant farmer in 1880 (his occupation in the 1880 federal census was identified as "farming"). He is listed in the 1880 Crawford County agricultural census as having only one cow and six hogs, valued at $43, in an estate valued at $58 for tax purposes.[16] When Walton died in 1897, he was still landless and had an estate worth only $85.

In most inventories, the phrase "household goods" referred to the aggregate value of possessions that were listed separately under categories such as kitchen, bedroom, and parlor. Sometimes, however, appraisers used "household goods" as a supplemental catchall category – another way of saying "miscellaneous." In these instances, appraisers did not list the items individually (Table 4.3). Although it is impossible to determine the types of possessions included in

12 Rebecca Hammack, *Last Will and Testament*, 1886, Crawford County, Probate Court, Miscellaneous Records of the Inferior Court, 1822–1900, Record Group 139, Subgroup 2, Series 1 (GDA); John Franklin, *Last Will and Testament*, 1886, Jasper County, Probate Court, Wills, 1809–1907, Record Group 179, Subgroup 2, Series 4 (GDA).

13 Uriah Miller, *Inventory and Appraisement*, 1892, Franklin County, Probate Court, Estate Records, 1786–1916, Record Group 159, Subgroup 2, Series 1 (GDA); *Ninth Census of the United States, 1870*, Georgia Roll M593–150, Page 85; *Tenth Census of the United States, 1880, Population*, Georgia Roll T9–147, Page 580; Uriah Miller is listed as Isaiah Miller in the 1880 census, but the fact he is living with Ludicy and Nancy Miller and the entry lists a 1797 birth date leaves little doubt that Uriah and Isaiah are one and the same.

14 Barney Hancock, "Petition of Harriett Hancock for twelve months support," 1896, Franklin County, Probate Court, Estate Records, 1786–1916, Record Group 159, Subgroup 2, Series 1 (GDA); Clark, Read, Cobb, and Irwin, *Code of the State of Georgia*, Pt. 2, Tit, 6, Chap. 3, Art. 2, §2632.

15 Clark, Read, Cobb, and Irwin. *Code of the State of Georgia*, Pt. 2, Tit, 6, Chap. 3, Art. 2, §2530; Robert S. Walton, *Petition of Mrs. Henrietta S. Walton for Twelve Months Support, April 4, 1898*, Crawford County, Ordinary Court Minutes, Book B (GDA); *Tenth Census of the United States, 1880, Population*, Georgia Roll T9–147, 693D.

16 Robert S. Walton, Crawford County, Property Tax Digests, 1877–1882, 3, 3135 (GDA).

TABLE 4.3. *Comparison of the Aggregate Value of Household Goods with Kitchen, Bedroom, and Parlor Assemblages by County*

	Household Goods (Inclusive)[a]	Household Goods (Supplemental)[b]	Kitchen	Bedroom	Parlor
Crawford					
Total	255.08	182.95	897.74	1,674.31	395.45
Average	51.016	36.59	34.53	63.16	25.92
Median	45.08	36.45	17.25	39.38	4.10
Cases	5	5	14	10	19
Jasper					
Total	178.02	78.02	872.19	1,383.80	166.00
Average	59.34	78.02	29.07	55.35	12.96
Median	50.00	78.02	18.18	19.00	3.63
Cases	2	1	13	10	16
Franklin					
Total	445.51	382.00	1,773.13	3,432.70	1,159.30
Average	44.55	63.67	21.11	45.30	26.77
Median	35.75	42.50	17.30	34.23	5.50
Count	10	7	14	10	56

[a] "Household goods" in this context refers to those situations where all household possessions were grouped into a single category.

[b] This usage refers to a general combined category used in addition to listing specific household items.

this general grouping, they were likely items of low value or very common things found throughout the house that could not readily be associated with any discrete room or function. Appraisers generally used this category with relatively wealthy decedents who had accumulated a higher-than-average number of personal possessions; estates for which the supplemental "household goods" category was used had twice the average value of household possessions, and the total value of these estates was well in excess of the 3-county average of $657. The 3 Jasper County estates with the additional household-goods category were valued at $1,542 on average; the 6 such estates in Crawford averaged $942 in appraised value, and the 6 in Franklin County ranged from $209 to $1,902.

The probate inventories reflect the types of housing available in the Georgia Piedmont as well as room function. Only one document, however, provided an explicit description of house plans in the sample counties: the loan application by James Bowman to C. P. N. Barker of Atlanta, Georgia. Bowman's newly built home, he wrote in the application, consisted of two large rooms with two "shed bed rooms attached . . . all well finished, [with] back and front verandas."[17] His tenant house, also recently built, was a different type of frame

[17] Bowman, "Application to C. P. N. Barker," 1.

structure, consisting of two single-family cells separated by a central chimney. This kind of double pen, "saddlebag" structure was typically built for agricultural workers and was most prevalent in North Georgia.[18] The two housing forms described in Bowman's application were among the most popular in the Georgia Piedmont, but there were many others; scholars have identified twenty-eight distinct vernacular house types and a wide range of styles built in Georgia between 1850 and 1910.

Houses tended to be small, with a minimal number of rooms. Many poor households lived in one- or two-room houses built in a variety of forms, including hall-and-parlor, saddlebag, dogtrot, and the central-hallway form, which was particularly popular in the nineteenth century.[19] Hall-and-parlor houses consisted of two rooms with a single entrance. Saddlebag houses also had two rooms, but they shared a central chimney. In central-hallway houses, two rooms flanked a corridor, with exterior chimneys providing heat to each cell; dogtrot houses were essentially the same, except that an open breezeway took the place of the central hallway. All of these small house types could be expanded by constructing a shed or an L-shaped addition (an "ell"), which would often double the number of rooms in the original house.[20]

Middling and upper-class farmers often built in a style known today as the "Georgian cottage," which was especially popular in the Georgia Piedmont. Similar to the four-room Bowman homestead, the Georgian cottage was "probably the single most popular and long-lived house type in Georgia."[21] Named for the symmetrical, eighteenth-century style it mimicked, the Georgian cottage had a square floor plan consisting of two pairs of rooms located on either side of a central hallway. A pair of chimneys served each pair of rooms, and the roof could be either gabled or hipped. Additional rooms often included a kitchen and bedroom at the rear of the house, and a parlor and another bedroom at the front. Although Georgian cottages were built over a long period of time, many went up between 1850 and 1890.[22]

Two-story houses were also popular in the rural Piedmont, especially the I-house and the plantation plain. I-houses were generally one room deep and two rooms wide, but the floor plan varied – it might be the central-hallway, hall-and-parlor, double-pen, or saddlebag form. As with single-story houses, I-houses could be expanded significantly with ell additions built onto the rear. Plantation plain homes were similar to I-houses but had an integral, single-story shed addition to the rear that provided one-third more rooms than

18 "House Types in Georgia," Unpublished manuscript on file with the Georgia Historic Preservation Division of the Georgia Department of Natural Resources, n. d., 4.

19 "House Types in Georgia," 5.

20 Mark Reinberger, "The Architecture of Sharecropping: Extended Farms of the Georgia Piedmont," in *Perspectives in Vernacular Architecture, Vol. 9: Constructing Image, Identity, and Place* (Knoxville: University of Tennessee Press, 2003): 122.

21 "House types in Georgia," 6; "Georgian" in this context refers to the English style that gained popularity in the eighteenth century.

22 Ibid., 6.

FIGURE 4.1. A typical rural, hall-and-parlor home near the town of Roberta in Crawford County, circa 1885. Courtesy, Georgia Archives, Vanishing Georgia Collection, image number crw001.

the basic I-plan. Although many Georgia families lived in plantation plain houses during the postbellum period, few new ones were constructed – most dated from between 1820 and 1850.[23] In all of these home types, the kitchen, bedrooms, and parlor were the primary rooms, whereas dining rooms, additional bedrooms, and other specialized rooms could be added when space was available.

Based solely on the value of items, Piedmont farm families had more invested in bedroom furnishings and accessories than in any other room of the house. Bedroom-related material accounted for 56 percent of the total appraised value of the estates from each of the three counties. While this may be because the average family in the region consisted of six members and owned four beds, it also suggests that bedrooms were significant spaces in the Georgia Piedmont home. Beds, mattresses, bedsteads, and chests of drawers accounted for most of the value. For example, the inventory of bedroom items for Jack Bellamy of Franklin County included two bedsteads, a chest with a lock, and a bible, worth a combined $13.50, or nearly half of the entire value of his household

[23] Ibid., 13.

goods.[24] Similarly, Philip McCarty, who owned 100 acres in Crawford County, had 5 beds and 1 crib, with a combined value of $15.80.[25] Finally, John McElhenney, a farmer with 1,392.5 acres in Jasper, had an impressive array of bedroom items, including 4 bedsteads, 18 counterpanes, 4 feather mattresses, 1 chest, 10 sheets, 12 quilts, 1 blanket, and several coverlets, worth $244 out of a household valued at $328.[26]

Despite the high average value of bedroom-related materials, bedrooms appear to have been conservatively if not sparsely furnished and decorated in the Georgia countryside in the late nineteenth century. Unlike the urban middle- and upper-class bedrooms of the late Victorian era, which were becoming multifunctional spaces that served as sitting and reception rooms in addition to sleeping quarters, farmers' bedrooms in the Georgia Piedmont remained private and functioned primarily as spaces for sleeping, washing, and dressing.[27] On occasion, they also served as birthplaces and rooms for the sick or dying. While some bedrooms were as spartan as the one belonging to T. L. Franks of Franklin County, with its bedstead and straw-filled mattress tick, fitted with an under sheet and covered with a counterpane, others, like the one belonging to Anna Malone of Jasper County, included a wardrobe, washstand, bureau, and bed with a mattress, quilts, and sheets.[28]

The inventories suggest that beds were often simple affairs.[29] Frequently describing them only as beds or bedsteads, appraisers occasionally noted the type of wood (e.g., pine, poplar, or walnut), construction features, such as turned posts, color (if painted), age (e.g., old), size (e.g., single, double, small), and height (e.g., high). Very few entries provided an indication of whether the bedsteads used springs to support the mattress – a recent innovation – or the more traditional rope or cord. In fact, no inventories from Crawford County mentioned rope, cord, or springs; Franklin inventories included three rope beds and five sets of springs; among the Jasper records were two instances of springs, one of rope. Mattress descriptions ran the gamut from straw to

[24] Jack Bellamy, *Inventory and Appraisement*, 1886, Franklin County, Probate Court, Estate Records, 1786–1916, Record Group 159, Subgroup 2, Series 1 (GDA).

[25] Philip McCarty, Inventory and Appraisement, 1896, Crawford County, Probate Court, Miscellaneous Records of the Inferior Court, 1822–1900, Record Group 139, Subgroup 2, Series 1 (GDA).

[26] John McElhenny, *Inventory and Appraisement*, 1883, Jasper County, Probate Court, Estate Case Files, 1809–1907, Record Group 179, Subgroup 2, Series 3 (GDA).

[27] Elizabeth Collins Cromley, "A History of American Beds and Bedrooms, 1890–1930," in *American Home Life, 1880–1930: A Social History of Spaces and Services* (Knoxville: University of Tennessee Press, 1992): 121, 130–131.

[28] T. L. Franks, *Inventory and Appraisement*, 1899, Franklin County, Probate Court, Estate Records, 1786–1916, Record Group 159, Subgroup 2, Series 1 (GDA); Anna B. Malone, *Inventory and Appraisement*, 1891, Jasper County, Probate Court, Estate Case Files, 1809–1907, Record Group 179, Subgroup 2, Series 3 (GDA).

[29] Atlanta Historical Society, *Neat Pieces: The Plain-Style Furniture of Nineteenth-Century Georgia* (Athens: University of Georgia Press, 2006): 81.

cotton to feather tick to spring. Cribs and cradles indicate the presence of small children, while the prevalence of bunk beds, cots, and trundle beds suggest that space was at a premium in many houses in the Georgia Piedmont. Bunk beds saved space, whereas cots and trundle beds could be brought out at night for sleeping and stowed out of the way during the day. Despite the paucity of description for beds, a bedstead and mattress was typically one of the most valuable possessions farmers owned, ranging in value from $10 to $25. The bed and bedding listed among John Kelly's Jasper County inventory in 1892 was appraised at $25, second in value to his prime mules, which averaged $50.[30]

Although the range of bed types and descriptions in the inventories were relatively narrow, appraisers provided greater detail about case furniture. The forms and styles found in the Georgia countryside were simple, and because of the conservative tastes of the makers and consumers, older forms persisted late into the nineteenth century.[31] Chests were the most prevalent form of case furniture in the three-county sample. Seventy-two percent of Jasper County decedents owned chests (n = 25), compared with 58 percent of Franklin County decedents (n = 52) and 42 percent of decedents in Crawford (n = 14). As with beds, appraisers provided little detail that would allow us to differentiate types or styles of chests owned in the Piedmont region. The few modifiers used included "large," "ordinary," "pine," and "spotted." While the simple descriptions may indicate that the pieces were of the ubiquitous six-board variety, more elaborate versions included blanket chests, chests-on-frames, and chests with legs and drawers, all of which were common throughout Georgia during the period.[32] The appraised values for chests ranged between $0.20 and $5.00, with an average of $1.00.

Larger pieces, such as wardrobes and clothespresses, which provided storage for clothes and other textiles before built-in closets became more common near the turn of the century, were particularly favored in the South.[33] Unlike in New England, where urban centers developed early and design trends became established and entrenched, Southern cities and towns could not support cabinetmaking until the eighteenth century, when English artisans who came to fill this void brought with them knowledge of the latest English designs and trends, including the designs for newer forms like the clothespress.[34]

30 John W. Kelly, *Inventory and Appraisement*, 1892, Jasper County, Probate Court, Estate Case Files, 1809–1907, Record Group 179, Subgroup 2, Series 3 (GDA).

31 Atlanta Historical Society, *Neat Pieces*, 10.

32 Ibid., 150–161.

33 Linen presses and clothespresses were large pieces of case furniture that provided shelves to store linens and other textiles, while wardrobes and armoires were tall storage cabinets that provided space to hang clothing that would crease easily or garments that were worn frequently. While both forms were common by the eighteenth century, wardrobes became more common by the late nineteenth century.

34 Ronald L. Hurst and Jonathon Prown, *Southern Furniture, 1680–1830: The Colonial Williamsburg Collection* (New York: Harry N. Abrams, 1997): 496.

The popularity of the clothespress persisted in the South well into the nineteenth century. Among our three-county sample, clothespresses were most commonly found in Franklin County, where 27 percent (n = 24) of the estates with household goods included a press. Five wardrobes were also identified among the Franklin decedents. Nineteen percent (n = 6) of Jasper inventories included at least one clothespress, while 16 percent (n = 5) listed a wardrobe. Oddly, just one clothespress and one wardrobe were included among the Crawford County sample, which may indicate that this type of furniture was not common there. These larger pieces were typically valued at between $1 and $5. Other similar pieces of furniture included a quilt safe (valued at $2.50) listed among John Jordan's Franklin County inventory in 1887, and a "closet and mirror" owned by L. B. Aultman, who died in Crawford County in 1901.[35]

Bureaus were also very popular in the Georgia Piedmont – equally so in each of the three counties, it seems, with 55 percent of the estates owning at least one. Nineteenth-century Georgians typically referred to chests of drawers as bureaus.[36] They were typically low pieces with legs and drawers and often a mirror or "glass" affixed to the back. Although bureaus represented a significant investment to acquire, appraisers used surprisingly few modifiers when listing them in inventories, perhaps suggesting that the form had become so accepted and standardized that any additional description beyond a value was considered unnecessary. The few entries with adjectives suggest that Piedmont bureaus were primarily constructed of native black pine and walnut (widely available throughout the region), while some had white tops fashioned from marble quarried in Cass, Cherokee, and Gilmer counties.[37] Because of their more elaborate construction, bureaus were appraised higher than most other furniture in the three counties, ranging from $2 to $10, with an average appraised value of $5.

Toiletry pieces round out the types of furniture typically found in bedrooms of the rural Georgia Piedmont. In nearly half of the estates, these consisted of a washstand with a bowl and pitcher for bathing. These were low-value items that ranged from $0.25 to $2.00 in assessed value, averaging $0.50. William A. Royston of Franklin had sixteen washstands with pitchers and bowls for his hotel at Franklin Springs.[38] "Chambers," one of which was "covered," appeared in three Jasper County inventories and one from Franklin and may represent chamber pots. Five decedents appear to have had more specialized toiletry furniture. Thomas Sims of Franklin owned a dressing table valued at

[35] John W. Jordan, *Inventory and Appraisement*, 1887, Franklin County, Probate Court, Estate Records, 1786–1916, Record Group 159, Subgroup 2, Series 1 (GDA); L. B. Aultman, *Inventory and Appraisement*, 1901, Crawford County, Probate Court, Miscellaneous Records of the Inferior Court, 1822–1900, Record Group 139, Subgroup 2, Series 1 (GDA).

[36] Atlanta Historical Society, *Neat Pieces*, 10.

[37] Ibid., 15.

[38] William A. Royston, *Inventory and Appraisement, 1891*; *Petition of D. A. Baker to the Heirs at Law of W. A. Royston, April 1896*, Franklin County, Probate Court, Estate Records, 1786–1916, Record Group 159, Subgroup 2, Series 1 (GDA).

$1.00, while Benjamin Persons and Samuel Tyler of Jasper had dressing tables valued at $1.00 and $1.10, respectively.[39] James Darden of Jasper County and Joe Danielly of Crawford owned items called "dressing cases." Darden's was appraised at $3.00, while Danielly, an African American, had one as part of an estate worth $1,050.[40] Because 4 of the 5 decedents who owned dressing cases and tables had estates valued in excess of $1,100, these may have been luxury items associated with affluence.[41]

The farm kitchen, arguably the heart of the household, served as the primary indoor workspace.[42] Food was stored, processed, prepared, and frequently eaten there. The typical decedent in each of the three counties owned kitchen furniture and equipment worth half the value of bedroom items. Crawford County estates had kitchen assemblages averaging $35 in value, Jasper decedents owned an average of $29 in kitchen items, and among Franklin decedents the average was $21. The median value for kitchen-related items in all three counties was $17.

The probate inventories indicate that kitchen furnishings were sparse and functional. Tables with chairs or benches for seating were an absolute necessity in the kitchen as a place to work and to eat. Like most other furniture in Georgia Piedmont households, tables were simple and appear to have been constructed of local pine and walnut. In estates with multiple tables, appraisers differentiated between them according to their function, identifying "kitchen," "farm," and "eating" tables among kitchen equipment and supplies. Some kitchens may have had multiple tables for specialized purposes like baking or dressing meat.[43] Although "dresser" was sometimes used to describe "dressing bureaus" beginning in the late nineteenth century, its usage in the Georgia Piedmont apparently refers to the more archaic meaning: a bench or piece of furniture where meat was "dressed," or prepared for cooking.[44] A dresser

[39] Thomas Sims, *Inventory and Appraisement*, 1896, Franklin County, Probate Court, Estate Records, 1786–1916, Record Group 159, Subgroup 2, Series 1 (GDA); Benjamin Persons, *Inventory and Appraisement*, 1885, Jasper County, Jasper County, Probate Court, Estate Case Files, 1809–1907, Record Group 179, Subgroup 2, Series 3 (GDA); Samuel B. Tyler, *Inventory and Appraisement*, 1888, Jasper County, Jasper County, Probate Court, Estate Case Files, 1809–1907, Record Group 179, Subgroup 2, Series 3 (GDA).

[40] James Darden, *Inventory and Appraisement*, 1881, Jasper County, Probate Court, Estate Case Files, 1809–1907, Record Group 179, Subgroup 2, Series 3 (GDA); Joe Danielly, *Inventory and Appraisement*, 1900, Crawford County, Probate Court, Miscellaneous Records of the Inferior Court, 1822–1900, Record Group 139, Subgroup 2, Series 1 (GDA).

[41] The estate of Thomas Sims was valued at $1,102, Benjamin Persons's was worth $1,886, James Darden had one appraised at $3,784, and Joe Danielly's was worth $1,050 at the time of his death.

[42] Sally McMurry, *Families and Farmhouses in Nineteenth Century America*, 70–73, 108, 127, 145.

[43] Atlanta Historical Society, *Neat Pieces*, 115.

[44] Hurst and Prown, *Southern Furniture*, 496.

could also refer to a table or a cupboard-type piece of furniture that provided storage as well as a workspace. As such, "dresser" appears only three times in the probate sample. Ora P. Randall of Franklin County had a dresser listed with a washstand and a bureau among his possessions, suggesting that the dresser and bureau differed.[45] The two other usages indicate that "dresser" referred to a kitchen work table in the Georgia Piedmont. James W. Gregory of Crawford County had a dresser listed with kitchen material, while David Brawner's appraisers listed a "dresser table" along with "crocking, knives, and forks" together on the same line of his Franklin County inventory.[46]

The typical Piedmont kitchen also had a cupboard for the secure storage of kitchen utensils, tableware, and foodstuffs.[47] These pieces were generally tall and rectangular, with a central door or double doors that opened into an enclosed space with shelves. Sometimes, drawers were located above, below or within the body of the cupboard. Only two cupboards were identified in Crawford, averaging $1.00 in value, while eight were identified among the inventories from Jasper County, worth an average of $1.53. Cupboards were most prevalent in Franklin County, where forty-one of eighty-nine estates with household goods owned one (n = 46%). Here, they averaged $2.32 in value. The trend suggests that cupboards were more popular farther north in the Piedmont.

Also common were food safes, constructed of wood and pierced tin to provide a cool, dry storage place for food (particularly baked goods). They allowed air to circulate and protected the food from insects and vermin.[48] Appraisers valued these pieces of furniture – also called "kitchen," "pantry," and "wood" safes in the inventories – from $0.45 to $6.00, averaging $1.00. Since indoor plumbing had not yet come to the Piedmont, many kitchens included water stands, which provided ready access to water needed for cooking or cleaning.[49] Most chairs found in the kitchen were either "split-bottom," made from woven oak splints, or "cane-bottom," woven from rush. The inventories from the three counties indicate that at least some of these were painted red or blue. John Dent of Crawford County even had three baby chairs listed among his possessions.[50] Two of these may have been highchairs to allow a toddler to eat at the same

45 Ora P. Randall, *Inventory and Appraisement*, 1896, Franklin County, Probate Court, Estate Records, 1786–1916, Record Group 159, Subgroup 2, Series 1 (GDA).

46 James W. Gregory, *Inventory and Appraisement*, 1906, Crawford County Probate Court, Miscellaneous Records of the Inferior Court, 1822–1900, Record Group 139, Subgroup 2, Series 1 (GDA); David Brawner, *Inventory and Appraisement*, 1887, Franklin County, Probate Court, Estate Records, 1786–1916, Record Group 159, Subgroup 2, Series 1 (GDA).

47 Atlanta Historical Society, *Neat Pieces*, 113,122; Hurst and Prown, *Southern Furniture*, 493–495.

48 Atlanta Historical Society, *Neat Pieces*, 130–132.

49 Ibid., 115.

50 John W. Dent, *Inventory and Appraisement*, 1880, Crawford County Probate Court, Miscellaneous Records of the Inferior Court, 1822–1900, Record Group 139, Subgroup 2, Series 1 (GDA).

height as the rest of the family, while the "low chair" was likely a smaller-scale version of an adult chair that accommodated the size of a child.

The equipment and supplies found in Georgia farm kitchens in the last quarter of the nineteenth century were much more varied than the furniture and included many more items that were manufactured beyond the local area. Perhaps the most important of these was the iron cookstove. Although foundries began mass-producing cookstoves in the 1830s, they did not achieve the efficiency, ease of use, or affordability to become truly popular until after the Civil War.[51] Half of the estates in the three counties considered in this survey included a cookstove. Appraisal values ranged from $0.65 to $32.00, depending on the stove's size, condition, and the associated utensils and fixtures. The average value of a stove in the Crawford County inventories was $8, while it was $6 in Jasper and Franklin counties. The 1897 Sears catalog lists fourteen cookstoves ranging in price from $5 to $50, including one that was intended specifically for Southern homes: the Southern Sunshine Cook, the cheapest stove Sears offered, was engineered to burn wood and came in several models. The main differences between the models were the size of the firebox (eighteen to twenty-four inches deep) and the pot-hole cover (seven to nine inches in diameter).[52] Three inventories from the probate sample provide an indication of which sizes were popular in the region. Richard Campbell, who died in Jasper County in 1881, and E. W. Turner, who died in Crawford five years later, both had "No. 7" cookstoves listed in their inventories, indicating pot holes of seven inches in diameter; William McEntire of Franklin County owned a "No. 8" stove.[53]

Stoves appear to have been widely adopted in the Georgia Piedmont by 1880, although several inventories provide convincing proof that hearth cooking was still practiced in some households. These inventories included specialized implements for hearth cooking, including pothooks, spiders, cast-iron bake ovens with lids, and tin-reflecting ovens. Pothooks were used to attach pots to fireplace cranes, while cast-iron spiders and bake ovens had legs that allowed them to stand above banked embers in the fireplace. Tin-reflecting ovens were convex convection-type roasters that reflected the heat of the fire onto meat attached to a spit. John Whittington of Crawford County owned a spider with

[51] Susan Strasser, *Never Done: A History of American Housework* (New York: Pantheon Books, 1982): 36–37; Ruth Schwartz Cowan, *More Work for Mother: The Ironies of Household Technology from the Open Hearth to the Microwave* (New York: Basic Books, 1983): 53–62.

[52] Fred L. Israel, *1897 Sears Roebuck & Co. Catalogue* (New York: Chelsea House Publishers, 1968, reprint), 119–124.

[53] Richard Campbell, *Inventory and Appraisement*, 1881, Jasper County, Probate Court, Estate Case Files, 1809–1907, Record Group 179, Subgroup 2, Series 3 (GDA); E. W. Turner, *Inventory and Appraisement*, 1886, Crawford County Probate Court, Miscellaneous Records of the Inferior Court, 1822–1900, Record Group 139, Subgroup 2, Series 1 (GDA); William C. McEntire, *Inventory and Appraisement*, 1887, Franklin County, Probate Court, Estate Records, 1786–1916, Record Group 159, Subgroup 2, Series 1 (GDA).

FIGURE 4.2. "The Home of the Farmer To-Day." Note the symbols of middle-class domesticity represented by the proliferation of tableware, the abundance of books, and the well-decorated interior. J. W. Fitz, *Profitable Farming in the Southern States*, p. 331, Courtesy of the Library of Virginia.

a lid and several ovens, as did Madison Bagwell of Franklin County, who had two spiders with lids, one tin-reflecting oven, and a cast-iron oven with a lid.[54]

While farmers in the Georgia Piedmont appear to have retained their commitment to older, conservative trends in household furnishings, the large number and wide variety of small kitchen implements in the inventories suggest that they were more easily persuaded to purchase smaller mass-produced goods. In particular, they bought items that were beyond their ability, or that of a local artisan, to produce: cast metal, glass, and some ceramics, as well as specialized equipment and items with precision parts. As with stoves, economy, efficiency, and affordability were key variables in the formula to convince thrifty, leery

[54] John W. Whittington, *Inventory and Appraisement*, 1881, Crawford County Probate Court, Miscellaneous Records of the Inferior Court, 1822–1900, Record Group 139, Subgroup 2, Series 1 (GDA); Madison Bagwell, *Inventory and Appraisement*, 1875, Franklin County Probate Court, Estate Records, 1786–1916, Record Group 159, Subgroup 2, Series 1 (GDA).

farmers to add a purchase to their account or to hand over their hard-earned cash. Cast-iron items, for example, were especially popular, since foundries had developed the capability to produce high-quality products in a myriad of forms at very affordable prices. Decedents in Crawford, Jasper, and Franklin counties owned iron skillets, griddles, muffin irons, waffle irons, teakettles, and pots and pans.[55] Lighter-gauge tin and iron graniteware were also produced in a wide range of forms and at a cost that nearly all could afford. While most of these items retailed between $0.10 and $1.00, depending on size and complexity, they appear to have retained much of their value in the probate inventories.[56] Examples of tin and graniteware found in the inventories of the three-county sample include tin pans, coffee pots, and wash pots, along with graniteware plates and cups. Finally, sausage grinders, coffee mills, spice mills, eggbeaters, and glass and metal casters represent a few of the more complex appliances assembled using precision-cast pieces.[57]

Perhaps more than any other kitchen item, tableware – ceramics, glass, and cutlery – reveals the incredible diversity of mass-produced goods and specialized forms made possible by industrialization. The inventories show that farmers living in the Georgia Piedmont at the end of the nineteenth century had access to many of the fruits of the consumer revolution that had begun in the eighteenth century and had expanded to touch virtually every sector of society.[58] When describing ceramics, appraisers did not elaborate on the quality or decoration, but they did often specify function. The only inventory in all three counties that mentioned a certain grade of ceramics was that of John Dent, of Crawford County – he owned five china saucers and two cups, in addition to one lot of cups and saucers, thirteen plates, one lot of seven dishes, at least two flat serving dishes, one large pitcher, soup plates, two butter dishes, and a teapot, valued at a combined total of $3.85.[59] Other appraisers, in addition to making generic listings of plates, dishes, bowls, and saucers, identified special pieces intended for butter, cake, fruit, pickles, preserves, steak, soup, and sugar, as well as pitchers intended for cream, molasses, and syrup. Appraisers also occasionally noted a pitcher's color (white) or size (small, large, and gallon-sized).

55 Strasser, *Never Done*, 41–48.

56 Israel, *1897 Sears Roebuck & Co. Catalogue*, 145; Strasser, *Never Done*, 42.

57 The rotary caster was a table ornament patented in 1862 that held between four and six cruets to hold vinegar, oil, and other condiments. The caster was typically produced of silver plate and held the bottles of cut or pressed glass in a circular frame attached to a footed base with a handle in the center. For example, see Henry E. Russell, *Illustrated Catalogue of American Hardware of the Russell and Erwin Manufacturing Company, 1865*. Reprint (New York: Association for Preservation Technology, 1980): 338.

58 Bushman, *The Refinement of America*, i–xix; James Deetz, *In Small Things Forgotten: An Archaeology of Early American Life* (New York: Doubleday, 1977).

59 John W. Dent, *Inventory and Appraisement*, 1880, Crawford County, Probate Court, Miscellaneous Records of the Inferior Court, 1822–1900, Record Group 139, Subgroup 2, Series 1 (GDA).

Glassware may provide a better indication of the degree to which urban middle-class values and ideals had infiltrated the Georgia Piedmont, as many glass pieces were essentially superfluous decorative items, intended for display and occasional use. Fourteen Franklin County estates, six in Jasper, and ten in Crawford listed glassware among the possessions, including sets of dishes, saucers, bowls, individual salts, syrup cruets, glasses, goblets, pitchers, and decanters, in addition to glass bottles, cans, and jars for fruit, honey, jelly, and pickles. James Darden of Jasper County, for example, owned a set of glass "cup plates," a set of glass dishes, four wine glasses, and two decanters, suggesting that he could entertain and even serve wine to his guests.[60] Likewise, appraisers called out specific types of cutlery in addition to generic forks, spoons, and knives: table cutlery, butter, carving, and cutting knives, tablespoons and teaspoons – some of which were silver or silver-plated. John Dent owned silver candlesticks and eight silver spoons, while Daniel Manley of Franklin County had two sets of silver-plated knives and forks in addition to sets of plates, dishes, glasses, and a tea set.[61]

While the glassware and cutlery in some inventories show that many Georgia farmers were participating in the culture of consumption, the utilitarian ceramics recorded in others suggest the persistence of conservative rural values and a continued commitment to local exchange. All three counties had access to locally made earthenware and stoneware within a two-county radius, and Crawford was well known for its pottery industry. The local potteries developed in the mid-nineteenth century and prospered well into the twentieth century.[62] Nearly 80 percent of all the estates with household goods included in the survey had what the locals called crockeryware or jugware. While three inventories from Franklin County include table crockery, most was purchased for use in processing and storing food.[63] Crocks, jugs, and jars of various sizes – small, large, four-gallon – were the most common forms listed in the inventories.

Locally made pottery came in a broad range of forms for nearly every conceivable processing and storage purpose. However, it is impossible to tell from the inventories which forms are represented, because the pottery is either listed generally in lots, generically as individual jugs or crocks, or so specifically by function that crock or jug are not used in the description. For example, the milk pan in James Aaron's Jasper County estate was very likely locally made

60 James Darden, *Inventory and Appraisement*, 1889, Jasper County, Probate Court, Miscellaneous Records of the Inferior Court, 1822–1900, Record Group 139, Subgroup 2, Series 1 (GDA); the glass "cup plates" were presumably saucers.

61 John W. Dent, *Inventory and Appraisement*, 1880, Crawford County, Ordinary Court Minutes, Book B. (GDA); Daniel J. Manley, *Inventory and Appraisement*, 1893, Franklin County, Probate Court, Estate Records, 1786–1916, Record Group 159, Subgroup 2, Series 1 (GDA).

62 John A. Burrison, *Brothers in Clay: The Story of Georgia Folk Pottery* (Athens: University of Georgia Press, 2008): 29–42.

63 Burrison, *Brothers in Clay*, 15–28.

earthenware, given that milk pans were a mainstay in the rural South's pottery tradition.[64] Likewise, the two "piggins" (pipkins) in William Reed's Franklin County estate represent an archaic earthenware form crafted by North Georgia potters: a small bowl with a handle, used to pour or serve liquids.[65] Other common forms included fruit jars, jugs, milk coolers, butter churns, cream pots, and syrup pitchers – the latter two forms are considered to be distinct to Georgia and North Carolina potters.[66]

Many kitchen items listed in the inventories suggest a high level of self-sufficiency among farm households – Piedmont farmers owned preserve kettles, sausage grinders and stuffers, and butter churns. While making preserves, sausage, and butter indicate the persistence of self-reliant ways and perhaps a resistance to obtaining processed goods through merchants or local exchange, at the same time they reflect the increased dependence on mass-produced consumer goods. The preserve kettle listed in David Henry's Franklin County estate was almost certainly a cast-iron kettle produced outside of the county and purchased from a merchant.[67] Likewise, roughly 10 percent of the probated households listing kitchen items included a sausage mill, a relatively cheap and widely available item in the years following the Civil War. The 1897 Sears catalog, for example, lists meat grinders from $1.35 to $2.35 and sausage stuffers from $0.22 to $4.95.[68] Butter churns, a quintessential symbol of rural self-sufficiency, were identified in nearly one-quarter of the inventories listing household goods. Yet even here, the inroads of the consumer revolution become apparent – Larkin Sewell of Franklin County used a churning machine and several others used patented churns, suggesting that a growing number of farmers saw the benefit of purchasing mass-produced items because they offered a low-cost way to improve efficiency.[69]

The inventories also make it possible to gauge how often formal dining took place in the Georgia Piedmont. Several types of furniture, while food-related, appear to have been associated with formal dining and may indicate that the decedent's house had a separate dining room. Pieces like sideboards and folding tables were associated more with serving food than with preparation, whereas corner cupboards were meant to store and display tableware in an attractive manner, as opposed to the plainer, more utilitarian cupboards found in kitchens.[70] Value alone indicates a difference, as corner cupboards were

64 Ibid., 64.
65 Ibid., 69.
66 Ibid., 64–65.
67 Henry F. David, *Inventory and Appraisement*, 1895, Franklin County Probate Court, Estate Records, 1786–1916, Record Group 159, Subgroup 2, Series 1 (GDA).
68 Israel, *1897 Sears Catalogue*, 116.
69 Larkin D. Sewell, *Inventory and Appraisement*, 1895, Franklin County Probate Court, Estate Records, 1786–1916, Record Group 159, Subgroup 2, Series 1 (GDA).
70 Atlanta Historical Society, *Neat Pieces*, 11; Hurst and Prown, *Southern Furniture*, 499–504.

typically valued at $4.00 and other cupboards at $2.32. Only three corner cupboards were identified in the sample, all of them in Franklin County.

Sideboards and slabs were essentially variations on a serving table. Long, shallow, and rectangular, slabs were used to serve food in dining rooms and, as such, represented a more genteel level of dining. The sideboard was a more developed version of the slab, with doors and drawers underneath the serving surface designed to store utensils or table linens.[71] One slab was identified in each of the three counties, averaging $1.50 in assessed value. Sideboards were much more prevalent, with two in Crawford County, five in Jasper, and seven in Franklin. The average appraised value in Crawford was $1.13, while it was $2.39 in Franklin and $3.75 in Jasper. Although they were not terribly expensive, slabs and sideboards appear to have been luxury items and perhaps even status indicators, as evidenced by the wealth level of the decedents who owned them. John McElmurry of Crawford County, who owned a sideboard, held more than 300 acres and had a total estate value of $1,187. All but 1 of the decedents with a sideboard in Jasper County owned more than 300 acres, and the average estate value among them was $1,388. In Franklin County, the average decedent who owned a sideboard held 275 acres of land and had an estate appraised at $417. Three of the 6 Franklin County decedents owned more than 300 acres and had estates worth an average of $586.

Certain types of tables also provide an indication of the existence of a dining room or, at the very least, the ownership of luxury items devoted to the social ceremony surrounding dining or entertaining visitors. Folding tables – or Pembroke tables, as they were commonly called – were identified in seven of the households.[72] They had originated in the 1770s, when English furniture makers developed them to serve as specialized tea or gaming tables.[73] The two folding leaves made these smaller pieces extremely versatile and portable, and they became very popular in the United States, where they were found mainly in dining rooms and parlors. John Dent of Crawford owned a folding table appraised at $10.00, while William Reed and Albert Bagwell of Franklin owned versions that had an average appraised value of $3.50.[74] Folding tables also appeared in the Jasper County inventories of Richard Campbell, James Darden, and James Williams, averaging $3.50 in appraised value.[75]

[71] Atlanta Historical Society, *Neat Pieces*, 11, 44; Hurst and Prown, *Southern Furniture*, 262–264.

[72] Atlanta Historical Society, *Neat Pieces*, 11.

[73] Hurst and Prown, *Southern Furniture*, 227 and 229.

[74] John W. Dent, *Inventory and Appraisal*, 1880, Crawford; William A. P. Reed, *Inventory and Appraisement*, 1893, Franklin County Probate Court, Estate Records, 1786–1916, Record Group 159, Subgroup 2, Series 1 (GDA). Albert G. Bagwell, *Inventory and Appraisement*, 1887, Franklin County Probate Court, Estate Records, 1786–1916, Record Group 159, Subgroup 2, Series 1 (GDA).

[75] Richard Campbell, *Inventory and Appraisement*, Jasper County, Probate Court, Estate Case Files, 1809–1907, Record Group 179, Subgroup 2, Series 3 (GDA); James Darden, *Inventory and Appraisement*, Jasper County, Probate Court, Estate Case Files, 1809–1907, Record Group

William Reed also owned a "drop table" valued at $1.00, which likely refers to a larger drop-leaf dining table.[76] Appraisers explicitly identified dining tables in 37 of the 155 households (n = 24%) that detailed estates' possessions. The average value of a dining table in Jasper County was $3.50, while they averaged $2.28 in Crawford and $5.92 in Franklin County. Ownership of dining tables was largely confined to the elite in Jasper County, as all but 2 of the decedents whose possessions included dining tables held between 300 and 1,000 acres, averaging 648 acres. In Crawford County, on the other hand, all of the dining tables that appeared in probate inventories belonged to the middling class – decedents who owned between 200 and 475 acres, with an average holding of 366 acres. Dining-table ownership in Franklin County also fell firmly in the middle tenure categories. Although ownership was more evenly distributed throughout the sample population in Franklin, nearly half of the tables (n = 45%) were part of estates that included between 250 and 450 acres of land, with an average tenure of 268 acres.

While the furnishings in Georgia Piedmont dining rooms correlated to an eighteenth- and early-nineteenth-century notion of expressing gentility and affluence, parlors reflected more up-to-date fashions and patterns of consumption. The concept of the American parlor developed out of ideals introduced from eighteenth-century England, where the well-off devoted space to entertaining and ostentatious displays of exotic goods and material wealth that established their affluence and their station in society.[77] The popularity of the parlor trickled down and spread through American society in the early decades of the nineteenth century, as Anglo-American industrial capacity expanded, making the latest products and fashions cheaper and more widely available. By the time of the Civil War, this trend had reached the middle and working classes and had even begun to pervade rural life.[78] The parlor reached the height of its popularity in America in the second half of the nineteenth century.[79] The evidence from the Georgia Piedmont, however, suggests that the parlors in farmhouses differed significantly from those in cities and towns. These farmers created social spaces that generally lacked the formality, clutter, and ostentatious display found in urban and suburban parlors. In fact, they frequently called such spaces sitting rooms rather than parlors. Essentially a simpler version of the parlor, the rural sitting room provided a communal

179, Subgroup 2, Series 3 (GDA); James M. Williams, *Inventory and Appraisement*, Jasper County, Probate Court, Estate Case Files, 1809–1907, Record Group 179, Subgroup 2, Series 3 (GDA).

76 Reed, *Inventory and Appraisement*, 1893, Franklin County.

77 Kenneth L. Ames, *Death in the Dining Room*, 9; Katherine Grier, "The Decline of the Memory Place: The Parlor after 1890," in *American Home Life, 1880–1930: A History of Spaces and Services* (Knoxville: University of Tennessee Press, 1992): 51–53.

78 McMurry, *Families and Farmhouses*, 152–155.

79 Grier, "The Decline of the Memory Place," 52.

FIGURE 4.3. "Hot Water Reservoir and Warming Oven, 1875." J. W. Fitz, *Profitable Farming in the Southern States*, p. 92. Courtesy of the Library of Virginia.

area beyond the workspace of the kitchen and farmyard, designed to heighten a family's refinement and morals through comfortable surroundings, tasteful decoration, and access to music and literature.[80]

In many respects, the most important piece of furniture in the country sitting room was the center table. The popular monthly magazine *Godey's Lady's Book* "idealized the center table as a device that promoted family solidarity and piety; its 'Center-Table Gossip' column, with its allusion to the prominent piece of furniture, was intended to encourage an exchange of ideas and information between family members, especially women."[81] Four estates in Crawford County (n = 12%) included center tables, three center tables were identified among the Jasper decedents (n = 9%), and Franklin County inventories included five center tables (n = 6%), including a marble-topped center table in the estate of the dentist, Dr. William Alexander, valued at $8.05.[82] The farmers in the probate sample who owned center tables were primarily of the

[80] McMurry, *Farms and Families*, 156.
[81] Ibid., 144.
[82] William L. Alexander, *Inventory and Appraisement*, 1890, Franklin County, Franklin County, Probate Court, Estate Bond Books, 1853–1880, Record Group 159, Subgroup 2, Series 37 (GDA).

middling sort in all 3 counties, owning an average of 131 acres and having an average estate value of $627.

Comfortable chairs were another key feature of the fashionable parlor or sitting room. In an urban setting, a middle-class parlor suite would include a matching sofa, gentleman's chair, lady's chair, and four smaller chairs.[83] Although it is impossible to determine whether the sitting-room furniture listed in the inventories matched, given the minimal descriptions appraisers provided, several inventories had enough seating to furnish a respectable sitting room. John Dent's inventory from Crawford County, for example, lists a group of furnishings that suggests a well-appointed sitting room. His appraisers recorded a hat rack, a couch with draping, a pair of fire dogs (andirons), eight "parlor chairs," one folding table with cover, about a dozen books, two spittoons, and another table with a cover – possibly a center table.[84] As in the rest of the United States, parlor chairs were common throughout Georgia by the mid-nineteenth century.[85] Other types of seating listed in the inventories include "sitting chairs," armchairs, a "spring chair," rocking chairs, lounges, couches, and sofas.[86] Three sofas averaging $3.00 in value, and four lounges appraised at $0.50 to $2.50, were identified in Jasper County, while a single sofa and six lounges, ranging in value from $0.10 to $3.50, belonged to Franklin County estates. Crawford County inventories contained two sofas, five couches, and a single lounge, all ranging between $0.25 and $5.00 in value. Rocking chairs were also prevalent, with five in Jasper, seven in Crawford, and twenty-four in Franklin. Appraisers valued rockers at anywhere from $0.40 to a whopping $10.00, the average being $2.50. The $10 rocker owned by Isaac Reeder might have been a newer upholstered rocking chair.[87]

The rigors of farm life may not have left much time for reading, but books and bookshelves were well represented among Piedmont farmers' possessions. Six Jasper County estates listed books (representing nearly 20 percent of the probated households), as did seven estates in Crawford (21 percent). The evidence from the inventories suggests that book ownership was greatest in Franklin County, where more than one-third (n = 33) of the estates itemizing household goods listed books. All of the decedents who owned books in Crawford held between 170 and 470 acres of land, while 4 of the 6 estates

[83] Ames, *Death in the Dining Room*, 190.

[84] John W. Dent, *Inventory and Appraisement*, 1880, Crawford County. Covers were commonly used to protect the surfaces of a wide range of finer pieces of furniture in the eighteenth and nineteenth century.

[85] Atlanta Historical Society, *Neat Pieces*, 90.

[86] Introduced into the United States in the mid-eighteenth century, the couch and sofa are distinct forms of seating. The names were not used interchangeably since a sofa is a bench with a full-length back and arms at either end, while a couch and lounge are generally a bench with no back and a single curved arm at the head end; Hurst and Prown, *Southern Furniture*, 147–148.

[87] Isaac N. Reeder, *Inventory and Appraisement*, 1895, Franklin County Probate Court, Estate Records, 1786–1916, Record Group 159, Subgroup 2, Series 1 (GDA).

FIGURE 4.4. "Mother's Recreation." Note the symbols of leisure depicted by the books and the toys in a well-appointed room with a side table set with a vase of flowers beneath a print or painting. J. W. Fitz, *Profitable Farming in the Southern States*, p. 382. Courtesy of the Library of Virginia.

with books in Jasper owned between 107 and 300 acres. In Franklin, however, book ownership was distributed fairly evenly, with at least one book-owning decedent in every tenure category.

Books were most often listed in bulk – as "lots," a "bookcase of books," or a "library." Individual titles were listed on a handful of occasions for books of especially high value. Religious themes were popular; each of the estates listing books included at least one Bible, and guides to Christian scripture and teachings were among the most common titles – for example, *Burkitt's Notes on the New Testament* (1825), by William Burkitt; *Clarke's Commentary* in six volumes (1831), by Adam Clarke; and *The Royal Path of Life (1882)*, by

T. L. Haines. Among secular books, many of the decedents preferred histories and reference works. James Darden of Jasper owned one volume on naval history and another on the history of the world, as well as an almanac, a dictionary, encyclopedias, and a book called *American Elegies* that presumably contained tragic poems.[88] In Crawford, John Dent's appraisers felt that *The Life of Washington* and the *Congressional* volume were worth mentioning in addition to the five "lots of books" appraised in bulk.[89] Among other titles, Sewell Larkin had a copy of *Burkitt's Notes* valued at $2, a copy of *King New American Family Physicians* (1857) valued at $1, and *Webster's Unabridged Dictionary*, appraised at $6; Milton Gillespie owned a Bible, a "Bible companion," one medical work, and two songbooks.[90] Three of the fifteen African-American decedents owned books, including Jack Bellamy, who owned a Bible; James Brown, who had a bookcase of books appraised at $0.50; and Barney Hancock, who owned one lot of books and a desk.[91] Surprisingly, all three of these decedents were from Franklin County, where the black population was lowest. Besides books, the most common printed matter listed in the inventories were maps – they were included in five estates in Franklin, five in Crawford, and three in Jasper.

For most families, all of the books they owned could be stored in a single bookcase, desk, or secretary that would likely have been located in a sitting room.[92] Although six decedents owned bookcases, the inventories list far more desks and secretaries, indicating that they were more commonly used to hold books, in addition to providing storage for personal papers and a place to work on accounts. Twelve percent (n = 11) of the decedents in Franklin County owned desks. Two of these were listed as bookcases and desks, suggesting that they were secretaries, while another was listed as a writing table. The Crawford inventories included five desks and one secretary, accounting for 15 percent (n = 5) of the decedents whose household possessions were itemized. Jasper County had the highest percentage of desk ownership, at 16 percent, with four desks and one secretary mentioned in the inventories. In Franklin, 5 of the decedents who owned desks held between 200 and 400 acres, while

88 Darden, *Inventory and Appraisement*, 1881, Jasper County.

89 Dent, *Inventory and Appraisement*, 1880, Crawford County.

90 Larkin D. Sewell, *Inventory and Appraisement*, 1895, Franklin County Probate Court, Estate Records, 1786–1916, Record Group 159, Subgroup 2, Series 1 (GDA); Milton M. Gillespie, *Inventory and Appraisement*, 1893, Franklin County Probate Court, Estate Records, 1786–1916, Record Group 159, Subgroup 2, Series 1 (GDA).

91 Jack Bellamy, *Inventory and Appraisement*, 1886, Franklin County Probate Court, Estate Records, 1786–1916, Record Group 159, Subgroup 2, Series 1 (GDA); James L. Brown, *Inventory and Appraisement*, 1894, Franklin County Probate Court, Estate Records, 1786–1916, Record Group 159, Subgroup 2, Series 1 (GDA); Barney Hancock, *Inventory and Appraisement*, 1898, Franklin County.

92 Atlanta Historical Society, *Neat Pieces*, 171.

5 others owned fewer than 200 acres. In Jasper, 2 of the 4 decedents who owned desks had large farms – 700 acres and 408 acres – but the other 2 owned between 50 and 150 acres. Crawford County showed a tighter pattern of desk ownership, in which 4 of the 5 decedents held between 200 and 400 acres.

Music became an important component of urban, middle-class parlor life during the second half of the nineteenth century. It provided entertainment for family and guests, and it became a way to communicate one's refinement.[93] The inventories from Crawford, Jasper, and Franklin counties reveal that farmers in the Georgia Piedmont shared a passion for music with their urban counterparts and engaged fully in the parlor-music culture that peaked in the 1890s. While instruments such as harmonicas, fiddles, and banjos fit the stereotype of the backcountry farmer, rural Georgians owned trumpets, bugles, violins, pianos, and the most important instrument in late-nineteenth-century parlor culture, organs. In fact, organs and pianos ($n = 16$) outnumbered all other instruments ($n = 7$) identified in the inventories by more than 2:1. The two pianos were by far the most valuable household items in the entire sample. William Royston of Franklin County owned a piano appraised at $225, and J. Fletcher Weatherbee of Crawford County owned a pianoforte valued at $250.[94] Remarkably, Weatherbee's pianoforte represented 84 percent of the total appraised value of his household goods. Royston, on the other hand, was in the top 3 percent of Franklin County decedents in terms of wealth, with real-estate holdings of 629 acres and an estate appraised at $1,206.

Nearly 10 percent of the decedents in the probate sample acquired a parlor organ for their home. Parlor organs were first produced early in the nineteenth century but did not become widespread until after mid-century, when improvements in design and manufacturing made them cheap and functional enough for average, middle-class consumers to indulge in. The popularity of the parlor organ took off in the 1850s, peaked in the 1890s, and declined rapidly early in the twentieth century, when upright pianos and phonographs presented affordable alternatives. Although the cost of an organ was considerable, it was a great deal cheaper than a piano. Even so, purchasing an organ was one of the biggest investments a Piedmont farmer would make, and the size of an organ meant that the rural consumer was committing a significant amount of living space to its placement in the home. Once the decision was made, however, the organ

93 Ames, *Death in the Dining Room*, 164–166; Donna R. Braden"'The Family That Plays Together Stays Together': Family Pastimes and Indoor Amusements, 1890–1930," in *American Home Life, 1880–1930: A Social History of Spaces and Services* (Knoxville: University of Tennessee Press, 1992): 154–156.

94 William A. Royston, *Inventory and Appraisement*, 1896, Franklin County; J. Fletcher Weatherbee, *Inventory and Appraisement*, 1887, Crawford County Probate Court, Miscellaneous Records of the Inferior Court, 1822–1900, Record Group 139, Subgroup 2, Series 1 (GDA).

became the centerpiece of the sitting room, with stylish details that fit current trends. Organs often had added appeal because of their association with sacred music, which appealed to the moral aspirations of many Victorian-era middle-class families, whether they lived in town or in the country.[95]

The appraised values of organs listed in the inventories ranged from $0.85 to $70.00, the average value being $25.00. Van Buren Horn of Crawford County had an organ appraised at $20.00, while William Campbell and Anna Campbell of Jasper had organs valued at $0.85 and $70.00, respectively. All of the Crawford and Jasper County decedents with organs were affluent – they either owned more than 400 acres of land or had estates appraised at more than $1,000. However, the Franklin County decedents who owned organs had landholdings ranging from 98 acres to 629 acres, with an average tenure of 305 acres and an average total estate value of $685. Furthermore, the distribution of ownership in Franklin cut across tenure classes, suggesting that parlor organs had a broad appeal to rural consumers.

The inventories from the three counties also provide an indication of how sitting rooms and other parts of the rural Piedmont homestead were decorated. Furnishings included candle stands, flower-stands, and small worktables with one drawer. Many rooms had fireplaces, as the presence of andirons, fenders, and other fireplace tools attests. On the walls, the decedents hung looking glasses (mirrors), photographs, and prints. Several inventories also listed window shades. J. Fletcher Weatherbee's sitting room, it seems, had a carpet and rug along with sofas, a center table, and a pianoforte.[96] Piedmont homes were lit by candles and oil lamps, and the inventories list many lighting accessories, such as lamp oil, wicks, and chimneys – items that farmers probably purchased from merchants, demonstrating their reliance on the market for their basic lighting needs. Some Piedmont farmers, however, still made their own candles, as the candle mold listed among Thomas Sanders's possessions suggests.[97] Likewise, the jug lamp included in Charles Reeder's Franklin County estate implies that utilitarian, locally made wares were still in use. On the other hand, James Blessingame of Crawford owned silver candlesticks, indicating (both to his contemporaries and to the historian) a certain level of sophistication and affluence.[98] Other lighting accessories mentioned in the inventories included chandeliers, hanging oil lamps, and swing lamps.

95 Ames, *Death in the Dining Room*, 150–155,160; Braden, "The Family That Plays Together," 155.

96 J. Fletcher Weatherbee, *Inventory and Appraisement*, 1887, Crawford County.

97 Thomas J. Sanders, *Inventory and Appraisement*, 1887, Crawford County Probate Court, Miscellaneous Records of the Inferior Court, 1822–1900, Record Group 139, Subgroup 2, Series 1 (GDA).

98 Charles Reeder, *Inventory and Appraisement*, 1895, Franklin County Probate Court, Estate Records, 1786–1916, Record Group 159, Subgroup 2, Series 1 (GDA); James G. Blessingame, *Inventory and Appraisement*, 1885, Crawford County Probate Court, Miscellaneous Records of the Inferior Court, 1822–1900, Record Group 139, Subgroup 2, Series 1 (GDA).

Another indicator of the extent to which Georgia Piedmont farmers engaged in the market for consumer goods is the variety of devices listed in the inventories intended to make work easier, especially those designed to measure or save time. The most obvious of these are clocks and watches. In a sense timepieces were luxury items, because of their high cost (especially watches), yet they also served the purpose of calibrating the day, which allowed a person to govern his or her schedule more precisely.[99] Magnolia Le Guin captured the joy that a functional purchase could provide when she wrote, "Ghu bought me a good stove and treated himself to a clock recently."[100] Clocks were well represented in the inventories for each tenure class, with more than half of the decedents owning at least one. They could be fairly expensive – the calendar clock James Reeves owned, appraised at $10, was the most valuable in the probate sample, while Philip McCarty owned an eight-day clock valued at $5.[101] Half of the decedents in Crawford County owned clocks (n = 17), along with 65 percent of those in Franklin, where the clocks ranged in value from $1 to $10. As for specific types, William Owen had a "common day clock," William McEntire owned a calendar clock (appraised at $8), Henry Stovall had a one-weight wall clock ($3), and William Rampley had an office clock for his mercantile enterprise.[102] In Jasper, 75 percent of the estates (n = 24) included at least one clock; Robert Minter had an eight-day clock, and Richard Campbell owned a wooden clock valued at $2.00.[103]

Watches represented a higher level of craftsmanship and wealth – only 10 percent of the probated individuals owned watches. Moreover, all of the watches appear to have been owned by men and produced in silver and gold, suggesting that they were as much status symbols as they were tools to help monitor one's schedule. Only two decedents in Jasper owned watches, while four men in Crawford County had at least one. The silver watch owned by

99 Mark Smith, *Mastered by the Clock: Time, Slavery, and Freedom in the American South* (Chapel Hill: University of North Carolina Press, 1997).

100 Le Guin, *Home-Concealed Woman*, 23.

101 James M. Reeves, *Inventory and Appraisement*, 1898, Crawford County Probate Court, Miscellaneous Records of the Inferior Court, 1822–1900, Record Group 139, Subgroup 2, Series 1 (GDA); Philip McCarty, *Inventory and Appraisement*, 1898, Crawford County Probate Court, Miscellaneous Records of the Inferior Court, 1822–1900, Record Group 139, Subgroup 2, Series 1 (GDA).

102 William Owen, *Inventory and Appraisement*, 1885, Franklin County Probate Court, Estate Records, 1786–1916, Record Group 159, Subgroup 2, Series 1 (GDA); William C. McEntire, *Inventory and Appraisement*, 1887, Franklin County; Henry F. Stovall, Sr., *Inventory and Appraisement*, 1900, Franklin County Probate Court, Estate Records, 1786–1916, Record Group 159, Subgroup 2, Series 1 (GDA); William Rampley, *Inventory and Appraisement*, 1898, Franklin County Probate Court, Estate Records, 1786–1916, Record Group 159, Subgroup 2, Series 1 (GDA).

103 Richard Campbell, *Inventory and Appraisement*, 1881, Jasper County, Probate Court, Estate Case Files, 1809–1907, Record Group 179, Subgroup 2, Series 3 (GDA); Robert J. Minter, *Inventory and Appraisement*, 1899, Jasper County, Probate Court, Estate Case Files, 1809–1907, Record Group 179, Subgroup 2, Series 3 (GDA).

Pleasant Duke of Crawford County was appraised at $25, making it the most valuable watch among all the probated estates.[104] Franklin County estates produced the highest number of watches, with eleven individual watch owners representing 12 percent of the decedents from the county. The average appraised value for a watch in Franklin County was $11.66, and all were silver watches with chains. Among the seventeen watches itemized in the probate sample, John Tabor's Waterbury watch was the only brand name listed.[105]

A similar blurring of the line between functional items and status items can be seen in gun ownership. Guns played a significant role in the history of the early United States and helped American men define their identities – especially in the South, where gun ownership was widespread because of the need for protection and for providing wild game for the table.[106] Guns' importance as a means of protection diminished as frontier conditions gave way to stable settlement; however, firearms continued to be used for hunting (particularly for deer, turkey, and rabbit) and remained popular throughout the nineteenth century. As much as 40 to 60 percent of the population had guns in some places, but gun ownership was by no means universal, primarily because of the significant cost of acquiring one.[107] Thirty-six percent of Franklin County estates with inventories itemizing household goods ($n = 32$) listed guns, while 42 percent of Crawford County decedents ($n = 14$) and nearly half of Jasper County decedents ($n = 15$) owned at least one firearm. Shotguns were the most common type, with seven single-barrel and fourteen double-barrel models mentioned in the inventories. Rifles were next, numbering fifteen, followed by thirteen pistols. Two smoothbore muskets were also identified, and the ten remaining firearms were simply listed as guns. Several inventories included specific descriptions of firearms. James Aaron of Jasper County owned a "silver mounted rifle," indicating that the mounts, including the trigger plate, butt plate, and all other metal except for the barrel, were silver or silver-plated.[108]

[104] Pleasant Duke, *Inventory and Appraisement*, 1890, Crawford County Probate Court, Miscellaneous Records of the Inferior Court, 1822–1900, Record Group 139, Subgroup 2, Series 1 (GDA).

[105] John F. Tabor, *Inventory and Appraisement*, 1887, Franklin County Probate Court, Estate Records, 1786–1916, Record Group 159, Subgroup 2, Series 1 (GDA).

[106] Anna L. Hawley, "The Meaning of Absence: Virginia's Southside Inventories in Surry County, Virginia, 1690–1715," in *Early American Probate Inventories* (Boston: Boston University, 1989): 23–32; Robert H. Churchill, "Gun Ownership in Early America: A Survey of Manuscript Militia Returns," *William and Mary Quarterly*, 3rd ser., 60, no. 3 (July 2003): 632–638; James Lindgren and Justin L. Heather, "Counting Guns in Early America," *William and Mary Quarterly*, 43, no. 5 (2002): 1777–1842; Hilliard, *Hog Meat and Hoecake*, 71–75.

[107] Churchill, "Gun Ownership in Early America," 634, 636; Nicolas W. Proctor, *Bathed in Blood: Hunting and Mastery in the Old South* (Charlottesville: University of Virginia Press, 2002): 85–86.

[108] James Aaron, *Inventory and Appraisement*, 1880, Crawford County Probate Court, Miscellaneous Records of the Inferior Court, 1822–1900, Record Group 139, Subgroup 2, Series 1 (GDA).

The rifle was appraised at only $1, however, suggesting that it was old or that the metal was silver-plated, not solid silver. Another Jasper decedent, James Darden, owned a Colt repeater worth $8.00, while appraisers listed a Smith & Wesson revolver valued at $5.60 among Robert Minter's possessions.[109] The only shotgun with a description beyond the number of barrels was a breechloader identified in Philip McCarty's Crawford County estate.[110]

The type of gun a person owned said something about him. The shotgun was considered to be a weapon that required skill and was favored by wealthier sportsmen, while poorer hunters preferred the rifle because it used less powder and shot.[111] The pattern of gun ownership in Franklin County reflects this: 6 of the 7 estates containing rifles or muskets belonged to farmers who owned between 100 and 201 acres, while 6 of the 7 shotguns were owned by decedents who held between 260 and 600 acres. Pistol ownership also correlated with upper-middle-class status, with the incidence in Crawford occurring exclusively among estates of between 300 and 550 acres. The 3 pistols in Jasper were in estates of farmers' with more than 200 acres, and the 2 Franklin County farmers who owned pistols held 190 acres and 500 acres.

While clocks, watches, and guns appear to have been primarily male-oriented technologies, sewing machines were decidedly part of the woman's sphere, even if they were listed among a man's possessions. Textile production was one of the first activities to industrialize in the United States, and cheap cloth manufactured in eastern mills quickly replaced homemade textiles during the second half of the nineteenth century, obviating the need for spinning and weaving equipment.[112] Sewing, however, remained an important and seemingly endless task in households throughout the nation. Next to the iron cookstove, the sewing machine was the labor-saving device that had the greatest impact on the lives of nineteenth-century women. Introduced in the 1840s, sewing machines continued to improve in quality and decrease in price as the century wore on, and they quickly became accessible to Americans at nearly all wealth levels.[113]

The probate data attest to the affordability of these devices by the 1880s and 1890s, revealing that the machines were concentrated in the lowest tenure

[109] Darden, *Inventory and Appraisement*, 1881, Jasper County; Robert J. Minter, *Inventory and Appraisement*, 1889, Jasper County.

[110] McCarty, *Inventory and Appraisement*, 1896, Jasper County.

[111] Proctor, *Bathed in Blood*, 21.

[112] Strasser, *Never Done*, 129.

[113] Elias Howe, Jr., a machinist from Spencer, Massachusetts, patented the first practical design for a home sewing machine in 1846. Within a decade, designs improved and prices decreased to a point where the personal sewing machine became widely accepted. The Singer Sewing Machine Company introduced the first electric home sewing machine in 1889. Grace Rogers Cooper, *The Sewing Machine: Its Invention and Development* (Washington, DC: Smithsonian Institution Press, 1976): 19.

classes in all three counties. Ten sewing machines were identified in Crawford County, with 4 owned by decedents holding fewer than 200 acres of land, and another 4 among estates with between 200 and 400 acres. Jasper County displayed a similar pattern, with 5 machines in estates of up to 100 acres and 4 in estates of between 101 and 400 acres. The pattern was clearest in Franklin County, however, where 18 estates of fewer than 200 acres included sewing machines, while the remaining 11 machines were owned by decedents who held between 201 and 800 acres. The average value of a sewing machine among the Franklin County inventories was $11.11, the cheapest being appraised at $2.50 and the most valuable at $20.00 (a Wheeler & Wilson model owned by William Farmer).[114] The average value of the twelve sewing machines in Jasper County was $13.06, while Crawford County's twelve machines had the highest average value, $16.10.

Strangely, all of the sewing machines set aside for widows from Crawford and Jasper counties (as part of the one year's support they were entitled to) were either listed without a value or appraised at very low values. This might represent a strategy among appraisers to undervalue the assets provided to widows in order to maximize the number of possessions they could retain as part of their widow's portion. No value was listed for the sewing machines set aside for the widows of Joe Danielly and Wiley Ray of Crawford County, while the sewing machine set aside for James Doster's widow in Jasper County was valued at $0.05 – a suspiciously low figure, considering that the average machine was appraised at more than $13.00.[115] Other details that appraisers noted about sewing machines included brand names (one Singer and one White), as well as the "domestic sewing machine" owned by John Dent and a "new house sewing machine" listed in William Owens's inventory.[116]

The evidence from the sample suggests that sewing machines were increasing in number in the three counties between 1880 and 1910, while spinning wheels and looms became less common. Only two looms (n = 6%) and two spinning wheels (n = 6%) were included in the Crawford County sample. Pleasant Duke's inventory listed a loom and cards valued at $4.00, as well as a spinning wheel valued at $0.50; Elijah Eubanks's loom and spinning wheel were worth

114 William H. Farmer, *Inventory and Appraisement*, Franklin County Probate Court, Estate Records, 1786–1916, Record Group 159, Subgroup 2, Series 1 (GDA).

115 Joe Danielly, *Inventory and Appraisement*, 1900, Crawford County; Wiley M. Ray, *Inventory and Appraisement*, 1897, Crawford County Probate Court, Miscellaneous Records of the Inferior Court, 1822–1900, Record Group 139, Subgroup 2, Series 1 (GDA); James Doster, *Inventory and Appraisement*, 1889, Jasper County, Probate Court, Estate Case Files, 1809–1907, Record Group 179, Subgroup 2, Series 3 (GDA).

116 John W. Dent, *Inventory and Appraisement*, 1880, Crawford County; William Owen, *Inventory and Appraisement*, 1885, Franklin County Probate Court, Estate Records, 1786–1916, Record Group 159, Subgroup 2, Series 1 (GDA).

$0.75 combined.[117] A single loom was identified in the Jasper County estate of William Rainey, while five other decedents (n = 16%) owned spinning wheels, worth $5.59 in all. Franklin County is another story, however. Here, 35 percent of the decedents owned sewing machines, 39 percent (n = 35) owned spinning wheels, and 18 percent (n = 16) owned looms. The average value of a loom in Franklin was $1.59, and that of a spinning wheel $0.89. Although it is difficult to determine how many of these spinning wheels and looms were still actually in use, the impressive numbers suggest a high degree of self-sufficiency through the production of homespun cloth. Magnolia Le Guin testified to the continued use of homemade cloth when she wrote in 1905, "I will sew up a bolt of homespun and perhaps make me a bleaching underskirt between now and Jan 1906 – (a time for the stork)."[118]

Washing machines were another household technology that had begun to appear in the Georgia Piedmont by the 1880s. Agitating, hand-cranked washing machines designed for home use were largely a development of the second half of the nineteenth century, and they retailed for between $2.50 and $3.50 by the end of the century.[119] The 3-county sample included a total of 6 washing machines, 5 of which belonged to middling farmers who owned between 250 and 350 acres of land. John Mauldin of Franklin County, the one exception, owned 500 acres. Albert Bagwell of Franklin County owned a washer valued at $0.50 in 1887, while Mauldin's was valued at $1.00 at his death in 1896.[120] Avoline Peurifoy's Jasper County estate also included a washing machine worth $0.50 when she died in 1882.[121] In Crawford County, William Sandefur's washing machine was appraised at $0.25, while Willis Scott and John Dent owned machines valued at $3.00 and $8.00, respectively, suggesting that these were newer or more advanced models than the washing machines owned by other decedents.[122]

The act of consumption in the rural South differed significantly from shopping in urban settings in the late nineteenth century. By the beginning of the 1870s,

117 Pleasant Duke, *Inventory and Appraisement*, 1890, Crawford County; Elijah Eubanks, *Inventory and Appraisement*, 1888, Crawford County Probate Court, Miscellaneous Records of the Inferior Court, 1822–1900, Record Group 139, Subgroup 2, Series 1 (GDA).

118 Le Guin, *A Home-Concealed Woman*, 181.

119 Strasser, *Never Done*, 116–117; Israel, *1897 Sears Catalogue*, 153.

120 Albert G. Bagwell, *Inventory and Appraisement*, 1887, Franklin County; John Mauldin, *Inventory and Appraisement*, 1896, Franklin County Probate Court, Estate Records, 1786–1916, Record Group 159, Subgroup 2, Series 1 (GDA).

121 Avoline Peurifoy, *Inventory and Appraisement*, 1882, Jasper County, Probate Court, Estate Case Files, 1809–1907, Record Group 179, Subgroup 2, Series 3 (GDA).

122 William Sandefur, *Inventory and Appraisement*, 1881, Crawford County Probate Court, Miscellaneous Records of the Inferior Court, 1822–1900, Record Group 139, Subgroup 2, Series 1 (GDA); John W. Dent, *Inventory and Appraisement*, 1880, Crawford County; Willis B. Scott, *Inventory and Appraisement, 1882*, Crawford County Probate Court, Miscellaneous Records of the Inferior Court, 1822–1900, Record Group 139, Subgroup 2, Series 1 (GDA).

the Southern mercantile system had become much more localized, and general stores had virtually displaced the factor system in which farmers bought supplies they needed on credit, using their expected cotton yield as collateral.[123] Although general stores continued to operate primarily on credit, they enabled farmers to deal with local merchants whom they knew from the community. By the end of the century, mail-order houses like Sears, Roebuck & Company, Montgomery Ward, and E. Butterick offered buyers in the country access – via the rail lines and depots – to a far greater range of consumer goods, often at discounts that local merchants could not match.[124] Estate auctions provided additional opportunities for acquisition in the Georgia Piedmont during the late nineteenth century, particularly for large items such as furnishings, livestock, and farm equipment. Occasional affairs only, auctions nevertheless provided an excellent alternative for acquiring goods at a discount.

Becoming a merchant was a way for farmers to diversify their operations, assuming they had the money to invest. The number of country stores in the South grew quickly during the years following the Civil War – by the turn of the twentieth century, an average county could boast 144, although competition was fierce and one-third of merchants failed within five years of entering the business.[125] Michael McDowell of Jasper County and William Royston of Franklin were the only decedents formally identified as merchants in the census data, yet the inventories of six other decedents included merchandise or other items (display cases, for example) that suggested they operated mercantile ventures in addition to farming. Five of the six were in Franklin County: merchandise was listed in the inventories of John Payne, Quillian Jordan, and Madison Bagwell, while James Hathcock's estate had twenty-five pages of stock enumerated.[126] Although there was no stock listed among William Rampley's possessions, two display cases and an office clock suggest that he ran a store of some kind.[127] William Minter of Jasper County also had merchandise, accounts, and notes listed in his estate.[128]

[123] Thomas D. Clark, "In the Southern Retail Trade after 1865," *Journal of Economic History* 3, Supplement: The Tasks of Economic History (December 1943): 39.

[124] Ibid., 87.

[125] Ayers, *The Promise of the New South*, 81 and 93.

[126] John W. Payne, *Inventory and Appraisement*, 1875, Franklin County Probate Court, Estate Records, 1786–1916, Record Group 159, Subgroup 2, Series 1 (GDA); Quillian Jordan, *Inventory and Appraisement*, 1887, Franklin County Probate Court, Estate Records, 1786–1916, Record Group 159, Subgroup 2, Series 1 (GDA); James Madison Bagwell, *Inventory and Appraisement*, 1875, Franklin County Probate Court, Estate Records, 1786–1916, Record Group 159, Subgroup 2, Series 1 (GDA); James H. Hathcock, *Inventory and Appraisement*, 1898, Franklin County Probate Court, Estate Records, 1786–1916, Record Group 159, Subgroup 2, Series 1 (GDA).

[127] William Rampley, *Inventory and Appraisement*, 1898, Franklin County Probate Court, Estate Records, 1786–1916, Record Group 159, Subgroup 2, Series 1 (GDA).

[128] William S. Minter, *Inventory and Appraisement*, 1897, Jasper County, Probate Court, Estate Case Files, 1809–1907, Record Group 179, Subgroup 2, Series 3 (GDA).

Regardless of size or locale, most Southern stores operated the same way. Drummers from wholesale firms in the larger cities usually supplied general stores twice a year, and store owners bought their merchandise on credit, just as they extended credit to the local clientele. Under these arrangements, merchants hoped that they would realize a profit when customers settled their accounts before the drummers returned with more goods. While merchants certainly accepted cash for purchases, they typically extended credit to local patrons for terms of 60, 90, or 180 days, and the customer paid interest in addition to the merchant's markup on the goods.

Although the range of products sold in general stores varied widely, the offerings were rather limited, especially in smaller, more rural establishments.[129] A Deed of Assignment from Franklin County, dated 1895, lists the contents of the W. A. Royston and Son store, providing a good indication of the types of products merchants were able to offer local customers.[130] Dry goods included calicos, worsted flannel, jeans, ginghams, sewing supplies, and suspenders. Stores also offered a variety of hardware, including small articles of hardware known as shelf goods. Groceries sold in bulk typically consisted of coffee, lard, and grits, while merchants also offered canned goods such as tomatoes, blackberries, oysters, peaches, sardines, potted hams, salmon, pepper, soap potash, and matches. Confections included candy, nuts, raisins, soda, and cream crackers. Patent medicines and staple drugs were also popular, as were clothing, crockery, glassware, and other household wares. The administrator engaged to oversee the assets in the Royston estate described the stock of goods as "being of the same quality usually kept and sold by merchants in small towns. The purchase of which stock goods is about $1,500."[131]

Dabney Holloway's account with A. M. & J. B. Robinson and Company of Monticello, Georgia, in Jasper County, provides a valuable portrait of the type of business Piedmont residents transacted with general stores in the closing years of the nineteenth century.[132] Holloway's account was included in the probate process because it remained open at the time of his death and was satisfied as part of the settlement of his estate. It lists purchases made between March 8, 1880, and March 19, 1881, a day after his death. The final transaction is represented by an addendum dated April 4, 1881, showing the return of one pair of red shoes. The account shows fourteen transactions between March and August of 1880, averaging $1.02 per transaction (omitting the single largest purchase – 200 pounds of sugar for $32.00 – as it would throw

[129] Ayers, *The Promise of the New South*, 90–91.

[130] William A. Royston, *A Deed of Assignment, D. A. Baker to Robert M. Turner, January 15, 1895*, Franklin County Probate Court, Estate Records, 1786–1916, Record Group 159, Subgroup 2, Series 1 (GDA).

[131] Royston, *Deed of Assignment*, 2.

[132] Dabney P. Holloway, *Mr. D. P. Holloway Bought of A. M. & J. B. Robinson & Co. of Monticello, Ga., 1881*, Jasper County, Probate Court, Estate Case Files, 1809–1907, Record Group 179, Subgroup 2, Series 3 (GDA).

off the mean). For the most part, the Holloway household bought items that could not be grown or produced on the farm, including medicine (laudanum, an opiate tincture, and hepatic compound); clothing (shoes, jean cloth, and a bank collar); farm-related items (horseshoes, leather wagon and breeching lines, and a buggy whip); sugar and tea; and incidentals such as matches, powder and shot, tobacco, and quires of paper comprised of twenty-five sheets. The purchase of white sheepskin gloves the day after Holloway's death in the spring of 1881 quite possibly represents pallbearer's gloves that were used at his funeral by a family member. The 10 percent interest charged on the account and the $2 credit applied against the balance hint at the complex pricing scheme merchants devised to maximize their profits on credit purchases.[133] In general, the types of goods Holloway acquired through the local store, the prices paid, his average expenditure, and the frequency of his purchases are typical of the spending patterns among Piedmont farmers in the final decades of the century.[134]

While store owners developed inscrutable systems for variable pricing and credit, especially for sharecroppers, they faced similarly coercive credit terms from their wholesalers, since they rarely had the cash on hand to pay for their stock upon delivery. The Deed of Assignment for William Royston's estate offers a rare glimpse into the precarious financial situation of many Southern general stores.[135] D. A. Baker, the estate administrator, was responsible for satisfying debts owed by the Royston and Son Mercantile Company to the Florence Alabama Wagon Company ($162.45), the Beck and Gregg Hardware Company of Atlanta ($117.00), S. W. Travers & Co. ($350.00), the Greenville Fertilizer Company ($2,300.00), the Marietta Guano Company ($260.00), Smith & Gilcreese ($575.00), and the Bank of Elberton ($350.00). The account books from the mercantile venture indicate that the business was owed approximately $10,592.95 in open accounts, notes, judgments, and mortgages at the time of William Royston's death, demonstrating the difficulty store owners frequently faced in getting customers to settle their accounts. Moreover, the administrator determined that only about $1,000.00 of the outstanding debt was "good," $5,000.00 was doubtful, and $4,599.95 was known to be bad and had been turned over to A. G. McMurray, Esq., for collection. D. A. Baker was instructed to "reduce the same to cash, as soon as the same can be... advantageously done," whether that was by employing a clerk to run the store until the stock was sold or by selling the remaining goods at auction, whatever "in his judgment may be best for the creditors of whose benefit this assignment is made."[136]

[133] Thomas D. Clark, "The Furnishing and Supply System in Southern Agriculture since 1865," *Journal of Southern History* 12, no. 1 (February 1946): 28–29.

[134] Ayers, *The Promise of the New South*, 90–91.

[135] Roytson, *Deed of Assignment*, 2.

[136] Ibid.

For Georgians with cash on hand, estate auctions offered a viable alternative to general stores for purchasing used items, particularly expensive consumer goods, at a significant savings. The average discount ranged from 7 percent to nearly 20 percent, which undoubtedly was as enticing to buyers then as it would be today. From the perspective of a decedent's household, an auction offered the liquidity of cash, which could be used to settle debts as well as providing widows and dependents with money to purchase necessary goods until they could recover from the death of a breadwinner. Nearly half of the estates (n = 100) in the aggregate probate sample were subjected to sale at auction. Property from 47 percent (n = 25) of Crawford County estates was auctioned off, compared to 40 percent (n = 25) of Jasper County estates and 38 percent (n = 50) of those in Franklin. Auctions were distributed fairly evenly across the tenure classes, suggesting that sale at public outcry was an accepted means of liquidating assets for households of all wealth levels. Land and personal property were rarely if ever sold together, as land was almost always passed to heirs unless debts could not be satisfied through the sale of personal property alone. Estate sales typically offered only a portion of the decedent's possessions – a group of items carefully selected to bring in just enough cash to provide for heirs or to pay off a debt. In situations where real estate was disposed of at auction, the sale was handled in the same way as personal property.[137]

Georgia law directed that personal property, with the exception of annual crops sent to market, be sold at public outcry in situations where the material assets needed to be converted to cash in order to pay debts.[138] The process to secure permission for an estate auction began when the administrator submitted a petition to the Clerk of the Ordinary providing a reason for the sale. For four weeks before the first hearing, the administrator would publish the petition in a county gazette to inform the public. If no objection was filed, the Ordinary issued an order allowing the sale. In addition to personal property, notes, bonds, judgments, accounts, and other debt instruments could be sold at auction after due diligence and with thirty days' notice of such sale being given at the courthouse door and at three additional public places in the county.[139] Once the order was granted, the auction was advertised yet again in a newspaper or gazette for forty days leading up to the sale date. Auctions were usually held on the first Tuesday of the month on the courthouse steps, between ten o'clock in the morning and four o'clock in the afternoon.[140] Although the estimated value of the goods to be auctioned was not made public, the appraisal figures listed

137 Clark, Read, Cobb, and Irwin, *Code of the State of Georgia*, Pt. 2, Tit, 6, Chap. 3, Art. 2, §2519.

138 Ibid., §2514–2517.

139 Clark, Read, Cobb, and Irwin, *Code of the State of Georgia*, Pt. 2, Tit, 6, Chap. 3, Art. 2, §2514–2517.

140 Ibid., §2514, §2519, §2588, and §3519.

TABLE 4.4. *Comparison of Aggregate Appraised and Sales Values for Crawford, Jasper, and Franklin Counties*

Category	Cases	Total Appraised Value ($)	Total Sales Value ($)	Average Appraised Value ($)	Average Sales Value ($)
Aggregate					
Household	36	1,084.6	973.7	30.1	27.0
Clocks/watches	18	73.5	61.2	4.1	3.4
Tools	62	3,106.2	2,858.4	50.1	46.1
Cotton planters	9	1,7.0	16.0	1.9	1.8
Mules	17	2,165.0	1,811.0	127.4	106.5
Livestock	46	5,545.0	4,779.8	120.5	104.0
Crawford County					
Household	5	213.6	265.3	42.7	53.1
Clocks/watches	0	0	0	–	–
Tools	13	853.1	880.3	65.6	67.7
Cotton planters	4	9.5	10.2	2.4	2.6
Mules	1	190.0	197.0	190.0	197.0
Livestock	8	845.0	780.1	105.6	97.5
Jasper County					
Household	7	158.0	82.1	22.6	11.7
Clocks/watches	5	21.0	12.1	4.2	2.4
Tools	12	886.1	880.7	73.8	73.4
Cotton planters	1	1.0	0.5	1.0	0.5
Mules	3	470.0	334.1	156.7	111.4
Livestock	7	718.7	687.7	102.7	98.2
Franklin County					
Household	24	713.0	626.3	29.7	26.1
Clocks/watches	13	52.5	49.1	4.0	3.8
Tools	37	1,367.0	1,097.5	36.9	29.7
Cotton planters	4	6.5	5.3	1.6	1.3
Mules	13	1,505.0	1,279.9	128.4	106.8
Livestock	31	3,981.3	3,312.1	115.8	98.5

in the inventories indicate how much the administrator expected each item to sell for. Administrators recorded detailed auction inventories describing the lots sold, the prices realized, and the names of successful bidders. These were presented to the Ordinary along with all of the other probate documents upon the conclusion of the estate administration.

The returns achieved at auction suggest that tools were in greater demand than household goods or livestock, given that they retained 93 percent of their appraised value on average (Table 4.4). Within that category, cotton planters typically brought in 95 percent of the administrator's estimate, indicating the high level of demand for such equipment.[141] The county-specific data, however, indicate discrete regional trends in the sale of mechanized equipment and specialized tools. While no cultivators went on the auction block in Jasper, in Crawford those implements realized 100 percent of their appraised value, and in Franklin they fetched double the amount for which they were listed. Planters also sold above list price in Crawford, going for 120 percent of their appraised value on average, compared to 50 percent in Jasper and 87 percent in Franklin. Few cotton gins went to auction, and the return they achieved varied: the one sold in Franklin realized 110 percent of its appraised value, compared to an average 78 percent return on the two sold in Crawford, and a paltry 36 percent return on the two sold in Jasper.

Smaller farm cotton gins and power engines brought in the highest dollar figures at auction. Gins, which allowed farmers to process their own cotton and that of neighbors (for a fee), sold for an average of $56. Engines could power threshers, gins, and other pieces of automated equipment, making them an invaluable alternative to high-cost manpower. They typically brought in 63 percent of the amount the administrator had estimated and exceeded the asking price (appraised value) by 125 percent in Jasper County. Wagons and cultivators also brought high returns in each county. It should come as no surprise that the most valuable farm stock was field equipment that faced such hard use during cultivation, harvest, and the preparation of cotton for sale.

Another type of farm stock, the tools needed to maintain field equipment and the structures on a farm, was also popular at auction. Typically these tools were sold in "lots" or "sets," suggesting they were calibrated or sized and required more care in manufacture. Tools like wrenches were especially useful for repairing wagons, gins, or other machines with moving parts. On average, mechanics' tools brought in 73 percent of their assessed value. In Jasper County, they typically brought a 93 percent return. Blacksmithing tools saw the highest demand of any farm-tool category: the 5 lots in Franklin County averaged 102 percent of their estimated value, the 6 lots in Crawford went for 105 percent, and the 3 lots in Jasper fetched 113 percent. Carpentry tools, on the other hand, did not do as well, realizing only a 59 percent return in Crawford and 66 percent in Franklin. In Jasper, however, carpentry tools achieved 93 percent of their appraised value at public outcry.

Household goods also brought a high rate of return at auction: an average of 90 percent in the three-county sample. The combined category of household furnishings and accessories returned only 52 percent of the administrators' estimates for 26 estates in Jasper County, but such items did much better in Crawford, fetching 88 percent of their assessed value, and in Franklin, where household goods achieved a return of 115 percent. Sewing machines, often the most valuable item among household goods, could be relied on to bring in a good return, with the 3 auctioned off in Franklin selling for 95 percent of their

[141] Ferleger, "Sharecropping Contracts."

appraised value, and the 3 in Crawford exceeding their estimated price, at 106 percent (no sewing machines were auctioned off in Jasper County). Although no clocks were put to auction in Crawford, the eight clocks auctioned in Franklin retained 94 percent of their estimated value, while the five in Jasper barely exceeded half of the list price.

Among household goods, sales data from auctions suggest that discretionary income was used in the kitchen first, followed by bedrooms. Stoves and larger pieces of furniture brought in the most cash for an estate. Stoves, which helped to sustain the labor force on the farm as well as to make time for the mistress of the farm, brought in $37 on average. Likewise, sewing machines were especially popular and averaged as much as $44 in Crawford, representing a 106 percent return on the estimate. Clocks also sold well and often brought as much as a plow.

Like household goods, livestock fetched an average 90 percent return on the appraised value, representing a bargain for the buyer. Mules and horses brought in the largest dollar amounts – no surprise, given that they were the engines that ran most of the agricultural enterprise for Piedmont farmers, pulling the plows and powering the threshers. Mules held the edge, probably because of their ruggedness and intelligence, features that were highly prized in the rocky foothills of the Smoky Mountains. The average mule in Crawford County sold for nearly $200, representing 115 percent of the estimated value, while the five auctioned in Franklin County averaged half that amount, with an average gavel price of $98 – a 20 percent discount from the appraised value. Jasper mules fell in between, with an average price of $111.35 (based on the sale of three animals), representing 71 percent of the appraised value. The pattern for horse sales was similar. Auction results indicate that horses were most expensive in Crawford, where four horses were sold for an average price of $68.00; the thirteen horses in Franklin County sold for approximately $66.68 per horse, 81 percent of the estimated value; a single horse in Jasper County sold for $40.00.

While pigs and chickens provided the lowest return among livestock, at 68 percent, sales seemed to favor the stock that could serve a family over a period of years. Hogs sold for better prices than pigs, indicating that animals bred for the table were favored over breeding stock, although both brought returns of between 86 and 116 percent on their appraised values. One estate auctioned pigs in Crawford, bringing an average price of $23.00 per pig, while the two estates offering pigs in Franklin got only $4.92 for them on average. The six estates that sold hogs in Franklin, on the other hand, received an average of $20.63 for each, and the two selling hogs in Jasper averaged $11.55.

Analyzing the demographics of the bidders at estate sales suggests that participants may have had motivations that extended beyond the promise of a discount or access to hard-to-find items. Family members, including widows, often bought back goods the deceased had previously owned. In fact, immediate family members participated in more than 90 percent of the estate sales in the probate sample. Their actual participation is probably even higher, given that this percentage reflects only family members who shared the name of the deceased and could be linked to the household at some point through census data. As such, it does not reflect married daughters or stepchildren who had different surnames. Moreover, relatives purchased a significant percentage of the lots in many cases, suggesting that they were trying to reacquire items for less than the appraised value. Henry David's widow and sons, for example, purchased 36 of the 175 lots auctioned off in Franklin County on April 2, 1888.[142] Likewise, the survivors of Elbert Baynes bought twenty-three of the forty-seven lots auctioned off in Jasper County in January 1887.[143] The widow Baynes purchased eighteen of the lots (all farm-related), including four mules, one bull, a syrup kettle, a gin-and-engine combination, wheat, and fodder. Eliza's two sons bought seven lots between them, including cottonseed, a Thomas harrow, a wagon, and plows.

The documents from the administrator's sale of David Brawner's Franklin County estate suggest that widows sometimes elected to take their portion of the estate from the auction, thereby maximizing their chances of acquiring more of the material assets than if they had made the selections from the appraisers' list. Brawner, a freedman, had done exceptionally well for himself by the time of his death in 1885. The inventory of his estate shows that he owned 100 acres of land and assets amounting to more than $900. Portions of his estate were auctioned off in two separate sales, suggesting that the administrator was trying to liquidate only enough of his belongings to arrive at a specific cash amount. David's widow, Hagar, bought corn and fodder in the first sale, held in November 1885, and $18 worth of seed and livestock in the second sale, in June 1886.[144] The bill for the second sale reports that her purchases in the amount of $18.00 were "set apart for the widow," and that the remainder of her petition for support would request the $209.65 in cash received for cotton sold by her agent, A. W. Gillespie.

The probate data from Crawford, Jasper, and Franklin counties show that, by the late nineteenth century, the expanding culture of consumerism and urban middle-class values had made significant inroads among the conservative yeoman farmers of the Georgia Piedmont. Yes, the furnishings and accessories in farm households remained, by and large, sparse and utilitarian. The highest priorities continued to be those pursuits or purchases that best provided for the family and supported the farming venture. Farm wives were quick to adopt

[142] Henry David, *Bill of Sale, April 2, 1888*, Franklin County, Probate Court, Homesteads, 1868–1904, Record Group 159, Subgroup 2, Series 23 (GDA).

[143] Elbert Baynes, *Bill of Sale, January 1, 1887*, Jasper County, Probate Court, Estate Case Files, 1809–1907, Record Group 179, Subgroup 2, Series 3 (GDA).

[144] David Brawner, *Bill of Sale, January 7, 1887*, Franklin County, Probate Court, Homesteads, 1868–1904, Record Group 159, Subgroup 2, Series 23 (GDA); David Brawner, *Bill of Sale, June 7, 1887*, Franklin County, Probate Court, Homesteads, 1868–1904, Record Group 159, Subgroup 2, Series 23 (GDA).

laborsaving devices like stoves, washing machines, and sewing machines, yet the prevalence of specialized kitchen tools and fashionable glassware, cruets, and other tableware suggests that the urge to consume made its way into the lives of farm families through the smallest, most innocuous objects. Likewise, dining rooms and parlors, rooms traditionally associated with social gatherings and ostentatious display, differed in subtle ways. Dining rooms continued to fit a pattern that was established in the early national period, with staid suites of dining tables, sideboards, and small serving tables. Sitting rooms, on the other hand, reveal clear evidence of a change in the perception of comfort, entertainment, and social display. Here, farmers in the middling tenure classes acquired the most current trappings of Gilded Age culture, including center tables, parlor organs, and upholstered chairs, despite the considerable prices.

Just as probate inventories suggest the ways in which farm families were embracing consumer culture, store accounts included in probate files indicate the persistence of an opposing, conservative tradition: the notion of limiting reliance on sources outside the family, especially when debt was involved. Furthermore, the data from estate sales reveal the shrewdness of Piedmont farmers, who recognized that these occasions represented an essential secondary market in used goods. Not only could farmers obtain a discount up front, they could also save money on taxes, since goods acquired at a cheaper price than the appraisal were worth less to the tax collector. Widows and heirs, for their part, understood that estate sales offered them the opportunity to acquire family assets at a lower price, thereby increasing the potential for maximizing the return on the appraised value of the estate. Estate sales also provided heirs with quick access to cash – arguably the greatest security to have in the extremely volatile economic climate of the time.

The data from the Georgia Piedmont reveal that farmers were keenly aware of the world of goods that existed beyond the county line. They were active consumers – albeit extremely selective ones – despite the ongoing economic pressures and uncertainties they faced. The evidence also suggests that farmers measured and displayed their success in different ways than their urban counterparts. While a parlor organ, a silver-plated caster, or a silver watch would be recognizable as symbols of affluence in the city, country folk were just as keenly aware that the ability to acquire a clock, a double-barrel shotgun, a prime mule, or a sulky plow sent an equally clear and powerful message.

5

Investing for Success in the Piedmont

James Chamberlain, formerly of western New York, eagerly put pen to paper in 1878 to offer a testimonial encouraging others to move to Georgia and experience the success he had achieved. He wrote that he was "well pleased with this country, and consider it unsurpassed in the United States for climate and healthfulness."[1] He was delighted with the land, the crops, the low taxes, the markets, and the length of the growing season. He also remarked that he was treated well by native Georgians, although they "take offense quicker, and the pistol and knife are more frequently handy than in the North."[2] But most importantly, he noted proudly that through "generous treatment" of the soil, he was able to produce 70 bales of cotton from 110 acres he purchased in Cobb County – "nine-tenths of it old worn land."[3] Chamberlain, if we are to believe the published account, was a yeoman farmer who was doing exceptionally well in the Georgia Piedmont in the years following the Civil War, and he succeeded despite being an outsider.

Chamberlain was not alone. According to Thomas Janes, the first Commissioner of Agriculture in Georgia, Chamberlain's reply was one of more than fifty received in response to a circular that the Department of Agriculture had distributed throughout the state, seeking endorsements from newcomers who were willing to praise the virtues of their adopted home. One

[1] Thomas P. Janes, *Georgia, from the Immigrant Settler's Stand-Point: Giving the Results of the Experience of Actual Settlers from Other States and Countries, Prefaced with an Account of the Natural Resources of Georgia and the Inducements to Immigrants and Capitalists* (Atlanta: Georgia Department of Argiculture), 35; The 1880 federal census lists a James I. Chamberlain living in Marietta, Georgia, in Cobb County in 1879; Bureau of Census. *Tenth Census of the United States, 1880, Population*, Marietta, Cobb County, Georgia. Roll 141, 202C; Enumeration District 37.

[2] Janes, *Georgia, from the Immigrant Settler's Stand-Point*, 35.

[3] Ibid., 35.

of the key missions of the Georgia Department of Agriculture when it was established in 1874 was to publish books and other promotional material that provided general information about the state of Georgia to its citizens, as well as "to supply Immigrants, actual and prospective, with accurate and reliable information on those subjects connected with Georgia in which it is believed they will feel a special interest."[4] Over the course of its first three decades, the Department of Agriculture issued at least twelve publications designed expressly to attract immigrants from throughout the United States and abroad to come settle in the Empire State of the South. These promotional pieces always carried the same message: Georgia was a land of unparalleled climate, bounty, and opportunity, where moral and enterprising people, both black and white, gladly welcomed outsiders, and where prosperity was entirely dependent on one's desire to succeed and willingness to work hard. Many of these pitches, however, ended with a note of realism for prospective immigrants, warning them to "not regard the present agriculturalists as knowing everything, nor yet fall into the contrary error of supposing they know nothing. In fact, they know much; yet the present is but a transition state, and they have not fully solved the problems of conformity to the new conditions of life and labor."[5]

While the handbooks and published testimonials were generally examples of unabashed boosterism, the recognition that many Georgians were struggling to solve "the problems of conformity to the new conditions of life and labor" was genuine, if a bit carefully worded. To be sure, emancipation forced whites and blacks throughout the South to quickly renegotiate rights in land and labor, as well as to begin adapting the social structure to accommodate people who were formerly considered chattel. Moreover, the expanding cotton economy added another dimension to the social and economic transformation, particularly in regions such as the Georgia Uplands, where cotton monoculture virtually displaced mixed agriculture during the postbellum period, shifting the focus from local and regional markets to engagement at the national level. The intensity of these changes varied from place to place; it was most profound in those areas where African Americans and plantations were concentrated, as well as in those locales that had largely existed outside of the cotton economy before the Civil War.[6]

4 Thomas P. Janes, *Hand-Book of the State of Georgia: Accompanied by a Geological Map of the State* (Atlanta: Russell Brothers, 1876), ii; The Georgia Department of Agriculture was the first state agency in the nation dedicated to encouraging the best agricultural practices in the state, as well as promoting Georgia's agricultural products in the marketplace.

5 Janes, *Hand-Book of the State of Georgia*, 15.

6 Jay Mandle, "The Plantation States as a Sub-Region of the Post-Bellum South," *Journal of Economic History* 34, no. 3 (September 1974): 732–738; David F. Weiman, "The Economic Emancipation of the Non-Slaveholding Class: Upcountry Farmers in the Georgia Cotton Economy." *Journal of Economic History* 45, no. 1 (March 1985): 71–72; Ferleger, "Self-Sufficiency and Rural Life on Southern Farms," 314–329.

Throughout the cotton South, this transformation generally meant an increase in the number of farms, a decrease in the average farm size, the rise of tenancy, and a greater dependence on credit. These changes often resulted in a decline in farmers' self-sufficiency, which translated into a cycle of dependency and poverty that was difficult to break and stood in the way of economic development. Scholars continue to debate the primary causes of the loss of self-sufficiency and their relative importance; however, most would agree that limited acreage, increased specialization in cotton, the high cost of credit, debt peonage, the paucity of improved technology, and predatory tenancy terms all factored into the formula promoting cotton monoculture over diversification.[7]

Ironically, given its expansion in the postbellum period, cotton had peaked as a big money crop in the 1850s – the memory of those high prices provided false hope to anxious planters and freedmen who expected it to bring salvation in the wake of the Civil War. However, "Cotton was a peculiarly unlucky crop" in the seventy-five years following the war – demand was down, and fertilizers were the only thing that kept the older cotton-producing regions in Georgia competitive with newer, fresher cotton land in Texas and the Mississippi Valley Uplands.[8] However, the commercial demand for cotton remained strong enough to encourage large-scale cultivation, and Georgia society was geared toward cotton production – it was the only thing that many planters knew how to grow. As a result, farmers living in the Cotton Belt between 1880 and 1910 were faced with a difficult choice: should they cultivate a profit-maximizing crop like cotton, or should they produce food crops that would help limit risk and provide for the household's needs directly?

Small farmers were at an immediate disadvantage, simply by not having the acreage necessary to grow an adequate number of food crops for home consumption in addition to enough cotton for market to realize a profit.[9] To make matters worse, the lack of ready cash made it necessary for farmers to seek high-interest credit from local banks and merchants; small farmers were especially vulnerable, since they often did not have the collateral necessary to negotiate favorable credit terms. As a result, merchants frequently were able to dictate the amount of cotton a farmer had to grow as part of the terms of the

[7] Mandle, "The Plantation States as a Sub-Region," 732–738; Gavin Wright and Howard Kunreuther, "Cotton, Corn, and Risk in the Nineteenth Century: A Reply," *Explorations in Economic History* 14, no. 2 (April 1977): 183; Ransom and Sutch, *One Kind of Freedom*, 154; Peter Temin, "Freedom and Coercion: Notes on the Analysis of Debt Peonage in *One Kind of Freedom*," *Explorations in Economic History* 16, no. 1 (January 1979): 56–63; Ferleger, "Self-Sufficiency and Rural Life," 327–328; Weiman, "The Economic Emancipation of the Non-Slaveholding Class," 71–72.

[8] The quote is by William N. Parker, "The South in the National Economy, 1865–1970," *Southern Economic Journal* 46, no. 4 (April 1980): 1022–1023.

[9] Wright, *The Political Economy*, 176–178; Wright, *Old South, New South*, 36–39; Lacy K. Ford, Jr., "Self-Sufficiency, Cotton, and Economic Development in the South Carolina Upcountry, 1800–1860," *Journal of Economic History* 45, no. 2 (June 1985): 265–266.

credit agreement.[10] Borrowers with little or no collateral used their farms or the future outcome of their cotton yield to secure loans, thereby assuming a much higher risk, since market trends were often volatile and growing conditions were anything but predictable. Likewise, tenants and especially sharecroppers were at the mercy of landlords who offered small plots and often imposed high quotas on the amount of cotton a tenant had to raise as part of the lease.[11] The lack of cash and close monitoring of farm practices by landlords also prevented the investment in newer farm technologies and the adoption of new crops or more progressive techniques of cultivation and farm management.[12]

Because farm size was directly linked to a farmer's income and level of wealth, tracing the pattern of asset ownership by tenure class (as revealed through probate data) shows how and when farmers diversified production, invested in labor-saving equipment, and felt comfortable enough to make more discretionary purchases. In addition, it is possible to identify the extent to which farmers were equipped to be self-sufficient and the degree to which they engaged in networks of consumption beyond the household. Finally, comparing households from the Lower Piedmont with those from the Uplands sheds light on the regional diversity that existed among the cotton-producing counties of Georgia because of differences in social structure, economic traditions, and physical environment.

The item-level investigation of assets listed in probate inventories from Crawford, Jasper, and Franklin reveals a picture of three Piedmont Counties that were agricultural in character and primarily devoted to the production of cotton by 1880. However, the tools, crops, and livestock listed in the inventories suggest a broad range of secondary production directed toward three possible strategies: to meet the household's needs and thereby ensure self-sufficiency; to diversify operations by venturing into the production for market of other crops and livestock; or to practice a trade that met neighbors' needs. When the data are broken down by tenure class (size of landholding, that is), other patterns become apparent, allowing us to better understand both how households organized themselves to achieve success and how the strategies for success differed as farmers progressed up the tenure ladder.

Comparing more advanced agricultural implements like harrows to core agricultural tools like plantation hoes and wagons provides an indication of the level at which farmers invested in more advanced technologies. For those farmers with the least amount of land and the fewest resources, the available

10 Ransom and Sutch, *One Kind of Freedom*, 157–162; Roger Ransom and Richard Sutch, "The 'Lock-In' Mechanism and Overproduction of Cotton in the Postbellum South," *Agricultural History* 49, no. 2 (April 1975): 406.

11 Gavin Wright, "Freedom and the Southern Economy," *Explorations in Economic History* 16, no. 1 (January 1979): 96–100.

12 Ferleger, "Self-Sufficiency and Rural Life," 327.

TABLE 5.1. *Aggregate Distribution of Hoes, Harrows, and Wagons from Crawford, Jasper, and Franklin Counties by Tenure Class*

Acreage	# Farms	# Hoes	Avg. # Hoes	# Harrows	Avg. # Harrows	# Wagons	Avg. # Wagons
1,000+	11	31	2.8	1	0.1	30	2.7
450–999	24	37	1.5	13	0.5	39	1.6
400–449	13	8	0.6	6	0.5	16	1.2
350–399	8	12	1.5	2	0.3	10	1.3
300–349	13	26	2.0	4	0.3	15	1.2
250–299	8	24	3.0	4	0.5	12	1.5
200–249	23	29	1.3	5	0.2	20	0.9
150–199	20	27	1.4	7	0.4	19	1.0
100–149	30	27	0.9	9	0.3	34	1.1
50–99	9	10	1.1	0	0.0	6	0.8
1–49	8	4	0.5	2	0.3	5.5	0.7
0/Blank	32	31	0.9	1	0.03	20.3	0.6
Total	199	266	1.3	54	0.3	227	1.1

tools were largely limited to the plow and the hoe; plows were used to break and turn the soil, while hoes were used for the finer work in cultivation. As the cotton and corn crop progressed during the season, farmers employed plows to control weeds, add soil to the rows, and ensure proper drainage, whereas hoes were essential for weeding and "chopping out" in close quarters to the cotton plants.[13] Hoes represented the most basic farm tool available for cultivation, and although they were cheap enough to be accessible to all tenure classes, they remained necessary even for farmers who could afford more advanced agricultural implements. Like hoes, wagons were among the first pieces of equipment a farmer acquired, because of the basic need for transportation and the broad range of utility a wagon brought to farm operations. Harrows, by comparison, represent the type of implement that farmers acquired to augment the basic tool kit. They were not essential for raising a crop, but they brought speed and efficiency to the process of preparing an even seed bed and controlling weeds between the rows during the growing season.

As might be expected, nearly all estates, regardless of tenure class, owned at least one hoe. The average number of hoes per estate was greatest among farmers owning between 250 and 350 acres and among those owning more than 1,000 acres (Table 5.1). The average farmer in our sample owned two hoes appraised at $3.00. Franklin County estates had the highest number, with 170 hoes (an average of 1.56 per decedent), while Jasper was second with 60 hoes (averaging 1.5 per estate), and Crawford had the fewest, with 36 hoes divided among three-quarters of the decedents. In Franklin County, hoes were

13 Ferleger, "Self-Sufficiency and Rural Life," 314–329.

most prevalent among households in the five middle tenure classes, ranging from 100 acres to 350 acres. Decedents owning parcels of 100–249 acres averaged 1.5 hoes per household, while those in the 250–299-acre tenure class averaged 4.2, and those in the 300–349 class owned 3.5. The pattern in Jasper was more diffuse, with 15 hoes evenly distributed among the six tenure classes (0–249 acres), a concentration of 17 hoes in the 300–349-acre tenure class, and 16 in the 450–499 class. In Crawford, 31 of the 36 hoes were concentrated in the upper three tenure classes, representing the 18 decedents who owned more than 400 acres of land.

Wagons, however, show a greater correlation to wealth: they gradually increased in number as the size of landholdings increased (Table 5.1). The average price of $23.86 for a wagon (calculated from the 156 wagons listed in the inventories) represented a financial obstacle for farmers in the lowest tenure classes, so they often secured the use of wagons by splitting the cost with others. Franklin County farmers Jeptha Atkinson, John Hemphill, and William Vandiver each owned 50 percent shares in wagons, while Rena Jordan, an African-American woman from Crawford, held a one-third share in a wagon, valued at $7.00.[14] The Franklin sample produced an average of 1 wagon per decedent from a total of 106 wagons, Crawford decedents owned an average of 1.3 wagons (65 total), and Jasper had the highest level of ownership, with an average of 1.4 from 56 wagons.

Harrows were identified in fifty-four estates from the three counties (Table 5.1). As with wagons, the incidence of harrows increased gradually on the way up the tenure ladder – from an average of 0.3 in the lowest tenure class (1–49 acres) up to 0.5 in the 450–499-acre class – suggesting a strong correlation between harrow ownership and wealth. The data from the individual counties are murkier. In Crawford, 2 estates in the 100–149-acre tenure class included harrows, while 4 harrows were associated with decedents who owned between 400 and 999 acres. The Jasper data reveal 3 areas of concentration, with 3 harrows among decedents in the third tenure class, 6 in the 3 tenure classes encompassing parcels from 200 to 349 acres, and 9 among the 13 decedents who owned more than 450 acres. The Franklin sample shows a concentration of 17 harrows among the 55 decedents who owned between 100 and 349 acres of land, and a second concentration of 9 harrows among the 20 estates owning between 400 and 999 acres. Overall, the data indicate that harrows were more prevalent in the Upper Piedmont than in Lower Piedmont counties like

[14] Jeptha Atkinson, *Inventory and Appraisement*, 1884, Franklin County, Probate Court, Estate Records, 1786–1916, Record Group 159, Subgroup 2, Series 1 (GDA); John Hemphill, *Inventory and Appraisement*, 1895, Franklin County, Probate Court, Estate Records, 1786–1916, Record Group 159, Subgroup 2, Series 1 (GDA); William Vandiver, *Inventory and Appraisement*, 1888, Franklin County, Probate Court, Estate Records, 1786–1916, Record Group 159, Subgroup 2, Series 1 (GDA); and, Rena Jordan, 1899, *Inventory and Appraisement*, Crawford County, Probate Court, Miscellaneous Records of the Inferior Court, 1822–1900, Record Group 139, Subgroup 2, Series 1 (GDA).

TABLE 5.2. *Aggregate Distribution of Plows from Crawford, Jasper, and Franklin Counties by Tenure Class*

Acreage	# Farms	# Plows	Avg. # Plows	# Dixie Plows	Avg. # Dixie Plows	# Double Plows	Avg. # Double Plows
1,000+	11	23	2.1	1	0.1	0	0.0
450–999	24	54	2.2	1	0.04	2	0.1
400–449	13	17	1.3	4	0.3	2	0.2
350–399	8	17	2.1	0	0.0	0	0.0
300–349	13	10	0.8	0	0.0	0	0.0
250–299	8	37	4.6	0	0.0	0	0.0
200–249	23	20	0.9	1	0.04	0	0.0
150–199	20	35	1.8	0	0.0	1	0.1
100–149	30	53	1.8	5	0.2	1	0.03
50–99	9	3	0.3	1	0.1	1	0.1
1–49	8	8	1.0	0	0.0	0	0.0
0/Blank	32	17	0.5	1	0.03	0	0.0
Total	199	294	1.5	14	0.1	7	0.04

Crawford. The higher incidence of harrows in Franklin corroborates the hypothesis that harrows were most commonly used in locales that fell outside of the plantation system prior to the Civil War but were incorporated into the cotton economy in the postbellum era.[15]

A total of 294 plows were identified in the Crawford, Jasper, and Franklin inventories (Table 5.2). Despite fluctuations that are probably attributable to sample size, the average number of plows per decedent increases slightly, from one to two, as the size of landholdings goes up. The variability in the aggregate sample is in large part because 31 of the 36 plows in Crawford are concentrated in the upper three tenure classes (more than 400 acres). The Jasper sample, on the other hand, produced 45 plows and a 1.5 plow-per-household average among the decedents across the eight tenure classes that include parcels from 100 to 999 acres in size. Franklin farmers typically owned 2 plows, with an average of nearly 2.5 in the 100–149-acre tenure class and among the owners of parcels larger than 350 acres. Appraisers specifically identified fourteen Dixie plows, meaning that less than 10 percent of households in the sample owned these models. Six belonged to farmers who held between 50 and 149 acres of land, and 6 were found among estates with more than 400 acres. While only 5 percent of the plows identified in Jasper and Franklin were Dixie plows, seven were identified in Crawford, representing nearly 15 percent of the households in the sample. Although the sample size is small, it is hard not to see some correlation between the higher incidence of lighter plows built expressly for

[15] Ferleger, "Self-Sufficiency and Rural Life," 322–323.

TABLE 5.3. *Aggregate Distribution of the Number and Dollar Value of Farm Tools and Cotton Planters from Crawford, Jasper, and Franklin Counties by Tenure Class*

Acreage	# Farms	Total Value Tools ($)	Average Value Tools ($)	Total # Cotton Planters	Average # Cotton Planters	Average Value Cotton Planters ($)
1,000+	11	3,909.0	355.0	7	0.64	0.6
450–999	24	3,315.0	138.0	8	0.33	0.3
400–449	13	1,785.0	137.0	4	0.31	0.4
350–399	8	501.0	63.0	1	0.13	0.19
300–349	13	1,259.0	97.0	6	0.46	0.67
250–299	8	554.0	69.0	2	0.25	0.11
200–249	23	1,587.0	69.0	1	0.05	0.9
150–199	20	1,146.0	57.0	2	0.10	0.8
100–149	30	1,738.0	58.0	10	0.34	0.7
50–99	9	386.0	43.0	3	0.33	0.43
1–49	8	266.0	33.0	0	–	–
0/Blank	32	1,081.0	36.0	3	0.09	0.18
Total	199	17,527.0	93.0	47	0.25	0.44

cotton farming with the lighter, sandier soils in Crawford (as contrasted with Jasper and Franklin, which have heavier, more clayey soils). Only seven double plows appeared in the aggregate sample, representing a 4 percent ownership rate among the decedents. Five of the seven double plows were identified in Franklin inventories, attesting to the need for quality implements to deal with the area's heavy soils with higher clay content.[16] Once again, the presence of more advanced plows in the Upland county of Franklin demonstrates a pattern in which counties outside of the traditional plantation districts invested more heavily in progressive labor-saving technologies.

While harrows increased the speed and ease with which one could tend crops, planters and cultivators represented even greater improvements (Table 5.3). Planters mechanized the sowing process, and cultivators could break the ground like plows, smooth the soil like harrows, and work close to the plants like hoes. There were walk-behind and riding models for both types of implement, depending on the farmer's budget and inclination. In addition, high-end cultivator models had interchangeable blades and other fittings that enhanced their

[16] USDA, "Major Land Resource Regions Custom Report for the South Atlantic and Gulf Slope Cash Crops, Forest, and Livestock for Crawford, Jasper, and Franklin Counties: Region 137, Carolina and Georgia Sand Hills, 136; Southern Piedmont; 133A, Southern Coastal Plain," *USDA Handbook* 296 (2006), 7, 11. http://soils.usda.gov/MLRAExplorer (accessed January 17, 2011).

adaptability.[17] A total of forty-seven cultivators and planters were identified in the probate sample from the three counties, suggesting that one in four decedents acquired one of these implements. Although none of the decedents in the first tenure class owned a cotton planter, the average number per farm for the rest of the tenure classes was somewhere between 0.05 and 0.33 – except for the 300–350-acre class, which averaged 0.46 planters per farm, and the highest class (1,000 or more acres), which averaged 0.64 planters. These statistics suggest that the number of planters needed on a farm was limited to two, irrespective of the size of the farm or the total amount invested in tools.

Cultivators and planters were quite common in the second and third tenure classes, with nearly half of the decedents who farmed between 50 and 149 acres owning one. Likewise, 46 percent of farmers in the 200–349-acre tenure class, and 66 percent of decedents who owned farms of 450 acres or more, possessed one of these advanced pieces of equipment. Crawford had the highest concentration of cultivators and planters, with 26.7, 20 of which were owned by farmers with more than 300 acres of land.[18] Within this group, the incidence of ownership increased from 50 percent in the seventh tenure class to one per decedent in the eleventh tenure class. In Jasper, 12.3 of the 17.3 cultivators and planters were concentrated in the five tenure groups ranging from 100 to 349 acres. Franklin had the fewest of these implements, at 23, 13 of which were owned by farmers with 50–249 acres of land. Eight were concentrated in the highest tenure class, where 36 percent of the decedents had either a planter or cultivator. Overall, the pattern of ownership of planters and cultivators suggests a stronger preference or ability in the Lower Piedmont to own one of these mechanized implements.

The aggregate pattern for cotton gins and engines suggests that these items were predominately associated with the tenure classes of 300 acres or more. Twenty-eight of 36 cotton gins and 8 of 10 steam traction engines were identified in the estates of decedents owning more than 300 acres, while the remaining 8 gins and 1 engine were scattered among the decedents who owned 50–249 acres. As with planters and cultivators, Crawford had the highest incidence, with eighteen gins and five engines. Fourteen of the gins and all but 1 of the engines belonged to decedents owning more than 400 acres in Crawford between 1880 and 1910. The pattern of ownership of cotton gins and engines in Jasper was strikingly similar to that found in Crawford, although the overall numbers were much lower. The 8 gins and 1.3 engines owned by Jasper decedents were associated with farms 300 acres and larger. A single engine was owned by a farmer in Jasper with more than 1,000 acres, and the estate with a one-third interest in an engine was in the seventh tenure class of 300–349 acres.

[17] Hurt, *American Agriculture*, 141–143.

[18] The percentages of equipment represent shares decedents owned in pieces of equipment. Examples of quarter, third, and half shares are common throughout artifact classes.

TABLE 5.4. *Aggregate Distribution of Livestock from Crawford, Jasper, and Franklin Counties by Tenure Class*

Acreage	# Farms	# Mules	Avg. # Mules	# Horses	Avg. # Horses	# Livestock	Avg. # Livestock
1,000+	11	79	7.2	17	1.6	501	45.6
450–999	24	49	2.0	43	1.8	728	30.3
400–449	13	32	2.5	7	0.5	457	35.2
350–399	8	13	1.6	3	0.4	151	18.9
300–349	13	14	1.1	11	0.9	147	11.3
250–299	8	8	1.0	9	1.1	214	26.8
200–249	23	17	0.7	16	0.7	253	11.0
150–199	20	12	0.6	15	0.8	299	14.9
100–149	30	35	1.2	20	0.7	496	16.5
50–99	9	2	0.2	5	0.6	65	7.2
1–49	8	1	0.1	3	0.4	48	6.0
o/Blank	32	22	0.7	16	0.5	338	10.6
Total	199	284	1.4	165	0.8	3,697	18.6

Franklin inventories included 10 cotton gins and 3.5 engines, representing 9 percent of the Franklin decedents. As in Crawford, the engines were all associated with planters who owned more than 300 acres. Cotton gins, however, did not follow the Crawford pattern and were more evenly distributed among the estates. Three were owned by decedents farming between 50 and 249 acres, while six were associated with the owners of more than 300 acres.

While mechanized farm implements like cultivators, planters, and cotton gins, and advanced technologies like portable steam traction engines, made farm work easier and more efficient, they also represented a significant monetary investment. Small farmers in particular assumed a considerable level of risk when they invested in such tools, because they had to spend a greater proportion of their resources to acquire them (Table 5.3). The average value of all the tools owned by a farmer in the first tenure class (1–49 acres) was just \$33; that figure rises to \$355 for farmers in the eleventh tenure class (more than 1,000 acres). Cotton planters represented 3 percent of the total value of tools for farmers owning between 50 and 249 acres, 2 percent for decedents in the 250–399 bracket, and 1 percent or less for farmers who owned more than 400 acres. While the costs associated with cotton planters may seem modest, the price of any advanced implement was considerable enough to cotton farmers in the Georgia Piedmont to represent a significant risk.

The aggregate pattern of distribution for animal stock tells a similar story (Table 5.4). A total of 284 mules and 165 horses were identified in the 3-county probate sample, and as farm size increased, so did the average number of mules and horses. The average number of mules per household was nearly double that of horses; leaving aside the very large farms (more than 1,000 acres), the tenure

TABLE 5.5. *Aggregate Distribution of the Number and Dollar Value of Livestock from Crawford, Jasper, and Franklin Counties by Tenure Class*

Acreage	# Farms	Total Value Livestock ($)	Average Value Livestock ($)	Total # Mules	Average # Mules	Average Value Mules ($)
1,000+	11	10,120.0	920.0	79	7.18	623.0
450–999	24	7,721.0	322.0	49	2.0	146.0
400–449	13	3,334.0	256.0	32	2.5	186.0
350–399	8	1,646.0	206.0	13	1.6	117.0
300–349	13	2,137.0	164.0	14	1.2	82.0
250–299	8	2,144.0	268.0	8	1.0	86.0
200–249	23	2,939.0	128.0	17	0.7	50.0
150–199	20	2,332.0	123.0	12	1.7	40.0
100–149	30	5,023.0	167.0	35	1.2	75.0
50–99	9	473.0	53.0	2	0.2	10.0
1–49	8	433.0	54.0	1	0.1	8.0
0/Blank	32	3,573.0	112.0	22	0.7	45.0
Total	199	41,875.0	225.0	284	0.9	123.0

class with the highest average number of mules was 400–449 acres (2.5 mules), while those farmers in the 450–499-acre bracket owned the highest average number of horses, at 1.8. Crawford inventories accounted for 170 mules, while the probate samples from Jasper and Franklin counties each listed 84. Horses appear to have been more important to farmers in the Upper Piedmont counties than in the Lower Piedmont – the 89 horses in the Franklin sample slightly outnumbered the 84 mules in that county by five, while among Crawford estates there were more than five times as many mules (170 mules 33 horses). Horse ownership in Jasper County seems at first to reflect the Upper Piedmont pattern, with the highest ratio of horses to decedents among the three counties, at 1:1 (forty-three horses identified in forty-three estates); however, the number of mules was more than double the number of households, indicating that, despite the high incidence of horse ownership in Jasper, mules were the predominant beast of burden, in keeping with the Lower Piedmont pattern reflected in Crawford County.

The broader category of livestock raised for food – including cattle, goats, swine, and fowl – shows a stronger correlation with tenure class than do horses and mules (Tables 5.4 and 5.5). The average number of farm animals increases from an average of 6 for the lowest class (1–49 acres) up to nearly 46 animals in the highest class (1,000+), with spikes in the third and fourth classes (100–149 and 150–199), and another spike in the sixth class (250–299 acres). Livestock values reinforce this pattern, increasing relatively steadily from the average investment of $54 in farm animals among farmers living on parcels of 1–49 acres, to an average of $322 among the 24 decedents in the tenth tenure

TABLE 5.6. *Aggregate Comparison of Farm Tools Reflected in the Inventories of Female Decedents from Crawford, Jasper, and Franklin Counties by Tenure Class*

Acreage	# Farms	# Hoes	Avg. # Hoes	# Harrows	Avg. # Harrows	# Wagons	Avg. # Wagons
1,000+	–	–	–	–	–	–	–
450–999	–	–	–	–	–	–	–
400–449	3	–	–	–	–	4	1.3
350–399	–	–	–	–	–	–	–
300–349	1	–	–	–	–	–	–
250–299	–	–	–	–	–	–	–
200–249	–	–	–	–	–	–	–
150–199	1	3	3	–	–	1	1
100–149	6	7		–	–	5.3	0.9
50–99	4	5	1.3	–	–	3	0.8
1–49	1	4	4	–	–	1	1
0/Blank	–	–	–	–	–	–	–
Total	16	19	1.8	–	–	14.3	0.9

Note: Average (mean) values do not include blank cases.

class of 450–999 acres. The value of farm stock among the 11 estates with more than 1,000 acres is significantly higher, with an average of $920. While Franklin had the largest number of livestock (1,515 animals), the average was 13.8 animals per decedent. Jasper had only 714 animals, but the average was slightly higher than in Franklin, at 17.85 per decedent. Crawford decedents had the highest average holding by far, with the 1,469 farm animals averaging out to 29.36 per household.

Sixteen of the eighteen female decedents included in the three-county sample had inventories with enough detail to facilitate analysis of assets owned at the time of death. Four of the women were from Crawford, two from Franklin, and nine from Jasper. Fifteen of the women were white, while one, Rena Jordan from Crawford, was African-American; all were widows.[19] Twelve of the women were identified in the 1880 federal census as "keeping house," while Caroline Sewell was listed as a domestic.[20] Rebecca Hammack and Milly Voiles were identified as farmers, and Rena Jordan was described as a farm laborer, although her estate included more than 200 acres of land in three parcels,

[19] Rena Jordan, *Inventory and Appraisement*, 1899, Crawford County, Probate Court, Miscellaneous Records of the Inferior Court, 1822–1900, Record Group 139, Subgroup 2, Series 1 (GDA).

[20] *Ninth Census of the United States*, 1870, Washington, DC: National Archives and Records Administration, Roll M593, 150, Franklin, Georgia, District 370, Page 91.

TABLE 5.7. *Aggregate Comparison of Livestock Reflected in the Inventories of Female Decedents from Crawford, Jasper, and Franklin Counties by Tenure Class*

Acreage	# Farms	# Mules	Avg. # Mules	# Horses	Avg. # Horses	# Animals	Avg. # Animals
1,000+	–	–	–	–	–	–	–
450–999	–	–	–	–	–	–	–
400–449	3	1	–	1	0.3	48	16
350–399	–	–	–	–	–	–	–
300–349	1	–	–	–	–	7	7
250–299	–	–	–	–	–	–	–
200–249	–	–	–	–	–	–	–
150–199	1	2	2	–	–	16	16
100–149	6	2	0.3	2	–	178	29.7
50–99	4	1	0.3	2	0.5	15	3.8
1–49	1	–	–	–	–	12	12
0/Blank	–	–	–	–	–	–	–
Total	16	6	0.4	5	.3	276	16.7

Note: Average (mean) values do not include blank cases.

as well as five cows with calves and nine head of cattle, suggesting that she was more than a laborer or tenant farmer.[21]

Twelve of the inventories were clustered in the four lowest tenure classes (between 1 and 199 acres of land). One estate was in the 300–349-acre class, while three were in the 400–499-acre class (Tables 5.6 and 5.7). Overall, the female decedents owned slightly more hoes (n = 1.8) than the average for all of the decedents (n = 1.8), but they owned fewer wagons. They also owned significantly more plows, including Dixie and double plows (Table 5.8). The female decedents owned 2.6 plows on average, compared to a 1.5 plow-per-decedent average for the entire probate sample. Likewise, the average numbers of Dixie and double plows in the sample at large were 0.01 for both categories, while women on average owned 0.12 of each type of those more advanced plows.

This pattern is reversed with more advanced implements. Women owned slightly fewer cultivators and planters than the average decedent in the sample (Table 5.9). A total of 5.66 cultivators and planters were identified among women's estates, producing a ratio of slightly more than 1:3 (cultivator or planter per female decedents), which falls short of the 0.39-per-decedent average for the aggregate sample. Furthermore, there were no engines and only a

[21] *Tenth Census of the United States*, 1880, Washington, DC: National Archives and Records Administration, Roll 142, Crawford, Georgia, District 521, Enumeration District 44, Page 635C; *Tenth Census of the United States*, 1880, Washington, DC: National Archives and Records Administration, Roll T9, 147, Franklin, Georgia, District 812, Enumeration District 28, Page 544.

TABLE 5.8. *Aggregate Comparison of Plows Reflected in the Inventories of Female Decedents from Crawford, Jasper, and Franklin Counties by Tenure Class*

Acreage	# Farms	# Plows	Avg. # Plows	# Dixie Plows	Avg. # Dixie Plows	# Double Plows	Avg. # Double Plows
1,000+	–	–	–	–	–	–	–
450–999	–	–	–	–	–	–	–
400–449	3	3	1	–	–	–	–
350–399	–	–	–	–	–	–	–
300–349	1	1	1	–	–	–	–
250–299	–	–	–	–	–	–	–
200–249	–	–	–	–	–	–	–
150–199	1	1	1	–	–	–	–
100–149	6	13	–	1	–	–	–
50–99	4	5	1.3	–	–	1	0.3
1–49	1	5	0.2	–	–	–	–
0/Blank	–	–	–	–	–	–	–
Total	16	28	2.6	1	0.1	1	0.1

Note: Average (mean) values do not include blank cases.

TABLE 5.9. *Aggregate Comparison of Mechanized Equipment Reflected in the Inventories of Female Decedents from Crawford, Jasper, and Franklin Counties by Tenure Class*

Acreage	# Farms	# Cultivators/ Planters	Avg. # Cultivators/ Planters	# Gins	Avg. # Gins	# Engines	Avg. # Engines
1,000+	–	–	–	–	–	–	–
450–999	–	–	–	–	–	–	–
400–449	3	–	–	–	–	–	–
350–399	–	–	–	–	–	–	–
300–349	1	–	–	–	–	–	–
250–299	–	–	–	–	–	–	–
200–249	–	–	–	–	–	–	–
150–199	1	–	–	–	–	–	–
100–149	6	3.7	0.6	–	–	–	–
50–99	4	2	0.5	1	0.3	–	–
1–49	1	–	–	–	–	–	–
0/Blank	–	–	–	–	–	–	–
Total	16	5.7	0.4	1	0.1	–	–

Note: Average (mean) values do not include blank cases.

single gin listed in the women's estate inventories, falling far short of the 18 percent of men who owned gins and the 5 percent who owned engines. The same pattern of women lagging behind the aggregate sample holds for mules and horses (Table 5.7). Female decedents owned 70 percent fewer mules and nearly 60 percent fewer horses on average than did their male counterparts. The overall pattern of livestock ownership among women, on the other hand, was nearly even with the aggregate sample population: an average of 16.65 farm animals per woman, compared to the overall average of 18.58 per decedent.

Nine of the fifteen African Americans' estates had enough data to permit further analysis of these decedents. This small group included three individuals from Crawford and six from Franklin – eight men and one woman. Represented in the group were five farmers, three farm laborers, and one blacksmith. The median estate value for these decedents was $406, which was 12 percent higher than the median estate value for the aggregate sample. Unlike the female decedents, African Americans fared less well in all ownership categories than did their white counterparts. While this is not surprising, it is striking, since the black decedents in the sample were among the most successful people in the three counties, judging from the estates of Barney Hancock and Joe Danielly. Barney Hancock left an estate consisting of more than 200 acres of land and $435 in personal possessions, including four mules, a cultivator, and a sulky plow.[22] Danielly, on the other hand, had an estate valued at $1,050 at the time of his death, which is nearly twice the average value for the aggregate sample.[23] While Joe Danielly, Sam Hall, and James Webster did not own land at the time of their death, Barney Martin and Barney Hancock were in the fifth tenure class, with 250 and 209.5 acres, respectively. The black decedents in the third tenure group included Rena Jordan, with 106.5 acres of land, James Brown (115 acres), and David Brawner (100 acres).

As a group, the African-American decedents owned fewer basic farming tools than did the aggregate probate population (Table 5.10). They owned 40 percent fewer hoes, 12 percent fewer harrows, and 29 percent fewer wagons on average. The only exceptions were Martin and Hancock, who both owned nearly triple the average number of hoes and nearly double the average number of wagons.[24] The trend continues with plows: the African-American decedents possessed 40 percent fewer plows on average, despite the fact that all but two decedents owned plows and Jack Bellamy owned two (Table 5.11).[25] Likewise, neither cotton gins nor engines were listed in the estates of African

[22] Barney Hancock, *Inventory and Appraisement*, Franklin County, 1898; Barney Hancock, Bill of Sale, Franklin County, 1898.

[23] Joe Danielly, *Inventory and Appraisement*, 1900, Crawford County, Probate Court, Miscellaneous Records of the Inferior Court, 1822–1900, Record Group 139, Subgroup 2, Series 1 (GDA).

[24] Barney Martin, *Inventory and Appraisement*, Crawford County, 1896.

[25] Jack Bellamy, *Inventory and Appraisement*, Franklin County, 1886.

TABLE 5.10. *Aggregate Comparison of Farm Tools Reflected in the Inventories of African-American Decedents from Crawford, Jasper, and Franklin Counties by Tenure Class*

Acreage	# Farms	# Hoes	Avg. # Hoes	# Harrows	Avg. # Harrows	# Wagons	Avg. # Wagons
1,000+	–	–	–	–	–	–	–
450–999	–	–	–	–	–	–	–
400–449	–	–	–	–	–	–	–
350–399	–	–	–	–	–	–	–
300–349	–	–	–	–	–	–	–
250–299	–	–	–	–	–	–	–
200–249	2	8	4	–	–	3	1.5
150–199	–	–	–	–	–	–	–
100–149	3	0.3	0.1	–	–	2.3	0.8
50–99	–	–	–	–	–	–	–
1–49	1	–	–	–	–	–	–
0/Blank	3	–	–	1	0.3	2	0.7
Total	9	8.3	0.9	1	0.1	7.3	0.8

Note: Average (mean) values do not include blank cases.

TABLE 5.11. *Aggregate Comparison of Plows Reflected in the Inventories of African-American Decedents from Crawford, Jasper, and Franklin Counties by Tenure Class*

Acreage	# Farms	# Plows	Avg. # Plows	# Dixie Plows	Avg. # Dixie Plows	# Double Plows	Avg. # Double Plows
1,000+	–	–	–	–	–	–	–
450–999	–	–	–	–	–	–	–
400–449	–	–	–	–	–	–	–
350–399	–	–	–	–	–	–	–
300–349	–	–	–	–	–	–	–
250–299	–	–	–	–	–	–	–
200–249	2	2	1	–	–	–	–
150–199	–	–	–	–	–	–	–
100–149	3	1	0.3	1	0.3	–	–
50–99	–	–	–	–	–	–	–
1–49	1	2	2	–	–	–	–
0/Blank	3	3	1	–	–	–	–
Total	9	8	0.9	1	0.1	–	–

Note: Average (mean) values do not include blank cases.

TABLE 5.12. *Aggregate Comparison of Mechanized Equipment Reflected in the Inventories of African-American Decedents from Crawford, Jasper, and Franklin Counties by Tenure Class*

Acreage	# Farms	# Cultivators/ Planters	Avg. # Cultivators/ Planters	# Gins	Avg. # Gins	# Engines	Avg. # Engines
1,000+	–	–	–	–	–	–	–
450–999	–	–	–	–	–	–	–
400–449	–	–	–	–	–	–	–
350–399	–	–	–	–	–	–	–
300–349	–	–	–	–	–	–	–
250–299	–	–	–	–	–	–	–
200–249	2	2	1	–	–	–	–
150–199	–	–	–	–	–	–	–
100–149	3	2.7	0.9	–	–	–	–
50–99	–	–	–	–	–	–	–
1–49	1	–	–	–	–	–	–
0/Blank	3	–	–	–	–	–	–
Total	9	4.7	0.5	–	–	–	–

Note: Average (mean) values do not include blank cases.

Americans (Table 5.12). They did, however, exceed the average with cultivators and planters, with a high incidence of ownership in the third and fifth tenure groups, suggesting that black farmers understood the value of advanced machinery over labor. Barney Hancock owned a cultivator and a planter, James Brown owned a cultivator, and Rena Jordan owned one planter and a two-thirds share in another.[26]

African Americans also owned more mules and livestock on average than did the rest of the sample population (Table 5.13). Sixteen mules were distributed among the nine African-American estates, producing an average rate of mule ownership of 1.8 for blacks, compared to 1.43 for the overall population. Four black estates listed horses, reflecting an average holding of 0.44 for the cohort. Horse ownership, however, was half the overall average, suggesting that African-American farmers preferred mules. Finally, the pattern of livestock ownership suggests a "safety first" strategy among many black decedents, because they kept more than the average number of farm animals. The average livestock holding for African-Americans was 20.11, compared to the sample-wide average of 18.58. The pattern becomes more distinctive when looking at the third tenure class, where the average holding of 33.67 was nearly twice the aggregate number. The average number of livestock for black farmers in the

[26] Barney Hancock, *Inventory and Appraisement*, Franklin County, 1898; James L. Brown, *Inventory and Appraisement*, Franklin County, 1894; Rena Jordan, *Inventory and Appraisement*, Crawford County, 1899.

TABLE 5.13. *Aggregate Comparison of Livestock Reflected in the Inventories of African-American Decedents from Crawford, Jasper, and Franklin Counties by Tenure Class*

Acreage	# Farms	# Mules	Avg. # Mules	# Horses	Avg. # Horses	# Animals	Avg. # Animals
1,000+	–	–	–	–	–	–	–
450–999	–	–	–	–	–	–	–
400–449	–	–	–	–	–	–	–
350–399	–	–	–	–	–	–	–
300–349	–	–	–	–	–	–	–
250–299	–	–	–	–	–	–	–
200–249	2	5	2.5	1	0.5	31	15.5
150–199	–	–	–	–	–	–	–
100–149	3	4	1.3	2	0.7	101	33.7
50–99	–	–	–	–	–	–	–
1–49	1	1	1	–	–	2	2
0/Blank	3	6	2	1	0.3	47	15.7
Total	9	16	1.8	4	0.4	181	20.1

Note: Average (mean) values do not include blank cases.

fifth tenure class was 15.50 – 29 percent higher than the three-county average of 11.00 animals.

To be sure, farm families in the Georgia Piedmont devoted most of their resources to agricultural production. But there was a life beyond the fields, and looking at the assemblages of non-farming items that decedents left behind provides important information about their lifestyles, how they organized their households, and how they spent their money apart from meeting basic needs. Moreover, examining the probate sample by tenure class makes it possible to identify discrete patterns of consumption at various rungs on the tenure ladder. The average estate value for the 3-county sample was $467.90, with $385.00 invested in farm assets and $83.00 (18 percent) in household items. Logically, the number and value of household items increased as the size of landholdings increased. Nearly all decedents, however, invested the largest percentage of their assets to meet basic household needs: kitchens held the greatest value, followed by bedroom-related items. Even so, a significant number of estates from each county included more discretionary possessions associated with social or leisure activities, many of which would have been conducted in parlor settings. Furthermore, some possessions – such as timepieces, organs, and silver-plated tableware – suggest that decedents were not necessarily averse to expressing affluence through consumption.

Of the three Piedmont counties in the sample, Crawford had been engaged longest in commercial cotton production and had the deepest roots in plantation society. As such, Crawford had the lengthiest exposure to the trade networks that not only carried cotton away to market but also brought in consumer goods. Crawford also had clearly defined socioeconomic strata before the Civil War, consisting of a small but influential planter minority that was vastly outnumbered by the yeoman and slave populations (which were approximately the same size). To mark their place in society, the planter elite routinely acquired luxury goods such as fine furnishings and tableware.[27] Although the war brought freedom for enslaved African Americans and financial ruin for many white cotton growers, the class boundaries that re-formed in the postbellum years largely perpetuated the model that had existed before, with a small, elite class of planters at the top of society and a mass of small-to-middling farmers scraping by and working desperately to hold onto what little they had. The only major change was that African Americans, rather than being slaves, entered the ranks of tenancy (overwhelmingly as sharecroppers) or became members of the yeomanry.

The Crawford County decedents in our sample were relatively evenly distributed by tenure class: ten estates of between 1 and 149 acres, nine estates holding between 150 and 299 acres, eight estates of 300–449 acres, and fourteen decedents with more than 450 acres, six of whom owned more than 1,000 acres. The distribution is somewhat top-heavy, as Crawford had the highest percentage of landowners in the highest two groups among the three counties, and none in the lowest group (1–49 acres). Estate values for farm and household goods combined ranged from $55.25 to more than $4,600.00, and those amounts increased steadily from the second tenure class to the eleventh, whose members typically had estates appraised at more than $2,600.00. The average estate in Crawford was worth $741, with $624 in farm assets and $117 in household goods (Table 5.14).

The Crawford probate sample included thirty-three inventories with enough detail to examine more fully the distribution of household assets. While several inventories combined some or all of the household assets into a single category, most listed individual items (Table 5.15). Moreover, goods listed at the item level could often be categorized according to function or the room where they were likely used (usually the kitchen, bedroom, or parlor). Ten of the inventories from Crawford listed a catch-all category labeled "household," ambiguously grouping items together. In all but one of these cases, that category included all items from the household, suggesting that appraisers may have believed it was better to provide a single overall value for household goods if they amounted to less than $100. While the appraised values of the "household" category ranged from $27 to $83, the average was $40.

Kitchen items were the most highly valued functional category in Crawford inventories, with an average appraised value of $52.00 derived from

[27] Joseph P. Reidy, *From Slavery to Agrarian Capitalism in the Cotton Plantation South: Central Georgia, 1800–1880* (Chapel Hill: University of North Carolina Press, 1992): 19, 31–32, 46–50; Lois Green Carr and Lorena S. Walsh, "The Standard of Living in the Colonial Chesapeake," *William and Mary Quarterly*, 3rd ser., 45, no. 1 (January 1988): 139–144.

TABLE 5.14. *Comparison of Total and Average Farm and Household Assemblage Values by Tenure Class for Crawford County Decedents*

Acreage	Cases	Total Farm Value ($)	Total Household Value ($)	Avg. Farm Value ($)	Avg. Household Value ($)	Avg. Combined Value ($)
1,000+	6	15,975.9	411.2	2,662.7	68.5	2,731.2
450–999	8	6,802.5	2,013.50	850.3	251.7	1,102.0
400–449	3	1,115.8	331.2	371.9	110.4	482.3
350–399	2	1,243.4	471.1	621.7	235.6	857.3
300–349	3	1,625.5	497.1	541.8	165.7	707.5
250–299	3	520.4	225.7	173.5	75.2	248.7
200–249	3	1,110.6	230.5	370.2	76.8	447.0
150–199	3	993.8	193.5	331.3	64.5	395.8
100–149	8	4,155.6	615.8	519.5	77.0	596.4
50–99	2	138.1	115.1	69.1	57.6	126.6
1–49	0	–	–	–	–	–
0/Blank	9	3,199.8	892.9	355.5	99.2	454.7
Total	50	36,881.4	5,997.6	624.3	116.6	740.9

Note: Average (mean) values do not include blank cases.

26 inventories, ranging from $9.80 to $127.10. Decedents who owned fewer than 200 acres typically had assemblages worth less than $20. Those who owned between 1 and 149 acres averaged $18.70 in kitchen items, while those with 150–299 acres typically had about $44.00 worth. The highest average, $82.30, was among individuals in the tenure classes from 300 to 499 acres; the figure decreased somewhat among larger estates, with members of the top two tenure classes (450 acres or more) owning on average $70.50 worth of kitchen material.

Bedrooms show a similar pattern. This category includes items related to bathing and personal hygiene that would have been kept in bedrooms (washstands, for example), in addition to beds, bureaus, and other furnishings and accessories associated with sleeping and dressing. While the bedroom items accounted for the largest sum total of any category in Crawford, that is because more decedents had bedroom items listed in their inventories than any other category of goods; the average appraised value was $34.80. The distribution of bedroom-assemblage values by tenure class reveals the same correlation between landownership and material possessions that is apparent with kitchen goods. Decedents in the bottom three tenure classes owned $18.70 worth of bedroom furnishings on average. This increased to $44.00 for those who owned between 150 and 299 acres, while those with 300–449 acres had the highest average once again, with $82.30 worth of bedroom items. The figure for the top two tenure classes dipped (as with kitchen-related possessions), averaging $70.50.

TABLE 5.15. *Distribution of Household Goods by Tenure Class for Crawford County*

Acreage	Household ($)	Average Household ($)	Kitchen ($)	Average Kitchen ($)	Bedroom ($)	Average Bedroom ($)	Parlor ($)	Average Parlor ($)
1,000+	–	–	105.3	52.7	216.2	36.0	26.4	13.2
450–999	166.8	83.4	176.9	88.4	185.6	23.2	5.6	2.8
400–449	27.0	27.0	43.3	21.7	45.3	15.1	0.5	0.3
350–399	36.5	36.5	127.1	127.1	145.5	72.8	42.7	21.3
300–349	50.8	50.8	149.0	101.2	248.9	41.5	6.0	1.5
250–299	45.3	45.3	90.3	90.3	38.1	19.1	7.4	3.7
200–249	70.1	35.1	98.9	32.9	109.9	54.9	4.3	1.4
150–199	–	–	–	9.8	34.0	17.0	5.3	2.6
100–149	2.0	2.0	69.8	17.5	435.5	62.2	14.0	3.5
50–99	50.0	50.0	19.9	19.9	33.6	16.8	0.2	0.2
1–49	–	–	–	–	–	–	–	–
0/Blank	35.0	35.0	53.7	10.7	167.5	23.9	279.6	93.2
Total	483.5	40.6	934.2	52.0	1,660.1	34.8	392.0	13.1

Note: Average (mean) values do not include blank cases. The household category refers only to those estates where household items were not listed individually or in functional/room-specific categories.

The Crawford County average of $13.10 for parlor furnishings represented nearly one-third the value of bedroom furnishings and nearly one-quarter the value of the average kitchen assemblage. Ownership of parlor furnishings correlates more strongly to wealth than does ownership of furnishings from the other room categories. Those who held fewer than 150 acres typically owned less than $2 worth of sitting-room furnishings or accessories, and those who owned between 150 and 299 acres owned less than $3 worth. The average jumped significantly, to $7.70 per decedent, for those in the next 3 tenure classes (300–449 acres), and it peaked at $8.00 per decedent for those who owned more than 450 acres.

The data regarding certain household items provide an indication of the extent to which farmers living in the Georgia Piedmont between 1880 and 1910 were investing in new technologies, spending money on non-essential purchases, or engaging in income-generating pursuits beyond farming (Table 5.16). Sewing machines and timepieces are particularly useful to consider, since they represent technological goods that were mass-produced by 1880 and were, as

TABLE 5.16. *Distribution of Sewing Machines, Timepieces, Books, and Cash by Tenure Class for Crawford County Decedents*

Acreage	Total Sewing Machine Value ($)	Avg. Sewing Machine Value ($)	Total Clock/ Watch Value ($)	Avg. Clock/ Watch Value ($)	Total Book Value ($)	Avg. Book Value ($)	Total Cash Value ($)	Avg. Cash Value ($)
1,000+	22.0	11.0	4.0	4.0	–	–	–	–
450–999	8.0	8.0	16.1	5.4	4.6	4.6	1,447.0	723.5
400–449	–	–	–	–	–	–	–	–
350–399	20.0	20.0	–	–	8.0	8.0	–	–
300–349	35.1	17.6	22.6	5.9	7.8	3.4	–	–
250–299	0.8	0.8	3.0	3.0	0.6	0.6	–	–
200–249	–	–	1.5	1.5	1.0	1.0	–	–
150–199	–	–	0.5	0.5	0.5	0.5	143.5	143.5
100–149	18.0	9.0	12.0	2.4	–	–	30.0	30.0
50–99	–	–	–	–	–	–	–	–
1–49	–	–	–	–	–	–	–	–
0/Blank	3.0	3.0	7.7	1.9	0.8	0.8	350.0	350.0
Total	106.9	9.9	67.4	3.1	23.3	2.7	1,970.5	1,247.0

Note: Average (mean) values do not include blank cases. For sewing machines, books, and cash, the calculation reflects only those inventories/farmers reporting the items/money in question; inventories not reporting the items/cash (zero values) are not included.

a result, relatively accessible and affordable. While timepieces had long been considered symbols of wealth and status in the United States, sewing machines became popular, despite their high price, because they enabled women to perform the traditional work of making and mending clothing far more quickly and effectively.[28] Twenty-six percent of the decedents (n = 10) from Crawford County with itemized inventories owned sewing machines, which ranged in appraised value from $8 to $20. That value generally increased with the size of landholdings, which suggests that wealthier decedents invested in better or more advanced machines. Among sewing-machine owners, Philip McCarty was the lowest on the tenure ladder, with 137 acres, perhaps indicating that most farmers in lower tenure classes could not afford the appliances, or that they deferred such purchases in favor of farm-related items or basic necessities.[29] McCarty's sewing machine was appraised at $9.00, while the average value of the four machines owned by decedents who held between 250 and 399 acres

[28] Mark P. Leone and Parker B. Potter, Jr., *The Recovery of Meaning: Historical Archaeology in the Eastern United States* (Washington, DC: Smithsonian, 1988): 204–242; Strasser, *Never Done*, 138–141.

[29] McCarty, *Inventory and Appraisement*, 1896, Crawford County.

was $12.80. Three decedents with more than 450 acres of land owned appliances worth about $9.50 each.

The American love affair with clocks began in the 1730s and became more pervasive in the nineteenth century, as they became more affordable. These precision instruments helped regulate the day and may have assisted their owners in establishing a work discipline.[30] While timepieces were hardly essential for bringing order to farming chores, ownership of a good clock or fine watch signified that a person was engaged in pursuits beyond farming – or at least that the bearer's time was valuable enough to measure.[31] Twenty decedents from Crawford (53 percent of those with itemized inventories) owned clocks, watches, or both – all of them held at least 100 acres of land. Appraised values ranged from $0.50 to $10.00, and averaged $3.10. Timepieces owned by farmers with 100–300 acres were worth an average of $1.86, while those who owned more than 300 acres had clocks and watches that were typically worth $5.10.

Like clocks, books had been a prized possession of many Americans since the mid-eighteenth century, but book ownership was not at all widespread until the early nineteenth century, when the quantity of printed matter increased and became more affordable.[32] The probate sample from Crawford suggests that at least one-quarter of the county population owned one or more books. The nine book-owning decedents were concentrated in the middle tenure classes, from 170 to 475 acres. The values of their books, which were appraised in lots, ranged from $0.50 to $8.00, with an average value of $3.60. All of the Crawford decedents who owned books were farmers by profession, except for John Avera, who was identified in the 1870 census as a schoolteacher.[33]

Jasper County is located in the central Piedmont region, approximately fifty miles northeast of Crawford. Situated on the margin between the Uplands and the Lower Piedmont, Jasper in the late nineteenth century shared similarities with both regions. While Jasper farmers grew food crops that were more commonly found on Upland farms, such as wheat, corn, and beans, they also developed a strong connection to the cotton economy early in the nineteenth century, as Crawford had. Despite its more northerly location, Jasper County was established fifteen years before Crawford, and farmers there were drawn into Georgia's cotton culture in the 1820s, thanks in large part to the

30 Smith, *Mastered by the Clock*; Leone and Potter, *The Recovery of Meaning*, 240.

31 John W. Avera, *Inventory and Appraisement*, 1896, Crawford County, Probate Court, Miscellaneous Records of the Inferior Court, 1822–1900, Record Group 139, Subgroup 2, Series 1.

32 Linda M. Kruger, "Home Libraries: Special Spaces, Reading Places," in *American Home Life, 1880–1930: A Social History of Spaces and Services* (Knoxville: University of Tennessee Press, 1992): 94–97.

33 *Ninth Census of the United States*, 1880, Georgia Roll 133–172, Page 415A, http://www.ancestry.com (accessed September 10, 2010).

TABLE 5.17. *Comparison of Total and Average Farm and Household Assemblage Values by Tenure Class for Jasper County Decedents*

Acreage	Cases	Total Farm Value ($)	Total Household Value ($)	Avg. Farm Value ($)	Avg. Household Value ($)	Avg. Combined Value ($)
1,000+	3	7,202.7	750.6	2,400.9	205.2	2,606.1
450–999	8	7,849.4	2,279.0	981.2	284.9	1,266.1
400–449	1	688.8	168.0	688.8	168.0	856.8
350–399	1	145.6	2.8	145.6	2.8	148.4
300–349	4	3,021.6	495.4	755.4	123.8	879.2
250–299	–	–	–	–	–	–
200–249	5	2,130.4	277.4	426.1	45.7	471.8
150–199	2	302.5	90.0	151.3	25.4	176.7
100–149	4	2,027.3	649.8	506.8	162.4	669.2
50–99	2	182.0	5.0	91.0	2.5	93.5
1–49	3	485.5	270.0	161.8	90.0	223.7
0/Blank	6	1,445.5	185.7	240.9	31.0	271.9
Total	39	25,481.3	5,173.7	595.4	101.2	696.7

Note: Average (mean) values do not include blank cases.

convenient means of shipping cotton to market provided by the Ocmulgee River.[34] Later in the 1820s, county residents wishing to take their crops to market could also rely on the Seven Islands Road that led to Macon. The transportation networks that connected Jasper with the state's major entrepôts also provided access to the rich variety of consumer goods pouring into ports along the coast by the early nineteenth century. Jasper had a larger slave population than did Crawford before the war, and the largest African-American population of all three counties following the war.

The values of farm and household goods in Jasper reveal the extent to which this central Piedmont county shared the plantation pattern reflected in the Crawford data (Table 5.17). The average value of farm goods in Jasper was $595.40, just $28.90 less than in Crawford, and the average value of household items was $15.40 less, at $101.20. The value of farm-related items increased with property size. Decedents who owned between 1 and 149 acres typically owned $253.20 in farm tools and livestock, while those with 150–299 acres held $288.70 in farm goods. The average value for estates with 300–449 acres was nearly double that of the previous tenure classes, at $529.93, while those with more than 450 acres typically owned more than three times the livestock and tools of those in the lower categories. Household goods reflected the same general pattern, increasing with the amount of land owned. The lower three tenure classes (1–149 acres) produced a combined average

34 Carnes, Harvey, and Malone, *History of Jasper County, Georgia*, 1–2, 41–42, 96–99.

TABLE 5.18. *Distribution of Household Goods by Tenure Class for Jasper County*

Acreage	Household ($)	Average Household ($)	Kitchen ($)	Average Kitchen ($)	Bedroom ($)	Average Bedroom ($)	Parlor ($)	Average Parlor ($)
1,000+	81	27	134	44.7	176	58.7	16	5.3
450–999	6	0.75	219	27.4	562	70.3	43	5.4
400–449	–	–	24	24	29	29	–	–
350–399	–	–	21	21	5	5	2	2.0
300–349	–	–	118	29.5	129	32.3	10	2.5
250–299	–	–	3	–	81	–	–	–
200–249	–	–	37	7.4	115	23	9	1.8
150–199	–	–	66	33	73	36.5	12	6.0
100–149	74	18.5	182	45.5	263	65.8	77	19.3
50–99	–	–	3	1.5	3	1.5	–	–
1–49	30	10	3	1	15	5	–	–
0/Blank	1	0.17	64	10.7	88	14.7	–	–
Total	**192**	**11.3**	**874**	**22.3**	**1539**	**31.1**	**169**	**6.0**

Note: Average (mean) values do not include blank cases. The household category refers only to those estates where household items were not listed individually or in functional/room-specific categories.

of $85.00 in household goods, while farmers in the next three groups (150–299 acres) owned less than half that amount, with an average of $35.55. The eight decedents who held between 300 and 449 acres typically owned $98.20 in household goods, while the eleven planters in the top two tenure classes (450 acres or more) averaged $245.05.

While the general trend in the value of farm-related assets and household goods in Jasper mirrors the pattern in Crawford, the distribution of assets reflected in the discrete categories of household items differed significantly (Table 5.18). For Crawford, the highest average values for household, kitchen, bedroom, and parlor assemblages were found in the tenure classes with more than 300 acres, while in Jasper the highest average values were concentrated among estates in the 1–149-acre range and in those larger than 450 acres. The inventories for three estates of 1,000 acres or more included a catch-all "household goods" category averaging $27.00 in value, in addition to household items listed individually, while four households in the third tenure class (100–149 acres) had a supplemental "household goods" listing, averaging $18.50 per estate. A similar pattern is reflected in the values of kitchen and bedroom

TABLE 5.19. *Distribution of Sewing Machines, Timepieces, Books, and Cash by Tenure Class for Jasper County Decedents*

Acreage	Total Sewing Machine Value ($)	Avg. Sewing Machine Value ($)	Total Clock/ Watch Value ($)	Avg. Clock/ Watch Value ($)	Total Book Value ($)	Avg. Book Value ($)	Avg. Cash Value ($)
1,000+	–	–	13.35	4.45	6	6	–
450–999	10.0	10.0	4	2	–	–	615.9
400–449	–	–	2.5	2.5	–	–	–
350–399	–	–	1	1	–	–	2,601.0
300–349	35.0	35.0	3	1	1	0.5	–
250–299	–	–	2	2	–	–	–
200–249	5.0	5.0	3.5	3.5	2	–	–
150–199	–	–	7.9	2.0	–	2	–
100–149	56.0	13.9	1	1	1	0.4	30
50–99	–	–	1	1	–	–	–
1–49	–	–	3	1.5	–	–	131.3
0/Blank	10.0	10.0	5	5	–	–	–
Total	116.0	14.8	47.3	2.2	10	2.2	844.6

Note: Average (mean) values do not include blank cases. For sewing machines, books, and cash, the calculation reflects only those inventories/farmers reporting the items/money in question; inventories not reporting the items/cash (zero values) are not included.

items, with the highest average values occurring in the 450–1,000-acre tenure classes, and the second highest found in estates in the 100–199-acre range. The pattern is reversed for the parlor category: the 7 estates in the 100–199-acre category averaged $9.03 in sitting-room furnishings, while the five estates with more than 450 acres typically had $5.03 in parlor items listed in their inventories. The existence of two concentrations of high-value assemblages across all the categories of household goods may suggest the presence of two levels of household formation: one representing the planter elite, who typically owned more than 450 acres, and the other a class of yeoman farmers who achieved success farming parcels of 100–200 acres.

Although the Jasper probate sample had approximately the same number of sewing machines and timepieces as the Crawford sample, there was significantly more cash listed in the Jasper inventories (Table 5.19). Nine decedents in Jasper owned sewing machines, which ranged in value from $0.05 to $25.50, with an average appraised value of $12.84. As in Crawford, sewing machines in Jasper were relatively evenly distributed among the tenure classes of 100 acres or more. Likewise, nineteen estates in Jasper included clocks or watches, compared to eighteen in Crawford. The Jasper pattern reveals at least one watch in each tenure class, with an average value of $2.20 among timepieces ranging in value from $1.00 to $5.35. Only six estates in Jasper listed books, while the Crawford sample included nine. These ranged in value from $0.20 for one lot of books owned by Robert Minter to $6.00 for eight lots of books listed among the possessions of James Darden.[35]

The Jasper sample also included six estates listing cash among the assets inventoried, compared to five decedents with cash in Crawford. In both counties, two estates with fewer than 200 acres had a combined total of less than $175. In Jasper, four decedents with more than 350 acres had a significant amount of cash at home at the time of their deaths. James Aaron had $233.70, Samuel Smith had $630.00, John Kelly had $984.00, and William Minter's inventory showed $2,601.00 in cash among his household possessions.[36] All four were farmers with no apparent involvement in any additional trades, which may suggest that these decedents were landlords, and the cash listed among their possessions had been collected as rent.

Franklin County is located ninety-six miles northeast of Jasper and firmly situated in the Upper Piedmont, or Uplands. The oldest of the three counties included in the probate sample for this study, Franklin was established in 1784 and settled largely by people who emigrated from the backwoods of Pennsylvania, Virginia, and North Carolina after the American Revolution, moving southward along the eastern foothills of the Appalachians in search of unclaimed fertile land.[37] These settlers brought with them a yeoman tradition of mixed agriculture on smaller landholdings that they worked primarily through the labor provided by members of the household, with few slaves. The statistical abstract for the 1840 United States census indicates the persistence of the yeoman tradition into the antebellum period. While cotton was certainly grown in Franklin, farmers there produced fewer than 300,000 pounds of it, while planters in Crawford and Jasper produced 4,556,905 and 5,058,680 pounds, respectively.[38] Although the Lower Piedmont counties of Crawford and Jasper out produced Franklin many times over in cotton, the Upland county could boast a wider variety of farm products, including tobacco, wheat, fruit, wax, and dairy. Furthermore, the home manufactures recorded for 1840 amount to $59,325 for Franklin, compared to $22,372 in Jasper, and only $12,665 in Crawford, suggesting a higher degree

35 Robert J. Minter, *Inventory and Appraisement*, 1899, Jasper County; James Darden, *Inventory and Appraisement*, 1881, Jasper County.

36 James Aaron, *Inventory and Appraisement*, 1880, Jasper County; Samuel R. Smith, *Inventory and Appraisement*, 1887, Jasper County; John W. Kelly, *Inventory and Appraisement*, 1892, Jasper County; William S. Minter, *Inventory and Appraisement*, 1897, Jasper County.

37 Jessie Julia Mize, *History of Franklin County, Georgia* (Fernandina Beach: Wolfe Publishing, 1986): 1225; Coleman, *A History of Georgia*, 92–93.

38 Department of State, *Compendium of the Enumeration of the Inhabitants and Statistics of the United States as Obtained at the Department of State, From the Returns of the Sixth Census, by Counties and Principal Towns, Exhibiting The Population, Wealth, and Resources of the Country* (Washington, DC: Thomas Allen, 1841): 184–185.

TABLE 5.20. *Comparison of Total and Average Farm and Household Assemblage Values by Tenure Class for Franklin County*

Acreage	Cases	Total Farm Value ($)	Total Household Value ($)	Avg. Farm Value ($)	Avg. Household Value ($)	Avg. Combined Value ($)
1,000+	2	2,882.4	221.9	1,441.2	110.9	1,552.1
450–999	11	7,555.2	1,692.6	686.8	153.9	840.7
400–449	5	3,155.9	1,407.5	631.2	281.5	912.7
350–399	1	63.9	131.9	63.9	131.9	195.8
300–349	6	3,448.6	819.1	574.8	136.5	711.3
250–299	6	3,067.7	596.9	511.3	99.5	610.8
200–249	10	2,838.1	823.4	283.8	82.3	366.1
150–199	17	3,281.9	1,923.5	218.8	128.2	347.0
100–149	17	2,561.4	593.5	365.9	84.8	450.7
50–99	9	2,108.7	455.9	234.3	50.7	285.0
1–49	8	1,036.5	279.0	129.6	34.9	164.4
0/Blank	16	3,120.8	854.2	195.1	53.4	248.4
Total	108	35,121.0	9,799.4	442.0	106.9	548.9

of self-sufficiency in Upland households.[39] Franklin retained its yeoman character as Georgia emerged from defeat at the end of the Civil War and began the process of rebuilding its economy and society.

The values of farm and household assemblages in Franklin between 1880 and 1910 indicate that the Upland phenomenon of smaller farms survived the war and persisted into the postbellum period even as the cotton economy spread northward (Table 5.20). In Crawford and Jasper counties, the land-tenure pattern shows sizable concentrations in the three lowest tenure classes, encompassing 1–149 acres (n = 25%), and in the two highest groups, estates more than 450 acres in size (n = 34%). In Franklin, on the other hand, 73 percent of the decedents owned between 1 and 299 acres, compared to approximately 40 percent of the decedents from Crawford and Jasper who were in this range. Moreover, 48 percent of the Franklin decedents were concentrated in the middle three tenure classes (100–249 acres), suggesting this was the predominant property size among successful yeoman farmers in the county.

Farm tools and livestock listed in the Franklin probate inventories ranged from a low average of $63.90 to a high average of $1,441.20 for the two decedents who owned more than 1,000 acres (Table 5.20). The average assemblage of farm goods for all estates was worth $442, which was 29 percent less than the average values for Crawford and Jasper. As in the other counties, the farm-assemblage values in Franklin increased gradually, corresponding to increases

[39] Department of State, *Compendium of the Sixth Census*, 185.

in the size of landholdings. Farm-related property in the lowest three tenure classes (1–149 acres) was appraised at $250 on average, which was roughly comparable to elsewhere in the Piedmont. The average farm-property value for the 150–299-acre tenure group, however, was 14 percent higher in Franklin than in Crawford and Jasper. There was even greater disparity between counties in the remaining tenure classes. Estates in the 300–449-acre class in Crawford and Jasper had farm property worth 22 percent more than that of comparably sized estates in Franklin, while among the largest landholders (450 acres or more), farm-property values were 38 percent higher in Crawford and Jasper.

The distribution of household goods in Franklin also reflects a concentration of wealth in the middle tenure classes, differing from the pattern shared by the two Lower Piedmont counties. The average value of household possessions in Franklin ranged from $46.30 for the eight decedents in the first tenure class (1–49 acres) to $182.10 for the two decedents in the eighth tenure class (350–399 acres) – across the entire Franklin sample, the average was $106.90, 74 percent less than in the other two counties. However, that disparity was not consistent across all tenure groups. While the average household-goods values in Crawford and Jasper were at least 16 percent higher for the lowest three (1–149 acres) and highest two (450 acres or more) tenure classes, the average in Franklin was more than 30 percent higher among farmers who held between 100 and 299 acres, indicating that middling landholders in the Uplands had a higher standard of living than did their peers in the Lower Piedmont.

Closer scrutiny of the different categories of household goods indicates where Franklin residents invested their discretionary income (Table 5.21). First of all, the low average value of $46.10 for the catch-all "household" category in Franklin closely matches the $40.60 average in Crawford; however, these values came from different segments of the population in the two counties. In Franklin, inventories that included this supplemental category were concentrated in the middling estates of 50–299 acres, whereas in Crawford the category appeared most frequently in estates larger than 300 acres. In terms of kitchen-related items, on the other hand, Franklin looks more like Jasper – the average value of kitchen goods in Crawford was $52.00, while it was $22.30 in Jasper and $20.50 in Franklin. In all three counties, the highest-value kitchen assemblages were concentrated in estates larger than 300 acres.

The average values of bedroom assemblages in Franklin ranged from $7.20 to $133.00. All three counties averaged more than $30.00 in bedroom-related possessions, but Franklin had the highest average, at $38.00, compared to $34.80 in Crawford and $31.10 in Jasper. Once again, the estates with the most valuable bedroom items in Franklin were concentrated in the middling tenure classes (100–299 acres), while in the other two counties, decedents who owned more than 300 acres had the most money invested in bedroom-related possessions. Parlor furnishings and accessories from individual estates ranged in value from $2 to $346 in Franklin. The average value of parlor goods in each county increased in value as the size of landholding increased, although

TABLE 5.21. *Distribution of Household Goods by Tenure Class for Franklin County Decedents*

Acreage	Household ($)	Average Household ($)	Kitchen ($)	Average Kitchen ($)	Bedroom ($)	Average Bedroom ($)	Parlor ($)	Average Parlor ($)
1,000+	35.0	35.0	36.0	18.0	64.0	32.0	4.0	2.0
450–999	112.0	56.0	390.0	35.5	429.0	39.0	320.0	29.1
400–449	–	–	69.0	13.8	134.0	26.8	15.0	3.0
350–399	–	–	144.0	72.0	266.0	133.0	91.0	45.5
300–349	–	–	76.0	12.7	200.0	33.3	57.0	9.5
250–299	40.0	20.0	54.0	9.0	284.0	47.3	54.0	9.0
200–249	0.10	0.1	281.0	28.1	333.0	33.3	346.0	34.6
150–199	223.0	44.6	252.0	14.8	640.0	37.6	28.0	1.6
100–149	305.9	102.0	310.0	18.2	702.0	41.3	176.0	10.4
50–99	83.0	83.0	34.0	3.8	65.0	7.2	2.0	0.2
1–49	–	–	83.0	10.4	86.0	10.8	17.0	2.1
0/Blank	56.5	28.3	157.0	9.8	229.0	14.3	49.0	3.1
Total	855.5	46.1	1,886.0	20.5	3,432.0	38.0	1,159.0	12.5

Note: Average (mean) values do not include blank cases. The household category refers only to those estates where household items were not listed individually or in functional/room-specific categories.

Franklin (n = $12.50) and Crawford (n = $13.10) had twice the average value of parlor furnishings found in Jasper County (n = $6.00). But once again the pattern in Franklin differs, in that parlor goods were fairly evenly distributed across the tenure classes, while they were absent from or minimally represented in the lower tenure classes in Crawford and Jasper. This might be further evidence that a higher standard of living prevailed among all tenure classes in the Upland county.

Parlor furnishings, sewing machines, timepieces, books, and cash owned by Franklin decedents reflect a more even pattern of distribution than in the Lower Piedmont counties (Table 5.22). Sewing machines were present in every tenure class in Franklin except for the lowest one (1–49 acres), unlike in the other two counties, where they were absent from roughly half of the estates. Although the average value of individual sewing machines was comparable in all three counties, the Franklin sample included more than three times as many machines as did the other two counties. Timepieces in the Franklin inventories displayed a similar pattern to sewing machines: they were consistently represented in

TABLE 5.22. *Distribution of Sewing Machines, Timepieces, Books, and Cash by Tenure Class for Franklin County Decedents*

Acreage	Total Sewing Machine Value ($)	Avg. Sewing Machine Value ($)	Total Clock/ Watch Value ($)	Avg. Clock/ Watch Value ($)	Total Book Value ($)	Avg. Book Value ($)	Total Cash Value ($)	Avg. Cash Value ($)
1,000+	12.9	12.9	4.0	2.0	5.0	5.0	–	–
450–999	49.8	9.95	14.0	1.4	28.0	2.9	–	–
400–449	30.7	10.2	5.0	1.3	4.0	4.0	825.0	825.0
350–399	2.0	2.0	2.0	2.0	13.0	4.3	348.0	348.0
300–349	81.3	16.3	3.0	1.0	5.0	2.5	284.0	95.0
250–299	25.5	8.5	3.0	1.0	13.0	6.5	69.0	21.0
200–249	30.0	15.0	8.5	1.1	15.0	2.5	806.0	269.0
150–199	40.3	10.1	7.0	1.0	10.0	5.0	171.0	171.0
100–149	57.0	11.4	11.0	1.2	56.0	8.0	14.0	14.0
50–99	33.0	11.0	4.0	1.0	–	–	–	–
1–49	–	–	4.0	1.3	3.0	1.3	13.0	13.0
0/Blank	22.0	7.3	12.0	1.2	10.0	3.2	3.0	3.0
Total	384.5	10.5	77.5	1.2	162.0	4.1	2,533.0	195.4

Note: Average (mean) values do not include blank cases. For sewing machines, books, and cash, the calculation reflects only those inventories/farmers reporting the items/money in question; inventories not reporting the items/cash (zero values) are not included.

each tenure class. Moreover, the average value of $1.20 remained relatively constant even as the size of landholdings increased. While Crawford and Jasper decedents of various wealth levels owned watches and clocks, the overall value of timepieces was higher in the Lower Piedmont counties, and there was a slight increase in value among the largest landholders.

Books were far more common in Franklin than in either of the other counties, judging by the probate inventories. The total value of books identified in the Franklin estates amounted to $162, compared to the totals of $10 in Jasper and $23 in Crawford. Likewise, the average book owner in Franklin owned $4.10 worth of books, while the average in Crawford was $2.70 and in Jasper $2.20. Like timepieces and sewing machines, books were represented in all but one tenure class (50–99 acres) in the Upland county, while their presence was more sporadic in the other two counties. Cash was also included more consistently in Franklin inventories than in the other county samples. Average cash holdings ranged from $3 to $825 in Franklin, and the amount tended to increase with the amount of land decedents owned. The overall average of $195.40 was far less than the $844.60 average in Jasper or the $1,247.00 average in Crawford. All of the Franklin decedents with cash were primarily engaged in agriculture, although the inventories of John Payne and

James Hathcock listed merchandise, indicating that they ran stores, while James Rumsey and James and Mary Ann Watkins had shoemaking tools.[40]

African Americans are poorly represented in the probate sample, despite the substantial size of their population in each county; this suggests that the overwhelming majority of blacks in Crawford, Jasper, and Franklin were very poor and fell well below the $500 threshold for inclusion in the probate process.[41] In many respects, the African Americans whose estates were probated between 1880 and 1910 were successful, because they had amassed enough land and personal possessions to satisfy outstanding debts and to leave assets to their heirs. Of the fifteen estates belonging to decedents of color in the three-county sample, only eight included household goods in an inventory. None of the three African-American estates' inventories from Jasper listed household goods, while two of the five from Crawford and six of the seven from Franklin did. Many black decedents were like Dow Walker, who had clearly done well for himself yet seems not to have acquired personal possessions aside from farm tools and livestock. Walker, a Crawford resident whom the census identified as "mulatto," died possessed of three mules, two horses, fifteen hogs, ten head of cattle, a steam engine, and a cotton press, yet neither the inventory nor the sale bill for his personal property listed any household goods.[42]

Further examination suggests that household goods were intentionally excluded from the seven African-American estates that make no mention of domestic items. Clues in the probate data suggest that this was accomplished through the use of wills to avoid appraisement or, more commonly, through petitions of support for widows or dependents, which often resulted in a pre-appraisement distribution of assets. Allen Clark and William Thomas of Jasper, for example, both had wills that dictated that their spouses receive their land and personal property. Clark even went so far as to specify that "the perishable

40 John W. Payne, *Inventory and Appraisement*, 1898, Franklin County; James H. Hathcock, *Inventory and Appraisement*, 1898, Franklin County; James A. Rumsey, *Inventory and Appraisement*, 1884, Franklin County; James Watkins, *Inventory and Appraisement*, 1900, Franklin County; Mary Ann Watkins, *Inventory and Appraisement*, 1890, Franklin County.

41 For an analysis of the problems confronting African Americans in Georgia, see Peggy G. Hargis and Patrick M. Horan, "The 'Low-Country Advantage' for African-Americans in Georgia, 1880–1930," *Journal of Interdisciplinary History* 28, no. 1 (Summer 1997): 27–46; Peggy G. Hargis, "Beyond the Marginality Thesis: The Acquisition and Loss of Land by African Americans in Georgia, 1880–1930," *Agricultural History* 72, no. 2 (Spring 1998): 241–262; Peggy G. Hargis, "Deeds, Mortgages, and the Conventions of Race," *Historical Methods*, 35, no. 2 (Spring 2002): 53–61.

42 Dow Walker, *Inventory and Appraisement*, 1894, Crawford County, Probate Court, Miscellaneous Records of the Inferior Court, 1822–1900, Record Group 139, Subgroup 2, Series 1 (GDA, Morrow, Georgia); Walker Dow, "Sale Bill of Personal Property Belonging to the Estate of Dow Walker, Dec'd, July 24, 1896," Crawford County, Probate Court, Miscellaneous Records of the Inferior Court, 1822–1900, Record Group 139, Subgroup 2, Series 1 (GDA).

property, viz. a buggy, mare, and household and kitchen furniture," be given to his wife Kate, "to dispose of as she pleases."[43] Both men had amassed several hundred acres of land and considerable numbers of farm tools, livestock, and household possessions. The case of Barney Hancock, on the other hand, seems like an example of the intentional use of a petition for support in order to safeguard household assets while farm tools and livestock were subjected to sale. Although Hancock's estate inventory simply includes an appraisement of $0.11 for "household goods," his widow Harriet received six beds and bedsteads, fifteen chairs, three tables, a desk, books, a stove, and "all household goods belonging to the estate" as part of her petition for twelve months of support.[44] None of these items was repeated in the inventory and appraisement completed later the same day. While it is difficult to draw firm conclusions from such a small sample, the results are undoubtedly suggestive.

Likewise, the disposition of household and farm assets reflected by the inventories of seven African-American decedents from Franklin County cannot be considered representative, but it does hint at a pattern of wealth demonstrated by successful African-American farmers in the postbellum period (Table 5.23). Overall, the average value of farm property for African-American decedents in Franklin was $326.40, which was 26 percent lower than the county average but in the middling range nonetheless; the average value of an African-American decedent's household goods was $30.60, more than 60 percent less than the county average. Half of the black decedents from Franklin owned between 1 and 100 acres, placing them in the lowest two tenure classes. However, considering tenure class and estate values together suggests a pattern that differentiates black decedents in Franklin from their white counterparts. While the single black estate in the first tenure class (1–49 acres) was appraised for nearly one-third less than most estates of comparable size, the two African-American estates in the second tenure class (50–99 acres) included farm assets worth 64 percent more than the county average, and household goods worth 21 percent more. This variance is repeated with the single African-American estate in the fifth tenure class (200–249 acres). Appraised at $405.80, Barney Hancock's assemblage of farm items was valued 30 percent higher than the average for his tenure group. While this pattern may reflect an anomaly from under sampling, it appears to suggest that black farmers in the lower tenure

43 Allen Clark, *Last Will and Testament of Allen Clark, col'd*, February 23, 1884, Jasper County, Probate Court, Estate Case Files, 1809–1907, Record Group 179, Subgroup 2, Series 3 (GDA); William Thomas, *Last Will and Testament of William Thomas*, January 12, 1907, Jasper County, Probate Court, Estate Case Files, 1809–1907, Record Group 179, Subgroup 2, Series 3 (GDA).

44 "Barney Hancock, "Petition of Harriett Hancock, widow of Barney Hancock, dec'd. for twelve months support out of estate of said dec'd and order appointing appraisers for selling a part of same," 2 November 1896 (GDA); Hancock, *Inventory and Appraisement*, November 2, 1896, Franklin County; Hancock, *Sale Bill for the Estate of Barney Hancock*, December 3, 1896, Franklin County.

TABLE 5.23. *Comparison of Total and Average Farm and Household Assemblage Values by Tenure Class for African-American Decedents in Franklin County*

Acreage	Cases	Total Farm Value ($)	Total Household Value ($)	Avg. Farm Value ($)	Avg. Household Value ($)	Avg. Combined Value ($)
1,000+	–	–	–	–	–	–
450–999	–	–	–	–	–	–
400–449	–	–	–	–	–	–
350–399	–	–	–	–	–	–
300–349	–	–	–	–	–	–
250–299	–	–	–	–	–	–
200–249	1	405.8	0.1	405.8	0.1	405.9
150–199	–	–	–	–	–	–
100–149	–	–	–	–	–	–
50–99	2	1,309.1	128.9	654.6	64.4	719.0
1–49	1	102.7	20.3	102.7	20.3	122.9
0/Blank	2	284.9	75.5	142.4	37.7	180.2
Total	**6**	**2102.5**	**224.8**	**326.4**	**30.6**	**357.0**

Note: Average (mean) values do not include blank cases.

classes invested more heavily than whites did, and that they found a strategy to achieve success and self-reliance on smaller parcels.

Among African-American estates in Crawford, the two inventories that reference household goods reflect the Franklin County pattern. Joe Danielly and Barney Martin had clearly achieved success as freedmen. Danielly acquired 100 acres of land and $936.50 worth of farm tools and livestock by the time of his death in 1900, while Martin owned 250 acres and farm assets valued at $180.00.[45] Martin's household goods were valued in a single non-itemized lot at $25.00, while the estate of Joe Danielly lists $113.50 worth of kitchen items and bedroom furniture. The appraisal returned for Danielly's estate totaled $1,050, making him one of the wealthiest Crawford decedents in the probate sample, yet his landholdings place him among the poorer farmers. Martin, conversely, owned enough land to qualify as a middling farmer, but the value of his personal possessions was below average for his tenure class (n = $248.70) at $205.00. Despite these incongruities, both men ranked high among the successful yeoman farmers of either race in Crawford, suggesting that there were multiple paths to success.

Looking at household assets by functional categories suggests how the pattern of acquisition and ownership differed for African Americans in the Georgia Uplands (Table 5.24). The value of $3.30 for kitchen-related items

[45] Joe Danielly, *Inventory and Appraisement*, 1900, Crawford County; Barney Martin, *Inventory and Appraisement*, 1896, Crawford County.

TABLE 5.24. *Distribution of Household Goods by Tenure Class for African-American Decedents in Franklin County*

Acreage	Household ($)	Average Household ($)	Kitchen ($)	Average Kitchen ($)	Bedroom ($)	Average Bedroom ($)	Parlor ($)	Average Parlor ($)
1,000+	–	–	–	–	–	–	–	–
450–999	–	–	–	–	–	–	–	–
400–449	–	–	–	–	–	–	–	–
350–399	–	–	–	–	–	–	–	–
300–349	–	–	–	–	–	–	–	–
250–299	–	–	–	–	–	–	–	–
200–249	–	–	–	–	–	–	–	–
150–199	–	–	–	–	–	–	–	–
100–149	–	–	43.9	21.9	69.0	33.5	9.5	4.8
50–99	–	–	–	–	–	–	–	–
1–49	–	–	3.3	3.3	16.3	16.3	0.8	0.8
0/Blank	25.0	25.0	16.4	16.4	9.8	4.9	16.0	16.0
Total	25.0	25.0	63.6	13.9	95.1	18.23	32.3	7.2

Note: Average (mean) values do not include blank cases.

in the lone black household in the first tenure class – that of Jack Bellamy of Franklin County – was 30 percent lower than the average for farms of that size, while the household's bedroom furnishings, appraised at $16.30, were worth 34 percent more than average. The Bellamys also had a higher level of value among parlor items – $0.80, compared to the average of $0.20. The pattern was reversed for the two African-American estates in the third tenure class. Here, the average kitchen value for black estates was $21.90, which was 17 percent above the countywide average. The average value for bedroom and parlor items in these African-American households, however, was lower than that of other estates in the same tenure class – 19 percent lower for the bedroom and 54 percent lower for the parlor. Despite the variance, it appears that African Americans had as much as 30 percent more household value than their white counterparts. This was probably reflected in both the quantity and the quality of their goods.

While the data from African-American households in Franklin confirm that blacks owned significantly less than whites, an analysis of household technology, books, and cash indicates the specific ways in which that economic disparity manifested itself (Table 5.25). No sewing machines were identified in any of the African-American estates' inventories, although thirty-two were

TABLE 5.25. *Distribution of Sewing Machines, Timepieces, Books, and Cash by Tenure Class for African-American Decedents in Franklin County*

Acreage	Total Sewing Machine Value ($)	Avg. Sewing Machine Value ($)	Total Clock/ Watch Value ($)	Avg. Clock/ Watch Value ($)	Total Book Value ($)	Avg. Book Value ($)	Total Cash Value ($)	Avg. Cash Value ($)
1,000+	–	–	–	–	–	–	–	–
450–999	–	–	–	–	–	–	–	–
400–449	–	–	–	–	–	–	–	–
350–399	–	–	–	–	–	–	–	–
300–349	–	–	–	–	–	–	–	–
250–299	–	–	–	–	–	–	–	–
200–249	–	–	–	–	–	–	–	–
150–199	–	–	–	–	–	–	–	–
100–149	–	–	–	–	1.0	1.0	–	–
50–99	–	–	–	–	–	–	–	–
1–49	–	–	–	–	–	–	–	–
o/Blank	–	–	1.0	1.0			3.3	3.3
Total	–	–	1.0	1.0	1.0	1.0	3.3	3.3

Note: Average (mean) values do not include blank cases. For sewing machines, books, and cash, the calculation reflects only those inventories/farmers reporting the items/money in question; inventories not reporting the items/cash (zero values) are not included.

found in white estates. Likewise, only a single clock and one lot of books were listed among the possessions of black decedents, whereas white estates in Franklin alone produced sixty-five clocks and thirty-nine lots of books. The value for the one clock owned by an African-American was comparable to the average for white decedents, while the appraisal of the single collection of books (Barney Hancock's) was 75 percent lower than the white average. Only a single black decedent had cash, in the amount of $3.30; sixteen white decedents in Franklin had an average of $195.40 in cash. These disparities suggest that African Americans owned fewer luxury items and expensive household appliances than did whites, and that, with little cash to spare, they needed to put everything they had into farming in order to be successful and self-sufficient.

The data from nearly 200 inventories reveal that tenure size correlated closely to wealth, as reflected in the type, quantity, and appraised value of household goods and tools that farmers acquired. The pattern of asset ownership is a sensitive indicator of regional variation and of how the standard of living varied by social class, county, and race. Furthermore, examining the relationship between land tenure and the ownership of specialized tools, labor-saving devices, and discretionary items provides insight into the level at which farmers were judged to be self-sufficient and successful.

Farm-related possessions owned by the decedents in each county display significant regional variation. Crawford and Jasper developed as plantation counties prior to the Civil War and had a much longer association with cotton monoculture, while Franklin County fit the Upland model, where self-reliant smallholders practiced mixed agriculture even after cotton became a large-scale commercial crop. Crawford and Jasper showed an ascending pattern of ownership, in which the largest and most valuable holdings of livestock, farm tools, and mechanized equipment were concentrated in the upper three tenure classes (400 acres or more). In Franklin, the most valuable assemblages of farm assets were concentrated in the middling tenure classes (100–299 acres) – this corresponds to the predominate pattern of tenure revealed in the census data, which shows that a plurality of farmers in Franklin County had farms in the 100–299-acre range. The farmers belonging to those tenure classes in which assets were concentrated, it appears, achieved enough success to invest in greater numbers of livestock and tools or in more advanced farm technology. As such, these data show that it was difficult for farmers to achieve self-sufficiency with fewer than 300 acres in Crawford and Jasper or with fewer than 100 acres in Franklin. Despite the small size of the sample from each county, the data also reveal regional preferences for tools and livestock. Lighter plows built for cotton farming were more prevalent in Crawford, where the soil was more friable than in Jasper and Franklin, which have more clayey soils. Planters and cultivators were also more common in Crawford than in the two counties to its north, and whereas mules were the preferred draft animal in the Lower Piedmont counties of Crawford and Jasper, horses outnumbered mules in the Upland county of Franklin.

In many respects, the distribution of household assets mirrors the pattern of ownership reflected by farm tools and livestock. In Crawford, the value of household possessions correlated strongly to landholding, with a concentration of value in the tenure classes of 450 acres and higher. Jasper revealed a similar concentration of value in the top three tenure classes, although there was a significant secondary grouping in the 100–200-acre range, suggesting the existence of an elite pattern and a yeoman pattern of asset ownership. The Franklin data indicate a pattern that is in keeping with the yeoman antecedents of the county: the value in household assets was concentrated in the middle tenure classes of 150–299 acres. Furthermore, the average assemblage of household items owned by these middling farmers was worth 30 percent more than that of farmers from the same tenure classes in the other two counties, which suggests a higher standard of living in Franklin. The pattern of ownership of discretionary items also supports this suggestion, as Franklin decedents possessed more sewing machines and books than their counterparts in Crawford and Jasper.

African Americans were significantly underrepresented in the samples from all three counties, yet the asset-ownership pattern represented in nine inventories provides tantalizing clues about the ways in which black farmers in the

Georgia Piedmont organized their households and defined success. Because an individual had to accrue more than $500 in personal possessions to require probate in the absence of a will, the African Americans in our sample were likely among the most successful in their respective counties. The paucity of data for African-American estates suggests either that black farmers were too poor to be involved in probate or that they successfully avoided the probate process through the pre-death transfer of assets (or some other means of ensuring payment of debts and equitable distribution of property to heirs). More than half of the probate cases involving black decedents excluded certain possessions from the appraisement and auction, especially household items, indicating that African Americans routinely used wills and petitions for support to protect certain assets and ensure their transmission to a spouse or dependents. More research needs to be completed to determine if this is in fact a well-defined pattern. Without sufficient data, it is difficult to ascertain whether the pattern reflects an economic strategy employed by both whites and blacks, a strategy employed primarily by African Americans to ensure that family members benefited from the wealth they had acquired, or simply a county-specific trend in probate.

For those African-American farmers whose possessions were itemized in probate inventories, the data confirm that even the most successful African Americans in the Georgia Piedmont were economically disadvantaged compared to their white neighbors. If the limited data from Franklin and Crawford are to be believed, blacks lucky enough to own land generally held fewer than 100 acres. In addition, the three-county sample suggests that black decedents' farm tools and household possessions were worth approximately 30 percent less than those of white decedents. Nevertheless, African Americans in the Georgia Piedmont took full advantage of their freedom and invested in their success. While the absence of mechanized equipment like gins and steam engines in the estate inventories of black farmers suggests that such technologies were beyond their financial means, they acquired the basic tools necessary to successfully raise cotton, and they worked their land more intensively than did white farmers. The limited data also suggest that they invested more in livestock than did whites, which enhanced their self-reliance. Despite considerable economic and social barriers, decedents of color like Barney Hancock and Barney Martin did well enough that their ownership of land, farm tools, and household goods made them among the most successful farmers in the Piedmont regardless of race.

Conclusion

> Azalia was a small town, but it was a comparatively comfortable one. For years and years before the war it had been noted as the meeting-place of the wagon-trains by means of which the planters transported their produce to market. It was on the highway that led from the cotton-plantations of Middle Georgia to the city of Augusta. It was also a stopping-place for the stage-coaches that carried the mails. Azalia was not a large town, even before the war, when, according to the testimony of the entire community, it was at its best; and it certainly had not improved any since the war. There was room for improvement, but no room for progress, because there was no necessity for progress. The people were contented. They were satisfied with things as they existed, though they had an honest, provincial faith in the good old times that were gone.[1]

Joel Chandler Harris's fictional town of Azalia could have been situated in Crawford, Jasper, Franklin, or anywhere in the Georgia Piedmont in the years following the Civil War. Harris contextualizes the town in terms of cotton, describing it as a meeting place for planters hauling their lint to market and a way station on a road that connected the plantations to one of Georgia's major cotton market cities. But Azalia is clearly a town in slow decline, its most successful days ended by a war that brought suffering and ruin to the community. Harris concedes that the Azalia that survived the war is in need of improvement, yet he quickly counters that there is no need for progress, because the residents realize that they cannot reestablish the era in which Azalia peaked – they are content to exist on the memories of the town's former prosperity.

While Harris's short story is largely a glib reconciliation piece in which Northerners and Southerners look beyond their past differences to realize and embrace shared ideals, his depiction of Azalia succinctly captures the situation

[1] Harris, "Azalia," in *Free Joe and Other Georgian Sketches*, 165.

for many rural communities in the Georgia Piedmont throughout the last third of the nineteenth century. The war had taken its toll in human lives, and what was not damaged or destroyed through military action was compromised by neglect. Furthermore, the war turned the Southern labor market on its ear with the emancipation of slaves. While roughly half of Piedmont families never owned slaves, the new postbellum reality placed them in direct competition with freedmen for land and resources. Newly emancipated African Americans, on the other hand, started with little or nothing to help them to succeed. Most farmers in the region looked to cotton to restore prosperity, but gone were the record prices of the late antebellum period. Expanding rail service and increased use of fertilizers made it possible to produce greater quantities of cotton, and to expand production into marginal areas to the north, yet the Southern staple experienced devastating periods of declining prices in the 1870s and again in the 1890s, resulting in financial ruin for many farmers.

Harris's paradox – how could people desire improvement but not progress? – can be addressed by examining the probate data, which makes it possible to move beyond aggregate-level regional analyses and focus more closely on household-level production and consumption among yeoman farmers. The probate inventories record the composition of household assets at the time of death, while estate sales and tax data show countywide trends in the acquisition of household assets over time. The pattern of asset ownership revealed through estate inventories and bills of sale from administrator's auctions indicates how farmers responded to the economic and social challenges of the postbellum period. It also suggests the extent to which farmers were engaged in cotton monoculture, the strategies they employed to achieve success, their approximate level of self-sufficiency, and how self-sufficiency varied according to wealth. Furthermore, probate inventories provide a lens into the world of rural Southern consumers and an opportunity to determine how much involvement they had in the burgeoning consumer culture of the late nineteenth century. The main questions related to consumption, as we have shown, focus on how Southern farmers mediated conservative provisioning traditions, the pressure to reinvest profits in the productive capabilities of the farm, and the desire to partake in the expanding world of consumer goods.

We selected the Georgia counties of Crawford, Franklin, and Jasper for this study because each had a large population of independent small-to-middling farmers who fit the yeoman mold. The counties also reflect different economic and cultural traditions, making it possible to compare and contrast patterns to better assess the impact of postbellum social and economic changes. The Lower Piedmont counties of Crawford and Jasper fit the plantation model of development. Cotton culture took hold early in the nineteenth century and flourished in the antebellum period; slavery became deeply and broadly entrenched. Society was characterized by the formation of a small planter elite that acquired large landholdings and relied on slave labor to achieve an economy of scale in cotton production that translated into great financial success. Smallholders in the Lower Piedmont, on the other hand, lived a more yeoman existence, balancing production for home use against cultivation for the market, perhaps at times employing one or two slaves.

Franklin County, on the other hand, was settled in the years following the American Revolution by a different breed of backcountry farmers, who hailed from the western frontiers of Pennsylvania, Virginia, and North Carolina. These newcomers to the Georgia Uplands farmed on a smaller scale and preferred to work in family units with only enough land to provide for the household. They practiced mixed agriculture and limited husbandry to meet the immediate needs of the household before committing any surplus to trade within the local area. In many respects, Franklin County remained isolated until after the Civil War because of its location in the Appalachian foothills, which reinforced the culture of self-sufficiency. The Upland environment was just different enough to discourage the widespread adoption of cotton as a cash crop. Patterns of slaveholding and land tenure reveal the extent to which the Uplands differed from the Lower Piedmont. Fewer than one-quarter of Franklin County households owned slaves in 1860, compared to 63 percent in Crawford and 56 percent in Jasper. In addition, 71 percent of Franklin slaveholders owned five or fewer slaves, while 52 percent of slaveholders in Crawford and 63 percent of Jasper slaveholders owned six or more slaves. The majority of Franklin County farmers held between 20 and 100 acres, while parcels of between 100 and 499 acres were most common in Crawford and Jasper.

Cotton bridged the differences between the Lower and Upper Piedmont traditions in the years following the Civil War. While the war brought an end to slavery, cotton became more important to the Georgia Piedmont economy in the postbellum period, because it offered a higher return than other crops, although it would never again command the prices of the late 1850s. In addition, the increased availability and use of fertilizers overcame the barriers of cooler temperatures, late-spring frosts, and a shorter growing season, promoting the spread of cotton culture into more northerly regions. The expansion of rail service throughout Georgia also had a significant impact, providing farmers in formerly isolated areas of the Georgia Uplands with a cost-effective means of shipping cotton to market.

While fertilizers and railroads brought the cotton economy of the Lower Piedmont to the Uplands, the end of slavery brought the Upland pattern of family farms operating on smaller parcels to the Lower Piedmont. Emancipation arguably had a greater impact in those regions where slaveholding was highest, as a large number of formerly enslaved laborers were introduced into the lowest ranks of commercial agriculture to make their own way. Although Crawford, Jasper, and Franklin retained some of their regional distinctiveness throughout the postbellum period, the conditions in the Upper and Lower Piedmont converged, as farmers in both regions became ever more dependent on credit and as increasing numbers of black and white farmers lost their financial independence, swelling the ranks of tenants and sharecroppers. The pattern of land tenure reveals the extent of the change in the Lower Piedmont counties. While most farmers in Crawford and Jasper held between 100 and 499 acres in 1860, the majority of farmers in all 3 counties operated on fewer than 100 acres by 1870. The average farm size continued to decrease between 1880 and 1910, as more families became enmeshed in debt and were pushed into tenantry.

The probate sample collected from Crawford, Jasper, and Franklin counties includes a broad cross section of the farmers who learned to successfully negotiate the economic and social challenges of postbellum Georgia. The sample represents approximately one-third of the decedents whose estates entered probate during the period because they owned more than $500 in assets, and they had more than one heir or creditor legally eligible to receive a distribution from the estate. The age distribution in the sample is relatively even, with decedents ranging from seventeen to ninety-five, producing an average age at death of sixty-one for the combined three-county group. The gender and racial composition of the data set is heavily weighted toward white males (n = 85%), with a representation of 8 percent for females and 7 percent for African Americans. These statistics confirm that women enjoyed few rights in property during the period and that few blacks were able to work their way up the tenure ladder to move beyond tenantry and into the ranks of farm owners. The figures are especially striking given the even gender balance that existed in all three counties during the period, and the sizable black population in each county (ranging from 22 percent in Franklin to 69 percent in Jasper).

Family-composition statistics also reflect regional differences between the Upper and Lower Piedmont. Nuclear-family households predominated in the Uplands, while extended and nuclear households were evenly balanced in Crawford County. Ninety percent of the decedents were listed as the head of a household in the census data recorded between 1879 and 1910, and 87 percent owned land. The average decedent owned between 150 and 499 acres – significantly more than the average landholding of around 100 acres indicated by the census data. Landholdings were also larger on average in Crawford and Jasper than in Franklin. The large percentage of decedents from the middling tenure classes in the sample suggests that the estates of yeoman farmers were most likely to be probated, since they had accumulated significant assets but did not typically make the effort to provide specific instructions about the distribution of their possessions through the use of a will.

The federal census data identify 86 percent of the 199 decedents as farmers, and the items in probate inventories and tax lists imply that the proportion actually farming at some level was as high as 93 percent. The ownership of tools and supplies suggests that virtually all of the farmers were committed to cotton production. Farmers acquired labor-saving devices as soon as they could afford them and especially favored multipurpose equipment (like horse-drawn cultivators), tools that brought speed and efficiency to farming (like planters), or tools that consolidated steps in a process (like threshers). Some choices in equipment reflected regional preferences – for instance, harrows were associated more with Franklin County, while cultivators were far more abundant in Crawford. Likewise, Crawford inventories included more of the lighter cotton plows than inventories from Jasper and Franklin, because of the sandier, more friable soils found in the latter two counties. Planters and cultivators were also more common in the Lower Piedmont than in the two counties to the north. Vibrators and separators, on the other hand, which were used to process wheat, were found most frequently on the middling and upper-class farms of Franklin, followed by Jasper; this reflects a continued commitment to mixed agriculture among those farmers who could afford to diversify their operations beyond the production of cotton. Livestock ownership shows a similar pattern of regional variability, in which mules predominated in the Lower Piedmont and horses outnumbered mules in the Uplands.

While acquiring an advanced piece of machinery helped a farmer save time and energy and increase production, another strategy Piedmont farmers employed to generate more income, balance risk, and augment self-reliance was to develop a skill or trade needed in the community. Spinning wheels, looms, and shoemaking equipment were present in some of the inventories, but these appear to have been used to fulfill household needs and contribute to self-sufficiency. While most farmers owned some carpentry, shop, or mechanics' tools, several had significant amounts of money invested in tools or owned such specialized equipment to strongly suggest that they were engaged in trades in addition to farming – at least eleven likely worked as blacksmiths and at least three as carpenters. Wealthier farmers in all three counties also engaged in logging, sawmill, and ginning operations as a means of diversifying production and augmenting their income-generating potential. Evidence of logging and sawmills was more common in Franklin, while Crawford had the most cotton gins. The probate data also indicate that middling farmers developed the largest operations and often invested a considerable amount of money in portable steam traction engines – arguably the most technologically advanced pieces of farm equipment represented in the inventories. The engines were used to power gins, saws, and threshers, and several inventories produced evidence to suggest that farmers saw the economy of scale that could be achieved by using an engine to develop capabilities in more than one pursuit.

Household possessions show that farmers throughout the Georgia Piedmont were shrewd if conservative consumers who placed a high priority on products that saved time and energy. They tended to invest most of their assets in farm stock, followed by livestock, and then household possessions. They were, however, keenly aware of popular trends in home furnishings and entertainment and were not against indulging on occasion. Houses were typically small, consisting of a kitchen, bedrooms, a sitting room or parlor, and perhaps a dining room. In general, furnishings were sparse and functional. Kitchens tended to contain more total furniture, and more valuable furniture, than any other room, given the presence of highly specialized items like stoves and food safes. Bedrooms also represented an area of high investment, because of the number of bedsteads and related items needed for families that ranged in size from three to nine members. Discrete collections of dining room furnishings appear in the middle tenure range and reflect a conservative adherence to early-nineteenth-century forms, including corner cupboards, sideboards, and folding serving tables. The presence of a dining suite also suggests that the owner likely engaged in social ceremony associated with entertaining. The incidence of sitting room furnishings, particularly upholstered chairs, center tables, and parlor organs, shows a recognition of middle-class urban values and an engagement in the consumer trends of the period. Surprisingly, the evidence from the inventories suggests that people from all wealth levels sought parlor accoutrements, although these furnishings were most heavily concentrated in the middling classes from 100 to 499 acres. Overall, sitting room furnishings were most prevalent in Franklin County inventories, as were books and sewing machines, perhaps suggesting a higher standard of living.

While the possessions listed in estate inventories represent consumer choices made by decedents, many of the probate cases also included lists of unpaid accounts from local stores and bills of sale from estate auctions, which provide direct evidence of purchases. The store accounts generally reflect a cautious and constrained pattern of expenditure – purchases are limited to grocery staples like salt and coffee, canned and dry goods, clothing, and incidentals like tobacco, candy, and paper. Although the store accounts and stock listings of merchants included in the probate sample provide no evidence for the purchase of bigger or more expensive consumables, it is certain that rural Georgians acquired larger items like farm equipment, stoves, and organs through local merchants and mail-order companies. The paucity of this information in the sample suggests that purchases of furniture and other high-ticket items were so infrequent as to be considered special-order items by customers and merchants alike. The returns from estate sales (administrator's auctions), which occurred in half of the cases in the sample, demonstrate that these were an important source for acquiring goods in the Georgia Piedmont. Estate sales constituted a crucial secondary market in used goods, where farmers could save an average of 10 percent (sometimes much more) on expensive items like farm equipment, livestock, and furnishings. Auctions were also an opportunity for widows and heirs to acquire family assets at a lower price, thereby maximizing the amount a widow could acquire under the legal limits for support derived from the estate, and limiting the tax liability. Moreover, liquidating an estate at auction was important for the cash it provided to settle accounts and ensure equitable distribution among heirs.

Overall, the pattern of acquisition reflected in probate inventories from Crawford, Jasper, and Franklin reveals that farmers were careful shoppers who placed the highest priority on acquiring the items that would enhance their productivity or ease the burden of household and farm chores. Yet the evidence clearly shows that these individuals were enticed by the expanding selection of consumer goods – non-essentials among the decedents' possessions included parlor furnishings, pocket watches, silver-plated castors with cruets, and more, showing that urban middle-class values pervaded Georgia Piedmont society. The evidence also demonstrates that rural Georgians adapted urban middle-class values to meet their needs and fit their world. Certain items, like parlor organs and silver watches, were visible symbols of refinement and success that any city dweller would have appreciated; in the Piedmont countryside, however, a clock, a shotgun, a blooded bull, or a sulky plow made for an equally potent status symbol.

While the range of goods listed in the inventories show Piedmont farmers to have been active and shrewd consumers, the distribution of asset ownership across tenure classes indicates the level at which farmers achieved success and self-reliance. The type and quantity of goods, as well as their appraised values, correlate closely to tenure class – as the size of landholding increased, so did the number, quality, and value of possessions. But the pattern of asset ownership varied significantly by region, class, and race. In Crawford and Jasper, for example, the quantity and value of farm tools and livestock increased with the amount of land owned – this suggests that the plantation pattern of wealth accumulation survived, with wealth concentrated among a small group of the largest estates (more than 400 acres). In Franklin, on the other hand, the bulk of farm assets was concentrated in the middling estates (between 100 and 299 acres), reflecting the perpetuation of a yeoman pattern of consumption. Moreover, the concentration of advanced machinery and labor-saving devices in the same tenure classes indicates the level at which farmers in both regions accumulated sufficient resources to invest in more aggressive strategies to generate profit and success. The concentrations of wealth suggest that farmers with fewer than 300 acres in Crawford and Jasper, and those with fewer than 100 acres in Franklin, struggled to make ends meet and were most likely to be drawn into a cycle of credit dependency. Quite simply, farmers below these thresholds were not able to realize a large enough profit to sustain their families and farms from season to season, nor were they able to grow enough foodstuffs for home consumption to offset the need to rely on local merchants and credit to provide for their families until the harvest was sold.

The distribution of household possessions across tenure classes reflects the same pattern as farm assets, with minor variations. The most valuable assemblages of household goods in Crawford were concentrated in estates of 450 acres or more; in Jasper, estates of that size were joined by a secondary cluster of estates with valuable household goods in the 100–200-acre range. This may indicate the presence of a sizeable yeoman population in the county, reflecting Jasper's position on the boundary between the Lower and Upper Piedmont. The distribution of household assets in Franklin mirrors the pattern in farm assets, where the highest values in the probate sample are concentrated among estates with 150–299 acres. Furthermore, the estates of middling farmers in Franklin were worth 30 percent more on average than those of their Lower

Piedmont counterparts – additional evidence that there was a higher standard of living in the Uplands.

The conclusions to be drawn from the cases of the few African Americans in the probate sample are much more tentative but are suggestive nonetheless. It is not surprising that blacks are so underrepresented, given the considerable economic and social challenges they faced during the period, yet the fifteen African Americans in the sample can be considered success stories by virtue of the fact that their estates were valuable enough to be probated. With that in mind, the pattern of asset ownership clearly demonstrates that blacks were significantly less well-off than were whites in the Georgia Piedmont. The average black decedent owned between 1 and 100 acres and had 30 percent less invested in farm assets and household possessions than did the average white decedent. However, the limited data suggest that African-American farmers acquired the basic tools needed for farming, invested more in livestock than did whites of comparable wealth, and worked their land more intensively than did most white farmers. Perhaps more telling, the data from their estates suggest that African Americans may have intentionally avoided the probate process. While the difficulty of accumulating at least $500 worth of assets is the primary reason for the scarcity of African Americans in the sample, in more than half of the African-American estates, goods listed in the appraisement inventories were excluded from the administrator's sales, indicating that they were likely distributed by means other than the probate process. Moreover, black decedents appear to have been more likely to use wills and petitions for support in order to retain select possessions, especially household goods.

Scholars who have not examined probate data have overlooked the role of the probate process in building and preserving wealth. Yeoman families who engaged in the probate process did so for several reasons, but paramount among them was the desire to safeguard estates in order to make sure that there would be an intergenerational transmission of assets. If families did not pay close attention to this process, the prospect of keeping their hard-earned wealth available for the next generation – whether in the immediate family or the extended family – would be threatened or diminished.

We argue that probate inventories and estate sales shed light on the ancillary productive activities engaged in by farmers. As documented in Chapters 3, 4, and 5, there is considerable evidence that farm families turned to non-crop activities to increase household incomes from farming. The presence of carpentry tools, shingle-making and blacksmithing tools, sewing machines, butchering equipment, and logging equipment suggests that these households were seriously engaged in market production.

These activities had gendered components. For men, logging after the harvest and before the next spring planting was common. Communities often had one or two butcher specialists who worked either for cash payments or for bartered goods, and whose roles included assisting with hog slaughtering throughout local areas. For women, owning a sewing machine offered other opportunities. The machines were quite expensive, and their purchase was likely financed on credit; so even if farm women initially used them for household needs, many were likely to take on sewing projects for pay. Like other products of women's at-home labor, such as butter, eggs, chickens, and honey, home-sewn goods were sold at local and distant markets, allowing farm households to take advantage of assets they owned that were inefficiently underutilized.

Unlike other accounts of rural Georgia during the postbellum period, we argue that Crawford, Jasper, and Franklin were connected to places where considerable market activity occurred, and that this connectedness gave farmers an increased likelihood of success. The possibility of selling all manner of goods at market – not just cotton – added complexity to the economic decision making in rural households. While we do not know if the existence of these markets increased individual productivity, it is fair to speculate that the hope that hard work would be rewarded – both in financial terms and in terms of being able to purchase consumer goods – may have been one reason so many people were able to significantly alter their household's pattern of consumption.

This exploration of the material world of the Georgia Piedmont between 1880 and 1910 clearly shows the extent to which farmers used the goods and livestock they acquired to mediate considerable economic and social challenges. The possessions listed in the inventories attest to the Piedmont farmers' full engagement in cotton production, but the inventories also provide compelling clues about the choices they made to balance the self-reliance of the household with the investments and risks necessary to gain a competitive edge. The evidence suggests that they understood the power of consumption in their struggle to succeed. They invested resources first and foremost in the farming operation – they knew it was important to acquire the right tools to grow cotton, and that more advanced machinery made it easier to expand production with less labor. They also employed a variety of strategies to enhance earning potential and to achieve a level of self-reliance that would reduce their dependence on merchants, who generally offered unfavorable credit terms. Some farmers diversified their crop regimes by growing wheat for market in addition to cotton and corn, while others raised mules and horses or purchased blooded bulls and cattle for dairy, meat, or perhaps to breed. Still others acquired the tools and skills necessary to practice trades in addition to farming, such as blacksmithing or carpentry, which were always in demand in rural communities. A few even amassed the necessary capital to invest in sophisticated ginning, logging, and milling operations powered by steam traction engines.

Farmers in the Georgia Piedmont approached household purchases in much the same way they invested in farm operations: the practical superseded the niceties. Kitchens received the greatest level of investment, especially in cast-iron stoves and other devices or implements that made food storage, processing, and preparation less of a chore. Beyond the kitchen, consumption was focused on meeting basic needs. Bedrooms were second in importance, judging from the appraisal values in the probate inventories, followed by dining rooms and parlors (or sitting rooms, as they were often called in the Piedmont). While parlors were, on the basis of the average level of expenditure, a comparatively low priority, a significant number of households in all but the lowest tenure class in each county had some sitting room–related goods, such as center tables, upholstered chairs, books, parlor organs, and other musical instruments. These items mark a departure from the spare, functional character of the rest of the typical Piedmont farmstead, which reflected an all-encompassing commitment to farming as well as severely limited discretionary funds. The presence of parlor goods among the possessions of rural Southerners reflects a cognizance of mainstream conventions of refinement and socializing, and a desire to emulate these ideals.

If Georgia Piedmont households were conservative in their habits and choices, it was probably because farm families lived from season to season, knowing that they could not control nature, credit, or the markets, and that there would be bad harvests just as surely as there would be good ones. Furthermore, most had limited means – they were careful to make the most of their resources, and they prioritized basic needs above all else. The evidence from the inventories and tax lists, however, shows that Piedmont farmers, white and black, were actively engaged in finding ways to improve their condition and provide the best for their families. They also found ways to communicate their success, their status, and their aspirations to others in the community, through the goods they bought for the home, used in the field, and wore into town. In short, the probate data from Crawford, Jasper, and Franklin counties reveal that farmers in the Georgia Piedmont, despite differences in region, class, and race, were keenly aware of the need for improvement, and that they showed creativity and persistence in trying to improve their lot in life. Contrary to Joel Chandler Harris's depiction of the imaginary town of Azalia, in reality Piedmont farmers recognized the need for improvement *and* were eager to embrace progress. While only some attained success, most felt it was within their reach and did everything they could to try to grasp it.

Bibliography

Primary Sources

Crawford County

Crawford County, Miscellaneous County Offices, Miscellaneous Original Documents, 1826–1928, Record Group 139, Subgroup 12, Series 10. GDA, Morrow, Georgia.

______, Ordinary Court, Annual Returns, Book J, 1858–1870. GDA, Morrow, Georgia.

______, Ordinary Court Minutes, Book A. GDA, Morrow, Georgia.

______, Ordinary Court Minutes, Book B. GDA, Morrow, Georgia.

______, Probate Court, Marriage Records of the Inferior Court, 1814–1930, Record Group 139, Subgroup 2, Series 2. GDA, Morrow, Georgia.

______, Probate Court, Miscellaneous Records of the Inferior Court, 1822–1900, Record Group 139, Subgroup 2, Series 1. GDA, Morrow, Georgia.

______, Property Tax Digests, 1877–1910, Vol. 3. GDA, Morrow, Georgia.

______, *Crawford County Sesquicentennial: Roberta, Georgia.* Commemorative Booklet Committee, November 16–19, 1972.

Franklin County

Franklin County, Probate Court, Estate Bond Books, 1853–1880, Record Group 159, Subgroup 2, Series 37. GDA, Morrow, Georgia.

______, Probate Court, Estate Records, 1786–1916, Record Group 159, Subgroup 2, Series 1. GDA, Morrow, Georgia.

______, Probate Court, Homesteads, 1868–1904, Record Group 159, Subgroup 2, Series 23. GDA, Morrow, Georgia.

______, Probate Court, Marriage Records, 1806–1905, Record Group 159, Subgroup 2, Series 3. GDA, Morrow, Georgia.

______, Property Tax Digest, 1878–1910. GDA, Morrow, Georgia.

______, Tax Collector, Tax Records, 1798–1896, Record Group 159, Subgroup 7, Series 80. GDA, Morrow, Georgia.

Jasper County

Jasper County, Probate Court, Estate Case Files, 1809–1907, Record Group 179, Subgroup 2, Series 3. GDA, Morrow, Georgia.

———, Probate Court, Marriage Records, 1816–1914, Record Group 179, Subgroup 2, Series 2. GDA, Morrow, Georgia.

———, Probate Court, Pony Homestead Exemptions, 1808–1903, Record Group 179, Subgroup 2, Series 11. GDA, Morrow, Georgia.

———, Probate Court, Wills, 1809–1907, Record Group 179, Subgroup 2, Series 4. GDA, Morrow, Georgia.

———, Property Tax Digests, 1878–1887 & 1895, Vol. 2. GDA, Morrow, Georgia.

———, Property Tax Digests, 1888–1910, Vol. 3, 1705. GDA, Morrow, Georgia.

———, Tax Collector, Miscellaneous Bound Volumes, 1864–1908, Record Group 179, Subgroups 7/10, Series 19/20. GDA, Morrow, Georgia.

State

Clark, Richard H., Thomas Read, Rootes Cobb, and David Irwin. *The Code of the State of Georgia*. Atlanta: Franklin Steam Printing House, 1867.

Georgia Department of Natural Resources, Historic Preservation Division. "House Types in Georgia." Atlanta: Georgia Department of Natural Resources, Historic Preservation Division, n.d., http://gashpo.org/assets/documents/housetypes.pdf (accessed: February 15, 2011).

Wright, William A., General Manager. *Report of the Comptroller General for the State of Georgia for the Year Ending September 30, 1890*. Atlanta: George W. Harrison, 1890.

———. *Report of the Comptroller General for the State of Georgia for the Year Ending September 30, 1895*. Atlanta: Franklin Publishing House, 1895.

———. *Report of the Comptroller General for the State of Georgia for the Year Ending September 30, 1900*. Atlanta: George W. Harrison, 1900.

———. *Report of the Comptroller General for the State of Georgia for the Year Ending September 30, 1910*. Atlanta: Charles P. Boyd State Printer, 1911.

Federal

Carleton, Mark Alfred. *Lessons from the Grain Rust Epidemic of 1904*. Washington, DC: GPO, 1905.

Hilgard, Eugene W. *Report on Cotton Production in the United States: Also Embracing Agricultural and Physico-Geographical Description of the Several Cotton States and of California*. Washington, DC: GPO, 1884.

Loughridge, Robert H. "Report on the Cotton Production of the State of Georgia, with a Description of the General Agricultural Features of the State," *Statistics of the Population of the United States at the Tenth Census, June 1, 1880*. Washington, DC: GPO, 1882.

U.S. Bureau of the Census. *Eighth Census of the United States, 1860: Population of the United States in 1860*; Compiled from the original returns of the Eighth Census, under the direction of the Secretary of the Interior by Joseph C. G. Kennedy, Superintendent of Census. Washington, DC: GPO, 1864.

———. *Eighth Census of the United States, 1860: Agriculture of the United States in 1860*; Compiled from the original returns of the Eighth Census under the direction of the Secretary of the Interior Joseph C. G. Kennedy, Superintendent of the Censusby Joseph C. G. Kennedy, Superintendent of Census. Washington, DC: GPO, 1864.

———. *Ninth Census of the United States, 1870: Agriculture of the United States in 1860*; Compiled from the original returns of the Ninth Census, under the direction of the Secretary of the Interior by Francis A. Walker, Superintendent of Census. Washington, DC: GPO, 1872.

———. *Report of the Mortality and Vital Statistics of the United States as Returned at the Tenth Census (June 1, 1880): Part I: Mortality and Vital Statistics by John S. Billings*. Washington, DC: GPO, 1885.

———. *Tenth Census of the United States, 1880: Population of the United States in 1880*. Washington, DC: GPO, 1883–1886.

———. *Tenth Census of the United States, 1880: Agriculture in the United States in 1880*. Washington, DC: GPO, 1882.

———. *Eleventh Census of the United States, 1890 Population of the United States in 1890*; Compiled from the original returns of the Ninth Census, under the direction of the Secretary of the Interior by Robert P. Porter, Superintendent of Census. Washington, DC: GPO, 1895.

———. *Twelfth Census of the United States, 1900: Vol. 1–2, Population of the United States in 1900*. Prepared under the supervision of William C. Hunt. Washington, DC: GPO, 1901–1902.

———. *Twelfth Census of the United States, 1900: Vol. 5–6, Agriculture in the United States in 1900*. Prepared under the supervision of Le Grand Powers; Pt. 1, Farms, Live Stock, and Animal Products; Pt. 2, Crops and Irrigation. Washington, DC: GPO, 1901–1902.

———. *Thirteenth Census of the United States, 1910: Vol. 1, Population of the United States in 1910*. Prepared under the supervision of William C. Hunt. Washington, DC: GPO, 1913.

———. *Thirteenth Census of the United States, 1910: Vol. 2–3, Reports by States, with Statistics for Counties, Cities and Other Civil Divisions, Alabama to Wyoming, Alaska, Hawaii, and [Puerto] Rico*. Washington, DC: GPO, 1913.

———. *Thirteenth Census of the United States, 1910: Vol. 5–7 Agriculture, 1909 and 1910, General Report and Analysis*. Washington, DC: GPO, 1913.

———. *Thirteenth Census of the United States, 1910: Vol. 6–8, Reports by States, with Statistics for Counties, Alabama to Wyoming, Alaska, Hawaii and [Puerto] Rico*. Washington, DC: GPO, 1913.

———. *Historical Statistics of the United States from Colonial Times to 1970, Part I*, Series K. Washington, DC: GPO, 1975.

U.S. Department of Agriculture. *Cotton and Cottonseed: Acreage, Yield, Production, Disposition, Price, Value by States, 1866–1952*. Washington, DC: Agricultural Marketing Service, 1955.

———. "Major Land Resource Regions Custom Report for the South Atlantic and Gulf Slope Cash Crops, Forest, and Livestock for Crawford, Jasper, and Franklin Counties: Region 137, Carolina and Georgia Sand Hills; 136, Southern Piedmont; 133A, Southern Coastal Plain," United States Department of Agriculture Handbook 296 (2006), 7, 11. http://soils.usda.gov/MLRAExplorer (accessed January 17, 2011).

U.S. Department of State. *Compendium of the Enumeration of the Inhabitants and Statistics of the United States as Obtained at the Department of State, From the Returns of the Sixth Census, by Counties and Principal Towns, Exhibiting The Population, Wealth, and Resources of the Country*. Washington, DC: Thomas Allen, 1841.

Wright, W. F. *The History of the Cowpea and Its Introduction into America*. Washington, DC: GPO, 1907.

Secondary Sources

Adams, Jane H. "The Decoupling of Farm and Household: Differential Consequences of Capitalist Development on Southern Illinois and Third World Family Farms." *Comparative Studies in Society and History* 30, no. 3 (July 1988): 453–482.

Aiken, Charles S. *The Cotton Plantation South since the Civil War*. Baltimore: The Johns Hopkins University Press, 1998.

Allen, Robert C. "Inferring Yields from Probate Inventories." *Journal of Economic History* 48, no. 1 (March 1988): 117–125.

Alston, Lee J., and Morton Owen Schapiro. "Inheritance Laws Across Colonies: Causes and Consequences." *Journal of Economic History* 44, no. 2, The Tasks of Economic History (June 1984): 277–287.

Alston, Lee J., and Kyle D. Kauffman. "Agricultural Chutes and Ladders: New Estimates of Sharecroppers and 'True Tenants' in the South, 1900–1920." *Journal of Economic History* 57, no. 2 (June 1997): 464–475.

Ames, Kenneth L. *Death in the Dining Room and Other Tales of Victorian Culture*. Philadelphia: Temple University Press, 1992.

Arp, Bill. *From the Uncivil War to Date, 1861–1903: Memorial Edition*. Atlanta: Hudgins Publishing, 1903.

Atlanta Historical Society. *Neat Pieces: The Plain-Style Furniture of Nineteenth-Century Georgia*. Athens: University of Georgia Press, 2006.

Ayers, Edward L. *The Promise of the New South: Life after Reconstruction*. New York: Oxford University Press, 1992.

Banks, Enoch Marvin. "The Economics of Land Tenure in Georgia." PhD diss., Columbia University, 1905.

Bankston, Emmie Carnes. *History of Roberta and Crawford County, Georgia*. Macon: Omni Press, 1976.

Barron, Hal S. *Mixed Harvest: The Second Great Transformation in the Rural North, 1870–1930*. Chapel Hill: University of North Carolina Press, 1997.

Barsby, Steven L. "Economic Backwardness and the Characteristics of Development." *Journal of Economic History* 29, no. 3 (September 1969): 449–472.

Bartley, Numan V. *The Creation of Modern Georgia*. Athens: University of Georgia Press, 1983.

Baughan, Denver Ewing, "Tarheel Talk." *American Speech* 32, no. 4 (December, 1957): 283–286.

Beck, John J. "Building the New South: A Revolution from Above in a Piedmont County." *Journal of Southern History* 53, no. 3 (August 1987): 441–470.

Bedell, John. "Archaeology and Probate Inventories in the Study of Eighteenth Century Life." *Journal of Interdisciplinary History* 31, no. 2 (Autumn 2000): 223–245.

Benson, Susan Porter. *Household Accounts: Working-Class Family Economies in the Interwar United States*. Ithaca: Cornell University Press, 2007.
Billings, Dwight B. "Class Origins of the 'New South': Planter Persistence and Industry in North Carolina." *American Journal of Sociology* 88, Supplement: Marxist Inquiries: Studies of Labor, Class, and States, (1982): S52–S85.
Blackburn, Graham. *Traditional Woodworking Handtools: An Illustrated Reference Guide for the Woodworker*. New York: Gramercy Books, 2000.
Blackmon, Douglas A. *Slavery by Another Name: The Re-Enslavement of Black Americans from the Civil War to World War II*. New York: Doubleday, 2008.
Blight, David W. *Race and Reunion: The Civil War in American Memory*. Cambridge: Belknap Press, 2001.
Bode, Frederick A., and Donald E. Ginter. *Farm Tenancy and the Census in Antebellum Georgia*. Athens: University of Georgia Press, 1986.
Bonner, James C. *A History of Georgia Agriculture, 1732–1860*. Athens: University of Georgia Press, 2009.
———. "Genesis of Agricultural Reform in the Cotton Belt." *Journal of Southern History* 9, no. 4 (November 1943): 475–500.
Braden, Donna R. "'The Family That Plays Together Stays Together': Family Pastimes and Indoor Amusements, 1890–1930." Chap. 6 in *American Home Life, 1880–1930: A Social History of Spaces and Services*. Knoxville: University of Tennessee Press, 1992.
Brandau, Rosemary. "The Butchering and Processing of Pork in Eighteenth-Century Williamsburg, Research Report RR-31." Williamsburg: Colonial Williamsburg Foundation, 1984.
Breen, T. H. "An Empire of Goods: The Anglicization of Colonial America, 1690–1776." *Journal of British Studies* 25, no. 4 (October): 467–499.
Brewer, John, and Roy Porter, eds. *Consumption and the World of Goods*. New York: Routledge, 1993.
Bronner, Simon J., ed. *Consuming Visions: Accumulation and Display of Goods in America, 1880–1920*. New York: W. W. Norton, 1989.
Brooks, Robert Preston. "The Agrarian Revolution in Georgia, 1865–1912." PhD diss., University of Wisconsin, 1914.
Burrison, John A. *Brothers in Clay: The Story of Georgia Folk Pottery*. Athens: University of Georgia Press, 2008.
Bushman, Richard. *The Refinement of America: Persons, Houses, Cities*. New York: Knopf, 1992.
Campbell, Colin. *The Romantic Ethic and the Spirit of Modern Consumerism*. Oxford: Basil Blackwell, 1987.
Carlton, David L. and Peter A. Coclanis. *The South, the Nation, and the World: Perspectives on Southern Economic Development*. Charlottesville: University of Virginia Press, 2003.
Carnes, Marcia Hayes, John P. Harvey, and Irene Roberts Malone, eds. *History of Jasper County, Georgia*. Fernandina Beach: Wolfe Publishing, 1984.
Carr, Lois Green, and Lorena S. Walsh. "Inventories and the Analysis of Wealth and Consumption Patterns in St. Mary's County, Maryland, 1658–1777." *Historical Methods* 13, no. 2 (1980): 81–104.
———. "Changing Lifestyles and Consumer Behavior in the Colonial Chesapeake." See 59–166 in *Of Consuming Interests: The Style of Life in the Eighteenth Century*.

Charlottesville: Published for the United States Capitol Historical Society by the University of Virginia Press, 1994.
———. "The Standard of Living in the Colonial Chesapeake." *William and Mary Quarterly*, 3rd ser., 45, no. 1 (January 1988): 135–159.
Carson, Cary. "The Consumer Revolution in Colonial British America, Why Demand?" See 483–700 in *Of Consuming Interests: The Style of Life in the Eighteenth Century*. Charlottesville: Published for the United States Capitol Historical Society by the University of Virginia Press, 1994.
Carson, Cary, Ronald Hoffman, and Peter J. Albert, eds. *Of Consuming Interests: The Style of Life in the Eighteenth Century*. Charlottesville: Published for the United States Capitol Historical Society by the University of Virginia Press, 1994.
Cashman, Sean Dennis. *America in the Gilded Age: From the Death of Lincoln to the Rise of Theodore Roosevelt*. 3rd ed. New York: New York University Press, 1993.
"Census Data Year 1850," (2004). *Historical Census Browser*. Retrieved December 10, 2010, from the University of Virginia, Geospatial and Statistical Data Center: http://fisher.lib.virginia.edu/collections/stats/histcensus/index.html.
"Census Data Year 1860," (2004). *Historical Census Browser*. Retrieved December 10, 2010, from the University of Virginia, Geospatial and Statistical Data Center: http://fisher.lib.virginia.edu/collections/stats/histcensus/index.html.
"Census Data for 1890, Agriculture" (2004). *Historical Census Browser*, retrieved December 10, 2010, from the University of Virginia, Geospatial and Statistical Data Center: http://fisher.lib.virginia.edu/collections/stats/histcensus/index.html.
Chappell, Edward A. "Slave Housing." *Fresh Advices: A Research Supplement*. Colonial Williamsburg Foundation, November 1982.
Churchill, Robert H. "Gun Ownership in Early America: A Survey of Manuscript Militia Returns." *William and Mary Quarterly*, 3rd ser., 60, no. 3 (July 2003): 615–642.
Clark, Christopher. "Household Economy, Market Exchange, and the Rise of Capitalism in the Connecticut Valley, 1800–1860." *Journal of Social History* 13, no. 2 (Winter 1979): 169–189.
Clark, Clifford E., Jr. "House Furnishings as Cultural Evidence: The Promise and Peril of Material Culture Studies." *American Quarterly* 43, no. 1 (March 1991): 73–81.
Clark, Thomas D. "In the Southern Retail Trade after 1865." *Journal of Economic History* 3, Supplement: The Tasks of Economic History (December 1943): 38–47.
———. "The Furnishing and Supply System in Southern Agriculture since 1865." *Journal of Southern History* 12, no. 1 (February 1946): 24–44.
Coale, Ansley J., and Norfleet W. Rives, Jr. "A Statistical Reconstruction of the Black Population of the United States, 1880–1970: Estimates of True Numbers by Age and Sex, Birth Rates, and Total Fertility." *Population Index* 39, no. 1 (January 1973): 3–36.
Cobb, James C. "Beyond Planters and Industrialists: A New Perspective on the New South." *Journal of Southern History* 54, no. 1 (February 1988): 45–68.
Cochrane, Willard W. *The Development of American Agriculture: A Historical Analysis*. Minneapolis: University of Minnesota Press, 1979.
Coleman, Kenneth, ed. *A History of Georgia*. Athens: University of Georgia Press, 1977.
———, ed. "How to Run a Middle Georgia Cotton Plantation in 1885: A Document." *Agricultural History* 42, no. 1 (January 1968): 55–60.

Collier, Peter. *Sorghum: Its Culture and Manufacture Economically Considered as a Source of Sugar, Syrup, and Fodder*. Cincinnati: Robert Clark & Company, 1884.

Cooper, Grace Rogers. *The Sewing Machine: Its Invention and Development*. Washington, DC: Smithsonian Institution Press, 1976.

Cooper, William J., Jr., and Thomas E. Terrill. *The American South: A History, Volume II*. 3rd ed. New York: McGraw Hill, 2002.

Cowan, Ruth Schwartz. *More Work for Mother: The Ironies of Household Technology from the Open Hearth to the Microwave*. New York: Basic Books, 1983.

Cromley, Elizabeth Collins. "A History of American Beds and Bedrooms, 1890–1930." See 120–141 in *American Home Life, 1880–1930: A Social History of Spaces and Services*. Knoxville: University of Tennessee Press, 1992.

Daniel, Pete. *Breaking the Land: The Transformation of Cotton, Tobacco, and Rice Cultures since 1880*. Urbana: University of Illinois, 1985.

Davis, A. H. *An Analysis of the Laws of Georgia since the Code of 1882*. Atlanta: Constitution Publishing Company, 1888.

De Canio, Steven J. *Agriculture in the Postbellum South: The Economics of Production and Supply*. Cambridge: MIT Press, 1974.

De Vries, Jan. "Between Purchasing Power and the World of Goods: Understanding the Household Economy in Early Modern Europe." Chap. 5 in *Consumption and the World of Goods*. London: Routledge, 1993.

Deetz, James. *In Small Things Forgotten: An Archaeology of Early American Life*. 1st ed. New York: Anchor Books/Doubleday, 1977.

Demos, John. *A Little Commonwealth: Family Life in Plymouth Colony*. New York: Oxford University Press, 1970.

Ditz, Toby L. "Ownership and Obligation: Inheritance and Patriarchal Households in Connecticut, 1750–1820." *William and Mary Quarterly*, 3rd ser., 47, no. 2 (April 1990): 235–265.

Duggar, John Frederick. *Southern Field Crops*. New York: Macmillan, 1911.

Dupre, Daniel. "Ambivalent Capitalists on the Cotton Frontier: Settlement and Development in the Tennessee Valley of Alabama." *Journal of Southern History* 56, no. 2 (May 1990): 215–240.

Farm Implement News Company. *Farm Implement News Buyer's Guide, 1888*. Chicago: Farm Implement News Company, 1888.

———. *Farm Implement News Buyer's Guide*. Chicago: Masonic Temple Publishers, 1914.

Ferleger, Louis. *Agriculture and National Development: Views on the Nineteenth Century*. Ames: Iowa State University Press, 1990.

———. "Capital Goods and Southern Economic Development." *Journal of Economic History* 45, no. 2, The Tasks of Economic History (June 1985): 411–417.

———. "Cutting the Cane: Harvesting in the Louisiana Sugar Industry." *Southern Studies* 23, no. 1 (Spring 1984): 42–59.

———. "Farm Mechanization in the Southern Sugar Sector after the Civil War." *Louisiana History* 23, no. 1 (Winter 1982): 21–34.

———. "Productivity Change in the Post-Bellum Louisiana Sugar Industry." See 147–171 in *Time Series Analysis*. New York: North-Holland Press, 1981.

———. "Science, Technology, and Farm Implements: Agricultural Research at the Alabama Experiment Station," *Agricultural History* 62, no. 2 (Spring 1988): 208–224.

______. "Self-Sufficiency and Rural Life on Southern Farms." *Agricultural History* 58, no. 3 (July 1984): 314–329.

______. "Sharecropping Contracts in the Late-Nineteenth-Century South." *Agricultural History* 67, no. 3 (Summer 1993): 31–46.

Fite, Gilbert C. *Cotton Fields No More: Southern Agriculture, 1865–1980*. Lexington: University Press of Kentucky, 1984.

Flynn, Charles L., Jr. *White Land, Black Labor: Caste and Class in Late Nineteenth-Century Georgia*. Baton Rouge: Louisiana State University Press, 1983.

Foner, Eric. *Nothing But Freedom: Emancipation and Its Legacy*. Baton Rouge: Louisiana State University Press, 1983.

Ford, Lacy K., Jr. "Rednecks and Merchants: Economic Development and Social Tensions in the South Carolina Upcountry, 1865–1900." *Journal of American History* 71, no. 2 (September 1984): 294–318.

______. "Self-Sufficiency, Cotton, and Economic Development in the South Carolina Upcountry, 1800–1860." *Journal of Economic History* 45, no. 2 (June 1985): 261–267.

Fox, Richard Wightman, and T. J. Jackson Lears, eds. *The Culture of Consumption: Critical Essays in American History, 1880–1980*. New York: Pantheon, 1983.

Fox-Genovese, Elizabeth. *Within the Plantation Household: Black and White Women of the South*. Chapel Hill: University of North Carolina Press, 1988.

______. "Women in Agriculture during the Nineteenth Century." See 267–302 in *Agriculture and National Development: Views on the Nineteenth Century*. Ames: Iowa State University Press, 1990.

Gallman, Robert. "Self-Sufficiency in the Cotton Economy of the Antebellum South." *Agricultural History* 44, no. 1 (January 1970): 5–23.

Gannett, Henry. "The Alleged Census Frauds in the South." *International Review* 10 (1881): 459–467.

Garrett, Martin A., Jr. "Evidence on the Use of Oxen in the Postbellum South." *Social Science History* 22, no. 2 (Summer 1998): 225–249.

______. "The Mule in Southern Agriculture: A Requiem." *Journal of Economic History* 50, no. 4 (December 1990): 925–930.

Gates, Frederick B. "The Georgia Land Act of 1803: Political Struggle in a One-Party State." *Georgia Historical Quarterly* 82, no. 1(Spring 1998): 1–21.

Gauthier, Jason G. *Measuring America: The Decennial Censuses from 1790 to 2000*. Washington, DC: U.S. Dept. of Commerce, 2002.

Genovese, Eugene. *The Political Economy of Slavery: Studies in the Economy and Society of the Slave South*. Middletown: Wesleyan University Press, 1989.

Gerster, Patrick, and Nicholas Cords, eds. *Myth and Southern History, Volume 2: The New South*. 2nd ed. Urbana: University of Illinois Press, 1989.

Gilmore, Glenda Elizabeth. *Gender and Jim Crow: Women and the Politics of White Supremacy in North Carolina, 1896–1920*. Chapel Hill: University of North Carolina Press, 1996.

Goodwyn, Lawrence. *The Populist Moment: A Short History of the Agrarian Revolt in America*. New York: Oxford University Press, 1978.

Grady, Henry Woodfin. *The Speeches of Henry W. Grady with a Short Biographical Sketch of His Life*. Atlanta, Georgia: Charles P. Byrd, 1895.

Gray, Lewis Cecil. *History of Agriculture in the Southern United States to 1860*. 2 vols. Gloucester: Peter Smith, 1958.

Greene, Jack P. *Pursuits of Happiness: The Social Development of Early Modern British Colonies and the Formation of American Culture*. Chapel Hill: University of North Carolina Press, 1988.

Grier, Katherine C. *Culture and Comfort: Parlor Making and Middle Class Identity, 1850–1930*. Washington, DC: Smithsonian Institution Press, 1997.

———. "The Decline of the Memory Place: The Parlor after 1890," See 49–74 in *American Home Life, 1880–1930: A History of Spaces and Services*. Knoxville: University of Tennessee Press, 1992.

Gutman, Herbert G., ed. *Work, Culture, and Society in Industrializing America: Essays in American Working-Class and Social History*. New York: Vintage Books, 1976.

Hahn, Steven. *The Roots of Southern Populism: Yeoman Farmers and the Transformation of the Georgia Upcountry, 1850–1890*. New York: Oxford University Press, 1983.

———. "Class and State in Postemancipation Societies: Southern Planters in Comparative Perspective." *American Historical Review* 95, no. 1 (February 1990): 75–98.

Haines, Michael R., and Richard H. Steckel, eds. *A Population History of North America*, New York: Cambridge University Press, 2001.

Hargis, Peggy G. "Beyond the Marginality Thesis: The Acquisition and Loss of Land by African Americans in Georgia, 1880–1930." *Agricultural History* 72, no. 2 (Spring 1998): 241–262.

———. "Name Games: Deeds, Mortgages, and the Conventions of Race." *Historical Methods* 35, no. 2 (Spring 2002): 53–61.

Hargis, Peggy G. and Patrick M. Horan. "The 'Low-Country Advantage' for African-Americans in Georgia, 1880–1930." *Journal of Interdisciplinary History* 28, no. 1 (Summer 1997): 27–46.

Harper, Roland M. "Development of Agriculture in Upper Georgia from 1850 to 1880." *Georgia Historical Quarterly* 6, no. 1 (March 1922): 3–27.

Harris, Joel Chandler. *Free Joe and Other Georgian Sketches*. New York: Charles Scribner's Sons, 1887.

Harris, J. William. "Crop Choices in the Piedmont before and after the Civil War." *Journal of Economic History* 54, no. 3 (September 1994): 526–542.

———. *The New South, New Histories*. New York: Routledge, 2008.

Hart, John Fraser. "Land Use Change in a Piedmont County." *Annals of the Association of American Geographers* 70, no. 4 (December 1980): 492–527.

Hawley, Anna L. "The Meaning of Absence: Virginia's Southside Inventories in Surry County, Virginia, 1690–1715." See 23–32 in *Early American Probate Inventories*. Boston: Boston University, 1989.

Headlee, Sue. *The Political Economy of the Family Farm: The Agrarian Roots of American Capitalism*. New York, Praeger, 1991.

Henretta, James A. "Families and Farms: Mentalité in Pre-Industrial America." *William and Mary Quarterly*, 3rd ser., 35, no. 1 (January 1978): 3–32.

Henry, William R. *Miscellaneous Estate Records of Crawford County, Georgia: Guardian Bonds, 1874–1906; Administrator's Bonds Book "2," 1874–1898; Appraisement and Sale Bills, 1881–1905*. Vol. 3. Warner Robins: Central Georgia Genealogical Society, 1989.

Hilliard, Sam Bowers. *Atlas of Antebellum Southern Agriculture*. Baton Rouge: Louisiana Sate University Press, 1984.

———. *Hog Meat and Hoecake: Food Supply in the Old South, 1840–1860*. Carbondale: Southern Illinois University Press, 1972.

———. "The Rails Come to Town." Chap. 9 in *Lavonia, Georgia: Then & Now, 1880–2005*. Compiled by the Lavonia Historic Preservation Commission and the Franklin County Resource, Conservation, and Development Council. Franklin Springs, Georgia: Lavonia Historic Preservation Commission and the Franklin County Resource, Conservation, and Development Council, 2005, 113–120.

Holbrook, Stewart H. *Machines of Plenty: Pioneering in American Agriculture*. New York: Macmillan, 1955.

Holmes, Marion B., ed. *Georgia Official and Statistical Register*. Atlanta: Perry Communications, 1978.

Holt, W. Stull. *The Bureau of the Census: Its History, Activities, and Organization*. Washington, DC: Brookings Institution, 1929.

Hurst, Ronald L., and Jonathon Prown. *Southern Furniture, 1680–1830: The Colonial Williamsburg Collection*. New York: Harry N. Abrams, 1997.

Hurt, R. Douglas. *American Agriculture: A Brief History*. West Lafayette: Purdue University Press, 2002.

Isaac, Rhys. *The Transformation of Virginia, 1740–1790*. Chapel Hill: University of North Carolina Press, 1982.

Israel, Fred L. *1897 Sears Roebuck & Co. Catalogue*. Reprint. New York: Chelsea House Publishers, 1968.

Izard, Holly V. "Another Place in Time: The Material and Social Worlds of Sturbridge, Massachusetts, from Settlement to 1850." PhD diss., Boston University, 1996.

Janes, Thomas P. *A Manual on the Hog*. Atlanta: James P. Harrison and Company, 1877.

———. *Hand-Book of the State of Georgia: Accompanied by a Geological Map of the State*. Atlanta: Russell Brothers, 1876.

———. *Georgia, from the Immigrant Settler's Stand-Point: Giving the Results of the Experience of Actual Settlers from Other States and Countries, Prefaced with an Account of the Natural Resources of Georgia and the Inducements to Immigrants and Capitalists*. Atlanta: Georgia Department of Agriculture, 1879.

Jones, Alice Hanson. "Estimating Wealth of the Living from a Probate Sample." *Journal of Interdisciplinary History* 13, no. 2 (Autumn 1982): 273–300.

———. "Wealth Estimates for the American Middle Colonies, 1774." *Economic Development and Cultural Change* 18, no. 4, pt. 2 (July 1970): i–x, 1–172.

Jones, B. W. *The Peanut Plant, Its Cultivation and Uses*. New York: Orange Judd, 1885.

Klein, Herbert. *A Population History of the United States*. New York: Cambridge University Press, 2004.

Kline, Ronald R. *Consumers in the Country: Technology and Social Change in Rural America*. Baltimore: The Johns Hopkins University Press, 2000.

Kruger, Linda M. "Home Libraries: Special Spaces, Reading Places." See 94–119 in *American Home Life, 1880–1930: A Social History of Spaces and Services*. Knoxville: University of Tennessee Press, 1992.

Kulikoff, Allan. "Households and Markets: Toward a New Synthesis of American Agrarian History." *William and Mary Quarterly*, 3rd ser., 50, no. 2 (April 1993): 342–355.

______. "The Transition to Capitalism in Rural America." *William and Mary Quarterly*, 3rd ser., 46, no. 1 (January 1989): 120–144.

Lanier, Sydney. "The New South," See 104–135 in *Retrospects and Prospects: Descriptive and Historical Essays*, 2nd ed. New York: Charles Scribner's Sons, 1899.

Le Guin, Magnolia Wynn. *A Home-Concealed Woman: The Diaries of Magnolia Wynn Le Guin, 1901–1913*. Charles A. Le Guin, ed. Athens: University of Georgia Press, 1990.

Leach, William. *Land of Desire: Merchants, Power, and the Rise of a New American Culture*. New York: Pantheon Books, 1993.

Leone, Mark P., and Parker B. Potter, Jr. *The Recovery of Meaning: Historical Archaeology in the Eastern United States*. Washington, DC: Smithsonian, 1988.

Lindert, Peter H. "An Algorithm for Probate Sampling." *Journal of Interdisciplinary History* 11, no. 4 (Spring 1981): 649–668.

Lindgren, James, and Justin L. Heather. "Counting Guns in Early America." *William and Mary Law Review* 43, no. 5 (2002): 1777–1842.

Lockridge, Kenneth. "A Communication." *William and Mary Quarterly*, 3rd ser., 25 (1968): 516–517.

Long, John H., and Peggy Tuck Sinko, eds. *Georgia: Atlas of Historical Boundaries*. Chicago: Newberry Library, 2010. http://publications.newberry.org/ahcbp/, (accessed January 5, 2011).

Lyman, Joseph B. *Cotton Culture*. New York: Orange Judd and Company, 1868.

Magrabi, Frances M., Young Sook Chung, Sanghee Sohn Cha, and Se-Jeong Yang. *The Economics of Household Consumption*. New York: Praeger, 1991.

Main, Gloria L. "Inequality in Early America: The Evidence from Probate Records of Massachusetts and Maryland." *Journal of Interdisciplinary History* 7, no. 4 (Spring 1977): 559–581.

______. "Many Things Forgotten: The Use of Probate Records in *Arming America*." *William and Mary Quarterly*, 3rd ser., 59, no. 1 (January 2002): 211–216.

______. "Personal Wealth in Colonial America: Explorations in the Use of Probate Records from Maryland and Massachusetts, 1650 to 1720." *Journal of Economic History* 34, no. 1, The Tasks of Economic History (March 1974): 289–294.

______. "Probate Records as a Source for Early American History." *William and Mary Quarterly*, 3rd ser., 32, no. 1 (January 1975): 89–99.

Mandle, Jay. "The Plantation States as a Sub-Region of the Post-Bellum South." *Journal of Economic History* 34, no. 3 (September 1974): 732–738.

______. *The Roots of Black Poverty: The Southern Plantation Economy after the Civil War*. Durham: Duke University Press, 1978.

Manning, J. Russell. *The Illustrated Stock Doctor and Live-Stock Encyclopedia*. Guelph, Ontario: World Publishing, 1881.

Martin A. Garrett, Jr. "Evidence on the Use of Oxen in the Postbellum South." *Social Science History* 22, no. 2 (Summer 1998): 225–249.

Martin, Ann Smart. "Makers, Buyers, and Users: Consumerism as a Material Culture Framework." *Winterthur Portfolio* 28, no. 2/3 (Summer–Autumn 1993): 141–157.

______. "Material Things and Cultural Meanings: Notes on the Study of Early American Material Culture." *William and Mary Quarterly*, 3rd ser., 53, no. 1 (January 1996): 5–12.

Martinez, Katherine, and Kenneth Ames, eds. *The Material Culture of Gender, The Gender of Material Culture.* Winterthur: Henry Francis du Pont Winterthur Museum, Distributed by University Press of New England, 1997.

Marx, Karl. *Capital: Volume 1, A Critique of Political Economy.* Translated by Ben Fowkes. New York: Penguin Press, 1992.

McCusker, John J., and Russell M. Menard. *The Economy of British America, 1707–1789.* Chapel Hill: University of North Carolina Press, 1985.

McDaniel, George W. *Hearth & Home: Preserving a People's Culture.* Philadelphia: Temple University Press, 1982.

McKendrick, Neil, John Brewer, and J. H. Plumb. *The Birth of a Consumer Society: Commercialization in the Eighteenth Century.* London: Europa Publications, 1982.

McMurry, Sally. *Families and Farmhouses in Nineteenth Century America: Vernacular Design and Social Change.* New York: Oxford University Press, 1988.

Messick, Denise P., J. W. Joseph, and Natalie P. Adams. *Tilling the Earth: Georgia's Historic Agricultural Heritage – A Context.* Report on file with the Georgia Department of Natural Resources, Historic Preservation Division. Stone Mountain: New South Associates, 2001.

Mize, Jessie Julia. *History of Franklin County, Georgia.* Fernandina Beach: Wolfe Publishing, 1986.

Morgan, James Oscar. *Field Crops for the Cotton-Belt.* New York: Macmillan, 1917.

Nesbitt, R. T. *Georgia: Her Resources and Possibilities.* Atlanta: Franklin Printing and Publishing, 1896.

Oemler, Dr. A. *Truck-Farming at the South: A Guide to the Raising of Vegetables for Northern Markets.* New York: Orange Judd Company, 1910.

Orser, Charles E., Jr. *The Material Basis of the Postbellum Tenant Plantation: Historical Archaeology in the South Carolina Piedmont.* Athens: University of Georgia Press, 1988.

Osterud, Nancy Grey. "She Helped Me Hay It as Good as a Man": Relations among Women and Men in an Agricultural Community." See 87–97 in "*To Toil the Livelong Day": America's Women at Work, 1780–1980.* Ithaca: Cornell University Press, 1987.

Overton, Mark, Jane Whittle, Darron Dean, and Andrew Hahn. *Production and Consumption in English Households, 1600–1750.* New York: Routledge, 2004.

Owsley, Frank L. *Plain Folk of the Old South.* Baton Rouge: Louisiana State University Press, 1949.

Parker, David B. *Alias Bill Arp: Charles Henry Smith and the South's "Goodly Heritage."* Athens: University of Georgia Press, 1991.

Parker, William N. "The South in the National Economy, 1865–1970." *Southern Economic Journal* 46, no. 4 (April 1980): 1019–1048.

Pease, Jane H. "A Note on Patterns of Conspicuous Consumption among Seaboard Planters, 1820–1860." *Journal of Southern History* 35, no. 3 (August 1969): 381–393.

Pennell, Sara. "Consumption and Consumerism in Early Modern England." *Historical Journal* 42, no. 2 (June 1999): 549–564.

Plumb, Charles S. *Judging Farm Animals.* New York: Orange Judd Company, 1919.

Potter, David. *People of Plenty: Economic Abundance and the American Character.* Chicago: University of Chicago Press, 1954.

Proctor, Nicolas W. *Bathed in Blood: Hunting and Mastery in the Old South*. Charlottesville: University of Virginia Press, 2002.

Prown, Jules David and Kenneth Haltman, eds. *American Artifacts: Essays in Material Culture*. East Lansing: Michigan State University Press, 2000.

Randolph, Mary. *The Virginia House-wife*. 1824; reprint. New York: Dover, 1993.

Range, Willard. *A Century of Georgia Agriculture, 1850–1950*. Athens: University of Georgia Press, 1954.

Ransom, Roger and Richard Sutch. "Debt Peonage in the Cotton South after the Civil War." *Journal of Economic History* 32, no. 3 (September 1972): 641–669.

______. "The 'Lock-In' Mechanism and Overproduction of Cotton in the Postbellum South." *Agricultural History* 49, no. 2 (April 1975): 405–425.

______. *One Kind of Freedom: The Economic Consequences of Emancipation*. New York: Cambridge University Press, 1977.

Raper, Arthur F. *Preface to Peasantry: A Tale of Two Black Belt Counties*. Chapel Hill: University of North Carolina Press, 1936.

Raper, Aurthur F., and Ira de Augustine Reid. *Sharecroppers All*. Chapel Hill: University of North Carolina Press, 1941.

Reidy, Joseph P. *From Slavery to Agrarian Capitalism in the Cotton Plantation South: Central Georgia, 1800–1880*. Chapel Hill: University of North Carolina Press, 1992.

______. "Slavery, Emancipation, and the Capitalist Transformation of Southern Agriculture, 1850–1910." See 229–266 in *Agriculture and National Development: Views on the Nineteenth Century*. Ames: Iowa State University Press, 1990.

Reinberger, Mark. "The Architecture of Sharecropping: Extended Farms of the Georgia Piedmont." See 116–134 in *Perspectives in Vernacular Architecture, Vol. 9: Constructing Image, Identity, and Place*. Knoxville: University of Tennessee Press, 2003.

Rubin, Julius. "The Limits of Agricultural Progress in the Nineteenth-Century South." *Agricultural History* 49, no. 2 (April 1975): 362–373.

Russell, Henry E., compiler. Russell and Erwin Manufacturing Company. *Illustrated Catalogue of American Hardware of the Russell and Erwin Manufacturing Company, 1865*. Reprint. New York: Association for Preservation Technology, 1980.

Ryan, Mary P. *Cradle of the Middle Class: The Family in Oneida County, New York, 1790–1865*. New York: Cambridge University Press, 1981.

Schmitz, Mark D., and Donald F. Schaefer. "Using Manuscript Census Samples to Interpret Antebellum Southern Agriculture." *Journal of Interdisciplinary History* 17, no. 2 (Autumn 1986): 399–414.

Scott, Thomas Allen. "Cobb County, Georgia, 1880–1900: A Socioeconomic Study of an Upper Piedmont County." PhD diss., University of Tennessee, 1978.

Shackel, Paul A. *Personal Discipline and Material Culture: An Archaeology of Annapolis, Maryland, 1695–1870*. Knoxville: University of Tennessee Press, 1993.

Shammas, Carole. "Anglo-American Household Government in Comparative Perspective." *William and Mary Quarterly*, 3rd ser., 52, no. 1 (January 1995): 104–144.

______. "Constructing a Wealth Distribution from Probate Records." *Journal of Interdisciplinary History* 9, no. 2 (Autumn 1978): 297–307.

______. "Consumer Behavior in Colonial America." *Social Science History* 6, no. 1 (Winter 1982): 67–86.

______. *The Pre-Industrial Consumer in England and America*. Oxford: Clarendon Press, 1990.

Silber, Nina. *The Romance of Reunion: Northerners and the South, 1865–1900*. Chapel Hill: University of North Carolina Press, 1993.

Simes, Lewis M., and Paul E. Basye. "The Organization of the Probate Court in America: I." *Michigan Law Review* 42, no. 6 (June 1944): 965–1008.

———. "The Organization of the Probate Court in America: II." *Michigan Law Review* 43, no. 1 (August 1944): 113–154.

Smith, Adam. *An Inquiry into the Nature and Causes of the Wealth of Nations*, Edwin Canaan, ed. Originally published 1776. Chicago: University of Chicago Press, 1977.

Smith, Algernon L. *The Story of the Continental Gin Company, 1900–1952*. Birmingham: Birmingham Publishing, 1952.

Smith, Daniel Scott. "Underregistration and Bias in Probate Records: An Analysis of Data from Eighteenth-Century Hingham, Massachusetts." *William and Mary Quarterly*, 3rd ser., 32, no. 1 (January 1975): 100–110.

Smith, Mark. *Mastered by the Clock: Time, Slavery, and Freedom in the American South*. Chapel Hill: University of North Carolina Press, 1997.

St. George, Robert Blair, ed. *Material Life in America, 1600–1860*. Boston: Northeastern University Press, 1988.

Strasser, Susan. *Never Done: A History of American Housework*. New York: Pantheon Books, 1982.

Tabor, Anna Belle Little. *History of Franklin County, Georgia*. Fernandina Beach: Wolfe Publishing, 2004.

Temin, Peter. "Freedom and Coercion: Notes on the Analysis of Debt Peonage in *One Kind of Freedom*." *Explorations in Economic History* 16, no. 1 (January 1979): 56–63.

———. "Patterns of Cotton Agriculture in Post-Bellum Georgia." *Journal of Economic History* 43, no. 3 (September 1983): 661–674.

Thompson, Eleanor, ed. *The American Home: Material Culture, Domestic Space, and Family Life*. Winterthur: Winterthur Museum, 1998.

Thompson, E. P. "Time, Work-Discipline, and Industrial Capitalism." *Past & Present*, no. 38 (December 1967): 56–97.

Trimble, Stanley W., and John Fraser Hart. "Commentary on 'Land Use Change in a Piedmont County,'" by John Fraser Hart. *Annals of the Association of American Geographers* 73, no. 2 (June 1983): 285–288.

Ulrich, Laurel Thatcher. "Housewife and Gadder: Themes of Self-Sufficiency and Community in Eighteenth-Century New England," See 21–34 in *"To Toil the Livelong Day": America's Women at Work, 1780–1980*. Ithaca: Cornell University Press, 1987.

Van Ame, Wales E. *Veterinary Obstetrics*. Fort Wayne: Wales E. Van Ame, 1903.

Veblen, Thorstein. *The Theory of the Leisure Class*. New York: Penguin Books, 1979.

Walker, Francis A. "Statistics of the Colored Race in the United States." *Publications of the American Statistical Association* 2, no. 11/12 (September–December 1890): 91–106.

Walsh, Lorena S. "Urban Amenities and Rural Sufficiency: Living Standards and Consumer Behavior in the Colonial Chesapeake, 1643–1777." *Journal of Economic History* 43, no. 1 (March 1983): 109–117.

Walton, Gary M., and James F. Shepherd, eds. *Market Institutions and Economic Progress in the New South*. New York: Academic Press, 1981.

Weatherill, Lorna. *Consumer Behavior and Material Culture in Britain, 1660–1760*. London: Routledge, 1988.
Weber, Max. *The Protestant Ethic and the Spirit of Capitalism*. Michael D. Coe, ed. New York: Dover Publications, 2003.
Weiman, David F. "The Economic Emancipation of the Non-Slaveholding Class: Upcountry Farmers in the Georgia Cotton Economy." *Journal of Ecomonic History* 45, no. 1 (March 1985): 71–93.
———. "Farmers and the Market in Antebellum America: A View from the Georgia Upcountry." *Journal of Economic History* 47, no. 3 (September 1987): 627–647.
Weiner, Jonathan M. "Class Structure and Economic Development in the American South, 1865–1955." *American Historical Review* 84, no. 4 (October 1979): 970–992.
Wetherington, Mark. *The New South Comes to Wiregrass Georgia, 1860–1910*. Knoxville: University of Tennessee Press, 1994.
Whatley, Warren C. "A History of Mechanization in the Cotton South: The Institutional Hypothesis." *The Quarterly Journal of Economics* 100, no. 4 (November 1985): 1191–1215.
White, William N. *Gardening for the South, or How to Grow Vegetables and Fruits*. New York: Orange Judd and Company, 1868.
Wilder, Sunnie, and William R. Henry. *Wills of Crawford County Georgia: Wills Book "A," 1835–1852; Wills Book "B," 1852–1894; Wills Book "C," 1894–1948 III*. Warner Robins: Central Georgia Genealogical Society, 1989.
Woodman, Harold D. "Class, Race, Politics, and the Modernization of the Postbellum South." *Journal of Southern History* 63, no. 1 (February 1997): 3–22.
Woodward, C. Vann. *The Burden of Southern History*. Baton Rouge: Louisiana State University Press, 1960.
———. *The Origins of the New South 1877–1913*. Baton Rouge: Louisiana State University Press, 1951.
———. "The Search for Southern Identity." See 119–132 in *Myth and Southern History, Volume 2: The New South*, 2nd ed. Urbana: University of Illinois Press, 1989.
———. *The Strange Career of Jim Crow*. New York: Oxford University Press, 1966.
———. *Tom Watson: Agrarian Rebel*. Savannah: Beehive Press, 1973.
Wright, Gavin. "Freedom and the Southern Economy." *Explorations in Economic History* 16, no. 1 (January 1979): 90–108.
———. "Note on the Manuscript Census Samples Used in These Studies." *Agricultural History* 44, no. 1 (January 1970): 95–99.
———. *The Political Economy of the Cotton South: Households, Markets, and Wealth in the Nineteenth Century*. New York: W. W. Norton, 1978.
———. *Old South, New South: Revolutions in the Southern Economy since the Civil War*. New York: Basic Books, 1986.
Wright, Gavin, and Howard Kunreuther. "Cotton, Corn, and Risk in the Nineteenth Century." *Journal of Economic History* 35, no. 3 (September 1975): 526–551.
———. "Cotton, Corn, and Risk in the Nineteenth Century: A Reply." *Explorations in Economic History* 14, no. 2 (April 1977): 183–195.
Young, Jeffrey Robert. *Domesticating Slavery: The Master Class in Georgia and South Carolina, 1670–1837*. Chapel Hill: University of North Carolina Press, 1999.

Images Bibliography

Fitz, J. W. Profitable Farming in the Southern States, Richmond, Virginia: Franklin Publishing Co., 1890.

Georgia Division of Archives and History, *Vanishing Georgia Collection* (GDA) Morrow, Georgia.

Jasper County. *Inventory and Appraisement of the Estate of Sampson Wagner of Jasper County, Deceased*, 1896. Probate Court, Estate Case Files, 1809–1907, Record Group 179, Subgroup 2, Series 3. GDA, Morrow, Georgia.

Metz, John D. Map of Georgia showing the location of Crawford, Jasper, and Franklin Counties in Relation to the Location of the Lower and Upper Piedmont Physiographic Regions, 2013.

______. *The Lynchburg Chilled and Hillside Plows: Manufactured by the Lynchburg Plow Co., Lynchburg, Virginia*, Lynchburg, Virginia: Lynchburg Plow Co., 1892.

______. *The Watt Plow Co.: Manufacturers and Dealers, Wholesale and Retail, in Agricultural Implements, Plows, Plow Castings, Baling Presses, Engines, Boilers, Saw Mills, Carriages, Buggies, Farm Wagons, Harness, Etc.*, Richmond, VA: Watt Plow Company, 1897.

Index